Statistical Reasoning for the Behavioral Sciences

Statistical Reasoning for the Behavioral Sciences

THIRD EDITION

Richard J. Shavelson
Stanford University

ALLYN and BACON
Boston   London   Toronto   Sydney   Tokyo   Singapore

This edition of *Statistical Reasoning* is dedicated to the memory of my dear friend and colleague Leigh Burstein.

Vice President, Publisher, Social Science: Susan Badger
Executive Editor: Sean W. Wakely
Editorial Assistant: Jennifer Normandin
Senior Production Administrator: Marjorie Payne
Manufacturing Buyer: Megan Cochran
Marketing Manager: Joyce Nilsen
Editorial-Production Service: Electronic Publishing Services Inc.
Cover Administrator: Linda Knowles

Copyright © 1996, 1988, 1981 by Allyn & Bacon
A Simon & Schuster Company
Needham Heights, Massachusetts 02194

Library of Congress Cataloging-in-Publication Data

Shavelson, Richard J.
   Statistical reasoning for the behavioral sciences / Richard J. Shavelson.—3rd ed.
     p.   cm.
   Includes Index.
   ISBN 0-205-18460-X
   1. Social sciences–Statistical methods. 2. Statitistics.
I. Title.
HA29.S5592   1995   95-42825
150'.72—dc20   CIP

Printed in the United States of America

10 9 8 7 6 5 4 3 2 1   00 99 98 97 96 95

Contents

Preface

A statistics textbook should communicate an understanding of the subject to its readers. The goal is for readers not only to know the meaning of statistical concepts, but also to be able to use these concepts to solve problems. To communicate meaning, I have used extensive verbal and visual exposition seldom found in statistics or mathematics textbooks. Knowing that concepts have certain meanings, however, does not guarantee that you "understand" statistics. Equally important is knowing *how* to use statistics to solve problems. This text, then, stresses both conceptual and procedural knowledge of statistics and the link between them.

With respect to conceptual knowledge, figures have been used to a greater extent than is usual in statistics texts. This has been done to provide visual representations of concepts that parallel and enhance verbal exposition. Moreover, sequences of pictures are used to represent concepts involving a process. These pictorial sequences are as close as I could come to what I wanted—a motion picture of the concepts at work.

As for procedural knowledge, the text contains *Procedures*, something like computational algorithms. Step by step, each problem identifies the information and computation needed to solve a well-defined class of problems. Moreover, Procedures are used to link the verbal and figural exposition of concepts to the working formulas of statistics.

The book also *integrates* statistics with the design of research in the behavioral sciences for three reasons:

1. To clarify the meaning of statistical concepts as well as to provide realistic problem applications from education, psychology, and sociology.

2. To familiarize readers with well-defined classes of problems that arise in behavioral research that can be solved by applying the concepts and procedures in this text.

3. To motivate readers by providing a *raison d'être* for statistics in their behavioral science curriculum.

ORGANIZATION

The book is divided into seven sections. Section I—Research and the Role of Statistics—contains two chapters, one on research design and statistics, and the other on a specific research study. Section II—Descriptive Statistics for Univariate Distributions—contains chapters on frequency distributions, descriptive statistics, and the normal distribution. Section III—Joint Distributions—contains two chapters, one on joint distributions and correlation and the other on linear regression.

Section IV—Reasoning Behind Statistical Inference—contains four chapters. The first in the section provides a conceptual introduction to statistical inference leading to the need for probability theory. The next chapter presents those aspects of probability theory needed to understand the inferential statistics contained in the remainder of the book. The third chapter in the section provides statistical tests for means and correlations in one- and two-sample designs using the normal distribution. And the last chapter in the section deals with power and sample size.

Section V—Statistical Tests for Between Subjects Designs—contains three chapters, one each on the *t* test, the one-way analysis of variance, and the factorial analysis of variance. Section VI—Statistical Tests for Within-Subjects and Mixed Designs—also contains three chapters, one each on the randomized-blocks analysis of variance, the split-plot analysis of variance, and the analysis of covariance. The last section, Section VII—Additional Topics: Correlational and Nonparametric Statistical Analysis, contains three chapters, one on multiple regression analysis, a second on chi square tests, and a third on other nonparametric statistical tests.

CHANGES FROM THE SECOND EDITION

This third edition clearly has its lineage in the first two editions. For example, like the first edition, it has a separate chapter describing behavioral research. Unlike the first edition, however, this chapter focuses on just one important study that has had both theoretical and practical impact on expectancy theory and education policy, and concludes with a brief review of research that followed from the original study. The chapters on analysis of variance, like the second edition, treat fixed-, mixed-, and random-effects models but in a much simpler (nontechnical) way. At reviewers' urging, like the first edition, planned comparisons for one-way and factorial designs may be found in the chapters on these topics along with post hoc comparisons. At reviewers' urging and unlike the first two editions, the dependent *t* test may be found in the same chapter with the independent *t* test. This sequencing follows teaching practice more closely. Finally, unlike the first two editions, Procedures are used frequently in the first thirteen chapters and then phased out of the text (and placed in the *Student Guide*) as they become cumbersome (e.g., factorial analysis of variance) and the use of a statistical package (primarily SPSS) is phased into the Exercises at the end of each chapter.

Throughout the text, hypothetical data based on recent research have been incorporated into the text and, where hypothetical data are based on studies presented in earlier editions, the findings are updated with results from more recent research. Moreover, increased attention has been paid as to when a particular statistical model is appropriate to a class of problems. For example, a table in Chapter 1 links the statistical tests presented throughout the text to the research designs described in that chapter. Finally, the number of formulas presented, especially computational formulas, has been reduced, and the more important or more frequently used formulas have been placed in a "Formula Glossary."

MAJOR FEATURES

The chapters on statistics (all but Chapters 1 and 2) are built around the major features of the book. Each chapter has the following general framework:

1. Outline of key topics covered in the chapter.
2. Conceptual overview of the major concepts presented in the chapter, usually couched in one or more research example, one's own intuition, or both.
3. Presentation of concepts verbally and pictorially.
4. Presentation of procedures involved in using the concepts until these procedures become overly laborious, and then presentation of statistical programs and their output in Exercises at the end of each chapter.
5. Presentation of example research problems after each major section in a chapter with detailed solutions at the end of the chapter.
6. Brief summary of the chapter.
7. Exercises drawing on published research with detailed answers including SPSS setups and output when hand computations become overly laborious.

The accompanying Instructor's Manual/Test Bank contains over 1,000 test items, all objectively scored, to assist in the creation of tests.

The *Student Guide* contains a summary of topics, study hints, a list of key words, and additional exercises. In order to complete the development of a general topic, items 3 through 6 are repeated throughout each chapter. *The* Student Guide *also contains a set of programs for use on either the Macintosh or Windows computer environment that provides the motion pictures of statistical procedures (simulations) that I couldn't use in the textbook, along with additional instructional tips.*

ACKNOWLEDGMENTS

Many different people have been involved in the development of the third edition and so deserve acknowledgment. I am deeply indebted to Patti Shavelson for her patient, careful proofreading of multiple drafts of the text's page proofs, and to Dr. Maria A. Ruiz-Primo for her careful review of each chapter, for her criticism and encouragement, for her patience, and for her relentless insistence on attention to details. I would also like to express my appreciation to the hundreds of students who, over a period of years, have participated in the pilot work on all three editions of the text at UCLA, UCSB, and other universities throughout the country. Instructors (especially Dr. Ali Reza Kiamanesh) and students have pointed out errors in the text and in the problems. They also helped work on rewording parts that were unclear. As a consequence, these errors and ambiguities have been eliminated from the text to the extent that is humanly possible.

I would also like to thank the staff at Allyn and Bacon—Laura Pearson, Marnie Greenhut, Jennifer Normandin, and Marjorie Payne, and the staff at Electronic Publishing Services Inc., especially Ruth Randall and Patty Andrews.

I am grateful to the Literary Executor of the late Sir Ronald A. Fisher, F.R.S., to Dr. Frank Yates, F.R.S., and to The Longman Group Ltd., London for permission to reprint Tables XXXIII, III, VII from their book *Statistical Tables for Biological, Agricultural and Medical Research* (6th edition, 1974). I am also grateful to the Literary Executor of the late Sir Ronald A. Fisher, F.R.S., and The Longman Group Ltd., London for permission to reprint Table V.B. from their book *Statistical Methods for Research Workers* (previously published by Oliver and Boyd, Ltd., Edinburgh, 1932).

The following reviewers were generous in their consideration of my manuscript: Rosemary Rosser, University of Arizona; Dennis Cogan, Texas Technical University; William Frankenberger, University of Wisconsin/Eau Claire; Lewis Aiken, Pepperdine University; Thomas E. Billimek, San Antonio College; Karen Swoope, Washington State University; Foster Brown, SUNY Oneonta; Dennis Sweeney, California University of Pennsylvania; Marie Fox, Metropolitan State College of Denver; Ralph DeAyala, University of Maryland; John Pittenger, University of Arkansas/Little Rock; Suzanne Dancer, University of Wisconsin/Milwaukee; Stephen Olejnik, University of Georgia; and William M. Stallings, Georgia State University. I want to thank them for their helpful suggestions.

Statistical Reasoning for the Behavioral Sciences

I RESEARCH AND THE ROLE OF STATISTICS

F rom the behavioral scientist's perspective, statistics are useful tools for unraveling the mysteries of data collected in research. In particular, statistics allow the researcher to summarize data and to distinguish between chance and systematic effects. Although the behavioral scientist's main interest lies in the substance of the study—a test of a theory, for example—there is an interplay between the substance, the design of the study, and the analysis of the data. Thus it seems appropriate to begin a text on statistics with issues of substance and design as well as statistics.

Substantive issues are the questions behavioral scientists are studying. For example, psychologists are examining the utility of concepts such as schema, thinking, and problem solving in explaining behavior. Sociologists are examining the effects of institutional demands on the role of women in society. And educators are examining the effects of information about students' backgrounds on teachers' expectations about student performance.

The design issue is one of matching the research design to the substantive question without changing the question or distorting it. The behavioral scientist must have a firm grasp on a variety of research designs, along with the logical and statistical rationale underlying them, and build the design most appropriate for the question being studied.

Once they have a research question, an appropriate design, the study run, and the data in hand, behavioral scientists rely heavily on statistical tools in seeking answers to their questions. These tools help to describe what happened in the study and to generalize the results from the observations made on the participants in the study to the larger group of people of interest to the researcher.

For most students in the behavioral sciences, the study of statistics becomes relevant when, and perhaps only when(!), something about a substantive area is understood and something about the design of research is understood. It is at this point that you are ready for answers to the question, "How do I make sense out of all the information I have collected?"

The purposes of Chapter 1, ambitiously stated, are to get you interested in doing behavioral research; to give you a brief review of topics on the design of research (with additional material included in the *Student Guide*) so that you become comfortable with research designs, and to provide you with an example of research that will arouse your interest in statistical methods. More humbly, the goal is to get you to the point where you can see the relevance of statistics to research in the behavioral sciences.

To this end, Chapter 1 presents material on designing and conducting research, along with a research example to whet your appetite for behavioral research. Design is discussed because the use of statistics in analyzing and interpreting data—the major topic of this textbook—depends on the type of research design used. The remaining chapters provide the statistical tools applicable to a wide variety of designs, always in the context of a concrete research example.

Research Design in the Behavioral Sciences

Research has been described as "doing one's damnedest to find answers to perplexing questions." This is not the usual textbook definition, but it is the definition used by most of us who are intimately involved in doing research. A more sober definition is that **research** is a systematic approach to finding answers to questions. This definition is fairly wide open, as it should be.

ROLE OF RESEARCH

There are many ways to systematically attempt to find answers to questions about human behavior. We might, for example, be interested in human emotion and whether different emotions (euphoria, anger) are due solely to different physiological states of a person, or due to a general physiological arousal plus a cognitive component for interpreting the arousal. Or we might investigate the influence of constructivist and behaviorist views of learning on the way children are taught, by systematically examining historical events. For example, we might compare teaching during the progressive education movement in the 1940s, the mathematics and science education reform after the launching of **Sputnik** in the late 1950s, and the constructivist movement following the publication of *A Nation at Risk* in the 1980s. Or we might proceed formally and logically by setting forth assumptions about, for example, the nature of memory and then work deductively from them to arrive at answers to our questions about how people learn. Or we might examine ordinary language systematically to find out how people view the world.

However, these examples are probably not the kinds of research that commonly come to mind for most of us. For some, "research" conjures up an image of a laboratory (Frankenstein's?) with microscopes, glass tubes, flasks, electrical discharges jumping from one pole to another, and smoke rising up from an "experiment." Others think of rats running mazes, monkeys communicating with experimenters, or college sophomores memorizing nonsense syllables. Still others think of experiments in natural settings, such as health maintenance organizations, or surveys such as the Kinsey report. When most of us think of research, then, we think of one possible type of research, exemplified by the **scientific method.** With this method, problems are formulated, hypotheses (alternative problem solutions) are identified using theory and/or direct observation, data are collected through observation and experimentation, and inferences are drawn about which hypothesis is most credible. That is, alternatives are tested by trying out each of them and seeing which ones work as expected.

This book focuses on the scientific method, only one of several approaches to research. It provides basic tools for helping to decide which of the possible alternative answers are best (in some sense) on the basis of empirical tests.

In some ways, researchers are like kids, though most of them won't admit it. Research questions are, for researchers, what puzzles or games are for kids. Researchers attempt to solve puzzles or win games by designing studies and finding answers. And most researchers have as much fun doing research as kids do playing games. This is not to say that the questions addressed by researchers are no more than games and that the answers provided are no more important than winning at Monopoly. Questions of the effects of schools on students' learning and self-concepts are indeed serious, and the answers must be as accurate as possible. Likewise, questions about the nature of human memory and information processing are important, and researchers are and should be held responsible for their answers. Research demands care, wisdom, accuracy, and doing one's damnedest, but it does not preclude having fun, too.

The purpose of this book is to let you in on the importance, excitement, and fun of research by providing some of the tools needed to begin to answer research questions. These tools involve the analysis and interpretation of data collected in behavioral research in areas such as psychology, sociology, and education.

PURPOSE OF EMPIRICAL RESEARCH

The purpose of empirical research in the behavioral sciences, in broad terms, is to provide answers to questions about behavior by using the scientific method. Throughout this book, the focus will be on examples that provide answers to questions about **human** behavior. Nevertheless, the methods presented apply also to studying the behavior of nonhumans.

Perhaps the best way to give you a flavor of this research is to describe it. A central question in psychology concerns whether or not concepts of "mind" such as memory, thinking, and problem solving are needed to explain behavior. Hull argued that such concepts were unnecessary in a theory of behavior, and conducted experiments to show that habit, strength, drive, and incentive could account for behavior. Tolman took the opposite position and argued that concepts involving the mind, such as "cognitive maps," were necessary to explain the behavior of rats running a maze. Watson disagreed. The concept of mind was unnecessary in explaining behavior; behavior could be controlled by controlling the environment in which a person was placed. Skinner followed the same line of reasoning and conducted experiments showing how behavior could be controlled by manipulating schedules of reinforcement. But as early as the 1950s, during the heyday of behaviorism, Simon and Newell's research was breaking new ground. They were modeling human information processing with computers. To model information processing, the computer models had to include concepts such as memory and problem solving. Today, psychologists and cognitive scientists use concepts such as mind in associationist computer models of how students learn school subjects. Moreover, cognitive scientists, educational psychologists, and sociologists, following the work of Vygotsky, are conducting research that shows how learning and the construction of knowledge is socially mediated. Presently, the research question is no longer mind versus no mind. Now that question has been replaced by the more sensible question of how environment and human cognitive, social, and emotional characteristics, taken together, influence observable behavior.

There is no limit to the research examples that could be given. You should now have some idea of the kinds of questions behavioral researchers attempt to answer. Moreover, you should see that the research and knowledge that the questions generate evolve as new theories challenge earlier ones, building on and sometimes changing them.

Regardless of the questions posed by researchers, the purposes of behavioral research, in more specific terms, are to **describe, predict,** and **control behavior.** Some questions call for **description of behavior.** For example, a politician might be interested in the preferences of voters on the issue of national versus private health care. A researcher might provide an answer to this question by describing past voting trends or by conducting a survey of voter preferences.

Some questions call for the **prediction of behavior.** For example, college administrators would like to predict the behavior (e.g., achievement) of students in order to decide whether or not to admit them to college. College entrance examination scores are collected for the purposes of predicting students' performance in college and, in this way, improving the accuracy of admissions decisions. With this information, the administrator admits those students who are predicted to be successful in that college.

Finally, some questions call for **control of behavior.** That is, they ask about a cause-and-effect relationship. For example, does the way a list of words is organized affect the number of words remembered? In order to answer this question, a researcher might randomly assign college sophomores in introductory psychology to an experimental group that studies a list of words arranged hierarchically or to a control group that studies the words arranged in a scrambled order. After some period of time, both groups of "subjects" would be asked to recall the words. The average number of words recalled by the two groups might then be compared to answer the question.

Process of Empirical Research

Research is a **process** of finding answers to questions. Whenever a process is described in writing (as opposed to **doing it**), it becomes static and idealized. In an attempt to overcome this problem, the interplay between the steps will be described, and a concrete example—

research into the effects of organization on remembering a list of words—will be used. However, it should be noted at the outset that the following is a deliberately simplified outline of what happens. In reality, the process is not so neat, and the researcher must have all the steps in mind at once and plan ahead.

The first step is to ask a question. This question will **identify a problem** and, with some hard thinking, the problem will become adequately defined so that it can be researched. In one of the preceding examples, we asked, "What is the effect of organization on remembering a list of words?" This question identified a problem. The selection of a list of words that could be arranged either hierarchically or in a scrambled fashion helped define the problem more precisely, as did the decision to have subjects recall the words once a period of time had elapsed after studying them.

The next step is to **review theories and past research,** which might suggest hypotheses about the solutions to the problem, that is, possible answers. For the example study, both past research and theory (e.g., Gagnè, Yekovich, & Yekovich, 1993; Thorndyke, 1977) suggested that words arranged in a logically ordered hierarchy would be remembered better than words not organized in any way. This work, then, led to the **hypothesis** that subjects studying a hierarchically organized list of words would recall more of the words than subjects studying an unorganized (scrambled) list of words. In general terms, a hypothesis is a statement about what you expect to actually happen in the experiment.

However, the actual process is not quite so neat. There is an interplay between these two steps. Reading some theory or research may suggest a problem to be researched. Or having identified a general problem, reviewing theories and past research may help define the problem more precisely. Reviewing past theory and research may lead to questions that challenge a presumed theory and result in research that attempts to disconfirm the existing theory and provide a basis for an alternative theory.

With a problem and one or more hypotheses in hand, the next step is to **design a study** in order to collect data (information) bearing on your hypotheses. In the design of the study, decisions are made about the "subjects" (people, students, groups of people, etc.) to be observed, the factors that are expected to influence the behavior of the subjects, the ways in which these factors will be controlled, and the ways in which the behavior of the subjects will be observed systematically (measured).

In the example study, subjects were to be college sophomores enrolled in introductory psychology. One factor was to be manipulated: the organization of the list of words (hierarchical or scrambled). Extraneous factors were to be controlled by flipping a coin to (randomly) assign subjects to either the organized list of words or the scrambled list. The behavior of the subjects was to be observed (measured) by counting the number of words correctly recalled from the list.

Of course, the way in which the research question is defined will influence the design of the research, as will prior research and theory. Again, there is an interplay between the steps in the research process.

Next, the design is implemented by **conducting** the study. In conducting the study, subjects' behavior is measured under each of the conditions of the study. In the example study, college sophomores were randomly assigned to the scrambled list of words or to the organized list. They read and studied a list either organized hierarchically or in scrambled order.

Then they were asked to recall these words, say, ten minutes after studying them. This step in conducting the study produces the data of interest.

The next step is to **summarize** the data in such a way that the summary sheds light on the question that started this whole process in motion. This is where statistics comes in. Statistics provide quantitative methods for summarizing and describing data. In the example study, the data—the number of words recalled correctly by each subject in the hierarchical- and scrambled-list groups—might be summarized by a statistic called an average, specifically the **mean.** The mean number of words recalled correctly by subjects in the organized-list group and the scrambled-list group might be used to summarize and describe the behavior of all the subjects in each group.

Finally, the data are **interpreted** in a manner relating to the original research question. Here, too, statistics come in handy. At this step, statistics are used to help decide whether the differences observed in the data may have been due to chance or to the experimental manipulation of list organization. In the example study, statistics could be used to determine whether the difference in mean number of words recalled between the hierarchical- and scrambled-list groups was due to chance or to the organization of the word lists.

To summarize, there are six general steps in conducting research:

1. Identify and define a research problem.
2. Formulate hypotheses on the basis of theory, research, or both.
3. Design the research.
4. Conduct the research.
5. Analyze the data.
6. Interpret the data as they bear on the research question.

ROLE OF STATISTICS IN BEHAVIORAL RESEARCH

The concepts and tools of statistics are involved either implicitly or explicitly throughout most of the research process. Statistics are involved in decisions about selecting subjects for a study, assigning subjects to different groups (if the design calls for this), describing the data collected in the study, and generalizing from the findings of the study. For example, in the study of the effect of organization on remembering a list of words, a decision was made to select college sophomores and **randomly** assign them (by flipping a coin) to either an organized or scrambled list of words. Moreover, once the study was conducted, the two groups of subjects were described and compared with regard to the average (mean) number of words recalled. Finally, attention was paid to the particular subjects in the study because, on the basis of their behavior, the researcher intended to draw inferences about the effect of the organization of the words on other people like them.

Statistics, then, play a number of major, interrelated roles in behavioral research. They set forth guidelines for summarizing and describing data. They also provide methods for drawing inferences from groups of subjects to larger groups of people. And they set forth guidelines for selecting subjects for a study, assigning them to groups (if called for in the design), and collecting data.

Descriptive Statistics

Descriptive statistics provide a picture of what happened in the study. More formally, the term **descriptive statistics** refers to a set of concepts and methods used in organizing, summarizing, tabulating, depicting, and describing collections of data. The data can be test scores, reaction times, or ratings; they can be ranks; or they can be indications of group membership (e.g., political party affiliation, personality type, sex). The goal of descriptive statistics is to provide a representation of the data that describes, in tabular, graphical, or numerical form, the results of research. For example, if one summarizes the number of words recalled by subjects in the scrambled-word group and in the organized-word group with a mean score for each group, one possible description of the performance of the subjects within each group is achieved. In order to ascertain the effects of organizing a list of words on recall, one can compute the means of the two groups. If organization has a facilitating effect on memory, the mean number of words recalled by subjects in the organized-word group should be greater than that in the scrambled-word group. Without descriptive statistics, data in the researcher's office would be overwhelming and uninterpretable. (Section II presents the concepts and tools for describing collections of data.)

Inferential Statistics

The term **inferential statistics** refers to a set of methods used to draw inferences about a large group of people from data available on only a representative subset of the group. In statistics, the large group of people is called a **population.** The subset of the large group is called a **sample.** The term inferential statistics refers to a set of methods used to draw inferences about a population from data available on a sample from the population.

Since the purpose of behavioral research is to provide answers to questions about human behavior, the researcher is interested in answers that may be true for populations, not just for samples of, say, 30 people. However, in behavioral research, it is usually impossible to observe an entire population (the population may be indefinitely large) or impractical to do so (the cost may be too great). Thus, the researcher must work inductively and infer the characteristics of populations from data gathered on samples from these populations. Thus, a sample of college sophomores was observed in the word-list study, not because the researcher was interested in those particular students, but because by observing their performance, she could infer something about the effects of organization on people's memories who were not observed (i.e., the population).

The validity of the inference from sample to population rests on the degree to which the subjects in the sample are representative of the people in the population. If you were interested in whether the voters in the United States wanted the federal government to set controls on the price of gasoline, common sense would tell you not to limit your sample to the top executives of the major oil companies. Clearly, these executives are not representative of voters in the United States. The representativeness of a sample is an important question, and it is addressed in statistics, as we shall see, by drawing a sample such that every person in the population has an equal chance of being included in the sample.

Random Sampling

When one makes inferences from the behavior of subjects in a sample to the behavior of people in the population, logic demands that the sample be representative of the population. Here the concept of random sampling plays an important role. **Random sampling** is the process of selecting subjects from a population such that each person in the population has an equal chance of being selected. Moreover, random sampling implies that the appearance of one subject in the sample is in no way affected by the appearance of any other subject. That is, random sampling implies that the selection of subjects in the sample is independent.

The concept of random sampling is theoretical. It can be approximated in reality by rolling dice, flipping coins, spinning roulette wheels, or drawing names from a hat. However, these methods are time-consuming and limited in their practical application to fairly small samples. For this reason, tables of random numbers have been generated that approximate randomness quite closely. They are tables of digits, 0 through 9, that are generated by a mechanical process with the criterion that each of the digits (0–9) has an equal chance of occurring at any one point in the table.

As an example of how the table of random numbers can be used to draw a random sample, consider the selection of subjects for the study of the effects of word-list organization on memory. Suppose 40 subjects were to be selected randomly from a sophomore class of 900 students. To each student in the class, a different three-digit number (ranging between 001 and 900) would be assigned. Next, a table of random numbers such as Table A at the end of this book would be used to select the 40 subjects. From that table, you would select 40 numbers (from 001 to 900) that would tell you which 40 subjects to include in your sample.

The process works as follows: With Table A open to, say, the first page, put your finger on the page with your eyes closed. Suppose you pointed to the number 48. This number tells you where to start collecting random numbers from the table. The 4 denotes the particular row on which you will start looking for random numbers and the 8 denotes the particular column—start at row 4 and column 8 of the table. Note that even though the numbers in the table are presented in pairs for ease of viewing (e.g., row 4 begins 40 07 20 . . .), treat each number as a separate column (in row 4, column 1 contains a 4, column 2 contains a 0, column 3 contains a 0, and so on). Moving along row 4, then, count over eight digits to the number in that column: 8. Beginning with that number, read across row 4 grouping the numbers in sets of three: 857, 209, 865, 371, ... Include in the sample those subjects with the identification numbers 857, 209, 865, 371, and so on, until 40 subjects are selected. Suppose you come across the number 901. Since there are only 900 students in the sophomore class, no one has this identification number, so it is disregarded. Now suppose that the number 857 (or any other number of a person who has already been included in the sample) comes up again. That number is also ignored.

The steps in using a table of random numbers (e.g., Table A) to draw a sample are summarized in Procedure 1-1. Throughout this text, "Procedures" are used to summarize step-by-step operations involved in applying concepts and tools in statistics. They may be used for quick references, as a check of your understanding of the ideas and tools, or both.

PROCEDURE 1-1 Steps in drawing a random sample of subjects

Operation	Example

1. Assign an identification number to each subject.

Name	ID Number
Sally	01
Tom	02
⋮	⋮
Linda	79
Debbie	80

2. Turn to the table of random numbers (Table A), place your finger anywhere on any page of the table, and locate any two-digit number.

Suppose you placed your finger on 33.

3. Find the number on the same page in the row represented by the first digit of the number located in step 2 and the column represented by the second digit of this number.

33—third row, third column. Find the number located in the third row and the third column on the same page.

4. Beginning with the place in the table found in step 3, group the digits into sets corresponding to the largest identification number.

Since 80 is the largest identification number, two columns are needed to select numbers from the table.

5. Begin reading across the row until you locate a number falling in the range of numbers assigned in step 1. (Ignore all numbers that are outside this range.)

  a. If a number has not been selected already, include the subject corresponding to that number in the sample.

  b. If a number has already been selected, ignore it and continue.

Suppose that six subjects are to be included in the sample. Beginning at the third row, third column, we identify the following two digit numbers:

93 (ignore)	96 (ignore)
07	83 (ignore)
46	66
85 (ignore)	69
87 (ignore)	90 (ignore)
87 (ignore)	47
55	

6. Continue the procedure in step 5 until the desired sample size has been reached.

The random sample will consist of individuals with the assigned identification numbers of 07, 46, 55, 66, 69, 47.

Example Problem 1.1

Out of a group of 50 students, draw a random sample of 8 students. (In choosing a starting point, suppose you turned to the first page of Table A and placed your finger on the number 45. Furthermore, suppose you decide to read across the appropriate row.) Answers to Example Problems are found at the end of the Chapter. Additional exercises are also provided at the end of this chapter. For a summary and additional practice on skills, see the *Student Guide*.

Relationship Between Descriptive and Inferential Statistics

Descriptions of both samples and populations are taken from descriptive statistics. When an index such as the mean is used to describe a characteristic of the sample, it is called a **statistic.** When an index such as the mean is used to describe a characteristic of a population, it is called a **parameter.** Thus, a parameter describes a population whereas a statistic describes a sample.

In behavioral research, we are interested in learning something about the population by inferring from the sample. After all, if we could describe the population thoroughly, there would be no need to draw the sample in the first place. When a statistic, computed from a sample, is used to estimate the population parameter, it is called an **estimator.** For example, the mean of a sample may be used to estimate the mean of the population. By using statistics as estimators of parameters, behavioral scientists draw inferences from sample data to the population.

Unfortunately, the value of a sample estimate of a parameter need not exactly equal the value of the parameter. This statement should come as no surprise, since the sample estimate is based only on a subset of subjects in the population. Likewise, from one sample to the next, the values of the estimators probably will vary. So errors may arise in estimating a parameter with a statistic. One very desirable characteristic of a sample statistic used as an estimator is called **unbiasedness.** An estimator is **unbiased** if for an indefinitely large number of random samples from a population, the mean of the sample estimates equals the value of the population parameter being estimated.

In sum, descriptive and inferential statistics are linked by the use of the sample statistic as an estimate of a population parameter. Estimators, then, are the cornerstone of the inferences made by behavioral scientists from sample to population. Although these terms may seem like a lot of unnecessary terminology, the terminology is essential to your ability to understand and apply concepts in statistics. Terms are also essential to your ability to communicate with others doing research. Finally, these terms provide an economical way for me to communicate with you. Without these terms and concepts, the writing would be (even more?) convoluted with long descriptions and distinctions. As you progress through this book, the terms will become familiar parts of your vocabulary, so don't worry about memorizing them now. (Just remember the location of this part of the chapter so you can refer to it when needed.)

SOME BASIC ELEMENTS IN DESIGNING RESEARCH

Two major elements in the design of research are the researcher's hypotheses and what is varied and what is measured (the variables) to test them. The hypotheses follow from theory and past research, and motivate the design of the study. The variables represent the embodiment of the hypotheses in terms of what the researcher can manipulate and observe. These two elements are considered in what follows.

Variables and Hypotheses

A **variable** is an attribute (characteristic, property) of an object or person that can change from one object to another or from person to person. Some examples of variables referring to objects are the **length** of a car, since cars differ in length; the **pronounceability** of a nonsense syllable, since some are easy to pronounce (e.g., "zeb") and others are not (e.g., "zxv"); the **organizational structure** of an institution, since some have rigid hierarchies and some do not; and the **degree of self-pacing** in instruction, since some teachers control the pace and others let students control the pace. Some examples of variables referring to persons are **height, weight, sex,** and **career aspirations.** Clearly, people differ on each of these variables. Furthermore, from these examples, it is probably obvious that a person or object may be described by any number of variables.

A **constant** is an attribute of an object or person that does not vary from object to object or from person to person. Constants are much more common in the physical sciences than in the behavioral sciences. In Einstein's famous equation for energy, $E = mc^2$, c is a constant (the speed of light). Regardless of the mass of an object (m), or the energy (E), the value of c does not change. Often in the behavioral sciences, the researcher "holds a variable constant." For example, because girls and boys differ in the rate at which they learn to read, often researchers will observe only girls or only boys in an experiment. The variable, sex, is held constant.

In an attempt to solve theoretical, social, and practical problems through empirical research, an expected solution to the problem is usually set forth for testing. It is based on theory, prior research, or both. This expectation is often called a hypothesis. A **hypothesis** is a tentative statement about the expected relationship between two or more variables. The hypothesis is tentative because its accuracy will be tested empirically. It can be quite formal and backed by a set of established facts; it can be a rough prediction backed by some tentative theory or set of studies, or it can be a best guess in the absence of adequate information. A hypothesis that motivated the study of the effects of organization on the recall of a list of words was: "There is a relationship between the **organization** of a list of words (organized versus scrambled) and the **number of words recalled.**"

When people or objects can be ordered on a variable (e.g., lowest to highest score on a driver's test), hypotheses may predict one of three relationships:

1. There is a positive relationship between variable X and variable Y: As X increases, Y also increases.
2. There is a negative relationship between variable X and variable Y: As X increases, Y decreases.
3. There is no relationship between variable X and variable Y: As X increases, Y varies unsystematically.[1]

For example, a hypothesis involving a positive relationship between two variables is: "There is a positive relationship between academic self-concept and college grades" (e.g., grade

---

[1]This hypothesis should not be confused with the "null hypothesis." The distinction will be discussed in Chapter 8.

point average: GPA). That is, as self-concept increases, so does GPA. A hypothesis involving a negative relationship is: "There is a negative relationship between scores on a measure of anxiety and scores on the solutions to complex problems." That is, as scores on anxiety increase, scores on problem solving decrease.

The process of hypothesis formulation can be illustrated with an example from research on teachers' expectations (see Chapter 2): "What is the effect of teachers' expectations on students' intellectual performance?" The symbolic interactionist theory of Cooley (1902) and Mead (1934) states, roughly, that the expectations of "significant others" affect a person's behavior. Since teachers represent significant others to students, the theory predicts that teachers' expectation will influence students' behavior. In addition, past research on experimenter bias in behavioral research (Rosenthal, 1966) supports this theory in that experimenters' expectations influenced the outcome of their experiments. So both theory and prior research suggest, by inference, a relationship between teachers' expectations and students' performance. Thus we have the following hypothesis:

> There is a relationship between a teacher's expectation concerning a student's intellectual performance and the student's actual intellectual performance.

Once the hypothesis has been developed deductively from a theory, inductively from a set of research studies, or both, several guidelines can be used to sharpen the focus of the hypothesis. They can be stated, briefly, as follows:

1. A hypothesis should predict a particular relationship between two or more variables.
2. A hypothesis should be stated clearly and unambiguously, usually in the form of a declarative sentence.
3. A hypothesis should be testable. That is, the hypothesis should be stated so that data can be collected to test it.

Example Problem 1.2

Which of the following represent adequate hypotheses? For those that do not, tell why.
  a. There is a positive relationship between a measure of socioeconomic status and scores on the Scholastic Aptitude Test.
  b. Positive attitudes about others are important in life.
  c. The number of hours spent in counseling is positively related to a clients' ratings of self-efficacy.
  d. Mental ability may be related to personality.
  e. Chess experts can recall the position of chess pieces during a game more accurately than chess novices.

Classification of Variables for Designing Research

Behavioral research focuses on the relationship between variables. Studies are designed, in part, for the purpose of observing the effects of certain variables (e.g., quality versus quantity of arguments in persuasive communication) on other variables (e.g., attitude change), or of describing the relationship between certain variables (e.g., years of experience) with some other variables (e.g., level of job performance rating). As a detailed example, consider the study of the effects of organization on subjects' recall of a list of words. The organization of a list of words was systematically varied (viz., hierarchical versus scrambled) in order to observe the effects of organization on the number of words recalled correctly from the list. Both **organization** and **number of words recalled** are variables. The former variable simply names categories (i.e., is "qualitative"); the latter indicates order with equal intervals (i.e., is "quantitative"). Furthermore, we are interested in the effect of the first variable, the "stimulus" of organization, on the second variable, the "response" (number of words recalled). Put another way, we are interested in the effect of the "independent variable" (stimulus) on the "dependent variable" (response). The relationship between the independent and dependent variables is assumed to arise due to an underlying, unobservable variable called an "intervening variable." In this case, the intervening variable posits a particular memory schema for words. Finally, researchers sometimes hold constant other variables not of direct interest. For example, suppose only male subjects' recall was studied. Hence, gender was held constant, and so it becomes a "control variable."

In any research study, an independent and dependent variable must be present. The researcher may not explicitly mention the intervening variable, and, consequently, it may go unnamed. But it's there. Finally, the researcher may or may not control other variables.

Independent Variables. An **independent variable** is a variable that is manipulated, measured, or selected by the researcher in order to observe its relation to the subject's "response" (i.e., dependent variable). An independent variable, then, is a variable that is employed to influence some other variable; it is an antecedent condition to observed behavior. In the word-list recall study, the independent variable—organization (hierarchical versus scrambled)—was systematically manipulated by the experimenter to see its effect on word recall. Specifically, a set of conceptually related words was organized hierarchically by the researcher and also was scrambled into a random order. An independent variable can also be measured and its relation to some other variable determined. For example, a measure of anxiety might be obtained on a sample of white-collar workers and the relation of anxiety to some other variable, such as job satisfaction, could be determined. In this case, the researcher measures the independent variable—anxiety—and relates it to a dependent variable, job satisfaction. Finally, an independent variable can be selected by the researcher. For example, classrooms might be selected for study because their organizational structures differ in some important way. This selection would permit the researcher to examine the relationship between classroom organization and, say, the frequency of behavior problems.

To summarize, an independent variable is employed because it is expected to influence another variable (some behavior). Independent variables can be manipulated (e.g., variation in list organization), measured (e.g., variation in level of anxiety), or observed (e.g., variation in classroom organization).

Control Variables. A **control variable** is any variable that is held constant in a research study by observing only one of its instances or levels. Control variables are used in research to neutralize the effects of variables that are not of central concern to the study, but that may affect the observed behavior. For example, in a study of reading, sex might be controlled, since it is known to be related to reading performance. In this case, only women (one instance or level of the sex variable) may be used.

Dependent Variables.   So far this term has been defined informally in these hypothetical experiments as the "response" to the independent variable (stimulus). More formally, a **dependent variable** may be defined as that variable that is observed and measured in response to an independent variable. This variable is expected to increase, decrease, or vary in some systematic fashion as the levels of the independent variable change. In the hypothetical study of word organization, the dependent variable was the number of words correctly recalled from the list. The words correctly recalled were observed and could be counted (i.e., measured).

Intervening Variables.   An **intervening variable** is a hypothetical variable that is not observed directly in research but, rather, is inferred from the relationship between the independent variable and the dependent variable. Its importance lies in its ability to explain the relationship between the independent and dependent variables under the conditions of the study **and** under conditions somewhat different from those set up in the study. In all types of behavioral research, intervening variables represent the foundation of theory. In psychological research, for example, a theory might posit that words are arranged in associative networks that are hierarchical. Although an associative network in a person's memory cannot be observed and measured directly (the network is a hypothetical variable posited by a theory), experiments can be conducted to determine whether people respond (dependent variable) under different conditions of learning words (independent variable) in ways predicted by the existence of an associative network. One of many possible experiments testing this intervening variable is the hypothetical experiment on the effects of the organization of a list of words on subjects' ability to recall words from that list correctly. Intervening variables are as numerous as there are theories. Some intervening variables that are familiar to most of us are learning, cognitive structure, achievement, group cohesiveness, intelligence, stages of moral development, and attitudes.

Example Problem 1.3 ▬▬▬▬▬▬▬▬▬▬▬▬▬▬▬▬▬▬▬▬▬▬▬▬▬▬▬▬▬▬▬▬▬▬▬▬▬▬▬

Identify the following variables (if present) in the following studies.
  a. Independent variable
  b. Control variable
  c. Intervening variable
  d. Dependent variable

Study 1. In a study of the effects of different types of legal arguments on jurors' perceptions of a defendant's guilt or innocence, subjects were randomly assigned to hear an argument that related to their daily experiences or to an argument of a more abstract and idealistic nature. Since the researcher felt that subjects with different amounts of education might react differently to these arguments, subjects were classified by education level and asked to rate the guilt or innocence of the defendant on a 12-point scale.

Study 2. A researcher studying child development hypothesized that breast feeding leads to a close mother-child relationship by increasing the warmth and intimacy between mother and child. In a test of this hypothesis, 3-year-old children who had been breast fed for 0, 1–3, or more than 3 months were identified. Then these children and their mothers were observed in an unstructured play situation for 2 hours. Observers rated the closeness of the relationship between mother and child.

Quantification of Variables

Numbers can be used to represent the levels of an attribute of an object or person. For example, the length of a car can be expressed in inches. The degree of organization of a word list can be expressed numerically: Most simply, a 1 might be assigned to the scrambled version and a 2 assigned to the hierarchically organized version. Likewise, the level of anxiety while taking a test might be expressed by the student's heart rate—the number of beats per minute—or by a score on an anxiety scale. And the sex of a person might be expressed numerically by assigning a 1 to males and a 2 to females.

From these examples, it is clear that the rules used to assign numbers to variables such as length or anxiety differ from those used to assign numbers to word-list organization or sex. For length and anxiety, the numbers represent an underlying continuum from zero length upward or from slow to fast heart rate. For list organization and sex, the numbers merely "stand for," "name," or "label categories of" differences on these variables.

Measurement is defined as the assignment of numbers to attributes of persons, objects, or events, according to logically acceptable rules. Different kinds of variables (attributes) require different rules for assigning numbers in order to express differences on those variables. There are some well-known rules for assigning numbers to variables. A particular set of rules defines a **scale of measurement,** and different sets of rules define different scales of measurement. Four kinds of scales of measurement are commonly used in characterizing variables in the behavioral sciences: nominal scale, ordinal scale, interval scale, and ratio scale. Each is described in what follows.

Nominal Scales.   A **nominal scale** uses numbers to stand for names or categories. These categories represent the way persons or objects differ. **Nominal measurement,** then, is a process of grouping persons or objects into classes and treating the members of each class as if they were the same with respect to some attribute. The particular number assigned to a class is completely arbitrary (see Figure 1-1). For example, numbers are used to identify different players on a football team, differences in the sex of subjects in an experiment (e.g., 1 = male; 2 = female), makes of cars (1 = Chevrolet, 2 = Plymouth, 3 = Ford), marital status (1 = married, 2 = widowed 3 = divorced, 4 = separated, 5 = never married), or treatment condition (1 = control, 2 = experimental). Since the numbers are no more than labels, arithmetic operations such as addition and subtraction with them imply nothing about the persons or objects themselves because the numbers were not assigned to reflect the order or size of the persons or objects.

Ordinal Scales.   An **ordinal measurement** is possible when degrees of an attribute can be identified. An **ordinal scale** uses numbers to **order** persons or objects on some continuum of, say, low to high. Thus, a teacher might order his students on an achievement continuum. The student who is highest in achievement would be assigned a 1, and the student who is lowest in a class of 30 would be assigned a rank of 30. Cars might be ordered as to their length, so that the shortest car was assigned the number 1, and the longest car was assigned the highest rank (see Figure 1-1).

An ordinal scale, then, provides information about the rank order of persons or objects on a variable. Its limitations can be shown by an example. Suppose three cars were ordered according to length: Honda Civic (1), Ford Escort (2), and Cadillac El Dorado (3). Even

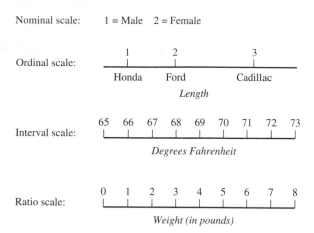

Nominal scale: 1 = Male   2 = Female

Ordinal scale:
1   2   3
Honda   Ford   Cadillac
Length

Interval scale: 65   66   67   68   69   70   71   72   73
Degrees Fahrenheit

Ratio scale: 0   1   2   3   4   5   6   7   8
Weight (in pounds)

FIGURE 1-1

Visual representation of the four kinds of measurement scales

though the numbers assigned to these three cars are equally spaced—1, 2, and 3—we cannot say that the Cadillac is as much longer than the Escort as the Escort is longer than the Honda. The rank ordering may indicate length intervals that are erratic or unequal. Although numbers standing for ranks can be manipulated arithmetically, the result of these operations cannot necessarily be interpreted as representing the amounts of some attribute that the persons or objects corresponding to the numbers possess. For example, the difference between the rank scores for a Cadillac and a Honda is $3 - 1 = 2$. Does this result mean that a Cadillac is twice as long as a Honda? No, it does not, because the result of the arithmetic does not reflect anything quantitative about the length of the two cars. In performing arithmetic operations on data measured on an ordinal scale, you should always ask, "Does the result have meaning with respect to the attribute measured?" (see Jones, 1971; Vellman & Wilkinson, 1993.)

Interval Scales. **Interval measurement** is possible when the differing levels of an attribute can be identified, and **equal distances** between the levels of the attribute can also be identified. For interval measurement, a unit of measurement such as degrees of temperature has been defined. An **interval scale** assigns a number to persons or objects such that the number of units of measurement is equal to the amount of the attribute possessed. An interval scale, then, is one for which the intervals between units (numbers) are equal, but the zero point is arbitrary (see Figure 1-1). For example, if temperature is measured in degrees Fahrenheit, the interval between 32°F and 33°F is equal to the interval between 85°F and 86°F; however, 0°F does not imply the absence of temperature. Indeed, 0°F is not the same as 0° Celsius.

There are many examples of interval scales for physical attributes of objects (e.g., temperature). There are fewer examples of interval measurements of attributes of people. However, many measures in the behavioral sciences involve paper-and-pencil instruments such as a test of spatial ability or a questionnaire on political attitude. The scores on these instruments are the numbers of correct responses (spatial ability) or the average of a series of ratings on, say, a 5-point scale (political attitude). While we are not always sure that these measurements have equal intervals, we proceed **as if** they did.

Interval measurements entail assigning numbers to levels of an attribute (e.g., temperature) such that equal differences in the numbers correspond to equal differences in the amount of an attribute measured. Thus, addition and subtraction of those numbers produce a result that is interpretable with respect to the actual amounts of the attribute. For example, yesterday the maximum temperature was 82°F, and the minimum temperature 60°F. The difference between the maximum and minimum temperatures, 22°F, is meaningful.

Ratio Scales.   It is also possible to form a scale such that the numbers represent equal intervals **and** there is a meaningful zero point on it. A **ratio scale** is an interval scale with a zero point that indicates the absence of the attribute measured. Some familiar examples of ratio scales are length, height, and weight (see Figure 1-1). Furthermore, a scale formed by counting, such as counting the number of students in a statistics class, provides values on a ratio scale.

Arithmetic operations with the numbers on a ratio scale produce results that are interpretable with respect to the actual amounts of an attribute. For example, a person weighing 250 pounds weighs 125 pounds more than a person weighing 125 pounds. Moreover, the former person weighs twice as much as the latter person.

In this text, the distinction between interval and ratio scales will not be maintained. Rather, for simplicity, we will speak of both types of scales as having, at least, interval properties.

Scale of Measurement and Statistical Analysis

There has been considerable debate about the application of statistical methods to the different scales on which data can be measured (see Mitchell, 1986). Some statistics books are even organized according to the scale of measurement. I am neutral on this issue (cf. Jones, 1971; Hays, 1994; and Vellman & Wilkinson, 1993):

> In developing procedures, mathematical statisticians have assumed that techniques involving numerical scores [etc.] . . . are to be applied where these numbers . . . are appropriate and meaningful within the experimenter's problem. If the statistical method involves the procedures of arithmetic used on numerical scores, then the numerical answer is formally correct. Even if the numbers are the purest nonsense, having no relation to real magnitudes or the properties of real things, the answers are still right *as* numbers [italics in original]. *The difficulty comes with the interpretation of those numbers back into statements about the real world* [italics mine]. If nonsense is put into the mathematical system, nonsense is sure to come out. [Hays, 1973, p. 88; see also Hays, 1994]

The problem, then, is not so much the match of statistical method and measurement scales. Rather, the problem is one of interpreting the results of a statistical analysis with respect to the attributes of people or objects measured in the study. "The experimenting psychologist [sociologist, educational researcher] must face the problem of the interpretation of statistical results *within psychology* and on *extramathematical grounds*" (Hayes, 1973, p. 89; italics in original). For this reason, little additional attention will be paid to the levels of measurement in this textbook (cf. Jones, 1971; Vellman & Wilkinson, 1993).

Example Problem 1.4

Indicate whether these variables are measured on a nominal, ordinal, or, at-least, interval scale.
 a. Score on a measure of introversion-extroversion
 b. Amount of annual income in dollars
 c. Ranking of teachers on enthusiasm
 d. Score on a law school admissions test
 e. Type of counseling technique

THREATS TO THE VALIDITY OF RESEARCH STUDIES[2]

As an answer to the question, "Does violence on television lead to aggressive behavior in children?" a researcher might examine the effects of televised violence, an independent variable with, say, three levels (none, some, much) on a measure of the aggressive behavior of children, the dependent variable. At the end of the study, the researcher would like to interpret the results as providing an answer, though not a complete one, to the question of televised violence and aggressive behavior. But suppose, indeed, the most aggressive children viewed the most violent TV program, whereas the least aggressive children viewed the program with no violence. Although the researcher might conclude that televised violence leads to aggressive behavior, an alternative, equally plausible explanation is that the children differed in aggressive behavior before viewing the programs. Put another way, it was not the independent variable that led to differences in the dependent variable. Rather, a third variable was responsible. In the design of research, then, it is crucial that alternative explanations be ruled out, as best as possible, so that the intended interpretation is the most plausible one or even the only possible interpretation.

The question of the interpretation of the results of a study is one of the most critical questions that can be asked. This is a question of the validity of a research study. The **validity** of a research study means the extent to which the interpretation of the results of the study follows from the study itself and the extent to which the results may be generalized to other situations with other people.

Some examples may bring home this notion of validity. Most of you have seen television commercials for deodorants. An old commercial for one brand of deodorant challenges viewers to conduct their own experiment. Put your old brand under your right arm and the new brand under your left in order to see which is better. The implication is that the new brand will work better because it is the better brand. However, there are several possible counterinterpretations. One possible interpretation is that since most people are right-handed and therefore the right arm sees more action than the left arm, the old and new brands are not tested under equivalent conditions. Another possible explanation is that an expectancy is set up—that the new brand will work. Thus, the expectancy and not the new brand

---

[2]This section and the next draw heavily from Campbell & Stanley (1963, 1966). You may want to refer to these and the work of Cook & Campbell (1979) for additional information.

caused the outcome. In short, there is a threat to the validity of this proposed study due to the design of the study itself.

A second example is provided by Neisser (1976) in a review of research on human perception. Most such research is conducted in a laboratory. A subject is placed in a darkened room, her head is held steady, and she is instructed to focus on a point directly in front of her. Then a stimulus is presented for a brief period of time (e.g., 200 msec), and the subject is asked to report what she saw in the stimulus. The research design itself rules out virtually all possible counterinterpretations for the proposed interpretation of the experiment. But as Neisser (and Brunswik [1955] long before him) pointed out, people do not normally perceive under these laboratory conditions. They usually are moving their bodies, their heads, or at the very least their eyes. Furthermore, the stimuli that they observe are much more complex than those in the laboratory. In other words, Neisser has raised questions about the validity of these findings in the laboratory in the sense of their generalizability to human behavior outside.

There are two ideas underlying the validity of a research study. The first idea is the validity of the interpretation of the results as in the deodorant example. The second idea is the generalizability of the findings to other settings and people as in the perceptual-laboratory example. The former is called internal validity, and the latter is called external validity.

The **internal validity** of a research study is the extent to which the outcomes of a study result from the variables that were actually manipulated, measured, or selected in the study rather than from other variables not systematically treated. In the study of the effects of televised violence, the internal validity of the study was threatened: children in the three groups differed as to their aggressive behavior **before** the study was begun. In the proposed deodorant study, two threats to the internal validity were identified: (1) the two brands of deodorant were not tested under equivalent conditions, and (2) an expectancy effect, not the effect of the deodorant, might have been the critical factor.

The **external validity** of a research study is the extent to which the findings of a particular study can be generalized to people or situations other than those observed in the study. In other words, external validity means the extent to which the findings of research can be generalized to the real world. An example of a threat to the external validity of laboratory studies was given in the description of some typical research on human perception. (For another perspective, see Mook, 1983.)

As might be expected, there is a trade-off between optimizing internal validity and optimizing external validity. In order to optimize internal validity, the researcher retreats to the laboratory, where all of the factors threatening internal validity can be controlled as best as possible. This research often produces interpretations of the results that are valid but do not generalize beyond the laboratory. In order to optimize external validity, the researcher travels into the real world. There she selects existing variations, such as hierarchically structured and "flat" private-sector organizations, and observes their effects, for example, on work productivity. While the organizational structures may be representative of the real world, the conclusions drawn are often open to counterinterpretations due to threats of internal validity.

There is disagreement on how to resolve this problem. Clearly, some middle ground must be struck. This middle ground depends upon the researcher's knowledge and choice of a research design that is appropriate for the problem under consideration. Some laboratory studies generalize even under restrictive conditions, some can be conducted under realistic conditions, and some field studies can control for threats to internal validity.

In the next section, different types of designs are described. These designs represent the tools the researcher has available in attempting to resolve this trade-off between internal and external validity.

For a detailed presentation of the threats to validity, see Chapter 1 of the *Student Guide.*

Example Problem 1.5 ▬▬▬▬▬▬▬▬▬▬▬▬▬▬▬▬▬▬▬▬▬▬▬▬▬▬▬▬▬▬▬▬▬

For each research design described, indicate whether there is a threat to (1) internal and/or (2) external validity, or (3) no threat to validity.

a. In a study of maze learning, rats are administered either a drug to enhance learning or a placebo. Each day, over a 2-week period, the rats are tested in the maze. To ensure that the experimental rats recover from the drug, these rats are separated from the control rats and kept in a climate-controlled laboratory, whereas the controls are placed in a basement with other rats.

b. In a study of memory structure on recall speed, subjects are asked to memorize a list of words. The list is either presented in a hierarchy according to word meaning or scrambled as to word meaning. Subjects are randomly assigned to one or the other condition and, after studying the words, are presented half the words on a computer and asked to recall (by striking appropriate keys) the word in the list most closely related. Response latency (time) is the dependent variable.

c. During the Truman (Democratic)/Taft (Republican) presidential race, a pollster carried out a telephone survey to determine the front-runner. He took a random sample of names from the phone book and found overwhelming support for Taft. (*Hint:* Telephones at the time were not as widely available as now.)

DESIGNS FOR BEHAVIORAL RESEARCH

A **research design** sets forth the independent, control, and dependent variables and specifies how subjects are sampled and assigned to conditions. Different types of research designs control for none, some, or almost all of the threats to internal and external validity; some represent alternative means for resolving the trade-off between internal and external validity.

Methods for Counteracting Validity Threats

Many of the designs use one or more of the following methods to counteract threats to internal validity:

1. One or more appropriate control groups.
2. Random assignment of subjects to groups.
3. Pretests in order to address the counterinterpretation that groups were not equivalent before the treatment was administered.

Control Group.   A **control group** is a group of subjects whose selection and treatment are exactly the same as those of the experimental group except that the control group does not receive the experimental treatment (i.e., the control group receives the neutral or null level of the independent variable). Note that this does not mean that the control group receives "no treatment." The control group is treated in exactly the same way as the experimental group, except that the control group receives a placebo or neutral treatment instead of the drug. For example, psychopharmacological research compares the behavior of rats that have received a drug (experimental group) with those who received a "sugar pill" (controls). Both groups are treated in exactly the same way except for the drug. Consider another example. Research on learning from prose material examines the effect of schematic overviews, called "advance organizers," on retention and understanding. The experimental group, before reading the prose material, reads a paragraph containing a conceptual framework that ties together the concepts presented in the material. A control group reads the prose material and in all other ways is treated exactly as the experimental group, except that the control group receives a placebo or neutral passage rather than an advance-organizer passage prior to reading the material.

The control group is very important in dealing with threats to internal validity. Since, for example, control and experimental groups can be treated in exactly the same way, both groups experience the same internal and external history. By the same internal history, I mean that the positive experimental effect cannot be discounted because they were treated in a special way. By the same external history, I mean that something that occurs outside the experiment that might have affected the experimental group's performance would also have affected the control group's performance. If the experimental group performs better than the control group, history cannot be used to explain the difference.

Random Assignment.   **Random assignment** is a method for assigning subjects to control and experimental groups. Random assignment should be distinguished from *random selection,* which is a method for selecting a sample of subjects from a population.

With random assignment, each subject has an equal and independent chance of being assigned to any of the groups in the study (assuming equal group sizes). By randomly assigning subjects to groups, the researcher is able, in the long run, to control for all factors not systematically varied or controlled in the experiment. The groups differ only by chance on all possible individual-difference variables prior to the initiation of the study. Random assignment is a particularly potent method for negating threats due to otherwise nonequivalence in groups. Procedure 1-2 describes the steps taken to randomly assign subjects to groups.

Pretests.   When random assignment of subjects to groups is impossible or undesirable, **pretests** can be used to examine the possibility of prior existing differences between groups and to statistically adjust for these differences. When pretests are used for this purpose, the following procedures should be followed:

1. Several different pretests should be used.
2. One of the pretests should be the same as or parallel to the posttest.
3. The pretests selected should be related to the dependent variable.

PROCEDURE 1-2 Steps in randomly assigning subjects to groups

Operation	Example

1. Assign an identification number to each subject.

Name	ID Number
Sally	01
Mary	02
Tom	03
Richard	04
Linda	05
Debbie	06
Cathy	07
David	08
Jon	09
Roger	10

2. Designate a number to represent each group in the study. A different number is used to represent each group. If there are k groups, k numbers will be used to "name" the groups.

Let 1 — experimental group
  2 = control group

3. Turn to the table of random numbers (Table A), place your number anywhere on the page, and locate any two-digit number.

Suppose you had placed your finger on 48.

4. Find the number on the same page in the row represented by the first digit of the number located in step 3 and the column represented by the second digit of this number.

48—fourth row, eighth column. Find the number located in the fourth row and the eighth column on the same page.

5. Begin reading down the column until you locate a 1 or 2, and assign the first subject to the group designated by that number.

If the first number located is a 1, assign subject 01 to the experimental group.

6. Continue step 5 until $1/k$ of the subjects have been assigned to one group (1/2 of the subjects if there are two groups, 1/3 of the subjects if there are 3 groups, etc.). Then continue assigning subjects to the remaining groups, using this process until all groups except one have been assigned $1/k$ subjects. Then assign the remaining subjects to the last group. (This process ensures that the groups will be of equal size.)

Subject	Group
01	1
02	2
03	2
04	1
05	1
06	1
07	1[a]
08	2
09	2
10	2

[a] At this point, $1/k$—or in this case, 1/2—of the subjects were assigned to the experimental group. The remaining subjects were assigned to the control group.

Example Problem 1.6

> Consider a study with a control group and two experimental groups. Randomly assign 15 subjects to the three groups so that each group contains 5 subjects. (In choosing a starting point, suppose you turned to page 1 of Table A, put your finger on the number 36, and decided to read down the appropriate column.)

Some words of warning are needed in using statistical adjustments for equating groups. Researchers, statisticians, and philosophers are by no means in agreement on the value of using statistical adjustments to equate groups that have not been formed randomly. The disagreement arises over the assumption that the variables used to make the statistical adjustment account for all the prior relevant differences between the groups. This assumption is often hard to swallow. There is no need to jump into the controversy; suffice it to say that some very important studies are conducted without random assignment (e.g., evaluations of federally funded programs such as Head Start)—studies that provide critical data for national policy decisions. To ignore such data because statistical adjustments are required to equate groups would not be "doing one's damnedest to provide answers to perplexing questions." If statistical adjustments are used with appropriate caution and if the interpretations of the results of these studies reflect this uncertainty, the use of these adjustments seems warranted.

Major Types of Research Designs

With these preliminary considerations about designs covered, let's consider four major types of research designs:

1. Preexperimental designs
2. Experimental designs
3. Quasiexperimental designs
4. Ex post facto designs

Of the four, experimental designs provide an ideal model for behavioral research in that they counteract all internal validity threats. The other three types of designs approximate, to a greater or lesser degree, experimental designs. A general description of each type of design follows. Details are found in the *Student Guide*.

Preexperimental Designs.   **Preexperimental designs** are designs that do not have an adequate control group and so are wide open to threats to internal validity. They are called "preexperimental" because they represent pieces of the ideal model, true experimental designs. Yet they do not provide results that are amenable to a single, most plausible interpretation.

One preexperimental design, the **one-shot case study,** uses one group to which a treatment is administered ("X," e.g., a new personnel policy in a large business), and then a measure is taken (i.e., a response observed—"O," e.g., job satisfaction) to gauge the impact of the treatment. Hence, a single sample is observed (workers in the business), and a measurement taken (satisfaction scale). One problem with this design is that some other factor, occurring at the same time the new policy was implemented, such as a bonus or change in a line manager, might account for the observed level of satisfaction. Another problem is that job incumbents may have been satisfied with their jobs before the policy change.

A second preexperimental design, the **one-group pretest-posttest design**, improves on the one-short case study by measuring before (O_1) and after a treatment (X) is applied (O_2). For example, satisfaction might be measured before and after the policy change is made. Unfortunately, this design does not deal with the fact that something else occurring within the business or in the local community might have caused the change in job satisfaction.

A third preexperimental design, the **intact-group comparison,** attempts to address the weakness of the one-group pretest-posttest design by providing a control group. Two groups are systematically selected, one receives the treatment (X) and the other doesn't. The satisfaction of the two groups is observed afterward (O). In our example, the policy might be applied to a group of workers in one unit of the business, but not to workers in another unit. If other factors within or outside the business account for the measured level of job satisfaction, the satisfaction of the control group should not differ from that of the experimental group. Unfortunately, this design has the problem that the control and experimental groups may not be equivalent. The two groups might differ, at the outset, before any policy is implemented.

Preexperimental designs, then, are loaded with threats to their internal validity. They lack two fundamental elements needed to ward off threats. They lack an appropriate control group, and they lack random assignment. One reason for presenting them here is that, as a "quick and dirty" method for collecting preliminary or "pilot" data, they may provide useful insights that can be incorporated into other research designs. Second, they provide good examples of what **not** to do if you want to obtain interpretable results from your research. And third, these designs sometimes show up in behavioral research. Perhaps if we "expose" them, their use will diminish.

Experimental Designs.   **Experimental designs** represent ideal models for the design of behavioral research in that they rule out virtually all threats to internal validity through the use of **control groups** and **random assignment.** These designs permit the researcher to make causal inferences about the effect of the independent variable on the dependent variable.

There are three prototypic experimental designs. The **posttest-only control-group design** calls for randomly (R) assigning subjects to a control or experimental group, administering the treatment (X) to the experimental group, but in all other ways treating the two groups identically, and then observing behavior (O). If this design were used in the business example, workers would be randomly assigned to either a control group not affected by the policy or an experimental group affected by the policy and, after a period of time, job satisfaction of the two groups would be measured (O).

The **pretest-posttest control-group design** parallels the posttest-only control-group design, but adds an observation prior to treatment implementation. For example, job satisfaction would be measured in the control and experimental groups prior to (O_1), as well as after (O_2), the new policy (X) is implemented for the experimental group.

The **factorial experimental design** also parallels the posttest-only control-group design, but incorporates a second independent variable. For example, suppose the members of the control and experimental groups had been drawn from each of three 8-hour shifts in the business. Now there are two independent variables: (1) personnel policy change or not (X_1), and (2) shift (morning, night, "graveyard"; X_2). Job satisfaction (O) would be measured after the policy was implemented.

Quasiexperimental Designs.   Often researchers are interested in studying human behavior in naturally occurring social settings such as classrooms, businesses, prisons, and homes. If at all possible, true experiments should be used. In some situations, it is either unfeasible or undesirable to assign subjects randomly (e.g., Cook & Campbell, 1979). In these cases, **quasiexperimental designs,** which include one or more **control groups,** but do **not** employ **random assignment,** provide an important alternative to true experiments. These designs attempt to rule out, as well as possible, threats to internal validity by collecting data that can be used to examine these threats. For example, with the **nonequivalent-control-group** design, subjects are not randomly assigned to the control and experimental groups, but receive a pretest (O_1), their respective treatment (experimental, X) or lack thereof (control, but otherwise treated in the same), and then a posttest (O_2). The pretest data are used to deal with the counterinterpretations that the differences between groups at posttest were due to differences at pretest, and not to the treatment effect. A second example of a quasiexperimental design is the **time series** design. Multiple observations are taken before and after a treatment is administered. The multiple pretreatment observations establish a control-group "baseline" and the multiple posttreatment observations establish a consistent change in response. Causal interpretations of the results of quasiexperiments are more tenuous than such interpretations of the results of true experiments. But they are much more tenable than causal interpretations from preexperimental designs.

Ex Post Facto Designs.   **Ex post facto designs** are most commonly used to describe relationships between two variables. For example, a study of the relationship between Scholastic Aptitude Test (SAT) scores and grade point average (GPA) in college is a type of ex post facto design called a **correlational design**. For a single sample of subjects, measures of SAT (O_1) and GPA (O_2) are collected. By convention, the variable measured first, SAT, is called the independent variable and the variable measured second, GPA, the dependent variable. Alternatively, two groups of subjects might be **selected** specifically (e.g., normal and schizophrenic individuals) and observed (e.g., their self-concepts might be measured, O). This design is called a **criterion-group design**—one group is the criterion and the other is compared to it. By convention, group membership is called the independent variable and the self-concept measure is the dependent variable.

These designs are called ex post facto because the researcher arrives at the scene **after the treatment has been administered.** Variations among scores or groups may have arisen either through differences in environments in which subjects find themselves, through differences in inheritance, or through some combination of the two. Interpretations that SAT caused GPA (or vice versa), or that being schizophrenic caused low self-concept (or vice versa), **are not warranted.** In general, ex post facto designs examine the degree of association between two or more variables; they do not examine the causal relationship. (For an exception to this rule, see the section "Correlation and Causality" in Chapter 6.)

Example Problem 1.7

Identify the type of design employed in the following studies:

a. Ms. Marple decides to use a programmed instruction method for teaching algebra to her third-period class. She gives the class an achievement test before using the new method. After using the method for 3 weeks, she administers an alternate form of the achievement test to determine the method's effectiveness.

b. In a study of the effects of marijuana use on driving skills, college students were randomly assigned to smoke two marijuana cigarettes in the laboratory or to smoke two placebo cigarettes that taste and smell like marijuana, but do not contain the drug. A short time later, subjects took a driving test in a simulator.

c. In a study of the effects of human relations programs designed to improve relations between different social and ethnic groups, two groups of students were identified: those who participated in such programs and those who did not. A measure of racial attitudes was administered to all students.

d. In a study of the relationship between mathematics achievement and attitude toward mathematics, a researcher collected two measures on all freshmen enrolled in a major university. All subjects completed a scale measuring attitudes toward mathematics during an orientation meeting. In addition, the scores for these students on the quantitative section of the SAT were collected.

e. A researcher interested in comparing the empathy of psychologists in different areas of specialization administered a measure of empathy to clinical psychologists and experimental psychologists. Since there is some evidence that men and women differ in empathy, the researcher measured empathy of both males and females.

RESEARCH DESIGN AND STATISTICS

Research examines how variation on an independent variable affects variation on the dependent variable. For example, variation in the way words are organized—the independent variable—affects the number of words recalled—the dependent variable. Suppose you found that when words were hierarchically organized, subjects recalled 12 words, on average. In contrast, when words were scrambled, they recalled only 8, on average. Does the difference of 4 words recalled, on average, represent a systematic effect of organization on recall? Did the difference arise by chance and, if the study were replicated, would subjects in the control group (scrambled words) have recalled the same number or more words than subjects in the experimental group? To answer this question, we need a "yardstick" that tells us when differences in behavior are due to chance and when they are due to a systematic relationship between the independent variable and the dependent variable. **Statistical tests** provide such a yardstick. They permit us to determine when differences in behavior are likely to have arisen due to chance and when these differences reflect a systematic relationship.

Research design and statistical tests, then, go hand in hand. Indeed, widely used statistical tests have been built to model particular, well-established research designs. Statistical models take into account the existence of control and experimental groups, randomization, and pre- and posttests. Research design, then, drives statistical modeling, not vice versa. Of course, there is, in reality, an interplay between the two. Knowledge of designs helps the researcher select appropriate statistical techniques and assumptions underlying statistical models guide researchers in designing experiments. This final section links well-known research designs to the statistical tests presented in this text.

In order to link designs to statistical tests, several pieces of information are needed. First, the designs need to be enumerated. This has been done in Table 1-1 for the designs described before. Next, we need to distinguish between variables measured on a nominal scale from variables measured on ordinal, interval, and ratio scales. That is, we need to distinguish independent and dependent variables that name or categorize persons and objects (nominal scale) from those that place a person or object in order according to some attribute (e.g., socioeconomic status; at least ordinal scale). Let's call the former scale "Categorized," and the latter "Quantified" (following Tatsuoka, 1992). The headings in Table 1-1 reflect this distinction. Indeed, for categorized independent variables, we specify the number of levels in the design: 1, 2, or more than 2 because different statistical tests have been developed specifically for differences in the number of levels of the independent variable. Finally, we need to consider the possibility of more than one independent variable, that is, factorial design, in which there are two or more categorized, independent variables.

Having specified the design, the scale of measurement, and the number of levels of the independent variable (and number of independent variables), Table 1-1 links statistical tests to designs. As can be seen, z and t tests can be used when there is one or two levels of a categorized independent variable (e.g., one-shot case study, pretest-posttest control-group design) and a quantified dependent variable. The chi square (χ^2) test can be used with the same designs when the dependent variable is categorized. As the number of independent variables goes from 2 to more than 2, various models of the Analysis of Variance (ANOVA) are used with quantified variables, and chi square is used with categorized variables.

Hopefully, this table makes clear the close link between the characteristics of the research design and the particular statistical tests that model the design. Note also that there is often more than one statistical test for a design. Selection of a statistical test for a given design depends on the assumptions that you are willing to make about the scale of the dependent variable, about the way the data were collected, about the way subjects were assigned to groups, and about certain statistical characteristics that you'll learn about.

SUMMARY

This chapter presents basic concepts related to behavioral research. The **steps** in conducting empirical research are presented. The role of **descriptive** and **inferential** statistics in describing and interpreting the outcome of research studies is discussed. Different **scales of measurement** and classification of **variables** for designing research are also covered. **Internal** and **external validity** of research studies and **designs** for conducting behavioral research are enumerated. The chapter concludes by linking the characteristics of research designs to the statistical tests covered in this textbook.

Table 1-1 Research Designs and Corresponding Statistical Tests in *Statistical Reasoning* (Chapter Numbers in Parentheses)

Research Design	Dependent Variable	Quantitative Independent Variable	Levels of Categorical Independent Variable(s)			Factorial
			1	2	>2	
Preexperimental						
One-shot case study X O	Quantitative		z-test (10) t-test (12)			
	Categorical		Chi Square (19)			
Pretest–Posttest O X O	Quantitative			t*-test (12) RBANOVA[1] (15) T test (20)		
	Categorical			Chi Square (19)		
Intact-group comparison X O O	Quantitative			z-test (10) t-test (12) ANOVA[2] (13) U-test (20)		
	Categorical			Chi Square (20)		
Experimental						
Posttest-only control-group R X O R O	Quantitative			z-test (10) t-test (12) ANOVA (13) U-test (20)	ANOVA (13) KWANOVA[3] (20)	
	Categorical			Chi Square (19)	Chi Square (19)	
Pretest–Posttest control group R O X O R O O	Quantitative	Pretest for covariate		RBANOVA (15) ANCOVA[4] (17)	RBANOVA (15) ANCOVA (17)	
	Categorical			Chi Square (19)	Chi Square (19)	
Factorial for example: R $X_{A_1B_1}$ O R $X_{A_1B_2}$ O R $X_{A_2B_1}$ O R $X_{A_2B_2}$ O	Quantitative	Covariate				ANOVA (14) RBANOVA (15) SPANOVA[5] (16) ANCOVA (17)
	Categorical					

[1]RBANOVA = Randomized Blocks Analysis of Variance
[2]ANOVA = Analysis of Variance
[3]KWANOVA = Kruskal-Wallis Analysis of Variance
[4]ANCOVA = Analysis of Covariance
[5]SPANOVA = Split Plot Analysis of Variance

Table 1-1 Continued

Research Design	Dependent Variable	Quantitative Independent Variable	Levels of Categorical Independent Variable(s)			
			1	2	>2	Factorial
Quasiexperimental[a]						
Non-equivalent control group	Quantitative					
O X O						
O O	Categorical					
Time series						
O O X O O						
Ex Post Facto[b]						
Correlational	Quantitative	zr-test (10)				
$O_x O_y$		t_β-test (18)				
		F_R-test (18)				
	Categorical					
Criterion group	Quantitative			z-test (10)	z-test (10)	ANOVA (14)
X_A O				t-test (12)	t-test (12)	RBANOVA (15)
X_B O				ANOVA (13)	ANOVA (13)	SPANOVA (16)
				U-test (20)	U-test (20)	ANCOVA (17)
	Categorical			Chi Square (19)	Chi Square (19)	

[a]Statistical models for quasiexperimental designs are beyond the scope of this textbook.

[b]In ex post facto designs, we do not speak of independent and dependent variables because the order of effect is not known. Rather, two variables are measured and their relationship statistically modeled.

ANSWERS TO EXAMPLE PROBLEMS

1. **20, 48,** 57, 20, 98, 65, **37, 11, 35,** 92, **39,** 54, 81, **33,** 67, **23.** The numbers in bold are the identification numbers of the subjects to be included in the sample.
2. a, c, and e are adequate hypotheses. b is not adequate because it only concerns one variable (attitudes) and is not testable. d is vague and does not predict a relationship clearly.
3. **Study 1:** Independent variables: type of legal argument and educational level. Dependent variable: rating of defendant's guilt or innocence. Control and intervening variables are not present.

    Study 2: Independent variable: length of breast-feeding. Control variable: 3-year-old children. Intervening variable: warmth, intimacy. Dependent variable: rating of closeness of mother-child relationship.

4. a. Interval scale
   b. At least interval (ratio) scale
   c. Ordinal scale
   d. Interval scale
   e. Nominal scale

5. a. (2) Threat to internal validity. Performance differences may have been due to "living conditions" and not a drug effect.
   b. (1) No serious threat to the internal validity of the study. Not clear whether the researcher wishes to generalize this to a practical situation or test a theory. Hence, external validity may or may not be an issue.
   c. (3) Threat to external validity. The sample did not represent the population of people to whom the pollster wanted to generalize, viz. all registered voters.

6.

Subject ID	Group	Subject ID	Group
01	2	09	2
02	3	10	3
03	3	11	1
04	1	12	1
05	2	13	**2**
06	2	14	**3**
07	3	15	**1**
08	1		

7. a. Preexperimental: pretest-posttest design.
   b. Experimental: posttest-only control-group design.
   c. Preexperimental: intact-group comparison design.
   d. Ex post facto: correlational design.
   e. Ex post facto: factorial criterion group (an answer of just criterion group would be fine).

EXERCISES

Exercises 1–2: For each of the studies described, identify the following. If the information does not apply to the study, write NA.

- a. Design of study
- b. Independent variable(s)
- c. Dependent variable
- d. Control variable
- e. Intervening variable
- f. Threat to internal validity
- g. Threat to external validity

1. Dr. Noah, a sociologist studying the effects of social networks in organizations, was interested in increasing the communication among staff in a small corporate office. She felt that one reason communication was so sparse was that staff were visually isolated in a geographic network of the office space. So, she rearranged desks into small groups of workers doing closely related work. Now workers could see and talk to one another. Three weeks prior to and following rearranging desks, she kept a daily record of the number of communications between pairs of workers. She found that the number of communications was significantly increased using this new arrangement.

2. Suppose instead that Dr. Noah: (a) grouped staff according to duties; (b) randomly assigned, for each duty area, staff to either a control group (no change in desk arrangement) or an experimental group (close contact); and (c) only observed communications after the treatment was implemented.

Exercises 3–5: Indicate the type of measurement scale on which each of the variables listed is measured.

3. Socioeconomic status (low, middle, high)
4. Time
5. Babe Ruth's baseball jersey number

ANSWERS TO EXERCISES

1. a. Time series
   b. Office arrangement
   c. Number of communications
   d. Small corporate office
   e. Visual isolation
   f. None evident, but something that co-occurred with the implementation of the treatment (like a pay raise!) might threaten internal validity.
   g. Limited to a single small corporate office. Findings may not generalize to other small corporate offices or other organizations.

2. a. Factorial experimental design
   b. Duty area and office arrangement

    c. Number of communications
    d. Small corporate office
    e. Visual isolation
    f. None evident
    g. Limited to a single small corporate office. Findings may not generalize to other small corporate offices or other organizations.

3. Ordinal
4. Ratio
5. Nominal

2 Statistics in Context: Research on Teacher Expectancy

- Teacher Expectancy: *Pygmalion in the Classroom*
- Data on Teacher Expectancy
- Epilogue to *Pygmalion*
- Summary
- Exercises
- Answers to Exercises

For most researchers, statistics are not ends in themselves but means to an end, such as theory building or policy analysis. Thus the subject of statistics, when taught out of the context of research it serves, is like an answer to a question you didn't ask and don't care about.

The role that statistics play in research is shown by giving particular emphasis to the fact that once the data are collected, the researcher is confronted with stacks of biographical information, tests, questionnaires, or physiological indices, notes about what happened, and so on. At this point, an uninformed, head-on attack on the unorganized data can result in little but frustration and fatigue. The need for knowledge and skills in statistics becomes readily apparent. That is, statistical tools help to organize, describe, and interpret data.

Statistics provide ways of organizing, summarizing, tabulating, depicting, and describing collections of data. And they provide ways of systematically drawing inferences about the possibility of differences between larger groups of people (*populations*) than just those observed in the study (*samples*). Without statistics, the researcher would have difficulty making sense of her data. When you see statistics at work organizing, clarifying, and helping you to interpret previously incomprehensible pieces of information, the mystery of the formulas will fall away to reveal useful research tools.

This chapter, then, provides a research context for studying statistics. It shows, by example, the role statistics can play in research in the behavioral sciences.

TEACHER EXPECTANCY: *PYGMALION IN THE CLASSROOM*

Do teachers' expectations of students' intellectual abilities influence students' behavior? Some say that one person's perception of another influences the way the other person behaves. To put the question more personally: Have you ever found yourself in a classroom where the teacher expects you to make mistakes? You *feel* that's what the teacher expects—and you do just what is expected. This is called an "expectancy effect." Intuition, at least for many of us, suggests a teacher expectancy effect: The way a teacher perceives a student influences the student's behavior. There is also some theory in sociology and social psychology that says that perceptions of significant others (e.g., teachers) influence people's behavior (e.g., students).

Although intuition and theory suggest this expectancy effect, the issue is not resolved. We still need to answer the question "Does the expectancy effect operate in classrooms?" In other words, if teachers are led to expect certain behavior from a student chosen randomly, does the student behave in the ways the teacher expects? To answer this question, suppose you decide to do a study on teacher expectancy. You select some classrooms, grades 1–6, at random and tell the teachers that on the basis of pretest information, 20 percent of the students in each class are expected to show tremendous academic and intellectual gains during the school year. Actually, the students you identified in each class as "bloomers" are selected at random; they wouldn't be expected to gain any more, on average, than the other students in the class. In order to determine whether the expectancy effect operated, you give all of the students in the classes a posttest at the end of the school year.

If there was an expectancy effect, students who were designated as "bloomers" should receive higher posttest scores—or higher gain scores (posttest minus pretest scores)—than the other students. If the expectancy effect did not occur, test scores for the two groups should be approximately the same. Suppose the test scores from your study look like those presented in Table 2-1. What can you conclude about the expectancy effect from your data? Should you summarize the data in the form of gain scores (posttest minus pretest scores)? How about a summary by grade level? By experimental (bloomers) and control group? By both grade and group? Would you look at some average score on the pretest and posttest for first and second graders in the experimental group? Would you be interested in how much the scores of third and fourth graders in the control group differ from each other? Suppose you found that the average gain score for fifth and sixth graders was 13.33 in the experimental group and 13.20 in the control group. Could you be sure that this slight difference represents a true difference between groups? Could you conclude that teacher expectancy influences students' intellectual performance? When you attempt to answer questions such as these, *descriptive statistical techniques will help you to **describe** your data, and inferential statistical techniques will help you to **infer** whether differences in means may have arisen from true differences or from chance.*

TABLE 2-1   Hypothetical IQ data for the teacher expectancy study

Grade Level	Experimental Group ("Bloomers")			Control Group		
	Student	Pretest	Posttest	Student	Pretest	Posttest
1	1	60	107	31	60	90
	2	85	111	32	75	99
	3	90	117	33	90	102
	4	110	125	34	105	114
	5	115	122	35	120	121
2	6	65	118	36	80	99
	7	79	115	37	85	95
	8	80	115	38	95	104
	9	95	116	39	99	108
	10	110	122	40	120	123
3	11	90	98	41	80	102
	12	93	103	42	100	106
	13	104	107	43	105	107
	14	108	100	44	110	111
	15	125	125	45	119	119
4	16	95	95	46	95	102
	17	100	108	47	99	102
	18	104	108	48	104	107
	19	106	104	49	110	116
	20	110	116	50	120	120
5	21	75	106	51	85	112
	22	88	106	52	90	110
	23	90	95	53	100	115
	24	105	115	54	110	119
	25	120	124	55	115	125
6	26	80	97	56	79	96
	27	95	102	57	100	120
	28	100	110	58	105	117
	29	110	98	59	106	110
	30	120	122	60	110	116

DATA ON TEACHER EXPECTANCY

Your hypothetical study and the patterns in the hypothetical data parallel a study and data reported by Rosenthal & Jacobson (1968) in *Pygmalion in the Classroom.* Actual studies will often be paraphrased in this book, and hypothetical data will be created that parallel the actual data but that will use smaller numbers and fewer cases (students, subjects) to make computations as easy as possible. For example, the data in Table 2-1 will be used throughout the book to exemplify different descriptive and inferential statistical techniques. However, for those of you who are interested in what the data say about teacher expectancy, one summary of data used by Rosenthal and Jacobson is presented in Table 2-2.

Rosenthal & Jacobson (1968, p. 121) concluded that "the evidence presented . . . suggests rather strongly that children who are expected by their teachers to gain intellectually in fact do show greater intellectual gains after one year than do children of whom gains are not expected." "Teachers' favorable expectations can be responsible for gains in their pupils' IQs and, for the lower grades, these gains can be quite dramatic" (p. 98).

Due to the important social and educational implications of the phenomenon of teacher expectancy, results of Rosenthal and Jacobson's study were widely distributed by the news media. Some example of reactions in the popular press are the following: "Here may lie the explanation of the effects of socio-economic status on schooling. Teachers of a higher socio-economic status expect pupils of a lower socio-economic status to fail" (Hutchins, *San Francisco Chronicle,* August 11, 1968). "The findings raise some fundamental questions about teacher training. They also cast doubt on the wisdom of assigning children to classes according to presumed ability, which may only mire the lowest groups into self-confining ruts" (*Time,* September 20, 1968).

TABLE 2-2   Average gain scores from the *Pygmalion* study (adapted from Rosenthal & Jacobson, 1968)

Grade Level	Experimental Group		Control Group		Difference in Gain (Experimental Gain Minus Control Gain)	Do Differences Represent True Differences Between Groups?[b]
	N^a	Gain	N	Gain		
1	7	+27.40	48	+12.00	+15.40	Yes
2	12	+16.50	47	+7.00	+9.50	Yes
3	14	+5.00	40	+5.00	.00	No
4	12	+5.60	49	+2.20	+3.40	No
5	9	+17.40	26	+17.50	.00	No
6	11	+10.00	45	+10.70	−.70	No
Grades 1–6 combined	65	+12.22	255	+8.42	+3.80	Yes

[a]N denotes the number of students' scores entering into the average score.
[b]Much of this textbook deals with deciding whether or not the differences may have arisen by chance or by a treatment's effect.

Before you reach these same conclusions, consider the following: In the actual study, the gain in the experimental group is due almost completely to a total of 19 first and second graders (see Table 2-2). Data for grades 3 and 5 do not show the expectancy effect. Data for grade 4 show a slight expectancy effect, and data for grade 6 show a slight disadvantage. Furthermore, there are good reasons to doubt the validity of these data, especially for grades 1 and 2 where the expectancy effect is the greatest. For example, the test used does not have adequate norms for the youngest children. Examination of scores for individual students suggests that the test may have been invalid at these younger age levels. For example, one subject had a pretest reasoning IQ of 17 and a posttest IQ of 148. In addition, when interviewed, teachers could not remember the names on the original list of "bloomers" and reported hardly having glanced at them. (For an excellent, thorough critique of *Pygmalion,* see Elashoff & Snow, 1971.)

EPILOGUE TO *PYGMALION*

Although a thorough analysis of *Pygmalion* casts doubts as to whether the study demonstrated the teacher expectancy effect (Elashoff & Snow, 1971; but see Rosenthal, 1973), subsequent research has found the effect (e.g., Braun, 1976, 1987). Not surprisingly, the mechanisms through which a teacher's expectations are communicated to a student and result in the student's success or failure are far more complex than originally envisioned by Rosenthal & Jacobson (1968). Braun (1987, p. 599) characterized the process as an expectancy cycle with no less than seven steps:

1. The teacher forms an expectation about a student based on observations, beliefs, and stereotypes, and that expectation differs from the teacher's expectations for other students.
2. The teacher, through interactions with the student, develops a "set" for acting toward the student, and holds different action sets for other students.
3. The teacher acts toward different students according to this set for acting.
4. The learner interprets the teacher's actions according to a set of beliefs he holds about himself and in relation to the teacher, and forms self-expectations about success or failure.
5. The learner acts on the teacher's actions in accordance with his expectations and perceptions of the situation.
6. The learner's actions provide new information for the teacher to confirm, modify, or refute the current set for acting toward the student.
7. The learner interprets his own actions, varying from acceptance of his act "as appropriate and caused by the teacher's action to a new inference about the self as a learner" (p. 599).

SUMMARY

This chapter describes the role of statistics in the context of a concrete example of behavioral research: research on teacher expectancy. The chapter shows how statistics can be used to describe data collected in the course of research, and the inferences that might be drawn on the basis of the data. The particular study described, *Pygmalion in the Classroom* (Rosenthal & Jacobson, 1968), highlights issues of drawing inferences from possibly questionable data, and the potential for overinterpretation of findings. The study, and the small data set generated to parallel the actual data reported by Rosenthal & Jacobson (1968), will be used throughout the textbook to illustrate statistical concepts and procedures.

EXERCISES

1. Identify the independent and dependent variables in the Teacher Expectancy Study as shown in Table 2-1.
2. What is the intervening variable in the Teacher Expectancy Study?

3. What type of a design—preexperimental, experimental, quasiexperimental, or ex post facto—is the Teacher Expectancy Study as shown in Table 2-1?

4. What statistical test might be used to test differences in performance across grade levels, groups, or both?

5. Elashoff & Snow (1971) claimed that the expectancy effect reported by Rosenthal & Jacobson (1968) was concentrated in grades 1–2, and not in the other grades. What evidence is there to support this claim? How many subjects was this finding based on?

ANSWERS TO EXERCISES

1. Independent variables: Group (Bloomers and Control), Grade Level (1–6), and Test Occasion (Pre- and Posttest). Dependent variable: IQ. Note: you might have said that the dependent variable is the pre- and posttest, or gain scores. That would have been OK.

2. The "expectancy effect."

3. True experimental design: Factorial.

4. Analysis of variance: ANOVA, SPANOVA, ANCOVA. (The RBANOVA probably wouldn't be used with the Expectancy Study design, but you don't know that yet.)

5. The average gain from pre- to posttest was greater in the experimental group than in the control group (experimental group average gain minus control group average gain): 15.40 and 9.50 IQ points in grades 1 and 2, respectively, and the only other positive difference (experimental-control) in posttest-pretest gain was 3.40 points in grade 4. The expectancy effect, then, was based on a total of 7 + 12 = 19 students or 31 students if you include grade 4.

II DESCRIPTIVE STATISTICS FOR UNIVARIATE DISTRIBUTIONS

I n this section, statistical methods are presented for summarizing and describing what has happened in a research study. More specifically, these methods summarize and describe data for each of the variables in a study.

Measures for each variable in a study, such as test scores, reaction times, and ratings, are first summarized in the form of a *data matrix*. This matrix is a table showing the scores for each subject on each variable.

From the data matrix, a *frequency distribution* can be constructed for each variable. This distribution tells us how many subjects earned each of the possible scores on the variable. When this distribution is graphed, a pictorial summary of the patterns in the data is obtained. Often data summarized this way look like a bell-shaped curve, sometimes called a normal distribution.

The data in the frequency distribution can be summarized even further in order to provide a clearer picture of what happened in a study. The average score (mean, mode, or median), for example, can be used to tell us where the center of the frequency distribution is. This average, then, provides a measure of the *central tendency* of the distribution. And a measure of the spread of the distribution (e.g., range, standard deviation) can be used to describe the variability of scores from subject to subject.

Since these statistical methods for summarizing data deal with one variable at a time, they are sometimes called univariate, descriptive statistics. And since all of the methods provide descriptions of a distribution of data, these statistical methods are applied to *univariate distributions*.

3 Frequency Distributions

The first step in dealing with a mass of data is, somehow, to organize it. The next step is to summarize the data in such a way that the important information is preserved and the unimportant information is discarded. In this chapter, you will discover how statistics can help you put together a picture that focuses on those aspects of the data that bear on research questions. For example, data can be organized by placing them into a data matrix. A *data matrix* is a table identifying each subject and showing his or her score on each variable in the study. Data from the matrix can then be readily summarized by a frequency distribution. A *frequency distribution* orders score values from lowest to highest and gives the number (frequency) of subjects earning each score value.

The purpose of this chapter is to teach you how to organize the information collected in a research study by using a data matrix and to build, display, and interpret different types of frequency distributions. Data in frequency distributions can be presented in tabular form or graphically as a *histogram* (a form of the familiar bar graph), a *frequency polygon* (a smooth-line curve), or a *stem-and-leaf plot*. Frequency distributions can also be represented by a *relative frequency distribution,* which gives the proportion of subjects earning each score value. Relative frequency distributions allow comparison of data from two or more samples of different sizes. Finally, the data can be represented as percentile scores, which are score values below which a certain percentage of scores fall. Graphically, percentiles can be displayed as a *cumulative relative frequency distribution.*

To make the presentation on distributions concrete, the hypothetical data from the teacher expectancy study—*Pygmalion in the Classroom*—will be used. Remember (from

Chapter 2) that Rosenthal & Jacobson (1968) wanted to find out whether teachers' perceptions of students' intellectual abilities actually influenced those students' intellectual performance. Several classes of students in grades 1–6 were selected at random. Teachers were told that several students in their classes were expected to show tremendous academic and intellectual gains during the school year. Actually, these "bloomers" were selected at random, so they should not have gained any more than any of the other students in the class. At the end of the school year, students were tested to see whether there were differences in intellectual performance between the "bloomers" and the other children.

DATA MATRIX

The process of examining data begins seriously when the data have been collected and your desk (or floor) is inundated with piles of tests and stacks of hastily scribbled notes about the conduct of the study. Somehow, this flood of information must be organized before you can make sense out of it. The data matrix provides a method. A **matrix** is defined as a rectangular arrangement of elements (e.g., persons, variables) into horizontal lines called rows and vertical lines called columns. These horizontal and vertical lines meet to form the *cells* of the matrix. A **data matrix** is a table or matrix of scores in which persons, subjects, or cases are listed on the rows of the table and the information collected on each subject (the variables) is listed along the columns of the table (see Table 3-1). Scores and other data for each individual are entered in the appropriate cells of the matrix. In this way, a convenient and easily read layout of the data is provided.

A data matrix for the experimental group in the teacher expectancy study is shown in Table 3-1. Notice that an identification number is assigned to each subject, beginning with

TABLE 3-1 Data matrix for the data from the hypothetical study of teacher expectancy (experimental group)

Cell	Persons	Column ↓ Treatment Group[a]	Variables Grade Level	Posttest	Cell	Persons	Column ↓ Treatment Group[a]	Variables Grade Level	Posttest
Row →	01	1	1	107	Row →	16	1	4	95
	02	1	1	111		17	1	4	108
	03	1	1	117		18	1	4	108
	04	1	1	125		19	1	4	104
	05	1	1	122		20	1	4	116
	06	1	2	118		21	1	5	106
	07	1	2	115		22	1	5	106
	08	1	2	115		23	1	5	95
	09	1	2	116		24	1	5	115
	10	1	2	122		25	1	5	124
	11	1	3	98		26	1	6	97
	12	1	3	103		27	1	6	102
	13	1	3	107		28	1	6	110
	14	1	3	100		29	1	6	98
	15	1	3	125		30	1	6	122

[a]Experimental group

1 and ending with the number corresponding to the last subject in the experimental group. Also, notice that a number is used to designate treatment group membership (1 = experimental group in this case) instead of a letter (e.g., E) or a label. In general, numerical designation of nominal variables should be used in constructing a data matrix. Using numerical designations allows you to transfer the data easily from the matrix to the computer for analysis. The steps for constructing a data matrix are summarized in Procedure 3-1.[1]

PROCEDURE 3-1 Construction of a data matrix, using all of the data from the hypothetical study of teacher expectancy (Table 3-1)

Operation_____ Example_____

1. List persons by subject number in rows of a matrix.

Begin with the lowest subject number and list in numerical order to the highest subject number.

Persons
1
2
3
⋮
58
59
60

2. Label the variables in the columns of the matrix.

		Variables	
Persons	Treatment	Grade Level	Posttest
1			
2			
3			
⋮			
58			
59			
60			

3. Assign numerical values to nonnumerical variables, and enter the appropriate value for each person in the appropriate column.

Often 0 and 1 or 1 and 2 are used when there are two levels of a variable (e.g., experimental group = 1; control group = 2). This procedure is often referred to as "coding."

		Variables	
Persons	Treatment	Grade Level	Posttest
1	1		
2	1		
3	1		
⋮	⋮		
58	2		
59	2		
60	2		

---

[1]This procedure and any subsequent procedure can be skipped if you are sure you can accurately carry out the steps involved.

Operation	Example

4. For numerical variables, enter the value for each person in the appropriate column.

		Variables	
		Grade	
Persons	*Treatment*	*Level*	*Posttest*
1	1	1	107
2	1	1	111
3	1	1	117
⋮	⋮	⋮	⋮
58	2	6	117
59	2	6	110
60	2	6	116

Example Problem 3.1

> Construct a data matrix for the control group in the teacher expectancy study, using the posttest data in Table 2-1. (*Hint:* Be sure to code the treatment level.) Additional exercises may be found at the end of this chapter. For a summary and additional practice problems, see the *Student Guide.*

FREQUENCY DISTRIBUTIONS

A frequency distribution is a method for summarizing and highlighting aspects of the data in the data matrix. By summarizing the critical features of the data, the distribution presents the mass of data in a more interpretable form than does a data matrix.

A **frequency distribution** is a tabular arrangement of score values showing the frequency with which each value occurs. In this definition, probably the only unfamiliar term is **score value.** It refers to any possible number (value) on a scale of numbers. For example, on a 10-item test, score values can range from 0 to 10. A "score" is a particular value earned by an individual. Score values are usually arranged with the lowest score value at the bottom of the table and the highest value at the top (see Table 3-2).

A frequency distribution, then, summarizes the data collected on a particular variable by arranging the score values in order of size or magnitude and indicating how often each is obtained. Notice that some information is lost in this process. Although we know how often a particular score value was earned, we lose information about the scores of specific individuals. The link, then, between subjects and their scores is lost. (The stem-and-leaf plot solves this problem. See below.)

Table 3-2 shows a frequency distribution using posttest scores for subjects ("bloomers") in the experimental group of the teacher expectancy study.[2] Notice that the frequency dis-

---

[2]Notice that posttest scores were chosen for examination in the frequency distribution. These data are sufficient to investigate the teacher expectancy effect; pretest data are helpful but not necessary. Since subjects were randomly assigned to either the experimental or the control group, we assume that any differences between the groups are due to chance. *Pretest information may be used to verify this reasoning.* If the random assignment

tribution quickly supplies some information about the performance of these subjects that is difficult to find in the data matrix. For example, posttest performance varied greatly among individual subjects; scores ranged from 95 to 125. The most frequently earned scores were 115 and 122. The steps in constructing a frequency distribution are described in Procedure 3-2.

TABLE 3-2   Frequency distribution of posttest scores from the hypothetical study of teacher expectancy (experimental group)

Score Value X	Tally	Frequency f	Score Value X	Tally	Frequency f
125	//	2	109		0
124	/	1	108	//	2
123		0	107	//	2
122	///	3	106	//	2
121		0	105		0
120		0	104	/	1
119		0	103	/	1
118	/	1	102	/	1
117	/	1	101		0
116	//	2	100	/	1
115	///	3	99		0
114		0	98	//	2
113		0	97	/	1
112		0	96		0
111	/	1	95	//	2
110	/	1			

PROCEDURE 3-2 Construction of a frequency distribution, using data from the experimental group in the hypothetical study of teacher expectancy (Table 3-1)

Operation	Example

1. List score values in descending numerical order from the highest at the top to the lowest at the bottom.

The highest score value is at the top; the lowest is at the bottom.

Score Value	Tally	Frequency
125		
124		
123		
:		
97		
96		
95		

worked and there is no systematic difference between the groups initially in intellectual performance, their average pretest scores should be approximately equal. Indeed, this result was found when average pretest scores were computed; they were 96.90 for the experimental group and 99.03 for the control group.

Operation	Example		
2. Working from the data matrix, count (tally) the number of times each score value occurs in the set of data.	*Score Value*	*Tally*	*Frequency*
	125	//	
	124	/	
	123		
	⋮	⋮	
	97	/	
	96		
	95	//	
3. Convert the number of tallies to Arabic numerals in the column labeled "frequency."	*Score Value*	*Tally*	*Frequency*
	125	//	2
	124	/	1
	123		0
	⋮	⋮	⋮
	97	/	1
	96		0
	95	//	2
4. Check the accuracy of your counting by adding the numbers in the frequency columns. The sum should equal the total number of scores you began with.	*Score Value*	*Tally*	*Frequency*
	125	//	2
	124	/	1
	123		0
	⋮	⋮	⋮
	97	/	1
	96		0
	95	//	2
			Sum = 30

Example Problem 3.2

    a. Using the data matrix from Example Problem 3.1, construct a frequency distribution of posttest scores for the control group in the teacher expectancy study.

    b. Compare this distribution with the frequency distribution for the experimental group in Table 3-2. Is the spread of scores roughly the same for both groups?

CLASS INTERVALS: A METHOD FOR GROUPING DATA

With a wide range of score values, as in Table 3-2 (see p. 47), patterns in the data are difficult to see. A common solution to this problem is to group score values together. For example, the scores in Table 3-2 have been grouped together in Table 3-3 so that three score values are placed in each group (e.g., [93, 94, 95]; [96, 97, 98]; [123, 124, 125]). By squeezing score values together, the distribution becomes more compact, and often clear patterns emerge. Notice that Table 3-3 is more economical, both in the time it takes to read the data and in the space the data occupy, than Table 3-2. We can see at a glance a pattern in the data: The most frequently earned scores fall in the interval 114–116, and other scores are spread out both above and below. Such information is more difficult to extract from Table 3-2.

TABLE 3-3   Frequency distribution using class intervals of posttest scores from the hypothetical study of teacher expectancy (experimental group)

(1) Class Interval	(2) f	(3) Real Limits	(4) Midpoint
123–125	3	122.5–125.5	124
120–122	3	119.5–122.5	121
117–119	2	116.5–119.5	118
114–116	5	113.5–116.5	115
111–113	1	110.5–113.5	112
108–110	3	107.5–110.5	109
105–107	4	104.5–107.5	106
102–104	3	101.5–104.5	103
99–101	1	98.5–101.5	100
96–98	3	95.5–98.5	97
93–95	2	92.5–95.5	94

The term given to a group of score values is **class interval.** Class intervals may be characterized by their size. The **size** of a class interval is simply the number of score values within it. The size of the class intervals in Table 3-3 is 3: Three score values are contained within each interval (e.g., the highest interval contains three score values: 123, 124, 125). (Notice that the size of the class intervals in Table 3-2 is 1. The score value and the class interval are the same.) The steps in constructing class intervals are presented in Procedure 3-3.

PROCEDURE 3-3 Steps in calculating the class interval, using the data from Table 3-2

Operation	Example
1. Choose the number of class intervals to be used. *As a rule of thumb, use 10–20 intervals. This recommendation represents a reasonable trade-off between having very few wide intervals (economy) and having intervals so wide that the data may be misrepresented (error; for details on the economy/error tradeoff, see the* Student Guide.).	Use 10 intervals
2. Find the range of the scores by subtracting the lowest score value from the highest.	$125 - 95 = 30$

Operation	Example
3. Divide the range (step 2) by the number of intervals (step 1) to find the size of the class interval (i): $$i = \frac{\text{Highest Score} - \text{Lowest Score}}{\text{Number of Class Intervals}}$$ *As a rule of thumb, interval sizes of 2, 3, 5, 10, or 20 points are preferred.*	$30/10 = 3$
4. Begin with the lowest score divisible by the interval size. (If the lowest score obtained in the data set is not divisible by the interval size, begin with the first number below the lowest score which is divisible by the interval size.) To obtain the highest score in any given interval: (a) subtract 1 from the interval size, and then (b) add this number to the lowest score in the interval. For example, if the interval size is 3, $3 - 1$, or 2, can be added to the lower score of the interval to obtain the highest score in the interval (e.g., the interval beginning with 93 ends with $93 + 2$, which equals 95.) *By convention, an interval is usually started with the lowest score divisible by the interval size.*	123–125 (123, 124, 125) 120–122 (120, 121, 122) $\vdots$ 96–98 (96, 97, 98) 93–95 (93, 94, 95)

Once class intervals have been formed for a set of data, a frequency distribution can be constructed with class intervals in the same way the distribution was constructed with individual score values (see Procedure 3-2). The only difference is that instead of counting the frequency of each score value (step 2 in Procedure 3-2), you determine the frequency with which scores fall within each *class interval*.

Example Problem 3.3

Use the posttest scores for the control group in the teacher expectancy study (see Example Problem 3.1) to:
  a. Construct a frequency distribution with 12 class intervals.
  b. Compare the frequency table you constructed with that for the experimental group (Table 3-3). Are there any major differences in the overall performance between the experimental and control groups?

Limits of Class Intervals

The next step in summarizing data is to construct a graph or pictorial representation of the frequency distribution. In order to construct a graph, we must establish the limits (boundaries) of each class interval. A class interval has two different types of limits: the score limits and the real limits. Both of these concepts will become important in the next section when methods for graphing frequency distributions are discussed.

Score Limits.   The **score limits** are defined as the highest score and the lowest score used in setting up a class interval. An illustration of the score limits for intervals of three points is shown in Figure 3-1a. Notice that the upper and lower score values mark the boundaries of each interval. For example, the lower score limit of the interval 93–95 is 93, and the upper score limit is 95.

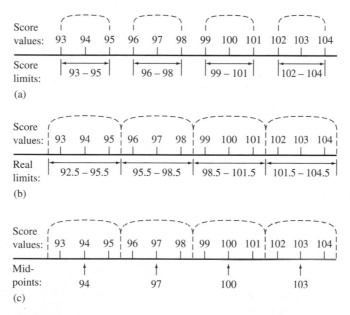

FIGURE 3-1
Illustration of score limits, real limits, and midpoints of the class intervals used for the teacher expectancy data.

Real Limits.   The intervals as defined by their score limits in Figure 3-1a do not meet. For example, the upper score limit of the first interval is 95 and the lower score limit of the second interval is 96. Nevertheless, scores of 95.1 and 95.4 would fall in the lowest interval, 93–95; scores of 95.5 and 95.8 would fall in the next interval, 96–98. Thus the real limits of these two intervals are 92.5–95.5 and 95.5–98.5. The **real limits** of a class interval are defined as the point falling exactly halfway between the two score values, indicating the upper boundary of one interval and the lower boundary of the other interval. The real limits of an interval, then, are

real lower limit = score limit − 0.5 (unit)

real upper limit = score limit + 0.5 (unit)

The term 0.5 (unit) needs some explanation. Measurements in the behavioral sciences are not perfect, and so they are rounded either when the measurement is taken or afterwards. SAT scores, for example, are rounded to whole numbers, although in theory a person's score could be 605.3. In this example, then, the *unit* used for the measurement is 1; namely, one SAT point. Hence 0.5 (unit) would be $0.5(1) = 0.5$. In contrast, suppose a measure of reaction time was accurate to one-tenth of a second and all reaction time scores were rounded to tenths (e.g., 2.1). In this case, the unit would be tenths, or 0.1. Thus $0.5(0.1) = 0.05$, and the real limits of a class interval such as 1.0–2.0 would be 0.95–2.05 (i.e., $1.00 - 0.05 = 0.95$ and $2.00 + 0.05 = 2.05$).

Figure 3-1b shows the real limits for class intervals used in the teacher expectancy study. Notice that adjacent intervals meet, so all possible score values are included in the intervals. For example, the lower real limit of the class interval 93–95 is 92.5; the upper real limit is 95.5.

Procedure 3-4 provides the steps in finding score limits and calculating real limits. The data are taken from the experimental group in the teacher expectancy study.

PROCEDURE 3-4 Steps in calculating the limits of a class interval, using the data from Table 3-3

Operation

1. Find *score limits* by identifying the lowest and highest score value of each interval.

Class Interval	Score Limits
123–125	123, 125
120–122	120, 122
⋮	⋮
96–98	96, 98
93–95	93, 95

2. Calculate *real limits* by identifying the point halfway between the upper score limit of a particular interval and the lower score limit of the next higher interval:

real lower limit = score limit − 0.5 (unit)
real upper limit = score limit + 0.5 (unit)

Notice that IQ scores are rounded to the nearest whole number, so that unit is 1. See the text for a discussion of the unit.

Class Interval	Score Limits	Real Limits
123–125	123, 125	122.5, 125.5
120–122	120, 122	119.5, 122.5
⋮	⋮	⋮
96–98	96, 98	95.5, 98.5
93–95	93, 95	92.5, 95.5

upper real limit of the interval 93–95 =
$95 + 0.5(1) = 95 + 0.5 = 95.5$

Example Problem 3.4

Using the frequency distribution with class intervals constructed in Example Problem 3.3, add a column labeled "real limits." Calculate the real limits of each interval.

Midpoints of Class Intervals

Since class intervals contain more than one score value, we need a single number to characterize an interval. The midpoint does this task. The **midpoint** of a class interval is defined as the score falling exactly midway between the possible numbers in the interval. To get a picture of the relationship between the midpoint and the class interval, see Figure 3-1c. The midpoint for the class interval with score limits 93–95 or real limits 92.5–95.5 is 94, the value falling exactly in the middle of the class interval. Procedure 3-5 provides the steps in calculating the midpoint using examples from the data for the experimental group. (Midpoints for each class interval are shown in column 4 of Table 3-3 on p. 49.)

PROCEDURE 3-5 Steps in calculating the midpoint of a class interval, using the data from Table 3-3

Operation	Example
1. Divide the *interval size* in half.	Since the interval size is 3, $3 \div 2 = 1.5$.
2. Add this value to the lower real limit of the interval.	For the interval 93–95: $92.5 + 1.5 = 94$.
3. Continue this process until a midpoint is computed for each interval.	

Class Interval	Real Limits	Midpoints
123–125	122.5–125.5	124
120–122	119.5–122.5	121
⋮	⋮	⋮
96–98	95.5–98.5	97
93–95	92.5–95.5	94

Example Problem 3.5

Using the frequency distribution for the control group constructed in Example Problem 3.3, add another column labeled "midpoint." Compute the midpoint for each class interval.

GRAPHICAL REPRESENTATIONS OF FREQUENCY DISTRIBUTIONS

Graphs are often used to present frequency distributions so that the shape of the distribution can be seen easily. Three types of graphs are commonly used for picturing data from a frequency distribution: the histogram, a version of the common bar graph (Figure 3-2 on the next page); the frequency polygon, a smooth-line curve (Figure 3-3a on p. 56); and the stem-and-leaf plot, a somewhat unconventional but informative variation on the histogram (Figure 3-4 on p. 58).

In constructing graphs, several general principles should be applied:

1. The two axes of the graph are constructed at right angles to each other. The vertical axis of a graph is called the **ordinate,** and the horizontal axis is called the **abscissa.**
2. The values of a variable are listed along the abscissa, and the frequencies are listed along the ordinate (e.g., Figure 3-2).
3. The figure is constructed so that it begins and ends with zero frequency (e.g., Figure 3-2).
4. Finally, the ordinate is drawn about two-thirds as long as the abscissa.

Histogram.   The histogram is a version of the familiar **bar graph** (see Figure 3-2). A **histogram,** then, is a graph in which each class interval is represented on the abscissa and the frequency of each class interval is represented by the height of the bar.

Figure 3-2 shows a histogram of the data from the experimental group in the teacher expectancy study. Notice that a rectangular bar is drawn such that the height of the bar denotes the frequency with which the class interval occurs. The width of each bar is the same, since all class intervals are of the same size. Finally, notice that class intervals with zero frequency immediately precede and follow the bars.

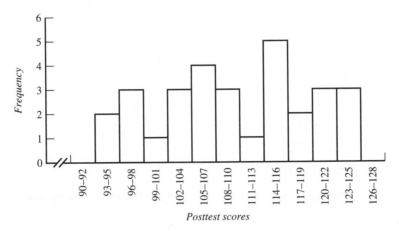

FIGURE 3-2
Histogram of the posttest scores for the experimental group in the hypothetical study of teacher expectancy (data from Table 3-3)

In constructing a histogram, list the frequencies on the ordinate and the class intervals (or score values if $i = 1$) on the abscissa. Be sure to label the abscissa and ordinate so that the reader knows the variable to which the data refer (abscissa) and the meaning of the values on the ordinate. In listing class intervals on the abscissa, use the *score limits.* Then, erect a bar over each class interval to a height corresponding to the frequency of the class interval. Thus, in Figure 3-2, the bar constructed over the interval 93–95 indicates that the frequency associated with the interval is 2. Although the abscissa is labeled with score intervals, in drawing the bars, use the lower and upper *real limits.* Then the bars touch one another. Steps in constructing a histogram are given in Procedure 3-6.

PROCEDURE 3-6 Steps in constructing a histogram, with examples from the data in Table 3-3

Operation	Example

1. Draw the axes of the graph.

   a. *Axes are perpendicular.*

   b. *The ordinate is usually two-thirds as long as the abscissa.*

2. Label the ordinate with frequency values at equal distances apart.

The lowest frequency is at the bottom, and the highest frequency is at the top.

3. Label the abscissa with score limits of the class intervals at equal distances apart.

The lowest score value is at the left, and the highest score value is at the right. Since the abscissa and ordinate meet at zero, the first break in the line indicates that the score values (abscissa) begin above zero; the second break indicates that intervals 99– 101 to 117–119 were omitted to save space.

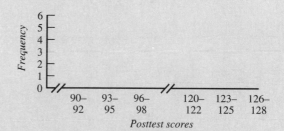

4. Draw a bar for each class interval to the height of the frequency as shown on the ordinate.

Draw bars of equal width and according to the real limits of the interval. For a more complete illustration, see Figure 3-2.

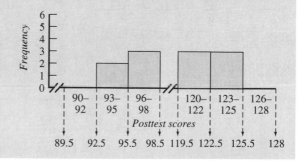

Example Problem 3.6 ▬▬▬▬▬▬▬▬▬

    Using the frequency distribution constructed in Example Problem 3.3, construct a histogram for the control group.

Frequency Polygon.   A **frequency polygon** is a graph in which each midpoint of each class interval (or score value if $i = 1$) is represented on the abscissa, the frequency of each midpoint is represented by the height of a point above it, and the points are joined by straight lines (see Figure 3-3a). Frequency polygons, like histograms, are used to graph a frequency distribution. They differ from histograms in that straight lines are used to show the relation between the levels of a variable and their frequencies instead of a series of connected bars. Actually, a frequency polygon is nothing more than a series of lines connecting the midpoints of the bars of a histogram (see Figure 3-3b).

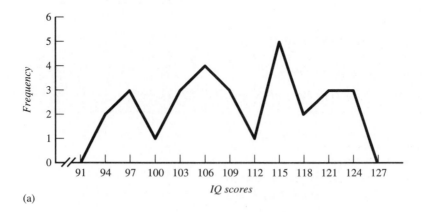

(a)

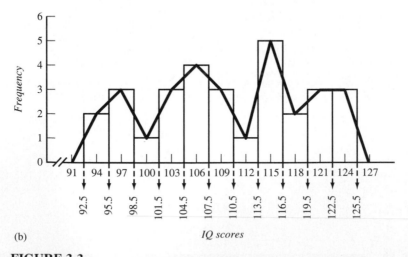

(b)

FIGURE 3-3

Frequency polygon and histogram of the posttest scores for the experimental group in the hypothetical study of teacher expectancy (data from Table 3-3)

Often the decision to use a histogram or a frequency polygon is arbitrary; they can be used interchangeably. In experiments with two (or more) groups (e.g., an experimental group and a control group), however, it is often desirable to portray the frequency distributions of both groups on one graph. In this case, the frequency polygon is preferred because it is easier to read. The steps in constructing a frequency polygon are summarized in Procedure 3-7.

PROCEDURE 3-7 Steps in constructing a frequency polygon from the data in Table 3-3

Operation	Example

1. Draw the axes of the graph.

   a. *Axes are perpendicular.*

   b. *The ordinate is two-thirds as long as the abscissa.*

2. Label the ordinate or vertical axis with frequency values.

The lowest frequency is at the bottom, and the highest frequency is at the top.

3. Label the abscissa or horizontal axis with midpoints of class intervals.

Begin with the midpoint of the class interval just below the lowest class interval with a frequency of 1 or more, and end with the midpoint of the class interval just above the highest class interval with a frequency of 1 or more. Indicate a break in the scale of values as shown in the example.

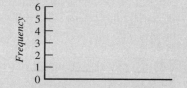

4. Plot a point over each midpoint at the height of the appropriate frequency as indicated on the ordinate.

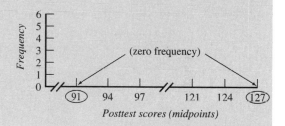

5. Connect the points with straight lines.

For a more complete illustration, see Figure 3-3.

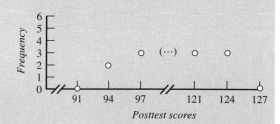

Using the frequency distribution constructed in Example Problem 3.1, draw a frequency polygon for the control group data.

Stem-and-Leaf Plot.   A limitation of traditional frequency distributions is that, in summarizing score values by the frequency with which they occur, information about students' individual scores is lost. This led the statistician, John Tukey (1977), to develop "quick and dirty" methods for exploring data that give the researcher a feel for each data point. The stem-and-leaf plot is one of Tukey's creations.

A **stem-and-leaf plot** combines the tabular frequency distribution with the histogram. This graphical display preserves the information contained in the data matrix, even when scores have been grouped to show patterns (see Figure 3-4). The **stem** in the stem-and-leaf plot is the "leftmost" digits in the numbers (Tatsuoka, 1992). For example, for a score of 95, the leftmost digit—the 10's digit or 9—would be listed in the left-hand column (see Figure 3-4). For the next-to-highest score, 124, the stem or leftmost digit—the 10's digit or 12 (12 10's)—would be listed. The **leaf** shows the units (or all but the leftmost). For 95, this would be 5; for 124, this would be 4. Since two students received a score of 95, we read the leaves: 9|55788. In addition, one other student received a score of 97 and two more students received a score of 98. Hence the additional leaves: 7, 8, and 8. For each student, there is a score in the stem-and-leaf plot. The stem-and-leaf plot provides a graphic representation and contains all of the scores in the data matrix. Moreover, the pattern of scores shown in Figure 3-4 parallels the patterns shown in Figures 3-2 and 3-3a, though different intervals were used.

		10's Digits of the Scores	1's Digits of the Scores	
9	55788	Stem ⟶ 9	55788 ⟵ Leaf
10	0234	10	0234
10	667788	10	667788
11	01	11	01
11	5556678	11	5556678
12	2224	12	2224
12	55	12	55
(a)			(b)

FIGURE 3-4
Stem-and-leaf plot (a) with descriptors (b)

There are many possible ways to create stem-and-leaf plots (see Tukey, 1977). Procedure 3-8 provides one basic approach.

PROCEDURE 3-8 Steps in constructing a stem-and-leaf plot using experimental group posttest data from Table 2-1

Operation_____   **Example**_____

1. List leftmost digits (stems) in ascending order.

   In the example, scores were grouped by sets of 5: 95–99, 100–104, . . . , 121–125 in order to provide a clear picture of the pattern.

Stem	*Leaf*
9	
10	
10	
11	
11	
12	
12	

2. Draw a line separating the stems from the leaves.

Stem	*Leaf*
9	
10	
10	
11	
11	
12	
12	

3. Write in the leaves such that each score is represented by its 1's digit.

Stem	*Leaf*
9	55788
10	0234
10	667788
11	01
11	5556678
12	2224
12	55

Example Problem 3.8 ▬▬▬▬▬▬▬▬▬▬▬▬▬▬▬▬▬▬▬▬

Using the control group posttest data in Table 2-1, construct a stem-and-leaf plot.

Shapes of Frequency Distributions

Frequency distributions can have a variety of shapes. The shape of any particular graph depends on the frequencies of class intervals being examined. Examples of several common types of distributions are shown in Figure 3-5.

One characteristic of a distribution is symmetry. A distribution is **symmetric** when the two halves of the distribution are mirror images of each other. Figures 3-5a-c, f show examples of symmetric distributions. Nonsymmetric distributions (e.g., Figures 3-5d, e) are sometimes described as skewed. A **skewed distribution** is a distribution in which one tail is longer than the other tail, relative to its central portion. In skewed distributions, most scores fall at one end of the scale and only a few scores at the opposite end. The distribution shown in Figure 3-5d is called a *positively skewed* distribution because the tail extends in the direction of the positive or higher end of the scale. This distribution indicates that most scores were low; however, a few scores were very high. Figure 3-5e shows a *negatively skewed* distribution; that is, the tail extends toward the negative or lower end of the scale. This distribution shows that most scores were high, but a few scores were quite low.

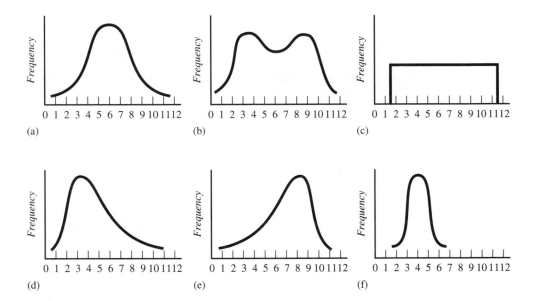

FIGURE 3-5
Common shapes of frequency polygons

Another characteristic of a distribution is its **modality**—the number of relative peaks it exhibits. (That is, the peaks must be higher than the neighboring values but not necessarily the same height.) For example, the flat distribution in Figure 3-5c has no peaks and is therefore often called a **rectangular distribution**. The bell-shaped curve in Figure 3-5a has one peak, and so it is called a **unimodal distribution**. The distribution in Figure 3-5b has two relative peaks, and so it is called a **bimodal distribution.** Note that it is possible to have a **multimodal distribution** with more than two peaks.

Finally, a distribution may be characterized by its **kurtosis**—its peakedness. (Kurtosis is the Greek word for peakedness.) Distributions that tend to be flat or broad are called **platykurtic** (e.g., Figure 3-5c is an extreme example). Distributions that tend to be very peaked are called **leptokurtic** (e.g., Figure 3-5f). And distributions that fall in between are described as **mesokurtic** (Figure 3-5a).

The Relative Frequency Distribution

In some studies, a comparison is made of the score distributions for two (or more) groups that differ in size. A direct comparison of frequencies by using a tabular frequency distribution or a frequency polygon is difficult to make. For example, a frequency of 5 in a group of 10 represents 50 percent of the subjects, whereas in a group of 20, it represents 25 percent of the subjects. The relative frequency distribution provides a means for comparing frequencies based on different group sizes. A **relative frequency distribution** is a frequency distribution in which the frequency of each score value or class interval is converted to a proportion by dividing the frequency by the total number of cases in the sample. (Either ungrouped score values or data grouped by class intervals may be used in relative frequency distributions; however, class intervals are preferred and will be used here.) *Relative frequencies,* then, are proportions; they can vary from 0 to 1. As will be shown in later chapters, relative frequency distributions can also be interpreted as probability distributions. Since probability distributions stand at the heart of inferential statistics, we will continually return to these distributions throughout the book.

The *Pygmalion* study illustrates a case where relative frequency distributions are useful in examining the data. It may be that, since younger children are often more impressionable and eager to please than older children, they may be more affected by their teachers' expectations of them. This hunch could be explored by constructing frequency distributions of posttest scores for subjects in the experimental and control groups at the primary grades (grades 1–2) and at the upper grades (grades 3–6). Since in the hypothetical study, the number of students in grades 1 and 2 is less than the number in grades 3–6, the data must be compared by using a relative frequency distribution.

Relative frequencies for the experimental group ("bloomers") in primary grades and upper grades are presented in Table 3-4. The relative frequencies show that in grades 1 and 2, most of the experimental "bloomers" tended to score relatively high (i.e., above 111). In grades 3–6, however, the majority of subjects tended to have somewhat lower scores

TABLE 3-4   Relative frequency distributions of the posttest scores for the experimental group students in grades 1–2 and grades 3–6 (teacher expectancy study)

Posttest Scores	Primary Grades (1–2)		Upper Grades (3–6)	
	f	*Rel. f*	*f*	*Rel. f*
123–125	1	.10	2	.10
120–122	2	.20	1	.05
117–119	2	.20	0	.00
114–116	3	.30	2	.10
111–113	1	.10	0	.00
108–110	0	.00	3	.15
105–107	1	.10	3	.15
102–104	0	.00	3	.15
99–101	0	.00	1	.05
96–98	0	.00	3	.15
93–95	0	.00	2	.10

(i.e., below 111). If only frequencies had been used, this difference in the distributions of scores would not have been so apparent.

The steps in constructing a relative frequency distribution are the same as those in constructing a frequency distribution except that relative frequencies are used instead of the original frequencies. Relative frequencies or proportions may be obtained by dividing the frequencies by the total number of subjects in the sample:

$$\text{relative frequency} = \frac{\text{frequency}}{\text{total number of subjects}}$$

For example, 1 out of the 10 first and second graders earned a score falling in the class interval 123–125 (Table 3-4). The relative frequency of the interval, then, is:

$$\text{relative frequency} = 1/10 = .10$$

The steps in constructing a frequency distribution can also be used to construct a relative frequency distribution. Just divide the frequencies in Procedure 3-2 by the total number of subjects.

Example Problem 3.9 ▬▬▬▬▬▬▬▬▬▬▬▬▬▬▬▬▬▬▬▬▬▬▬▬▬▬▬▬▬▬▬▬

a. Construct a relative frequency distribution of posttest scores for the control group in primary grades (1–2) and upper grades (3–6). (*Hint:* These data are shown in your data matrix constructed in Example Problem 3.1. Use the same class intervals you used in Example Problem 3.3.)

b. Compare the relative frequency distributions for grades 1–2 with grades 3–6 in the experimental group and in the control group.

c. Is the pattern of posttest scores in the control group between primary and upper grades the same as in the experimental group?

Relative Frequency Polygons

For easy comparisons of relative frequency distributions, **relative frequency polygons** can be constructed. These graphs are constructed exactly as frequency polygons are, except that relative frequencies are listed on the ordinate. Figure 3-6 shows the relative frequency polygons for the experimental group in grades 1–2 and grades 3–6. It is clear from this figure that younger children tended to earn higher scores, and older children tended to earn somewhat lower scores. The steps for constructing a relative frequency polygon are the same as those for constructing a frequency polygon, except that relative frequencies are listed on the ordinate. Hence, the steps are as summarized in Procedure 3-7. Just remember to use relative frequencies on the ordinate and not frequencies.

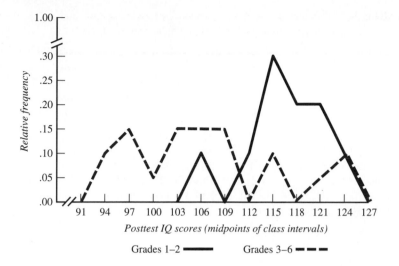

FIGURE 3-6
Relative frequency polygons for the posttest data from Table 3-4 ("Bloomers")

Example Problem 3.10

Using the relative frequency distributions constructed in Example Problem 3.9, construct relative frequency polygons in one graph for control group data at primary and upper grades.

The Cumulative Frequency Distribution

A **cumulative frequency distribution** is a distribution that shows the number of scores falling below a certain point on the scale of scores. It provides a basis for computing certain statistics, such as percentiles, which indicate the percentage of subjects scoring *below* a particular score. And it provides another method for comparing the scores in two or more groups.

The **cumulative frequency** of a score value or class interval is defined as the number of cases falling *below the upper real limit* of that class interval. The cumulative frequency of posttest scores for the experimental group in the teacher expectancy study is shown in Table 3-5. (Ignore columns 5 and 6 for the moment.)

A cumulative frequency distribution is usually constructed from a frequency distribution as in Table 3-5, column 2. From this column, cumulative frequencies are readily calculated by a process of successive addition of entries in the frequency column (as in column 4). The steps in constructing a cumulative frequency distribution are summarized in Procedure 3-9.

TABLE 3-5   Cumulative frequency distributions for the experimental group ("bloomers") in the hypothetical study of teacher expectancy

(1) Class Interval	(2) f	(3) Upper Real Limit	(4) Cumulative Frequency (cf)	(5) Cum. Prop.	(6) Cum. %
123–125	3	125.5	27 + 3 = 30	1.00	100
120–122	3	122.5	24 + 3 = 27	.90	90
117–119	2	119.5	22 + 2 = 24	.80	80
114–116	5	116.5	17 + 5 = 22	.73	73
111–113	1	113.5	16 + 1 = 17	.57	57
108–110	3	110.5	13 + 3 = 16	.53	53
105–107	4	107.5	9 + 4 = 13	.43	43
102–104	3	104.5	6 + 3 = 9	.30	30
99–101	1	101.5	5 + 1 = 6	.20	20
96–98	3	98.5	2 + 3 = 5	.17	17
93–95	2	95.5	0 + 2 = 2	.07	7

PROCEDURE 3-9 Steps in constructing a cumulative frequency distribution (data from Table 3-5)

Operation

1. Identify the real upper limit of each score value or class interval.
Construct a cumulative frequency distribution from a tabular frequency distribution.

Example

Class Interval	f	Upper Real Limit
123–125	3	125.5
120–122	3	122.5
117–119	2	119.5
⋮	⋮	⋮
99–101	1	101.5
96–98	3	98.5
93–95	2	95.5

2. Calculate the cumulative frequencies by *successive* addition. Begin with the observed frequency of the lowest score or interval.

Class Interval	f	Upper Real Limit	cf
123–125	3	125.5	
120–122	3	122.5	
117–119	2	119.5	
⋮	⋮	⋮	
99–101	1	101.5	
96–98	3	98.5	
93–95	2	95.5	2

Operation

3. Add the frequency of the bottom interval to the frequency of the second to find the cumulative frequency of the second interval.

4. Add the cumulative frequency of the second class interval to the frequency of the third interval to find the cumulative frequency of the third interval.

5. Continue this process of successive addition until you reach the highest score or class interval.

6. Check the accuracy of the successive additions by noting the cumulative frequency of the highest interval. This value should equal the total number of cases (N).

Example

Class Interval	f	Upper Real Limit	cf
123–125	3	125.5	
120–122	3	122.5	
117–119	2	119.5	
⋮	⋮	⋮	
99–101	1	101.5	
96–98	3	98.5	5
93–95	2	95.5	2

Class Interval	f	Upper Real Limit	cf
123–125	3	125.5	
120–122	3	122.5	
117–119	2	119.5	
⋮	⋮	⋮	
99–101	1	101.5	6
96 98	3	98.5	5
93–95	2	95.5	3

Class Interval	f	Upper Real Limit	cf
123–125	3	125.5	30
120–122	3	122.5	27
117–119	2	119.5	24
⋮	⋮	⋮	
99–101	1	101.5	6
96–98	3	98.5	5
93–95	2	95.5	2

Example Problem 3.11

Construct a cumulative frequency distribution for the control group from the frequency distribution constructed in Example Problem 3.3. Identify the upper real limit and cumulative frequency of each class interval.

Cumulative Frequency Polygons

The cumulative frequency distribution is commonly graphed in the form of a cumulative frequency polygon. The **cumulative frequency polygon** is a graph with *cumulative frequencies* listed on the ordinate and the *upper real limits* of class intervals listed on the abscissa (see Figure 3-7).

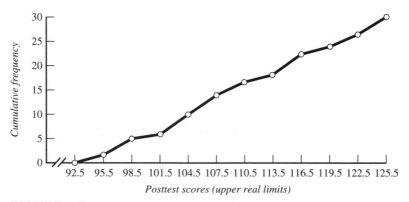

FIGURE 3-7

Cumulative frequency polygon of the posttest scores for the experimental group in the teacher expectancy study (data from Table 3-5)

The trend of the cumulative frequency curve is always rising. It never drops down, since cumulative frequencies are formed by successive addition and can never be less than the cumulative frequency of the preceding interval. The form of the curve is generally not a straight line but is S-shaped. These properties are illustrated in Figure 3-7, which shows the cumulative frequency curve for the experimental group in the expectancy study. This graphical representation is also useful in comparing the cumulative frequency distributions of two or more groups that are equal in size. For example, plotting the cumulative frequency curves of two groups, such as an experimental and control group, on the same set of axes provides a unique way of comparing differences between the groups. The closer together the two curves are, the more similar the performance of the two groups is. The steps for constructing a cumulative frequency polygon are summarized in Procedure 3-10.

PROCEDURE 3-10 Steps in constructing a cumulative frequency polygon (data from Table 3-5)

Operation	Example

1. Draw the axes of the graph.
  a. *Axes are perpendicular.*
  b. *The ordinate usually is two-thirds as long as the abscissa.*	

Operation	Example

2. Label the ordinate with cumulative frequency values.
Begin with zero at the bottom, and end with the highest cumulative frequency at the top.

3. Label the abscissa with upper real limits of score values or class intervals.
Begin with the upper real limit of the interval just below the lowest class interval, and end with the highest interval. Indicate a break in the scale of values, as shown.

4. Plot a point over each upper real limit at the height of the appropriate cumulative frequency as shown on the ordinate.

5. Connect the points with straight lines.
For a more complete illustration, see Figure 3-7.

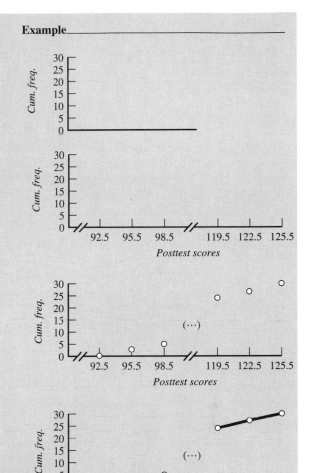

Example Problem 3.12

Using the cumulative frequency distribution in Example Problem 3.11, construct a cumulative frequency polygon with the control group data.

Cumulative Proportions and Percentages

It is easier to interpret the statement "80 percent of the subjects in the experimental group of the expectancy study received a posttest score below 119.5" than the statement "The cumulative frequency for a score of 119.5 is 24." So it is often useful to convert cumulative frequency distributions to cumulative proportions or percentages in order to interpret the cumulative frequencies more easily. A **cumulative proportion** is defined as the cumulative frequency divided by the total number of subjects in the group. A **cumulative percentage** is defined as a cumulative proportion multiplied by 100:

cumulative proportion = cumulative frequency/total number of subjects

cumulative percentage = cumulative frequency $\times$ 100/total number of subjects

A cumulative proportion indicates the proportion of subjects with scores below a particular value. A cumulative percentage, or **percentile score,** indicates the percentage of subjects falling below a particular value. For example, a percentile score of 75 indicates that 75 percent of the subjects received lower scores. Finally, just like relative frequencies, cumulative proportions or percentage distributions can be used to compare groups based on different sample sizes.

Cumulative proportions and percentages are shown in columns 5 and 6 of Table 3-5 on p. 64. They can be calculated directly from the cumulative frequencies in the table. The cumulative proportion of the class interval 117–119 is the cumulative frequency of the interval (24) divided by the total number of subjects (30): 24/30 = .80. The cumulative percentage of this class interval is simply the cumulative proportion multiplied by 100: .80 $\times$ 100 = 80. In this way, cumulative proportions and percentages can be found from cumulative frequencies for all class intervals. Thus cumulative proportion and percentage distributions can be constructed.

Example Problem 3.13 ▬▬▬▬▬▬▬▬▬▬▬▬▬▬▬▬▬▬▬▬▬▬▬▬▬▬▬▬

Using the cumulative frequency distributions that you constructed in Example Problem 3.11, calculate the cumulative proportions and cumulative percentages of each class interval.

PERCENTILES

Percentile scores or ranks are familiar to probably every college student, since these scores are often reported to indicate the student's relative standing on a test. The popularity of percentile ranks lies in their interpretability. Jane's percentile score of 95, for example, means that she scored higher than 95 percent of her peers on the test. Because of the wide use of percentile scores in educational and psychological testing, you may want to pay particularly close attention to how they are obtained.

Percentiles can be read directly from a graph of a cumulative percentage distribution such as that for the experimental group in the expectancy study shown in Figure 3-8. From this curve, any posttest score in this group can be converted to its percentile rank. For example, in order to determine the percentile rank of a posttest score of, say, 113.5, the score value of 113.5 is located on the abscissa and a perpendicular line is extended until it intersects the curve. The percentile is then obtained from the scale on the ordinate by reading directly across to the left. From Figure 3-8, a raw score of 113.5 has a percentile rank of 57.

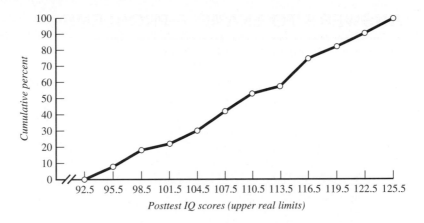

Posttest IQ scores (upper real limits)

FIGURE 3-8
Percentile scores for the experimental group in the teacher expectancy study

Example Problem 3.14

Construct a graph using percentiles for the control group. (You will need to refer to the cumulative percentage distribution constructed for these data in Example Problem 3.13.)

SUMMARY

This chapter provides procedures for beginning to describe and summarize a set of data. First, data are entered into a *data matrix*. Then a *tabular frequency distribution* is constructed to summarize the frequency with which each score value (for ungrouped data) or class interval (for grouped data) occurs. In addition, a *relative frequency distribution* may be constructed if data from two or more groups of unequal size are to be compared. Or a *cumulative frequency distribution* may be constructed if cumulative frequencies, proportions, or percentages are of interest. These frequency distributions can then be represented graphically to highlight the shape of the distribution, using a *histogram,* a *frequency polygon,* a *stem-and-leaf plot,* a *relative frequency polygon* (if a relative frequency distribution has been constructed), a *cumulative frequency polygon* (if a cumulative frequency distribution has been constructed), or a *cumulative percentage polygon* (if cumulative percentages are of interest). Note, however, that in many cases, firm conclusions about research questions cannot be drawn until further statistical analyses are made on the data.

ANSWERS TO EXAMPLE PROBLEMS

1.

Persons	Treatment[a]	Grade	Posttest
31	2	1	90
32	2	1	99
33	2	1	102
34	2	1	114
35	2	1	121
36	2	2	99
37	2	2	95
38	2	2	104
39	2	2	108
40	2	2	123
41	2	3	102
42	2	3	106
43	2	3	107
44	2	3	111
45	2	3	119
46	2	4	102
47	2	4	102
48	2	4	107
49	2	4	116
50	2	4	120
51	2	5	112
52	2	5	110
53	2	5	115
54	2	5	119
55	2	5	125
56	2	6	96
57	2	6	120
58	2	6	117
59	2	6	110
60	2	6	116

[a]1 = experimental group, 2 = control group

2. **a.**

Score Value X	Tally	Frequency	Score Value X	Tally	Frequency
125	/	1	107	//	2
124		0	106	/	1
123	/	1	105		0
122		0	104	/	1
121	/	1	103		0
120	//	2	102	////	4
119	//	2	101		0
118		0	100		0
117	/	1	99	//	2
116	//	2	98		0
115	/	1	97		0
114	/	1	96	/	1
113		0	95	/	1

a. Continued

Score Value X	Tally	Frequency	Score Value X	Tally	Frequency
112	/	1	94		0
111	/	1	93		0
110	//	2	92		0
109		0	91		0
108	/	1	90	/	1

b. Scores are about equally spread out in two groups; control group scores are somewhat lower. Most frequently earned scores were 115 and 122 in the experimental group and 102 in the control group.

3. **a.**

(1) Class Interval	(2) f	(3) Real Limits	(4) Midpoint
123–125	2	122.5–125.5	124
120–122	3	119.5–122.5	121
117–119	3	116.5–119.5	118
114–116	4	113.5–116.5	115
111–113	2	110.5–113.5	112
108–110	3	107.5–110.5	109
105–107	3	104.5–107.5	106
102–104	5	101.5–104.5	103
99–101	2	98.5–101.5	100
96–98	1	95.5–98.5	97
93–95	1	92.5–95.5	94
90–92	1	89.5–92.5	91
	Sum = 30		

b. The pattern of frequencies in each class interval of the two groups is quite similar.

4. See column 3 of 3a.
5. See column 4 of 3a.
6.

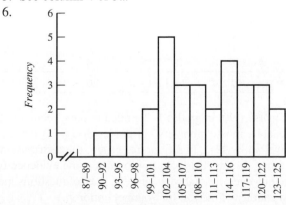

Posttest scores

7.

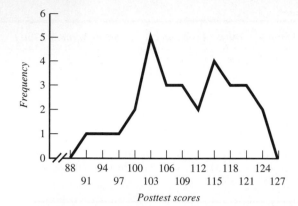

Posttest scores

8.

9	0
9	5699
10	22224
10	6778
11	00124
11	566799
12	0013
12	5

9. **a.**

Posttest Scores	Grades 1–2		Grades 3–6	
	f	*Rel. f*	*f*	*Rel. f*
123–125	1	.10	1	.05
120–122	1	.10	2	.10
117–119	0	.00	3	.15
114–116	1	.10	3	.15
111–1i3	0	.00	2	.10
108–110	1	.10	2	.10
105–107	0	.00	3	.15
102–104	2	.20	3	.15
99–101	2	.20	0	.00
96–98	0	.00	1	.05
93–95	1	.10	0	.00
90–92	1	.10	0	.00
Sum	10	1.00	20	1.00

b. Most "bloomers" (.90) in grades 1–2 tended to have relatively high posttest scores (i.e., above 111); most "bloomers" in grades 3–6 (.75) tended to have somewhat lower scores (below 111). In the control group, the distributions for the two grade levels are fairly similar. This pattern provides some evidence for our hunch. (This conclusion, however, is somewhat suspect, due to questions mentioned in Chapter 2 about the validity of the test for younger children.)

10.

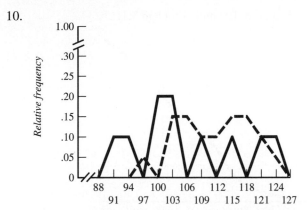

Posttest scores (midpoints of class intervals)

———— Grades 1–2
– – – Grades 3–6

11.

(1) Class Interval	(2) f	(3) Upper Real Limit	(4) Cum. f	(5) Cum. Prop.	(6) Cum. %
123–125	2	125.5	30	1.00	100
120–122	3	122.5	28	.93	93
117–119	3	119.5	25	.83	83
114–116	4	116.5	22	.73	73
111–113	2	113.5	18	.60	60
108–110	3	110.5	16	.53	53
105–107	3	107.5	13	.43	43
102–104	5	104.5	10	.33	33
99–101	2	101.5	5	.17	17
96–98	1	98.5	3	.10	10
93–95	1	95.5	2	.07	7
90–92	1	92.5	1	.03	3

12.

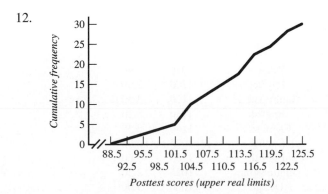

Posttest scores (upper real limits)

13. See columns 5 and 6 of Example Problem 3.11.

14.

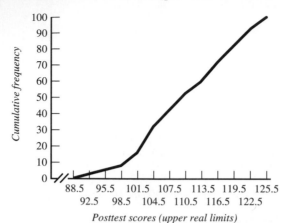

Posttest scores (upper real limits)

EXERCISES

In an editorial in the *Santa Barbara News-Press,* Linda Seebach (1993) argued that low SAT scores reflect much more than a gender gap. She pointed out that females tended to earn higher grades in math and science courses, when they were in those courses. But the reality of the situation is that women do not have the same access as men to these courses. In a study of the relationship between gender, SAT scores, and course grades, Goldman, Schmidt, Hewitt, & Fisher (1974) collected the following data at the University of California (UC) that bear on Seebach's point:

TABLE E-1 Hypothetical data on sex, undergraduate major, Scholastic Aptitude Test Score, and grade point average for four University of California campuses (after Goldman et al., 1974).

Campus[a]	Sex	Major	SAT	GPA
UCLA	M	Physics	1050	2.90
	M	Physics	1200	2.00
	M	Anthropology	1100	3.50
	M	English	1130	3.20
	M	Chemistry	1160	2.50
	F	English	1075	2.90
	F	English	1100	3.60
	F	Engineering	1025	2.30
	F	Design	1000	3.00
	F	Biology	1000	2.50

TABLE E-1 Continued

Campus[a]	Sex	Major	SAT	GPA
UCD	M	Physics	1175	2.90
	M	Engineering	1125	3.20
	M	Biology	1100	3.00
	M	Engineering	1150	2.70
	M	Biology	1200	2.50
	F	Chemistry	1120	2.50
	F	Sociology	1090	3.30
	F	Sociology	1100	3.00
	F	English	1085	2.90
	F	Anthropology	1125	3.20
UCI	M	Physics	1125	2.70
	M	Biology	1175	2.90
	M	Chemistry	1200	3.20
	M	Biology	1100	2.90
	M	Engineering	1150	3.00
	F	Sociology	1090	3.10
	F	Design	1060	2.90
	F	English	1050	2.70
	F	Anthropology	1175	3.00
	F	English	1100	3.20
UCSD	M	Physics	1150	2.70
	M	Chemistry	1185	2.80
	M	Engineering	1200	3.10
	M	Biology	1160	3.00
	M	English	1200	3.40
	F	Biology	1150	2.50
	F	Sociology	1100	3.00
	F	Anthropology	1120	3.10
	F	Anthropology	1080	2.90
	F	Design	1150	3.50

[a]UCLA = Los Angeles, UCD = Davis, UCI = Irvine, UCSD = San Diego

Use these data to carry out the following:

1. Construct a data matrix for the tabled data.
2. Construct a frequency distribution for SAT scores from the data matrix using ungrouped data (i.e., $i = 1$).
3. Construct a frequency distribution for SAT scores from the data matrix using grouped data with 10 intervals.
4. Add to the frequency distribution constructed in 3 above, columns containing real limits and midpoints.
5. Construct a histogram for grouped SAT scores.
6. Construct a frequency polygon for grouped SAT scores.
7. Construct a stem-and-leaf plot for SAT scores.
8. Construct relative frequency polygons for males and females. Is there a gender difference on SAT scores?

9. Construct a cumulative frequency distribution for SAT scores.
10. Construct a cumulative frequency polygon using SAT scores.
11. Construct a cumulative percentage frequency polygon using SAT scores.
12. In this sample (a) an SAT score of 1150 corresponds to (approximately) what percentile score? (b) What SAT score corresponds to a percentile score of (approximately) 85?

ANSWERS TO EXERCISES

1.

Persons	Campus[a]	Sex[b]	Major[c]	Score
01	1	1	1	1050
02	1	1	1	1200
03	1	1	5	1100
04	1	1	7	1130
05	1	1	2	1160
06	1	2	7	1075
07	1	2	7	1100
08	1	2	4	1025
09	1	2	8	1000
10	1	2	3	1000
11	2	1	1	1175
12	2	1	4	1125
13	2	1	3	1100
14	2	1	4	1150
15	2	1	3	1200
16	2	2	2	1120
17	2	2	6	1090
18	2	2	6	1100
19	2	2	7	1085
20	2	2	5	1125
21	3	1	1	1125
22	3	1	3	1175
23	3	1	2	1200
24	3	1	3	1100
25	3	1	4	1150
26	3	2	6	1090
27	3	2	8	1060
28	3	2	7	1050
29	3	2	5	1175
30	3	2	7	1100
31	4	1	1	1150
32	4	1	2	1185
33	4	1	4	1200
34	4	1	3	1160
35	4	1	7	1200
36	4	2	3	1150
37	4	2	6	1100
38	4	2	5	1120
39	4	2	5	1080
40	4	2	8	1150

[a]1 = UCLA, 2 = UCD, 3 = UCI, 4 = UCSD (any numbers could be used for nominal variable)
[b]1 = male, 2 = female (any numbers could be used for nominal variable)
[c]1 = physics, 2 = chemistry, 3 = biology, 4 = engineering, 5 = anthropology, 6 = sociology,
   7 = English, 8 = design (any numbers could be used for nominal variable)

2.

Score Value[a]	Frequency	Score Value	Frequency
1200	5	1100	7
1195	0	1095	0
1190	0	1090	2
1185	1	1085	1
1180	0	1080	1
1175	3	1075	1
1170	0	1070	0
1165	0	1065	0
1160	2	1060	1
1155	0	1055	0
1150	5	1050	2
1145	0	1045	0
1140	0	1040	0
1135	0	1035	0
1130	1	1030	0
1125	3	1025	1
1120	2	1020	0
1115	0	1015	0
1110	0	1010	0
1105	0	1005	0
		1000	2

[a] The SAT scores reported here change by 5 points, so the frequency distribution increments score values by 5 points to save space. If you incremented by 1 point (a bit tedious), that's okay.

3.–4.

Class Interval	Frequency	Real Limit	Midpoint
1200–1220	5	1199.5,1220.5	1209.5
1180–1199	1	1179.5,1199.5	1189.5
1160–1179	5	1159.5,1179.5	1169.5
1140–1159	5	1139.5,1159.5	1149.5
1120–1139	6	1119.5,1139.5	1129.5
1100–1119	7	1099.5,1119.5	1109.5
1080–1099	4	1079.5,1099.5	1089.5
1060–1079	2	1059.5,1079.5	1069.5
1040–1059	2	1039.5,1059.5	1049.5
1020–1039	1	1019.5,1039.5	1029.5
1000–1019	2	999.5,1019.5	1009.5

Note: There are 11 intervals because 1200 falls just above the 10th class interval (1180–1199).

5.

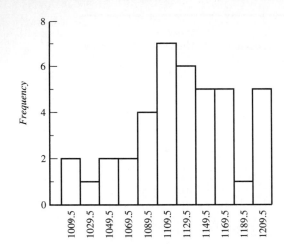

6.

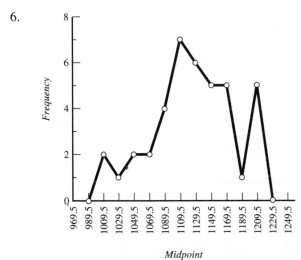

7.

10	00
10	2
10	55
10	67
10	8899
11	0000000
11	222223
11	55555
11	66777
11	8
12	00000

8.

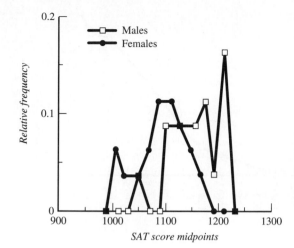

9.

Upper Real Limit	Cumulative Frequency
1209.5	40
1199.5	35
1179.5	34
1159.5	29
1139.5	24
1119.5	18
1099.5	11
1079.5	7
1059.5	5
1039.5	3
1019.5	2

10.

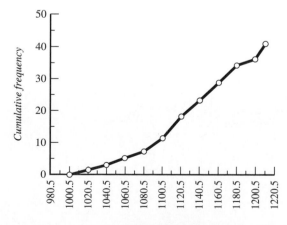

11.

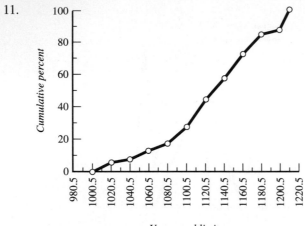

12. From the graph in 11:

    a. About the 73rd percentile
    b. About 1180

4

Measures of Central Tendency and Variability

Frequency distributions provide an important picture of the sample data that bear on a research question. However, distributions, like raw data, provide too much information for easy interpretation. In addition to a distributional representation of the data, we need ways of describing the important features of the distribution. This chapter presents two important concepts for describing distributions—central tendency and variability—and provides the skills necessary to calculate and interpret measures of these concepts.[1]

The *central tendency* of a distribution is an "average" or "typical" score value in the distribution. Put another way, the central tendency of a distribution describes the location of the center of the distribution by indicating one score value that represents the "average" score. Three measures of central tendency are commonly used:

1. The *mode*—the score value that occurs most frequently in the distribution
2. The *median*—the score value that divides the distribution into the lower and upper 50 percent of the scores
3. The *mean*—the "center of gravity" of the distribution, such that the "weight" of the scores above the mean exactly balance the "weight" of the scores below it

---

[1]These measures are sample statistics; they describe the central tendency and variability of a set of scores collected on a *sample* of subjects. However, as mentioned in Chapter 1, researchers are usually interested in generalizing to the population from which the sample was drawn. Since it's usually not feasible to collect information about an entire population and calculate the population parameters directly, these sample statistics are used as estimates of population parameters. This point will become clearer in Chapter 8.

The *variability* of a distribution describes the spread or range of scores in the distribution. Four measures are commonly used to describe the variability of a distribution:

1. The *range*—the highest score minus the lowest score
2. The *semi-interquartile range*—one-half the difference between the score values at the 75th and 25th percentiles
3. The *standard deviation*—an average variability of scores in the distribution measured in units of the original score scale
4. The *variance*—an average variability of scores in the distribution measured in squared units of the original score scale

RESEARCH EXAMPLE: ATTRIBUTIONAL INTERVENTION TO REDUCE AGGRESSION

Hypothetical data from an intervention to reduce peer-directed aggression of aggressive African-American boys (Hudley & Graham, 1993) are used to illustrate how measures of central tendency and variability describe data more economically than a frequency distribution. Before turning to these statistics, though, we set the context with this research.

Much of behavioral research has, as its aim, theory building. From a theory, predictions are made about how people will behave in certain situations. These predictions are then tested empirically—that is, by observation and experiment. The data obtained bear directly on the accuracy of the predictions and thus indirectly on the validity of the theory. For example, the *Pygmalion* study was based on social psychological theory and empirical evidence (Rosenthal, 1966). Nevertheless, its major impact was *not on conclusions* about the theory, but on *decisions* about socioeducational *policy*. For example, some school districts abandoned the use of intelligence tests partly in response to the *Pygmalion* findings.

Research on attribution theory (e.g., Weiner, 1986, 1991) has led not only to advances in the theory, but also to interventions developed to test the theory. A study by Hudley & Graham (1993) provides a good example of theory testing with considerable practical significance. They noted that childhood aggression persists over time and predicts low academic achievement, school dropout, juvenile delinquency, and adult criminality and pathology. Furthermore, many of these correlates of aggression are prevalent among minorities, especially African-American boys. Thus, "the 20-year-old black male dropout, gang member, or convict is often the 10-year-old boy labeled as aggressive by teachers and peers" (Hudley & Graham, 1993, p. 124).

Attribution theory provides a basis for considering why aggression might arise and how it might be ameliorated in inappropriate situations. This theory is concerned with the perceived causes of events and behaviors. Within attribution theory, a consistent finding is that aggressive boys have a bias to perceive their peers as acting with hostile intent, particularly in situations in which the cause of an event or behavior is ambiguous.

> For example, when a child is instructed to imagine that a peer spilled milk on him or her in the lunchroom, and no other information is given, the student labeled as aggressive is more likely to state that the peer did this "on purpose" than is his or her nonaggressive counterpart. Such biased attributions of intent are then thought to lead to retaliatory behavior. (Hudley & Graham, 1993, p. 125)

Attribution theory goes beyond biased perceptions of intent. This theory links intent with emotion, emotion to behavior. Aggressive boys are biased to perceive ambiguous behavior as maliciously intended, which tends to elicit anger, and anger leads to aggressive behavior (Weiner, 1991):

$$\begin{array}{ccccc}
\text{Ambiguous} & \longrightarrow & \text{Biased Intent} & \longrightarrow & \text{Emotion} & \longrightarrow & \text{Aggressive} \\
\text{Situation} & & \text{Perception} & & \text{(Anger)} & & \text{Behavior}
\end{array}$$

Hudley and Graham reasoned that, if biased attributions stimulate a motivational sequence leading to aggression, changing boys' attributions of intent in ambiguous situations would lead to a reduction in anger that in turn should lead to a reduction in aggressive behavior. To test this hypothesis, they created an experimental, 12-session intervention "specifically to train aggressive African-American males to infer nonhostile intent following ambiguous peer provocation" (p. 125). Before and after the intervention, data were collected on (a) aggressive boys' intent attributions and anger in ambiguous situations, (b) teacher ratings of aggressive behavior, and (c) the number of disciplinary referrals.

Hudley and Graham also included two additional groups in their study. One received *attention training* to deal with the possible effects of simply participating in a special program. The other received no special attention in order to deal with issues of history concurrent to the conduct of the study.

To carry out the study, African-American boys, about 10.5 years of age on average, were divided into two groups: aggressive and nonaggressive. (The authors provide convincing evidence, based on both teacher and peer measures, of the aggressiveness of the aggressive boys.) Then the aggressive and nonaggressive boys were randomly assigned to one of the three groups: experimental, attention, and control. This produced a 2 (aggression) by 3 (group) factorial design with 24 aggressive boys and 12 nonaggressive boys in each group. However, to simplify matters, the simulated data in Table 4-1 has 6 aggressive and 6 nonaggressive boys in each group.

At both pre- and posttest, each subject responded to a questionnaire that presented story themes that described negative outcomes occurring to the subject by a hypothetical peer provocateur. The negative outcomes included damage to one's property, physical harm, and social rejection. The stories varied as to the provocateur's intent: hostile, ambiguous, prosocial, or accidental. For each story, subjects made six responses: (a) three elicited judgments of the provocateur's *intent,* for example, "Do you think he did this on purpose?" (from surely not = 1 to yes for sure = 7); (b) two dealt with *emotion,* including how angry the subject felt and how much the subject blamed the provocateur (not at all = 1 to very much = 7); and (c) the last was to select one of six *behaviors* for dealing with the situation ranging from "do something nice for the other kid" (1) to "have it out then and there" (6). For now, we'll focus on the intent data, combining responses to the three items.

Hypothetical data are presented in Table 4-1.[2] Are aggressive boys' perceptions of a provocateur's intent more aggressive at pretest than nonaggressive boys' perceptions? Did

---

[2]I would like to thank Professor Cynthia Hudley for providing thorough descriptive statistics from the Hudley & Graham (1993) study. These statistics served as the basis for a simulation that produced the hypothetical data in this table.

the experimental intervention work for aggressive boys compared to attention training and control? Did the intervention increase or decrease nonaggressive boys' perceptions of an actor's intent as aggressive? Did the intervention decrease aggressive boys' biased perceptions of intent under ambiguous causal conditions as it was designed to do? These questions

TABLE 4-1   Listing of hypothetical data on boys' perception of negative intent: Ambiguous situation (after Hudley & Graham, 1993)

Subject ID	Aggressiveness[a]	Group[b]	Pretest	Posttest
01	1	1	6	3
02	1	1	4	1
03	1	1	4	2
04	1	1	5	2
05	1	1	4	2
06	1	1	5	1
07	1	2	7	6
08	1	2	6	6
09	1	2	3	5
10	1	2	4	3
11	1	2	6	4
12	1	2	6	6
13	1	3	3	4
14	1	3	4	4
15	1	3	5	5
16	1	3	5	5
17	1	3	3	4
18	1	3	5	7
19	2	1	2	2
20	2	1	4	4
21	2	1	2	3
22	2	1	3	1
23	2	1	3	4
24	2	1	5	4
25	2	2	3	4
26	2	2	2	2
27	2	2	4	3
28	2	2	6	6
29	2	2	4	3
30	2	2	4	5
31	2	3	4	5
32	2	3	4	2
33	2	3	5	4
34	2	3	2	3
35	2	3	4	4
36	2	3	4	4

[a] 1 = Aggressive, 2 = Nonaggressive
[b] 1 = Experimental, 2 = Attention, 3 = Control

are difficult to answer from the data matrix provided. What's needed, at least in the beginning, are descriptive statistics. These statistics help you to summarize or describe your data, and to find patterns.

The hypothetical study and the patterns in the simulated data (if you can find them!) parallel the study and data reported by Hudley & Graham (1993). Figure 4-1 (next page) summarizes the results of the actual study for aggressive boys (Hudley & Graham, 1993, p. 130). Recall that the study focused on reducing aggressive boys' perceptions of aggressive intent of a provocateur in causally ambiguous situations. In this figure, average scores for each of the three groups—experimental, attention, and control—are plotted at pre- (occasion 1) and posttest (occasion 2). For completeness, I've included not only the intent data from the ambiguous situation, but also data from the other three situations: hostile and prosocial intent, and accidental. Clearly, the intervention (experimental group) had its intended effect (Figure 4-1a): perception of aggressive intent in ambiguous situations dropped dramatically from pre- to posttest. In the authors' words:

> [T]he attributional intervention influenced aggressive subjects' judgments in the ambiguous stories only. Ratings of the other three causal conditions did not change significantly from pre- to posttest for any treatment group. (Hudley & Graham, 1993, p. 131)

The authors conclude:

> Compared to their counterparts in the attention training and control groups, aggressive subjects in the attribution retraining program [experimental] showed marked reduction in . . . the bias to presume hostile intent. (p. 135)

MEASURES OF CENTRAL TENDENCY

In reporting findings from Hudley & Graham (1993), "average" scores for each group at pre- and posttest were presented in Figure 4-1. It is now time to formalize this notion of "average" as a family of descriptive statistics.

The "average" or "typical" score value in a distribution shows the **central tendency** of the distribution. Measures of central tendency describe a frequency distribution by indicating one score value that represents the center of the distribution or the "average" score in a group of persons. This value can also be thought of as representing the *location* of a distribution on a scale of score values. This location can then be used to compare different distributions. For example, frequency polygons varying in central tendency (and variability) are shown in Figure 4-2.[3] We can see that distributions *A* and *B* have approximately the same location since they center at approximately the same point on the scale. Distribution *C* centers on a somewhat lower point on the score scale and thus differs in location. The location of these distributions can be compared by using measures of central tendency: mode, median, and mean.

---

[3]Throughout the remainder of this text, many of the figures will be smoothed, even if they represent data from a sample, in order to make concepts as clear as possible.

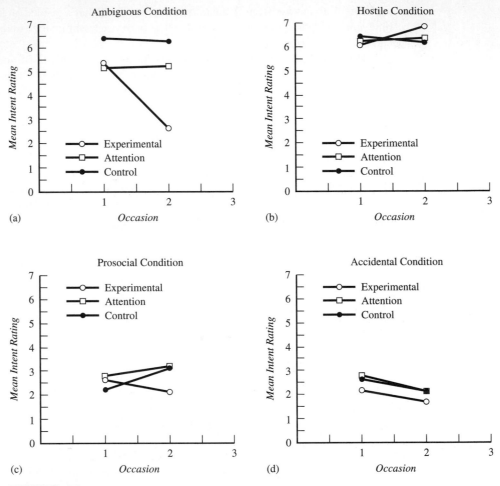

FIGURE 4-1

Average scores for the experimental, attention, and control groups across four situational conditions: ambiguous, hostile, prosocial, and accidental

The Mode

The **mode** is defined as that score value that is obtained most often. When data are grouped into class intervals, the mode is taken to be the midpoint of the interval that contains the most cases. This measure is referred to as the **crude mode.**

The pre- and posttest modes for hypothetical ratings of aggressive boys' perceptions of the provocateur's intent are shown in Table 4-2 (ignore the rows for median and mean for now). From the frequency distributions and modes in Table 4-2, there appears to be some evidence of a change in perceptions from pretest to posttest with less aggression perceived at posttest than at pretest. For example, low (less aggression) ratings of 1 and 2 are observed at posttest but not at pretest. Moreover, the modal score at pretest is 4.50 and the modal value at posttest is 4.00.

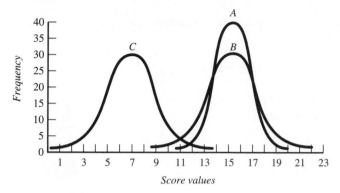

FIGURE 4-2
Three frequency polygons differing in central tendency, variability, or both

TABLE 4-2   Frequency distribution and central tendency measures of intent judgments at pretest and posttest, using the data in Table 4-1 for aggressive boys when the provocateur's intent is ambiguous (ignoring group)

Intent Judgment	Frequency	
	Pretest	Posttest
7	1	1
6	4	3
5	5	3
4	5	4
3	3	3
2	0	2
1	0	2

Measure of Central Tendency	Pretest	Posttest
Mode	4.50	4.00
Median	5.00	4.00
Mean	4.72	3.94

In order to find the mode, begin with a frequency distribution. The mode is simply the score value that occurs most frequently in the distribution. For reference, the steps in finding the mode of a frequency distribution are given in Procedure 4-1, where pretest data in Table 4-2 are used as an example. (If necessary, refer to Procedures 3-4 and 3-5 to review calculation of the real limits and the midpoint of a class interval.)

PROCEDURE 4-1 Steps in calculating the mode with an example from intent judgments of aggressive boys (data from Table 4-2)

Operation	Example

Operation

1. Construct a frequency distribution with score values or class intervals.

2. If scores are used (data are *not grouped* into class intervals), the mode is the score value most frequently obtained, 4 in this case.

3. If data are grouped into class intervals, find the midpoint of the interval with the maximum frequency. The value of the midpoint is the crude mode. See Procedure 3-5.

4. When there are two score values or class intervals containing the most cases, then proceed as follows:

   a. If the values are *adjacent*, locate the real limit separating the two values or intervals (cf. Procedure 3-4). For adjacent score values, the value of this real limit is the mode (4.5 in this case); for class intervals, this value is the crude mode.

   b. If the values are *not adjacent* (bimodal distribution), locate the two score values most frequently earned; these are the modes (3 and 6 in this case). If the intervals are not adjacent, locate the midpoints of the two intervals with greatest frequency; these are the crude modes.

Example

Posttest Intent	f
7	1
6	3
5	3
4	4
3	3
2	2
1	2

Mode = 4

Pretest Intent	f
7	1
6	4
5	5
4	5
3	3
2	0
1	0

Hypothetical Intent Data	f
7	1
6	5
5	4
4	0
3	5
2	3
1	0

Example Problem 4.1

The frequency distribution of intent judgments of nonaggressive boys in ambiguous situations is shown in Table 4-3.

a. Find the mode at pre- and posttest.

b. Do nonaggressive boys change their perceptions of the provocateur's intent from pre- to posttest based on the modes?

c. Compare and describe differences in intents between nonaggressive and aggressive boys.

TABLE 4-3   Frequency distribution of intent judgments, using the data in Table 4-1 for non- aggressive boys

Intent Judgment	Frequency	
	Pretest	*Posttest*
7	0	0
6	1	1
5	2	2
4	8	7
3	3	4
2	4	3
1	0	1

Although the mode can be useful when a quick estimate of central tendency is needed, it has several limitations. First, the mode is unduly affected by chance factors unless the number of subjects (N) in the sample is very large. When N is small, a shift in the scores of one or two subjects may move the mode several points on the score scale. For example, if, at pretest, one boy rated the provocateur's intent as 4 instead of 5, the mode would be 4.00 and not 4.50 (Table 4-2). If this boy rated the intent as 6 instead of 5, the distribution would be bimodal (see Table 4-2 on p. 87). So the mode may not accurately represent the central tendency of this distribution because of the small sample size.

Second, when data are grouped into class intervals, the crude mode can only fall at the midpoint of the interval. Thus, the value of the crude mode will depend upon the particular size of the intervals used, even though the data set is the same.

Finally, the mode is an especially poor representation of frequency distributions in which the frequencies for the intervals containing the most cases are nearly the same. For such "flat" or rectangular distributions (see Figure 3-5c), a shift of just one or two cases moves the crude mode.

The Median

The median is a more useful and informative measure of central tendency than the mode. The **median** is defined as the point or score value below which 50 percent of the scores fall. Notice that according to this definition, the median coincides with the 50th percentile of a distribution. Figure 4-3 shows the medians of several distributions with different shapes.

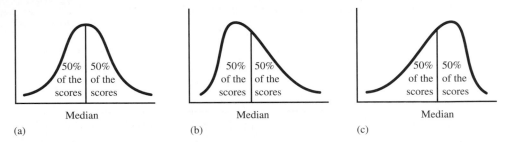

FIGURE 4-3
Medians of several distributions with different shapes: (a) symmetric distribution; (b) positively skewed distribution; (c) negatively skewed distribution

The median is generally used as a measure of the central tendency of distributions that are drastically *asymmetric* (skewed). These distributions often contain extreme scores (see Figures 4-3b, c). The median is particularly useful as a measure of central tendency for such distributions because it is fairly insensitive to extreme scores. (This point will be elaborated when the relationships between the three measures of central tendency are discussed.)[4]

The medians for the hypothetical data on aggressive boys' perceptions of a provocateur's negative intent in ambiguous situations are shown in Table 4-2. The median perceived intent decreased from pretest (5.00) to posttest (4.00). This finding is consistent with the decrease in modal ratings from 4.50 to 4.00.

In calculating the median, recall that it is the score value below which 50 percent of the subjects fall. When the scores are arranged in order of magnitude, the median is the score value that corresponds to the middle subject, or the score value that divides the subjects into two groups with equal numbers in either group. If there is an odd number of subjects, the median corresponds to the score value of the subject exactly in the middle of the range of score values. For example, in the set of scores 2, 3, 4, 5, 6, the median is 4, the score value earned by the subject in the middle of the range of scores. If there is an even number of subjects, the median is the score value halfway between the scores of the two middle subjects. For example, in the set of scores 1, 2, 3, 4, 5, 6, the median is 3.5, the score value halfway between the two middle scores (3 and 4).

When the median is calculated from scores grouped into class intervals, the following general formula can be used:

---

[4]The median is also sometimes used as the dividing point in experiments in which the researcher wants to divide a sample of subjects into two groups on the basis of some individual-difference variable, such as high and low self-concept or high and low verbal ability. However, this "median split" procedure has several drawbacks and is usually not recommended (Maxwell & Delaney, 1993). For example, it treats a subject whose score is just below the median as more similar to a subject whose score is far below the median than to a subject whose score is just above the median. Other statistical procedures presented later in this book, such as regression, permit analysis of the effects of an individual-difference variable without these limitations.

$$\text{median} = X_{ll} + \frac{i\left(N/2 - cf_{ll}\right)}{f_i} \tag{4-1}$$

where:

> X_{ll} = lower real limit of the interval that contains the median
>
> i = interval size
>
> N = total number of scores
>
> cf_{ll} = cumulative frequency of the interval below the interval containing the median
> (see Procedure 3-9)
>
> f_i = frequency of the interval containing the median

Although this formula may look ominous, it does just what the easier counting procedure does. It says to identify the interval that contains the median. This step is not hard to do, since the median lies in the interval below which half the scores fall. The term X_{ll} then, refers to the lower real limit of that interval. Next, it says to find the number of scores in the critical interval below the median ($N/2 - cf_{ll}$). Here $N/2$ is (roughly) the rank of the middle person in the distribution and cf_{ll} is the total number of persons below the interval containing the median. Finally, i/f_i simply distributes the frequency of scores evenly over each score value in the interval. For reference, the steps in calculating the median for a set of scores grouped by class intervals ($i > 1$) are summarized in Procedure 4-2.

PROCEDURE 4-2 Steps in calculating the median from grouped data

Operation_____   Example_____

1. Arrange data in a frequency distribution. The example shows grouped data.

   For simplicity N = 20 and only a few intervals are used.

Class Intervals	f	cf
45–49	3	20
40–44	5	17
35–39	7	12
30–34	3	5
25–29	2	2
		20

2. Determine the value of the frequency below which 50 percent of the cases fall by dividing N by 2:

   $f_{50} = N/2$

   If $N = 20$, $f_{50} = 20/2 = 10$

3. Beginning at the bottom of the distribution, add the values in the frequency column until the halfway point ($f_{50} = 10$) is reached.

   The median will fall in the interval, 35–39 since the tenth and eleventh subjects lie in this interval.

Operation	Example
4. Use Formula 4-1 for calculating the median:	

$$\text{median} = X_{ll} + \frac{i\left(N/2 - cf_{ll}\right)}{f_i}$$

where:

X_{ll} = lower real limit of the interval which contains the median	The lower real limit of the interval 35–39 is 34.5.
i = interval size	The interval size is 5.
N = total number of scores	$N = 20$
cf_{ll} = cumulative frequency of the interval below the interval containing the median (see Procedure 3-9)	The cumulative frequency of the interval *below* (i.e., the interval 30–34) is 5.
f_i = frequency of the interval containing the median	The frequency of the interval containing the median (35–39) is 7.
5. Insert appropriate values into Formula 4-1 and solve.	$34.5 + \dfrac{5\left(20/2 - 5\right)}{7} = 34.5 + 3.57 = 38.07$

Example Problem 4.2 ▬▬▬▬▬▬▬▬▬▬▬▬▬▬▬▬▬▬▬▬▬▬▬▬▬▬▬

    a. Calculate nonaggressive boys' median intent ratings at pre- and posttest. (See Table 4-3 for data.)

    b. Do nonaggressive boys change their perceptions of the provocateur's intent from pre- to posttest based on the median?

    c. With the median as a measure of central tendency instead of the mode, do your conclusions change?

The Mean

The most basic and frequently used measure of central tendency is the arithmetic mean. It is also the measure of central tendency most familiar to you, since it is the same as the "average" you learned to calculate in elementary school. The arithmetic **mean** is defined as the sum of the scores divided by the number of scores that entered that sum. When we express this definition as a formula, special notation—summation notation—is used. The Σ (an oversized Greek capital letter sigma) is used to denote the operation of summing or adding up a group of numbers. And the capital letter X is used to represent any score on a particular variable. Thus, ΣX means the sum of the values of X. If N is used to denote the number of scores entering the sum, then ΣX can be written as:

$$\sum X = X_1 + X_2 + \cdots + X_N$$

The notation ΣX simply represents the verbal statement, "Add up all of the N scores." With this notation, the formula for the mean can be written as shown next.

$$\bar{X} = \frac{\sum x}{N}$$ (4-2)

where:

$\bar{X}$ = mean of a set of scores on variable X (read "X-bar")

N = total number of scores entering the sum

This formula, read in verbal form, says that the mean ($\bar{X}$) equals the sum (Σ) of the scores (X) divided by the number of scores entering the sum (N). Often summation notation is written even more precisely to indicate exactly which persons' scores enter the sum. In this case, p stands for any person from the first person up to the Nth person, and we write:

$$\sum_{p=1}^{N} X_p = X_{p=1} + X_{p=2} + \cdots + X_{p=N}$$
$$= X_1 + X_2 + \cdots + X_N$$

The embellished summation symbol is read as "the sum of X sub p from $p = 1$ to N." In this more detailed notation, the formula for the mean is:

$$\bar{X} = \frac{\sum_{p-1}^{N} X}{N}$$

Throughout this book, summation notation will be used to express formulas. In order to be able to read and use these formulas, you should review the presentation of summation notation in Appendix 1 if you are not already familiar with the notation.

If scores are ordered along a scale of score values, the mean will fall directly at the "balance point" or "center of gravity" of the distribution, as shown in Figure 4-4. This figure looks like a seesaw, with the mean as the point of balance for all scores on either side of it. If the mean were subtracted from each score in the distribution, some of the differences $X - \bar{X}$ would be positive, some zero, and some negative, with the positive scores exactly canceling the negative scores. So the mean can be described more formally as *that point in a distribution such that the algebraic sum of the differences of all scores from the point is zero.*

Figure 4-4 shows hypothetical scores for seven subjects. The mean of this distribution is 6. Notice that the sum of the differences of all scores from this mean on the right is +9, and on the left it is −9. These values sum to 0, as expected.

The analogy between the mean and the balance point of a seesaw illustrates another important characteristic of the mean: It is very sensitive to extreme scores at one or the other end of the range. The hypothetical test scores from Figure 4-4 are shown in the first column

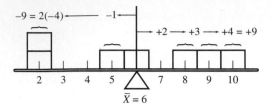

FIGURE 4-4
An illustration of the mean as the point of balance of a seesaw

(labeled "X") of Table 4-4. The mean of this distribution is 6. Column 2 (labeled "X^*") contains the same set of scores except for one extremely large score, 38. This one extreme score is sufficient to shift the mean from 6 to 10. Thus, by the addition of one extreme score, or more weight to one end of the seesaw, the balance is shifted radically. The balance point must be moved toward the extreme score, or toward the end with the new weight, to achieve a new balance.

The means for the hypothetical intent judgments of aggressive boys are shown in Table 4-2. Notice that means in this group closely parallel the other measures of central tendency. Again, aggressive boys' perceptions of negative intent in ambiguous settings decrease, on average, from a mean of 4.72 at pretest to a mean of 3.94 at posttest. This finding is consistent with findings using the mode and median.

The steps for calculating a mean from raw scores are summarized in Procedure 4-3, using posttest intent judgments of aggressive boys in the experimental condition (see Table 4-1).

TABLE 4-4   Comparison of means of two distributions, one of which contains an extreme score

X	X^*
10	38
9	9
8	8
6	6
5	5
2	2
2	2
$\sum X = 42$	$\sum X^* = 70$
$\bar{X} = 6$	$\bar{X}^* = 10$

PROCEDURE 4-3 Steps in calculating the mean from raw scores (data from Table 4-1)

Operation	Example
1. Obtain data for Formula 4-2 $$\bar{X} = \frac{\sum X}{N}$$	Data from aggressive boys' posttest intent judgments: Experimental group

Subject	Judgment
1	3
2	1
3	2
4	2
5	2
6	1

2. Find $\sum X$ by adding all raw scores:
$$\sum X = X_1 + X_2 + \cdots + X_N$$

$$\sum X = 3 + 1 + \cdots + 1 = 11$$

3. Divide $\sum X$ (step 2) by N to find $\dfrac{\sum X}{N}$

$$\bar{X} = \frac{11}{6} = 1.83$$

Example Problem 4.3

 a. Calculate the mean of the nonaggressive boys' intent judgments in the experimental condition at pre- and posttest (see Table 4-1 for data).
 b. Do your conclusions from Example Problem 4.2 change?
 c. Compare and discuss these findings with those for aggressive boys

Averaging Means

Suppose a teaching assistant gives his instructor the mean final exam scores for each of her two statistics classes. Suppose further that the instructor wishes to obtain a measure of the average performance of all her students, regardless of class. She could, of course, obtain the final examination scores for students in both classes and calculate a mean over all these scores. Suppose, however, that she is looking for a simpler way or that she doesn't have all the scores handy. Could she use the mean of the two means to obtain a measure of the average performance of her students? This procedure is only appropriate when the means are based on samples of equal size. In that case, the means have equal weights, since they are based on the same sample size (N). Suppose, for instance, that the mean final examination score was 77 in class 1 and 83 in class 2, and that each class had the same number of students (say, 25). In this case, the mean for all students in both classes is simply the mean of the two separate class means:

$$\frac{77 + 83}{2} = 80$$

For the formula for the average of two or more means based on samples of equal size, some additional notation needs to be introduced. Notice that if we take the average of the group means, the summation is over different groups and not over persons (p). So let i refer to any group and k refer to the last group: $i = 1, 2, \ldots, k$. Then, the formula for the average of two or more means based on equal sample sizes is as given in Formula 4-3.

$$\text{avg } \bar{X} = \frac{\sum\limits_{i=1}^{k} \bar{X}}{k} \tag{4-3}$$
$$= \frac{\bar{X}_1 + \bar{X}_2 + \cdots + \bar{X}_k}{k}$$

In words, this notation says: "Take the sum of the means over all of the (k) groups and divide that sum by the number of groups entering it." Notice that now the precise notation on the summation symbol is essential. It says that this is a sum over groups (and not persons). Again, you should consult Appendix 1 so that you can read and use the formulas in this book.

Suppose, however, that this instructor's classes were *unequal* in size. In this more common case, a *weighted mean* must be computed—that is, means based on a larger sample are weighted more heavily than those based on a smaller number of cases. Because the instructor knows the mean and number of students for each class, she knows how to recover the sum of all the individual scores in each class (even if they are not readily available). Here's how: Recall from Formula 4-2 that

$$\bar{X} = \frac{\sum X}{N}$$

Using the standard algebraic device of multiplying both sides of the equation by N, we find that $\sum X = N\bar{X}$. If, in this way, the instructor calculates the sum of individual scores ($\sum X$) for each of the two classes and adds these sums, she will obtain the sum of scores for all students in both classes. Now, if this total sum is divided by the total number of students in the two classes, the mean score for all students will be obtained.

For example, suppose that the mean final examination score was 77 in class 1 and 83 in class 2, but this time there were 30 students in class 1 and 20 in class 2. Because the classes are unequal in size, a weighted mean must be computed. First, the instructor could calculate the sum of all scores for class 1 ($\sum X = N\bar{X} = 30 \times 77 = 2310$) and for class 2 ($\sum X = N\bar{X} = 20 \times 83 = 1660$). Then, the mean for all students in both classes can be obtained by adding these two sums and dividing by the total number of students:

$$\frac{2310 + 1660}{30 + 20} = \frac{3970}{50} = 79.4$$

The weighted mean for these two classes of unequal size is somewhat lower than the mean for the two classes of equal size. This result makes sense, since the larger class received a lower mean score. This procedure for calculating a weighted mean can be summarized as in Formula 4-4.

$$
\bar{X}_w = \frac{\displaystyle\sum_{i=1}^{k} N_i \bar{X}_i}{\displaystyle\sum_{i=1}^{k} N_i}
$$

$$
= \frac{N_1\bar{X}_1 + N_2\bar{X}_2 + \cdots + N_k\bar{X}_k}{N_1 + N_2 + \cdots + N_k}
$$

(4-4)

where:

$\bar{X}_w$ = weighted mean

k = number of means being combined

N = number of scores (cases) entering into a mean

$\bar{X}_i$ = sample mean for group i

Note that if $N_1 = N_2 = \cdots = N_k$, Formula 4-4 reduces to Formula 4-3.

The steps in computing the weighted mean are summarized in Procedure 4-4.

PROCEDURE 4-4 Steps for averaging k means, based on samples of *unequal* size (hypothetical data)

Operation	Example
1. Look up the general formula for the weighted mean: $\bar{X}_w = \dfrac{\sum_{i=1}^{k} N_i \bar{X}_i}{\sum_{i=1}^{k} N_i}$	
2. Multiply each mean ($\bar{X}$) by its sample size (N) to obtain $N_1\bar{X}_1, N_2\bar{X}_2, \ldots, N_k\bar{X}_k$.	Mean exam scores for three classes ($k = 3$): N $\bar{X}$ $N\bar{X}$ 30 77 2310 20 83 1660 25 80 2000
3. Add $N_1\bar{X}_1, N_2\bar{X}_2, \ldots, N_k\bar{X}_k$: $N_1\bar{X}_1 + N_2\bar{X}_2 + \cdots + N_k\bar{X}_k$	$2310 + 1660 + 2000 = 5970$

Operation	Example
4. Add $N_1, N_2, \ldots, N_k$ to find the total N: $N_1 + N_2 + \cdots + N_k$	$30 + 20 + 25 = 75$
5. Divide the result of step 2 by the result of step 3: $\dfrac{N_1 \bar{X}_1 + N_2 \bar{X}_2 + \cdots + N_k \bar{X}_k}{N_1 + N_2 + \cdots + N_k}$	$\dfrac{5970}{75} = 79.6$

Example Problem 4.4

    a. An instructor taught four introductory classes one year. The mean scores of these classes on the final examination were (a) 71, (b) 76, (c) 79, and (d) 81. The number of students enrolled in these classes were (a) 22, (b) 30, (c) 35, and (d) 28. Find the mean of the final examination scores for all students enrolled in this instructor's classes.

    b. Suppose you wanted to combine the mean pretest and posttest intent judgments of aggressive boys in the experimental group. Could you just take the mean of the two means or do you need to take a weighted mean? Justify your answer.

Relationship Among Measures of Central Tendency

There is no one best measure of the central tendency of a distribution. The preferred measure depends on the shape of the distribution and on what you are trying to communicate about the distribution. For example, if the distribution is symmetric, as in Figure 4-5a, the values of the mean, mode, and median are equal, so any one of the three will tell the same story. With symmetric or nearly symmetric distributions, often the mean or median is preferred to the mode since the mode is the least stable measure of central tendency. Most often in practice, the mean is used, because the researcher not only wants to describe the distribution of scores in the sample but also wants to draw inferences from the sample to the population. In this case, the mean is mathematically more tractable than the median. For this and other reasons, mathematical statistics has taken the mean as the focus of most of its inferential methods.

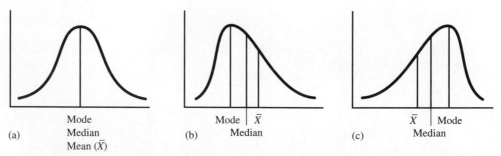

FIGURE 4-5

Relative position of measures of central tendency in three distributions: (a) symmetric (bell-shaped) distribution; (b) distribution with a few extremely high scores (positively skewed); (c) distribution with a few extremely low scores (negatively skewed)

However, in some cases, the median or mode may be preferred to the mean as a measure of central tendency. In distributions with a few extremely high scores (positively skewed distributions), such as that shown in Figure 4-5b, the mode, the median, and the mean have different values. Extreme scores usually have their greatest effect on the mean, a smaller effect on the median, and the least effect on the mode. Because the mean has to balance the distribution, it is pulled out toward the extreme scores of the tail. Thus, in a distribution with a few extremely high scores, the mean has the highest value of all the measures of central tendency. The median has an intermediate value. The mode, or most frequently earned score, has a somewhat lower value than the median. Similarly, in distributions with a few extremely low scores (negatively skewed distributions), such as that shown in Figure 4-5c, the mean is pulled out toward the extreme scores and has the lowest value of all the measures of central tendency. The median has a somewhat higher value, and the mode has the highest value of all the measures of central tendency. Thus, in asymmetric distributions in which there are very high or very low scores, the mean is less representative of most scores than the other measures of central tendency, and so the median is usually preferred. The mode is appropriate when a quick, approximate estimate of central tendency is desired; however, as already mentioned, it is rarely used in drawing conclusions from behavioral research because of its instability.

MEASURES OF VARIABILITY

Another way to characterize a frequency distribution is by the *spread* of scores in the distribution. The greater the differences between scores earned by different people, the more spread out (or scattered) the scores are in a distribution. The more tightly the scores cluster together, the smaller the spread of scores in the distribution. The **variability** of a distribution is the general term for the spread of scores in it.

Distributions may be the same with respect to central tendency (location on a score scale) but differ considerably with respect to variability. Three hypothetical distributions of scores were shown in Figure 4-2. Notice that scores in classes *A* and *B* have the same central tendency but differ in variability. How do classes *B* and *C* compare on central tendency and variability?

The Range

For measures of variability, an index is needed that indicates the spread or distance of scores along the score scale. The range is one such measure of spread. It is the easiest to compute and, probably, to understand. It is simply the difference between the highest and the lowest score in the distribution. Formally, the **range** is defined as the highest score in the distribution minus the lowest score; see Formula 4-5.

$$\text{range} = X_{\text{highest}} - X_{\text{lowest}} \qquad\qquad (4\text{-}5)$$

The range of intent judgments of all 18 aggressive boys (ignoring treatments) is presented in the first row of Table 4-5 at pre- and posttest. (Ignore the other rows for the moment.) Notice that the range is considerably smaller at pretest than at posttest. This result may have occurred because boys in the experimental group lowered their intent judgments at posttest whereas boys in the other two groups did not.

TABLE 4-5   Measures of variability for intent judgments of aggressive boys, using data from Table 4-1

Measure of Variability	Pretest	Posttest
Range	4.00	6.00
SIQR	0.92	1.33
Standard deviation	1.18	1.81
Variance	1.39	3.28

Although the range is easy to compute, it is seldom used as the only measure of variability, for several reasons. First, it is based only on the two most extreme scores in the distribution, which makes it highly unstable. For example, the range might differ greatly in two groups of subjects just because one subject in one of the groups earned an extremely high score. Second, the range does not fully reflect the pattern of variation in the distribution. For example, if there is one extreme score in a distribution, the range of scores will be very large when, in fact, all of the other scores might cluster together.

Example Problem 4.5

a. Calculate the range of intent judgments of nonaggressive boys at pre- and posttest. (See Table 4-1 for data.)
b. Are the ranges for nonaggressive boys at pre- and posttest similar to those of aggressive boys?

The Semi-Interquartile Range

The semi-interquartile range (SIQR) also provides a measure of the spread of scores along a score scale. More specifically, the SIQR provides a measure of the spread of the middle 50 percent of the scores. Formally, the **semi-interquartile range** is defined as half the difference between the scores at the 75th and 25th percentiles; see Formula 4-6.

$$SIQR = \frac{Q_3 - Q_1}{2}$$ (4-6)

where:

Q_3 = score at the 75th percentile (i.e., top of the third quarter)
Q_1 = score at the 25th percentile (i.e., top of the first quarter)

Figure 4-6 shows the SIQR for a symmetric and an asymmetric distribution. Notice that the extreme scores in Figure 4-6 have much less of an influence on the SIQR than they have on the range.

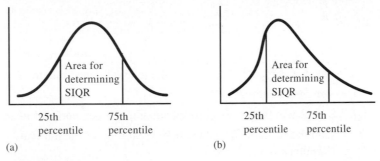

(a)   (b)

FIGURE 4-6
Symmetric and asymmetric distributions, with the spread for determining the semi-interquartile range (SIQR) indicated

In calculating the SIQR, determine the score values corresponding to the 25th and 75th percentiles. As an example of how this calculation is done, suppose the following data were collected on a sample of 20 subjects (only a few class intervals are used to simplify the example):

Class Interval	f	cf
35–39	1	20
30–34	2	19
25–29	9	17
20–24	6	8
15–19	2	2

In order to find the score values corresponding to the 25th and 75th percentiles, we must first find the cumulative frequencies corresponding to these percentiles. Then the score values corresponding to these cumulative frequencies can be calculated as shown in Procedure 4-5.

1. Find the cumulative frequencies:

$$cf = \frac{\text{percentile rank} \times N}{100}$$

Thus

$$cf_{25} = \frac{25 \times 20}{100} = 5$$

$$cf_{75} = \frac{75 \times 20}{100} = 15$$

2. Find the score at each percentile by using Formula 4-7:

$$\text{score at percentile } (Q) = X_{ll} + \frac{i(cf - cf_{ul})}{f_i} \qquad \text{(4-7)}$$

where:

X_{ll} = value of the lower real limit of the interval containing the *cf* of interest

i = size of the interval

cf = cumulative frequency corresponding to the percentile of interest

cf_{ul} = cumulative frequency at the upper real limit of the interval *below* the interval containing the *cf*

f_i = frequency of the interval containing the *cf*

Thus

$$Q_1 = 19.5 + \frac{5(5 - 2)}{6} = 22.00$$

$$Q_3 = 24.5 + \frac{5(15 - 8)}{9} = 28.39$$

Once Q_1 and Q_3 are known, the semi-interquartile range can be calculated from Formula 4-6.

$$SIQR = \frac{Q_3 - Q_1}{2} = \frac{28.39 - 22.00}{2} = 3.20$$

The steps in calculating the SIQR are reviewed in Procedure 4-5. In your review of these steps, note that in finding Q_1 and Q_3 with data in class intervals, we assume that the frequency of each score value is equal to the frequency of every other score value within the interval. If this assumption does not hold, Q_1 and Q_3 may be slightly in error. But this error is negligible.

PROCEDURE 4-5 Steps in computing the semi-interquartile range (example taken from Table 4-1, aggressive boys' posttest intent judgments)

Operation	Example
1. Look up Formula 4-6 for calculating the *SIQR*:	This example uses score values, not class intervals.

$$SIQR = \frac{Q_3 - Q_1}{2}$$

where:

Q_3 = score at the 75th percentile

Q_1 = score at the 25th percentile

Operation		**Example**			

2. Construct a cumulative frequency distribution. *(See Procedure 3-8 for the steps.)*

Score Value	f	Upper Real Limit	cf
7	1	7.5	18
6	3	6.5	17
5	3	5.5	14
4	4	4.5	11
3	3	3.5	7
2	2	2.5	4
1	2	1.5	2

3. Calculate the cumulative frequency corresponding to Q_3 (score at the 75th percentile):

$$cf = \frac{\text{percentile rank} \times N}{100}$$

$$cf = \frac{75 \times 18}{100} = 13.5$$

4. Compare Q_3 by inserting the appropriate values into Formula 4-7:

$$\text{Score at percentile} = X_{ll} + \frac{i(cf - cf_{ul})}{f_i} \quad \textbf{(4–7)}$$

$$Q_3 = 4.5 + \frac{1(13.5 - 11)}{3} = 5.33$$

where:
X_{ll} = value at the lower real limit of the interval containing the cf of interest

$X_{ll} = 4.5$

i = interval size

$i = 1$

cf = cumulative frequency corresponding to the percentile of interest

$cf = 13.5$ (computed in step 3)

cf_{ul} = cumulative frequency at the upper real limit of the interval *below* the interval containing the cf

$cf_{ul} = 11$

f_i = frequency of the interval containing the cf

$f_i = 3$

5. Calculate the cumulative frequency corresponding to Q_1 (score at the 25th percentile; see step 3).

$$cf = \frac{25 \times 18}{100} = 4.5$$

6. Compute Q_1 by inserting the appropriate values into Formula 4-7 (see step 4).

$$Q_1 = 2.5 + \frac{1(4.5 - 4)}{3} = 2.67$$

$X_{ll} = 2.5$
$i = 1$
$cf = 4.5$ (see step 5)
$f_i = 3$

7. Insert the appropriate values in Formula 4-6 (see step 1), and solve.

$$SIQR = \frac{5.33 - 2.67}{2} = 1.33$$

The semi-interquartile range for aggressive boys' intent judgments at pre- and posttest is shown in Table 4-5 (on p.100). Notice that the semi-interquartile range increases from pre- to posttest as does the range. However, as a measure of spread, the SIQR has a magnitude that is considerably smaller than the magnitude of the range. Because the SIQR focuses on the middle 50 percent of the scores, it is much less affected by extreme scores than is the range. For this reason, the semi-interquartile range is often preferred to the range and is often used as a measure of variability in skewed distributions that have a few extremely high or extremely low scores (see Figure 4-6b). Given a skewed distribution, then, the median is often used to measure its central tendency, and the semi-interquartile range is often used to describe and measure its variability.

Example Problem 4.6

    a. Calculate the semi-interquartile range for the intent judgments of nonaggressive boys at pre- and posttest (see Table 4-1 for data).
    b. Does the variability change from pre- to posttest?
    c. Does the pattern of variability change when the SIQR is used rather than the range? If so, how?
    d. Is there a difference at posttest between the SIQR of aggressive and nonaggressive boys? If so, what might explain the difference?

The Standard Deviation

The most commonly used measure of the variability of scores in a distribution is the standard deviation. It is an index of the variability (spread) of scores about the mean of a distribution, something like the average dispersion or deviation of the scores (X) about their mean $(\bar{X})$. The greater the spread of scores, the greater is the standard deviation. For example, in Figure 4-2 the scores in distribution A cluster about the mean of the distribution, and the scores in distribution B are spread out. The standard deviation for distribution A, then, would be less than the standard deviation for distribution B.

More formally, the **standard deviation** may be defined as the square root of the average squared deviation of scores from the mean of the distribution, measured in units of the original score scale. This definition is reflected in the **deviation score formula** for the standard deviation, Formula 4-8.

$$s = \sqrt{\frac{\sum (X - \bar{X})^2}{N - 1}}$$

         (4-8)

In this formula, $\sum (X - \bar{X})^2$ represents the sum of the squared deviations of each person's score from the mean. By dividing $\sum (X - \bar{X})^2$ by $N - 1$, we get (approximately) an average of the squared deviations. Finally, by taking the square root of this average, we get a measure of variability in the original measurement units. That is, since we squared $X - \bar{X}$, we have to take the square root to get back to the original measurement units.

At first glance, this formula is somewhat awesome. In order to give you a feeling about how it works, let's start from the beginning and build the formula. Don't be alarmed—no sophisticated mathematical concepts are needed.

To begin, recall that the major limitation of the range as a measure of the variability of scores in a distribution is that it is based on two extreme, often unstable scores. Another way to measure the spread of scores in a distribution might be to consider the variability of each of the scores in the distribution about the central tendency of the distribution. More specifically, then, we might begin to develop this measure of variability, the standard deviation, by subtracting the mean—the most stable measure of central tendency—from each of the scores in the distribution. This process produces deviation scores that can be represented as $x = X - \bar{X}$. These deviation scores provide a measure of the *distance* of each raw score from the mean of the distribution.

Since we want a measure that takes all deviation scores into account, the most obvious next step would be to sum up the deviation scores. This process gives us Σx or $\Sigma (X - \bar{X})$. However, since the mean is the balance point of the distribution, we know that this attempt is doomed to failure: $\Sigma (X - \bar{X}) = \Sigma x = 0$. Back to the drawing board! The difficulty in summing deviation scores is that the ones with positive (+) signs cancel out the ones with negative (–) signs, leaving us with zero.

One possible way around this problem is simply to ignore the sign of the deviation scores. In this case, we would be summing the absolute values of the deviation scores. This procedure provides a measure of variability called the *average deviation*. The average deviation has some history as a measure of variability; however, it is seldom used today because it is unsuitable for use in other statistical analyses.

Another way to do away with the nuisance of the signs of the deviation scores canceling each other is to square each deviation score. This procedure will work because the square of a negative number is positive, as is the square of a positive number. We now have the sum of the squared deviation scores: $\Sigma (X - \bar{X})^2 = \Sigma x^2 \neq 0$ unless all of the scores are exactly equal to the mean. This procedure turns out to be useful for our own purposes as well as applicable to other statistical analyses.

We now have a measure of variability that takes all of the deviation scores into account. The next problem is to get some measure of the "average" amount of variability about the mean of the distribution. This average can be obtained by dividing the sum of squared deviation scores, $\Sigma (X - \bar{X})^2 = \Sigma x^2$, by $N - 1$:

$$\frac{\Sigma (X - \bar{X})^2}{N - 1} = \frac{\Sigma x^2}{N - 1}$$

This formula will give us something like the average dispersion of scores in the distribution about the mean; it is defined as the variance (see the section, "The Variance," below).[5]

---

[5]I assume that you are interested in learning statistics as tools that can be used to answer research questions. As a consequence, I have sidestepped certain statistical developments that are not directly germane to you. The use of $N - 1$ in the denominator of the expression $\Sigma (X - \bar{X})^2/(N - 1)$ is a case in point. Formally, this term, called the variance, is defined as the mean of the squared deviation of scores about $\bar{X}$: $\Sigma (X - \bar{X})^2/N$. Thus, it is an

The last problem is to return the measure of variability back to the original score scale. (Remember each deviation score was squared.) This problem can be solved by taking the square root. Thus, we have Formulas 4-8 a, b.

$$s = \sqrt{\frac{\sum(X - \bar{X})^2}{N - 1}} \qquad \text{(4-8a)}$$

$$= \sqrt{\frac{\sum x^2}{N - 1}} \qquad \text{(4-8b)}$$

The result matches the formula for the standard deviation given at the beginning of this section.

In order to show how to calculate a standard deviation and to keep things simple, consider the standard deviation of a sample of three scores—1, 2, 3. Two preliminary calculations have to be made:

$$\bar{X} = \frac{1 + 2 + 3}{3} = 2$$

$$\sum(X - \bar{X})^2 = (X_1 - \bar{X})^2 + (X_2 - \bar{X})^2 + (X_3 - \bar{X})^2$$
$$= (1 - 2)^2 + (2 - 2)^2 + (3 - 2)^2$$
$$= 1 + 0 + 1 = \sum x^2$$

With these preliminary calculations made, the appropriate values can be entered into the formula for the standard deviation, with the following result:

$$s = \sqrt{\frac{\sum x^2}{N - 1}} = \sqrt{\frac{2}{3 - 1}} = \sqrt{1} = 1$$

The square root of the average squared deviation of the set of scores about their mean—the standard deviation—is 1 score point.

For reference, the steps in calculating a standard deviation are given in Procedure 4-6.

---

average of the squared deviation of scores about the sample mean. However, in answering research questions, we are seldom interested in describing the sample as an end in itself. Rather, we are interested in the sample because it gives us some insight into the nature of the population. That is, we typically use sample statistics as estimators of population parameters (see Chapter 1). Thus, the sample mean is used to estimate the population mean, and the sample variance is used to estimate the spread of scores in the population—the population variance. When the sample variance is used to estimate the population variance, it is defined as $\sum (X - \bar{X})^2/(N - 1)$. This definition produces an unbiased estimate of the population variance, whereas $\sum (X - \bar{X})^2/N$ produces a biased estimate (see Chapter 1; see Hays [1973, pp. 283–284] for the derivation). So, we have opted to define the sample variance as $\sum (X - \bar{X})^2/(N - 1)$. This definition provides for a simplification of notation and presentation of new concepts when we take up material on inferential statistics. It also allows you to focus on those aspects of statistics that provide tools for answering research questions.

PROCEDURE 4-6 Steps in calculating the standard deviation using deviation scores

Operation	Example

1. Look up Formula 4-8 for calculating the standard deviation from deviation scores:

Scores: 2, 4, 6.

$$s = \sqrt{\frac{\sum (X - \bar{X})^2}{N-1}} = \sqrt{\frac{\sum x^2}{N-1}}$$

2. Set up a table with the following four columns: X, $\bar{X}$, x, x^2.

X	$\bar{X}$	x	x^2

3. List all raw scores in the column labeled X.

X	$\bar{X}$	x	x^2
2			
4			
6			

4. Calculate the mean and list it in the column labeled $\bar{X}$.

X	$\bar{X}$	x	x^2
2	4		
4	4		
6	4		

5. Subtract the mean ($\bar{X}$) from each raw score (X) to obtain the deviation score (x): $x = X - \bar{X}$. List each deviation score in the column labeled x.

X	$\bar{X}$	x	x^2
2	4	-2	
4	4	0	
6	4	2	

6. Square each deviation score (x). List the values of the squared deviation scores in the column labeled x^2.

X	$\bar{X}$	x	x^2
2	4	-2	4
4	4	0	0
6	4	2	4

7. Sum the squared deviation scores to obtain $\sum x^2$.

X	$\bar{X}$	x	x^2
2	4	-2	4
4	4	0	0
6	4	2	4
			$\sum x^2 = 8$

8. Divide $\sum x^2$ by $N-1$.

$8 \div 2 = 4.00$

This value is defined as the variance.

9. Take the square root of the value obtained in step 8.

$\sqrt{4.00} = 2.00$

As mentioned earlier, the greater the variability of scores in the distribution, the larger the standard deviation of the distribution. The standard deviations of aggressive boys' intent judgments are presented in Table 4-5 (on p.100). They are larger at posttest than at pretest. This pattern was also reflected in the corresponding ranges and SIQRs for these conditions. These statistics suggest that something has happened across the three treatment groups that has increased the variability of scores at posttest.

The standard deviation has several advantages over the range and SIQR as a measure of variability. Although both the range and the SIQR are defined relative to the total distribution of scores, the former focuses on only two scores, and the latter focuses on 50 percent of the scores. In contrast, the standard deviation uses each score in the distribution in providing a measure of variation among scores. It is a more *stable* measure of variation than the range or the SIQR. Furthermore, when referred to the normal distribution, the standard deviation permits a precise interpretation of scores in the distribution (see Chapter 5). Lastly, many statistical tests rely on the standard deviation to represent the variability of scores in a set of data.

Example Problem 4.7

    a. Use the deviation score formula to calculate the standard deviation of nonaggressive boys' intent judgments at pre- and posttest.

    b. Are the standard deviations of this group similar to those of the aggressive boys (see Table 4-5)? Explain.

The Raw Score Formula

An alternative to calculating the standard deviation from deviation scores is to calculate it directly from raw scores. A **raw score formula,** Formula 4-9, is presented here because you may see it used in statistics books by itself or in the development of other statistics.[6]

---

[6]The following proof demonstrates the equivalence of the deviation score formula and raw score formula for calculating the standard deviation s of a distribution:

Step	Reason
$\sum x^2$	
$= \sum (X - \bar{X})^2$	Definition of a deviation score
$= \sum (X^2 - 2X\bar{X} + \bar{X}^2)$	Expansion of a polynomial
$= \sum X^2 - 2\sum X\bar{X} + \sum \bar{X}^2$	Distribution of summation sign
$= \sum X^2 - 2N\bar{X}^2 + \sum \bar{X}^2$	Substitution $\sum X = N\bar{X}$. Thus, $2\sum X\bar{X} = 2(N\bar{X})\bar{X} = 2N\bar{X}^2$
$= \sum X^2 - 2N\bar{X}^2 + N\bar{X}^2$	Effects of summation over a constant
$= \sum X^2 - N\bar{X}^2$	Combination of terms
$= \sum X^2 - N\left(\sum X / N\right)^2$	Definition of a mean

$$s = \sqrt{\frac{\sum X^2 - \dfrac{\left(\sum X\right)^2}{N}}{N - 1}}$$

(4-9)

The Variance

Another commonly used measure of variability is the variance. The **variance** is defined as the average squared deviation of scores about their mean. It is denoted as s^2, since it is equal to the square of the standard deviation s. The deviation score formula for the variance is given in Formula 4-10.

$$s^2 = \frac{\sum (X - \bar{X})^2}{N - 1}$$

(4-10a)

$$= \frac{\sum x^2}{N - 1}$$

(4-10b)

The raw score formula for the variance is given in Formula 4-11.

$$s = \frac{\sum X^2 - \dfrac{\left(\sum X\right)^2}{N}}{N - 1}$$

(4-11)

The variance is mentioned here because it is frequently used in more advanced statistical tests, such as the analysis of variance, and will be referred to in later sections of this book.

The variances of intent judgments are shown in Table 4-5 (on p. 100). To calculate the variance, simply square the standard deviation.

Comparison of Measures of Variability

In general, the standard deviation is the most commonly used measure of variability. It has several desirable characteristics. First, it is as stable as the variance, and more so than the range. Furthermore, the standard deviation, unlike the variance, is directly interpretable in

---

$$= \sum X^2 - \left(\sum X\right)^2 / N \qquad \text{Combination of terms}$$

$$s = \sqrt{\frac{\sum x^2}{N - 1}} \qquad \text{Definition}$$

$$= \sqrt{\frac{\sum X^2 - \left(\sum X\right)^2 / N}{N - 1}} \qquad \text{Substitution}$$

terms of actual score units. Finally, the standard deviation (like the variance) is used in inferential statistics, whereas the range and semi-interquartile range are not. The virtue of the
range is that it provides a quick, rough estimate of variability. The major advantage of the
semi-interquartile range is that it is relatively unaffected by extreme scores. Thus, the SIQR
is often used to describe skewed distributions.

SUMMARY

This chapter presents measures that can be used to describe the *central tendency* and *variability* of a distribution of scores. Measures of central tendency—the *mode*, the *median*, and
the *mean*—describe the location of a distribution on a score scale. Indexes of variability—
the *range*, the *semi-interquartile range*, the *standard deviation*, and the *variance*—describe
the spread of scores in the distribution.

ANSWERS TO EXAMPLE PROBLEMS

1. **a.** $\text{Mode}_{\text{pretest}} = 4.00$; $\text{Mode}_{\text{posttest}} = 4.00$

    b. On average (where average is defined by the mode), nonaggressive boys did not
    change their perceptions of the provocateur's intent in ambiguous situations. How-
    ever, individuals did change their ratings.

    c. The aggressive boys, on average, decrease their perceptions of negative intent from
    pretest (4.50) to posttest (4.00). The posttest mode for aggressive boys is at the level
    of negative intent perceived by nonaggressive boys at both pre- and posttest.

2. **a.** $\text{Median}_{\text{pretest}} = 4.00$; $\text{Median}_{\text{posttest}} = 4.00$

    b. On average (where average is defined by the median), nonaggressive boys did not
    change their perceptions of the provocateur's intent in ambiguous situations. How-
    ever, individuals did.

    c. No, both measures of central tendency produce the same result.

3. **a.** $\text{Mean}_{\text{pretest}} = 3.17$; $\text{Mean}_{\text{posttest}} = 3.00$

    b. No. As measured by the mean, the nonaggressive boys' perceptions of negative
    intent are, on average, stable from pre- to posttest. However, the mean provides a
    systematically lower score value for central tendency (about 3) than does either the
    mode or median (4.00). The mean is influenced by extreme scores (such as 1 in these
    data) more than either the mode or median.

    c. Whereas the mean intent judgment for nonaggressive boys remains fairly stable,
    such judgments for aggressive boys decrease, but the decrease does not go as low
    as the intent judgment of nonaggressive boys.

4. **a.**
$$\bar{X}_w = \frac{N_1\bar{X}_1 + N_2\bar{X}_2 + N_3\bar{X}_3 + N_4\bar{X}_4}{N_1 + N_2 + N_3 + N_4}$$
$$= \frac{(22)(71) + (30)(76) + (35)(79) + (28)(81)}{22 + 30 + 35 + 28}$$
$$= 77.2$$

    b. Simply take the mean of the two group means—sample sizes are the same.

5. **a.** $Range_{pretest} = 4.00$; $Range_{posttest} = 5.00$

    b. The range at pretest is the same; at posttest, the range is greater for the aggressive than for the nonaggressive boys.

6. **a.** $SIQR_{pretest} = 0.82$; $SIQR_{posttest} = 0.83$

    b. No

    c. Yes. The range shows an increase (4.00 to 5.00) and the SIQR is stable.

    d. Yes. The SIQR is greater for aggressive boys. Perhaps this reflects an effect of the experimental treatment on aggressive boys while the other two conditions may not have changed, thus increasing the variability at posttest.

7. **a.** Calculate SD with the Deviation Score Formula.

    $S_{pretest} = 1.15$ $S_{posttest} = 1.25$

    b. No. Again, the pre- and posttest standard deviations are about the same for the nonaggressive boys whereas the posttest standard deviation is greater than the pretest standard deviation for the aggressive boys, perhaps reflecting an experimental treatment effect.

EXERCISES

Use the data from the study of the relationship between student sex and SAT scores (Chapter 3 Exercises) to:

1. Construct a separate data matrix for students' SAT scores in the humanities (English, design), the social sciences (anthropology, sociology), and the sciences (physics, chemistry, biology, engineering). (*Note:* include information on campus, sex, and major for future use.)
2. Calculate and compare the mode, median, and mean SAT score for each group.
3. Calculate the combined mean SAT score for the humanities and social sciences and compare this mean with the mean of the sciences.
4. Calculate and compare the range, interquartile range, and standard deviation of SAT scores for each group.

ANSWERS TO EXERCISES

1.   *HUMANITIES*

Original Persons	ID	Campus[a]	Sex[b]	Major[c]	Score
04	01	1	1	7	1130
06	02	1	2	7	1075
07	03	1	2	7	1100
09	04	1	2	8	1000
19	05	2	2	7	1085
27	06	3	2	8	1060
28	07	3	2	7	1050
30	08	3	2	7	1100
35	09	4	1	7	1200
40	10	4	2	8	1150

[a] 1 = UCLA, 2 = UCD, 3 = UCI, 4 = UCSD
[b] 1 = male, 2 = female
[c] 7 = English, 8 = design

SOCIAL SCIENCES

Original Persons	ID	Campus[a]	Sex[b]	Major[c]	Score
03	01	1	1	5	1100
17	02	2	2	6	1090
18	03	2	2	6	1100
20	04	2	2	5	1125
26	05	3	2	6	1090
29	06	3	2	5	1175
37	07	4	2	6	1100
38	08	4	2	5	1120
39	09	4	2	5	1080

[a] 1 = UCLA, 2 = UCD, 3 = UCI, 4 = UCSD
[b] 1 = male, 2 = female
[c] 5 = anthropology, 6 = sociology.

SCIENCES

Original Persons	ID	Campus[a]	Sex[b]	Major[c]	Score
01	01	1	1	1	1050
02	02	1	1	1	1200
05	03	1	1	2	1160
08	04	1	2	4	1025
10	05	1	2	3	1000
11	06	2	1	1	1175
12	07	2	1	4	1125
13	08	2	1	3	1100
14	09	2	1	4	1150
15	10	2	1	3	1200
16	11	2	2	2	1120
21	12	3	1	1	1125
22	13	3	1	3	1175
23	14	3	1	2	1200
24	15	3	1	3	1100
25	16	3	1	4	1150
31	17	4	1	1	1150
32	18	4	1	2	1185
33	19	4	1	4	1200
34	20	4	1	3	1160
36	21	4	2	3	1150

[a] 1 = UCLA, 2 = UCD, 3 = UCI, 4 = UCSD
[b] 1 = male, 2 = female
[c] 1 = physics, 2 = chemistry, 3 = biology, 4 = engineering

2.

Group	Mode	Median	Mean
Humanities	1100	1092.50	1095.00
Social Sciences	1100	1100.00	1108.89
Sciences	1150, 1200	1150.00	1138.10

The average SAT scores—as indexed by the mode, median, and mean—are quite similar for the humanities and social sciences. The average for the sciences appears to be somewhat higher than the other two groups. Given the similarity among the three indices of central tendency, the distribution of scores for each of the groups is, roughly, symmetric.

3. $\dfrac{(10 \times 1095) + (9 \times 1108.89)}{10 + 9} = 1101.58$

Students' SAT scores in the sciences are, on average, higher than students' in the social sciences and humanities combined.

4.

Group	Range	Interquartile[a] Range	Standard Deviation
Humanities	200	35.00	55.88
Social Sciences	95	15.00	28.59
Sciences	200	27.50	57.00

[a]Rounding: For the social sciences, for example: $(1120 - 1090)/2 = 15.00$

The variation in SAT scores—as indexed by the range, interquartile range, and standard deviation—of the social sciences appears to be considerably smaller than that of either the humanities or sciences, which appear to be fairly close.

The Normal Distribution

A curious thing happens when data are summarized in a frequency polygon. Regardless of the characteristic being measured (e.g., achievement, personality, height), often this distribution looks like a bell (as in Figure 5-1) and so is described as a *bell-shaped curve*. The curve is roughly symmetric, with the most frequently earned scores at the middle of the distribution. The mean, mode, and median provide about the same numerical values as measures of the central tendency of the distribution. Often this bell-shaped curve can be modeled by a normal distribution. The **normal distribution** is a mathematical idealization of a particular type of symmetric distribution; it is a mathematical curve that provides a good model of relative frequency distributions found in behavioral research. Since the normal distribution serves as a model for much of the data collected in behavioral research, it plays a critical role in statistics.

This chapter examines the normal distribution and its properties in some detail. The purposes of this chapter are (1) to introduce you to the properties of the normal distribution and (2) to provide you with the concepts and skills to identify areas under the normal curve corresponding to particular scores.

115

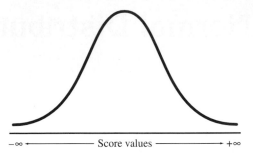

FIGURE 5-1
The normal distribution or bell-shaped curve

RESEARCH EXAMPLE: DISPARITY IN WOMEN'S AND MEN'S COLLEGE GRADES

Hypothetical data from a study of the disparity in college grades earned by men and women are used to illustrate the use or interpretation of the normal distribution in behavioral research. Before turning to the normal distribution, we set the context with research.

Did you know that when college grades of men and women of equivalent aptitude are compared, the women tend to earn higher grades than the men? For example, Keller, Crouse, & Trusheim (1993) studied gender differences in freshman grades in 290 college courses at a mid-Atlantic university and found that, on average, female students earned grades .10 grade point above male students.

In the literature on sex differences in higher education, there have been several "explanations" of this finding. One proposed explanation is that a different standard is used for grading men and women; perhaps men are graded harder than women. A second explanation is that the same grading standard is used for men and women and that the difference in grades is due to "typically feminine" traits. For example, in its most pejorative form, the reasoning has been that women, being more docile, may follow their instructor's directions more closely than men. Hence, they attend class more regularly, turn in assignments on time more often, and are more responsive to the instructor's criticisms of their work. Still another proposed explanation has been that the difference in grades may stem from women's highly developed "clerical traits." In this view, their work may be neater than the men's, it may be more artistic, or it may be more tedious in detail. Regardless of the exact nature of the explanation, it has "typically female," nonacademic-related characteristics.

A plausible, but often overlooked, alternative explanation is that the apparent disparity in grades between men and women of equal ability is due to differences in the grading practices in different fields of study and not due to some inherent or learned characteristic of women. For example, Keller et al. (1993) found that the apparent .10 grade-point advantage of women over men disappeared when Scholastic Aptitude Test (SAT) scores and high-school grade point averages (HSGPAs) were taken into consideration. Moreover, they found that:

• Females tended to enroll in courses that awarded higher grades, on average, than did males

- Courses with higher female enrollments tended to be those in which "higher SAT scores and HSGPAs are relatively less important for earning higher grades" (p. 705)

Finally, Goldman et al. (1974) found that grading standards are more stringent in the biological and physical sciences than in the humanities and social sciences so that, perhaps, the grade difference is due to gender-related course taking. Keller et al. (1993, pp. 706–707) provide support for this conjecture. They found GPA advantages for females or males in the following courses:

Female Advantage	*Male Advantage*
Nutrition and dietetics	Statistics
Recreation and park administration	Anthropology
Food and resource economics	History
African-American studies	Physics
French	Chemical engineering
Linguistics	Chemistry
Russian	Computer and information sciences
Italian	Electrical engineering
Spanish	Geography
Art, continuing education	Economics

It may be, then, that a greater percentage of women than men enroll in the humanities and social sciences, but a greater percentage of men than women enroll in biology and the physical sciences.

In order to check out this explanation, suppose you collect information on men's and women's choices of academic majors, grade point averages, and aptitude test scores. If your hunch is correct, these data should show that men and women tend to choose different academic majors, that women tend to major in the humanities and social sciences whereas men tend to major in the biological and physical sciences, and that men and women of similar ability have similar grade point averages when the major field is taken into account.

Data from your hypothetical study are presented in Table 5-1 for male and female undergraduates from four campuses of the University of California. Do these data support your hypothesis that men and women choose different major fields and that men and women of similar aptitudes have similar grade point averages when the major field is taken into account? In an attempt to answer these questions, descriptive statistics can be used to summarize the data in your study.

This hypothetical study and the patterns in the hypothetical data parallel a study and data reported by Hewitt & Goldman (1975). They collected data on all undergraduates enrolled at four campuses of the University of California for whom complete data on the following measures were available: major, GPA, and SAT scores. The final sample numbered over 13,000 students.

Hewitt and Goldman sought answers to two major questions. First, "Do men and women tend to choose different majors?" Actual data showing the numbers of men and women choosing four majors at UCLA are presented in Table 5-2. A similar pattern occurred at the three other universities. From these and other data, Hewitt and Goldman concluded that gender and major field were related at all four schools.

TABLE 5-1   Hypothetical data on sex, undergraduate major, and grade point average for four University of California campuses

Campus[a]	Student	Sex	Major	GPA[b]	SAT[c]
UCLA	1	M	Physics	2.90	1050
	2	M	Physics	2.00	1200
	3	M	Anthropology	3.50	1100
	4	M	English	3.20	1130
	5	M	Chemistry	2.50	1160
	6	F	English	2.90	1075
	7	F	English	3.60	1100
	8	F	Engineering	2.30	1025
	9	F	Design	3.00	1000
	10	F	Biology	2.50	1000
UCD	11	M	Physics	2.90	1175
	12	M	Engineering	3.20	1125
	13	M	Biology	3.00	1100
	14	M	Engineering	2.70	1150
	15	M	Biology	2.50	1200
	16	F	Chemistry	2.50	1120
	17	F	Sociology	3.30	1090
	18	F	Sociology	3.00	1100
	19	F	English	2.90	1085
	20	F	Anthropology	3.20	1125
UCI	21	M	Physics	2.70	1125
	22	M	Biology	2.90	1175
	23	M	Chemistry	3.20	1200
	24	M	Biology	2.90	1100
	25	M	Engineering	3.00	1150
	26	F	Sociology	3.10	1090
	27	F	Design	2.90	1060
	28	F	English	2.70	1050
	29	F	Anthropology	3.00	1175
	30	F	English	3.20	1100
UCSD	31	M	Physics	2.70	1150
	32	M	Chemistry	2.80	1185
	33	M	Engineering	3.10	1200
	34	M	Biology	3.00	1160
	35	M	English	3.40	1200
	36	F	Biology	2.50	1150
	37	F	Sociology	3.00	1100
	38	F	Anthropology	3.10	1120
	39	F	Anthropology	2.90	1080
	40	F	Design	3.50	1150

[a]UCLA = University of California, Los Angeles; UCD = University of California, Davis; UCI = University of California, Irvine; UCSD = University of California, San Diego

[b]GPA = grade point average

[c]SAT = Scholastic Aptitude Test (verbal and mathematics combined)

TABLE 5-2   Major-field choices of male and female undergraduates at UCLA (data from Hewitt & Goldman,
1975)

	Major Field			
Sex	*Physics*	*Engineering*	*English*	*Design*
Male	108	345	94	17
Female	8	12	253	60

The second question was whether or not men and women showed differences in academic achievement when their major field was taken into account. They found that, in general, women did tend to have higher grade-point averages than men of similar ability. However, these diffrences were drastically reduced or entirely eliminated when the major field
was considered. The authors concluded: "It seems very clear that men and women tend to
major in different college fields. This difference in major field is sufficient to account for
much, if not most, of the apparent 'overachievement' of college women" (Hewitt & Goldman, 1975, p. 329).

A frequency polygon summarizing the distribution of hypothetical GPAs is shown in
Figure 5-2. About half the GPAs fall above the mean, and about half fall below (give or take
a few). This distribution resembles the bell-shaped curve in Figure 5-1. About two-thirds
of the GPAs in this sample fall between one standard deviation above and one standard deviation below the mean. Few GPAs fall at the extremely high or extremely low ends of the
GPA scale.

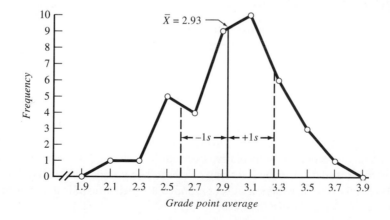

FIGURE 5-2
Distribution of hypothetical grade point averages, where $\bar{X} = 2.93$ and $s = .33$ (data from
Table 5-1)

THE NORMAL DISTRIBUTION: AN OVERVIEW

The normal distribution does not actually exist. It is not a fact of nature. Rather, it is a mathematical model—an idealization—that can be used to represent data collected in behavioral research. (See the Technical Appendix at the end of this chapter for mathematical details.) For example, the distribution of heights of people in a population can be modeled reasonably well with the normal distribution. Most people are about average in height, but a few are quite short and a few are quite tall. Likewise, the normal distribution serves as a reasonably accurate model of the frequency distribution of cognitive ability scores. However, as is often the case in science, the observed data and the abstract mathematical model almost never fit exactly.

The major value of the normal distribution lies in its ability to serve as a reasonably good model of many natural phenomena. In fact, scores on many measures used in the behavioral sciences are distributed so that the normal distribution provides a good model of their frequency distributions.

The normal distribution has particular importance in inferential statistics as a probability distribution. One reason is that when measures on large samples of natural phenomena such as height, weight, and cognitive ability are represented as a frequency distribution, the normal distribution provides a reasonably good model of the frequency distribution. Hence, the distribution of the true magnitudes of a trait such as cognitive ability may be thought of as being normally distributed in the *population*. A second reason is that there is a close connection between the sample size and the distribution of means calculated for many samples of subjects drawn from the same population. As the sample size increases, the distribution of sample means can be approximated by the normal distribution even though the distribution of scores in the population is not normal. And a third reason is that the normal distribution may provide a good approximation to other theoretical distributions that are more difficult to work with in determining probabilities.

PROPERTIES OF THE NORMAL DISTRIBUTION

The mathematical model for the normal distribution implies that the normal distribution will have a set of properties that characterize it. Other nonnormal distributions may have some of these properties. However, only those distributions following the mathematical rule for the normal distribution are normal distributions.

One property of the normal distribution is that it is *unimodal*. In a large frequency distribution, the most frequently observed value of X is that value of X falling exactly at the mean of the distribution. The greater the distance between X and the mean, the smaller the frequency with which X occurs. This fact results in the characteristic bell shape.

A second property of the normal distribution is that it is *symmetric* about its mean; that is, if you folded the distribution along its mean, the two sides of the distribution would coincide exactly. The distribution of scores above the mean, then, is a mirror image of the distribution of scores below the mean.[1]

---

[1]This property is also implied by the working part of Formula TA5-1: $(X - \mu)^2/2\sigma^2$. Since the difference between X and μ is squared, a score below the mean ($X - \mu$ negative) has exactly the same effect on Formula TA5-1 as its counterpart above the mean ($X - \mu$ positive). For example, suppose $\mu = 5$ and that scores one unit

Since the normal distribution is unimodal and symmetric about its mean, a third property of the normal distribution is that *the mean, mode, and median of the distribution are all equal.* Since the mode is the most frequent value of X, the mean and mode are the same. Since the distribution is symmetric, half the scores fall above the mean and half below. Thus, the median equals the mean, which equals the mode.

A fourth property of the normal distribution is that it is *asymptotic.* That is, the curve never touches the abscissa.[2] This property arises from the fact that the normal distribution is continuous for all values of a variable (X) from $-\infty$ to $+\infty$. Thus, each conceivable nonzero interval of real numbers will occur with some probability.

All normal distributions possess the four properties discussed before, since these properties all follow from the mathematical model on which the normal distribution is based. A closer look at the mathematical rule for the normal distribution in the Technical Appendix indicates that its mean and variance are not fixed. That is, different normal distributions can be obtained by applying the rule defining the normal distribution to distributions with different means and variances. For example, Figure 5-3 shows three normal distributions based on sample data. The distributions in Figures 5-3a, b have the same variance ($s^2 = 100$) and different means ($\bar{X}_a = -40$; $\bar{X}_b = +20$). The distributions in Figures 5-3b, c have the same mean (+20) and different variances ($s_b^2 = 100$; $s_c^2 = 25$). Finally, the distributions in Figures 5-3a, c have different means and variances. Despite these differences, however, they are all normal distributions. Thus, the mathematical model for the normal distribution actually defines a family of distributions. These normal distributions may differ in their means and variances, but they all have the properties of the normal distribution in common. Since these distributions resemble each other in this way, they are often referred to as a **family of normal distributions.**

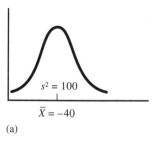
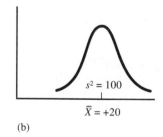
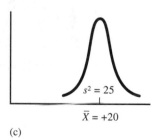

$s^2 = 100$ $s^2 = 100$ $s^2 = 25$

$\bar{X} = -40$ $\bar{X} = +20$ $\bar{X} = +20$

(a)   (b)   (c)

FIGURE 5-3

Normal distributions based on sample data with different means (a and b) and different variances (b and c)

---

below and above μ (4 and 6, respectively) are considered. Then $(4 - 5)^2 = (-1)^2 = 1$ and $(6 - 5)^2 = 1$. Both scores will produce the same value, so that the distribution is symmetric. One caution here is in order. Although the normal distribution is symmetric, there are also many other mathematical rules that can form symmetric distributions.

[2]Even if the distance between X and μ is infinite, the working part of the equation, $e^{-(X-\mu)^2/2\sigma^2}$, will never be zero.

AREAS UNDER THE NORMAL DISTRIBUTION CURVE

Since 100 percent (a proportion of 1.00) represents an entire quantity, the total area underneath the curve of any distribution is 100 percent, or 1.00. When this area is divided into parts, the relative frequency or proportion or percentage of scores falling in some part of the distribution can be determined. For example, as shown in Figure 5-4, approximately one-third (.3413) of the scores in the normal distribution fall between the mean and one standard deviation above the mean. Since the normal distribution is symmetric, approximately one-third of the scores fall between the mean and one standard deviation below the mean. Thus, approximately two-thirds (or approximately 68 percent) of the scores in a normal distribution fall in the interval ranging from one standard deviation below the mean to one standard deviation above the mean: .3413 + .3413 = .6826, or 68.26 percent (see Figure 5-4).

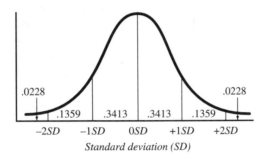

FIGURE 5-4
Areas under the curve of a normal distribution

In order to illustrate the importance of the normal distribution in interpreting score values, suppose you earned a score of 20 correct out of 32 on a statistics examination. Your first feeling might be panic, since this score is not close to 32. After calming down, your next thought might be that the test was difficult for everyone else, so you might try peeking at test scores earned by your fellow students. However, not until the instructor puts the distribution of scores on the board will you know exactly where your score stands with respect to other students' scores. Suppose, instead, the teacher returned your test with a note that a score of 20 fell 2 standard deviations above the mean of the class. *Assuming that the distribution of scores on the test can be represented by the normal distribution,* this information will tell you exactly where you stand with respect to other students. Since a score of 2 standard deviations above the mean is greater than 98 percent of the scores earned by other students (see Figure 5-4: .0228 + .1359 + .3413 + .3413 + .1359 = .9772, or 97.72 percent), now you know that you actually did extremely well on the exam.

One important feature of the normal distribution, then, is that when it is used appropriately as a model of the distribution of test scores, it permits us to interpret these scores and other measures (dependent variables in our research) with reference to the part of the distribution in which a particular score falls. For example, Scholastic Aptitude Test (SAT) scores have a mean of 500 and a standard deviation of 100. A person with a score of 400 has earned a score 1 standard deviation below the mean and hence has scored higher than about 16 percent of the students who have taken the examination.

A second feature of the normal distribution, one that will become quite important later in this book, is that it is a probability distribution. Thus, the area under the normal curve can be used to determine probabilities. Since the normal distribution is so commonly used in measurement and statistics and since skills in working with the normal distribution as well as other distributions are needed throughout this text, methods for finding areas under the normal curve will be covered in some detail.

STANDARD SCORES

Introduction

In behavioral research, many different scales of measurement are used to measure the outcome of a study. For example, scholastic aptitude is often measured on a scale with a mean of 500 and a standard deviation of 100; reaction time may be measured in seconds or even milliseconds; and tests developed for specific research purposes usually contain 50 questions or less and may have means of 20 or 30 with standard deviations of less than 10 points. For the interpretation of scores from these measures, it is helpful to transform the raw scores into a standard type of score that shows a person's *relative* status in a distribution of scores. Remember that we were able to tell how well you did on a hypothetical statistics examination, relative to your classmates, by knowing that your score of 20 fell 2 standard deviations above the mean. This example suggests that we need only a method for determining how far a score falls above or below the mean in terms of standard deviations in order to render an interpretable score from any one of many measurements made in behavioral research.

This reasoning suggests that we need to determine the distance of a score from its mean and then convert that distance into the number of standard deviations that the score falls above or below the mean. In short, we need to get a **standard score,** a score indicating the *relative standing* of the raw score in a distribution. Put another way, a standard score tells how many standard deviations a raw score falls above or below the mean of the distribution.

Formula for a Standard Score

In developing the logic behind a formula for calculating a standard score, we will use a simple example. Suppose that Charlie received a score of 70 on a test that has a mean of 50 and a standard deviation of 10. How many standard deviation units is this GPA above the mean? You've probably figured it out already, but let's follow the reasoning behind the standard score. First, find the distance between Charlie's score and the mean:

70 − 50 = +20, or 20 points above the mean

The next step is to convert this measure of distance into the number of standard deviations that this distance covers—that is, into standard deviation units. How many standard deviations does 20 points above the mean cover? Since the standard deviation is 10, the distance can be divided by 10 in order to find the number of standard deviation units that the score of 70 lies above the mean of 50:

$$20 \div 10 = 2.00$$

This procedure tells us that the score of 70 lies 2.00 standard deviations above the mean.

This procedure for computing a standard score, usually referred to as a z **score,** is summarized by the following formula.

$$z = \frac{X - \bar{X}}{s} = \frac{x}{s} \qquad\qquad (5\text{-}1)$$

Charlie's z score, corresponding to a raw score of 70 on a test with a mean of 50 and a standard deviation of 10, is:

$$z = \frac{70 - 50}{10} = \frac{20}{10} = 2$$

For reference, the steps in computing a z score are summarized in Procedure 5-1 using the hypothetical GPA data from the study of men's and women's achievement in college.

PROCEDURE 5-1 Steps in computing a z score (example data taken from Figure 5-2)

Operation	Example
1. Use Formula 5-1: $z = \dfrac{X - \bar{X}}{s} = \dfrac{x}{s}$	To find the z score for a GPA of 3.50:
2. Compute $\bar{X}$ and s if they are not given. *See Procedures 4-3 and 4-6.*	$\bar{X} = 2.93$ $s = .33$
3. Insert the appropriate values into Formula 5-1 and solve for z.	**a.** Insert 3.50 for X. **b.** Insert 2.93 for $\bar{X}$. **c.** Insert .33 for s. $z = \dfrac{3.50 - 2.93}{.33} = \dfrac{.57}{.33} = 1.73$ Interpretation: A GPA of 3.50 lies 1.73 standard deviations above the mean.

A z score contains two important pieces of information about the corresponding observed score. The *magnitude* of the z score tells how many standard deviations the observed score lies from the mean. The *sign* of the z score indicates whether the observed score lies above the mean (z is positive) or below the mean (z is negative).

The z scores also have other important characteristics. First, the mean of the distribution of z scores will always be zero regardless of the value of the mean of the original score distribution:

$$\bar{z} = \frac{\sum z}{N} = \frac{1}{N} \sum \frac{X - \bar{X}}{s}$$
$$= \frac{1}{Ns} \sum (X - \bar{X}) = 0$$

The mean is zero because, as you know, the mean is that point in a distribution at which the algebraic sum of the difference of each score (X) from the mean ($\bar{X}$) is zero [i.e., $\sum(X - \bar{X}) = 0$]. Second, the variance of z scores, s_z^2, always equals 1. Therefore, the standard deviation of z scores, s_z, also equals 1.[3] The upshot of these characteristics is that regardless of the scale of measurement, z scores always refer to a distribution with a mean of 0 and a standard deviation of 1.

Although transforming raw scores to z scores changes the mean and standard deviation of the frequency distribution, this transformation does not alter the shape of it. The frequency of a particular z score is exactly equal to the frequency of its corresponding raw (X) score. If the shape of the original frequency distribution is symmetric, the shape of the distribution of z scores will be as well. Likewise, if the original distribution is skewed, so will be the distribution of z scores. Finally, if scores in a theoretical distribution such as the normal distribution are transformed to z scores, the exact shape given by the mathematical rule for the theoretical distribution will not be changed. Only the mean and standard deviation of the theoretical distribution will be changed to 0 and 1, respectively.

---

[3]This characteristic of z scores is not obvious. Here's a proof that $s_z^2 = 1$:

$$s_z^2 = \frac{\sum (z - \bar{z})^2}{n - 1} \qquad \text{by definition}$$

$$= \frac{\sum z^2}{n - 1} \qquad \text{since } \bar{z} = 0$$

$$= \frac{\sum (X - \bar{X})^2 / s^2}{n - 1} \qquad \text{by substitution}$$

$$= \frac{1}{s^2} \left[\frac{\sum (X - \bar{X})^2}{n - 1} \right] \qquad \text{by rearranging terms}$$

$$= \left(\frac{1}{s^2} \right) s^2 \qquad \text{by definition of } s^2$$

$$= 1$$

Standard Scores and the Standard Normal Distribution

When the sample frequency distribution can be modeled accurately by the normal distribution, the relative frequency, or the proportion of scores falling in some area of the distribution, can be determined. If we are to use the normal distribution for this purpose (and others), it might seem that a different normal distribution would be needed for every frequency distribution with a different mean and standard deviation. Since the normal distribution is a family of distributions, each member is defined by its mean and standard deviation. Fortunately, this is not the case. If raw scores are converted to z scores, then regardless of the original score scale and its mean and standard deviation, the distribution of z scores will have a mean of 0 and a standard deviation of 1. Thus, if we convert raw scores to z scores, the z scores can be referred to just one member of the family of normal distributions—the member with mean equal to 0 and standard deviation equal to 1. The normal distribution with a mean of 0 and a standard deviation of 1 is called the **standard normal distribution.**

The standard normal distribution can be used as follows: Remember that Charlie earned a score of 70 on a test with a mean of 50 and a standard deviation of 10. By converting Charlie's score of 70 to a z score of +2, we can use the standard normal distribution to determine, say, the percentage of scores falling below Charlie's score of 70 (assuming the scores are accurately modeled by the normal distribution). From Figure 5-4, we find that Charlie's score is greater than 97.72 percent of the scores in the distribution (i.e., .0228 + .1359 + .3413 + .3413 + .1359 = .9772, and .9772 × 100 = 97.72 percent).

Example Problem 5.1

What is the z score corresponding to a GPA of 2.65 in Figure 5-2?

USING THE STANDARD NORMAL DISTRIBUTION

The normal distribution permits interpretation of scores with reference to where they fall in the distribution. For example, Figure 5-4 shows that when the standard normal distribution is divided into standard deviation units, the proportion (percentage) of scores falling in each area of the distribution can be determined: Approximately 34 percent of the scores fall between the mean and 1 standard deviation above the mean, and so on. However, for the interpretation of scores, Figure 5-4 is of limited usefulness because z scores may take on values other than just whole numbers. For this reason, Table B at the end of the book gives proportions of area under the standard normal distribution that correspond to each possible z score (rounded to two decimal places). In examining Table B, notice that the first column lists z scores. Columns 2–4 give areas corresponding to particular areas under the normal distribution. For example, column 2 identifies the area between the mean and the z score listed in column 1. Thus, the area between a z score of 1.00 and the mean is .3413. (Note that this value agrees with Figure 5-4.)

Several types of questions can be answered by using z scores and Table B. For example:

1. What proportion of scores fall between the mean and a given raw score?
2. What proportion of scores fall above (or below) a given raw score?
3. What proportion of scores fall between two raw scores?
4. What raw score falls above (or below) a given percentage of scores?

Each of these questions is discussed in turn, along with the step-by-step procedure for answering them. The main reason for the following "exercise" is that an understanding of subsequent chapters will depend on your skill in finding areas under the normal curve.

What Proportion of Scores Fall Between the Mean and a Given Raw Score?

In answering this question, first convert the raw score to a z score. Next, locate the z score in column 1 of Table B. And then refer to column 2 (area from mean to z) to find the proportion of scores. For example, Charlie's score of 70 in a distribution with a mean of 50 and a standard deviation of 10 corresponds to a z score of:

$$z = \frac{70 - 50}{10} = 2$$

From column 2 in Table B, the proportion of cases falling between Charlie's z score of 2 and the mean is .4772.

Suppose Bart, a fellow student of Charlie's, earned a score of 42. What proportion of the scores fall between 42 and the mean of 50? First, calculate a z score for Bart:

$$z = \frac{42 - 50}{10} = \frac{-8}{10} = -.80$$

Next, find a z score in Table B corresponding to .80. (Note that you ignore the sign of z in using Table B, since the normal distribution is symmetric. So the proportion of scores between the mean and a positive score will also be the proportion of scores between the mean and a negative score of the same magnitude.) Then refer to column 2 of the table to find the proportion of scores between −.80 and the mean; this value is .2881.

For reference, the steps in finding the proportion of scores between a raw score and the mean are given in Procedure 5-2. Note that throughout the remainder of this chapter, we assume that the normal distribution is a valid model of the frequency distributions providing the data for examples.

PROCEDURE 5-2 Steps for identifying the proportion of scores falling between the mean and a given observed score (example GPA data taken from Figure 5-2)

Operation

1. Convert the observed score to a z score by using Formula 5-1:

$$z = \frac{X - \bar{X}}{s}$$

   The observed score must be converted to a z score in order to use the standard normal distribution.

2. Draw a picture of the normal distribution, and block out the area to be identified.
   This figure helps define the problem and determine the column in Table B that provides the needed information.

Example

To identify the proportion of scores falling between the mean and a 3.70 GPA, first compute z:

$$z = \frac{3.70 - 2.93}{.33} = 2.33$$

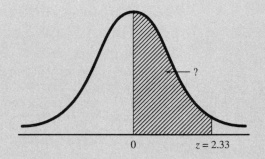

3. Turn to Table B at the end of the book.

   a. If z is *positive*, locate z in column 1 and read across to column 2.
   Note that the area blocked off in the figure above column 2 in Table B corresponds to the area blocked off in step 2.

   b. If z is *negative*, ignore the sign of z and follow step **a**.

   This procedure is possible because the normal distribution is symmetric. The area between the mean and a particular positive z score (e.g., 1.50) is equal to the area between the mean and the same z score with a negative sign.

The proportion of cases falling between the mean and a z score of 2.33 is approximately .49 (actually .4901), or 49%.

If $z = -2.33$, area $= .4901$, since the area between $\bar{X}$ and -2.33 is the same as the area between $\bar{X}$ and $+2.33$.

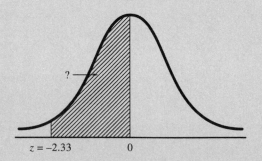

Example Problem 5.2

Identify the proportion of scores in Figure 5-2 falling between the mean and a GPA of 2.25.

What Proportion of Scores Fall Above (or Below) a Given Raw Score?

In answering this question, first convert the raw score to a z score. Next, draw a picture of a normal distribution and shade in the area you are looking for. For example, Figure 5-5 shows the area above Charlie's z score (shaded). Then use column 4 to find the area in the smaller tail of the distribution if that is the area you shaded, or column 3 to find the area in the larger tail if that is what you have shaded (.0228).

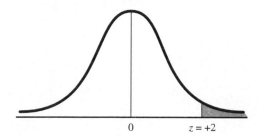

FIGURE 5-5
Area under the curve of a normal distribution above Charlie's z score

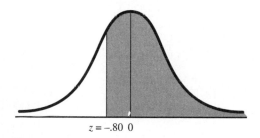

FIGURE 5-6
Area under the curve of a normal distribution above Bart's z score

What is the proportion of cases falling above Bart's score of 42? The z score corresponding to Bart's score of 42 has been calculated: $z = -.80$. Next, draw a picture representing the answer to the question. Since Bart's score falls below the mean and we are interested in scores above Bart's, we have the diagram shown in Figure 5-6. (Note that the sign of z is ignored when we use Table B. But it is *not* ignored when we draw Figure 5-6.) With the area of the larger tail shaded, column 3 is used to find the proportion, which is in this case .7881. For reference, the steps in finding the proportion of scores above (or below) a given raw score are summarized in Procedure 5-3.

PROCEDURE 5-3 Steps for identifying the proportion of scores falling above (or below) a given observed score (example data from Figure 5-2)

Operation	Example

Procedures for scores above the mean:

1. Convert the observed score to a z score, using Formula 5-1:

$$z = \frac{X - \bar{X}}{s}$$

The observed score must be converted to a z score in order to use the standard normal distribution.

2. Draw a figure of the normal distribution, and block out the area to be identified.

This picture helps define the problem and determine the column in Table B that provides the needed information.

To identify the proportion of scores falling above (or below) a GPA of 3.50, first compute z:

$$z = \frac{3.50 - 2.93}{.33} = 1.73$$

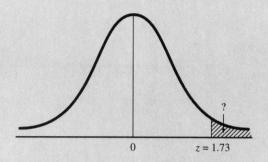

3. Turn to Table B.

   a. If the area to be identified represents the *smaller* tail of the curve, locate z in column 1 and read across to column 4.

   Note that the area blocked off in the figure above column 4 in Table B corresponds to the shaded area in step 2.

Area $= .0418$. The proportion of scores falling above a z score of 1.73 is approximately .04, or 4%.

   b. If the area to be identified represents the *larger* tail of the curve, locate z in column 1 and read across to column 3.

   Note that the area blocked off in the figure above column 3 in Table B corresponds to the shaded area in the example to the right.

The proportion of scores falling below $z = 1.73$ is .9582—the area of the larger tail of the curve.

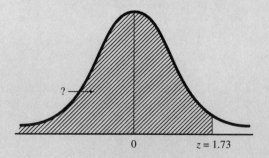

Operation_____   **Example**_____

Procedures for scores below the mean:

1. Convert the observed score to a *z* score, using Formula 5-1:

$$z = \frac{X - \bar{X}}{s}$$

The observed score must be converted to a z score in order to use the standardized normal distribution.

2. Draw a figure of the normal distribution, and block out the area to be identified.
The picture helps to define the problem and determine the column in Table B that provides the needed information.

To identify the proportion of cases falling below (or above) a GPA of 2.60, first compute *z*:

$$z = \frac{2.60 - 2.93}{.33} = \frac{-.33}{.33} = -1$$

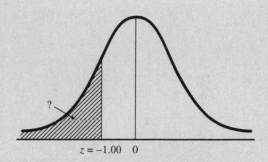

$z = -1.00 \quad 0$

3. Turn to Table B.

  a. If the area to be *identified represents the smaller portion* of the curve, locate $|z|$ (i.e., the value of *z* ignoring the sign) in column 1 and read across to column 4.
  Note that since the normal distribution is symmetric, the area below a z score of −1.00 is equal to the area above a z score of 1.00.

Area = .1587. The proportion of scores falling below $z = -1.00$ is .1587—the area in the smaller portion of the curve.

  b. If the area to be identified represents the *greater portion* of the curve, locate $|z|$ (i.e., the value of *z* ignoring the sign) in column 1 and read across to column 3.
  Note that since the normal distribution is symmetric, the area above a z score of −1.00 is equal to the area below a z score of 1.00.

Area = .8413. The proportion of scores falling above $z = -1.00$ is .8413—the area in the greater portion of the curve.

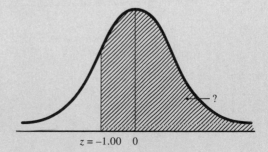

$z = -1.00 \quad 0$

Example Problem 5.3

Using the data given in Figure 5-2, identify the proportion of cases falling above a GPA of 2.75.

What Proportion of Scores Fall Between Two Raw Scores?

In answering this question, first transform the two raw scores into z scores. Second, draw a normal distribution, locate the two z scores on the abscissa, and shade in the area between them. Finally, find the proportion of scores falling below each of the z scores and subtract the smaller area from the larger area to find the proportion of scores.

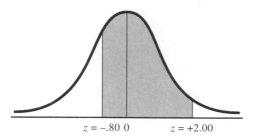

$z = -.80 \quad 0 \qquad z = +2.00$

FIGURE 5-7
Area under the curve of a normal distribution falling between Bart's and Charlie's z scores

For example, what proportion of scores fall between Bart's and Charlie's scores of 42 and 70, respectively? The first step is to convert these raw scores to z scores. This step has been done: −.80 and +2.00. Next, as shown in Figure 5-7, draw a normal distribution and shade in the area between the two scores. Now, find the area below both z scores. The area to the left of $z = 2.00$ is the area in the larger tail. So column 3 in Table B can be used to find this area: .9772. The area to the left of $z = -.80$ is the area in the smaller tail. So column 4 in Table B can be used to find this area: .2119. Finally, subtract the smaller area from the larger area in the distribution: $.9772 - .2119 = .7653$. For reference, the steps in finding the proportion of scores between two raw scores are summarized in Procedure 5-4.

PROCEDURE 5-4 Steps for identifying the proportion of scores falling between two observed scores (example GPA data from Figure 5-2)

Operation	Example
1. Convert each observed score to a z score, using Formula 5-1: $$z = \frac{X - \bar{X}}{s}$$ *Observed scores must be converted to z scores in order to use the standardized normal distribution.*	To identify the proportion of scores falling between a GPA of 2.40 and a GPA of 3.20, first compute z for each GPA: $$z_{\text{GPA}=2.40} = \frac{2.40 - 2.93}{.33} = -1.61$$ $$z_{\text{GPA}=3.20} = \frac{3.20 - 2.93}{.33} = .82$$

Operation

Example

2. Draw a graph of the normal distribution and block out the area to be identified. Note that the area identified is not directly given in Table B.

   This graph helps define the problem and determine the column(s) in Table B that provide the needed information.

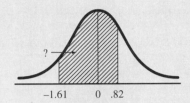

3. If at least *one* of the z scores is positive, locate the area of interest as follows:

   a. Identify the area below the highest z score, using column 3 of Table B.
   This area contains the area to be identified as well as some area to the left that is not of interest.

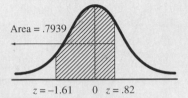

Since the area to the left of a positive z score always constitutes the greater portion of the curve, it is found in column 3 of Table B.

   b. Identify the area to the left of the lower z score, using the appropriate column of Table B (see step 3 of Procedure 4-3 to identify the appropriate column).
   This area represents the area not *of interest contained in the figure for step a.*

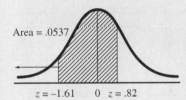

Since this area in this example constitutes the smaller portion of the curve, it is found in column 4 of Table B.

   c. Subtract the area located in the figure for step b from that located in the figure for step a.
   This difference represents the area to be identified.

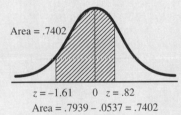

The proportion of cases falling between z scores of -1.61 and $.82$ is approximately $.74$, or 74%.

Operation	Example

4. If *both* z scores are *negative*, locate the area of interest as follows:

    a. Identify the area to the left of the z score with the lowest negative value (i.e., the value closest to zero) by locating $|z|$ (the value of z ignoring the sign) in column 1 and reading across to column 4.

    This area contains the area to be identified as well as some area to the left that is not of interest.

Suppose we wish to identify the proportion of scores falling between z scores of -1.00 and -2.30.

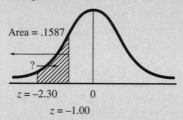

Since the area below a negative z score always constitutes the smaller portion of the curve and since the normal curve is symmetric, this area can be found by locating the area in column 4 corresponding to $|z|$.

    b. Identify the area to the left of the z score with the highest negative value (i.e., the value farthest from zero) by locating $|z|$ in column 1 and reading across to column 4 of Table B.

    This area represents the area not *of interest contained in the figure for step a.*

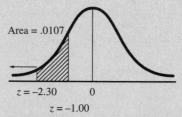

Since the area below a negative z score always constitutes the smaller portion of the curve and since the normal curve is symmetric, this area is found in column 4 of Table B corresponding to $|z|$.

    c. Subtract the area located in the figure for step b from that located in the figure for step a.

    The difference represents the area to be identified.

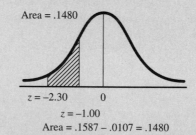

Area = .1587 − .0107 = .1480

The proportion of cases falling between a z scores of -1.00 and -2.30 is approximately .15, or 15%.

Example Problem 5.4

       Using the data given in Figure 5-2, identify the proportion of scores falling between a GPA of 3.00 and 3.35.

What Raw Score Falls Above (or Below) a Given Percentage of Scores?

In answering this question, first draw a picture of a normal distribution and shade in the area (percentage of scores) to be found. Next, convert the given percentage to a proportion by dividing it by 100. Then, turn to Table B and find the column corresponding to the shaded area of your diagram. Read down this column to find the proportion of scores corresponding to the shaded area, and then read to the left of column 1 to find the z score corresponding to this area. Now you know the values of z, $\bar{X}$, and s. Since $z = (X - \bar{X}) \div s$, you need to find X, the score above (or below) a given percentage of scores. In order to find X, you can use the following formula.[4]

$$X = s \cdot z + \bar{X} \qquad\qquad\qquad (5\text{-}1a)$$

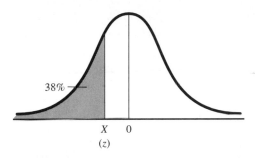

38%

X 0
(z)

FIGURE 5-8
Area under the curve of a normal distribution below 38 percent of the scores

For example, what raw score falls above 38 percent of the scores in Charlie's class? To answer this question, first draw a picture. In doing so, note that 50 percent of the scores fall below the mean of the normal distribution (mean = median), so the shaded area of the distribution will be in the small tail below the mean, as shown in Figure 5-8. Next, convert 38 percent to a proportion by dividing by 100: $38 \div 100 = .38$. Then, turn to column 4 in Table B, the column providing proportions in the smaller tail, and read down to .3783 (as close as we can get to .3800 in the column). Now read the z score in column 1 corresponding to .3783: $z = .31$. Since this z score corresponds to the lower tail of the distribution, it is negative: $z = -.31$. With the following information available—$z = -.31$, $\bar{X} = 50$, $s = 10$—

---

[4]We have:

$$\frac{X - \bar{X}}{s} = z \qquad\qquad \text{Formula 5-1; definition of a } z \text{ score}$$

$$X - \bar{X} = sz \qquad\qquad \text{multiply both sides of the equation by } s$$

$$X = sz + \bar{X} \qquad\qquad \text{Formula 5-1a; add } \bar{X} \text{ to both sides of the equation}$$

the raw score falling above 38 percent of the scores in Charlie's class can be found with Formula 5-1a:

$$X = (10)(-.31) + 50 = -3.1 + 50 = 46.9$$

A raw score of 46.9 falls above 38 percent of the scores in Charlie's class. For reference, the steps in finding a raw score falling above (or below) a given percentage of scores in a normal distribution are given in Procedure 5-5.

PROCEDURE 5-5 Steps for identifying the raw score that falls above (or below) a given percentage of scores (example data taken from Figure 5-2)

Operation

1. Draw a graph of the normal distribution, blocking out the area to be identified.
   This figure helps define the problem and determine the column of Table B that provides the needed information.

Example

To identify the observed GPA that falls above 85% of the GPAs in this sample:

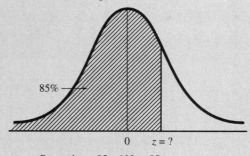

Proportion = 85 ÷ 100 = .85

2. Convert the given percentage to a proportion by dividing by 100.

3. Read down the appropriate column in Table B, locate the nearest proportion to that identified in step 2, and locate z by reading across to column 1.
   This procedure locates the z score corresponding to the proportion of interest.

   a. If the area represents the *greater* portion of the curve, read down column 3.

   b. If the area represents the *smaller* portion of the curve, read down column 4.

   From column 3 of Table B, the closest value to .85 is .8508. This area corresponds to a z score of 1.04.

4. Check the graph constructed in step 1 to determine whether z is positive or negative.
   z will be positive if z is above $\bar{X}$ and negative if z is below $\bar{X}$.

   In this case, z is positive.

   $$z = 1.04$$

Operation	Example
5. Convert z to X by using Formula 5-1a:	
$X = s \cdot z + \bar{X}$	$X = .33(1.04) + 2.93 = 3.27$
	A GPA of 3.27 falls above 85% of the GPAs in this sample.

Example Problem 5.5

Using data given in Figure 5-2, determine the raw score that falls below 60 percent of the GPAs.

SUMMARY

This chapter describes the *normal distribution*—a mathematical model that fits a lot of behavioral science data—and its properties in some detail. In addition, the concept of a *standard score* (z score) is presented, along with procedures for computing z scores. Finally, the *standard normal distribution* is presented along with methods for using z scores to identify areas in this distribution. These concepts and skills will become particularly important in later chapters when inferential statistics are considered.

TECHNICAL APPENDIX

The normal distribution is defined by the somewhat forbidding Formula TA5-1.

$$y = \frac{1}{\sqrt{2\pi\sigma^2}} e^{-(X-\mu)^2/2\sigma^2} \qquad \text{(TA5-1)}$$

where:

y = ordinate on the graph
X = observed score
μ = mean of the distribution in the population
σ^2 = variance of the distribution in the population
π = 3.1416 (rounded)
e = 2.7183 (rounded)

(*Note:* When the normal distribution is used as an idealized representation of data, μ and σ will be used instead of $\bar{X}$ and s. The rationale for this notation is explained in Chapter 8.) This equation defines the relative frequency with which particular values of X occur in a normal distribution. It says that these frequencies depend on two parameters—the mean (μ) and the variance (σ^2) of the distribution in the population—and two constants—pi (π = 3.1416) and the base of the natural system of logarithms (e = 2.7183).

In this formula, it turns out that X is the only term that takes on different values once μ and σ^2 are specified. Thus, the working part of this equation is the exponent where X appears:

$$e^{-(X-\mu)^2/2\sigma^2}$$

As the distance between X and μ becomes increasingly large, the value of the expression above, which is less than 1, becomes increasingly small, according to Formula TA5-2.

$$e^{-(X-\mu)^2/2\sigma^2} = \frac{1}{e^{(X-\mu)^2/2\sigma^2}} \qquad \text{(TA5-2)}$$

Thus, the greater the distance between particular values of X and the mean of the distribution μ, the lower the relative frequencies with which these values of X occur. See Formula TA5-1a.

$$y = \frac{1}{\sqrt{2\pi\sigma^2}} \cdot \frac{1}{e^{(X-\mu)^2/2\sigma^2}} \qquad \text{(TA5-1a)}$$

When the score value X equals the mean μ, the exponent becomes zero, and we have Formula TA5-3.

$$e^{-(X-\mu)^2/2\sigma^2} = e^{-0} = \frac{1}{e^0} = \frac{1}{1} = 1 \qquad \text{(TA5-3)}$$

In this case, the curve is at the maximum, according to Formula TA5-4.

$$y = \frac{1}{\sqrt{2\pi\sigma^2}} \cdot 1 \qquad \text{(TA5-4)}$$

ANSWERS TO EXAMPLE PROBLEMS

1. $z = \dfrac{2.65 - 2.93}{.33} = -.85$

2. a. $z = \dfrac{2.25 - 2.93}{.33} = -2.06$

b.

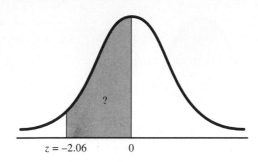

$z = -2.06$ 0

c. Area = .4803 (see column 2)

3. **a.** $z = \dfrac{2.75 - 2.93}{.33} = -.55$

b.

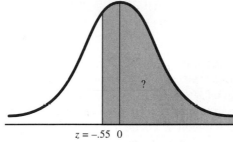

$z = -.55 \quad 0$

c. Area = .7088 (see column 3)

4. **a.** $z_{GPA}(3.00) = \dfrac{3.00 - 2.93}{.33} = .21$

$z_{GPA}(3.35) = \dfrac{3.35 - 2.93}{.33} = 1.27$

b.

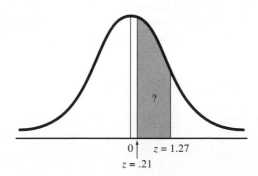

$0 \uparrow \quad z = 1.27$
$z = .21$

c. Area below $z = 1.27$ is .8980 (see column 3). Area below $z = .21$ is .5832 (see column 3). Difference in areas: .3980 − .5832 = .3148.

5. **a.**

z = ? 0

b. Proportion of interest = 60 ÷ 100 = .60
c. Nearest proportion in column 3 = .5987; corresponding z score = .25
d. Since z is below $\bar{X}$, z is negative: $z = -.25$
e. $X = .33(-.25) + 2.93 = 2.85$

EXERCISES

During the 1980s, the Department of Defense, in conjunction with each of the services, conducted a massive study of military job performance. What was remarkable about this study was that, unlike most such studies of job performance that use supervisors' ratings, this study actually sampled tasks from military jobs and observers evaluated job incumbents' performance. (For details, see Wigdor & Green, 1991.) One finding in the analysis of data on both Navy machinist mates and Marine Corps infantry was that the distribution of performance scores was normal. For our purposes, we can put the scores on a scale with a mean of 50 and a standard deviation of 10. Use this information to answer the following questions.

1. What is the z score corresponding to an observed performance score of 55?
2. What proportion of performance scores fall between the mean and a performance score of 55?
3. What proportion of scores fall above a performance score of 55?
4. What percent of scores fall between performance scores of 40 and 55?
5. What performance score falls below 10 percent of all performance scores?

ANSWERS TO EXERCISES

1. $z = \dfrac{X - \bar{X}}{s} = \dfrac{55 - 50}{10} = \dfrac{5}{10} = .50$
2. From Table B: 19.15 percent
3. From Table B: .3085
4. $z = \dfrac{X - \bar{X}}{s} = \dfrac{40 - 50}{10} = \dfrac{-10}{10} = -1.00$

Area below highest z score ($z = .50$) = 69.15. Area to the left of the lower z ($z = -1.00$) score (small area) = 15.87. Subtract the latter (smaller) area from the former (larger) area: $69.15 - 15.87 = 53.28$. Alternatively, you could do the following. Find the percent between $z = -1$ and the mean (34.13) and add that to the percent between $z = .5$ and the mean (19.15) = 53.28.

5. Note that we are looking for a performance score in the upper part of the curve since 90 percent of the scores will fall below it. In this case, we find the z score that corresponds to 90 percent below z: $z = 1.28$. Then, $X = s \cdot z + \bar{X} = 10 \cdot 1.28 + 50 = 62.80$.

III DESCRIPTIVE STATISTICS FOR JOINT DISTRIBUTIONS

S ection II dealt with *univariate distributions*—distributions summarizing one variable at a time (e.g., the frequency distribution of achievement test scores). Statistics such as means and standard deviations were used to describe these distributions. In this section, attention is focused on *joint distributions*—distributions in which *two variables are considered simultaneously*. These distributions arise from data collected in correlational studies—studies in which the researcher is interested in the relationship between two variables.

Joint distributions are used to summarize the relationship between two variables. Just as univariate distributions could be described by means and standard deviations, joint distributions can be described by a *correlation coefficient*—a single number describing the relationship between two variables—and a *regression equation*—an equation describing a functional relationship between two variables.

In a correlational study, the researcher is interested in the relationship between two continuous variables such as scores on an achievement test and scores on an anxiety inventory. In the study of men's and women's achievement in college, for example, one concern was the relationship between Scholastic Aptitude Test (SAT) scores and college grade-point averages (GPA). The relationship between the two variables could be described by a *correlation coefficient*. The correlation coefficient provides a measure of the strength of association between two variables. Or, put another way, the correlation coefficient provides an index of how closely two variables "go together."

In studies of the relationship between two variables, it is also possible to describe the approximate *functional relationship* between two variables. The term *functional relationship* refers to a statement something like the following: "As scores on the achievement test increase one point (at a time), scores on the anxiety inventory decrease three points (at a time)." Or the functional relationship between SAT scores and GPA in the study of men's and women's achievement might be described as follows: "As scores on the SAT increase by 50 points, GPA increases by .10 point." (Note that the GPA usually ranges from 0 to 4 points, whereas SAT scores usually range from 200 to 800 points.) Our concern with functional relationships, then, is a concern with predicting how much of a change in one variable is associated with a change in the second variable. This functional relationship is described by an equation called a *regression equation*.

The next chapter describes how to represent and interpret joint distributions, and how to compute and interpret correlation coefficients. Chapter 7 describes how to represent, compute, and interpret functional relations.

6

Joint Distributions and Correlation Coefficients

- Research Example: The Psychological Belief Scale and Student Achievement
- Joint Distributions
- Correlation Coefficients
- Development of the Correlation Coefficient: An Intuitive Approach
- The Squared Correlation Coefficient, r_{XY}^2
- Spearman Rank Correlation Coefficient
- Sources of Misleading Correlation Coefficients
- Correlation and Causality
- Summary
- Answers to Example Problems
- Exercises
- Answers to Exercises

In correlational studies, the researcher is interested in the question "What is the relationship between variable X and variable Y?" If X represents scores on the Scholastic Aptitude Test (SAT) and Y represents college grade point averages (GPAs), the research question can be stated as follows: "What is the relationship between scores on the SAT and GPAs?" This was one of the research questions posed in the study of men's and women's achievement in college. If X represents scores on a measure of self-concept and Y represents scores on a measure of peer popularity, the research question in this correlational study can be stated as follows: "What is the relationship between scores on the self-concept measure and scores on the peer popularity measure?"

In all cases, correlational studies focus on answering the question "How are scores on one measure associated with scores on another measure?" In a correlational study, two measures—representing the two variables of interest—are given to one group of subjects. The subjects' scores on both measures are summarized, and the relationship between the scores on the two measures is examined.

The first step in examining the relationship between scores on two measures is to arrange them in the form of a joint distribution. A **joint distribution** is a distribution in which a pair of scores for each subject is represented. A next step is to summarize the relationship represented by a joint distribution with a single number—by a correlation coefficient. A **correlation coefficient** is a descriptive statistic that represents both the magnitude of the relation between two variables (ranging from 0 to |1|),[1] and the direction of the relation (positive or negative).

RESEARCH EXAMPLE: THE PSYCHOLOGICAL BELIEF SCALE AND STUDENT ACHIEVEMENT

Throughout this section, hypothetical data based on a study of the congruence between students' and instructors' beliefs and student achievement are used to illustrate the concepts presented (see Table 6-1).[2] Intuition and perhaps prior experience suggest that it is easier to learn from teachers who have the same beliefs as we do than from teachers with opposing beliefs. At least, we have earned higher grades in classes with instructors who share our beliefs than in classes with instructors who do not. For example, if your beliefs tend toward humanism, you might do better in an introductory psychology class with an instructor who shares this belief than in a class taught by a behaviorist, and vice versa.

In order to test these predictions (intuitions), suppose you develop a short "Psychological Belief Scale" and give it to instructors and students on the first meeting of introductory psychology classes. At the end of the semester, you collect the students' scores on course examinations. Intuition leads you to predict that those students whose beliefs are closest to their instructor's beliefs will earn the highest examination scores. You also predict that exam scores should decrease as the difference between the students' and their instructors' beliefs increases. Hypothetical data bearing on these predictions are presented in Table 6-1 for three introductory psychology classes at three different colleges. Are these data consistent with your predictions? Should you combine the data for all three classes and compare the average belief score and average achievement score? Or should your analysis be more specific and compare students' beliefs and final-examination scores in each class separately?

This hypothetical study and the patterns in the hypothetical data parallel a study and data (see Figure 6-1) reported by Majasan (1972; for a concise, accessible overview, see Cronbach, 1975). In order to measure beliefs about the study of psychology, he developed a scale in which each item offered a humanistic (H) or behavioristic (B) alternative. For example: "The central focus of the study of human behavior should be (a) the specific principles that apply to unique individuals (H); (b) the general principles that apply to all individuals (B)." Instructors in introductory psychology classes and their students received the scale at the beginning of the course. A high score on the belief scale indicated a behavioristic orientation; a low score indicated a humanistic orientation. The achievement score was

---

[1]The symbol, |1|, is read "absolute value of 1." Absolute value ignores the sign (+ or −).

[2]Large samples are needed for correlational studies. However, for ease of illustration and computation, we use small samples.

TABLE 6-1   Tabular form of a joint distribution: Relationship between belief scores and exam scores in three introductory psychology classes (hypothetical data)

Class 1			Class 2			Class 3		
(1) ID	(2) Belief Score	(3) Exam Score	(1) ID	(2) Belief Score	(3) Exam Score	(1) ID	(2) Belief Score	(3) Exam Score
1	3	7	1	2	1	1	8	10
2	4	6	2	2	5	2	7	8
3	6	9	3	7	10	3	3	2
4	5	10	4	6	9	4	5	6
5	8	2	5	9	3	5	7	9
6	9	3	6	3	4	6	2	2
7	6	10	7	7	9	7	4	5

Instructor's Belief Score

| 6 | | | 7 | | | 8 | | |

the students' total scores earned on all class examinations. (We'll call this total of all examination scores, the "exam score," for brevity.) Actual data from 3 of the 12 classes in the study are presented in Figure 6-1. The lines in the figure represent the relationship between scores on the belief scale (briefly, "belief scores") and exam scores. Since each instructor gave a different examination, the number of items, and thus the magnitude of students' scores, differed from one class to the next. Therefore, all exam scores were converted to standard scores that show how far above (+) or below (−) the class average a particular exam score falls.

In 11 of the 12 classes, Majasan found that exam scores were highest for students whose beliefs corresponded closely with their instructors. In the one class that did not support his prediction, examinations were not used. Rather, the only available measure of achievement in this class, taught by a humanist, was the student's grade on an independent project.

What might account for the higher achievement of students whose beliefs corresponded closely to those of their instructors? One theory is that teachers and students with similar beliefs about psychology have similar cognitive structures (i.e., similar organizations of concepts and ideas). Teachers may be able to communicate the subject matter more effectively to students with cognitive structures similar to their own. The higher achievement of these students may be a result of this increased effectiveness of communication (see Runkel, 1956). Further research studies are needed, however, to test this speculation.

JOINT DISTRIBUTIONS

Recall that a **joint distribution** is a distribution in which a pair of scores for each subject is represented. Joint distributions can be represented either by a table or a graph. Both representations are described here.

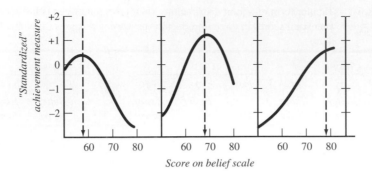

FIGURE 6-1
Relationship between students' beliefs and exam scores in three representative classes (the arrow denotes the instructor's belief score)

Tabular Representation

Table 6-1 is a tabular representation of a joint distribution. Consider the data for class 1. The identification number for each student in the class is listed in the first column. In the second column, each student's score on variable X (belief score) is entered. Finally, in the third column, each subject's score on variable Y (exam score) is entered. In correlational studies, the identification of scores on one measure as variable X and scores on the other measure as variable Y is arbitrary. Often, variable X represents the first measure taken, and variable Y represents the second measure. Or variable X may represent the variable on which predictions are based, and variable Y the outcome or criterion predicted.

Since the arrangement of scores in Table 6-1 is somewhat obvious, this procedure may seem trivial at first glance. However, note that when subjects' scores are arranged in this manner, it is possible to get an idea of the relationship between the two sets of scores. For example, by examining the X and Y scores for each subject in class 1, we see that the general pattern in the data for class 1 is as follows: (1) low belief scores are associated with moderately high exam scores (subjects 1 and 2); (2) moderate belief scores are associated with high exam scores (subjects 3, 4, and 7); and (3) high belief scores are associated with low exam scores (subjects 5 and 6).

When scores in class 2 are examined, we see that as belief scores increase, so do exam scores with one exception: Subject 5 received a belief score of 9 and an exam score of 3. Finally, comparison of scores in the third class reveals that as belief scores increase, so do exam scores without exception.

When the number of subjects is small, the tabular form of the joint distribution can be used, with some difficulty, to identify relationships between two variables. When the number of subjects is large, this tabular display is almost impossible to use. Regardless of the number of subjects, it would be much easier to find patterns in the data with a graphical representation of the relationship between scores on two variables. This graphical representation would provide a *picture* of how the two variables "go together."

Graphical Representation

A graphical representation of a joint distribution is called a **scatterplot.** It provides a picture that shows pairs of scores for each of the subjects in a group.

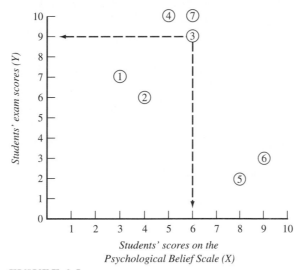

FIGURE 6-2
Scatterplot of the scores for the subjects in class 1 (data from Table 6-1)

In the scatterplot of the scores for the seven subjects in class 1, presented in Figure 6-2, each point represents one subject. In order to show that each point represents one subject, we plot each point as a circle surrounding the subject's identification number. If a line is drawn from a point in the scatterplot perpendicular to the abscissa (horizontal axis), the score on the belief scale for that particular subject can be read. If a line is drawn from the same point perpendicular to the ordinate (vertical axis), the same subject's exam score can be found. For example, the belief score for subject 3 is 6, and the exam score for this subject is 9 (broken lines in Figure 6-2). The steps in constructing a scatterplot are summarized in Procedure 6-1. Data from class 3 are used as an example.

PROCEDURE 6-1 Steps in constructing a scatterplot (example data taken from class 3 in Table 6-1)

Operation	Example
1. Draw the axes of the graph. *Axes are perpendicular; the ordinate is usually two-thirds the length of the abscissa.*	

Operation

Example

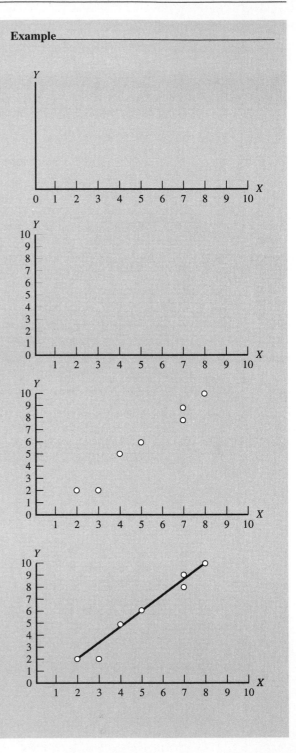

2. Label the abscissa with score values of the X variable.
Begin with the lowest score value at the far left and the highest score at the far right.

3. Label the ordinate with score values of the Y variable.
Begin with the lowest possible score at the bottom and the highest possible score at the top.

4. Plot one point for each subject in the following way:

    a. A line drawn from the point perpendicular to the abscissa crosses the abscissa at the subject's score on the X variable.

    b. A line drawn from the point perpendicular to the ordinate crosses the ordinate at the subject's score on the Y variable.

5. Draw a line to highlight the pattern of the data if there is a systematic trend or pattern.

Example Problem 6.1

In the study of men's and women's college achievement described in Chapter 5, SAT scores and GPAs were collected on a large number of undergraduates at four University of California campuses. Table 6-2 shows hypothetical data for one campus (UCLA).
a. Construct a scatterplot of these data.
b. Describe the relationship between SAT scores and GPAs

TABLE 6-2   Hypothetical SAT scores and GPAs (data from Table 5-1)

Student	SAT	GPA
1	1050	2.90
2	1200	2.00
3	1100	3.50
4	1130	3.20
5	1160	2.50
6	1075	2.90
7	1100	3.60
8	1025	2.30
9	1000	3.00
10	1000	2.50

The relationship between scores on two variables, such as scores on the belief scores (variable X) and exam scores (variable Y), is revealed by the points in the scatterplot. In addition, scatterplots for different groups of subjects can be compared to see whether the relationships between the variables are the same in each group. Scatterplots for classes 1, 2, and 3 are shown in Figure 6-3. Lines are drawn on the scatterplots to highlight the pattern in the data.

For classes 1 and 2, a curved line best describes the relationship between belief and exam scores. In other words, as belief scores increase, so do exam scores, up to some point ($X = 6$ for class 1 and $X = 7$ for class 2). Then, as belief scores increase further, exam scores decrease. Since a curved line best fits this relationship, the relationship between belief scores and exam scores is called a **curvilinear relationship.**

For class 3, as belief scores increase, exam scores also increase. A straight line best fits the pattern of scores on the two measures. This relationship between the two sets of scores is called a **linear relationship.**

Figure 6-3 also highlights an important problem that arises in correlational studies. The problem is that a few "deviant points," or **outliers,** on the scatterplot can drastically change the pattern of the relationship between two variables, especially when the number of subjects is small. For example, we concluded that the relationship between beliefs and achievement was curvilinear in classes 1 and 2. But suppose the starred point in the scatterplot for class 2 represents a chance occurrence—for example, that particular student might have been ill at the time the final exam was given. If that subject is ignored, the relationship between beliefs and achievement in class 2 is no longer curvilinear; it is linear. The nature of the relationship is substantially changed.

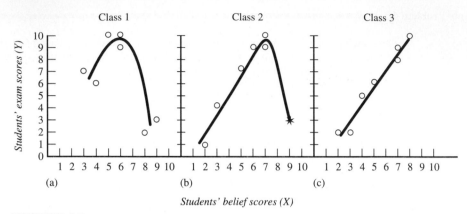

FIGURE 6-3
Comparison of scatterplots for each of the three classes in the study (data from Table 6-1)

In any correlational study, then, the data should be cast into a scatterplot and the scatterplot should be examined for deviant points. If such outliers are found, the data can first be analyzed with the outliers included in the data and then with them deleted. If the pattern changes, the researcher must decide what to do with the outliers. The decision of whether to include or ignore outliers will depend on the questions that the researcher wishes to answer and the information available. If a decision is made to ignore outliers, the researcher should give a full description—a kind of case study—of each subject representing an outlier.

Figure 6-4 presents the intriguing data in the Majasan study. It is the same as Figure 6-3 except that it contains information about the belief score of each of the three instructors. Notice that those students whose belief score tend to agree with their instructor's belief score also tend to earn the highest exam scores. The greater the difference between the student's and the instructor's beliefs, the lower the student's exam score. This relationship between students' and instructors' beliefs and student achievement holds for all instructors, even though the instructors obtained different scores on the belief scale.

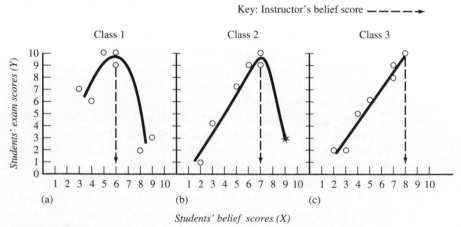

FIGURE 6-4
Scatterplots for three classes with instructor's belief score superimposed

CORRELATION COEFFICIENTS

The relationship between two variables can be described numerically, as well as graphically by a scatterplot. The statistic that describes this relationship is called a correlation coefficient. The **correlation coefficient** is a measure of the strength of association between two variables. It reflects how closely scores on two variables go together. The more closely two variables go together, the stronger the association between them and the more extreme the correlation coefficient.

There are many different types of correlation coefficients. Most coefficients have been developed to measure the strength of relationship between two variables that show a *linear relationship* in a scatterplot. (See Figure 6-5 for examples of linear relationships.) This chapter focuses on the most widely used measure of the strength of relationship between two linearly related variables—the Pearson product-moment correlation coefficient.

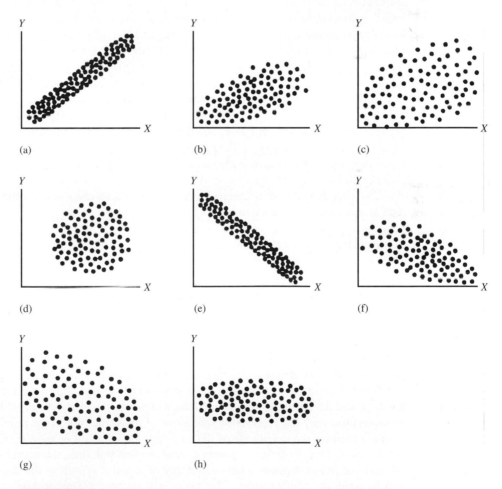

FIGURE 6-5
Scatterplots of some possible linear relationships between two variables

When a correlation coefficient is used to describe a linear relationship, the coefficient can take on values from −1.00 to +1.00. The *sign* of the correlation indicates the *direction* of the relationship between two variables. A **positive relationship** means that low scores on X go with low scores on Y whereas high scores on X go with high scores on Y. In other words, it indicates that as scores on X increase, scores on Y also increase. A **negative relationship** means that as scores on X increase, scores on Y decrease. That is, low scores on one measure go with high scores on the other measure, and vice versa.

The absolute *magnitude* or size of the correlation coefficient—that is, ignoring the plus or minus sign—indicates the strength of the relationship between the two variables. A correlation of +.95 reflects a very strong relationship between X and Y. A correlation of −.95 also reflects a very strong relationship. A correlation coefficient of 0 indicates that there is no linear relationship.

The correlation coefficient is a *descriptive statistic* used to summarize the relationship between two variables represented in a joint distribution. (In Chapter 10, the correlation coefficient is treated as an estimator of a parameter.) Figure 6-5 shows a series of joint distributions in which each set of variables has a linear relationship. Notice that in Figures 6-5a–c, the points in the scatterplot rise from left to right. As scores on X increase, scores on Y increase. There is a positive relationship between X and Y. Therefore, the correlation between X and Y will be positive. The points in Figures 6-5e–g fall from the upper left of the joint distribution to the lower right. As scores on X increase, scores on Y decrease. There is a negative relationship between X and Y. Therefore, the correlation between X and Y will be negative, and the correlation coefficient will always be preceded by a minus sign. Finally, in Figures 6-5d, h, as scores on X increase, scores on Y may either increase or decrease; there is no relationship between X and Y. The correlation coefficient will be zero.

Two characteristics of a scatterplot provide important clues to determining the magnitude of a correlation coefficient:

1. The slope of the scatterplot
2. The degree to which the points in the scatterplot cluster about an imaginary line representing the slope

Consider first the slope of the scatterplot. If the scatterplot can be represented by a line drawn either parallel to the abscissa (a horizontal line) or perpendicular to the abscissa (a vertical line), the magnitude of the correlation is zero. Notice that in Figure 6-1d, a horizontal or vertical line can be used to represent the scatterplot. If the slope of the line is *not* horizontal or vertical to the abscissa, the magnitude of the correlation coefficient is not zero.

If the slope of the scatterplot is not horizontal or vertical, the correlation coefficient is not zero; and the magnitude of the coefficient depends upon how closely the points cluster about an imaginary line representing the slope of the scatterplot. If the points cluster tightly about the line, the magnitude of the correlation coefficient is high. If they scatter way out, it is low. This clustering of points around the line and, thus, the magnitude of the correlation coefficient depends on the variability of X and Y as well as the degree of association between the two variables. This point will become clearer in later sections of this chapter.

Figures 6-5a, e show points tightly clustered about the slope; the magnitude of the correlation coefficient summarizing these two scatterplots would be high (.80 or above). They would differ only in sign (plus and minus, respectively). The points in Figures 6-5b, f cluster somewhat more widely about the slope, so the magnitude of the correlation summarizing these two scatterplots would be moderate (.40 to .60). Finally, the points in Figures 6-5c, g scatter widely about the slopes of the scatterplots. The magnitude of the correlation coefficient summarizing those two scatterplots would be low (.30 or less).

Notice that in Figure 6-5h, even though the points cluster tightly about the slope of the scatterplot, the slope is parallel to the abscissa. When a horizontal slope is found, the correlation coefficient is zero regardless of how tightly the scores cluster. What this result means is that as scores on X increase, *scores on Y do not systematically change.* Hence, the correlation between X and Y is zero. Similarly, when a vertical slope is found, the correlation coefficient is zero regardless of how tightly the scores cluster. What this result means is that as scores on Y increase, *scores on X do not systematically change.* Hence, the correlation between X and Y is zero.

DEVELOPMENT OF THE CORRELATION COEFFICIENT: AN INTUITIVE APPROACH

Up to this point, a scatterplot has been used to get "eyeball" estimates of the magnitude and sign of the correlation coefficient. Now, let's develop a statistic—the correlation coefficient—that describes the relationships shown in Figure 6-5. In order to clarify the ideas presented, we will use the data shown in Table 6-3 as an example.

Since a joint distribution or scatterplot shows how two variables *go together,* the measure of the relationship between these variables should show how the scores go together (how they covary). In order to see how scores covary, we begin by comparing the SAT score

TABLE 6-3   Relationships between Scholastic Aptitude Test scores and grade point averages at Bart Farguart College

Student	SAT X	GPA Y	Scatterplot
1	450	2.40	
2	500	3.12	
3	525	3.05	
4	650	3.19	
5	760	3.74	
Σ	2885.00	15.50	
$\overline{X}$	577.00	3.10	
s	126.08	.48	

and the GPA for the first student. In making the comparison, we encounter a major problem immediately. The variables are measured on different score scales. GPA is measured on a 4-point scale, but SAT scores can be as high as 800 points. A direct comparison, then, is impossible. The first step toward solving this problem of comparing scores on different measurement scales is to represent each score on each variable as a deviation score. This deviation score would provide a measure of how far each score on each measure is from the mean for that variable. For example, subject 1's deviation score on the SAT is:

$$x = X - \bar{X} = 450 - 577 = -127$$

Her deviation score on the GPA is:

$$y = Y - \bar{Y} = 2.40 - 3.10 = -.70$$

This step seems to be a reasonable beginning. We now know that student 1 earned scores below the mean of each variable. This rescaling is completed for the scores of the other four subjects in columns b–g in Table 6-4.

We are now in a position to get a measure of how the two sets of deviation scores go together or covary. By multiplying each student's x score by his y score, a measure of covariation is obtained for each person. This product is called a **cross product.** The cross product for each person is shown in column h of Table 6-4. Notice that when a subject's scores on both measures deviate markedly from the mean for that measure (i.e., |x| and |y| are large), the cross products are large. (See subjects 1 and 5 in Table 6-4.) When subjects' scores on both measures are close to their respective means (i.e., |x| and |y| are small), the cross product is small. (See subjects 2, 3, and 4 in Table 6-4.) Thus, this procedure gives us a measure of the covariation between X and Y for each person.

Ultimately, however, we are interested in describing the relationship between X and Y over the entire group rather than for particular individuals. Thus, we need to obtain a measure of the average covariation between pairs of scores for all students. To obtain a measure of the average covariation between pairs of scores, we add the cross products (xy) and divide by $N - 1$, where N is the number of persons. (See footnote 5 in Chapter 4 for an explanation of why $N - 1$ and not N is used to obtain this average. See also the discussion of degrees of freedom in Chapter 12.) In our example, the sum of the cross products is 213.65.

TABLE 6-4   Covariance of Scholastic Aptitude Test scores and grade point averages at Bart Farguart College

(a)	*(b)*	*(c)*	*(d)* x $X - \bar{X}$	*(e)*	*(f)*	*(g)* y $Y - \bar{Y}$	*(h)*
Student	X	$\bar{X}$	$X - \bar{X}$	Y	$\bar{Y}$	$Y - \bar{Y}$	xy
1	450	577	−127	2.40	3.10	−.70	88.90
2	500	577	−77	3.12	3.10	.02	−1.54
3	525	577	−52	3.05	3.10	−.05	2.60
4	650	577	73	3.19	3.10	.09	6.57
5	760	577	183	3.74	3.10	.64	117.12
Σ	2885.00	2885.00	0	15.50	15.50	0	213.65

(In adding the cross products, be sure to pay attention to the *sign* of each cross product.) To obtain the average covariation, divide this sum by $N - 1 = 4$:

$$213.65 \div 4 = 53.41$$

Let's summarize briefly. To get a measure of covariance—how scores covary—we converted raw scores to deviation scores to obtain a measure of how far each score deviated from the mean. Then, to get a measure of the covariation of pairs of scores, we found the cross product of each subject's deviation scores by multiplying each subject's deviation score on variable X by his deviation score on variable Y. Then to find the average covariation between X and Y over all subjects, we summed the cross products and divided by $N - 1$.

At this point the statistic called the covariance has been obtained. The **covariance** is the sum of the cross products of the deviation scores divided by $N - 1$ or, in other words, the average of the sum of the cross products of deviation scores on two variables.[3] The formula for the covariance Cov_{XY} is given next.

$$\text{Cov}_{XY} = \frac{\sum(X - \bar{X})(Y - \bar{Y})}{N - 1} = \frac{\sum xy}{N - 1} \qquad \textbf{(6-1)}$$

In the formula, Cov_{XY} stands for the covariance of variables X and Y. The covariance is a measure of how two variables go together, or *covary*. The other symbols should be familiar to you. By inserting information from Table 6-4 into the formula, we get:

$$\begin{aligned}
\text{Cov}_{XY} &= \frac{\sum xy}{N - 1} \\
&= \frac{(-127 \times -.70) + (-77 \times .02) + (-52 \times -.05) + (73 \times .09) + (183 \times .64)}{5 - 1} \\
&= \frac{213.65}{4} = 53.41
\end{aligned}$$

The covariance measures the direction and magnitude of relationship between two variables. However, the covariance has one severe limitation. Its magnitude depends upon the variability of scores on X and on Y. If the scores are quite spread out on both X and Y, then $X - \bar{X}$ and $Y - \bar{Y}$ will be quite large, and so will be the sum of their cross products, $\sum(X - \bar{X})(Y - \bar{Y})$. In short, the magnitude of the covariance depends upon the standard deviation of X and the standard deviation of Y. Thus, it is impossible, for example, to compare the six possible covariances obtained from a set of four different measures such as

---

[3]Incidentally, the variance is a special case of a covariance. The variance is the covariance of a variable with itself.

$$\text{Cov}_{XX} = s_X^2 = \frac{\sum(X - \bar{X})(X - \bar{X})}{N - 1} = \frac{\sum x^2}{N - 1}$$

achievement, verbal aptitude, self-concept, and anxiety. Differences in covariances may be due to differences in relationships between pairs of variables, differences in standard deviations, or both.

A last step, then, must be taken in order to develop a measure of the relationship between X and Y that is not influenced by differences in measurement scales: the correlation coefficient. Variable X and variable Y must be corrected for differences in standard deviation. This correction can be made by dividing the covariance by the product of the standard deviation of X and the standard deviation of Y.[4]

$$\text{correlation}(X, Y) = r_{XY} = \frac{\text{Cov}_{XY}}{s_X s_Y} \qquad \text{(6-2)}$$

This value, r_{XY}, is called the **Pearson product-moment correlation coefficient.** It is defined as the covariance of X and Y divided by the product of the standard deviation of X and the standard deviation of Y. It has just those properties of correlation coefficients described in the beginning of the chapter:

1. It provides a measure of the strength of association between two variables.
2. It describes a linear relationship between two variables.
3. It can take on values from −1.00 to +1.00, where the absolute magnitude provides an index of the strength of the relationship between the two variables and the sign indicates the direction of the relationship.

The correlation between SAT scores and GPAs sampled at Farguart College, then, can be found by using information from Tables 6-3 and 6-4. From Table 6-4, the sum of cross products is 213.65. So $\text{Cov}_{XY} = 213.65 \div (5 - 1) = 53.41$. From Table 6-3, $s_X = 126.08$ and $s_Y = .48$. Thus,

$$r_{XY} = \frac{\text{Cov}_{XY}}{s_X s_Y} = \frac{53.41}{(126.08)(.48)} = \frac{53.41}{60.52} = .89$$

---

[4]This equating of X and Y for standard deviations amounts to converting scores on X to z_X scores and scores on Y to z_Y scores. As you know from Chapter 5, z scores have unit standard deviations: $s_{z_X} = s_{z_Y} = 1$. Therefore, the correlation coefficient can be thought of as a covariance of z_X and z_Y scores—i.e., a measure of the average covariation between z_X and z_Y scores over all pairs of scores. Mathematically, it works like this:

$$r_{XY} = \frac{\text{Cov}_{XY}}{s_X s_Y} = \frac{\frac{\sum xy}{N-1}}{s_X s_Y} = \frac{\frac{1}{N-1} \sum xy}{s_X s_Y} = \frac{1}{N-1} \frac{\sum xy}{s_X s_Y}$$

$$= \frac{1}{N-1} \sum \left[\frac{X - \bar{X}}{s_X} \cdot \frac{Y - \bar{Y}}{s_Y} \right] = \frac{1}{N-1} \sum (z_X z_Y) = \frac{\sum (z_X z_Y)}{N-1}$$

$$= \text{Cov}_{z_X z_Y}$$

The correlation between scores on the SAT and GPAs is .89. This statistical finding corresponds to what one might expect from eyeballing the scatterplot in Table 6-2. The points show a linear relationship with a positive slope, indicating that the correlation is positive. (*Note:* If the covariance had been negative, the correlation coefficient would have been negative also.) Finally, the points cluster closely about an imaginary straight line drawn through them; the magnitude of the correlation coefficient is what we expected from an eyeball analysis.

In computing the Pearson correlation, the first step is to make a scatterplot of the two variables of interest. If the scatterplot can be approximated by a straight line, Formula 6-2, called the *deviation-score formula,* can be used to calculate the correlation coefficient.[5]

For reference, the steps in computing this correlation coefficient are shown in Procedure 6-2, using data from class 3 in the Majasan study.

PROCEDURE 6-2 Steps in calculating the Pearson product-moment correlation r_{XY} using deviation scores (data from class 3 of the Majasan study; see Table 6-1)

Operation	Example

1. Look up the *deviation score formula:*

$$r_{XY} = \frac{\text{Cov}_{XY}}{s_X s_Y}$$

2. Draw a scatterplot to check that X and Y are *linearly* related.
See Procedure 6-1 for constructing a scatterplot.

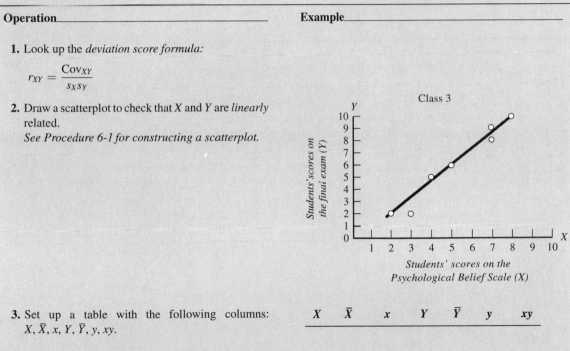

3. Set up a table with the following columns: $X, \bar{X}, x, Y, \bar{Y}, y, xy$.

X	$\bar{X}$	x	Y	$\bar{Y}$	y	xy

---

[5]If the scatterplot cannot be described as linear, the Pearson product-moment correlation coefficient may not provide the best measure of the relationship between X and Y. For curvilinear relationships, the correlation ratio, η (eta), should be used (e.g., Kirk, 1982).

Operation	Example

4. For each subject, enter the scores on variables X and Y in the appropriate columns.

X	$\bar{X}$	x	Y	$\bar{Y}$	y	xy
8			10			
7			8			
3			2			
5			6			
7			9			
2			2			
4			5			

5. Calculate the means of X and Y, and enter the values in the columns labeled $\bar{X}$ and $\bar{Y}$.
See Procedure 4-3 for calculating a mean.

X	$\bar{X}$	x	Y	$\bar{Y}$	y	xy
8	5.14		10	6.00		
7	5.14		8	6.00		
3	5.14		2	6.00		
5	5.14		6	6.00		
7	5.14		9	6.00		
2	5.14		2	6.00		
4	5.14		5	6.00		

6. Calculate deviation scores for the X and Y variables by subtracting the mean from each raw score:

$$x = X - \bar{X}$$
$$y = Y - \bar{Y}$$

X	$\bar{X}$	x	Y	$\bar{Y}$	y	xy
8	5.14	2.86	10	6.00	4.00	
7	5.14	1.86	8	6.00	2.00	
3	5.14	−2.14	2	6.00	−4.00	
5	5.14	−.14	6	6.00	.00	
7	5.14	1.86	9	6.00	3.00	
2	5.14	−3.14	2	6.00	−4.00	
4	5.14	−1.14	5	6.00	−1.00	

7. Multiply each subject's deviation score x for the variable X by his or her deviation score y for variable Y to obtain the cross product for each subject (xy).
Pay attention to the signs of x and y when multiplying.

X	$\bar{X}$	x	Y	$\bar{Y}$	y	xy
8	5.14	2.86	10	6.00	4.00	11.44
7	5.14	1.86	8	6.00	2.00	3.72
3	5.14	−2.14	2	6.00	−4.00	8.56
5	5.14	−.14	6	6.00	.00	.00
7	5.14	1.86	9	6.00	3.00	5.58
2	5.14	−3.14	2	6.00	−4.00	12.56
4	5.14	−1.14	5	6.00	−1.00	1.14

8. Sum the cross products to obtain $\sum xy$.
Pay attention to the sign of each cross product when summing.

X	$\bar{X}$	x	Y	$\bar{Y}$	y	xy
8	5.14	2.86	10	6.00	4.00	11.44
7	5.14	1.86	8	6.00	2.00	3.72
3	5.14	−2.14	2	6.00	−4.00	8.56
5	5.14	−.14	6	6.00	.00	.00
7	5.14	1.86	9	6.00	3.00	5.58
2	5.14	−3.14	2	6.00	−4.00	12.56
4	5.14	−1.14	5	6.00	−1.00	1.14

$$\Sigma xy = 43.00$$

Operation	Example
9. Divide $\sum xy$ (found in step 8) by $N - 1$ to obtain: $$\text{Cov}_{XY} = \frac{\sum xy}{N-1}$$ *This value is known as the covariance.*	$$\frac{43.00}{6} = 7.17$$
10. Calculate the standard deviations (s_X and s_Y) of X and Y. *See Procedure 4-6 for calculating a standard deviation.*	$s_X = 2.27$ $s_Y = 3.21$
11. Multiply s_X by s_Y.	$(2.27)(3.21) = 7.29$
12. Divide Cov_{XY} (found in step 9) by $s_X s_Y$ (found in step 11) to obtain: $$r_{XY} = \frac{\text{Cov}_{XY}}{s_X s_Y} = \frac{\dfrac{\sum xy}{N-1}}{s_X s_Y}$$	$$\frac{7.17}{7.29} = .98$$

The scatterplot in Procedure 6-2 shows a linear relationship between scores on the Psychological Belief Scale and exam scores in class 3. The correlation between these variables is .98. This correlation coefficient is consistent with an eyeball analysis of the scatterplot. The slope of the points in the scatterplot is not horizontal; it rises from the lower left to upper right. Hence, the correlation should not be zero; it should be positive. The points in the scatterplot cluster closely about the imaginary line, indicating a linear relation. The correlation coefficient, then, should be positive and large in magnitude, which means that there is a very strong relationship between belief scores and exam scores. Since a high score represents a strong belief in behaviorism, the correlation coefficient tells us that the greater the student's belief in behaviorism, the higher her exam score in class 3.

Example Problem 6.2

Using hypothetical SAT and GPA data from the study of men's and women's college achievement in Table 6-2, compute the correlation between SAT scores and GPAs.

Whereas the deviation-score formula (6-2) makes sense conceptually, an alternate formula works directly from raw scores, not deviation scores; is computationally less time-consuming; and is often used in computer programming. It is presented here only because you might see this version of the Pearson correlation presented in another statistics book, or in a manual for a calculator, or a computer statistics package.

$$r_{XY} = \frac{N\left(\sum XY\right) - \left(\sum X\right)\left(\sum Y\right)}{\sqrt{\left[N\sum X^2 - \left(\sum X\right)^2\right]\left[N\sum Y^2 - \left(\sum Y\right)^2\right]}} \qquad \text{(6-3)}$$

where:

    N = number of subjects

    X = score on variable X

    Y = score on variable Y

THE SQUARED CORRELATION COEFFICIENT, r_{XY}^2

Recall that the Pearson product-moment correlation coefficient provides a measure of the strength of association between X and Y. The larger the absolute value of r_{XY}, the stronger the relationship between X and Y. The square of r_{XY}, $r^2{}_{XY}$, is called the **coefficient of determination.** The square of the correlation coefficient—the coefficient of determination—can be interpreted as the proportion of variability in Y that can be accounted for by knowing X, or the proportion of variability in X that can be accounted for by knowing Y.

    The concept of percentage of variance needs to be explained. The scores on the belief scale (X) vary from one subject to another, as do scores on the exam scores (Y). This variability on each measure can be described by the standard deviation (s_X and s_Y) or the variance (s_X^2 and s_Y^2). The variability in X is due to two factors: (1) predictable differences between subjects (i.e., differences in beliefs) and (2) random error (i.e., unsystematic differences between subjects unrelated to differences in beliefs, such as fatigue, inattention, misunderstanding of instructions, etc.). Similarly, the variability in Y is also affected by these two factors. Thus the correlation coefficient might be thought of as a ratio, with the numerator representing the common variability or covariability between X and Y (covariance), and the denominator representing the total possible variability of X and Y ($s_X s_Y$). When this coefficient is squared, the result is a ratio of variances, with the **common variance** shared by X and Y in the numerator, and the total variance in the denominator:

$$r_{XY}^2 = \frac{(\text{Cov}_{XY})^2}{s_X^2 s_Y^2} = \frac{\text{shared variance}}{\text{total variance}}$$

In other words, r_{XY}^2 gives the proportion of the total variance shared by X and Y. Put still another way, r_{XY}^2 is the proportion of variance in Y predictable from X, or vice versa. The actual **percentage of variance** in Y accounted for by X can be found with the following formula.

percentage of variance in Y accounted for by knowing $X = r_{XY}^2 \times 100$ **(6-4)**

With a correlation of .98, the percentage of variance in exam scores (Y) accounted for by belief scores (X) is:

$$(.98)^2 \times 100 = .96 \times 100 = 96 \text{ percent}$$

Figure 6-6 provides a pictorial representation of the concept of percentage of variance accounted for. The circle labeled X represents the variability of scores on X, and the circle labeled Y represents the variability of scores on Y. The greater the overlap of circles, (1) the greater the common variance shared by X and Y (i.e., the stronger the relationship between X and Y), (2) the greater the percentage of variance in Y that is accounted for by knowing X, and (3) the greater the percentage of variance in X that is accounted for by knowing Y. For example, Figure 6-6a represents the case in which X and Y do not share variability in common; they are independent and $r^2_{XY} = 0$. Figure 6-6b shows the case in which X and Y share a moderate percentage of variance in common—that is, X is moderately predictable from Y, and Y is moderately predictable from X. Finally, Figure 6-6c represents the percentage of variance in exam scores accounted for by variability in belief scores—96 percent. In this case, almost all the variability in Y is accounted for by variability in X, and vice versa.

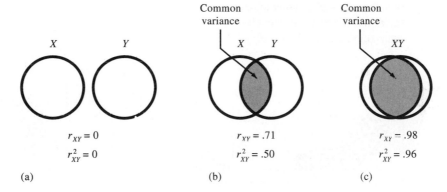

FIGURE 6-6
Percentage of variance in Y (or X) accounted for by knowing X (or Y)

Example Problem 6.3 ▬▬▬▬▬▬▬▬▬▬▬▬▬▬▬▬▬▬▬▬▬▬▬▬▬▬

Using hypothetical SAT and GPA data from the study of men's and women's college achievement (Table 6-2):
   a. Compute the coefficient of determination.
   b. Interpret the coefficient of determination.

SPEARMAN RANK CORRELATION COEFFICIENT

The Pearson correlation coefficient is a measure of the *linear* relationship between X and Y. However, linearity is not always found for data in the behavioral sciences. As we saw, the relationship between belief scores and exam scores in psychology classes may be curvilinear.

Several cases of curvilinearity can be distinguished. Some examples are provided in Figure 6-7. In Figures 6-7a, b, the scatterplots just miss being linear; they are *weak* examples of curvilinear relationships. (More marked curvilinear relationships are shown in Figures 6-7c, d.) The scatterplots in Figures 6-7a, b show Y to be *monotonically* related to X. A **monotonic relationship** is one in which an increase in scores on one variable is always accompanied by an increase in scores on a second variable (monotone increasing) or by a decrease in such scores (monotone decreasing). Put another way, a monotonic relationship is one where the scatterplots (curves) are everywhere increasing or everywhere decreasing. In Figure 6-7a, Y decreases at a faster rate (steeper slope) for low values of X and continues to decrease, though at a slower rate (less steep slope), for high levels of X. In this case, Y is described as a **monotonically decreasing function** of X. In Figure 6-7b, just the reverse occurs. Initially, Y increases at a slower rate for low values of X and continues to increase, though at a faster rate, for high values of X. In this case, Y is described as a **monotonically increasing function** of X. The Spearman rank correlation can be used when a nonlinear, monotonically increasing or decreasing function describes the relation between X and Y. Furthermore, the Spearman coefficient can be used when the original data are ordinal, as with ranks (e.g., a teacher's ranking of students as to their achievement and cooperation in class).

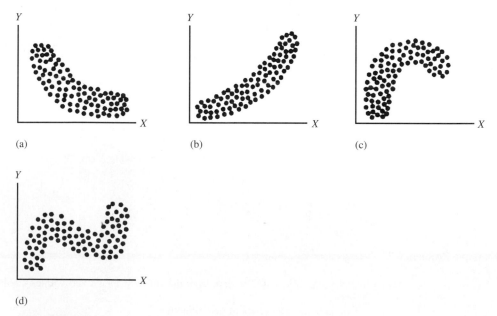

FIGURE 6-7
Examples of several curvilinear relationships between two variables

When a monotonic relationship between X and Y exists, scores on continuous variables are converted to scores representing each person's rank on the variables (from lowest = 1, next lowest = 2, . . ., highest = N). When scores are converted to ranks, a scatterplot of the monotonic relationship between X and Y is converted to a scatterplot of rank scores that is *linear*. With a linear relationship of rank scores, the **Spearman rank correlation coefficient** r_S can be computed.[6] It is the Pearson coefficient for ranks. It reflects the magnitude and direction of the relationship between X and Y.

As an example, consider some hypothetical data on the relationship between scores on an extroversion scale and scores on a humor scale (presented in Table 6-5). The scatterplot in this table shows that Y is a monotonically increasing function of X. Hence, the usual

TABLE 6-5   Data bearing on the relationship between scores on extroversion (X) and humor (Y)

Person	Extroversion X	Humor Y	Scatterplot of X and Y
1	1	4	
2	1	8	
3	2	10	
4	3	14	
5	4	15	
6	5	16	
7	6	17	
8	7	18	
9	8	18	

TABLE 6-6   Rank order data bearing on the relationship between extroversion (X) and humor (Y)

Person	Extroversion X	Humor Y	Scatterplot of Ranks on X and Y
1	1.5	1	
2	1.5	2	
3	3	3	
4	4	4	
5	5	5	
6	6	6	
7	7	7	
8	8	8.5	
9	9	8.5	

[6]In using r_S, the X and Y variables are assumed to be measured on at least an ordinal scale.

product-moment coefficient on the original scores may not be appropriate. The rank order correlation, then, is an appropriate correlation coefficient for these data.

Ranks on X and Y are shown in Table 6-6 along with the scatterplot of the ranked data. Notice the difference between the scatterplots in Tables 6-5 and 6-6. The monotonic relation between scores on X and Y in Table 6-5 has been converted to a linear relation between ranks on X and Y in Table 6-6.

With scores on X and Y transformed to rank scores on X and Y, a correlation can be computed with the Pearson formula,[7] which, with rank order data, gives Spearman's correlation r_S (Formula 6-5).

$$r_S = \frac{\text{Cov}_{XY}}{s_X s_Y} \tag{6-5}$$

where X and Y are ranks.

For reference, the steps in calculating r_S are given in Procedure 6-3.

PROCEDURE 6-3 Steps in computing the Spearman rank correlation coefficient r_S, using data from Table 6-5 as an example

Operation	Example			
			Rank	*Rank*
1. Set up a table with the following columns: X, Y, Rank on X, Rank on Y.	*X*	*Y*	*on X*	*on Y*
Note that r_S is appropriate for (a) variables measured on at least an ordinal scale or (b) continuous variables with a monotonically increasing or decreasing relationship, as shown in Figures 6-3a, b.				

---

[7] The common form of the rank order correlation,

$$r_S = 1 - \frac{6 \sum d_p^2}{N(N^2 - 1)}$$

(where d_p^2 is the square of the difference between each person's rank on X and Y), is derived from the product-moment correlation (Formula 6-2). It is the equivalent to the product-moment correlation using rank order data with untied ranks (i.e., no two subjects have the same rank on X, Y, or both; see Siegel [1956] for the mathematical derivation). Since the common form of the formula assumes no ties in ranks but the Pearson formula used with ranks permits ties, the latter is presented in the text.

Operation	Example

2. Enter the X and Y scores for each subject.
List the X scores in order from smallest to largest. Note that, because X and Y are almost perfectly correlated, the scores are also ordered from smallest to largest. This is not typical of most correlations in behavioral research.

X	Y	Rank on X	Rank on Y
1	4		
1	8		
2	10		
3	14		
4	15		
5	16		
6	17		
7	18		
8	18		

3. Convert scores on X to ranks. (Then convert scores on Y to ranks.)

  a. 1 = lowest score
  2 = next lowest score
  $\vdots$
  N = highest score
  Note that each person's X and Y scores are converted to their corresponding ranks on each variable.

X	Y	Rank on X	Rank on Y
1	4	1.5	1.5
1	8	1.5	2.5
2	10	3.5	3.5
3	14	4.5	4.5
4	15	5.5	5.5
5	16	6.5	6.5
6	17	7.5	7.5
7	18	8.5	8.5
8	18	9.5	8.5

  b. If two scores are tied for a rank, average the ranks and assign the average rank to both scores.

On X, there are two scores of 1, which are tied for ranks of 1 and 2. The ranks of 1 and 2 are averaged $[(1+2)/2 = 1.5]$, and this average rank is assigned to both scores of 1 on X.

Rank on X	$\bar{X}$	x	Rank on Y	$\bar{Y}$	y	xy
1.5	5	−3.5	1	5	−4	14.5
1.5	5	−3.5	2	5	−3	10.5
3	5	−2	3	5	−2	4.5
4	5	−1	4	5	−1	1.5
5	5	0	5	5	0	0.5
6	5	1	6	5	1	1.5
7	5	2	7	5	2	4.5
8	5	3	8.5	5	3.5	10.5
9	5	4	8.5	5	3.5	14.5

Operation	Example

4. Sum xy. Then calculate the correlation between the ranks on X and Y, using the Pearson correlation. Steps are given in Procedure 6-2.

$$r_S = \frac{\text{Cov}_{XY}}{s_X s_Y}$$

where X and Y are ranks. Recall from Formulas 6-1 and 4–7 that:

$$\text{Cov}_{XY} = \frac{\sum xy}{N - 1}$$

$$s = \sqrt{\frac{\sum x^2}{N - 1}}$$

$$\text{Cov}_{XY} = \frac{\sum xy}{N - 1} = \frac{59}{8} = 7.375$$

$$s_X = \sqrt{\frac{\sum x^2}{N - 1}} = \sqrt{\frac{59.5}{8}} = \sqrt{7.44} = 2.73$$

$$s_Y = \sqrt{\frac{59.5}{8}} = \sqrt{7.44} = 2.73$$

$$r_S = \frac{\text{Cov}_{XY}}{s_X s_Y} = \frac{7.375}{(2.73)(2.73)} = .9899$$

The correlation between ranks on extroversion (X) and humor (Y) is .99. This correlation is consistent with an eyeball analysis of the scatterplot in Table 6-6. First, the slope of the scatterplot goes from the lower left to the upper right. Hence, the correlation coefficient is different from zero and should be positive (+). Second, most of the points in the scatterplot fall on an imaginary straight line. Therefore, the correlation coefficient should be large in magnitude.

Recall that r_S is the appropriate correlation coefficient for variables measured on an ordinal scale or for variables measured on interval scales where a weak curvilinear relationship is found—for example, monotonically decreasing or monotonically increasing functions, as shown in Figures 6-7a, b. (The Spearman rank order correlation is not appropriate for marked curvilinear relationships such as those shown in Figures 6-7c, d; see footnote 5.) The rank order correlation is interpreted in the same way as the product-moment correlation: The sign of the coefficient indicates the direction of the relationship between the two variables, and the absolute magnitude of the coefficient indicates the strength of association between the two variables.

Example Problem 6.4

Table 6-7 reports hypothetical ratings of workers on performance and enthusiasm that were obtained in a study of a sales firm. Compute the correlation between these variables.

a. Construct a scatterplot.

b. Decide on and calculate a correlation coefficient.

TABLE 6-7   Hypothetical rankings of workers based on performance and enthusiasm

Worker	Performance	Enthusiasm
1	3	4
2	4	3
3	1	1
4	6	5
5	5	5
6	2	4
7	1	2
8	3	3

SOURCES OF MISLEADING CORRELATION COEFFICIENTS

Sometimes researchers and users of research are all too confident in correlations. When low correlations are found, they are tempted to conclude that there is little or no relationship between the variables; when high correlations are obtained, they are tempted to conclude that there is a strong relationship. However, certain characteristics of the sample data may lead to spuriously low or high correlation coefficients and thus distort the true relationship between the variables. In particular, we will show the following:

1. *Restriction of the range* of values on one of the variables may reduce the magnitude of the correlation coefficient.
2. Use of *extreme groups* may inflate the correlation coefficient.
3. *Combining groups* with different means on one or both variables may have an unpredictable effect on the correlation coefficient.
4. *Extreme scores* may have a marked effect on the correlation coefficient, especially if the sample size is small.
5. A *curvilinear relationship* between X and Y may account for a near-zero Pearson correlation coefficient.

To help avoid interpreting spurious correlations, always examine scatterplots before interpreting them.

Restriction of Range

A low correlation coefficient may result from a **restriction of the range** of values of one of the variables. This effect becomes especially important when one is interpreting correlations based on *selected* groups of individuals. For example, suppose that a college admissions officer is interested in the relationship between SAT scores and GPA in the first year of college. If students taking the SAT were admitted to college without regard to these scores, a scatterplot of the relationship between SATs and GPAs might resemble the hypothetical scatterplot shown in Figure 6-8a. The correlation is probably about .60—that is, there is a positive, moderately strong relationship between these variables. Now consider the fact that most major colleges and universities only admit students with SAT scores of 1000 or above. The vertical line in Figure 6-8b represents this admission policy, which results in restricting the range of scores, as shown in Figure 6-8c. Notice that an imaginary straight line fitted to the circular scatterplot in Figure 6-8c would almost be flat, suggesting a low correlation. Since freshman grades are available only for students admitted to college, the admissions officer might erroneously conclude that there is little relationship between SAT scores and freshman GPAs.

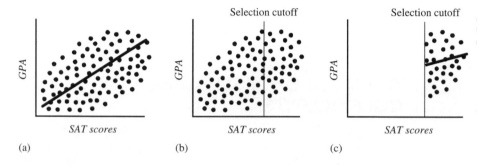

(a)   (b)   (c)

FIGURE 6-8
Illustration of the effect of restricting the range of X (e.g., SAT) scores on the correlation between X and Y (e.g., GPA)

Thus, one must be cautious in interpreting correlations based on selected groups. Variances or standard deviations of measures on which a correlation coefficient is calculated should be checked in order to determine whether restriction of range has occurred. Small variances or standard deviations for these measures may suggest a restriction of range and signal that caution must be taken in interpreting the correlation coefficient.

Extreme Groups

Researchers sometimes use **extreme groups**—that is, they select subjects with extreme scores on a certain variable (X) in order to study whether subjects who differ on this dimension also differ in other ways (Y). For example, a researcher might be interested in whether subjects who differ in need for achievement (X) also show differences in other personality traits, such as anxiety (Y). Thus she might select subjects who scored very high or very low on need for achievement and correlate these scores with their scores on a test of anxiety. This procedure may result in a larger correlation coefficient than would be obtained if subjects with moderate scores on need for achievement had also been included. A larger correlation coefficient results because subjects with very extreme scores on one variable may also tend to have very extreme scores on the other variable. Subjects with moderate scores on one variable may also tend to have moderate scores on the other variable. However, the variability of the moderate score on the Y variable may be greater than the variability of the extreme scores on the same variable. Because of the larger spread of scores in the middle of the joint distribution, the points do not cluster as tightly around an imaginary straight line as they do at the extremes. Thus, correlation coefficients based on extremely high and extremely low scores usually tend to be higher than those that also take moderate scores into account.

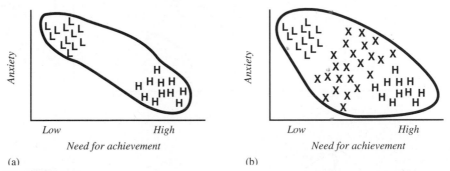

FIGURE 6-9

Illustration of the effects of extreme groups on r_{XY}, where H = high need for achievement, X = moderate need for achievement, and L = low need for achievement: (a) when extreme groups only are used, $r_{XY} = -.80$; (b) when moderates scores are also included, $r_{XY} = -.60$

   The effect of extreme groups is illustrated in Figure 6-9a. A scatterplot of hypothetical scores for need for achievement and anxiety is shown for a sample that contained only subjects with extreme scores on need for achievement. The points on the scatterplot cluster tightly around an imaginary line representing the slope of the scatterplot. The correlation is negative and strong—about −.80. The figure shows that subjects who score extremely low on need for achievement tend to score extremely high on anxiety; subjects who score very high on need for achievement tend to score very low on anxiety. Figure 6-9b shows how the correlation is affected when scores falling in the intermediate range on need for achievement are included. In this case, the points cluster less tightly around the imaginary line drawn to represent the slope of the scatterplot; the coefficient is reduced to about −.60. Thus, caution must be used in making general statements about the degree of association between two variables based on correlation coefficients that are computed on subjects with extreme scores on one of the variables.

Combining Groups

In general, caution should be taken in interpreting a correlation coefficient based on subjects that represent samples from two or more populations. In such cases, the correlation coefficient for the combined sample may be quite misleading, for two reasons. First, differences in means may produce a misleading correlation coefficient even if the relationship between the variables is the same in each group (see Figures 6-10a, b, f). Second, the relationship between variables may differ from group to group (see Figures 6-10c, d, e). For example, suppose a school district is interested in the relationship between reading and mathematics achievement. The correlation coefficient will provide a measure of this relationship over all subgroups of students (e.g., boys and girls; native English and Spanish speakers) in the district. Notice, though, that this correlation may be influenced by differences in the means of the subgroups on X, on Y, or both. Or it may be influenced by the fact that the relation between X and Y is not the same for all of the subgroups.

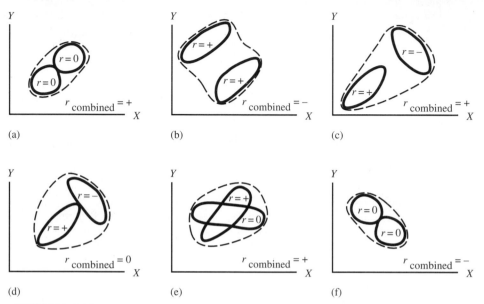

FIGURE 6-10

Examples of the effect on r_{XY} when groups with different means and different relationships between X and Y are combined

    Figures 6-10a–f show the effects of combining groups with different means and/or different relationships between X and Y on the correlation coefficient. Figure 6-10a shows how a positive correlation may be obtained by combining groups with different means when, within each group, there is no systematic relationship between X and Y. Figures 6-10b–f show the results of some other possible combinations of groups with different means. In general, if a sample consists of subjects whose scores tend to fall into two different groups with different means, correlation coefficients should be computed separately for each group.

Outliers

As shown earlier in this chapter, a few outliers (deviant points) on the scatterplot can change the nature of the relationship between two variables. For example, the scatterplot of class 2 in the Majasan study (Figure 6-3) shows that a curved line best describes the relationship between the two variables. In other words, there is a curvilinear relationship between variables X and Y in this group. However, notice that if the one outlier is ignored, the relationship between the variables is best described by a straight line. The relationship between the variables is linear now.

    Not only can extreme scores change the nature of the relationship between the two variables (linear versus curvilinear), but they may also change the *direction* and *magnitude* of the correlation coefficient, particularly if the sample size is small. For example, the scatterplot in Figure 6-11 shows the relationship between scores on variables X and Y. The correlation between these scores is negative and moderately large ($r = -.48$). However, suppose the one subject who scored extremely high on variable X and extremely low on variable Y (denoted by * in Figure 6-11) is ignored. When this one subject is excluded from the sample, the correlation is low and in the opposite direction ($r = .05$). In general, extreme scores only have such a drastic effect on the correlation coefficient when the number of subjects is small and the extreme scores deviate markedly from the general cluster. With a reasonably large number of subjects (e.g., $N = 100$), the effect of the outlier is unlikely to be dramatic.

If such outliers are found, the researcher must decide whether to include or ignore them in the data analysis. If a decision is made to ignore outliers, a full description—a kind of case study—should be given for each subject representing an outlier.

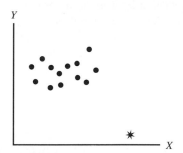

FIGURE 6-11
An illustration of the effects of an extreme score on r_{XY}

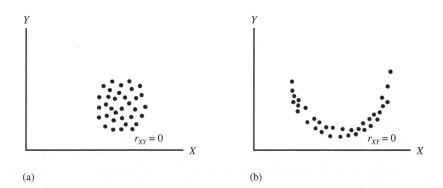

(a)   (b)

FIGURE 6-12
Two examples of an approximately zero Pearson product-moment correlation (after Glass & Stanley, 1970)

Curvilinearity

When a low or near-zero correlation is obtained between two variables, one is tempted to conclude that there is no relationship between the two variables under study. However, recall that the correlation coefficients calculated in this chapter are meaningful only for a linear relationship between X and Y. Thus, a correlation of zero indicates only that there is no *linear* relationship between the variables. Yet, X and Y may be closely related in a curvilinear fashion and r_{XY} may be low. For example, Figure 6-12 shows two scatterplots that have correlation coefficients of zero. In one case (Figure 6-12a), X and Y lack any systematic relationship, but in the other case (Figure 6-12b), X and Y are curvilinearly related. Thus, data should be cast into a scatterplot before one computes a correlation coefficient. If the relationship to be described is curvilinear, the eta coefficient should be used (see footnote 5).

CORRELATION AND CAUSALITY

A single correlation is a measure of association between two variables. In the absence of additional information, the correlation coefficient cannot tell us anything about the causal relation between the two variables. However, correlations can tell us something about causal relationships among a set of variables. This section provides the logic underlying causal interpretations of patterns of correlations. The presentation is conceptual only, and reading it will not give you the skills needed to do the statistical analyses suggested here. Nevertheless, this topic is an extremely important one in behavioral research, and so you should at least be familiar with it.

A true experiment is characterized by random assignment of subjects to one or more experimental groups and to one or more control groups; the researcher manipulates one or more independent variables in order to make inferences about the effects of the independent variables on the dependent variable (see Chapter 1). Although causality cannot be proved empirically, support for some kind of causal influence can be inferred from true experiments with some degree of certainty. The procedures of the experiment help rule out alternative interpretations to the experimenter's assertion that the independent variable caused the change in the dependent variable.

In correlational studies, the researcher does not systematically manipulate the independent variable to observe its effect on the dependent variable; rather, he *selects* two variables to see how they covary in a group (random sample) of subjects. Subjects cannot be randomly assigned to different levels of the variables; rather, nature or experience has already performed the "treatment" at the time of the study, and the researcher observes a group of subjects on two variables. For example, in a study of the relationship between sex and self-concept, nature has assigned subjects to the sex variable (male or female), and experience has assigned them to the self-concept variable (degree of positive self-concept). Hence, the experimenter cannot randomly assign subjects to the levels of the variables. Finally, since nature has performed the "treatments" prior to the researcher's observation, correlational studies do not have control groups. The procedures of a correlational study, then, make it impossible to verify that the correlation coefficient is a measure of causality between two variables. *A single correlation coefficient cannot be interpreted as a measure of causality. There are too many alternative hypotheses that cannot be ruled out* (cf. Chapter 1).

Indeed, there are three rival hypotheses about the causal relationship between two correlated variables X and Y: (1) X causes Y, (2) Y causes X, or (3) the relation between X and Y is caused by some third variable Z. For example, in the Majasan study of the relation between beliefs (X) and achievement (Y), did behavioristic beliefs (X) cause high achievement (Y)? Or did high achievement (Y) cause behavioristic beliefs (X)? Or did some other variable (Z)—such as the knowledge gained from courses with content related to the psychology course—cause the relation between beliefs (X) and achievement (Y) in class 3?[8] The nature of the correlation study does not permit us to decide which is the correct interpretation.

Even though a single correlation coefficient cannot be interpreted as a measure of the causal relationship between X and Y, causal inferences can be made from the correlational studies. The key to examining the causal relationship between X and Y is to include in a correlational study a third variable (Z) that challenges the hypothesized causal relationship. In the Majasan study, for example, suppose we wanted to test the hypothesis that beliefs (X) caused achievement in introductory psychology (Y). There are a number of rival hypotheses to the proposed causal interpretation. One such hypothesis is that achievement (Y) caused beliefs (X). However, this hypothesis can be discounted because of the order in which the data were collected—viz., beliefs were measured at the beginning of the semester, before students studied psychology, and achievement in introductory psychology was measured throughout the course. A second, more plausible rival hypothesis is that knowledge gained from courses with similar content caused the observed correlation between beliefs and achievement. A third variable (Z) representing this rival hypothesis might then be measured in the study. For example, grade point average in related courses might be used as the third variable Z.

With three variables in the correlational study, a number of **causal models** (possible causal relationships between X, Y, and Z) might be postulated. Suppose, on the basis of common sense and some psychological or sociological theory, we expect achievement to be caused by both beliefs (X) and knowledge from related courses (Z). This predicted causal relation can be represented as a model with arrows corresponding to the direction of the causal links:

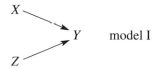

model I

Model I states that X causes Y, Z causes Y, but X and Z are not causally related.

A rival model of the causal relationship might assert that beliefs (X) caused both achievement (Y) and grades in related courses (Z). This model can be written as:

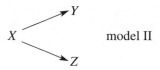

model II

---

[8]Only variable Z may not be enough to account for the causal relation. Two or more such variables may be needed. However, for simplicity, only one extra variable is considered here.

Still another plausible model asserts that the causal relationship between beliefs (X) and achievement (Y) is mediated by grades in related courses (Z). In this case, beliefs have an indirect effect on achievement through grades in other courses:

$$X \rightarrow Z \rightarrow Y \qquad \text{model III}$$

Finally, a fourth model might account for the observed relation between beliefs (X) and achievement (Y) as being due to the fact that knowledge from related courses (Z) caused both X and Y:

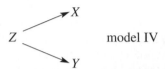

model IV

In order to determine whether model I provides an accurate representation of the causal relation between beliefs and achievement, the researcher can fit the data from the correlational study with model I and each of the three competing models to see whether the data fit the proposed model better than the rival models.[9] If they do not, doubt is cast on the proposed model; and further conceptual and empirical work are needed to clarify the causal relation between X and Y.

In the examination of causal relations in correlational studies, then, both theory and data are combined. On the basis of theory, certain rival hypotheses can be eliminated (e.g., temporal order), and causal relations within a proposed model can be justified. Then, data from the study can be used to test whether the proposed model or some alternative provides the most accurate representation of the causal relationship (see, e.g., Blalock, 1964; Davis, 1985; Duncan, 1975; Pedhazur, 1982).

SUMMARY

This chapter presents the concept of a joint distribution, a distribution showing the relationship between two variables, X and Y. The chapter provides both tabular and graphical representations of the joint distribution. The chapter also provides a summary coefficient, the *correlation coefficient,* for describing the relationship shown in a joint distribution. Procedures are provided for calculating and interpreting the correlation coefficient, a measure of the strength and direction of association between two variables. Two types of correlation coefficients are presented: the *Pearson product-moment correlation coefficient,* used when X and Y are linearly related, and the *Spearman rank order correlation coefficient,* a special case of the Pearson coefficient, used when X or Y is measured on an ordinal scale or when X and Y are monotonically related. Then, several *sources of misleading correlation coefficients* are discussed. Finally, the relation between correlation and causality is discussed.

---

[9]For example, model I accounts for a greater proportion of the variance in Y than does model IV.

ANSWERS TO EXAMPLE PROBLEMS

1. **a.**

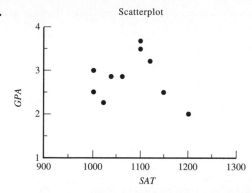

Scatterplot

b. The scatterplot looks slightly negative, mainly due to one data point: Student 2 has a relatively high SAT score of 1200 and a low GPA of 2.00. A negative relation between SAT scores and GPAs is unexpected since, in very large samples, the correlation is positive. See the section, "Sources of Misleading Correlation Coefficients," in this chapter for possible explanations.

2. $r = -.127$

3. **a.** Coefficient of determination $= r^2 = (-.127)^2 = .016$

   b. The proportion of variation in GPAs that can be accounted for by variation in SAT scores is .016. Put another way, 1.6 percent of the variance in GPAs is accounted for by variation in SAT scores. The proportion of variation accounted for is negligible.

4. **a.**   Original data   Ranked data

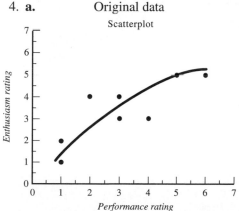

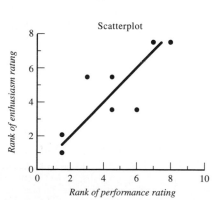

b. The original data are not linear but monotonic. Consequently, transforming original scores to ranks created the linear relation shown in the second scatterplot. Consequently, the Spearman rank correlation was used to calculate the correlation:

$r_s = .810$. If you calculated the correlation using the original scores, you would have found $r = .821$.

EXERCISES

Unless otherwise indicated, use the following data from the first-grade bloomers in the Study of Teacher Expectancy (data from Table 2-1):

Student	Pretest	Posttest
1	60	107
2	85	111
3	90	117
4	110	125
5	115	122

1. Construct a scatterplot of the bloomers' data.
2. Calculate the correlation between pretest and posttest scores.
3. Calculate the coefficient of determination.
4. Interpret the coefficient of determination.
5. In a consumer survey of new models of cars, a random sample of car buyers was asked to rank order the newest economy models of the major car manufacturer with respect to their attractiveness. In addition, background information was also collected, including age. In correlating age with model preference, what correlation coefficient would you use and why?
6. In Example Problems 6.1 and 6.2, you found a negative relation between SAT scores and GPAs. What might explain the negative correlation?

ANSWERS TO EXERCISES

1.

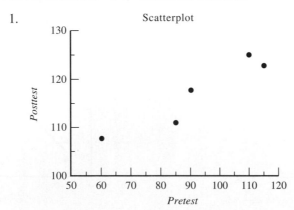

Scatterplot

2. $r = .946$
3. Coefficient of determination = $r^2 = (.946)^2 = .895$
4. Variation in pretest scores account for a large proportion (.895) of the variance in posttest scores, or vice versa. Put another way, about 90 percent of the variance in

posttest scores is accounted for by variance in the pretest scores. This correlation and coefficient of determination are high but not surprising since pre- and posttest scores are usually highly correlated, especially when the measure is IQ and the time span is less than a year.

5. Spearman rank correlation because one of the variables is rank.

6. There are three possible reasons (aside from the fact that they're hypothetical data!): (1) The sample size is very small ($N = 10$) and correlations based on small samples are not reliable. (2) There may be an outlier in the data. In fact, when subject 2 is omitted, the correlation goes from $-.127$ to $+.336(!)$. (3) The data are based on a selected sample of students: those students who were admitted to UCLA. The lowest SAT score is 1000, suggesting that the range of scores on this variable has been restricted by the admissions process.

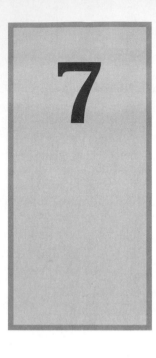

Linear Regression

- Establishing a Systematic Relationship Between Variables
- Prediction of Y from X: Intuitive Approach
- Prediction Using Linear Regression
- Errors in Prediction
- Linear Regression Equation for Predicting X from Y
- Percentage of Variance
- Summary
- Answers to Example Problems
- Exercises
- Answers to Exercises

One goal of science is **prediction.** Theories are built to predict one variable from other variables. For example, the force on an object can be predicted perfectly by knowing its mass and acceleration. In many cases, of course, prediction is less than perfect. For example, weather conditions such as rainfall can be predicted from barometric pressure and other indicators but, sometimes, not very reliably. Prediction is as important a goal in the behavioral sciences as in other sciences. For example, job performance as a typist can be predicted from scores on a typing test, but of course not perfectly. College grade point averages can be predicted from scores on the Scholastic Aptitude Test, but again not perfectly. Such a functional relationship does not imply that one variable causes the other. It only says that values of one variable can be predicted by knowing values of the other. For example, a functional relationship can be specified between college GPA and scores on SAT so that a student's GPA can be predicted from knowledge of her SAT score. This relationship does not suggest, however, that a high GPA, say, is caused by a high SAT score.

Much of the research and theory building in the behavioral sciences, then, is aimed at not only providing an index of the relationship between two variables, as the correlation coefficient does, but also improving predictions by specifying a functional relationship between two variables. This functional relationship is based on data collected from the same subjects on the "predictor" variable—the variable with which predictions are to be made (e.g., SAT scores)—and on the "outcome" variable—the variable to be predicted (e.g., GPAs). Once the functional relationship between the two variables is specified, scores on the predictor variable can be used to predict scores on the outcome variable for similar individuals. The purpose of this chapter is to present a technique for specifying the functional relationship that statistically predicts one variable (e.g., GPAs) from another variable (e.g., SAT scores) and to provide the skills necessary to compute and interpret the descriptive statistics involved in prediction.

ESTABLISHING A SYSTEMATIC RELATIONSHIP BETWEEN VARIABLES

If we are to predict one variable from another, there must be some **systematic relationship** between the two variables. And as you know from Chapter 6, both the joint distribution and the correlation coefficient provide information about the relationship between two variables. If there is a systematic relationship between X and Y, the points in a scatterplot will form a pattern, and the correlation coefficient will not be zero. In this case, one variable (Y) is some function of the other variable (X), and the functional relation between X and Y can be found. This functional relationship tells us how many score points Y is expected to change if scores on X change by a certain number of points. For example, the relationship between SAT scores and GPAs, as shown in Figure 7-1, is systematic. This strong, positive, linear relationship is reflected by the correlation between the scores on the two variables: $r_{XY} = .89$. As SAT scores increase, GPAs tend to increase. This result suggests that if a person's SAT score were known, his or her GPA could be predicted because of the systematic relationship between SAT scores and GPA. Furthermore, this systematic relationship between scores on the SAT and GPA can be translated into a functional relationship that goes something like this: For every 100-point increase in SAT scores, there is an increase of .3 point in GPA.

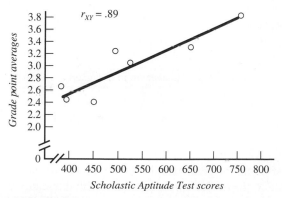

FIGURE 7-1
Scatterplot of scores on the Scholastic Aptitude Test (SAT) and grade-point averages (GPAs)

In Majasan's study (see Chapter 6 for a review), achievement in introductory psychology was systematically related to students' beliefs about psychology (humanistic versus behavioristic). In class 3, the relationship between beliefs and achievement was linear and positive (Figure 7-2a); the points fall along a straight line rising from the lower left to upper right. The correlation coefficient is .98. If we know a person's score on the belief scale, his or her exam score can be predicted almost exactly. This systematic relationship can be translated into the following functional relationship: For every increase of 1.39 points on the belief scale, exam scores are expected to increase by 1 point.

In another class, the relationship between beliefs and achievement was curvilinear (Figure 7-2b); the points fall along a curved line. Since there is a systematic relationship between X (beliefs) and Y (achievement), exam scores can still be predicted from belief scores. The prediction would go something like this: For scores below $X = 5.5$, exam scores are predicted to increase; for scores above $X = 5.5$, exam scores are predicted to decrease. In this more complicated case, a functional relationship can be specified mathematically, but the techniques are beyond the scope of this book.

The purpose of this chapter is to formalize these notions about prediction. In particular, this chapter translates the statement "Exam scores can be predicted from belief scores" into an equation that predicts an exam score from a belief score. In this discussion, only the *linear* (straight-line) case is considered, where X and Y are continuous[1]; the process of fitting such a straight line is called **linear regression.**

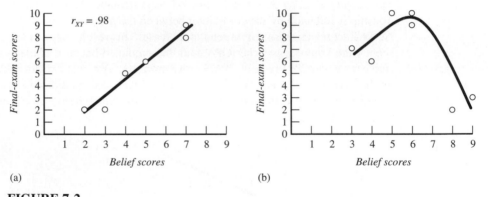

FIGURE 7-2
Scatterplot of scores on the belief scale and final exam in two classes of Majasan study

PREDICTION OF *Y* FROM *X:* INTUITIVE APPROACH

In the development of a rule for predicting a person's score on some variable Y from his score on some variable X, the obvious place to start is with the scatterplot of X and Y. The scatterplot contains the information needed to develop the prediction rule. But of course, the scatterplot is something like an inkblot; what is seen depends on who is doing the looking. One way to reduce this potential ambiguity is to simplify matters by looking at scatterplots with a few points, all of which fall on a straight line. Three such scatterplots

---

[1]Other textbooks such as Draper & Smith (1981) provide treatments of the case of prediction with curvilinear relationships.

are presented in Figure 7-3. In Figure 7-3a, all points lie on a horizontal line; in Figure 7-3b, all points lie on a line rising from left to right; and in Figure 7-3c, all points lie on a line descending from left to right.

A second way to reduce the ambiguity in looking at a scatterplot in order to develop a rule for predicting Y from X is to recall those factors that influence the sign and magnitude of a correlation coefficient in a scatterplot. Two factors are important:

1. The slope of the scatterplot
2. The degree to which the points in the scatterplot cluster about a line representing the slope

Armed with the scatterplots in Figure 7-3 and the critical features of a scatterplot that give rise to a systematic relationship between X and Y, we can develop a rule that specifies the **functional relation** between X and Y, which in turn will enable us to predict Y from X. To begin, consider what is known about the scatterplot in Figure 7-3a. First, all points lie on a straight line. Second, as the values of X increase, Y stays the same. Third, since the line is flat, it has zero elevation or slope. In this case, perfect prediction is possible (even without knowing X), and a prediction rule can be stated: Regardless of a person's score on X, predict a Y score of 6—the mean, $\bar{Y}$, of Y—for each person. Although this situation seems like too simple a case to be useful, it is quite important in the development of a general prediction rule. First, it points out two critical factors that must be included in the prediction rule: (1) the mean of the Y variable, $\bar{Y}$, and (2) the slope of the imaginary line in the scatterplot. Second, it points out that if the slope is zero, the rule should predict $\bar{Y}$ for each value of X. In short, Figure 7-3a shows that any rule for predicting Y from X must include a piece of information pertaining to the mean of Y and another, separate piece of information pertaining to the slope of the line in the scatterplot.

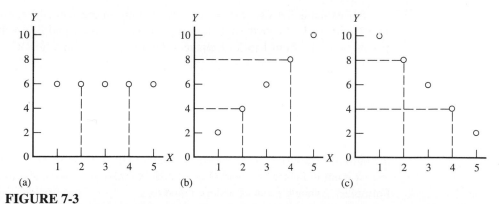

FIGURE 7-3

Scatterplots of hypothetical errorless data: (a) zero slope; (b) positive slope; (c) negative slope

Next, consider the case presented in Figure 7-3b. There is a perfect, positive relationship between X and Y. Furthermore, there is a clear pattern in the relationship between X and Y: If $X = 1$, $Y = 2$; if $X = 2$, $Y = 4$, . . . ; if $X = 5$, $Y = 10$. This pattern in the relationship between X and Y, reflected in Figure 7-3b as a positive slope (rising from left to right), can be summarized as follows: As X increases 1 point, Y increases 2 points. This result suggests that the **slope** of the scatterplot indicates how much of a change in Y is associated with a unit change in X. Or put a slightly different way, the slope tells us how many points Y changes if X changes by 1 point. In the development of a rule for predicting Y from X, then, information is needed about the magnitude and direction of the slope of the imaginary line.

In order to determine the magnitude and direction of the slope—how rapidly Y changes with a unit change in X—we can divide the change in Y by the change in X, as indicated in Formula 7-1.

$$\text{slope} = \frac{\text{change in } Y}{\text{change in } X} \qquad\qquad \textbf{(7-1)}$$

And in order to determine the change in Y and the change in X, we can use the values for two score pairs falling on the imaginary straight line in the scatterplot in Figure 7-3b. Let's denote a pair of scores X and Y as (X, Y). If (X_1, Y_1) represents one point on the scatterplot and (X_2, Y_2) represents the second point, then the equation for the slope of the data points is as given in Formula 7-2.

$$\text{slope} = \frac{Y_2 - Y_1}{X_2 - X_1} \qquad\qquad \textbf{(7-2)}$$

For example, let (X_1, Y_1) be the lowest point in the scatterplot, so that $X_1 = 1$ and $Y_1 = 2$; and let (X_2, Y_2) be the next lowest point, so that $X_2 = 2$ and $Y_2 = 4$. Then as X changes 1 unit (as X goes from 1 to 2), Y changes 2 units (Y goes from 2 to 4):

$$\text{slope} = \frac{Y_2 - Y_1}{X_2 - X_1} = \frac{4 - 2}{2 - 1} = \frac{2}{1} = 2$$

No matter which pair of points is selected from the points on the imaginary straight line, the ratio of their changes will be the same and will equal the slope. Thus, if (X_1, Y_1) is the lowest point in Figure 7-3b and (X_2, Y_2) is the highest point, then inserting these values in Formula 7-2 should produce a slope equal to 2:

$$\text{slope} = \frac{Y_2 - Y_1}{X_2 - X_1} = \frac{10 - 2}{5 - 1} = \frac{8}{4} = 2$$

A rule for predicting Y from X, then, should include information about the mean of Y, information about the slope of the imaginary line describing the scatterplot, and, of course, information about a person's relative standing on X. This rule would then add to or subtract from the mean of Y a value that depends on the slope of the imaginary straight line and how far above or below $\bar{X}$ the person's score X stands. The rule can be stated in the following form:

$$\begin{pmatrix} \text{predicted} \\ \text{score on} \\ Y \end{pmatrix} \quad \text{equals} \quad \begin{pmatrix} \text{the mean} \\ \text{of } Y \end{pmatrix} \quad \text{plus} \quad \begin{pmatrix} \text{an increment or} \\ \text{decrement based on} \\ \text{the slope and the} \\ \text{person's standing} \\ \text{on } X \text{ relative to} \\ \text{the mean of } X \end{pmatrix}$$

This rule is mathematically stated in Formula 7-3.

$$\hat{Y} \;=\; \bar{Y} \;+\; \frac{Y_2 - Y_1}{X_2 - X_1} \;\cdot\; (X - \bar{X}) \tag{7-3}$$

$$\underset{\substack{\text{predicted} \\ \text{score on } Y}}{} \quad \underset{\text{mean of } Y}{} \quad \underset{\text{slope}}{} \quad \underset{\substack{\text{relative} \\ \text{standing on } X}}{}$$

Notice that a carat (^) has been placed above Y to denote a *predicted score* of Y.

Now, let's apply this formula to the data in the scatterplots in Figure 7-3. The rule for predicting Y from X in the scatterplot in Figure 7-3a was to predict $\bar{Y}$ regardless of X. If Formula 7-3 is correct, it should make the same prediction. From the scatterplot in Figure 7-3a, $\bar{Y}$ is known to be 6 and $\bar{X}$ is known to be 3. In order to calculate the slope, let's use the lowest and highest points in the scatterplot: (1, 6) and (5, 6). (Remember that we reasoned the slope should be zero because the points fell on a horizontal line.) Finally, let's determine the predicted Y score for X scores of 2 and 4:

$$\hat{Y}_{\text{for } X=2} = 6 + \frac{6-6}{5-1}(2-3) = 6 + 0(-1) = 6 + 0 = 6$$

$$\hat{Y}_{\text{for } X=4} = 6 + \frac{6-6}{5-1}(4-3) = 6 + 0(+1) = 6 + 0 = 6$$

So far so good. Now let's apply the formula to the data in the scatterplot in Figure 7-3b. In looking at these data, we developed a rule for predicting Y from X that said: For every increase of 1 point in X, increase Y by 2 points. Thus, if one point on the scatterplot is X = 1 and Y = 2, then if X = 2 for a second point, $\hat{Y}$ will equal 2 + 2, or 4. Formula 7-3 should make the same prediction. In using this equation, note that $\bar{X} = 3$ and $\bar{Y} = 6$. Again, in calculating the slope, let's use the lowest and highest points in the scatterplot:

$$\hat{Y}_{\text{for } X=2} = 6 + \frac{10 - 2}{5 - 1}(2 - 3) = 6 + 2(-1) = 6 + (-2) = 4$$

$$\hat{Y}_{\text{for } X=3} = 6 + \frac{10 - 2}{5 - 1}(3 - 3) = 6 + 2(0) = 6$$

Again, Formula 7-3 predicts accurately. As a final test, let's use this equation to predict the Y scores in the scatterplot in Figure 7-3c from the X scores. Note that the slope of the points in this figure is negative, so that the slope calculated in Formula 7-3 should also be negative:

$$\hat{Y}_{\text{for } X=2} = 6 + \frac{2 - 10}{5 - 1}(2 - 3) = 6 + (-2)(-1) = 8$$

$$\hat{Y}_{\text{for } X=4} = 6 + \frac{2 - 10}{5 - 1}(4 - 3) = 6 + (-2)(+1) = 4$$

The data in Figure 7-3 have led to the development of a prediction rule that fits a straight line to the scatterplot. This straight line passes through each of the points in the scatterplot. This observation can be verified by drawing a straight line through any two values of predicted Y scores and determining whether this line passes through the other three points in the scatterplot. For example, data from Figure 7-3c led to a predicted Y of 8 for $X = 2$ and a predicted Y of 4 for $X = 4$. Thus if this line were graphed, it would pass from upper left to lower right on the graph and it would include the following points (pairs of scores): (1, 10), (2, 8), (3, 6), (4, 4), (5, 2). These points correspond precisely to the scatterplot in Figure 7-3c. The prediction rule, then, tells us the following when there is a linear relation between X and Y:

1. A straight line can be fitted to the data in the scatterplot.
2. The functional relation between the predicted Y score and the predictor variable X specifies the nature of the straight line and takes the form $\hat{Y}_X = \bar{Y} + b(X - \bar{X})$, where b is the slope.
3. For each value of X, the predicted Y score lies on the straight line fitted to the scatterplot.

PREDICTION USING LINEAR REGRESSION

In the ideal case shown in Figure 7-3, all pairs of scores (points) fell on a straight line. Although these data were used to develop an equation for a straight line intuitively, the relationship between X and Y could have been described directly by the general mathematical equation for a straight line, given in Formula 7-4.

$$Y = a + bX \tag{7-4}$$

where:

$a = Y$ intercept

$b =$ slope of the line

The **Y intercept** a is the score value of Y when X equals zero (see Formula 7-5). The slope b of the line has the same definition as given in Formula 7-2. It specifies the amount of change in Y for a unit change in X:

$$\text{slope} = b = \frac{Y_2 - Y_1}{X_2 - X_1}$$

where:

$(X_1, Y_1), (X_2, Y_2) =$ any two points on the straight line

Formula 7-4 can be applied to the data in Figure 7-3b to predict Y from X. In the scatterplot in Figure 7-3b, the intercept—the value of Y when X equals zero—is zero. (Just extend the line below the lowest data point.) The slope has already been calculated: $b = 2$. The predicted value of Y for $X = 3$ is:

$$\hat{Y}_{X=3} = 0 + 2(3) = 6$$

In the scatterplot of Figure 7-3a, the intercept is 6. The slope has already been calculated: $b = 0$. The predicted value of Y for $X = 3$ is:

$$\hat{Y}_{X=3} = 6 + 0(3) = 6$$

Finally, in the scatterplot of Figure 7-3c, the intercept is 12 ($a = 12$), the slope is -2 ($b = -2$), and the predicted value of Y for $X = 3$ is:

$$\hat{Y}_{X=3} = 12 + (-2)(3) = 12 - 6 = 6$$

Development of the Equation for Linear Regression

In the special case in which all of the points in a joint distribution fall along a straight line, Formula 7-4 can be used to predict Y from X. The line developed by this equation gives the predicted values of Y for each value of X. Both a and b in the equation can be determined from the data available in the joint distribution. However, data in a joint distribution almost never fall on a straight line; rather, the points often tend to cluster along a straight line. Some of the points may fall on the line, others will not. This more usual case is shown in Figure 7-4a. If the intercept of Y (i.e., a) is defined as the value of Y when X equals zero, which value of Y should be chosen when X equals zero? If the slope is the rate of change in Y divided by the rate of change in X, which pair of points should be chosen in order to use Formula 7-2 to calculate the slope?

The problem, in short, is that when all the points in a joint distribution do *not* fall on a straight line, it is not clear how we determine the value of a and b in Formula 7-4:

$$Y = a + bX$$

The solution to this problem is to specify that some criterion should be met in estimating *a* and *b* and then determine the values of *a* and *b* that meet it. The **criterion of least squares** is used to estimate *a* and *b* in prediction studies. It states that *a* and *b* should be determined so as to minimize the variability of points about the line fitted to the joint distribution. Thus, in fitting a straight line to the data in Figure 7-4a, we place the line in Figure 7-4b in the swarm of points so that the mean squared distance of the points from the line is as small as possible. (In Figure 7-4b, note that the distance from a point to the regression line is measured by drawing a perpendicular line to the abscissa, not to the slope.) This criterion is called the criterion of least squares because the regression line is fitted to the swarm of points in the scatterplot so that the sum of the squared deviations between the points and the regression line [i.e., $\Sigma(Y - \hat{Y})^2$] is minimized.

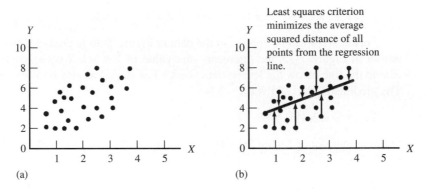

FIGURE 7-4

Scatterplot of *X* and *Y*: (a) original data; (b) illustration of the least squares criterion in fitting a regression line to the scatterplot

When the criterion of least squares is applied to the general equation for a straight line, the following estimates of *a* and *b* are found (for details on this estimation, see Draper & Smith, 1980).

$$a = \bar{Y} - B_{Y \cdot X}\bar{X} \tag{7-5}$$

$$b_{Y \cdot X} = \frac{\mathrm{Cov}_{XY}}{s_X^2} \tag{7-6}$$

where:

$a = Y$ intercept

$b_{Y \cdot X} =$ slope of the line predicting *Y* from *X* (read "*Y* dot *X*")

If, in the general equation for a straight line $(Y = a + bX)$, a is replaced by its definition, the result is Formula 7-7a.

$$\hat{Y} = \bar{Y} - b_{Y \cdot X}\bar{X} + b_{Y \cdot X}X \qquad\qquad \textbf{(7-7a)}$$

If the terms on the right side of Formula 7-7a are rearranged, the result is Formula 7-7b.

$$\hat{Y} = \bar{Y} + b_{Y \cdot X}X - b_{Y \cdot X}\bar{X} \qquad\qquad \textbf{(7-7b)}$$

Finally, notice that both X and $\bar{X}$ are multiplied by b. So b can be factored out to arrive at a general equation (Formula 7-7) for predicting Y from X.

$$\hat{Y} = \bar{Y} + b_{Y \cdot X}(X - \bar{X}) \qquad\qquad \textbf{(7-7)}$$

The equation in Formula 7-7 is called a **linear regression equation.** It is used to predict the values of one variable (Y) from the values of another variable (X). It is similar to Formula 7-3, which was developed intuitively.

$$\hat{Y} = \bar{Y} + \frac{Y_2 - Y_1}{X_2 - X_1}(X - \bar{X})$$

The one exception is that $b_{Y \cdot X}$ in Formula 7-7 is estimated by Cov_{XY}/s_X^2. However, if all of the points in a joint distribution fall on a straight line, the two measures of the slope of the regression line are the same.

Interpretation of the Components of the Linear Regression Equation

The purpose of the equation for linear regression is to specify a functional relation between X and Y so that Y can be predicted from X. The regression equation accomplishes this specification by fitting a straight line or **regression line** to the points in a joint distribution, using the criterion of least squares. The prediction is accomplished in that *for each value of X, the regression line gives the predicted value of Y.*

There are two components in the linear regression equation that accomplish the task of fitting a straight line to a scatterplot: (1) $\bar{Y}$ and (2) $b_{Y \cdot X}(X - \bar{X})$. The first component, $\bar{Y}$, provides the information needed to adjust the regression line to the *height*, or *elevation*, of the swarm of points in the joint distribution. The second component, $b_{Y \cdot X}(X - \bar{X})$, provides the information needed to adjust the slope of the regression line. The second component also provides information on how much to increase or decrease $\bar{Y}$ in order to obtain a predicted value of Y from a particular value of X.

The criterion of least squares leads to a definition of the slope $b_{Y \cdot X}$, which looks somewhat different from the one given in the intuitive approach. So some additional discussion is needed. The slope using the criterion of least squares is (Formula 7-6)

$$b_{Y \cdot X} = \frac{\text{Cov}_{XY}}{s_X^2}$$

The numerator is the covariance of X and Y. It provides information on the degree to which changes in Y are associated with changes in X—that is, how much X and Y covary. The denominator, s_X^2, is the variance of X. This ratio adjusts the rate-of-change information, Cov_{XY}, so that it corresponds to a unit increase in X. Thus, the slope has the same interpretation using the least squares formula as it does using the change formulas given earlier in Formulas 7-1 and 7-2. That is, the *slope* provides information on *how many units Y increases for every one-unit increase in X*.

An alternative way of defining the regression slope $b_{Y \cdot X}$ is in terms of the correlation coefficient. Since the correlation coefficient is defined as (Formula 6-2)

$$r_{XY} = \frac{\text{Cov}_{XY}}{s_X s_Y}$$

this equation can be solved for the covariance of X and Y as follows:

$$\text{Cov}_{XY} = (r_{XY})(s_X)(s_Y)$$

By substituting $(r_{XY})(s_X)(s_Y)$ into the equation for the regression slope, we get Formula 7-6a.

$$b_{Y \cdot X} = \frac{(r_{XY})(s_X)(s_Y)}{s_X^2} = r_{XY} \frac{s_Y}{s_X} \qquad \text{(7-6a)}$$

This new formula states that the slope adjusts the correlation—a measure of how X and Y go together—according to how large an increase in Y results from a unit increase on the X scale (s_Y/s_Y). Again, it tells us how many units to increase Y for every increase in X of one unit.

Finally, the slope of the regression line, $b_{Y \cdot X}$, can also be calculated directly from raw scores using Formula 7-6b. This formula is presented only for completeness. You may see it in other statistics books, or in calculator or statistical software manuals.

$$b_{Y \cdot X} = \frac{N \left(\sum XY \right) - \left(\sum X \right) \left(\sum Y \right)}{N \sum X^2 - \left(\sum X \right)^2} \qquad \text{(7-6b)}$$

Application of the Regression Equation

Enough talk about the regression equation for a while; how is it applied? The steps in applying the regression equation will be described with the help of the data from class 3 in the Majasan study.

In using linear regression, we assume that X and Y are approximately linearly related. This assumption can be checked by examining the scatterplot of X and Y to ensure that a straight line provides an appropriate description of the data.[2] (See Figure 7-2a.) If the scatterplot shows a linear relation between X and Y, Formula 7-7 can be used to fit a regression line to the data:

$$\hat{Y} = \bar{Y} + b_{Y \cdot X}(X - \bar{X})$$

For each X score, this formula generates a predicted Y score. These predicted Y scores can be plotted on the scatterplot. There is a point on the scatterplot for each X, $\hat{Y}$ pair. If these points are connected by a straight line, it forms a "regression line." The imaginary lines drawn onto scatterplots in Chapter 6 are no longer imaginary: they're regression lines. The regression line shows visually the predicted Y score for every X value observed.

Calculating the Regression Slope. To use this formula, the next step is to calculate the statistics in it. In Table 7-1, the mean and standard deviation of X and Y have been calculated along with the covariance and correlation of X and Y. The only value needed in the equation but not provided in Table 7-1 is the slope $b_{Y \cdot X}$. This value can be calculated by using either Formula 7-6 or 7-6a. From Formula 7-6, we have:

$$b_{Y \cdot X} = \frac{\text{Cov}_{XY}}{s_X^2} = \frac{7.17}{(2.27)^2} = 1.39$$

TABLE 7-1   Descriptive statistics for the data from class 3 in the Majasan study

	Belief Score				**Final Exam Score**			
X	$\bar{X}$	x	x^2	Y	$\bar{Y}$	y	y^2	xy
8	5.14	2.86	8.18	10	6	4	16	11.44
7	5.14	1.86	3.46	8	6	2	4	3.72
3	5.14	−2.14	4.58	2	6	−4	16	8.56
5	5.14	−.14	.02	6	6	0	0	.00
7	5.14	1.86	3.46	9	6	3	9	5.58
2	5.14	−3.14	9.86	2	6	−4	16	12.56
4	5.14	−1.14	1.30	5	6	−1	1	1.14
Σ 36	36	0	30.86	42	42	0	62	43.00

$$s_X = \sqrt{\frac{30.86}{6}} = 2.27 \qquad s_Y = \sqrt{\frac{62}{6}} = 3.21$$

$$\text{Cov}_{XY} = \frac{\sum xy}{N-1} = \frac{43}{6} = 7.17 \qquad r_{XY} = \frac{\text{Cov}_{XY}}{s_X s_Y} = \frac{7.17}{2.27 \times 3.21} = .98$$

---

[2]There are statistical tests that can be used in deciding whether a straight line provides a good fit of the points in a scatterplot. If a straight line is not an appropriate fit, consult advanced texts on regression analysis to determine the appropriate model for fitting a curvilinear regression line to the data.

And from Formula 7-6a, we have

$$b_{Y \cdot X} = r_{XY} \frac{s_Y}{s_X} = (.98)\frac{3.21}{2.27} = 1.39$$

Procedure 7-1 summarizes the steps in computing $b_{Y \cdot X}$ with Formula 7-6a, the most commonly used form of this equation.

PROCEDURE 7-1 Steps in computing $b_{Y \cdot X}$ by using the correlation coefficient (data taken from Table 7-1)

Operation	Example
1. Look up Formula 7-6a: $b_{Y \cdot X} = r_{XY} \dfrac{s_Y}{s_X}$	
2. Compute $r_{XY}, s_Y,$ and s_X. *See Procedures 6-2 and 4-6, respectively, to review procedures for these calculations.*	$r_{XY} = .98$ $s_Y = 3.21$ $s_X = 2.27$
3. Insert the appropriate values into Formula 7-6a and solve.	$b_{Y \cdot X} = (.98)\dfrac{3.21}{2.27} = 1.39$

Calculating a Predicted Y from X.   Now that $b_{Y \cdot X}$ has been calculated, the symbols in the regression equation (7-7) can be replaced by their respective values for predicting achievement from belief:

$$\hat{Y} = 6 + 1.39(X - 5.14)$$

Then, for any X score, replace X with its value and calculate the predicted Y. For $X = 2$, we have

$$\hat{Y}_{X=2} = 6 + 1.39(2 - 5.14) = 6 + (-4.3\,6) = 1.64$$

For a person whose belief score is 2, we should predict his exam score to be 1.64.

Drawing a Straight Line onto a Scatterplot.   In order to draw a straight line onto a scatterplot, we need to calculate a predicted score for each of two X scores. (Recall that two points are necessary to draw a straight line.) Any two values of X can be used, but having them some distance apart increases the accuracy with which we can draw the line. Using data from Table 7-1, let's select $X = 2$ and $X = 8$ and calculate the corresponding predicted Y scores:

$$\hat{Y}_{X=2} = 6 + 1.39(2 - 5.14) = 6 + (-4.36) = 1.64$$
$$\hat{Y}_{X=8} = 6 + 1.39(8 - 5.14) = 6 + 3.98 = 9.98$$

These two points—($X = 2$, $\hat{Y} = 1.64$) and ($X = 8$, $\hat{Y} = 9.98$)—are used to draw the regression line in Figure 7-5. Notice that the points in the scatterplot cluster tightly about the regression line, as expected from a correlation of .98 between X and Y.

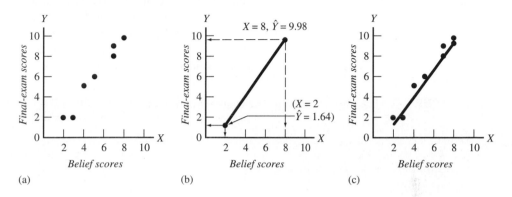

(a)   (b)   (c)

FIGURE 7-5

Scatterplot for the data from class 3 in the Majasan study: (a) original data; (b) regression line; (c) scatterplot with the regression line

The data in Figure 7-6 are taken from a hypothetical study of the relation between anxiety and task performance. One theory of anxiety predicts a negative relationship between anxiety (X) and performance on a complex cognitive task (Y). Data in this figure support the prediction: $r_{XY} = -.77$, $b_{Y \cdot X} = -.57$. In order to draw the regression line in Figure 7-6b, we must determine the predicted Y scores for two values of X:

$$\hat{Y}_{X=2} = 9.55 + (-.57)(2 - 10.5) = 14.4$$
$$\hat{Y}_{X=19} = 9.55 + (-.57)(19 - 10.5) = 4.7$$

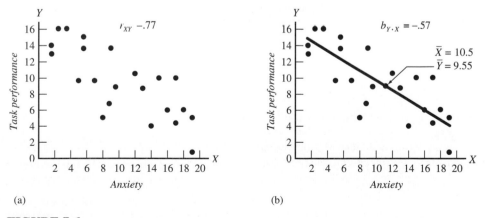

(a)   (b)

FIGURE 7-6

Scatterplot of scores earned on a measure of anxiety and on a measure of performance on a complex cognitive task: (a) original data; (b) scatterplot with the regression line

These two sets of points—$(X = 2, \hat{Y} = 14.4)$ and $(X = 19, \hat{Y} = 4.7)$—are used to draw the regression line.

When a regression line is drawn on a scatterplot, it can be used to predict Y from any value of X. For example, for an anxiety score of 10.5 (the mean of X), the predicted performance score is 9.55 (the mean of Y). Thus, *in order to determine the predicted score $\hat{Y}$ from any value of X, you can use the regression equation to provide the value, or you can read $\hat{Y}$ directly from a scatterplot in which the regression line has been drawn.* The steps for calculating the regression line are summarized in Procedure 7-2.

PROCEDURE 7-2 Steps for computing the regression line (data from Table 7-1)

Operation

1. Verify that assumptions have been met by examining the following:
   a. Measurement scale of X and Y

   b. Scatterplot of X and Y
   See Procedure 6-1 to review the procedure for constructing a scatterplot.

   a. *Variables X and Y are continuous variables (i.e., scores can theoretically assume an infinite number of values).*
   b. *The relationship between X and Y is linear.*

2. Look up Formula 7-7:
$$\hat{Y} = \bar{Y} + b_{Y \cdot X}(X - \bar{X})$$

3. Compute $\bar{Y}$ and $\bar{X}$ and s_Y and s_X.
See Procedure 4-3 to review procedures for calculating a mean, and Procedure 4-6 for calculating a standard deviation.

4. Compute $b_{Y \cdot X}$ by using Formula 7-6a,
$$b_{Y \cdot X} = r_{XY} \frac{s_Y}{s_X}$$
See Procedure 7-1 for using this formula.

5. Insert appropriate values into Formula 7-7 and solve.
Values of $\hat{Y}$ for two values of X are computed so that the regression line can be plotted.

Example

a. Belief scores and exam scores represent continuous variables.

b.

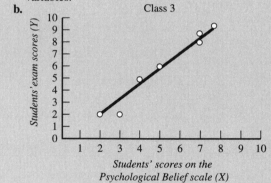

Students' scores on the Psychological Belief scale (X)

$\bar{Y} = 6$

$\bar{X} = 5.14$

$b_{Y \cdot X} = 1.39$

For $X = 2$,
$$\hat{Y} = 6 + 1.39(2 - 5.14) = 6 + (-4.36) = 1.64$$

The predicted exam score for a belief score of 2 is 1.64.
For $X = 8$,
$$\hat{X} = 6 + 1.39(8 - 5.14) = 6 + 3.98 = 9.98$$

The predicted exam score for a belief score of 8 is 9.98.

Operation	Example
6. Plot the regression line.	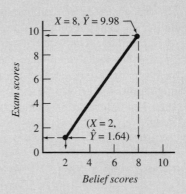

Example Problem 7.1

The data reported in Table 7-2 were obtained in a study of predictors of job success.

    a.   Compute $b_{Y \cdot X}$.
    b.   Calculate the linear regression equation for predicting job performance from the simulation test.
    c.   Compute values of $\hat{Y}$ for $X = 1$ and $X = 6$.
    d.   Using the two points computed in part c, plot the regression line for Y on X.

TABLE 7-2   Hypothetical scores on simulated and actual job performances

Performance on Job Simulation Test X	Actual Performance on Job Y
2	5
3	4
3	6
4	9
5	7

$\bar{X} = 3.40$	$r_{XY} = .64$	$\bar{Y} = 6.20$
$s_X = 1.14$	$\text{Cov}_{XY} = 1.40$	$s_Y = 1.92$

ERRORS IN PREDICTION

It does not take Sherlock Holmes to realize that not all of the points in Figures 7-5c and 7-6b fall on the regression line. In fact, most of the points do not fall exactly on the line even in Figure 7-5c, where $r_{XY} = .98$. Since the regression line represents the predicted value of Y for each value of X and the points in the joint distribution represent the actual values of Y for each value of X, *the discrepancy between the points and the regression line constitutes an* **error in prediction** *of Y from X.*

Standard Error of Estimate

Figure 7-7 reproduces Figure 7-5c and highlights the discrepancy between the predicted values of Y on the regression line and the actual values of Y represented by the points in the figure. The numerical value of the discrepancy is obtained by subtracting the predicted value of Y from the actual value of Y for a given value of X: discrepancy $= Y - \hat{Y}$. This discrepancy shows the magnitude of the error of estimating Y from a particular value of X. For example, the predicted Y score for an X score of 3 is 3.03. The actual value of Y is 2. The prediction is in error by $2 - 3.03 = -1.03$ points; the minus sign indicates that the actual value fell below the predicted value.

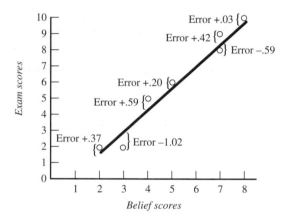

FIGURE 7-7

Errors in predicting the exam scores from the belief scores for class 3 in the Majasan study

One possible measure of the amount of error involved in estimating Y from X would be to add up the discrepancy scores and divide this sum in order to get an "average discrepancy score" as an index of error. However, as might be expected, the algebraic sum of the positive and negative discrepancy scores is zero.

The solution to this problem is analogous to the solution for the standard deviation. The discrepancy scores can be squared and summed, and then divided by N. (Actually, $N - 2$ is used when we estimate the parameter.) Finally, the square root can be taken to return this average value to the original scale of measurement.

This measure of the error in predicting Y from X is called the **standard error of estimate;** it is an index of the magnitude of error made in estimating Y from X. The formula can be written as shown in Formula 7-7.

$$s_{Y \cdot X} = \sqrt{\frac{\sum (Y - \hat{Y})^2}{N - 2}} \qquad\qquad (7\text{-}7)$$

where:

$s_{Y \cdot X}$ = standard error of estimate[3]

Y = actual value(s) of Y for a given value of X

$\hat{Y}$ = predicted value Y for a given value of X

$N - 2$ = number of observations minus 2^4

In order to determine the standard error of estimate for the data in Figure 7-7, we square the discrepancy scores in the figure, and these squares are then summed. This sum of the squared discrepancy scores is divided by $N - 2$, and then the square root of this value is taken:

$$s_{Y \cdot X} = \sqrt{\frac{(.37)^2 + (-1.02)^2 + (.59)^2 + (.20)^2 + (.42)^2 + (-.59)^2 + (.03)^2}{5}}$$

$$= \sqrt{\frac{2.0908}{5}} = \sqrt{.42} = .65$$

An alternative formula, computationally much easier than Formula 7-7, is given in Formula 7-8.

$$s_{Y \cdot X} = s_Y \sqrt{1 - r_{YX}^2} \qquad\qquad (7\text{-}8)$$

Since r_{XY}^2 equals the proportion of variance in Y predictable from X, $1 - r_{XY}^2$ represents the proportion of variance in Y that is *not* predictable from X—that is, the error in prediction. Multiplying $\sqrt{1 - r_{XY}^2}$ by s_Y adjusts the error to the scale of measurement of the variable being predicted.

From Table 7-1, we know that $r_{XY} = .98$ and $s_Y = 3.21$. Since r_{XY} equals r_{YX}, we can insert these values into Formula 7-8, obtaining:

$$s_{Y \cdot X} = 3.21\sqrt{1 - (98)^2} = 3.21\sqrt{1 - .9604} = 3.21\sqrt{.0396} = .64$$

The difference between .65 and .64 is minor and is due to the fact that in Formula 7-7, we divided by $N - 2$, whereas in Formula 7-8, there is an implicit division by $N - 1$. The steps in computing $s_{Y \cdot X}$ by using Formula 7-8 are summarized in Procedure 7-3.

---

[3]The similarity of the symbols used for the standard error of estimate ($s_{Y \cdot X}$) and the standard deviation (s_X or s_Y) is intentional. Both are essentially measures of variability, as will become clear in the next section.

[4]Note that $N - 2$ rather than N is used to calculate the "average" of the squared discrepancy scores. Although the standard error is defined as the mean of the squared deviations of the points from the regression line, the formula given here provides a statistic that is used as an estimator. Hence, the denominator reflects an adjustment for degrees of freedom (see Chapter 12 on degrees of freedom).

PROCEDURE 7-3 Steps in calculating $s_{Y \cdot X}$ by using the correlation coefficient (data taken from Table 7-1)

Operation	Example
1. Look up Formula 7-8: $s_{Y \cdot X} = s_Y \sqrt{1 - r_{YX}^2}$ **2.** Compute s_X and r_{YX}. *See Procedures 4-6 and 6-2 for making these calculations.*	$s_Y = 3.21$ $r_{YX} = .98$
3. Insert the appropriate values into Formula 7-8 and solve.	$s_{Y \cdot X} = 3.21\sqrt{1 - (.98)^2} = 3.21\sqrt{1 - .9604}$ $= 3.21\sqrt{.0396} = .64$

For completeness, the standard error of estimate can also be calculated directly from raw scores by using Formula 7-9:

$$s_{Y \cdot X} = \sqrt{\frac{1}{N(N-2)} \left\{ N \sum Y^2 - \left(\sum Y \right)^2 - \frac{\left[N \sum XY - \left(\sum X \right)\left(\sum Y \right) \right]^2}{N \sum X^2 - \left(\sum X \right)^2} \right\}} \qquad (7\text{-}9)$$

Example Problem 7.2

Calculate the standard error of estimate for predicting actual job performance from performance on the job simulation test. (See Table 7-2 for data.)

Interpretation of the Standard Error of Estimate

The standard error of estimate for a joint distribution is analogous to the standard deviation for a univariate distribution. Just as the standard deviation provides a measure of the dispersion of scores about the mean of a univariate distribution, the standard error of estimate provides a measure of the dispersion of points about the regression line.

The analogy can be carried even further. The regression line can be thought of as a *moving mean*. At each value of X, theoretically there can be an indefinitely large number of Y values. The mean of these Y values, $\overline{Y}$ for a given X, falls on the regression line. The standard error of estimate, then, is the standard deviation of actual Y scores about the mean of Y for a given value of X. Thus, for the standard error of estimate, we write $s_{Y \cdot X}$, which can be read as the standard deviation of Y for a given value of X.

This reasoning is reflected in Figure 7-8. The predicted Y score is the mean of the Y scores at a particular value of X. Thus, the regression line, representing the predicted Y scores, can be thought of as a line of means. If the standard deviation of Y scores about $\hat{Y}$ at each level of X were calculated and averaged, this average standard deviation of Y at each value of X would be the standard error of estimate.

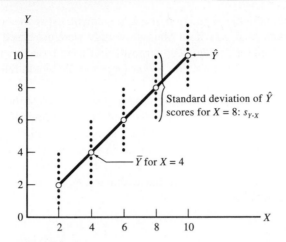

FIGURE 7-8
Interpretation of the standard error of estimate as the average standard deviation of Y scores about their predicted Y scores

If the Y values are normally distributed about their mean—$\hat{Y}$ in the joint distribution—the standard error of estimate can be used to mark off the areas in the normal distribution. From Table B at the back of the book, we know that about 68 percent of the scores in the normal distribution fall between 1 standard deviation below the mean and 1 standard deviation above the mean. Thus, 68 percent of the Y scores at a particular $\hat{Y}$ will fall within ± 1 standard error of estimate. The relation of the standard error of estimate to the normal distribution and the joint distribution is shown in Figure 7-9.

The standard error of estimate was .64 for the data from Majasan's study of the relation between beliefs in psychology and achievement in introductory psychology. It is

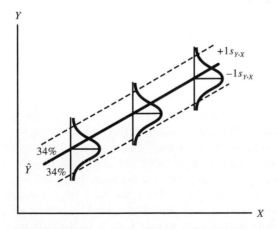

FIGURE 7-9
Relationship of the standard error of estimate to the normal distribution

reasonable to assume that in the population, the achievement test scores are normally distributed; so if the hypothetical data from Majasan's study were not based on seven hypothetical observations (used for pedagogical purposes) but were based on 1000 cases, then approximately 68 percent of the raw scores in this large sample would fall within $\pm s_{Y \cdot X}$, or $\pm.65$ point, of the predicted Y score.

Table B also shows that 95 percent of the cases in the normal distribution fall between 1.96 standard deviation units below the mean and 1.96 standard deviation units above the mean. (Note that these values amount to virtually 2 standard deviations above and below the mean. Recall our earlier discussion in Chapter 5 in which we stated that approximately 95 percent of the cases fall within ± 2 standard deviations.) Thus, assuming normality, 95 percent of the observed Y scores would fall within $\pm 1.96 \, s_{Y \cdot X}$, or $\pm 1.96 \times .65 = \pm 1.27$ points of the predicted value of Y.

LINEAR REGRESSION EQUATION FOR PREDICTING X FROM Y

Linear regression establishes a functional relationship between X and Y. In this relationship, X may be written as a function of Y or Y may be written as a function of X:

$$X = f(Y) \qquad Y = f(X)$$

Since linear regression is most often used in *prediction studies* in the behavioral sciences and since X is typically used to label the predictor variable that is measured prior to the outcome variable, the functional relation of interest is usually the one defining Y as a function of X.

The equation for predicting Y from X, then, can be used to predict college grade point averages from Scholastic Aptitude Test scores. Since SAT scores are measured prior to college GPAs, SAT scores are labeled X and GPAs are labeled Y. In prediction research, then, we are interested primarily in the functional relation predicting Y from X and therefore tend to ignore the functional relation predicting X from Y.

In some research, however, the focus is not on prediction of one variable (Y) from another variable (X). Rather, the focus is on identifying the functional relation between two variables. In this case, predicting X from Y is just as important as predicting Y from X. The researcher, then, is interested in both of the functional relations written before. In this case, scores on either variable might be labeled X; neither variable occurs prior to the other.

For example, a researcher might be interested in describing the functional relation between scores on the Stanford-Binet Intelligence Test and scores on the Wechsler Intelligence Test. In this case, scores on either measure might be labeled X; neither variable occurs prior to the other. And the researcher is probably just as interested in the relation of X to Y as she is in the relation of Y to X. Likewise, a researcher may want to describe the functional relation between scores on measures of trait and state anxiety. Again, either measure could be labeled X, since neither occurs prior to the other and the researcher is probably just as interested in relating state anxiety to trait anxiety as she is in relating trait anxiety to state anxiety.

An equation for predicting X from Y could be developed in exactly the same way that the equation for predicting Y from X was developed. The only change would be that in the formula for predicting X from Y with a straight line ($X = a + bY$), the least squares estimates of a and b would be found by minimizing the mean squared distance between subjects' actual scores on X and their predicted scores on X (i.e., $X - \hat{X}$). With this change made, the linear regression equation for predicting X from Y is as given in Formula 7-10.

$$\hat{X}_Y = \bar{X} + b_{X \cdot Y}(Y - \bar{Y}) \tag{7-10}$$

Now let's compare the equation for predicting X from Y (7-10; often stated as "regressing X on Y") with the equation for predicting Y from X (7-7; "regressing Y on X").

$$\hat{X}_Y = \bar{X} + b_{X \cdot Y}(Y - \bar{Y}) \quad \text{and} \quad \hat{Y}_X = \bar{Y} + b_{Y \cdot X}(X - \bar{X})$$

This comparison reveals three major differences between the two equations:

1. The mean used as the starting point of the regression equation ($\bar{X}$ and $\bar{Y}$)
2. The distance of the score on the predictor from the mean on the predictor [$(Y - \bar{Y})$ or $(X - \bar{X})$]
3. The slope ($b_{X \cdot Y}$ or $b_{Y \cdot X}$)

The first two differences are obvious. The mean of X (or Y) tells us about the scale on which X (or Y) is measured and adjusts the predicted value to that scale. The deviation of Y from $\bar{Y}$ or X from $\bar{X}$ tells us about an individual's standing (relative position) on the variable used to make the prediction. The third difference, the slope $b_{X \cdot Y}$ and $b_{Y \cdot X}$, requires some further explanation.

Recall that the slope is a measure of how much the predicted variable changes as a consequence of a one-unit change in the predictor variable. For example, $b_{Y \cdot X}$ tells how much Y changes for each one-unit increase in X. Similarly, $b_{X \cdot Y}$ tells how much X changes for each unit increase in Y. Suppose Y changes drastically for each unit change in X. In this case, the slope for predicting Y from X ($b_{Y \cdot X}$) will be relatively large. Conversely, if X were predicted from Y, then X would show a very small change for each unit increase in Y. Thus, $b_{X \cdot Y}$ would be relatively small. The reason for this difference in size is also illustrated by the following formula (Formula 7-6),

$$b_{Y \cdot X} = \frac{\text{Cov}_{XY}}{s_X^2}$$

and by Formula 7-11a.

$$b_{X \cdot Y} = \frac{\text{Cov}_{XY}}{s_Y^2} \tag{7-11a}$$

where:

$b_{Y \cdot X}$ = slope for predicting Y from X

$b_{X \cdot Y}$ = slope for predicting X from Y

Note that the denominator of each equation contains the variance of the variable used to make the prediction. Thus, the equation for $b_{Y \cdot X}$ contains the variance of X (s_X^2) in the denominator, and the equation for $b_{X \cdot Y}$ contains the variance of Y (s_Y^2) in the denominator. The process of dividing Cov_{XY} by the variance of the variable used to make the prediction adjusts the increase in the predicted variable to a one-unit increase in the predictor variable. Suppose, again, that the variance of X is much smaller than the variance of Y. It follows, then, that $b_{Y \cdot X}$ will be relatively large, since Cov_{XY} is divided by a relatively small number (s_X^2). Thus for each increase of one unit in X, Y will increase drastically. Conversely, $b_{X \cdot Y}$ will be relatively small, since Cov_{XY} is divided by a relatively large number (s_Y^2). That is, for an increase of one unit in Y, X will increase only slightly. If $s_X = s_Y$, then $b_{Y \cdot X} = b_{X \cdot Y}$; and the slopes will be the same.

In order to show this relationship between the two slopes pictorially, Figure 7-10 presents the regression line for predicting Y from X ($b_{Y \cdot X}$) and the regression line for predicting X from Y ($b_{X \cdot Y}$) for two variables, where $r_{XY} = .60$, $\text{Cov}_{XY} = 9.6$, $\bar{X} = 4$, $\bar{Y} = 6$, $s_X = 2.00$, and $s_Y = 8.00$. Before examining this figure closely, let's make some predictions about the slopes from these descriptive statistics. Notice that s_Y is four times greater than s_X. Thus for a small change in X, there will be a large change in Y. Therefore, we predict that $b_{Y \cdot X}$ will be large compared with $b_{X \cdot Y}$. Put another way, if $r_{XY} = 1$, a unit change in X would lead to a four-unit change in Y. However, since r_{XY} is considerably less than 1 in this example, the change will not be 1 to 4; it will be less.

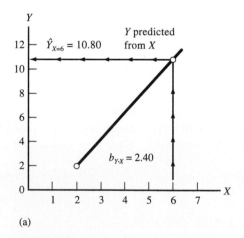

(a)

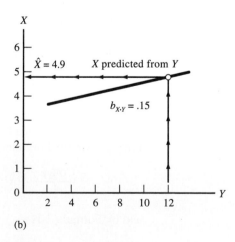

(b)

FIGURE 7-10

Regression lines: (a) for predicting Y from X; (b) for predicting X from Y

In order to check this reasoning, we can calculate the two regression slopes:

$$b_{Y \cdot X} = \frac{\text{Cov}_{XY}}{s_X^2} = \frac{9.6}{2^2} = 2.40$$

$$b_{X \cdot Y} = \frac{\text{Cov}_{XY}}{s_Y^2} = \frac{9.6}{8^2} = .15$$

When we are predicting Y from X, $b_{Y \cdot X}$ tells us that for an increase of 1 point on X, Y increases by 2.40 points. When we are predicting X from Y, $b_{X \cdot Y}$ tells us that for an increase of 1 point on Y, X increases by .15 point.

These calculations verify our reasoning. The slope coefficient for predicting Y from X ($b_{Y \cdot X}$) is considerably larger than the one for predicting X from Y ($b_{X \cdot Y}$). Since $b_{Y \cdot X}$ is greater than $b_{X \cdot Y}$, the regression line for predicting Y from X is steeper than that for predicting X from Y. (See Figure 7-10.)

Example Problem 7.3

Use the data in Table 7-2.
    a. Compute $b_{X \cdot Y}$.
    b. Calculate the general linear regression equation for X on Y.
    c. Compute X for $Y = 8$ and $Y = 3$.
    d. Plot the regression line for X or Y on the same scatterplot you constructed in Example Problem 7.1d.
    e. How do you account for the different slopes?

PERCENTAGE OF VARIANCE

In Chapter 6, the proportion of variability in one variable that could be accounted for by knowing the variability in the second variable was found by squaring the correlation coefficient. For example, in the study of the relationship between simulated and actual job performance (Table 7-2), we found that r_{XY} was .64. Therefore, the proportion of variability in state anxiety that is accounted for by knowing trait anxiety is found by squaring r_{XY}:

$$r_{XY}^2 = (.64)^2 = .41$$

The proportion of variance in actual job performance accounted for by simulated-job performance is .41.

To obtain the **percentage of variance** accounted for by X, multiply the proportion by 100:

$$r_{XY}^2 \times 100 = (.64)^2 \times 100 = .41 \times 100 = 41\%$$

Thus, 41 percent of the variance in actual job performance is accounted for by job-simulation performance (see Figure 7-11).

In Chapter 6 the predictable variability—the variability that could be accounted for—was represented by the slope of an imaginary straight line fitted to a scatterplot. This imaginary straight line is now known to you as a regression line. Since the regression line provides information about the predictable variability, there should be some relation between the slope and the proportion of variance in one variable that can be accounted for by knowing variability in the second variable. This is the case, as shown in Formulas 7-12 and 7-12a.

$$\text{proportion of variance} = r_{XY}^2 = (b_{X \cdot Y})(b_{Y \cdot X}) \tag{7-12}$$

$$\text{percentage of variance} = 100 r_{XY}^2 = 100(b_{X \cdot Y})(b_{Y \cdot X}) \tag{7-12a}$$

The data from the study of job performance (Table 7-2) can be used to demonstrate the equivalence implied in Formulas 7-12 and 7-12a (see also Figure 7-11).

$$\text{proportion of variance} = (.64)^2 = (.38)(1.08) = .41$$

$$\text{percentage of variance} = 100(.41) = 41\%$$

Thus 41 percent of the variance in actual job performance can be predicted from simulated job performance.

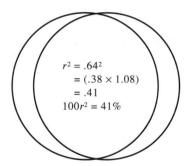

$r^2 = .64^2$
$= (.38 \times 1.08)$
$= .41$
$100r^2 = 41\%$

FIGURE 7-11
Percent of variance in actual job performance accounted for by a simulated job-performance test

SUMMARY

This chapter presents statistical techniques for specifying the *functional relationship* between two variables so that scores on one variable can be predicted from scores on the other. Procedures for computing a *linear regression equation* for predicting Y from X and for calculating the *standard error of estimate* to measure the error in predicting Y from X are discussed. Finally, procedures for identifying the *proportion* or *percentage of variance* in one variable accounted for by the other are described.

ANSWERS TO EXAMPLE PROBLEMS

1. **a.** $b_{Y \cdot X} = (r_{S \cdot Y}) \dfrac{s_Y}{s_X} = (.64) \dfrac{1.92}{1.14} = 1.08$

   b. $\hat{Y} = \bar{Y} + b_{Y \cdot X}(X - \bar{X}) = 6.2 + 1.08(X - 3.4)$

   c. $\hat{Y}_{X=1} = 6.2 + 1.08(1 - 3.4) = 3.61$

   $\hat{Y}_{X=6} = 6.2 + 1.08(6 - 3.4) = 9.01$

   d.

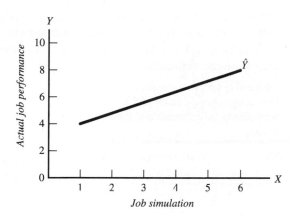

Job simulation

2. $s_{Y \cdot X} = s_Y \sqrt{1 - r_{YX}^2} = 1.92 \sqrt{1 - (.64)^2} = 1.48$

3. **a.** $b_{X \cdot Y} = (r_{YX}) \dfrac{s_X}{s_Y} = (.64) \dfrac{1.14}{1.92} = .38$

   b. $\hat{X}_Y = \bar{X} + b_{X \cdot Y}(Y - \bar{Y}) = 3.4 + (.38)(Y - 6.2)$

   c. $\hat{X}_{Y=8} = 3.4 + (.38)(8 - 6.2) = 4.08$

   $\hat{X}_{Y=3} = 3.4 + (.38)(3 - 6.2) = 2.18$

   d.

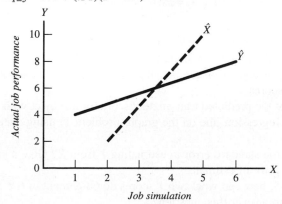

Job simulation

e. The difference in slopes is due to the difference between $s_X = 1.44$ and $s_Y = 1.92$. The predictor with the smaller standard deviation (variance) will have the steeper slope. Compare Formulas 7-6 and 7-10.

EXERCISES

Psychologists have long studied anxiety. . . you know, that feeling you get just before taking a statistics test. Their research has led them to distinguish between just-before-the-statistics-test anxiety from a more general state in which some people are just more anxious than others. The former is called *state* anxiety—produced by a particular environmental condition such as the statistics test. The latter is called *trait* anxiety, a condition that generalizes across situations. Table 7-3 reports hypothetical data on measures of trait and state anxiety for a sample of college sophomores. Use these data to work the exercises.

TABLE 7-3   Data and descriptive statistics from a hypothetical study of the relationship between trait and state anxiety

State Anxiety (X)	Trait Anxiety (Y)
5	4
4	5
10	9
6	3
6	6
8	5
9	10
7	7
8	8
10	9

$\bar{X} = 7.30$ $r_{XY} = .80$ $\bar{Y} = 6.60$
$s_X = 2.37$ $Cov_{XY} = 3.91$ $s_Y = 2.07$

1. Graph the relationship between trait (X) and state anxiety.
2. Calculate the regression slope for predicting Y from X.
3. Interpret the regression coefficient ($b_{Y \cdot X}$) in terms of state-anxiety scores predicting trait-anxiety scores.
4. Calculate the predicted trait-anxiety score for a subject with an X score of 5.
5. Plot the regression line on the graph (problem 1) using state-anxiety scores of 5 and 10.
6. What is the standard error in estimating Y from X? Give a simple interprettion of the stardard error of estimate.
7. For X = 5, between what two Y scores do 68 percent of the cases lie? What must you assume to answer this question?

8. Calculate the percentage of variance in trait anxiety accounted for by variance in state anxiety using regression slope coefficients. Interpret this finding.
9. Why does $b_{X \cdot Y}$ have a steeper slope than $b_{Y \cdot X}$?

ANSWERS TO EXERCISES

1.

2. $$b_{YX} = \frac{3.91}{(2.37)^2} = \frac{3.91}{5.62} = .70$$

3. For every 1 point increase in state anxiety, trait anxiety increases .70 point.
4. $\hat{Y}_{X=5} = 6.6 + 7(5 - 7.3) = 4.99$
5. $\hat{Y}_{X=10} = 6.6 + 7(10 - 7.3) = 8.49$

6. $s_{Y \cdot X} = 2.07\sqrt{1 - (.80)^2} = (2.07)(.60) = 1.24$. The standard error of estimate indicates the standard deviation of Y scores about a predicted Y score for a particular X score (1.24 in this example). For example, for $X = 5$, the standard error indexes the standard deviation of Y scores about the predicted Y score.
7. $6.18 - 1.24 = 4.94$ and $6.18 + 1.24 = 7.42$

8. Percentage of variance $= (b_{Y \cdot X})(b_{X \cdot Y}) = (.70)(.91) = .64$

   Note: $b_{X \cdot Y} = \dfrac{3.91}{(2.07)^2} = .91$

9. Because the standard deviation of X is smaller than that of Y.

REASONING BEHIND STATISTICAL INFERENCE

The first three sections have focused on designing research and summarizing and describing what happened to subjects in that research. However, research seldom stops at the point where a lot is known about the particular subjects in the study. Rather, it attempts to generalize from the behavior of the subjects in the study to what is probably true of the behavior of similar people in general.

Psychologists and sociologists build theories by generalizing from the results of a particular study or series of studies to what might be true of human behavior in general. Educators, making recommendations on how to improve education, generalize from the results of a particular study or series of studies to what is probably true for all students like the ones observed in the studies. And politicians may base their policies, in part, on generalization from the results of a particular study to what might be true for an entire population of people.

Research ideally operates by randomly selecting samples from a population and observing the behavior of subjects in the sample. On the basis of the observed behavior (e.g., described as a mean or variance), an inference is drawn to what is probably true in the population. This sampling procedure is the basis of statistical inference. In this section of the text, the underpinnings of a large variety of inferential (statistical) tests are presented.

8

Statistical Inference: By Intuition

In behavioral research, inferences (generalizations) are drawn from the behavior of a small group of people to the behavior of people in the larger group of interest. This larger set of people is called a *population,* and the smaller subset is called a *sample.* In order to infer from sample to population, researchers follow a standard set of procedures underlying statistical inference. A random sample of subjects is drawn from a population. In a *random sample,* each person in the population has an equal chance of being included in the sample. Over many such samples, then, the behavior of the subjects in the typical sample is representative of the behavior of the people in the population.

Descriptive statistics play an important role in this sampling scheme. Recall from Chapter 1 that *statistics* (e.g., mean, variance, correlation) are measures describing a sample, and *parameters* are measures describing a population (mean, variance, correlation). Moreover, statistics can be used to estimate parameters. Not surprisingly, when a statistic is used to estimate a parameter, it is called an *estimator.* A sample mean, then, is an estimator; it can be used to estimate the mean of a population. Likewise, a sample variance can be used to estimate the population variance and a sample correlation the population correlation. By using statistics as estimators of parameters, behavioral scientists draw inferences from sample data to the population of interest. Unfortunately, the value of a sample estimate of a parameter may not exactly equal the value of the parameter. After all, the sample estimate is based only on a small subset of subjects from the population. So errors may arise in inferring characteristics of the population (i.e., values of parameters) from sample statistics. A major contribution of statistical theory is to enable researchers to indicate the probability that their inferences are in error.

In this chapter, the basic concepts underlying statistical inference are presented. The chapter is conceptual, and it is intended to give you an overview of how statistical inference operates. Subsequent chapters will provide the skills for drawing inferences from sample data.

STATISTICAL INFERENCE AND PAST EXPERIENCE

One way to get an idea of what statistical inference is all about is to draw on past experience. For example, have you ever met a person that you liked immediately? On the basis of a limited sample of information—looks, dress, initial behavior—you draw the inference that Charlie's a nice guy. Or perhaps you've met someone you didn't like right off. Again, you're drawing an inference about that person in general from a limited set of observations.

Consider another example. Jujyfruits are chewy candies I ate as a kid. They come in several different flavors. Some of the candies are red (cherry), some yellow (lemon), some black (licorice), some orange (orange), some purple (grape), and some green (lime). Suppose the red (cherry) Jujyfruits are my favorites. But the company that makes the candy skimps on the number of cherry candies in the box. I drew this generalization, of course, by inference after having eaten the candy from numerous boxes. (Although this is an example of an inference, I make no claim that it is a *valid* inference. Valid inferences are the focus of the remaining sections of this chapter.)

One last example should bring the concept of inference home: the weather report. Weather forecasters sample wind conditions, temperature, and barometric pressure and infer from these and other observations what the weather will be. From my sample of weather reports, I infer that the forecasts are often incorrect. (Again, I make no claim that this is a valid inference, although most people would agree with it.)

The common element in each of these examples is that people draw generalizations or inferences about themselves, other people, and the world in general from a limited sample of information (observations, data). Sometimes these inferences are valid and sometimes they are not (Shavelson et al., 1977; Tversky & Kahneman, 1974). Statistical inference refers to a particular procedure for making inferences or generalizations from a limited sample of data.

The procedures of statistical inference differ from the intuitive procedures used in everyday life in that they involve random sampling. The great value of random sampling is that we can determine the sort of representativeness of a sample to be expected in the long run. So the validity of statistical inference can be readily evaluated, but the validity of everyday, intuitive inferences cannot be.

STATISTICAL INFERENCE FROM THE RESEARCHER'S PERSPECTIVE[1]

In research, a group of "subjects" is observed, and the researcher attempts to draw valid generalizations or inferences from this sample to a population of people like the subjects observed in the research. For example, a researcher might collect television ratings from

[1]For an informative discussion of the ideas presented in the following sections, and more, see Hahn & Meeker (1993).

1000 households and attempt to generalize what she finds from this small group to all households. In other words, research works from the particular to the general. We almost always deal with a limited number of data and attempt to make valid generalizations by inference from these data. We use samples because there is not time enough, energy enough, or money enough to make all possible observations of interest. And even if there were, all possible observations probably could not be made, because they are not available at one point in time. So a limited number of observations must be used to make inferences about the larger group of observations of interest. If the observed data are representative of this larger group, then conclusions drawn from our data will generalize to the larger group—that is, they will be valid. If the sample data are not representative of the larger group to which the researcher wants to generalize, conclusions drawn about this larger group may not be valid.

To make these abstract ideas more concrete, consider two studies, one described previously. In Rosenthal & Jacobson's (1968) study of teacher expectancy (the *Pygmalion* study), a sample of 320 elementary school students was randomly assigned to either the experimental (expectancy) group or the control group. Data were collected on these students before and after teachers were provided information about the expected intellectual performance of their students. By inference from these sample data, Rosenthal and Jacobson made the following generalization: "The evidence presented . . . suggests rather strongly that children who are expected by their teachers to gain intellectually in fact do show greater intellectual gains after one year than do children of whom gains are not expected." Thus from a sample of 65 students in the expectancy group and 255 in the control group, in grades 1–6, Rosenthal and Jacobson drew an inference to *all children*. This inference is unusually broad, especially because students in a convenient elementary school, and not a random sample, participated.[2] Nevertheless, it points out one purpose of research noted earlier: to reach important generalizations by making inferences from a limited number of observations (i.e., sample data).

In a study of the development of moral judgment from childhood to adulthood, Weiner & Peter (1973) drew a sample of children and adults ranging in age from 4 to 18 years. All subjects read stories in which the *intent* of the actor and the *outcome* of the actor's behavior were varied. After each story, the subjects judged whether the actor should be rewarded or punished for his or her acts. Using sample data from 300 subjects drawn from five different age levels, Weiner and Peter reached the following generalization: "A progressive decline [was found] in use of objective outcome information and an increment [was found] in the use of subjective intent information, given both positive and negative outcomes and intents, until the age of 18." Note that at this point, Weiner and Peter no longer have in mind just the 300 subjects they observed in their study; rather, they infer from these subjects to a whole

---

[2]Note that *random assignment* addresses *internal* validity—Does the causal interpretation of the findings follow from the conduct of the study?—by enabling the researcher to rule out *selectivity,* the argument that the observed outcome was caused by prior existing differences between groups. *Random selection* addresses *external* validity—Are the subjects in the sample representative of the larger group to which the researcher wishes to infer?—by giving each subject in the population an equal (or proportionate) chance of being included in the sample. Consequently, even though Rosenthal and Jacobson randomly assigned subjects to "bloomers" or controls, the generalization of findings to all students rests formally on random sampling grounds, or as is often true in behavioral research, on less formal grounds that the convenient sample is representative of a population of interest (e.g., Cornfield & Tukey, 1956; Cook & Campbell, 1979; Mook, 1983).

population of people, aged 4 to 18 years. This example points out, once again, that one intent of research is to reach important generalizations by making inferences from sample data.

From these studies, the intent of behavioral research becomes quite clear: to go beyond data describing a particular sample and reach important generalizations that apply to a larger group of people, the population. In order to reach these generalizations, the researchers in each study followed a set procedure for drawing statistical inferences from sample data. These procedures are set forth in the remainder of this chapter and in Chapters 9 through 12.

A MODEL OF STATISTICAL INFERENCE

In a way, people operate like intuitive statisticians. They draw inferences about themselves, other people, and the world in general from sample data. Although they act as if their sample data were representative of a class of data to which they wish to make inferences, in real-life situations, these data may or may not be representative or valid. In behavioral research, an attempt is made to obtain representative data in order to make valid generalizations from a small sample to a larger class of data. To do so, the researcher follows steps prescribed by a statistical model of inference.

One model of statistical inference takes the following form: We assume an indefinitely large—perhaps infinite—set of observations we would like to know about (e.g., achievement test scores for all third graders in the United States or reaction times for all college sophomores in a memory experiment). This *set of observations* is called a **population.**[3] The population is so large that all possible observations cannot be made, so a subset of all possible observations must be drawn. This subset of observations on a more limited number of people is called a **sample.** A sample, then, is a *subset* or *part of a population.* Inferences about the population are drawn from information found in the sample.

When one draws inferences from the sample to the population, the statistical model requires that the sample be random.[4] A **random sample** is a sample drawn so that each member of the population has an equal and independent chance of being included in the sample. Throughout this textbook, we assume that samples are random. This assumption of random selection of subjects from the population represents an ideal situation. When it is satisfied, sample findings can be generalized to a known population. For example, political opinion surveys and the Nielsen ratings of television programs may approximate this ideal, since it is not too difficult to phone or mail questionnaires to people throughout the country. However, researchers often are not able to randomly select subjects, due to logistical, financial, and time constraints. In this case, samples may be selected for convenience

---

[3]In some cases, the populations may be finite and small. The statistical methods presented in this textbook do not apply to that case. For an outstanding treatment of finite statistics, see Cochran (1966). As Glass & Stanley (1970, p. 241) point out: "For the purposes of statistical inference it is generally not necessary to worry about the distinction between finite and infinite populations whenever the size of the population is more than 100 times greater than the sample taken from the population."

[4]Various techniques other than simple random sampling are available for drawing samples and making inferences from these samples to populations. See, for example, Cochran (1966).

or availability (e.g., volunteers, college sophomores). For example, Rosenthal and Jacobson used subjects at one elementary school in their study of teacher expectancy because they were readily available. (Jacobson was associated with the school district in which the study was conducted.) Likewise, Weiner and Peter used subjects from local schools in their study of moral judgments. As Cornfield & Tukey (1956) pointed out, when available samples are used, inferences from the sample should be made to the accessible population—that is, the population of subjects like those observed in the study. (The validity of these inferences can be tested by replicating the study with a new sample.) Notice that the accessible population may differ from the population to which the researcher wishes to generalize. In reporting the results of a study, researchers should be careful to point out the limits of their generalizations.

In drawing inferences about a population, we are interested in describing the characteristics of the population—such as its central tendency or variability—using the characteristics of the sample. Descriptive measures of the characteristics of the *population*—such as the mean or variance—are called **parameters.** Descriptive measures of the characteristics of the *sample* are called **statistics.** Parameters, then, describe populations; statistics describe samples. The importance of this distinction, if not already apparent, will become apparent in the remainder of this chapter. As a convention for maintaining this distinction, parameters are denoted by Greek letters, and statistics are denoted by Latin letters. For example, the population mean (a parameter) is denoted by the Greek letter μ (mu); the sample mean (a statistic) is denoted by the Latin letter $\bar{X}$ (with a bar). The population variance is denoted by σ^2 (sigma square); the sample variance is denoted by s^2.

When a statistic is used to **estimate** a parameter, it is called an estimator. For example, the sample mean is often used as an estimator of the population mean. An **estimator,** then, is a statistic defined by some formula for combining scores from sample data. The sample mean, $\bar{X} = \sum X \div N$, is a statistic that is used as an estimator of the population mean μ. The value of a particular sample mean is taken as our "best estimate" of the value of μ. Likewise, the sample variance s^2—defined by the formula $s^2 = \sum x^2 \div (N-1)$—is used to estimate the population variance σ^2. The value of a particular sample variance is taken as our best estimate of σ^2.

Since a sample provides only a small subset of data from a population, it is highly unlikely for, say, a particular sample mean to equal exactly the population mean. Indeed, $\bar{X}$ and μ probably will not be the same, since all sorts of factors of which the researcher is unaware may make the particular sample mean a poor representation of the population mean. Such factors are lumped together and called chance or random effects. Just as chance factors give rise to differences between a sample mean and the population mean it is intended to estimate, they also give rise to differences in means from one sample to the next, all of which were drawn from the same population. So, although sample statistics such as $\bar{X}$ are used as our best guess of a population parameter such as μ, this estimate may be in error due to random effects. Thus, knowing something about the characteristics of estimators such as $\bar{X}$ and s^2 is important.

Three important characteristics of estimators are (1) unbiasedness, (2) consistency, and (3) relative efficiency. Each is discussed briefly here. Note that estimators may possess one, some, or all of these characteristics.

An estimator is said to be *unbiased* in estimating a parameter if, for an indefinitely large number of random samples from a population, the mean of the estimator equals the value of the parameter being estimated. If many samples are randomly selected from a population, and a sample mean $\bar{X}$ calculated for each sample, the mean of the sample means will equal μ. A sample mean, then, is an unbiased estimator of the population mean μ. Likewise, the sample variance $s^2 = \sum x^2 \div (N-1)$ is an unbiased estimator of σ^2, because the mean of the sample variances, calculated for an extremely large number of samples from a population, equals σ^2. If, instead, the formula $\sum x^2 \div N$ for a sample variance is used, the sample variance will be a *biased* estimator of σ^2. It is biased because the average value of this sample variance, calculated over an indefinitely large number of random samples, is *less than or equal to* the population variance.

A *consistent* estimator tends to get closer and closer to the parameter it estimates as sample size increases. The sample mean is a consistent estimator of the population mean; if the sample included the entire population, the sample mean would equal the population mean. The sample mean, then, is both an unbiased and consistent estimator of the population mean. The sample standard deviation s is also a consistent estimator of the population standard deviation σ, but it is biased. The larger the sample, the more closely s estimates σ, but it never equals σ.

The *efficiency* of an estimator is the degree to which the estimate of a population parameter varies from sample to sample. Put another way, the efficiency of an estimator is the precision with which it estimates a parameter. The *relative efficiency* of an estimator is the ratio of the variance of that estimator to the variance of another estimator of the same population parameter. For example, suppose we are interested in estimating the mean of a normal population. If a large number of random samples were drawn from this population and the mean and median for each sample were calculated, both would provide unbiased estimates of μ. But the variance of sample means would be less than the variance of sample medians. Hence, relative to the median, the sample mean is a more efficient estimator of μ.

From this discussion, we see that in the long run (i.e., over many samples), sample statistics tell us what we want to know about the parameters they estimate. And some statistics are "better" estimators than others. Also clear is that on the basis of limited evidence from a single sample, our estimate of a parameter may be in error. This issue of error is a central problem addressed by inferential statistics—given sample data, what should we conclude is true of the population? In describing how inferential statistics addresses this problem, we take a hypothesis-testing approach in this chapter.[5]

Example Problem 8.1 ▬▬▬▬▬▬▬▬▬▬▬▬▬▬▬▬▬▬▬▬▬▬▬▬

In a market study of a new TV "soap," *Slippery Rock,* 500 households were randomly telephoned in the late morning and the adult at home was invited to a special viewing of the new soap. These adults viewed and then rated *Slippery Rock* on a scale from 0 to 10 ("would never view" to "would never turn off"). The sample mean rating was 6.9 with a standard deviation of .90. Based

[5]This approach, instead of one using estimation and confidence intervals, is taken for pedagogical reasons. It may be easier for you to conceptualize statistical inference initially from a hypothesis-testing approach than from an estimation approach. In subsequent chapters, both approaches are presented.

on past research on a very large number of such viewings, the overall average for soaps is known to be 7.4. The researcher wanted to test the hypothesis that *Slippery Rock* differed from the average soap.

a.   What statistics were reported for the study?

b.   Which statistic was used as an estimator in the study?

c.   What are three important characteristics of this estimator?

d.   What population parameter was estimated?

STATISTICAL INFERENCE IN BEHAVIORAL RESEARCH

In behavioral research, statistical inference can be used to help answer two somewhat similar, commonly posed questions about a population:

—*Case I.* Does a particular sample of observations belong to a hypothesized population of observations?

—*Case II.* Do observations taken on two groups of subjects differ from one another? That is, do the two sets of observations represent samples from identical populations or from different populations?

In case I research, sample data are drawn to determine whether the data came from some hypothesized population. For example, the average score on an intelligence test is 100 in the general population. A psychologist might wonder whether the mean IQ of clients at community-based clinics is 100. So a random sample of clients from the clinics is given an intelligence test, and the mean of the sample is calculated and used to estimate the population parameter. If the sample mean is close to 100, the psychologist might conclude that the clients belong to the general population with IQ 100. If, however, the sample mean deviates from 100 drastically, he might conclude that the clients differ from the general population.

In case I research, then, a particular population is hypothesized (e.g., the general population with mean IQ 100). This hypothesis about the population is usually based on previous research findings, on theory, and/or on the researcher's best hunch about the nature of the population. A sample of subjects is drawn randomly. An inference is made from sample data as to whether the subjects were drawn from the hypothesized population *or* from some alternative population. In our example, the inference is whether the clients were drawn from the general population with mean 100 or another population with a different average IQ.

Case II research addresses the question "Do observations on two groups of subjects differ from one another?" In this case, two sets of observations are made. The problem, then, is to infer whether the two groups represent samples from identical or different populations. If the samples were drawn from common populations, then the researcher should conclude from her sample data that the populations do not differ from one another. If the samples were drawn from different populations, then the researcher should conclude from her sample data that the population means differ from one another. For example, suppose that subjects are randomly assigned either to an experimental group that received text material in a logical sequence or to a control group that received the material in a scrambled sequence. After reading the text, subjects in both groups are tested for recall of the text. The researcher is interested in whether there was an effect due to the sequence. To answer this question, she compares the sample data for both groups. Prior to reading the material, the two samples represented populations with the same mean. If, after the subjects have read the material, the mean scores of the two groups are similar, the inference is that both groups still represent populations with the same mean. Thus the researcher concludes that the treatment did not have an effect. If the means differ greatly, the inference is that the groups represent samples from populations with different means. In this case, the researcher concludes that there was a treatment effect.

These two types of research questions, case I and case II, are extremely common in research in the behavioral sciences. The two examples that follow illustrate in further detail the types of research questions associated with case I and case II studies. In addition, steps are provided for answering the research questions posed—a procedure known as hypothesis testing.

HYPOTHESIS TESTING AND STATISTICAL INFERENCE

Case I—Does the Sample Belong to a Hypothesized Population?

Suppose, for example, that a state board of education wanted to estimate the mean reading level of its high school seniors—that is, the entire population (see Figure 8-1a). Since testing all of the high school seniors in the state at one time is difficult and costly, a random sample of seniors is tested in the spring. From this sample of test scores, the mean of the sample score distribution is calculated (see Figure 8-1b). This statistic is used to estimate the mean of the entire population of scores for high school seniors in the state (see Figure 8-1c).

The next question the state board might ask about the mean reading level of its high school seniors is whether it differs from that of high school seniors in the entire United

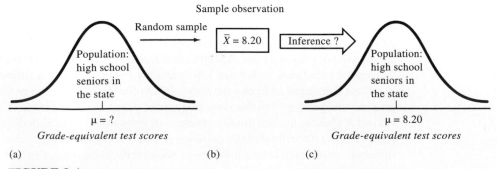

Sample observation

Random sample

$\bar{X} = 8.20$ Inference ?

Population: high school seniors in the state

Population: high school seniors in the state

$\mu = ?$

$\mu = 8.20$

Grade-equivalent test scores

Grade-equivalent test scores

(a)   (b)   (c)

FIGURE 8-1

Schematic representation of the steps involved in statistical inference from sample data to the population

States. Suppose that from national test norms, the mean reading level of high school seniors is known to be 7.89 on a grade-equivalent scale. The question of interest, then, is: *How likely are we to observe a sample mean of 8.20 or greater when, in fact, the sample was drawn from a population with a mean of 7.89?*

The answer to this question will help the board decide whether the high school seniors in this particular state are similar in reading level to high school seniors across the United States. Clearly, if a sample mean of 8.20 or greater is likely to occur when random samples are drawn from a population with $\mu = 7.89$, the conclusion that the seniors are similar to those in the country as a whole seems to be warranted. However, if a sample mean of 8.20 or greater is quite unlikely to occur when the population mean is 7.89, the conclusion that high school seniors in this state differ in reading level from seniors in other states seems reasonable. In short, should we infer that the sample data were drawn from a population with $\mu = 7.89$, or should we conclude that they were drawn from a different population with $\mu > 7.89$ (μ greater than 7.89)? This problem of inference is shown in Figure 8-2c (a and b are the same as in Figure 8-1).

In reaching a decision on whether a sample mean differs from some known or expected population mean, we use the following strategy: The hypothesis to be tested is set forth. This hypothesis is called the **null hypothesis** (denoted H_0). For the reading study, the null hypothesis would be H_0: $\mu = 7.89$.

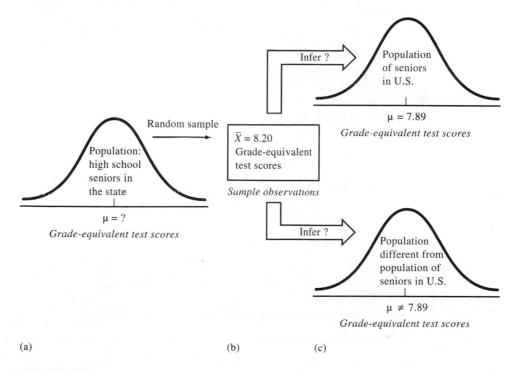

(a)   (b)   (c)

FIGURE 8-2

Schematic representation of the steps involved in inference—case I ($\overline{X}$ represents the sample mean; μ represents the population mean)

An **alternative hypothesis** (denoted H_1) is also stated. It may take one of three forms:

1. The population mean is not equal to some specified value (H_1: $\mu \neq 7.89$). This is often called a "nondirectional" alternative hypothesis.
2. The population mean is less than some specific value (H_1: $\mu < 7.89$).
3. The population mean is greater than some specific value (H_1: $\mu > 7.89$).

These last two forms are often called "directional" alternative hypotheses.

The choice of an alternative hypothesis is not arbitrary. If theory, prior research, or (preferably) both suggest that μ may be less than or greater than the value specified in the null hypothesis, a directional alternative hypothesis should be used. In the absence of such evidence, the nondirectional alternative hypothesis should be used. From the sample mean (e.g., $X = 8.20$), the researcher decides whether or not to reject the null hypothesis. A decision not to reject the null hypothesis lends no support to the alternative hypothesis. However, a decision to reject the null hypothesis indirectly confirms the alternative hypothesis. The following discussion enumerates the steps in hypothesis testing. (See the Spring 1993 issue of the *Journal of Experimental Education* for an informative debate about approaches to hypothesis testing, as well as whether or not to hypothesis test at all. See especially Levin's [1993] article.)

1. Assume that the sample was drawn from the known or expected population. This assumption is equivalent to saying that the seniors in this particular state have the same reading level as seniors in the United States. This assumption that is to be tested is known as the *null hypothesis* H_0. The null hypothesis is denoted as:

   H_0: μ = some specific value

   where:

   H denotes "hypothesis"
   0 denotes "null"
   μ denotes the population mean

In our example, H_0: $\mu = 7.89$, or in words, the average reading level of seniors in the state is 7.89—the average reading level of seniors in the country.

2. Test the assumption of the null hypothesis against an *alternative hypothesis* H_1. The alternative hypothesis asserts that the sample differs from the population specified in the null hypothesis. That is, it asserts that the sample is drawn from a *different* population than the one specified in the null hypothesis. The alternative hypothesis is denoted as:

   H_1: $\mu \neq$ some specified value ($\neq$ denotes "not equal")

   or:

   H_1: $\mu >$ some specified value ($>$ denotes "greater than")

   or:

   H_1: $\mu <$ some specified value ($<$ denotes "less than")

In our example (research on reading level), the alternative would be H_1: $\mu \neq 7.89$, or in words, the average reading level of seniors in the state is different from 7.89—the average reading level of seniors in the country.

3. In order to test the null hypothesis, draw a random sample of subjects from the population of interest (high school seniors in the state).

4. From the sample mean (and other statistics), decide whether or not to reject the null hypothesis that the reading level of the population of seniors in the state is the same as in the country.[6] If you decide not to reject the null hypothesis, you decide that the difference between the sample mean and the hypothesized population mean was likely to be due to chance. If you decide to reject the null hypothesis, you decide that a difference as large as or larger than that between the sample mean and the hypothesized population mean was unlikely to have arisen by chance. In this case, you accept the alternative hypothesis that the average reading level of high school seniors in the state differed from the average reading level of seniors in the United States.

Example Problem 8.2

The researcher conducting the market study of the soap, *Slippery Rock*, wanted to test the hypothesis that viewers' ratings of *Slippery Rock* differed from the overall average rating of soaps in general. Use the information in Example Problem 8.1 to:
a. Set forth a null hypothesis for this study.
b. Set forth and justify an alternative hypothesis for this study.

Case II—Are Two Groups Drawn from Populations with Equal Means?

In a study to determine the effect of organization on remembering and recalling a list of words, a random sample of 100 college sophomores was drawn from a population of sophomores (Figures 8-3a, b). Half of these sophomores were randomly assigned to the experimental group ($n_E = 50$) and half to the control group ($n_C = 50$; see Figure 8-3c). Note that at this point in the study, no "treatment" had been given. Thus, the two samples should look very similar and each should provide a picture of what the entire population of sophomores looks like. In this way, sophomores in the experimental group and the control group began the experiment on equal footing.

Next, both groups of sophomores were presented a list of related words to learn. The list was arranged in its proper hierarchical form for the experimental group and in a scrambled order for the control group. After studying the words, the sophomores were asked to recall as many of the words as possible. Figure 8-3d indicates that the mean number of words recalled in the experimental group was greater than in the control group.

---

[6]Specific procedures for making this decision will be discussed at length in Chapter 10. Our concern here is with the nature of the inferences that are drawn from research. Note that the decision is "not to reject" rather than "to accept" H_0. The reason for this distinction is explained at length in Chapter 10.

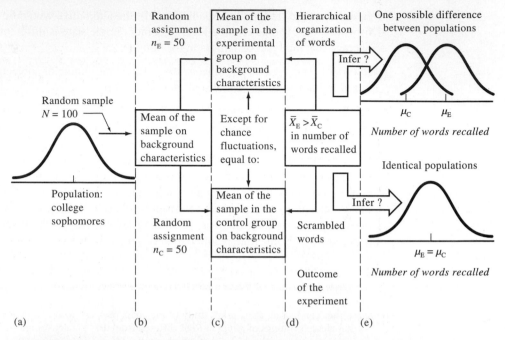

FIGURE 8-3
Schematic representation of the steps involved in statistical inference from a true experiment ($\bar{X}$ represents the sample mean; μ represents the population mean; E represents the experimental group; C represents the control group)

From these sample statistics, we must decide between one of two alternatives:

1. The two groups represent populations with a common mean. In this case, the conclusion drawn from the experiment is that organization did not affect recall.
2. The two samples represent populations with different means—that is, there were differences between the groups in recall. In this case, the conclusion is that organization did affect recall.

If the difference between the sample distributions of the experimental and control groups was likely to occur by chance, we should decide that there was no treatment effect and conclude that both samples (groups) belong to the same population. If the difference was not likely to occur by chance, we should decide that there was a treatment effect and conclude that the samples (groups) represent different populations. This decision is made by inferring from the sample data to the population or populations (see Figure 8-3e).

The problem of deciding whether the two samples—experimental and control groups—belong to populations with a common mean or different means is the fundamental problem addressed by statistical inference. The problem is to decide whether the observed differences between sample means may have arisen by *chance* or whether the observed differences arose because after the experimental treatment, the two samples represent two different populations.

This element of chance introduced into the sample observations suggests that we can never be absolutely sure of the true state of affairs in the population. The best we can do is state *how likely* we are to observe sample differences as large or larger than the ones we have observed if the samples were drawn from the same population. If the observed sample differences are *likely* to arise by sampling from the same population, we infer the sample data represent the same population—that is, there was no treatment effect. However, if the observed sample differences are quite *unlikely* to arise by sampling from the same population, we infer that the sample data represent different populations—that is, there was a treatment effect.

The steps in reaching a decision about whether sample differences represent differences in populations are similar to the steps in case I. There are differences, however, in the hypotheses and procedures, since a different research question is being asked. The steps in hypothesis testing are given in the following discussion.

1. Assume that the samples represent populations with the *same* mean. This assumption is equivalent to the assumption that there is no treatment effect. This assumption is the *null hypothesis* H_0, and it predicts *no difference* between the population means from which the two sets of observations were taken. (Recall that in case I, H_0 also predicted *no difference*; however, it predicted no difference between the population from which one set of sample observations was drawn and a hypothesized population.) The null hypothesis is denoted as:

   H_0: $\mu_E = \mu_C$

   where:

   H denotes the "hypothesis"
   0 denotes "null"
   μ denotes the population mean from which the sample was drawn
   E and C denote experimental and control groups, respectively

   Or in words, the mean of the experimental population equals the mean of the control population.

2. Test the null hypothesis against an *alternative hypothesis* H_1. The alternative H_1 asserts that the null hypothesis is incorrect; in the example, it asserts that the two samples represent different populations. The alternative hypothesis is denoted as:

   H_1: $\mu_E \neq \mu_C$

   (the mean of the experimental group is not equal to the mean of the control group), or:

   H_1: $\mu_E > \mu_C$

   (the mean of the experimental group is greater than the mean of the control group), or:

   H_1: $\mu_E < \mu_C$

(the mean of the experimental group is less than the mean of the control group). Thus, H_1 specifies a difference between the means of the populations.

3. To test these hypotheses, draw a random sample of subjects from some known population. Then randomly assign the subjects in this sample to either the experimental or the control group.[7]

4. Perform the experiment—that is, introduce the independent variable, or "treatment"—and observe the outcome, or dependent variable, in each group.

5. From the sample data, decide whether or not to reject the null hypothesis. If you decide *not* to reject the null hypothesis, you decide that the observed differences between the experimental and control group were *likely to have arisen by chance.* If you decide to reject the null hypothesis, you decide that the observed differences between the experimental and control group after the treatment were *quite unlikely to have arisen by chance.* In this case, you accept the alternative hypothesis that there was a "treatment effect."

Example Problem 8.3

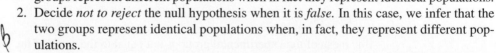

The researcher conducting the market study of the soap, *Slippery Rock,* also showed a highly acclaimed (but, alas, no longer aired) soap, *Santa Barbara,* to a second random sample of household adults for comparison purposes. The audience rated *Santa Barbara* 8.6, on average, with a standard deviation of 1.04. Use this information and that in Example Problem 8.2 to:
a. Set forth a null hypothesis for this comparison.
b. Set forth and justify an alternative hypothesis for this study.

ERRORS IN STATISTICAL INFERENCE

In making inferences about what is true of the populations, we can never be certain that our decision to reject or not reject the null hypothesis will be correct. The possibility of making the wrong decision (i.e., making an error) is always there. An error can be made in two ways:

1. Decide to *reject* the null hypothesis when it is *true.* In this case, we infer that the two groups represent different populations when in fact they represent identical populations.
2. Decide *not to reject* the null hypothesis when it is *false.* In this case, we infer that the two groups represent identical populations when, in fact, they represent different populations.

---

[7]Case II procedures are also used to compare two groups of subjects who differ on some personal characteristic such as sex or high or low anxiety prior to the study. In this case, subjects are not randomly assigned to levels of the treatment; the treatment has been performed by nature. The question answered by these hypothesis-testing procedures is whether or not the observations (e.g., reaction times in a memory study) drawn from these groups represent populations with the same or different means. This point will be discussed at length in later chapters.

TABLE 8-1   Decision matrix: to reject or not to reject the null
hypothesis—that is the question

| | *True State of Affairs in the Population* | |
Decision	*Identical Populations*	*Different Populations*
Identical Populations (Not Reject H_0)	Correct decision	Error
Different Populations (Reject H_0)	Error	Correct decision

This decision problem is represented in Table 8-1. The *true state of affairs* in the population—the state of affairs that we attempt to find out about through our sample data—is that the *populations are either identical* (null hypothesis) *or different* (alternative hypothesis). From the sample data, we can decide that the observed differences between the two groups represent populations with identical means (not reject H_0) or that the observed differences between the two groups represent different population means (reject H_0). The cells in this 2×2 decision matrix indicate the conditions under which a correct decision is made and the conditions under which an incorrect decision is made.

As we have seen in our discussion of the concepts involved in statistical inference, the decision about whether or not to reject the null hypothesis has depended on *how likely the observed differences in sample data were to arise by chance.* The notion of chance was not explained in this chapter. Furthermore, no criterion was given for deciding how large a difference between the two sets of sample data is necessary in order to conclude that the differences between sample data were unlikely to arise by chance. In a sense, the remainder of this book deals with the definition of chance and the decision about whether sample data arose by chance or from true differences. Specifically, the next two chapters develop the concept of chance and provide methods for determining whether sample data arose by chance. Chapter 11 presents methods for estimating the magnitude of errors in our decisions.

SUMMARY

This chapter introduces basic concepts underlying *statistical inference* such as *random sampling, sample, population, statistic, parameter,* and *estimator.* With these concepts, researchers can make valid inferences about a population from a limited sample of data. Two types of questions about populations are presented that are commonly posed in behavioral research. Case I: Does a particular sample of observations belong to a hypothesized population of observations? And case II: Do observations taken on two groups of subjects represent differences in populations? Procedures, called *hypothesis testing,* for answering these questions are presented. Finally, possible *errors* that can be made in statistical inference are presented.

ANSWERS TO EXAMPLE PROBLEMS

1. **a.** The sample mean (6.9) and standard deviation (.90).
   b. The sample mean.
   c. The sample mean is unbiased, consistent, and efficient.
   d. The population mean, μ.

2. **a.** H_0: $\mu = 7.4$.
   Note: if you used the sample mean, instead of the population mean, in the null hypothesis (viz. H_0: $\mu = 6.9$), this represents a serious misconception. Hypotheses are about population parameters, *not* sample statistics. We use sample statistics to estimate these parameters. Estimators give us a window into what the population might look like.
   b. H_1: $\mu = 7.4$. **[equals not]** In the absence of prior research, there are no grounds to assert a directional alternative hypothesis.

3. **a.** H_0: $\mu_{\text{Slippery Rock}} = \mu_{\text{Santa Barbara}}$
   b. H_1: $\mu_{\text{Slippery Rock}} \neq \mu_{\text{Santa Barbara}}$ **[equals not]** Again, in the absence of prior comparative research, there are not grounds to assert anything other than a non directional alternative hypothesis.

EXERCISES

A humorist, Ashley Brilliant (1994, p. 11), recently wrote:

> If you are as skeptical about most reports of "extrasensory perception" as I have always been, you will probably find the following hard to believe. But this . . . actually happened to me.
> Sometime between midnight and 3 a.m. on the night of February 23–24, 1994, I woke from what seemed an unusually vivid dream, and, as I sometimes do on such occasions, I tried to write it down. All I managed to write was: "Dinah Shore Commits Suicide." . . . I had no idea why I would be dreaming about Dinah Shore. She had not recently been in the news, and I had scarcely even been aware of her as a TV personality.
> Four hours later, at 11:30 a.m. . . . I heard a news report on the radio: Dinah Shore had just died.

Reports of "ESP" are daily occurrences, even by novelists. They have largely been dismissed as scientifically unfounded. Nevertheless, no less a prestigious journal than the *Psychological Bulletin* has recently published a review of a certain ESP literature (Bem & Honorton, 1994), and concluded that one experimental procedure, the ganzfield procedure, had produced big enough, replicable ESP effects to warrant "bringing this body of data to the attention of the wider psychological community" (p. 5).

The ganzfield procedure[8] recognizes that reports of the *psi* phenomenon—"anomalous processes of information or energy transfer" (Bem & Honorton, 1994, p. 4)—occur during meditation, hypnosis, dreaming, and other altered states of consciousness. By reducing

---

[8]This description of the ganzfield procedure is taken directly from Bem & Honorton (1994, pp. 5–6).

external sensory stimuli, so the reasoning goes, "noise" is reduced and the psi signal can be detected.

With the ganzfield ("total field") procedure, the *receiver* is placed in a reclining chair in an acoustically isolated room. Ping-pong ball halves are taped over the eyes and a red floodlight directed toward the eyes to produce an undifferentiated visual field. Headphones play white noise to produce an similar auditory field. To reduce somatic "noise," the subject typically undergoes a series of progressive relaxation exercises at the beginning of the experimental session. The *sender* is secluded in a separate, acoustically isolated room where a visual stimulus is randomly selected from a large set of stimuli (brief videotape, art, photograph). One stimulus is randomly selected as the target for the session. "While the sender concentrates on the target, the receiver provides a continuous verbal report of his or her ongoing imagery and mentation, usually for about 30 minutes" (Bem & Honorton, 1994, p. 5). At the end of the session, the receiver is presented with (usually) four alternative stimuli and rates the degree to which each matches the imagery and mentation experienced during the session. If the receiver rates the target highly, it is scored a "hit." Thus, just by chance, the hit rate should be .25—guessing randomly one of four stimuli. In one research summary, 82 percent (23 of 28) of the senders scored hits.

1. What statistic is reported for this study?
2. What population parameter might this statistic estimate?
3. Set forth a null hypothesis for the ganzfield study.
4. Set forth and justify an alternative hypothesis.

ANSWERS TO EXERCISES

1. A percent: 82 percent
2. The percent of receivers in the population who "hit" on the sender's imagery and mentation.
3. H_0: percent = .25
4. The alternative hypothesis depends on your skepticism (see the discussion in Bem & Honorton, 1994). If you are a skeptic:

   H_1: percent ≠ .25

   If you tend to believe in the possibility, you're probably less skeptical (Bem & Honorton, 1994) and you might then venture a one-tail alternative:

   H_1: percent > .25

9

Probability Theory and Mathematical Distributions

As pointed out in Chapter 8, behavioral research, ideally, operates by randomly selecting samples from a population and observing the behavior of subjects in the sample. On the basis of the observed behavior (described by a sample statistic such as mean or a variance), an inference is drawn to what is probably true in the population. Without observing the behavior of every person in the population, however, researchers can never be absolutely certain that the inference from sample to population is correct. The best that can be done is to indicate the chance that the inference is incorrect. Or put another way, the best researchers can do is to indicate the probability that their inferences are correct.

The purposes of this chapter are to introduce, formally, the concept of probability and to provide you with skills in finding probabilities by a counting procedure or from probability distributions. In order to keep the technical discussions at a minimum, we present just the bare bones of probability theory (see Hays, 1994, for a more complete introduction). Throughout some of the more technical parts of the presentation here, keep in mind that the goal of this chapter is to provide you with something more than an intuitive understanding of the question underlying statistical inference: "How likely are we to get the sample results assuming that the null hypothesis is true?"

AN INTUITIVE APPROACH TO PROBABILITY

Most people are fairly good intuitive statisticians. They have a reasonably clear concept of probability without any formal education on the topic. When you ask people what the probability of rain is, they can answer the question—perhaps almost as well as the weather forecaster. The purpose of this section is to extend your knowledge about probability by adding some concepts in probability theory.

What is the probability of tossing a fair coin—one for which a head or a tail is equally likely to occur—and getting heads? Most people will probably answer that there is a "50–50 chance." This statement is usually expressed as a proportion in probability theory: ".50." This response is the same one you would get if you used probability theory to answer the question. Probability theory would reason as follows (assuming equally likely outcomes):

1. What are the possible outcomes in flipping a coin? Heads or tails.
2. Of all possible outcomes, how many ways can I toss a head? One.
3. The probability of heads, then, is given by the number of ways the favored outcomes occur (i.e., one way—heads) divided by the total number of possible outcomes (two ways—heads or tails): 1/2 = .50.

Points 1 through 3 are summarized in Table 9-1a. Note that a frequency distribution can be constructed (column 5 of Table 9-1a). Along the abscissa are the possible outcomes: "not heads" or "heads." Along the ordinate is the number of ways an outcome can occur. Notice that a *relative frequency distribution* can also be constructed. The frequencies from the frequency distribution are divided by N, the total number of outcomes possible. These relative frequencies can be read as probabilities. Thus, the relative frequency distribution can be used as a *probability distribution*.

Let's try estimating another probability, one that may hit closer to home. What is the probability of guessing on a true–false test and getting the right answer? To get you into a guessing frame of mind (if you aren't already there), try answering this question:

T   F   Johnny Bench hit two home runs in the fifth game of the 1975 World Series.

Most of you probably guessed at the answer to the question. For those of you who know Johnny Bench, you know that he was quite capable of hitting home runs, so you might take an "educated guess" and say true. But many of you could just as easily have flipped a coin: heads I say true, tails I say false. In this case, you're guessing at random. You are as likely to guess heads as tails. Finally, some baseball buffs will know the correct answer: false. (Tony Perez hit two home runs in the fifth game.)

Now, the question again: What is the probability of guessing (*randomly*) on a true–false test and getting the right answer? Most students will readily say "50–50," or expressed as a proportion, ".50." Or since guessing randomly is the same as flipping a coin—heads you're right and tails you're wrong—you can get the answer. Probability theory would use the same three steps as described before:

1. List the possible, equally likely outcomes of guessing on the test (right or wrong).
2. Determine how many of those outcomes will give a right answer (one).
3. Calculate the probability of a right answer as the number of ways the favored outcome occurs (i.e., the right answer) divided by the total number of outcomes 1/2 = .50). This reasoning is also summarized in Table 9-1b.

TABLE 9-1 Theoretical distributions of outcomes of three experiments

Example	Number of Equally Likely Possible Outcomes	Number of Favored Outcomes	Probability $(p) = \dfrac{\text{No. of Favored Outcomes}}{\text{No. of Possible Outcomes}}$	Theoretical Frequency Distribution	Theoretical Relative Frequency Distribution (Probability Distribution)
a. Flipping a fair coin	2 — heads, tails	Tossing heads: 1	$p(\text{heads}) = \dfrac{1}{2} = .50$		
b. Guessing on true–false	2 — right, wrong	Guessing correctly: 1	$p(\text{right}) = \dfrac{1}{2} = .50$		
c. Rolling a die	6 — 1, 2, 3, 4, 5, 6	Rolling a 2: 1	$p(2) = \dfrac{1}{6} = .17$		

Now let's try a last example with a potentially bigger payoff. What is the probability of getting a 2 by rolling a die? Good gamblers—and many not-so-good gamblers—will quickly answer "one out of six" or "1/6" or ".17." By using the three steps in probability theory, we find the same conclusion:

1. What are the possible, equally likely outcomes of rolling a die? (There are six: 1, 2, 3, 4, 5, and 6.)
2. Of all possible outcomes, how many will give a 2? (One: a 2 occurs only once in the list of possible outcomes.)
3. The probability of getting a 2 by rolling a die is given by the number of ways the favored outcome occurs (i.e., 1) divided by the total number of outcomes (i.e., 6): $1/6 = .17$.

This reasoning is summarized in Table 9-1c. Notice that on the abscissa of the frequency distribution and on the relative frequency distribution (*probability distribution*), the possible values of rolling a die are either "2" or "not 2." There is one way to get a 2; there are five ways to get "not 2."

Example Problem 9.1 ▬▬▬▬▬▬▬▬▬▬▬▬▬▬▬▬▬▬▬▬▬▬▬▬▬▬▬▬▬▬▬▬▬▬▬

What is the probability of guessing right (*randomly*) on a four-alternative, multiple-choice question? (If necessary, refer to Table 9-1 for help.)

A MORE FORMAL APPROACH TO PROBABILITY

At this point, our intuition can be summarized formally in probability theory. Flipping a coin, guessing on a true–false question, rolling a die, and guessing on a multiple-choice question are all examples of trials that produce an **outcome:** heads or tails; right or wrong; and 1, 2, . . . , 6. All possible individual outcomes of a trial are collectively called the **outcome space** (*OS*) of the experiment. The outcome space for the coin experiment is $OS = \{H, T\}$; the outcome space for the true–false item experiment is $OS = \{R, W\}$; and the outcome space for the die experiment is $OS = \{1, 2, 3, 4, 5, 6\}$. In short, the outcome space corresponds to the set of all possible outcomes.

An event (*E*) is any specific combination of possible, individual outcomes. Put another way, an **event** is a subset of the outcome space. In the coin experiment, we were interested in the event heads. In the true–false experiment, we were interested in the event correct. In the die experiment, we were interested in the event 2. In short, events correspond to what we were calling the favored outcome(s).

Note that the unfavored outcome is also an event but not the one of interest. For example, for the event 2 in the die experiment, there is another event, not 2. The event not 2 includes the following outcomes: 1, 3, 4, 5, and 6. In notation form:

$OS = \{1, 2, 3, 4, 5, 6\}$

$E(2) = \{2\}$

$E(\text{not } 2) = \{1, 3, 4, 5, 6\}$

Similarly, some other event can be selected in the die experiment. For example, what outcomes would be included in the event even numbers on the roll of a die?

$OS = \{1, 2, 3, 4, 5, 6\}$

$E(\text{even numbers}) = \{2, 4, 6\}$

At this point, probability can be defined in a formal way. Under the assumption of a finite or countably infinite outcome space with equally likely outcomes, the **probability p** of an event is defined as the number of outcomes in the event divided by the number of outcomes in the outcome space.[1]

$$p(E) = \frac{\#E}{\#OS} \qquad\qquad (9\text{-}1)$$

where:

$\#E$ = number of outcomes in the event

$\#OS$ = number of outcomes in the outcome space

The probability of rolling a 2, then, is $p(2) = 1/6 = .17$; the probability of not rolling a 2 is $p(\text{not } 2) = 5/6 = .83$; and the probability of rolling an even number is $p(\text{even}) = 3/6 = .50$. The steps in computing the probability of an event are summarized in Procedure 9-1, using the die experiment as an example.

PROCEDURE 9-1 Steps in computing the probability of an event

Operation	Example
1. Look up Formula 9-1: $p(E) = \dfrac{\#E}{\#OS}$ *where:* $\#E$ = number of outcomes in the event $\#OS$ = number of outcomes in the outcome space	Die experiment: What is the probability of rolling a 2 in one throw?
2. Identify the number of outcomes in the event ($\#E$).	$\#E = 1$ (there is only one way to roll a 2).
3. Identify the number of outcomes in the outcome space ($\#OS$).	$\#OS = 6$ (there are six possible outcomes from rolling a die).
4. Divide $\#E$ by $\#OS$.	$\dfrac{1}{6} = .17$ The probability of rolling a 2 in one throw is .17.

[1]The word "countably," means that each outcome or event can be associated with one and only one of the "natural" or counting numbers.

I'M TOO BUSY TO DO ALL THAT COUNTING

In each of the examples, it was easy to count the outcomes in the outcome space and in an event. However, when four or five true–false questions are considered, or when two or three dice are rolled, the counting gets quite tedious. In general, as the number of repetitions increases, the amount of counting needed to specify the outcome space increases dramatically.

Addition and Multiplication Rules of Probability

Two rules of probability—the addition and multiplication rules—eliminate some of the cumbersome counting. The addition rule is used to find the probability of two events combined. For example, we might ask, "What is the probability of tossing two dice with the outcome that the first die comes up 3 (one event), or the second die comes up odd (second event), or both come up (a 3 on the first die and an odd on the second)?" For those of you who aren't gamblers, how about this: Suppose your statistics instructor has a policy that, to pass the course, you must get a passing grade on either the midterm (one event) or final (second event). Of course you won't be penalized if you pass both tests! What is the probability that you pass at least one test and receive a passing grade? In both these examples, the *addition rule* of probability can be used to answer the questions. Moreover, the addition rule provides a definition of what is meant by "mutually exclusive" events, an important concept in statistics.

The multiplication rule addresses the independence of two events. For example, we can ask, "What is the probability of tossing two coins and both coming up heads (the first coin coming up heads is one event; the second coming up heads is the other)?" Of perhaps greater relevance to behavioral scientists is determing whether, for instance, gender is independent of political party affiliation. So we might ask, "Is the probability of being female (the first event) independent of being a Republican (the second event)?" In both these examples, the *multiplication rule* provides a mechanism for answering these questions.

Probability theory, then, can be used to answer both sets of questions. Let's see how.

Addition Rule.   The addition rule is helpful in finding probabilities when there are *two events* and we are interested in knowing the *probability* that *at least one* of the two events occurs. That is, the addition rule helps us find the probability that one event (A) or another event (B), or both (A and B) occur. For example, consider passing the statistics midterm as one event (A) and passing the final as a second event (B). The additive rule helps us find the probability of receiving a passing grade in the course—that is, the probability that passing the midterm, the final, or both occurs.

Let's consider the following question in detail to see how the addition rule works: "What is the probability of tossing two dice with the outcome that the first die comes up 3 (call this event A), or the second die comes up odd (1, 3, 5—event B), or both come up (a 3 on the first die and a odd on the second)?" Intuition, as well as some knowledge, leads us to say that the probability of a 3 on the first die is 1/6, and the probability of an odd on the second is 3/6. Moreover, the probability of getting a 3 on the first die *and* an odd on the second can occur 3 ways [{3, 1}, {3, 3}, {3, 5}] out of a total of 36 ways [{1, 1},

{1, 2}, . . ., {6, 5}, {6, 6}. So the answer, at first blush, is: $1/6 + 3/6 + 3/36 = 6/36 + 18/36 + 3/36 = 27/36 = .75$. Unfortunately our logic is a bit faulty; we're guilty of counting the same thing twice, as shown in Figure 9-1. That is, "both A and B"—3 and odd—may count toward event A and toward event B. It has been double counted. So, to be fair, we should add the probability of event A with the probability of event B and then subtract out, just once, the probability of "both A and B": $1/6 + 3/6 − 3/36 = 6/36 + 18/36 − 3/36 = 21/36 = .58$.

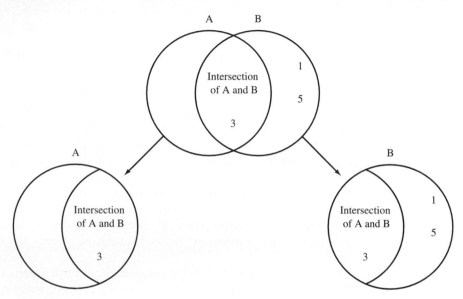

FIGURE 9-1
Schematic representation of the additive rule: dice experiment

This reasoning leads to the general **addition rule:** *The probability of event A or event B or both is equal to the probability of event A plus the probability of event B minus the intersection of event A with event B (A intersect B).* In our example, we say that the probability of the event "3" with the first die, or the probability of the event "odd" with the second, or both is equal to the probability of rolling a 3 with the first die plus the probability of rolling an odd number with the second minus the intersection of 3 and odd: $6/36 + 18/36 − 3/36 = .58$.

Now try this one. A new pill has been shown to be very successful in relieving headaches. However, a study showed that 5 percent of those taking the pill developed a rash, 10 percent got a runny nose, and 12 percent got both symptoms. What is the probability of getting at least one symptom, based on this study?

First, recognize the following: p(rash) = .05, p(runny nose) = .10, and p(both) = .12. The probability of at least one symptom, then, is $.05 + .10 − .12 = .03$!

Consider one final example before leaving the topic. What is the probability of rolling a 3 with the first die and an even {2, 4, 6} with the second? Notice that the first event, "3," does not intersect the second event, "even." There is no way you can get *both* 3 and even—3 is not an even number. In this case, the probability of the intersection of 3 and even is zero: p(A intersect B)—you can't have both a 3 and even—is 0. When two events do not intersect, we speak of **mutually exclusive events.** *Two events are mutually exclusive if they do not share any outcomes in common.* In this case, the additive rule is the sum of the probabilities of the two events: p(A) + p(B).

Example Problem 9.2 ▬▬▬▬▬▬▬▬▬▬▬▬▬▬▬▬▬▬▬▬▬▬▬▬

Suppose you throw two dice. Event A is a 2 on die 1 and Event B is a 6 on die 2.
  a. Find p(A intersect B)
  b. Find the probability of event A or event B or both.

▬▬▬

Multiplication Rule.   The multiplication rule is useful in finding the probability of two (or more) independent events occurring. Let's model the question, "What's the probability of tossing two coins and both coming up heads?" Assuming the coins are fair so that a head or a tail is equally likely, and the toss of one coin has no bearing on (is *independent* of) the toss of the other, we could write the outcome of both trials as follows:

Trial (Coin)

1	2

H ⟨ H
⟨ T

T ⟨ H
⟨ T

The outcome space now contains four equally likely outcomes: (1) get a head with coin 1 and a head with coin 2 {HH}, (2) get a head with coin 1 and a tail with coin 2 {HT}, (3) get a tail with coin 1 and a head with coin 2 {TH}, and (4) get a tail with coin 1 and coin 2 {TT}. The event, two heads, can occur only once: {HH}. The probability of tossing two fair coins and both coming up heads, then, is 1/4 = .25. Suppose you tossed three coins. What do you think would happen? The outcome space contains eight equally likely outcomes (you can extend the preceding model if you like): {HHH}, {HHT}, {HTH}, {HTT}, {THH}, {THT}, {TTH}, and {TTT}. The probability of tossing three fair coins and getting all heads is 1/8 = .125.

Note that there's a regularity in our findings. The probability of tossing heads with a single coin is 1/2. This is $p(H)^1$. The probability two coins coming up heads is (1/2) × (1/2) = 1/4. This is $p(H)^2$. And the probability of three coins coming up heads is (1/2) × (1/2) × (1/2) = 1/8. This is $p(H)^3$. Can you predict what the probability of four coins coming up heads will be without counting the entire outcome space?

This regularity is summarized by the **multiplicative rule:** *The probability that event A, which has a probability [p(A)] of occurring on any one trial, will occur n times in n inde-*

pendent trials is: $p(A) \cdot p(A) \cdots p(A) = p(A)^n$. In terms of the coin tossing experiment, the probability of tossing heads, which has a probability $[p(A) = 1/2]$ of occurring on any one trial, will occur n times in n independent trials is: $(1/2) \cdot (1/2) \cdots (1/2) = (1/2)^n$. With four coins, we have: $(1/2)^4 = (1/2) \cdot (1/2) \cdot (1/2) \cdot (1/2) = 1/16$.

Example Problem 9.3

Consider a three-item, multiple-choice test with four alternatives. What is the probability of guessing randomly on each item and getting all three items correct?

Probability Distribution

The addition and multiplication rules of probability only go so far in relieving us of having to count up the outcomes in the outcome space and in the event. To do more calls for additional help. This is where a probability distribution comes in handy. As a first example, consider a fairly small outcome space such as that produced by guessing on a two-item, true–false test. By "guessing," I mean that outcomes (right, wrong) on each item are equally likely and that a guess on one item has no effect whatsoever on the response to the second item (i.e., guesses on the item are independent). The outcome space, then, contains four equally likely outcomes (see Table 9-2). Furthermore, there are three possible score values on a two-item, true–false test: 0, 1, 2 (see Table 9-2). These score values can be considered events. There is only one way to obtain a score value of zero—both answers must be wrong. Thus, there is one outcome in the event zero correct: $E(0 \text{ correct}) = \{WW\}$. A score value of 1 can be obtained by answering either the first or second item correctly. Thus, there are two outcomes in the event 1 correct: $E(1 \text{ correct}) = \{RW, WR\}$. Finally, there is only one way to obtain a score value of 2—both answers must be correct. So there is one outcome in the event 2 correct: $E(2 \text{ correct}) = \{RR\}$.

TABLE 9-2 Representation of guessing on the two-item, true–false test in probability terms

Outcomes on First Item	*Outcomes on Second Item*	*Total Number of Items Correct (Score Value)*
R	R	2 (RR)
	W	1 (RW)
W	R	1 (WR)
	W	0 (WW)
	#OS = 4	

From this information, the probability of getting each event or score value can be found:

$$p(E = 0) = \frac{\#E}{\#OS} = \frac{1}{4} = .25$$

$$p(E = 1) = \frac{\#E}{\#OS} = \frac{2}{4} = .50$$

$$p(E = 2) = \frac{\#E}{\#OS} = \frac{1}{4} = .25$$

This counting is summarized in Figures 9-2a, b. Figure 9-2a shows the three possible events or score values—0, 1, and 2—on the abscissa and the number of outcomes or frequency with which each score value can occur on the ordinate.

Example Problem 9.4

Suppose you roll two dice.
    a. Represent the outcome space for rolling the two dice.
    b. What is the probability of rolling a 7?

Like any frequency distribution, Figure 9-2a can be converted into a *relative frequency distribution* by dividing each frequency value (number of outcomes in an event) by *N*, the total number of outcomes in the outcome space (see Figure 9-2b). In symbol form, the relative frequency is given by Formula 9-1a.

$$\text{relative frequency} = \frac{\text{number of outcomes on ordinate}}{\text{number of outcomes in } OS} = \frac{\#E}{\#OS} \qquad \textbf{(9-1a)}$$

At this point, the value of a relative frequency distribution should be clear. *By converting a frequency distribution into a relative frequency distribution, we form a **probability distribution**.* See Formula 9-1b.

$$P(E) = \text{relative frequency of } E = \frac{\#E}{\#OS} \qquad \textbf{(9-1b)}$$

Now, let's derive the probability distribution for scores on a three-item test. First, the outcome space needs to be enumerated. As shown in Table 9-3, there are eight possible, equally likely outcomes: RRR, RRW, RWR, RWW, WRR, WRW, WWR, WWW.

Four events (four score values) can be observed with a three-item test: E(score value $= 0$), E(score value $= 1$), E(score value $= 2$), E(score value $= 3$). In short, a person can get a score ranging from 0 to 3 on a three-item, true–false test. There is one outcome associated with a score of 0: $E(0) = \{WWW\}$. There are three outcomes associated with (ways to get) a score of 1: $E(1) = \{RWW, WRW, WWR\}$. Likewise, there are three outcomes associated with a score of 2: $E(2) = \{RRW, RWR, WRR\}$. Finally, there is only one way to

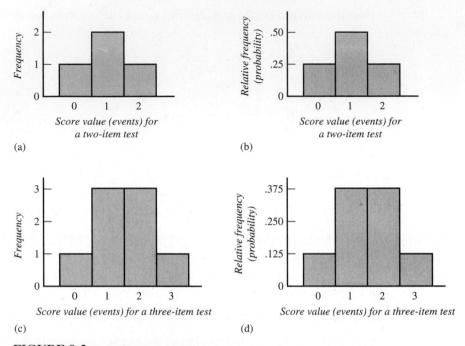

FIGURE 9-2
Frequency distributions and probability distributions: (a, b) for two items; (c, d) for three items

guess correctly on all the items: $E(3) = \{RRR\}$. These frequencies, or numbers of outcomes, associated with the events (score values) are the same as those shown in Figure 9-2c, as expected.

TABLE 9-3 Representation of guessing on the three-item, true–false test in probability terms

	Outcomes On		Number of Items
First Item	Second Item	Third Item	Correct (Score Value)
	R	R	3 (RRR)
		W	2 (RRW)
R		R	2 (RWR)
	W	W	1 (RWW)
	R	R	2 (WRR)
		W	1 (WRW)
W		R	1 (WWR)
	W	W	0 (WWW)
#OS = 2	#OS = 4	#OS = 8	

In order to convert the frequency distribution in Figure 9-2c into the probability distribution in Figure 9-2d, we must calculate the probability of each event:

$$p(E = 0) = \frac{\#E}{\#OS} = \frac{1}{8} = .125$$

$$p(E = 1) = \frac{\#E}{\#OS} = \frac{3}{8} = .375$$

$$p(E = 2) = \frac{\#E}{\#OS} = \frac{3}{8} = .375$$

$$p(E = 3) = \frac{\#E}{\#OS} = \frac{1}{8} = .125$$

These probabilities are placed on the ordinate of a graph and the score values are placed on the abscissa to form Figure 9-2d.

A lot of time and tedious counting could have been saved if we already had the probability distribution for guessing randomly on the three-item, true–false test. Figure 9-2d can be used to find the answer to the following question: "What is the probability of getting a score of 1 correct by guessing on a three-item, true–false test?" From this figure, the probability of a score of 1 is .375. Likewise, the probabilities of the scores 0, 2, and 3 can be found (.125, .375, and .125, respectively). Moreover, the probability of getting a score of two *or more* can be found by adding the probabilities for a score of 2 and a score of 3: .375 + .125 = .500.

Example Problem 9.5 ▀▀

Draw the relative frequency distribution for the roll of two dice and show that the probability of rolling a 7 is .17.

MATHEMATICAL DISTRIBUTIONS

At this point, three conclusions can be made about probability distributions. First, as the number of items on a true–false test increases, the amount of counting needed to determine the size of the outcome space and the event of interest increases greatly. A 10-item, true–false test has an outcome space of 1024 outcomes. This conclusion also holds as the number of dice rolled increases, as the number of coins flipped increases, as the number of multiple-choice questions increases, and, in general, as the number of trials increases.

Second, the number of outcomes increases in an orderly, lawlike manner as the number of trials (coins, true–false items, etc.) increases. For example, a toss of one coin produces an outcome space of 2, a toss of two coins produces an outcome space of 4, a toss of three coins produces an outcome space of 8, and a toss of four coins produces an outcome space of 16 outcomes. Thus, the counting process we have just gone through can be modeled mathematically (i.e., described by a mathematical formula), and the probability of each event of interest can be calculated directly without counting.

Third, reading probabilities from a probability distribution is a lot easier and less time-consuming than calculating probabilities by counting. Mathematical models that produce probabilities instead of our doing a lot of counting, then, are worthy of consideration.

When a distribution is derived from a mathematical model, it is referred to as a **mathematical distribution.** A very common mathematical model is the **binomial expansion.** It models situations in which each trial is independent of every other trial, two outcomes are possible on each trial, and the probability of success is the same from one trial to the next. Some examples are tossing coins (each coin is a trial), guessing on a true–false test (each item is a trial), or rolling dice (each die is a trial), and, for example, getting an even number or not. The mathematical distribution produced by the binomial expansion is called the binomial distribution; it can be used as a probability distribution for tossing coins or guessing on tests.

The purpose of developing the binomial distribution here is threefold: (1) to give you a sense of what a probability distribution is, (2) to show you that mathematical distributions can be used as probability distributions, and (3) to show you that these distributions provide information about the probability of an event. To begin, the binomial expansion is probably most familiar to you as presented in your elementary algebra course. There you were taught to expand an expression such as $(a + b)^2$ as follows:

$$(a + b)^2 = a^2 + 2ab + b^2$$

If, in this expression, a is replaced by the probability of success (p), b by the probability of not success (q), and the power (2 in this case) by the number of trials (N), then the binomial expansion can be written as shown in Formula 9-2.

Binominal expansion $= (p + q)^2$ **(9-2)**

For $(p + q)^2$, the expansion of Formula 9-2 results in three probabilities, each corresponding to one of three possible score values (0, 1, or 2):

$$p^2 + 2pq + q^2$$
$$\updownarrow \quad \updownarrow \quad \updownarrow$$
$$2 \quad 1 \quad 0$$

Notice that p^2 gives the probability of success on both trials ($p \cdot p$), q^2 gives the probability of failure on both ($q \cdot q$), and $2pq$ gives the probability of success on one trial (p) and of failure on the other (q) multiplied by the number of ways this event can happen.

To see how the binomial expansion can be used to produce a binomial distribution, consider a two-item, true–false test in which the examinee guessed the answer to each item. The probability of guessing correctly on an item is one-half, and the probability of guessing incorrectly is also one-half. Moreover, there are two items on the test, so there are two trials ($N = 2$). In this case, the binomial expansion can be written as:

$$(p+q)^2 = \left(\frac{1}{2}+\frac{1}{2}\right)^2$$

Notice that on a two-item test, the examinee can receive one of three scores: 0, 1, 2. The binomial expression, then, should produce a probability for each of the three possible score values. This is exactly what happens:

$$\left(\frac{1}{2}+\frac{1}{2}\right)^2 = \left(\frac{1}{2}\right)^2 + 2\left(\frac{1}{2}\right)\left(\frac{1}{2}\right) + \left(\frac{1}{2}\right)^2$$

$$= \frac{1}{4} + \frac{1}{2} + \frac{1}{4}$$

score: 2   1   0

If the results of this binomial expansion are cast into a relative frequency distribution with score values (0, 1, 2) on the abscissa and relative frequencies (1/4, 1/2, 1/4) on the ordinate, the result is a **binomial distribution** (shown in Figure 9-2b).

The binomial distribution can be found for any number of trials (N) and for any different values of p and q. (Note that $p + q = 1.00$.) The general form of the binomial expansion is given below followed by an example of a five item, true–false test.

$$(p+q)^N = p^N + Np^{N-1}q + \frac{N(N-1)}{1\times 2}p^{N-2}q^2 + \frac{N(N-1)(N-2)}{1\times 2 \times 3}p^{N-3}q^3 + \cdots + q^N$$

$$(p+q)^5 = p^5 + 5p^4q + \frac{5\times 4}{1\times 2}p^3q^2 + \frac{5\times 4 \times 3}{1\times 2 \times 3}p^2q^3 + \frac{5\times 4 \times 3 \times 2}{1\times 2 \times 3 \times 4}pq^4 + q^5$$

$$\left(\frac{1}{2}+\frac{1}{2}\right)^5 = \left(\frac{1}{2}\right)^5 + 5\left(\frac{1}{2}\right)^4\left(\frac{1}{2}\right) + 10\left(\frac{1}{2}\right)^3\left(\frac{1}{2}\right)^2 + 10\left(\frac{1}{2}\right)^2\left(\frac{1}{2}\right)^3 + 5\left(\frac{1}{2}\right)\left(\frac{1}{2}\right)^4 + \left(\frac{1}{2}\right)^5$$

$$= .0313 \qquad .1563 \qquad .3125 \qquad .3125 \qquad .1563 \qquad .0313$$

Score: 5   4   3   2   1   0

Example Problem 9.6

Consider a three-item, multiple-choice test with four alternatives on each item. Assuming guessing (independently) on each item (something we've all done?):
a. Use the binomial expansion to calculate the probability of each possible score on the test.
b. Graph the results as a probability distribution.

Actually, the binomial distribution is not one distribution but rather a whole family of distributions that depends on two parameters: (1) N, the number of trials in an experiment, and (2) p, the probability of success on any one trial. To see that there is a family of binomial distributions, compare the true–false example with the multiple-choice example. Figure 9-3 presents three binomial distributions in which p(success) = 1/2 and N = 3, 10, and infinity. Notice that as the number of trials increases, the binomial distribution becomes increasingly bell-shaped. In fact, when N = infinity (e.g., an infinite number of coin tosses) and p = 1/2, the binomial distribution becomes a *normal distribution* (Figure 9-3c).

Like the binomial distribution, the **normal distribution** is a family of mathematical distributions. It is particularly important because this theoretical distribution can be used to model many kinds of data collected in the behavioral sciences. Applications of the normal distribution are discussed extensively in the next chapter.

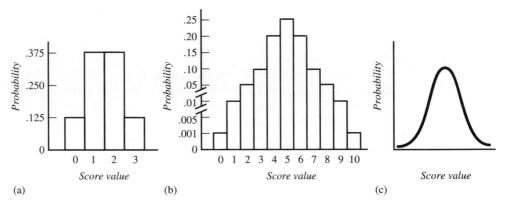

(a)   (b)   (c)

FIGURE 9-3

Binomial distributions with probability = .50: (a) for 3 trials; (b) for 10 trials; (c) for an infinite number of trials

The purpose in mentioning normal distributions here is that they, too, like the binomial distribution, could be derived mathematically or by counting—given enough time. We do not intend to take the time. However, after the development of the binomial distribution, you should have a sense of what a probability distribution is, recognize that mathematical distributions can be used as probability distributions when they are represented as relative frequency distributions, and realize that these distributions provide information about the probability of an event.

TO ANSWER THE QUESTION "HOW LIKELY?"

By now, you may be having some difficulty remembering why we got into probability theory. If you think back to the previous chapter, you will remember that in answering research questions with empirical data, the researcher can never be absolutely certain his answer is correct. Rather, the best that can be done is to collect data and state how likely those data are to arise if the null hypothesis is true. In order to make statements about how likely sample results are to occur under the null hypothesis, we had to develop some probability theory. Having developed the theory, we can apply it in answering the question. In fact, the remainder of this book deals just with this problem: "How likely are we to get the sample results under the null hypothesis?"

In order to show how the probability theory developed in this chapter can be used to answer the question "How likely?" consider an example using a true–false test. Suppose that a 10-item, true–false test is given to subjects after some experimental treatment. Perhaps the first question the researcher would like to answer is whether or not the subjects were guessing on the test. Her null hypothesis, then, is that the subjects were guessing— that is, that their performance was due to chance alone. Her alternative hypothesis is that they were not guessing.

Under the null hypothesis—that the subject's performance is due to chance or random guessing—we can think of each subject's score as being drawn from a binomial distribution in which the number of trials (N) is equal to 10 and the probability of success on each trial (p) is 1/2. The theoretical distribution for the number of correct responses under the null hypothesis is shown in Figure 9-3b. The null hypothesis is that subjects are guessing and should get about half of the true–false items correct ($10 \div 2 = 5$):

H_0: $\mu = 5$

The alternative hypothesis is that subjects' performance is not due to chance; that is, they are not randomly guessing. Thus the research hypothesis can be formally stated as follows:

H_1: $\mu \neq 5$

In a test of this hypothesis, suppose a single subject is drawn at random from the population proposed under the null hypothesis (the population of persons guessing at random), given the experimental treatment, and then tested. The question of interest is: "How likely is it that this subject could have obtained her score if she were actually guessing?" Suppose the person earned a score of 10 on the test. Under the null hypothesis that this person was guessing, how likely is she to obtain a score of 10 correct out of 10 possible? Intuition says that this event is *quite unlikely.* However, we can do better. Using the probability distribution under the null hypothesis (Figure 9-3b), we see that if the person were guessing, the probability of her earning a score of 10 would be 0.001. Quite unlikely! From this sample data, we should decide to reject the null hypothesis that the person was guessing. We therefore accept the alternative hypothesis that the person was not guessing at random.

Although there are many variations on this theme, this example can serve as a basis for all statistical inference. Assuming the null hypothesis is true, a probability distribution can be identified. Sample data are collected. Then the question is asked: "How likely would we be to get these sample data if they were drawn from the probability distribution identified under the null hypothesis?" If they are likely to arise from the hypothesized distribution, the null hypothesis is not rejected. If they are quite unlikely to arise under the null hypothesis (i.e., the probability is quite low), the null hypothesis should be rejected with the conclusion that the research hypothesis is correct. The chance of being incorrect in this case is quite small, depending on the criterion used to decide whether or not to reject the null hypothesis.

SUMMARY

This chapter presents basic concepts and skills in *probability theory* that are necessary to understand how that theory is used in making statistical inferences. Procedures for calculating *probabilities* are presented, and the use of *probability distributions* such as the *binomial* and *normal distributions* is discussed. Finally, the use of probability theory in statistical inference is illustrated.

ANSWERS TO EXAMPLE PROBLEMS

1. Intuition says: 1/4, or .25. This is consistent with probability theory: (1) there are four possible equally likely outcomes in guessing; (2) of these possible outcomes, only one will give the correct answer; (3) the probability of guessing correctly is given by the number of ways the favored outcome occurs ("right") over the total number of outcomes—1/4, or .25. This is shown in the table below. Note also that the abscissa of the frequency distribution and probability distribution is labeled right and wrong (there are three ways to guess wrong).

2. **a.** $p(A \text{ intersect } B) = 1/36 = .03$

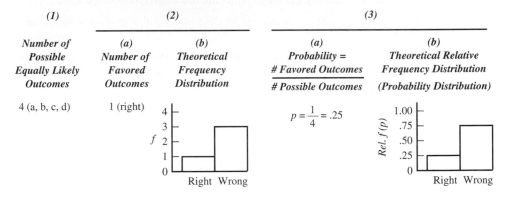

(1)	*(2)*		*(3)*	
Number of Possible Equally Likely Outcomes	*(a) Number of Favored Outcomes*	*(b) Theoretical Frequency Distribution*	*(a) Probability = # Favored Outcomes / # Possible Outcomes*	*(b) Theoretical Relative Frequency Distribution (Probability Distribution)*
4 (a, b, c, d)	1 (right)		$p = \dfrac{1}{4} = .25$	

   b. $p(A \text{ or } B \text{ or Both}) = 6/36 + 6/36 - 1/36 = 11/36 = .31$

3. The probability of correctly responding to an item is 1/4. The probability of correctly responding at random to all three items is given by the multiplicative rule:
   $(1/4)^3 = 1/64 = .016.$

4. **a.**

First Die	Second Die
	1
	2
1	3
	4
	5
	6
	1
	2
2	3
	4
	5
	6
⋮	⋮
	1
	2
6	3
	4
	5
	6
$OS = 6$	36

   b. $p(7) = 6/36 = 1/6 = .17$

5.

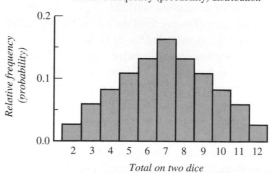

Relative frequency (probability) distribution

6. **a.**

Binomial Expression	Binomial Expansion	Probability	Score Value
$\left(\frac{1}{4} + \frac{3}{4}\right)^3$	$\left(\frac{1}{4}\right)^3$	.02	3
	$+ 3\left(\frac{1}{4}\right)^2\left(\frac{3}{4}\right)$	.14	2
	$+ 3\left(\frac{1}{4}\right)\left(\frac{3}{4}\right)^2$	.42	1
	$+ \left(\frac{3}{4}\right)^3$	.42	0

b.

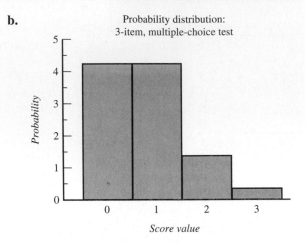

Probability distribution:
3-item, multiple-choice test

Score value

EXERCISES

The following exercises begin to build up your card-playing skills by asking you questions about the probability of certain events (e.g., getting dealt four aces with a well-shuffled deck of cards!). Assume a regular, well-shuffled (randomized) deck of cards (no jokers, no wild cards) unless otherwise specified.

1. What is the probability of being dealt a red card off the top of the deck?
2. What is the probability of being dealt a face card off the top of the deck?
3. What is the probability of being dealt an ace off the top after the first shuffle of the cards and then an ace after the second shuffle?
4. What is the probability of being dealt an ace off the top after the first shuffle of the cards or a red card after the second shuffle, or both?
5. Suppose that a new game of cards, called "Turtle" for some unknown reason, uses only clubs from a regular deck of cards. Moreover, only aces (as 1) and cards (clubs) numbered 2 through 5 are used. The game is played with two well-shuffled decks (1 through 5 of clubs). What is the probability that the sum of the two cards delt off the top of the decks would be 4?
6. Draw a probability (relative frequency) distribution for the possible outcomes in 5.
7. Consider a card game where the player receives a score of 1 if a diamond is dealt off the top of a well-shuffled deck, otherwise a 0. With four decks of cards, calculate the probability of each possible score in the game.
8. Graph the results in 7 as a probability distribution.

ANSWERS TO EXERCISES

1. There are 52 cards in a deck, half of them (26) red: p(red) = 26/52 = .50.
2. There are a total of 12 face cards in a deck (jack, queen, and king of clubs, diamonds, hearts, spades. p(face card) = 12/52 = .23.

3. The probability of getting an ace on the first trial is 4/52 = 1/13 and the probability on the second trial is 1/13. By the multiplicative rule, p(ace on two trials) = $(1/13)^2$ = 1/169 = .006.

4. First find p(A intersect B): Two aces are red cards (diamond, heart). So, p(ace intersect red card) = 2/52 = .04. Next determine p(ace, or red card, or both) = p(ace) + p(red card) − p(ace intersect red card) = 4/52 + 1/2 − 2/52 = 4/52 + 26/52 − 2/52 = 28/52 = .54.

5. There are 25 possible outcomes of drawing cards off two decks of 5 cards each (1 off deck 1, 1 off deck 2; 1 off deck 1, 2 off deck 2; . . . ; 5 off deck 1, 5 off deck 2). Event 4 can occur only 3 times (1 off deck 1, 3 off deck 2; 2 off deck 1, 2 off deck 2; and 3 off deck 1, 1 off deck 2). So, p(4) = 3/25 = .12.

6.

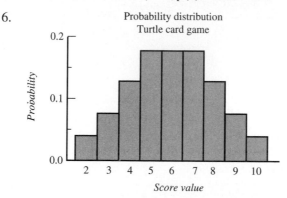

Probability distribution
Turtle card game

7. The probability of randomly drawing a diamond is 13/52 = .25. So the probability of not drawing a diamond is 39/52 = .75. So p = .25 and q = .75. With 4 decks of cards, the binomial expansion can be worked out as follows:

$$\left(\frac{1}{4} + \frac{3}{4}\right)^4 = \left(\frac{1}{4}\right)^4 + 4\left(\frac{1}{4}\right)^3\left(\frac{3}{4}\right) + \frac{4 \times 3}{1 \times 2}\left(\frac{1}{4}\right)^2\left(\frac{3}{4}\right)^2$$

$$+ \frac{4 \times 3 \times 2}{1 \times 2 \times 3}\left(\frac{1}{4}\right)\left(\frac{3}{4}\right)^3 + \left(\frac{3}{4}\right)^4$$

$$= .0039 + 4(.0156)(.75) + 6(.0625)(.0625)$$

$$+ 4(.25)(.4219) + .3164$$

$$= .0039 + .0234 + .0468 + .4219 + .3164$$

Score: 4   3   2   1   0

8.

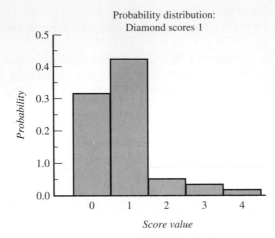

Probability distribution:
Diamond scores 1

10 Statistical Inference Using the Normal Distribution

- Basic Concepts Underlying Hypothesis Testing
- Statistical Inference about a Population Mean
- Applications of Hypothesis Testing: Inference about a Population Mean
- Statistical Inference about a Difference between Population Means
- Application of Hypothesis Testing: Inference about a Difference between Population Means
- Statistical Inference about a Population Correlation Coefficient
- Statistical Inference about a Difference between Population Correlation Coefficients
- Summary
- Answers to Example Problems
- Exercises
- Answers to Exercises

In this chapter, statistical procedures are developed to test hypotheses arising out of case I and case II research questions. Case I research asks: "Does a particular sample belong to a specified population?" For example, we might ask whether the heart rate of long-distance runners is, on average, the same as the heart rate of individuals in the general population, about 72 beats per minute. The null hypothesis would assert that there is no difference in heart rates. The alternative hypothesis might state that the average heart rate of runners is lower than that in the general population. To test the null hypothesis, a random sample of long-distance runners would be drawn from the population and their resting heart rates measured.

Case II research asks: "Do two samples belong to the same population?" For example, we might ask—as was done in the study of teacher expectancy (Chapter 2)—whether teachers' expectations of students' intellectual performance actually have an effect on students' performance. The null hypothesis would assert that the two groups would not differ, on average, in performance. The alternative hypothesis might conjecture that, on average, students expected to perform highly would do so. To test the null hypothesis, a random sample of 60 elementary school children might be drawn from a population of elementary school children. Half would be randomly assigned to the experimental group (labeled "bloomers") and half to the control group ($n_{Experimental} = n_{Control} = 30$). Teachers might be told that children in the experimental group were expected to show exceptional intellectual progress over the school year. At the end of the year, students in both groups might receive a test of intellectual ability to see if there is a performance difference.

BASIC CONCEPTS UNDERLYING HYPOTHESIS TESTING

Two fundamental ideas underlie statistical tests for case I and II research. The first idea is that the null hypothesis is *assumed* to be true until it is shown to be false. In case I research, this means that the difference between the sample mean heart rate of runners and the mean heart rate in the general population (72 bpm) is *assumed* to be due to chance. The greater the difference between the sample mean and the hypothesized population mean, the lower the probability that the difference is due to chance (all other things being equal, of course). If the difference is extremely large, we should conclude that the difference is not due to chance (i.e., reject the null hypothesis) and the sample was drawn from a different population than the general population (see Figure 10-1).

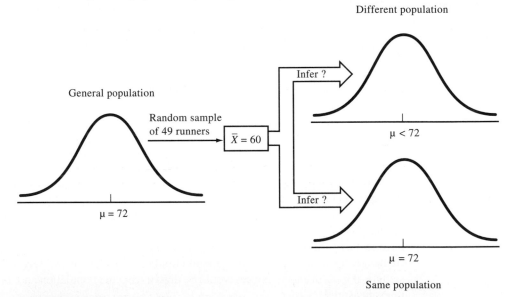

FIGURE 10-1
Schematic of inference from case I research (example: long-distance runners' heart rate)

In case II research, the assumption that the null hypothesis is true until shown to be false means that we assume that there is no difference between the population means of the experimental and control groups. A difference between the sample means of the experimental and control groups, then, must have arisen by chance. The greater the difference between sample means, the less likely it is that the difference is due to chance. If the sample difference is extremely large, we should conclude that the difference is not due to chance and the experimental and control samples were drawn from populations with different means (see Figure 10-2).

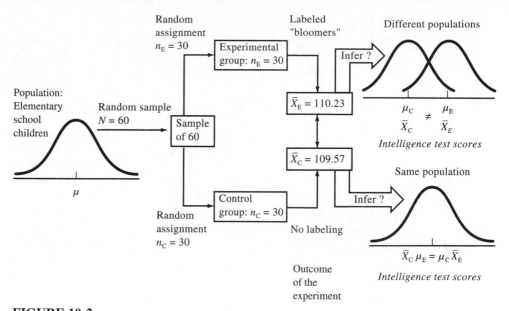

FIGURE 10-2
Schematic of inference from case II research (example: teacher expectancy study)

The second idea allows us to come to grips, formally, with statements like "due to chance," "the lower the probability," and the like. Stated for case I research, the idea is that a piece of research uses just one sample out of an indefinitely large number of samples that could have been taken from the population specified under the null hypothesis. Furthermore, if a large number of samples were drawn from this population, each sample mean would not be exactly the same value as most of the others. Rather, the sample means would differ from one another and from the mean of the population. (Assuming the null hypothesis is true, this variation in means from one sample to the next happens because the samples are small relative to the indefinitely large population.) In order to determine whether the particular sample mean obtained in a research study actually was drawn from the population specified in the null hypothesis, we need to know how much "bounce" to expect in means from one sample to the next. That is, we need to know about the distribution of means sampled from that population.

Imagine a frequency distribution with values of *sample means* on the abscissa and relative frequencies on the ordinate (see Figure 10-3a). This distribution shows the relative frequency of each possible sample mean value for a given sample size. It is called a *sampling distribution of means.* A sample mean can be located on the abscissa to determine whether it falls in the center of the distribution or at the extreme ends of the distribution. The farther the sample mean lies from the center of the sampling distribution—the farther it is from the hypothesized population mean value—the greater the chances are that the discrepancy is not due to chance but represents a systematic difference. The sampling distribution of means, then, serves as a yardstick for determining just how deviant a sample mean is from the hypothesized population mean under the null hypothesis.

A parallel argument can be made for case II research. Rather than talk about a single sample mean, we speak of a single sample *difference-between-means* (e.g., $\bar{X}_{Experimental}$ −

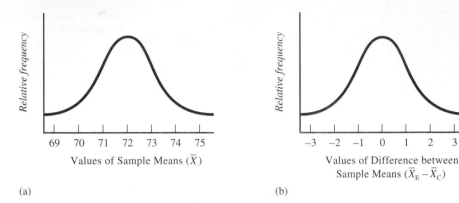

FIGURE 10-3

(a) Sampling distribution of means (example: long-distance runners' heart rate) and (b) sampling distribution of differences between means (example: teacher expectancy study)

$\bar{X}_{\text{Control}}$). This sample difference between means will probably not equal 0, the hypothesized difference between population means under the null hypothesis of "no difference." Assuming the null hypothesis is true, this difference arises from "sampling error": Not all subjects in the two populations (experimental and control) are included in the (small) samples. Furthermore, the mean differences will vary from one sample to the next for the same reason. In order to determine whether the particular sample mean difference obtained in a research study actually was drawn from the populations specified in the null hypothesis, we need a model of how much "bounce" in sample mean differences to expect when the samples are drawn from identical populations.

Now imagine a frequency distribution with values of *sample-mean-differences* on the abscissa ($\bar{X}_{\text{Experimental}} - \bar{X}_{\text{Control}}$) and relative frequencies on the ordinate (Figure 10-3b). This distribution shows the relative frequency of each possible sample mean difference value for a given sample size. It is called a *sampling distribution of differences between means*. A sample mean difference can be located on the abscissa to determine whether it falls in the center of the distribution or at the extreme ends of the distribution. The farther the sample difference lies from the center of the sampling distribution—the farther it lies from the hypothesized mean population difference of 0—the greater the chances are that the discrepancy is not due to chance but represents a systematic difference. The sampling distribution of differences between means, then, serves as a yardstick for determining just how deviant a sample difference is from the hypothesized difference of 0 under the null hypothesis.

The ideas presented in this chapter form the bedrock of statistical inference. You should try your "damnedest" to understand them. To reiterate, so far, the first idea is that the null hypothesis is assumed to be true until shown to be false. This assumption allows us to specify a particular population from which, we hypothesize, we are sampling. The second idea is that a research study typically uses just one sample out of an indefinitely large number of samples that could have been taken. The third idea is that any particular sample may not give a precise picture of what is true in the population. Because the sample constitutes only a small portion of the population, it can be in error. This error might arise due to faulty measurements, due to a disproportionately large number of subjects with certain characteristics in this particular sample ("luck of the draw"), or some combination of the two. The fourth idea is that we need a way to determine just how much sampling error to expect if we draw repeated samples of a certain size from a population. One way to do this is to repeatedly draw samples from the same population (specified by the null hypothesis), calculate an estimator such as the mean for each sample, and plot the sample means, as shown in Figure 10-3a. The spread of this "sampling distribution of means" tell us just how much error—bounce in the sample means—to expect from one sample to the next. Finally, everything I've said about sampling a single mean applies directly to sampling means from two identical populations (assuming the null hypothesis is true) and calculating their differences (see Figure 10-3b). Instead of thinking about sampling a single mean, think about sampling a single difference between means. This may help you get your mind around this idea of a difference between means.

It turns out that we do not need to go to the bother of repeatedly sampling from a population to know about the sampling distribution of means. As you will see very soon, the normal distribution provides a good model for the sampling distribution. To see how this works, I begin by developing, in some detail, the rationale for using the normal distribution as a sampling distribution of means and then show how the normal sampling distribution permits us to test hypotheses and draw inferences. Next, exactly the same ideas are applied to differences between means. Finally, I show how the normal sampling distribution can be used to test hypotheses about correlations, and differences between correlations.

STATISTICAL INFERENCE ABOUT A POPULATION MEAN

Recall that researchers set out to reject the null hypothesis and gain support for the alternative hypothesis. A decision about H_0, based on sample data, bears on what the population of subjects, students, observations, and so on looks like. In order to decide, we need to know what to expect in a study if the null hypothesis is actually true. In making inferences about the mean of a population from a sample mean, we need a *model to indicate just how much variability to expect in sample means drawn randomly from the population under the null hypothesis.* From this model of chance sample means, we can decide whether or not our sample mean was within the expected range. If it is expected, the null hypothesis cannot be rejected.[1] If it is unexpected—unlikely to arise by chance sampling under the null hypothesis—we might decide to reject the null hypothesis and conclude that our alternative hypothesis is true.

Sampling Distribution of Means

A model that characterizes the variability of sample means drawn from a population specified by the null hypothesis is the sampling distribution of means. It works as follows: In theory, an indefinitely large number of samples could be drawn from the population specified

---

[1]We speak of not rejecting the null hypothesis rather than accepting it because even though we cannot reject the null hypothesis on the basis of sample data, we do not know that its value is exactly that of the true population mean. After all, we could be off by a few tenths of a point or even more.

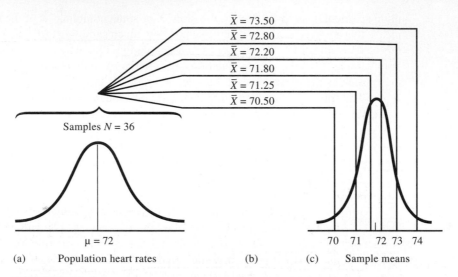

$\bar{X} = 73.50$
$\bar{X} = 72.80$
$\bar{X} = 72.20$
$\bar{X} = 71.80$
$\bar{X} = 71.25$
$\bar{X} = 70.50$

Samples $N = 36$

$\mu = 72$

70 71   72 73   74

(a)   Population heart rates   (b)   (c)   Sample means

FIGURE 10-4

The concept of a sampling distribution of means: (a) theoretical population of heart rates (HRs) with a mean μ_{HR} equal to 72 beats per minute and a standard deviation σ_{HR} of 9 bpm; (b) six means that were drawn randomly from the population with $\mu_{HR} = 72$ and $\sigma_{HR} = 9$; each mean is based on a sample of 36 subjects' heart rates; (c) sampling distribution of means based on samples of size 36

by the null hypothesis. Furthermore, in theory, a mean could be calculated for each sample. For example, suppose the null hypothesis is that the mean heart rate (HR) in the population is 72 (Figure 10-4a). Due to sampling error, the sample means drawn from this population will differ from one another (Figure 10-4b). Nevertheless, they will cluster around the central value—the population mean: $\mu = 72$ (Figure 10-4c).

In order to get a picture of the variability in sample means that could be expected from sampling under the null hypothesis, we could plot the sample means as a frequency polygon with the abscissa representing the values of the sample means and the ordinate representing the frequency or relative frequency with which each value is observed. Such a theoretical distribution is called a **sampling distribution of means.** The theoretical sampling distribution of means for samples of 36 subjects, each drawn from the population specified by the null hypothesis, is shown in Figure 10-4c. Notice that the mean of the sampling distribution of means is equal to the population mean and that the variability of the sample means (Figure 10-4c) is much less than the variability of the HRs themselves (Figure 10-4a). This result happens because there are more scores in the middle of a score distribution than at the ends of the distribution, so that the sample mean is more likely to be based on these middle scores than on the extreme scores. (We will return to this point shortly.) *The sampling distribution, then, provides a model of the variability of sample means* based on samples of 36 subjects from the population specified by the null hypothesis.

To illustrate how the sampling distribution of means is used in research, consider the hypothetical study of long-distance runners' heart rates. Researchers want to know whether the population of runners they plan to randomly sample has a mean HR of 72, like the general population, or whether the subjects represent a population with a mean HR different from (less than) 72. They begin by stating the null and alternative hypotheses: H_0: μ_{HR} = 72; and H_1: $\mu_{HR} \neq 72$ (or H_1: $\mu_{HR} < 72$). Then a sample of 36 runners is drawn randomly and its mean HR calculated. In our example, the sample mean was 65. Under the assumption that the null hypothesis is true, the sampling distribution shown in Figure 10-4c suggests that the sample mean is most likely to fall within the range of 70.5 to 73.5. Is a sample mean of 65 or less a likely outcome under the null hypothesis? What is the basis for your decision?[2]

The importance of the sampling distribution of means is that it provides a model of what is likely to occur if the null hypothesis is true. Conceptually, this model is formed by assuming that repeated, random samples of size N can be drawn from a population specified under the null hypothesis. The sample for a study, then, is just one of many that might have been drawn. If a mean is calculated for each sample, these sample means will differ from one another just by chance. These differences give rise to errors in inferring from the sample to the population. By taking repeated samples, we can specify just how much variability to expect among sample means. Using this variability as a yardstick, we can determine how likely it is that an observed sample mean in a research study arose under the null hypothesis. If, according to the yardstick, the mean falls close to the hypothesized population mean, the null hypothesis should not be rejected. If the mean does not fall close to the hypothesized population mean, a decision to reject H_0 should be made.

Characteristics of the Sampling Distribution of Means

From mathematical statistics, we know that if repeated random samples of size N are drawn from a normally distributed population, the distribution of sample means has the following characteristics:

1. It will be normally distributed.
2. It will have a mean equal to the population mean.
3. It will have a standard deviation—called the standard error of the mean—equal to the population standard deviation divided by the square root of the sample size.

Furthermore, if N is large, the **central limit theorem** (see what follows) states that the sampling distribution of means will be approximately normal, even though the population is not normally distributed.

Shape of the Sampling Distribution.   For samples of 30 subjects or more, the sampling distribution of means will be approximately normal for a wide variety of differently shaped population distributions. As stated before, if the distribution of scores in the population is normal, so will be the sampling distribution of means, regardless of N. However, if there is no available information about the shape of the distribution of scores in the population, the **central limit theorem** states that as the sample size increases, the shape of the sampling distribution of means becomes increasingly like the normal distribution. For a sample of size 30, the normal distribution provides a reasonably good approximation of the

---

[2]The outcome is unlikely since this sample mean falls way below the hypothesized population.

sampling distribution of means. So $N = 30$ is used, as a rule, for inferring the shape of the sampling distribution.

The relation between sample size and shape of the sampling distribution of means is shown in Figure 10-5. Figure 10-5a shows the distribution of scores in the population. A population distribution that is flat or rectangular rather than normal was intentionally chosen to show that even in this case, with samples of size 30 or more, the sampling distribution of means approaches normality. Figure 10-5b shows the sampling distribution of means based on a sample size of 2. Notice that the distribution has slight peaks in the center. Figure 10-5c shows the sampling distribution based on samples of size 4. The distribution is becoming increasingly symmetric about the population mean. Finally, Figure 10-5d shows the sampling distribution based on samples of size 36. This sampling distribution of means can be described as normal.

Mean of the Sampling Distribution.   The mean of the sampling distribution of means is the population mean. It is the population mean because the sample mean is an unbiased estimator of the population mean. That is, for random samples from any population, the long-run average of the sample means will equal the population mean.

Standard Error of the Mean.   The standard deviation of sample means in a sampling distribution of means is called the **standard error of the mean.** It provides an index of how much the sample means vary about the population mean (the mean of the sampling distribution). Thus it provides information about the amount of error likely to be made by inferring the value of the population mean from a sample mean. The greater the variability among sample means, the greater the chance is that the inference about the population mean from a single sample mean will be in error.

The standard error of the mean ($\sigma_{\bar{X}}$) is a function of the population standard deviation (σ) and the sample size (N), as shown in Formula 10-1.

$$\sigma_{\bar{X}} = \frac{\sigma}{\sqrt{N}}$$ (10-1)

Formula 10-1 indicates that as N increases, $\sigma_{\bar{X}}$ decreases, since σ is the same regardless of sample size. This relationship between sample size and the standard error makes intuitive sense if we take note of two things:

1. The mean is greatly influenced by extreme scores.
2. There are usually more scores near the center of a distribution than at the extremes.

In a small sample (e.g., $N = 4$), most of the scores would fall around the population mean, but one extreme score would greatly influence the value of a sample mean. Thus, from sample to sample (of $N = 4$), considerable variability between means should be expected. However, in a large sample (e.g., $N = 121$), the existence of a few extreme scores might be balanced by scores at the other extreme of the distribution and greatly outweighed by the large number of scores close to the population mean. In this case, the differences between sample means should be small.

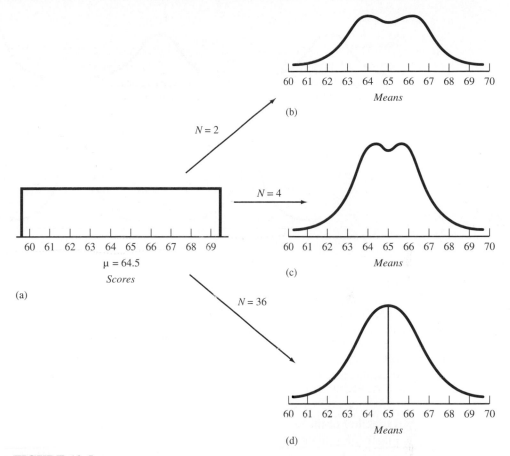

FIGURE 10-5

Relationship between sample size and the shape of the sampling distribution of means (after Clarke et al., 1965): (a) frequency distribution of scores in the population; (b) sampling distribution from samples of size 2; (c) sampling distribution from samples of size 4; (d) sampling distribution from samples of size 36

In order to illustrate the importance of this relationship between sample size and standard error, consider the sampling distributions shown in Figure 10-6. Figure 10-6a shows the distribution of scores in some hypothetical population with a mean equal to 50 and a standard deviation of 10 points. Figure 10-6b shows the distribution of means based on a sample size of 1. Notice that this sampling distribution of means is the same as the population distribution, since there is no difference between a mean based on one score and the score itself. Figure 10-6c shows a sampling distribution based on samples of size 2. The variability of this sampling distribution is less than that of the population distribution. Figure 10-6d shows a sampling distribution based on samples of size 16. The variability of this distribution is considerably smaller than that of the preceding sampling distributions. The

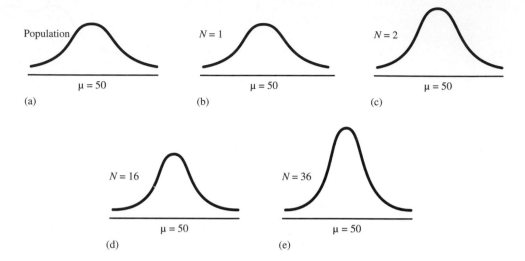

FIGURE 10-6

Relationship between sample size and the standard error of the mean (samples drawn from a population with scores normally distributed): (a) distribution of scores in a hypothetical population with $\mu = 50$, $\sigma = 10$; (b) sampling distribution of means based on sample sizes of $N = 1$; $\sigma_{\bar{X}} = 10/\sqrt{1} = 10$; (c) sampling distribution of means based on sample sizes of $N = 2$; $\sigma_{\bar{X}} = 10/\sqrt{2} = 7.07$; (d) sampling distribution of means based on sample sizes of $N = 16$; $\sigma_{\bar{X}} = 10/\sqrt{16} = 2.50$; (e) sampling distribution of means based on sample sizes of $N = 36$; $\sigma_{\bar{X}} = 10/\sqrt{36} = 1.67$

 variability of the sampling distribution based on samples of size 36 is the smallest of all. Finally, if a sample of "size infinity" were drawn, the standard error would equal zero. *As sample size increases, the standard error of the mean decreases.* The larger the sample, on the average, the smaller is the error made in inferring the population mean from a sample mean.

Example Problem 10.1 ━━━

The results of a statewide testing program of high school seniors in California showed a mean of 50 and standard deviation of 14 on a measure of mechanical ability. Suppose a large number of samples of 49 seniors were drawn at random and a mean calculated for each sample.

   a. What *shape* will this sampling distribution of means take?

   b. What is the *mean* of this sampling distribution of means?

   c. What is the standard error of the mean (i.e., the standard deviation of the sampling distribution of means)?

Sampling Distribution as a Probability Distribution. The sampling distribution of means can be used as a probability distribution to answer questions about how likely a particular sample mean is to arise under the null hypothesis. Recall that in the previous chapter, probability was defined as the relative frequency of an event. Thus, a frequency distribution of scores can be converted into a probability distribution by converting it to a relative frequency distribution. Since the sampling distribution is a frequency distribution for means, means are sampled and not scores. An event is defined as a mean equal to or less than a particular value. Thus, the probability of an event—a sample mean—is:

$$p(\text{event}) = p(\bar{X} \leq \text{particular value})$$

$$\approx \frac{\text{frequency of (sample means} \leq \text{particular value)}}{\text{total number of means sampled}}$$

$$= \text{cumulative relative frequency}$$

Suppose 200 sample means were drawn and 10 of them were less than or equaled 55. The probability of observing a sample mean less than or equal to 55, then, is:

$$p(\bar{X} \leq 55) = \frac{\text{frequency of (sample means} \leq 55)}{\text{total number of means sampled}} = \frac{10}{200} = .05$$

The probability of observing a sample mean less than or equal to 55 is the cumulative relative frequency of that event—that is, $10/200 = .05$. Thus, by converting the sampling distribution of means to a cumulative relative frequency distribution, we can use this distribution as a probability distribution. Since the sampling distribution is a normal distribution with a mean equal to μ under the null hypothesis and a standard deviation (standard error) equal to $\sigma_{\bar{X}}$, this distribution can be used to find probabilities and answer the question "How likely was this sample mean to arise, assuming the null hypothesis is true?"

Finding Probabilities in the Sampling Distribution of Means

The sampling distribution of means is approximately normal for sample sizes of 30 or more. With this rule of thumb, we usually need not worry about the shape of the distribution of scores in the population. When the area under the normal curve is considered as relative area (cumulative relative frequency), it may be interpreted as probability (see Figure 10-7a). And when the area is divided into blocks of 1 standard deviation each, as in Figure 10-7b, the probabilities in various parts of the distribution are known. For example, the relative area beyond 2 standard errors (standard deviations) above the mean is .0228; the probability of observing a sample mean 2 standard errors or more above the population mean specified in the null hypothesis is .0228 (Figure 10-7b).

In order to use Table B at the end of the book to find the probabilities under the normal curve, we must convert the means on the abscissa of the sampling distribution of means to z scores in a manner analogous to converting raw scores to z scores (Formula 5-1):

raw scores: $$z = \frac{X - \bar{X}}{s}$$ *x - moyenne de l'échantillon*

écart -type " "

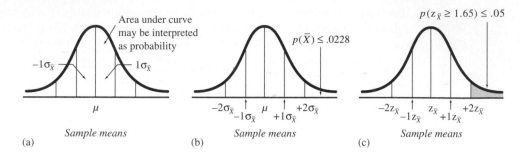

FIGURE 10-7

Sampling distribution of means as a probability distribution: (a) sampling distribution of means as a probability distribution with mean μ and standard error (standard deviation) $\sigma_{\bar{X}}$; (b) probabilities may be found by dividing the normal sampling distribution into standard error (standard deviation) units; (c) probabilities may be found in the unit normal distribution by transforming to $z_{\bar{X}}$ scores

For sample means, we use Formula 10-2.

$$z_{\bar{X}} = \frac{\bar{X} - \mu}{\sigma_{\bar{X}}}$$ **(10-2)**

Notice that the z scores corresponding to means in the sampling distribution are denoted by $z_{\bar{X}}$, which reminds us that we are dealing with a sampling distribution of means and not raw scores. Furthermore, note that $\sigma_{\bar{X}}$ indicates how many standard errors (standard deviations in a sampling distribution) a sample mean falls below or above the mean μ of the distribution. Hence the statistical test based on the normal distribution is called the $z_{\bar{X}}$ test.

In order to become familiar with using the sampling distribution of means as a probability distribution, consider a sampling distribution with $\mu = 50$ and $\sigma_{\bar{X}}$ (Figure 10-8a). What is the probability of observing a sample mean of 55 or above? The conceptual problem is shown in Figure 10-8b. First, convert the sample mean of 55 to $z_{\bar{X}=55}$:

$$z_{\bar{X}} = \frac{55 - 50}{5} = \frac{5}{5} = 1$$

Note that we are dealing with the upper tail of the sampling distribution and that we need to know the relative area in the small portion of the normal distribution. Using Table B, locate a score of 1 in the left column, and find the relative area under the smaller portion of the curve—in this case, .1587. Finally, since relative area can be interpreted as probability, the probability of observing a sample mean of 55 or more is .1587. Procedure 10-1 summarizes these steps.

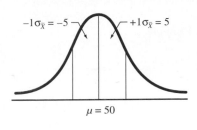 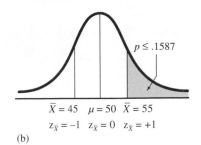

(a)   (b)

FIGURE 10-8
Finding probabilities by using the normal sampling distribution of means: (a) sampling distribution of means with $\mu = 50$ and $\sigma_{\bar{X}} = 5$; (b) probability of observing a sample mean equal to or greater than 55 shown in the shaded area

---

PROCEDURE 10-1 Steps in identifying the probability of observing a sample mean at or above (below) some value

Operation	Example
1. Convert $\bar{X}$ to $z_{\bar{X}}$ by using Formula 10-2: $$z_{\bar{X}} = \frac{\bar{X} - \mu}{\sigma_{\bar{X}}}$$	Example 1: What is the probability of observing a sample mean of 55 or more if $\mu = 50$ and $\sigma_{\bar{X}} = 5$? $$z_{\bar{X}} = \frac{55 - 50}{5} = 1$$ Example 2: What is the probability of observing a sample mean of 38.40 or less if $\mu = 50$ and $\sigma_{\bar{X}} = 5$? $$z_{\bar{X}} = \frac{38.40 - 50}{5} = \frac{-11.60}{5} = -2.32$$ Example 3: What is the probability of observing a sample mean of 60 or more or 40 or less? $$z_{\bar{X}=60} = \frac{60 - 50}{5} = 2.00$$ $$z_{\bar{X}=40} = \frac{40 - 50}{5} = -2.00$$
2. Specify the tail of the sampling distribution to be identified.	Example 1: 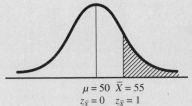

Operation_____   Example_____

Example 2:

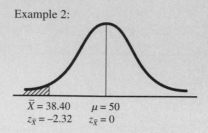

$\bar{X} = 38.40$ $\mu = 50$
$z_{\bar{X}} = -2.32$ $z_{\bar{X}} = 0$

Example 3:

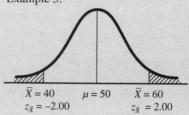

$\bar{X} = 40$ $\mu = 50$ $\bar{X} = 60$
$z_{\bar{X}} = -2.00$ $z_{\bar{X}} = 2.00$

3. Using Table B, locate the probability of $z_{\bar{X}}$.
See Procedure 5-3 for a review.

Example 1: Since the area to be identified constitutes the smaller portion of the curve, locate a z score of 1 in the first column of Table B and read across to column 4: $p = .1587$. The probability of observing a sample mean of 55 or more under $H_0 : \mu = 50$ is .16.

Example 2: This area also constitutes the smaller tail of the curve. Since the normal distribution is symmetric, the area above a score of 2.32 is the same as that below a score of -2.32. From column 4 of Table B, $p = .0102$. The probability of observing a sample mean of 38.40 or less under $H_0 : \mu = 50$ is .01. Quite improbable!

Example 3: First, locate the area above a $z_{\bar{X}}$ score of 2.00 (small tail of curve) by locating a $z_{\bar{X}}$ of 2.00 in column 1 of Table B and reading across to column 4. This probability is $p = .0228$. Since the normal curve is symmetric, the area below a $z_{\bar{X}}$ score of -2.00 is equal to the area above a $z_{\bar{X}}$ score of 2.00. Thus, this probability is also .0228. To find the total probability, simply sum these values: $p = .0228 + .0228 = .0456$. The probability of observing a sample mean of 60 or more or 40 or less under $H_0 : \mu = 50$ is about .05.

Example Problem 10.2

Suppose $\mu = 20$ and $\sigma_{\bar{X}} = 2$. What is the probability of observing the following sample means?
  a. 26 or greater
  b. 16 or less
  c. 16 or less or 24 or more

Significance Level α: What Do You Mean, "Unlikely"?   Since the sampling distribution of means can be modeled by a normal probability distribution, this distribution can be used to answer the question "Assuming the null hypothesis is true, what is the probability of obtaining a sample mean as large or larger than the one observed?" If sample means of this size or greater are quite *unlikely* to be observed (i.e., quite improbable), a decision to reject the null hypothesis should be made. However, if sample means are likely to arise under the null hypothesis, a decision not to reject the null hypothesis should be made.

The problem, then, is to define operationally what is meant by *unlikely*. By convention, an unlikely sample result—for example, a sample mean at or above (below) some extreme value—is defined as one whose probability of occurrence is less than or equal to a fixed small quantity: .05 or .01. This convention grew out of experimental settings in which the error of rejecting a true H_0 was very serious. For example, in medical research, the null hypothesis might be that a particular drug produces undesirable effects. Deciding that the medicine is safe (i.e., rejecting H_0) can have serious consequences. Hence, conservatism is desired. Often in behavioral research, however, the consequences are not so dire. For example, suppose an instructor is to select one of two texts of approximately equal cost. The instructor might conduct a study to determine which book leads to greater achievement, satisfaction, or both. In this case, the instructor might be willing to reject the null hypothesis on the basis of a probability less than or equal to .25. If, in fact, there is no true difference between the texts, the "error" of selecting one over the other is not particularly serious. If the decision is correct, teacher and students alike benefit. Some wisdom, then, should be exercised in setting the level of significance (see "Trade-Off between Level of Significance and Power of the Statistical Test" in Chapter 11).

This definition of an unlikely sample result in probability terms is called the **level of significance** of the statistical test. The level of significance is often denoted by the Greek letter α (alpha): $\alpha = .05$ or $\alpha = .01$. It leads to the following decision rule: *Reject the null hypothesis if the probability of obtaining a sample mean at or beyond a certain value is less than or equal to .05 (or .01); otherwise, do not reject the null hypothesis.*

Reject H_0 if $p \leq .05$ (or .01).

Do not reject H_0 if $p > .05$ (or .01).

This decision rule, then, defines an unlikely event in a research study as one that occurs 5 times in 100 or less (.05) or 1 time in 100 or less (.01) assuming the null hypothesis is true. Thus, the rule implies that we are willing to make an error 5 times in 100 (or 1 time in 100) and reject the null hypothesis when it is actually true. The probability of making this error—rejecting a true null hypothesis—is denoted by the level of significance α. When $\alpha = .05$, this value means that we are willing to make an error by rejecting a true null hypothesis in 5 studies out of 100. This margin of error seems reasonable since it is much more probable that extreme sample means are drawn from an alternative population with a different mean. Note also that when we set $\alpha = .05$, a correct decision *not to reject the null hypothesis* will be made 95 times in 100 $(1 - .05 = .95)$.

Significance Level and the Sampling Distribution of Means.   The significance level defines unlikely sample means as those that would occur in no more than, say, 5 samples in 100 if the null hypothesis were true. Since the sampling distribution of means for $N = 30$ can be modeled by a normal probability distribution, the level of significance can be marked off in the sampling distribution. It is marked off by identifying that part of the sampling distribution beyond which the probability of observing a sample mean is less than .05. In order to find this part of the sampling distribution, identify the critical value of $z_{\bar{x}}$ beyond which 5 percent of the sample means fall (i.e., $p \le .05$); this critical value of $z_{\bar{x}}$ is often called $z_{\bar{X}\text{ critical}}$. From Table B, $z_{\bar{X}\text{critical}}$ equals 1.65 for $\alpha = .05$. Figure 10-9a shows a sampling distribution with $\mu = 50$ and $\sigma_{\bar{x}} = 5$ in which $\alpha = .05$ is denoted by the shaded area. A sample mean falling in the shaded area would lead to a decision to reject the null hypothesis H_0: $\mu = 50$. Likewise, Figure 10-9b shows the level of significance at $\alpha = .01$ in the lower tail of the sampling distribution; $z_{\bar{X}\text{critical}}$ equals -2.33. A sample mean falling in this shaded area would lead to a decision to reject the null hypothesis $\mu = 50$. Notice that as the level of significance becomes more stringent, the area under the distribution leading to a rejection of the null hypothesis becomes smaller.

The only problem now is to decide which tail of the normal distribution to use as the critical region for rejecting the null hypothesis. As shown in the next section, this decision is not as arbitrary as Figure 10-9 suggests.

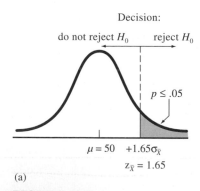
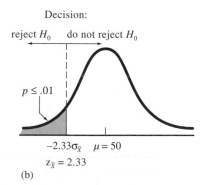

FIGURE 10-9
Critical regions for rejecting the null hypothesis: (a) level of significance $\alpha = .05$ in the upper tail; (b) level of significance $\alpha = .01$ in the lower tail

Example Problem 10.3

Suppose a study was conducted with $\alpha = .05$ so that $z_{\bar{X}\text{ critical}} = 1.65$. What decision would you make about H_0 if the observed (calculated) value of $z_{\bar{x}}$ is as follows?
   a.   1.90
   b.   1.50

The Alternative Hypothesis and the Tail You Seek

The tipoff about which tail to seek in the sampling distribution is given by the alternative hypothesis. Recall from Chapter 8 that there are three possible alternative hypotheses that can be posed as a rival to the null hypothesis:

H_1: $\mu > 50$

H_1: $\mu < 50$

H_1: $\mu \neq 50$

The first two hypotheses are **directional;** they indicate the direction of the difference between the mean of the population under the null hypothesis and the mean of the population under the alternative hypothesis. *If the alternative hypothesis predicts the true population mean to be above the mean in the null hypothesis, the critical region for rejecting the null hypothesis lies in the upper tail of the sampling distribution* (Figure 10-10a). *If the alternative hypothesis predicts the true population mean to be below the mean in the null hypothesis, the critical region for rejecting the null hypothesis lies in the lower tail of the sampling distribution* (Figure 10-10b). Directional hypotheses are sometimes called **one-tail hypotheses** because the critical region for rejecting the null hypothesis falls in only one tail of the probability distribution.

The third alternative hypothesis, H_1: $\mu \neq 50$, is **nondirectional.** It predicts that the true mean does not equal the mean in the null hypothesis, but it does not say whether it is below or above. Thus, we must consider the critical region to be either tail of the distribution. *If the alternative hypothesis is nondirectional, the critical region for rejecting the null hypothesis lies in both tails of the sampling distribution.*

In order to test the null hypothesis against a nondirectional alternative hypothesis at α = .05, mark off critical regions in both tails of the distribution as $\alpha/2 = .05/2 = .025$. (See Figure 10-10c.) We use $\alpha/2$ because we want to mark off no more than a total of 5 percent of the normal sampling distribution as a critical region for testing the null hypothesis: .025 + .025 = .05. Note that if we marked off both tails at α = .05, we would have actually marked off 10 percent of the distribution: .05 + .05 = .10. By using $\alpha/2$, we set the significance level at α = .05. Nondirectional alternative hypotheses are sometimes called **two-tail hypotheses** because the critical region for rejecting the null hypothesis lies in both tails of the probability distribution.

Basis for Choosing a One-Tail or Two-Tail Test.   The choice of a directional or nondirectional hypothesis depends upon how much is known about the phenomena being studied. If a *theory* predicts the direction of the outcome of a study, a directional alternative hypothesis may be used. If there is strong *empirical evidence* (i.e., prior research studies) suggesting the direction of the outcome of a study, a directional alternative hypothesis may also be used. Of course, if both theory and empirical evidence suggest the outcome of a study, a directional research hypothesis should be used. But whenever there is doubt about the outcome of a study, either because prior research has yielded conflicting outcomes or because theory inadequately predicts the outcome, a nondirectional alternative hypothesis should be used. When in doubt about whether to use a directional or nondirectional hypothesis, use a nondirectional hypothesis. Null hypotheses rejected on the basis of the two-tail hypothesis will also be rejected with a one-tail hypothesis. In decisions about whether or

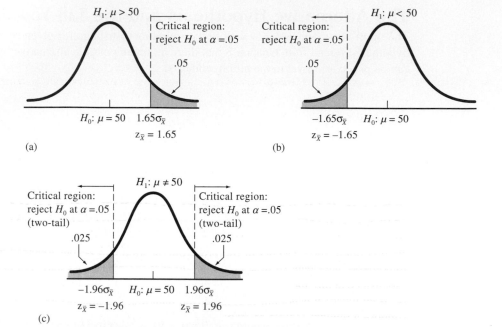

FIGURE 10-10

Critical regions of the sampling distribution of means for rejecting H_0 under directional (one-tail) and nondirectional (two-tail) research hypothesis when $\alpha = .05$; (a) directional H_1 (one-tail test); (b) directional H_1 (one-tail test); (c) nondirectional H_1 (two-tail test)

not to reject the null hypothesis, conservatism is usually preferred (but see the beginning of the section "Significance Level α").

The following question often arises: "What if you test a one-tail hypothesis and the sample mean turns out to be significantly far from H_0 in the *opposite* direction?" The answer to this question can be seen from a precise statement of the null hypothesis for a directional statistical test:

H_0: $\mu \leq$ some value

H_1: $\mu >$ some value

or

H_0: $\mu \geq$ some value

H_1: $\mu <$ some value

Once the null hypothesis is stated in its fullest form, we see that a sample mean falling in an extreme but opposite direction falls within the domain of the null hypothesis, and so the null hypothesis should not be rejected.[3] Furthermore, if this situation happens, it raises seri-

---

[3]In testing the null hypothesis of, say, H_0: $\mu \leq 50$, we actually test the exact hypothesis, H_0: $\mu = 50$. If H_0 can be rejected by using the largest value of μ (50), it will also be rejected for all values of the population mean less than 50.

ous doubts about the basis for originally specifying the directional hypothesis. A two-tailed test should have been used from the start.

Example Problem 10.4

    a. Suppose that H_0: $\mu = 10$, H_1: $\mu \neq 10$, and $\alpha = .05$. What is $z_{\bar{X}\,\text{critical}}$?
    b. Suppose that H_0: $\mu = 15$, H_1: $\mu < 15$, and $\alpha = .05$. What is $z_{\bar{X}\,\text{critical}}$?

APPLICATIONS OF HYPOTHESIS TESTING: INFERENCE ABOUT A POPULATION MEAN

At this point, the concepts in the preceding section can be put together in order to test hypotheses with data from a study. Recall that the hypothesis and significance level are established *before* the study is conducted. The logic of hypothesis testing demands that they be. (Obviously, it is not fair to look at your data first and then decide H_0, H_1, and α.) Then, suppose a random sample of 30 or more subjects is drawn from a population and a sample mean calculated. Finally, for our statistical model, the act of drawing a random sample of 30 or more subjects and calculating a sample mean implies that the sampling distribution of means will be approximately normal with mean equal to μ and standard error equal to $\sigma_{\bar{X}}$. Furthermore, the sampling distribution can be considered a normal probability distribution and can be used to determine the probability of a sample mean at or beyond a certain value given the null hypothesis.

From the sample data, a decision is made to reject or not reject the null hypothesis. Statistically, the decision is made by comparing the $z_{\bar{X}}$ value for the observed sample mean with the $z_{\bar{X}\,\text{critical}}$ value. If $z_{\bar{X}\,\text{observed}} \geq z_{\bar{X}\,\text{critical}}$, reject the null hypothesis. The steps in this reasoning are given in Table 10-1.

Case I research addresses the question, "Does the sample belong from a population with μ equal to some specific value, or was the sample drawn from some alternative population?" Recall the study of long-distance runners' heart rates. We suspected that runners would have lower heart rates, on average, than the general population ($\mu = 72$ bpm and $\sigma = 9$). The null hypothesis for this study, then, is:

H_0: $\mu = 72$

Based on our hunch (and other empirical research), a plausible alternative hypothesis is:

H_1: $\mu < 72$

In testing the null hypothesis, let's set the level of significance at .05 ($\alpha = .05$).

Since the alternative hypothesis is directional, one tail—the *lower* tail—of the sampling distribution corresponds to the critical region. The critical value of $z_{\bar{X}}$ is a negative 1.65 (-1.65; see Figure 10-11). If $z_{\bar{X}\,\text{observed}}$ is less than or equal to $= -1.65$, we should decide to reject the null hypothesis.

TABLE 10-1 Correspondence between the steps in hypothesis testing and the features of the statistical model

Steps in Hypothesis Testing	*Features of the Statistical Model*
1. Assume the null hypothesis is true: $H_0: \mu$ = specific value	**1.** Identifies the population from which the sample is assumed to be drawn: 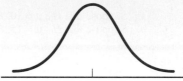 *Distribution of scores in population*
2. State an alternate hypothesis that, if the null hypothesis is rejected, will be accepted: $H_1: \mu \neq$ specific value, or $H_1: \mu <$ specific value, or $H_1: \mu >$ specific value	**2.** Identifies the alternative population from which the sample may be drawn; also provides the information needed for establishing a rule for deciding whether or not to reject H_0 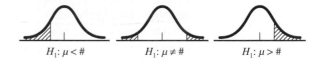 $H_1: \mu < \#$ $H_1: \mu \neq \#$ $H_1: \mu > \#$
3. State a decision rule: Reject H_0 if the probability is less than or equal to .05; otherwise, do not reject H_0	**3.** Identifies a critical value of $z_{\bar{x}}$ in the sampling distribution which corresponds to a probability of .05
4. Draw a random sample of $N \geq 30$ from the population, and calculate a sample mean	**4.** Identifies the nature of the sampling distribution of means: **a.** Normal distribution **b.** Mean equal to μ **c.** Standard error equal to $\sigma/\sqrt{N}$
5. From the sample data, decide whether or not to reject the null hypothesis	**5.** Is $|z_{\bar{x}\,observed}|$ equal to or greater than $z_{\bar{x}\,critical}$? If so, reject H_0; otherwise, do not reject H_0

For a test of the null hypothesis, a random sample of 36 long-distance runners was drawn from the population. The mean heart rate was 65 bpm. In order to decide whether or not to reject the null hypothesis on the basis of this sample result, we need to transform the observed sample mean into a score as follows:

$$z_{\bar{X}_{observed}} = \frac{\bar{X} - \mu}{\sigma_{\bar{X}}} = \frac{65 - 72}{9/\sqrt{36}} = \frac{-7}{1.5} = -4.67$$

Since $z_{\bar{X} \text{ observed}}$ falls way below $z_{\bar{X} \text{ critical}}$, the decision is made to reject the null hypothesis, accept the alternative, and conclude that the mean heart rate for long-distance runners is lower than in the general population.

The steps in hypothesis testing are summarized in Procedure 10-2 for a hypothetical study of the reading level of high school seniors in a particular state. A state school board wanted to determine whether the average reading level of its high school seniors was above the national average of 7.87 (with a standard deviation of 1.10). A random sample of 100 seniors took the reading test and the mean reading score was found to be 8.20.

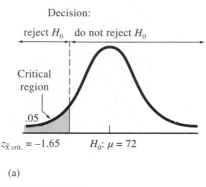
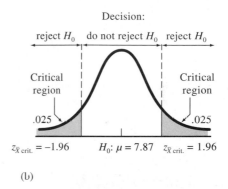

(a)   (b)

FIGURE 10-11

Critical regions for rejecting the null hypothesis in the long-distance runner study: (a) critical region for rejecting H_1 (one-tail test); (b) critical region for rejecting H_1 (two-tail test)

PROCEDURE 10-2 Steps in hypothesis testing (one-tail test with $\alpha = .05$)

Operation	Example
1. Specify the null and alternative hypotheses: H_0: μ = particular value	H_0: $\mu = 7.87$
a. H_1: μ > particular value, or	H_1: $\mu > 7.87$
b. H_1: μ < particular value *Since the direction of difference between the population mean and a particular value is specified, the alternative hypothesis is directional, or one-tail.*	
2. Specify the decision rule with a one-tail test at $\alpha = .05$ **a.** Reject H_0 if $z_{\bar{X} \text{ obs.}} \geq z_{\bar{X} \text{ crit.}} = 1.65$	**a.** Reject H_0 if $z_{\bar{X} \text{ observed}} \geq 1.65$

Operation	Example
b. Do not reject H_0 if $z_{\bar{X} \, obs.} < z_{\bar{X} \, crit.} = 1.65$	**b.** Do not reject H_0 if $z_{\bar{X} \, observed} < 1.65$ 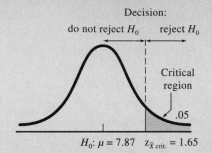

3. Compute $z_{\bar{X} \, observed}$ by using Formula 10-2:

$$z_{\bar{X}} = \frac{\bar{X} - \mu}{\sigma_{\bar{X}}}$$

where:

$$\sigma_{\bar{X}} = \frac{\sigma}{\sqrt{N}} \quad \text{(Formula 10-1)}$$

4. Make a decision (see step 2) and reach a conclusion.

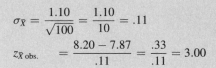

$$z_{\bar{X} \, obs.} = \frac{8.20 - 7.87}{.11} = \frac{.33}{.11} = 3.00$$

For a one-tail test with $\alpha = .05$, $z_{\bar{X} \, critical} = 1.65$. Since $z_{\bar{X} \, observed} > z_{\bar{X} \, critical}$, reject H_0. Conclude that the mean grade-equivalent reading level of seniors in the state is greater than that of seniors nationwide.

In deciding whether or not to reject the null hypothesis in the runner study, we might have taken a conservative turn and based our decision about H_0: $\mu = 72$ on a two-tail test. One change is that the alternative hypothesis is stated in its nondirectional form:

$$H_1: \mu \neq 72$$

A second change is the specification of the critical region (Figure 10-11b). Furthermore, since we want to keep α at .05, each tail is marked off at:

$$\alpha/2 = .05/2 = .025$$

$z_{\bar{X} \, critical}$ corresponding to .025 is 1.96 (Table B). Our decision rule for rejecting the null hypothesis is as follows:

Reject H_0 if $z_{\bar{X} \, observed}$ is greater than or equal to 1.96 or less than or equal to −1.96; that is, reject H_0 if $|z_{\bar{X} \, observed}| \geq 1.96$. Otherwise do not reject H_0.

Since $z_{\bar{X} \, observed} = -4.67$, it is greater than $|z_{\bar{X} \, critical}|$, reject the null hypothesis. In accepting the alternative hypothesis, conclude that the mean heart rate of long-distance runners is lower than that in the general population. The steps in carrying a nondirectional test are summarized in Procedure 10-3 using the high school reading example.

PROCEDURE 10-3 Steps in hypothesis testing (two-tail test at $\alpha = .05$)

Operation	Example

1. Specify the null and alternative hypotheses:

H_0: μ = particular value

H_1: $\mu \neq$ particular value

Since the direction of difference between the population mean and a particular value is not specified, the alternative hypothesis is nondirectional, or two-tailed.

H_0: $\mu = 7.87$

H_1: $\mu \neq 7.87$

2. Specify the decision rules with $\alpha = .05$ (two-tail):

a. Reject H_0 if:

$|z_{\bar{X} \text{ obs.}}| \geq z_{\bar{X} \text{ crit.}} = 1.96$

a. Same as operation 2a.

b. Do not eject H_0 if:

$|z_{\bar{X} \text{ obs.}}| < z_{\bar{X} \text{ crit.}} = 1.96$

b. Same as operation 2b.

3. Compute $z_{\bar{X} \text{ observed}}$, using Formula 10-2:

$$z_{\bar{X}} = \frac{\bar{X} - \mu}{\sigma_{\bar{X}}}$$

where:

$\sigma_{\bar{X}} = \frac{\sigma}{\sqrt{N}}$ (Formula 10-1)

$$\sigma_{\bar{X}} = \frac{1.10}{\sqrt{100}} = \frac{1.10}{10} = .11$$

$$z_{\bar{X} \text{ obs.}} = \frac{8.20 - 7.87}{.11} = \frac{.33}{.11} = 3.00$$

4. Make a decision (see step 2) and reach conclusions.

Two-tail test at $\alpha = .05$: $z_{\bar{X} \text{ critical}} = 1.96$. Since $|z_{\bar{X} \text{ observed}}| > z_{\bar{X} \text{ critical}}$, reject H_0. Conclude that the mean grade-equivalent reading level of seniors in the state differs from the nationwide mean.

(Note that H_0 was rejected by using both a one- and a two-tail test. This will not always happen, as mentioned before and discussed further in Example Problem 10.5.)

Example Problem 10.5 ▬▬▬▬▬▬▬▬▬▬▬▬▬▬▬▬▬▬▬▬▬▬▬▬▬▬▬▬▬▬▬▬▬▬▬▬

The mean score of a sample of 49 seniors enrolled in a particular vocational education program was 53.4 on a measure of mechanical ability. The principal of the program wants to test the hypothesis that seniors from her school are superior in mechanical ability to seniors in general throughout the state. State norms show that mean mechanical ability is 50 with a standard deviation of 14.

a. Test the principal's hypothesis at $\alpha = .05$, using the format for a one-tail test shown in Procedure 10-2 and noting hypotheses, decision rules, computation, decision, and conclusion.

b. Suppose the principal did not have sufficient evidence to warrant a directional hypothesis. Perform a two-tail test with $\alpha = .05$ using the format shown in Procedure 10-3.

c. Compare conclusions based on the one-tail and the two-tail test. Are they the same or different? Why?

Confidence Intervals

Suppose a friend offered you the following choice in making a bet for a pitcher of beer: (1) You say that Mt. Everest is 29,000 feet high or (2) you say that Mt. Everest is between 29,000 and 31,000 feet high. Which bet would you prefer making? Probably you would choose the latter bet since it allows you a fair margin for error; there is a good chance that the true height falls within the interval. Suppose this character offers you another pair of bets: that, in the 1969 NCAA basketball championships, UCLA beat Purdue by (1) 20 points or (2) between 15 and 25 points. You would probably prefer the latter bet, since there is a greater probability that the true difference falls within the interval than that you will hit the true difference by making a **point estimate** of 20 points. In sum, you could be more certain of winning the bet by choosing an interval that included the point estimate of the true value than by choosing the bet with only the point estimate and no margin for error.

Interval Estimates for a Population Mean. These betting situations are somewhat analogous to point estimation and interval estimation (confidence intervals). The reasoning goes something like this for case I situations: A sample is drawn randomly from a population, and the sample mean is calculated. This step is equivalent to drawing a sample mean from a sampling distribution of means. This sample mean is interpreted as an estimate of the true population mean. However, since the estimate is based on sample data, the estimate may be in error. The magnitude of the error in estimating μ from $\bar{X}$ depends on how much sample means differ from one another on repeated sampling from the population—in short, on the standard error of the mean $\sigma_{\bar{X}}$. The smaller the standard error, the smaller is the error likely to arise in estimating μ from $\bar{X}$.

The sample mean is the best *point estimate* of the population mean, but as with the bet about the height of Mt. Everest, a single point estimate can easily be in error. In estimating the true value of the population mean, just as in estimating the true height of Mt. Everest, we would like to hedge our bets by constructing an interval in which the population mean is likely to fall. In this way, we could increase our confidence by supposing that our **interval estimate** contained the population mean.

In order to understand the rationale underlying the **confidence interval,** let's assume, for the moment, that we are omniscient and know that the mean of a certain population on an English proficiency test is 50, with a standard deviation of 20. For samples of size 100, Figure 10-12a shows the corresponding sampling distribution of means. (Notice that $\sigma_{\bar{X}} = 20/\sqrt{100} = 2$.) Now suppose we took a particular random sample of 100 subjects and found the mean proficiency score to be 50.7. This step amounts to selecting randomly a mean from the sampling distribution. As ordinary mortals—we are no longer omniscient—our best estimate of the mean proficiency score in the population, μ, is 50.7. But just to be sure we have not made a mistake about the value of μ, we decide to hedge our bet by saying that μ falls within 2 standard errors on either side of this sample mean:

μ falls within the interval: $\bar{X} \pm 2\sigma_{\bar{X}}$

This statement is a reasonably conservative proclamation—2 standard deviations account for a large part of the area under a normal distribution. The result of constructing the confidence interval about the sample mean is:

μ falls within the interval: $50.7 \pm (2)(2)$

or:

$46.7 \le \mu \le 54.7$

In words, this inequality says that we are reasonably certain that the mean proficiency score in the population falls within an interval such as 46.7 and 54.7. Figure 10-12 shows the sampling distribution of means and provides a visual representation of the confidence interval constructed about the sample mean of 50.7. Notice that in this case, the interval actually includes μ = 50.

Suppose we draw another mean randomly from the sampling distribution in Figure 10-12a. This time the sample mean is 55. Again, our single best estimate of μ is the sample

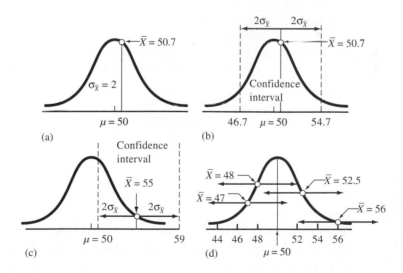

FIGURE 10-12

Confidence intervals for μ: (a) sampling distribution of means: (b) confidence interval about $\bar{X} = 50.7$: (c) confidence interval about $\bar{X} = 55$; (d) confidence intervals for each of four randomly sampled means

mean, but to be on the safe side, we construct a confidence interval 2 standard errors above and below the sample mean:

$$55 \pm 2(2)$$

$$51 \leq \mu \leq 59$$

In this case, the interval says that we are confident that the population mean falls within an interval such as 51 and 59. If we become omniscient for the moment, we are bound to have an all-knowing grin on our faces because we know that drawing a sample mean of 55—$2\frac{1}{2}$ $\sigma_{\bar{X}}$'s beyond μ—was quite unlikely and that even the wide confidence bands do not include μ in this case.

Figures 10-12b, c exemplify an important point about the use and interpretation of confidence intervals. A confidence interval constructed about a single, randomly sampled mean either does or does not include the population mean μ. Since we are not omniscient, we can never be absolutely sure that a particular confidence interval includes μ. Therefore, we must resort to a statement about the probability that a confidence interval includes μ. The reasoning goes something like this: Suppose we select a large number of means randomly from Figure 10-12a and construct confidence intervals for each mean. Since most of the randomly sampled means will fall within ±2 standard errors of μ, most of the confidence intervals constructed within ±2 standard errors of the sample mean will include the population mean μ. This situation is shown in Figure 10-12d for a few randomly sampled means. Notice that almost all of the confidence intervals in the figure include μ.

The probability statement, then, is about randomly sampled means and the intervals constructed about them. Since 95 percent of the sample means fall roughly within 2 standard errors of the population mean ($1.96\sigma_{\bar{X}}$ to be exact), approximately 95 out of 100 sample confidence intervals will include μ. Or put another way, *over all possible randomly sampled means, the probability is .95 that the population mean falls within the interval given in Formula 10-3a.*

$$\bar{X} - 1.96\sigma_{\bar{X}} \leq \mu \leq \bar{X} + 1.96\sigma_{\bar{X}} \tag{10-3a}$$

This confidence interval is called the *95 percent confidence interval* (CI$_{.95}$). Its two boundaries, $\bar{X} - 1.96\sigma_{\bar{X}}$ and $\bar{X} + 1.96\sigma_{\bar{X}}$, are called the *95 percent confidence limits*. The steps in constructing the 95 percent confidence interval are summarized in Procedure 10-4, using the sample of scores for the 100 subjects on the English proficiency test (see page 272).[4]

---

[4]Once actual values—confidence limits—are obtained, the probability statement no longer refers to the particular values, since the interval either does or does not include μ. Rather, we can say that the probability is, for example, approximately .95 that the true value of μ is covered by an interval *such as* that between the particular confidence limits in our data.

PROCEDURE 10-4 Steps in constructing the 95 percent confidence interval

---

Operation	Example
1. Identify the values of $\bar{X}$ and σ.	From a sample of scores for 100 subjects on an English proficiency test, $\bar{X} = 50.7$ and $\sigma = 20$.
2. Compute $\sigma_{\bar{X}}$ by using Formula 10-1: $$\sigma_{\bar{X}} = \frac{\sigma_X}{\sqrt{N}}$$	$$\sigma_{\bar{X}} = \frac{20}{\sqrt{100}} = \frac{20}{10} = 2.0$$
3. Compute the 95 percent confidence interval by inserting the appropriate values into Formula 10-3a and solving: $$\bar{X} - 1.96\sigma_{\bar{X}} \le \mu \le \bar{X} + 1.96\sigma_{\bar{X}}$$	$$50.7 + (1.96)(2.0) \le \mu \le 50.7 + (1.96)(2.0)$$ $$50.7 - 3.92 \le \mu \le 50.7 + 3.92$$ $$46.78 \le \mu < 54.62$$ Over all possible samples, the probability that a randomly sampled confidence interval like this one includes the true population mean μ is .95. The confidence limits are 46.78 and 52.86.

The *99 percent confidence interval* (CI.99) is given by Formula 10-3b.

$$\bar{X} - 2.58\sigma_{\bar{X}} \le \mu \le \bar{X} + 2.58\sigma_{\bar{X}} \tag{10-3b}$$

The value of 2.58 corresponds to the upper and lower area of .005 (i.e., .01/2) in the normal distribution (Table B). The procedures for constructing the 99 percent confidence interval are identical to those for constructing the 95 percent confidence interval, except that $\sigma_{\bar{X}}$ is multiplied by 2.58 rather than 1.96 (see Formula 10-3a). If the 99 percent confidence interval is constructed for the sample data from the English study, we have:

CI.99: $$50.7 - 2.58(2.0) \le \mu \le 50.7 + 2.58(2.0)$$
$$50.7 - 5.16 \le \mu \le 50.7 + 5.16$$
$$45.54 \le \mu \le 55.86$$

Over all possible samples, the probability that a randomly sampled confidence interval, such as the one above, includes the true population mean μ is .99.

By comparing the limits for CI.99 with the confidence limits for CI.95 (Procedure 10-4), we see that increasing our confidence from .95 to .99 increases the width of the interval.

The price of greater confidence, then, is a wider confidence interval. If we want to be perfectly confident, a 100 percent confidence interval could be constructed:

$$\bar{X} - \infty\sigma_{\bar{X}} \leq \mu \leq \bar{X} + \infty\sigma_{\bar{X}}$$

However, this interval is, perhaps, a bit large for our needs. You never get something for nothing—or hardly ever, anyway.

Example Problem 10.6 ▬▬▬▬▬▬▬▬▬▬▬▬▬▬▬▬▬▬▬▬▬▬▬▬▬▬▬▬▬▬▬▬

Construct the 95 percent and 99 percent confidence intervals for μ given the following information:

$$\bar{X} = 30, \quad \sigma_{\bar{X}} = 4$$

Relationship Between Confidence Intervals and Hypothesis Testing

Two-Tail Tests.   In hypothesis testing, the focus is on whether a sample mean was obtained from a population specified by the null hypothesis or whether the sample mean was drawn from some alternative population. Put another way, hypothesis testing focuses on how likely we are to observe the sample mean—a point estimate of the population mean—under the null hypothesis. For a two-tail test, by convention, a sample mean was likely to arise if it were no more than 2 standard errors above or below the population mean. (Actually, we use 1.96 standard errors.) A sample mean is deemed unlikely if it lies at or beyond 2 (or 1.96) standard errors of the mean of the population designated by the null hypothesis. Figure 10-13a provides a pictorial representation of the hypothesis-testing strategy for this two-tail alternative hypothesis with $\alpha = .05$. As this figure shows, the area for rejecting the null hypothesis lies in both tails of the sampling distribution of means.

When we construct a confidence interval, the focus is on the range of values that have a high probability of including the population mean. Thus, the 95 percent confidence interval will include the population mean for all randomly sampled means falling within 2 (1.96) standard errors of the true population mean. This focus is represented pictorially in Figure 10-13b. Notice that all but one of the intervals include μ. In the long run, 95 out of 100 randomly sampled means will fall within 2 (1.96) standard errors of either side of μ. In hypothesis testing, then, 95 out of 100 times we will reach the correct decision not to reject the null hypothesis.

From Figure 10-13c, we see that any confidence interval centered more than $1.96\sigma_{\bar{X}}$ away from μ will *not* include the value of $\mu = 7.87$. In general, then, if a sample mean falls in the $\alpha = .05$ (two-tail) region for rejecting the null hypothesis in the hypothesis-testing framework, then the 95 percent confidence interval constructed about this sample mean will not contain the hypothesized population mean. Likewise, if a mean falls in the $\alpha = .01$ (two-tail) rejection region, the 99 percent confidence interval constructed about this sample mean will not contain the hypothesized population mean. In short, if the $(1 - \alpha)$ percent confi-

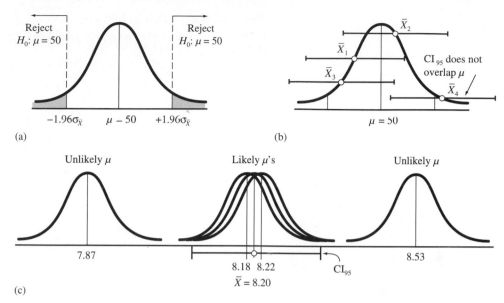

(a)

(b)

(c)

FIGURE 10-13

Representations of the focus of hypothesis testing and confidence intervals: (a) focus of hypothesis testing—assumes H_0 is true until it is shown to be false; (b) relation between hypothesis testing and confidence intervals; (c) some likely and unlikely estimates of the sampling distribution from which $\bar{X} = 8.20$ was sampled ($\sigma_{\bar{X}} = .10$ in all cases)

dence interval constructed about a sample mean does not include μ under the null hypothesis, then the hypothesis test at $\alpha/2$ will lead to a decision to reject the null hypothesis.

Perhaps a concrete example will bring this point home. In the study of reading achievement, the null hypothesis was that $\mu = 7.87$. The population standard deviation was 1.10. From a random sample of 100 seniors, $\bar{X} = 8.20$. With $N = 100$ and $\sigma_{\bar{X}} = .11$, we have:

$$z_{\bar{X} \text{ observed}} = \frac{8.20 - 7.87}{.11} = 3.00$$

Since $z_{\bar{X} \text{ observed}}$ is greater than 1.96, it exceeds $z_{\bar{X} \text{ critical}}$ ($\alpha = .05$, two tail), and we should decide to reject the null hypothesis. This situation is represented pictorially in Figure 10-14a.

The $1 - \alpha$ ($1 - .05$) or 95 percent confidence interval can be constructed by using Formula 10-3a (see Procedure 10-4 for the computational steps):

$$\text{CI}_{.95}: \quad 8.20 - 1.96(.11) \leq \mu \leq 8.20 + 1.96(.11)$$
$$7.984 \leq \mu \leq 8.416$$

This situation is shown in Figure 10-14b. As we can see from the figure or from the lower confidence limit, the 95 percent confidence interval does not include the hypothesized population mean of 7.87. Thus we should decide to reject the null hypothesis. For the two-tail case, then, either the method of hypothesis testing or a confidence interval estimation can be used to test the null hypothesis.

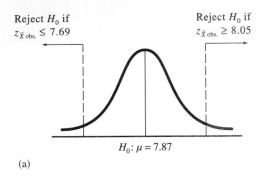

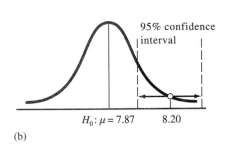

(a)

(b)

FIGURE 10-14

Pictorial representations of hypothesis testing and confidence intervals for the hypothetical study of reading achievement: (a) hypothesis testing ($\alpha = .05$, $\sigma_{\bar{X}} = .11$); (b) 95 percent confidence interval

Incidentally, one-tail tests, by their nature, do not have an analog with symmetric confidence intervals. That is, if there is good reason to perform a one-tailed test, the confidence interval, too, should take advantage of this information. Hence, the confidence interval should be unidirectional, also.

Example Problem 10.7

Use the data in Example Problem 10.5.
   a. Construct 95 percent confidence limits for the sample mean.
   b. What decision would you make about H_0 from these results?
   c. Compare this decision with the decision in Example Problem 10.5b based on hypothesis-testing procedures.

STATISTICAL INFERENCE ABOUT A DIFFERENCE BETWEEN POPULATION MEANS

Case II research asks, "Might the observed difference between the sample means of an experimental and control group be due to chance, or does the difference represent a difference in population means due to systematic treatment effect? The hypothetical study of teacher expectancy summarized at the beginning of this chapter (see Figure 10-2) is a good example of case II research. Based on the sample difference between experimental and control group means ($\bar{X}_{\text{Experimental}} - \bar{X}_{\text{Control}} = 110.23 - 109.57 = .66$), we must decide whether the two groups represent populations with a common mean (hence no treatment effect) or represent populations with different means (due to a treatment effect).

In order to decide whether the observed difference in sample means arose by chance, we must first specify a sampling distribution for difference between sample means assuming the null hypothesis is true. A *sampling distribution of differences between means* is a theoretical distribution with values of differences between sample means [($\bar{X}_{Experimental}$ − $\bar{X}_{Control}$) or ($\bar{X}_1 − \bar{X}_2$)] on the abscissa and probabilities on the ordinate. Once the sampling distribution is specified, it can be used as a probability distribution in deciding whether the difference between sample means was likely to occur under the null hypothesis.

Sampling Distribution of Differences Between Means

At this point, let's conceptualize what is going on in a case II study, assuming the null hypothesis is true (Figure 10-15a). From a population, two random samples of size *n* (number of subjects in each of the two groups) are drawn, a mean score for each group is calculated, and the **difference between the means** is found by subtracting one sample mean from the other: $\bar{X}_1 − \bar{X}_2$. Theoretically, at least, this study could be replicated over and over again by drawing pairs of random samples from the population and finding the difference ($\bar{X}_1 − \bar{X}_2$) between the sample means of the two groups. If it were, the difference between pairs of sample means would be expected to vary from one replication of the study to the next. A picture of the variability between differences in sample means is obtained when the differences between means are graphed in the form of a frequency polygon, with the values of $\bar{X}_1 − \bar{X}_2$ on the abscissa and the frequency with which each value of $\bar{X}_1 − \bar{X}_2$ is observed on the ordinate (Figure 10-15b).

This frequency distribution shows a sampling distribution of the differences between means. It shows the variability that is expected to arise from randomly sampling differences between pairs of means from the population under the null hypothesis. Since it is a frequency distribution, it can be converted into a relative frequency distribution and treated as a probability distribution. Formally, a **sampling distribution of differences between means** is a theoretical probability distribution with differences between sample means ($\bar{X}_1 − \bar{X}_2$) on the abscissa and probabilities on the ordinate. By treating the sampling distribution of differences between means as a probability distribution, we can answer such questions as "What

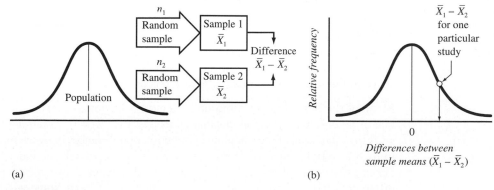

(a)   (b)

FIGURE 10-15
Making inferences about differences between means: (a) finding the difference between two sample means, assuming the null hypothesis is true; (b) differences between sample means ($\bar{X}_1 − \bar{X}_2$)

is the probability of observing a difference between sample means $(\bar{X}_1 - \bar{X}_2)$ as large or larger than the observed sample difference, assuming that the null hypothesis is true?"

In the study of teacher expectancy, the difference between the means of the experimental and control groups, $\bar{X}_E - \bar{X}_C$, represents a random sample from a sampling distribution of differences between means. Such a sampling distribution can be used to answer the question, "If the null hypothesis is true, what is the probability of observing a difference between sample means equal to $\bar{X}_E - \bar{X}_C$ or greater?" If the probability is greater than .05, the null hypothesis (in this case, "no treatment effect") cannot be rejected. If the probability is .05 or less, the null hypothesis can be rejected and the conclusion is that teacher expectancy improves intellectual ability.

Characteristics of the Sampling Distribution of Differences Between Means

In order to use the sampling distribution of differences between means as a probability distribution, first, we need to assume that the null hypothesis is true, and, second, we need to know something about the nature of this sampling distribution. According to mathematical statistics, if repeated random samples of size n are drawn from a normally distributed population, the sampling distribution of the difference between means has the following characteristics:

1. It is normally distributed.
2. It has a mean equal to zero (i.e., since the samples are taken from the same population, $\mu_1 = \mu_2$ and $\mu_1 - \mu_2 = 0$).
3. It has a standard deviation called the **standard error of the difference between means.**

For samples of size approximately 30 or more ($n \geq 30$), the *central limit theorem* states that for a wide variety of different population distributions, the sampling distribution of the differences between means will be approximately normal. Furthermore, the mean of the sampling distribution will still equal zero, and the variability of sample means will still equal the standard error of the difference between means.

Shape of the Sampling Distribution.   As sample size increases, the sampling distribution of differences between means becomes increasingly close to the normal distribution. If the difference between sample means, $\bar{X}_1 - \bar{X}_2$, is thought of as a single mean representing this difference, $\bar{X}_d$, then Figure 10-15 shows the effect of increasing sample size on the shape of the sampling distribution of differences between means.

Mean of the Sampling Distribution.   In most behavioral research, the null hypothesis is that of no difference between population means: $\mu_1 - \mu_2 = 0$. Assuming the null hypothesis is true, the mean of the sampling distribution of differences between means will be equal to $\mu_1 - \mu_2 = 0$. In order to see this intuitively, suppose we take an indefinitely large number of pairs of sample means and calculate the difference between each pair. Some of the differences will be positive (i.e., $\bar{X}_1 > \bar{X}_2$, so that $\bar{X}_1 - \bar{X}_2 > 0$), some will be zero ($\bar{X}_1 = \bar{X}_2$, so that $\bar{X}_1 - \bar{X}_2 = 0$), and some will be negative ($\bar{X}_1 < \bar{X}_2$, so that $\bar{X}_1 - \bar{X}_2 < 0$). Since the sample pairs are drawn from what amounts to the same population, the same number of positive differences as negative differences would be expected in the long run. Thus, when we calculate the mean of the sampling distribution of differences between means, the positive and negative sample differences should cancel each other out and the mean of the distribution should be zero.

Standard Error of the Difference Between Means.   Subtracting pairs of sample means can be conceived of as subtracting sample means drawn from two identical sampling distributions, each with a standard error (standard deviation of sampling distribution of sample means) equal to $\sigma_{\bar{X}}$. The error involved in calculating differences between sample means, then, will depend on the standard error of the mean in one sampling distribution ($\sigma_{\bar{X}_1}$) as well as that in the other sampling distribution ($\sigma_{\bar{X}_2}$) is an additive combination of these two individual errors in estimating the means: The *standard error of the difference between means* is defined in Formula 10-4.

$$\sigma_{(\text{difference between } \bar{X}_1 \text{ and } \bar{X}_2)} = \sigma_{\bar{X}_1 - \bar{X}_2} = \sqrt{\sigma_{\bar{X}_1}^2 + \sigma_{\bar{X}_2}^2} \qquad (10\text{-}4)$$

As mentioned earlier, this error is the error involved in estimating the difference between population means from sample means. Put another way, it is the standard deviation of the difference between means. These conclusions are represented graphically in Figure 10-16a.

For the study on the effects of teacher expectancy, the sampling distribution of the difference between means is approximately normally distributed, since $n_E = n_C = 30$ and $N = 60$. Under the null hypothesis, the mean of this sampling distribution is zero. Suppose that $\sigma_E = \sigma_C = 10$.[5] Then the standard error of the difference between means is found by using Formula 10-4 as follows:

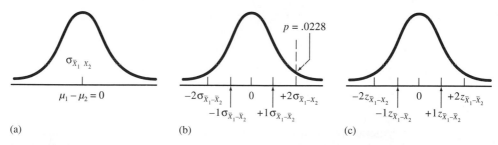

(a)   (b)   (c)

FIGURE 10-16
Characteristics of the sampling distribution of the difference between means: (a) normally distributed with mean $\mu_1 - \mu_2 = 0$ and standard error of the difference $\sigma_{\bar{X}_1 - \bar{X}_2}$; (b) probabilities may be found by dividing the normal distribution into standard error units; (c) probabilities may be found in the unit normal distribution by transforming to $z_{\bar{X}_1 - \bar{X}_2}$ scores

---

[5]Under the null hypothesis, sample 1 and sample 2 are drawn randomly from identical populations, each with a standard deviation of σ. Thus, if the population standard deviation for sample 1 is σ_1 and for sample 2 is σ_2, then $\sigma_1 = \sigma_2 = \sigma$.

$$\sigma_{\bar{X}_E - \bar{X}_C} = \sqrt{\sigma_{\bar{X}_E}^2 + \sigma_{\bar{X}_C}^2}$$

The first step is to find $\sigma_{\bar{X}_E}$ and $\sigma_{\bar{X}_C}$.

$$\sigma_{\bar{X}_E} = \frac{\sigma_E}{\sqrt{n_E}} = \frac{10}{\sqrt{30}} = \frac{10}{5.48} = 1.82$$

and:

$$\sigma_{\bar{X}_C} = \frac{\sigma_C}{\sqrt{n_C}} = \frac{10}{\sqrt{30}} = \frac{10}{5.48} = 1.82$$

So:

$$\sigma_{\bar{X}_E - \bar{X}_C} = \sqrt{(1.82)^2 + (1.82)^2} = \sqrt{3.31 + 3.31}$$
$$= \sqrt{6.62} = 2.57$$

Example Problem 10.8

What is the standard error of differences between means ($\sigma_{\bar{X}_E - \bar{X}_C}$) if $\sigma_E = 8$, $\sigma_C = 8$, $n_E = 64$, and $n_C = 64$?

The Sampling Distribution of the Difference Between Means as a Probability Distribution

We know from the central limit theorem that for sample sizes n_1, $n_2 \geq 30$, the sampling distribution of the difference between means is approximately normal (Figure 10-16a). When the frequency polygon is converted to a relative frequency polygon, the areas under the curve in this normal distribution may be interpreted as probabilities. And when the area is divided into blocks of 1 standard deviation each, as in Figure 10-16b, the probabilities corresponding to the various parts of the normal distribution can be seen. For example, the relative area beyond 2 standard deviations (standard errors of the difference between means) above the mean is .0228; the probability of observing a difference between sample means of 2 or more standard errors (deviations) above the mean is .0228 (Figure 10-16b).

If we are to use Table B to find probabilities under the normal curve, the differences between means on the abscissa of the sampling distribution must be converted to z scores in a manner analogous to converting raw scores to z scores (Chapter 5). For raw scores, we use Formula 5-1:

$$z = \frac{X - \bar{X}}{s}$$

For the sample difference between means, we use Formula 10-5.

$$z_{\bar{X}_1 - \bar{X}_2} = \frac{\overbrace{(\bar{X}_1 - \bar{X}_2)}^{\substack{\text{Difference} \\ \text{in sample} \\ \text{means } (\bar{X}_d)}} - \overbrace{(\mu_1 - \mu_2)}^{\substack{\text{Difference} \\ \text{in population} \\ \text{means } (\mu_d)}}}{\sigma_{\bar{X}_1 - \bar{X}_2}} \qquad (10\text{--}5)$$

Notice that the z score corresponding to the difference between means in the sampling distribution is denoted by $z_{\bar{X}_1 - \bar{X}_2}$, or $z_{\bar{X}_E - \bar{X}_C}$ for experimental and control groups. This notation reminds us that we are dealing with a sampling distribution of the differences between means and not raw scores. Furthermore, note that $z_{\bar{X}_1 - \bar{X}_2}$ tells us how many standard errors the difference between sample means falls above or below $\mu_1 - \mu_2 = 0$. Figure 10-16c shows this sampling distribution marked off in units of $z_{\bar{X}_1 - \bar{X}_2}$.

In order to practice using the sampling distribution of the difference between means as a probability distribution, consider a few examples. In the study of teacher expectancy, under the null hypothesis the sampling distribution of the difference between means is approximately normal ($n_E = n_C = 30$ and $N = 60$) with a mean equal to zero and a standard error of the difference between means, $\sigma_{\bar{X}_E - \bar{X}_C}$, equal to 2.57 (see the preceding section). What is the probability of observing a difference between sample means of 3.00 points or more (i.e., $\bar{X}_E - \bar{X}_C \geq 3.00$)? Should the null hypothesis be rejected? This problem is shown conceptually in Figure 10-17a. In answering this question, we first set forth the null and alternative hypotheses along with the level of significance: H_0: $\mu_E - \mu_C = 0$; H_1: $\mu_E - \mu_C > 0$; $\alpha = .05$. Next, we convert the difference between means ($\bar{X}_E - \bar{X}_C$) to a $z_{\bar{X}_E - \bar{X}_C}$ score, using Formula 10-5:

$$z_{\bar{X}_E - \bar{X}_C} = \frac{(\bar{X}_E - \bar{X}_C) - (\mu_E - \mu_C)}{\sigma_{\bar{X}_E - \bar{X}_C}} = \frac{3.00 - 0}{2.57} = 1.17$$

Then we use Table B to find the relative area under the normal curve corresponding to the smaller portion of the upper tail of the curve. For a z of 1.17, this area is .1210. The probability of observing a difference of 3 points or greater between sample means is .1210, or .12. Since .12 is greater than α, the null hypothesis should not be rejected.

In hypothesis testing, the z_{critical} value corresponding to α is commonly found from Table B, and z_{observed} is compared with it in order to decide whether to reject the null hypothesis. For example, suppose we wished to identify the critical value of $z_{\bar{X}_E - \bar{X}_C}$ beyond which the probability is .05 or less of observing a difference between sample means *above* the

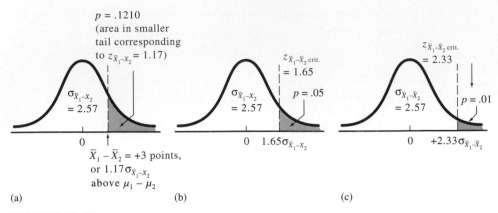

FIGURE 10-17
Conceptual representation of the problem of determining probability with the sampling distribution of differences between means

difference between population means—that is, above zero. This question can be interpreted as follows: "What is the $z_{\bar{X}_E-\bar{X}_C}$ at or above which 5 percent of the differences between sample means fall?" This problem is presented conceptually in Figure 10-17b. Referring to Table B, we see that the $z_{\bar{X}_E-\bar{X}_C}$ value corresponding to .05 of the area in the upper tail of the curve is 1.65. Hence, the critical value of $z_{\bar{X}_E-\bar{X}_C}$ is 1.65, and the probability of observing a difference of $z_{\bar{X}_E-\bar{X}_C} \geq 1.65$ between sample means is .05.

Example Problem 10.9

a.   What is the probability of observing a difference between sample means equal to or greater than 2.50 if the sampling distribution of differences between means is approximately normal, with a mean equal to zero and $\sigma_{\bar{X}_1-\bar{X}_2} = 1.20$?

b.   What is the critical value of $z_{\bar{X}_1-\bar{X}_2}$ beyond which the probability is .01 or less of observing a difference in sample means above the difference between population means (i.e., above zero)?

APPLICATION OF HYPOTHESIS TESTING: INFERENCE ABOUT A DIFFERENCE BETWEEN POPULATION MEANS

With the nature of the sampling distribution of the differences between means specified under the null hypothesis, this sampling distribution can be used as a probability distribution for testing hypotheses about differences between group means. At this point, the steps in hypothesis testing are analogous to the steps in case I research. As an example, consider the study on teacher expectancy. In this case, the null hypothesis was that there would be no difference between mean intelligence scores of the control group and the experimental group:

$$H_0: \mu_E - \mu_C = 0$$

The alternative hypothesis, based on symbolic interactionist theory and prior research, was that the mean intelligence of the experimental group is greater than that of the control group:

$$H_1: \mu_E - \mu_C > 0$$

In testing the null hypothesis, let's use $\alpha = .01$ as the level of significance.

Since the research hypothesis is directional, one tail of the sampling distribution of the difference between means—the upper tail—is identified as a critical region in Figure 10-17c. The critical value of $z_{\bar{X}_E - \bar{X}_C}$ that identifies the small portion of the upper tail is 2.33 (see Table B).[6] Note that we now speak of $z_{\bar{X}_E - \bar{X}_C}$ and not $z_{\bar{X}}$, since we are dealing with the sampling distribution of the *difference between two means*. If $z_{\bar{X}_E - \bar{X}_C \text{ observed}}$ is greater than $z_{\bar{X}_E - \bar{X}_C \text{ critical}}$, the null hypothesis should be rejected.

The observed sample means are 110.23 for the experimental group and 109.57 for the control group; the standard error of the means is 2.57. In order to decide whether to reject the null hypothesis, we convert these sample data to a z score, using Formula 10-5:

$$z_{\bar{X}_E - \bar{X}_C \text{ observed}} = \frac{(\bar{X}_E - \bar{X}_C) - (\mu_E - \mu_C)}{\sigma_{\bar{X}_E - \bar{X}_C}}$$

Since $\mu_E - \mu_C = \mu_D = 0$ under the null hypothesis, this equation can be rewritten as in Formula 10-5a:

$$z_{\bar{X}_E - \bar{X}_C \text{ observed}} = \frac{(\bar{X}_E - \bar{X}_C)}{\sigma_{\bar{X}_E - \bar{X}_C}} \tag{10-5a}$$

Thus we obtain:

$$z_{\bar{X}_E - \bar{X}_C \text{ observed}} = \frac{110.23 - 109.57}{2.57} = \frac{.66}{2.57} = .26$$

Since $z_{\bar{X}_E - \bar{X}_C \text{ observed}}$ does not exceed $z_{\bar{X}_E - \bar{X}_C \text{ critical}}$, the decision is made *not* to reject the null hypothesis. The steps for conducting tests of one- and two-tail hypotheses are summarized in Procedure 10-5. Example data are taken from the hypothetical study of teacher expectancy.

---

[6]The same critical values of z are used for both case I and case II research, since the alternative hypothesis in both types of research designs refers to the same parts of the normal distribution.

PROCEDURE 10-5 Steps in hypothesis testing—case II (example data from the hypothetical study of teacher expectancy)

Operation	Example

Operation

1. Specify the null and alternative hypotheses:

$$H_0: \mu_1 - \mu_2 = 0$$

For a two-tail test:

$$H_1: \mu_1 - \mu_2 \neq 0$$

For a one-tail test:

$$H_1: \mu_1 - \mu_2 > 0$$

or

$$H_1: \mu_1 - \mu_2 < 0$$

Subscripts E and C (for *experimental* and *control* groups) many be substituted if the mnemonic helps.

2. Specify a decision rule at α:

   a. For a one-tail test at $\alpha = .01$, reject H_0 if

   $$\left| z_{\bar{X}_1 - \bar{X}_2 \text{ obs.}} \right| \geq z_{\bar{X}_1 - \bar{X}_2 \text{ crit.}} = 2.33$$

   Do not reject H_0 if

   $$\left| z_{\bar{X}_1 - \bar{X}_2 \text{ obs.}} \right| < z_{\bar{X}_1 - \bar{X}_2 \text{ crit.}} = 2.33$$

   b. For a two-tail test at $\alpha = .01$, reject H_0 if

   $$\left| z_{\bar{X}_1 - \bar{X}_2 \text{ obs.}} \right| \geq z_{\bar{X}_1 - \bar{X}_2 \text{ crit.}} = 2.58$$

   Do not reject H_0 if

   $$\left| z_{\bar{X}_1 - \bar{X}_2 \text{ obs.}} \right| < z_{\bar{X}_1 - \bar{X}_2 \text{ crit.}} = 2.58$$

3. Draw a random sample of N subjects from the population of interest. Randomly assign each subject to one of the two groups. Conduct the study and collect the data.

Example

In the teacher expectancy study, a one-tail test was conducted as follows:

$$H_0: \mu_E - \mu_C = 0$$

$$H_0: \mu_E - \mu_C > 0$$

$$\alpha = .01$$

Reject H_0 if

$$\left| z_{\bar{X}_E - \bar{X}_C \text{ obs.}} \right| \geq 2.33$$

Do not reject H_0 if

$$\left| z_{\bar{X}_E - \bar{X}_C \text{ obs.}} \right| < 2.33$$

Sixty elementary school children are selected and randomly assigned to the experimental or control groups. Experimental subjects are labeled as "bloomers," and control subjects are not labeled. Intelligence test scores are collected at the end of the school year, and the following data are obtained:

$$\bar{X}_E = 110.23$$

$$\bar{X}_C = 109.57$$

Assume that it is known that:

$$\sigma_E = \sigma_C = 10$$

(See the example in the section "Standard Error of the Difference Between Means.")

Operation

Example

4. Compute $\sigma_{\bar{X}_1 - \bar{X}_2}$ by using Formula 10-4:

$$\sigma_{\bar{X}_1 - \bar{X}_2} = \sqrt{\sigma_{\bar{X}_1}^2 + \sigma_{\bar{X}_2}^2}$$

$$\sigma_{\bar{X}_E} = \frac{\sigma_E}{\sqrt{n_E}} = \frac{10}{\sqrt{30}} = \frac{10}{5.48} = 1.82$$

$$\sigma_{\bar{X}_C} = \frac{\sigma_C}{\sqrt{n_C}} = \frac{10}{\sqrt{30}} = \frac{10}{5.48} = 1.82$$

$$\sigma_{\bar{X}_E - \bar{X}_C} = \sqrt{(1.82)^2 + (1.82)^2}$$
$$= \sqrt{3.31 + 3.31} = \sqrt{6.62} = 2.57$$

5. Compute $z_{\bar{X}_1 - \bar{X}_2 \text{observed}}$ by using Formula 10-5a:

$$z_{\bar{X}_1 - \bar{X}_2 \text{observed}} = \frac{\bar{X}_1 - \bar{X}_2}{\sigma_{\bar{X}_1 - \bar{X}_2}}$$

$$z_{\bar{X}_E - \bar{X}_C \text{obs.}} = \frac{110.23 - 109.57}{2.57}$$
$$= \frac{.66}{2.57} = .26$$

6. Make a decision about whether or not to reject H_0 (see step 2), and draw a conclusion about the outcome of the experiment.

Since $|z_{\bar{X}_E - \bar{X}_C \text{observed}}| < z_{\bar{X}_E - \bar{X}_C \text{critical}}$ $(.26 < 2.33)$, we do not reject H_0. We conclude that there is insufficient evidence in the sample data to reject the null hypothesis. This conclusion does not mean that the null hypothesis is true—the sample difference was .66 and not 0—but the evidence is not strong enough to allow us to reject H_0. It is just too likely that a sample difference of .66 arose when the true difference is zero.

Example Problem 10.10

In a study of the effects of special class placement on the achievement of educably mentally retarded (EMR) children, 36 EMR children were randomly assigned to special education classes and 36 were randomly assigned to regular classes. The following results were obtained:

$$\bar{X}_{SC} = 50, \quad \bar{X}_{RC} = 48$$

Assume that:

$$\sigma_{SC} = 5, \quad \sigma_{RC} = 5$$

where:

SC = special class
RC = regular class

Using Procedure 10-5, test the null hypothesis at $\alpha = .01$ (two-tail).

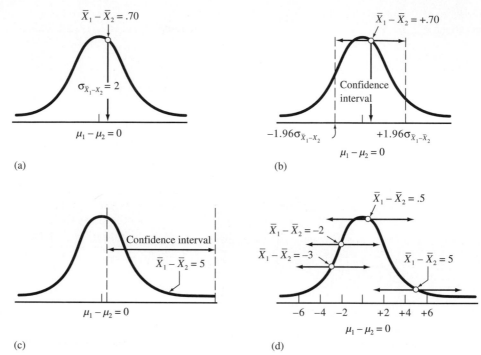

FIGURE 10-18
Confidence intervals for $\mu_1 - \mu_2$: (a) sampling distribution of differences between means; (b) confidence interval about $\bar{X}_1 - \bar{X}_2 = .70$; (c) confidence interval about $\bar{X}_1 - \bar{X}_2 = 5$; (d) confidence intervals for each of four randomly sampled differences between means

Confidence Intervals for a Difference between Means

The logic behind and the procedures for constructing a confidence interval for differences between population means is the same as that for a single population mean. As a reminder of this logic and these procedures, suppose we randomly sample a difference between means from the sampling distribution of differences in Figure 10-18a. (The sample, then, is drawn from a distribution with $\mu_1 - \mu_2 = 0$ and $\sigma_{\bar{X}_1 - \bar{X}_2} = 2$.) For this sample, the difference between means is +.70 point. This difference is our single best estimate of $\mu_1 - \mu_2$. However, recognizing that the sample difference might be in error, we can construct a confidence interval to hedge our bet (see Figure 10-18b). The form for a 95 percent confidence interval is given in Formula 10-6.

$$CI_{.95} = \text{(mean difference)} \pm 1.96 \times \text{(standard error)} \qquad \textbf{(10-6)}$$

For our example, we have:

$$CI_{.95} = .7 \pm (1.96)(2)$$

Thus:

$$-3.22 \le \mu_1 - \mu_2 \le 4.62$$

The probability, then, is approximately .95 that the difference between population means lies within an interval *such as* −3.22 to +4.62.

Notice that this statement does *not* mean that the *particular interval* contains $\mu_1 - \mu_2$. For a specific confidence interval, the probability is 0 or 1 that it contains $\mu_1 - \mu_2$, since the particular interval either does or does not contain the difference. This point is illustrated in Figure 10-18c. Here a difference of 5 points was randomly sampled from the sampling distribution with $\mu_1 - \mu_2 = 0$; this difference is an unlikely occurrence. The 95 percent confidence interval ($CI_{.95}$) is:

$$5 \pm (1.96)(2)$$

or

$$1.08 \le \mu_1 - \mu_2 \le 8.92$$

Although the probability is approximately .95 that an interval *such as* 1.08 to 8.92 contains $\mu_1 - \mu_2$, this particular interval does not contain the true value, 0.

Since 95 out of 100 randomly sampled differences between means will fall within ± 1.96 standard errors of $\mu_1 - \mu_2$, most confidence intervals will include the true value of $\mu_1 - \mu_2$. However, we never know exactly which ones do and which ones do not. This situation is shown in Figure 10-18d for a few randomly sampled differences between means.

The 95 Percent Confidence Interval.   The 95 percent confidence interval ($CI_{.95}$) for $\mu_1 - \mu_2$ is defined by Formula 10-6a.

$$(\bar{X}_1 - \bar{X}_2) \pm 1.96\sigma_{\bar{X}_1 - \bar{X}_2} \qquad\qquad \textbf{(10-6a)}$$

The $CI_{.95}$ can also be written as shown in Formula 10-6b.

$$(\bar{X}_1 - \bar{X}_2) - 1.96\sigma_{\bar{X}_1 - \bar{X}_2} \le \mu_1 - \mu_2 \le (\bar{X}_1 - \bar{X}_2) + 1.96\sigma_{\bar{X}_1 - \bar{X}_2} \qquad \textbf{(10-6b)}$$

In the hypothetical study of the teacher expectancy effect, the difference between the expectancy group's mean and the control group's mean was $110.23 - 109.57 = .66$. The standard error of the difference between means, $\sigma_{\bar{X}_1 - \bar{X}_2}$, was 2.57 (see Procedure 10-5). The 95 percent confidence interval is constructed by inserting the appropriate values into Formula 10-6b:

$$\text{CI}_{.95}: \quad .66 - 1.96(2.57) \le \mu_1 - \mu_2 \le .66 + 1.96(2.57)$$
$$.66 - 5.04 \le \mu_1 - \mu_2 \le .66 + 5.04$$
$$-4.38 \le \mu_1 - \mu_2 \le 5.70$$

The probability is .95 that a randomly selected confidence interval such as this one includes the true difference between population means.

The 99 Percent Confidence Interval.   The 99 percent confidence interval (CI$_{.99}$) for $\mu_1 - \mu_2$ is defined by Formula 10-7.

$$(\bar{X}_1 - \bar{X}_2) \pm 2.58\sigma_{\bar{X}_1 - \bar{X}_2} \qquad \qquad \textbf{(10-7)}$$

The CI$_{.99}$ can also be written as shown in Formula 10-7a.

$$(\bar{X}_1 - \bar{X}_2) - 2.58\sigma_{\bar{X}_1 - \bar{X}_2} \le \mu_1 - \mu_2 \le (\bar{X}_1 - \bar{X}_2) + 2.58\sigma_{\bar{X}_1 - \bar{X}_2} \qquad \textbf{(10-7a)}$$

The 99 percent confidence interval for the data from the hypothetical study on teacher expectancy is:

$$\text{CI}_{.99}: \quad .66 - 2.58(2.57) \le \mu_1 - \mu_2 \le .66 + 2.58(2.57)$$
$$.66 - 6.63 \le \mu_1 - \mu_2 \le .66 + 6.63$$
$$-5.97 \le \mu_1 - \mu_2 \le 7.29$$

Example Problem 10.11

Suppose $\bar{X}_E = 56$, $\bar{X}_C = 53$, and $\sigma_{\bar{X}_E - \bar{X}_C} = 1.50$. Construct a 95 percent confidence interval and a 99 percent confidence interval around the observed difference between sample means.

STATISTICAL INFERENCE ABOUT A POPULATION CORRELATION COEFFICIENT

As you might suspect, statistical tests using the normal distribution are not limited to hypotheses about means. One widely used test is the test of the null hypothesis that the population correlation coefficient, ρ_{XY}, equals zero: H_0: $\rho_{XY} = 0$. Another test is that the population correlation coefficient equals some specified value (e.g., .30):

H_0: $\rho_{XY} =$ some specified value.

Indeed, the former test is a special case of the latter where the specified value is zero.

Test of ρ_{XY} = Specified Value

The purpose of the test for ρ_{XY} = specified value is to determine whether or not the observed value of r_{XY} was sampled from a population in which the linear relationship between X and Y is some specified value.

A test of the null hypothesis $\rho_{XY} = 0$ helps the researcher decide whether or not two variables, X and Y, are linearly related in the population. If, however, on the basis of theory, prior research, or both, the relation between X and Y is expected to be positive and moderately high, a test of $\rho_{XY} = 0$ would be trivial. For example, theory and prior research suggest that the relationship between scores on measures of verbal, quantitative, and spatial ability should be about .30 since the average correlation between many such tests is about this value. So a test of $\rho_{XY} = .30$ would be more important in this case than a test of $\rho_{XY} = 0$.

In order to decide whether or not to reject the null hypothesis (e.g., $\rho_{XY} = 0$ or $\rho_{XY} = .30$), we need to know something about the sampling distribution of the correlation coefficient r_{XY}. To provide an intuitive feel for the sampling distribution of r_{XY}, suppose that a random sample of 50 subjects is taken from a population in which the correlation between X and Y is zero: $\rho_{XY} = 0$. If, for the 50 subjects, the correlation between their X and Y scores is calculated, r_1 should be close to zero but not necessarily equal zero. This result is due to sampling error. And so if the difference between r_{XY} and $\rho_{XY} = 0$ is measured in standard error units, the difference will not be zero either. Suppose a second sample of 50 subjects is drawn and r_2 is calculated. Again, r_2 may not equal zero exactly (it will probably not equal r_1 either), and the distance between r_{XY} and $\rho_{XY} = 0$, measured in standard error units, will not be zero. Suppose this procedure of randomly sampling 50 subjects, calculating r_{XY}, and measuring the difference between r_{XY} and $\rho_{XY} = 0$ in standard error units was carried out an indefinitely large number of times. In this case, a frequency distribution could be constructed with observed values of the distance between r_{XY} and $\rho_{XY} = 0$ on the abscissa and frequencies on the ordinate. This frequency distribution would represent the sampling distribution of r with $\bar{r}_{XY}$, the mean value of r_{XY} equal to ρ_{XY}, which is equal to zero (see Figure 10-19).

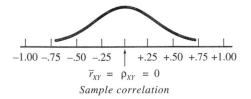

$$\bar{r}_{XY} \; = \; \rho_{XY} \; = \; 0$$

Sample correlation

FIGURE 10-19
Sampling distribution of the Pearson product-moment correlation coefficient for $\rho_{XY} = 0$

However, when ρ_{XY} is positive (e.g., $\rho = .30$), the sampling distribution of r_{XY} is negatively skewed. When ρ_{XY} is negative (e.g., $\rho = -.25$), the sampling distribution is skewed in the positive direction. In order to develop a general statistical test, then, we must do something so that both types of null hypotheses—$\rho_{XY} = 0$ and ρ = specified value—can be tested. This result is accomplished by a transformation. Since skewed distributions can often be transformed into approximately normal distributions by taking a logarithmic transformation of the data, a log transformation of r_{XY} is made. With this transformation, the sampling distribution of r_{XY} is approximately normal, regardless of whether the sample correlation is drawn from the population with $\rho_{XY} = 0$ or $\rho_{XY} =$ some specific value.

The logarithmic transformation used on r_{XY} is Fisher's **Z** transformation, given by Formula 10-8.

$$\mathbf{Z} = 1.1513 \, \log_{10}\left(\frac{1+r}{1-r}\right) = .5 \, \log_e\left(\frac{1+r}{1-r}\right) \qquad \textbf{(10-8)}$$

The standard error of the sampling distribution of r_{XY} when it has been transformed to **Z** is given in Formula 10-9.

$$s_Z = \frac{1}{\sqrt{N-3}} \qquad \textbf{(10-9)}$$

In order to test whether or not an observed correlation r_{XY} differs from the hypothesized value of the population parameter ρ_{XY}, we use the normal sampling distribution when r_{XY} and ρ_{XY} are transformed to **Z**'s, as in Formula 10-10.

$$z_{r\,\text{observed}} = \frac{\mathbf{Z}_r - \mathbf{Z}_\rho}{s_Z} \qquad \textbf{(10-10)}$$

The null and alternative hypotheses for a nondirectional alternative hypothesis are:

$H_0: \rho_{XY} =$ specified value

$H_1: \rho_{XY} \neq$ specified value

In the case of a directional alternative hypothesis, the null and alternative hypotheses are:

$H_0: \rho_{XY} =$ specified value $H_0: \rho_{XY} =$ specified value

$H_1: \rho_{XY} <$ specified value   or $H_1: \rho_{XY} >$ specified value

Three assumptions are made in testing the null hypothesis:

1. Independence of each pair of scores
2. Bivariate normality
3. $N \geq 30$

The assumption of independence means that the score for any particular student is independent of the score of every other student. The assumption of bivariate normality implies that for each value of X, the values of Y are normally distributed; for each value of Y, the values of X are normally distributed and X and Y are linearly related (see Figure 10-20).

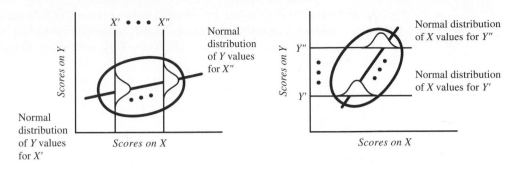

(a) Regression of Y on X (b) Regression of X on Y

FIGURE 10-20
Visual representation of the assumptions of bivariate normality

Bivariate normality can be examined in several ways. Perhaps the easiest way is to inspect a scatterplot to verify linearity and then plot separate frequency distributions for the X scores and the Y scores. If these distributions are roughly normal in form (bell-shaped, approximately 34 percent of the scores between the mean and 1 standard deviation above and below the mean, etc.), the significance test may be used. If these distributions are not normal in form, the assumption of bivariate normality has not been met. If the distributions are skewed or are otherwise nonnormal, a nonparametric analog to the product-moment coefficient, such as Spearman's rank order correlation coefficient (r_s), should be used (see Chapter 6).

Computational Formula and Statistical Test.   The formula for testing the null hypothesis of ρ_{XY} = specified value is given by Formula 10-10a.[7]

$$z_r = (\mathbf{Z}_r - \mathbf{Z}_\rho)\sqrt{N - 3} \qquad\qquad \textbf{(10-10a)}$$

In order to use this formula, we must transform the correlation coefficients, r_{XY} and ρ_{XY}, to Fisher's $\mathbf{Z}$'s. We do so by finding the Fisher's $\mathbf{Z}$ corresponding to the values of r_{XY} and ρ_{XY} in Table I in Appendix II. In this table, the values of r_{XY} are listed in one column and their $\mathbf{Z}$ transformation is listed in the next column.

---

[7]This formula is an algebraic equivalent to the conceptual Formula 10-10:

$$z_{r\ observed} = \frac{\mathbf{Z}_r - \mathbf{Z}_\rho}{s_Z} \qquad \text{(Formula 10-10)}$$

$$= \frac{\mathbf{Z}_r - \mathbf{Z}_\rho}{1} \Big/ \sqrt{N - 3}$$

$$= (\mathbf{Z}_r - \mathbf{Z}_\rho)\sqrt{N - 3} \qquad \text{(Formula 10-10a)}$$

As an example of how to use this formula, suppose a study of the relationship between inductive reasoning and analogies was conducted. A random sample of 103 subjects was given a measure of inductive reasoning (X). Then, they were given 30 analogies to solve (Y), which took the following form:

Washington is to 1 as Lincoln is to _____.

(a) 5
(b) 10

[The answer is (a).] The sample correlation between inductive reasoning and analogies was found to be .68.

Prior to the study, the researcher's null hypothesis was:

$$H_0: \rho_{XY} = .30$$

since this was the average correlation found between measures of human abilities. However, the researcher's alternative hypothesis was:

$$H_1: \rho_{XY} > .30$$

since she had a theory linking these two variables more closely than just any two variables reflecting human abilities. Finally, α was set at .05.

In using Formula 10-10a, we first transform $r_{XY} = .680$ and $\rho_{XY} = .300$ into Fisher's $\mathbf{Z}$'s, using Table I:

$$\mathbf{Z}_{r=.680} = .829 \quad \text{and} \quad \mathbf{Z}_{\rho=.300} = .310$$

These values, then, along with the sample size ($N = 103$) can be placed in the formula, and the observed value of z_r can be found:

$$
\begin{aligned}
z_{r\ observed} &= (\mathbf{Z}_r - \mathbf{Z}_\rho)\sqrt{N - 3} \\
&= (.829 - .310)\sqrt{103 - 3} \\
&= (.519)(10) \\
&= 5.19
\end{aligned}
$$

Decision Rules for the Statistical Test.   Since this statistical test uses the normal distribution as a model of the sampling distribution of z_r, the decision rules can be stated specifically as in Table 10-2.

In our example, $z_{r\ observed}$ was 5.19. If the one-tail test ($H_1: \rho_{XY} > .30$) is made at $\alpha = .05$, $z_{r\ critical}$ is 1.65. Since $z_{r\ observed}$ exceeds $z_{r\ critical}$, the null hypothesis should be rejected. In the population, the correlation between scores on inductive reasoning and analogies is greater than .30.

A study of the relationship between achievement motivation and performance in school (grade-point average) was conducted. Theory and prior research suggested that the correlation between these variables is positive and moderately high (around .5). The observed

TABLE 10-2 Decision rules for the inductive reasoning vs. analogies study

Test	α	Do Not Reject H_0 If	Reject H_0 If
Nondirectional	.05	$\lvert z_{r\,obs.}\rvert < 1.96$	$\lvert z_{r\,obs.}\rvert \geq 1.96$
	.01	$\lvert z_{r\,obs.}\rvert < 2.58$	$\lvert z_{r\,obs.}\rvert \geq 2.58$
Directional	.05	$\lvert z_{r\,obs.}\rvert < 1.65$	$\lvert z_{r\,obs.}\rvert \geq 1.65$
(in predicted	.01	$\lvert z_{r\,obs.}\rvert < 2.33$	$\lvert z_{r\,obs.}\rvert \geq 2.33$
direction)			

correlation in this study, based on 63 subjects, was .75. The procedures for testing whether the correlation between these variables is .50 in the population are summarized in Procedure 10-6.

PROCEDURE 10-6 Steps in testing the null hypothesis ρ_{XY} = specified value (data from the hypothetical study of achievement motivation)

Operation

1. Specify the hypotheses:

   H_0: ρ_{XY} = specified value

   H_1: $\rho_{XY} \neq$ specified value (nondirectional)

or

   H_1: $\rho_{XY} <$ specified value (directional)

or

   H_1: $\rho_{XY} >$ specified value

2. Specify the level of significance.

3. Specify the decision rule.

4. Collect the data.

5. Verify the assumptions.
   a. Independence of score pairs
   b. Bivariate normality
   c. $N \geq 30$

6. Transform the values of r and ρ to Fisher's Z using Table I.

7. Insert the appropriate values into Formula 10-10a and solve:

   $z_{r\,obs.} = (\mathbf{Z}_r - \mathbf{Z}_\rho)\sqrt{N - 3}$

   where:

   $\mathbf{Z}$ = Fisher's transformation of correlations given in Table I

Example

   H_0: ρ_{XY} = .50

   H_1: $\rho_{XY} \neq$ .50

Let α = .05.

   a. Do not reject H_0 if $\lvert z_{r\,observed}\rvert < 1.96$.
   b. Reject H_0 if $\lvert z_{r\,observed}\rvert \geq 1.96$.

For the purposes of this computational model, assume that all assumptions can be verified.

   $r = .75$ so $\mathbf{Z}_r = .973$

   $\rho = .50$ so $\mathbf{Z}_\rho = .549$

   $z_{r\,obs.} = (.973 - .549)\sqrt{63 - 3} = (.424)(7.75)$

   $= 3.29$

Operation	Example
8. State the conclusions.	Since $\lvert z_{r\ observed} \rvert > 1.96$, we reject H_0. We conclude that the relationship between achievement motivation and school performance is greater than the specified value of $\rho_{XY} = .50$.

Since $z_{r\ observed}$ exceeds $z_{r\ critical}$, the null hypothesis should be rejected. The relationship between achievement motivation and school performance is greater than .50 in the population. If the null hypothesis were not rejected, we could conclude that there was insufficient evidence to reject the null hypothesis that the correlation was .50.

The hypothesis, H_0: $\rho_{XY} = 0$, is tested so frequently that tables have been worked out so that $z_{r\ observed}$ does not have to be calculated. Rather, with the sample correlation in hand, the null hypothesis can be tested by referring to Table G in Appendix II. All that need be done to test H_0: $\rho_{XY} = 0$ is to compare $r_{XY\ observed}$ with $r_{XY\ critical}$ based on sample size (actually, based on degrees of freedom: $df = N - 2$). For example, suppose we wanted to test this null hypothesis against a directional alternative (say, H_1: $\rho > 0$). To do so, we draw a random sample of , say, 102 subjects from a population, collect measures of X and Y from the sample, and calculate the sample correlation to be .24. Then $r_{observed} = .24$ can be compared with $r_{critical(.05, df = 100)} = .1638$. (*Note: $df = 102 - 2 = 100$.*) Since the observed correlation exceeds the value of the critical correlation, the null hypothesis should be rejected and the conclusion drawn that, in the population, there is a positive correlation, and our best point estimate of that correlation is .24.

Example Problem 10.12 ▬▬

A researcher was interested in the relationship between attitudes about school and achievement. A random sample of 52 third graders was given a measure of liking for school (X). They were then given an achievement test at the end of the school year (Y). The correlation between these measures was .50. Test whether these two variables are independent at $\alpha = .05$. Include the following items in your answer.
  a. Null and alternative hypotheses
  b. Values of Fisher's **Z** corresponding to r and ρ
  c. Computation of $z_{r\ observed}$
  d. Decision rule
  e. Conclusions

Testing H_0: $\rho_{XY} = 0$ for Two or More Correlations Based on the Same Sample

Often in correlational studies, more than two measures are collected on the same group of subjects. For example, suppose the following measures were collected on 82 subjects: GPA, self-concept, and locus of control (internal vs. external). In this case, three different correlations can be calculated. Table 10-3 presents a *correlation matrix* (table) for these three

TABLE 10-3 Matrix of correlations between GPA, self-concept, and locus of control ($N = 82$)

	(1) *GPA*	*(2)* *Self-Control*	*(3)* *Locus of Control*
(1) GPA	1.00	.40	−.56
(2) Self-Control	.40	1.00	−.64
(3) Locus of Control	−.56	−.64	1.00

variables. Notice that the main diagonal of the matrix—upper left to lower right—contains 1's. The correlation of a variable with itself is always 1.00. Notice also that the correlations below the main diagonal are a mirror image of the correlations above the main diagonal. They are mirror images because the correlation between variable 1 and variable 2 is the same as the correlation between variable 2 and variable 1. Thus, we say that a correlation matrix is symmetric; and in the case of three variables, we have three different coefficients that might be tested to decide whether or not $\rho_{XY} = 0$ in each case. (For four variables, there are six different correlations; for five variables, ten correlations, etc.)

In order to test all of the correlations in the matrix at, say, $\alpha = .05$, we need to take into account that more than one statistical test is being conducted on data from the same group of subjects. This accounting is necessary since sampling errors associated with one of the coefficients will also be associated with the other coefficients.

To be sure that we are testing at a given level of α when more than one coefficient is involved, we should use Table H in Appendix II. The observed correlations r_{XY} can be compared against the critical values in this table in order to decide whether or not to reject H_0: $\rho_{XY} = 0$. It's as easy as that! Table H gives the critical values of r ($\alpha = .05$ and .01, two-tail) when 2, 3, 4, . . . , 25 variables are involved. In this table, the rows correspond to the degrees of freedom for the correlation coefficient ($N - 2$), the columns correspond to the number of variables, and the entries in the table are the critical values of r at $\alpha = .05$ and .01. In the example correlation matrix with three variables, let's test H_0: $\rho_{XY} = 0$ for each at $\alpha = .01$ (two-tail). Since these correlations are based on 82 subjects, there are $82 - 2 = 80$ degrees of freedom. The critical value of r can be found from Table H by finding the row corresponding to 80 and the column corresponding to three variables:

$$r_{\text{critical}(.01/2,80)} = .330$$

Since all three correlations in Table 10-3 exceed the critical value, the null hypothesis of $\rho_{XY} = 0$ can be rejected for all three. (Notice that with the negative correlations, the absolute value of r_{XY} is compared with the critical value.) The correlation between GPA and self-concept is greater than zero; the correlation of these two variables with locus of control is less than zero.

The effect of using Table H for determining r_{critical} when three or more variables are involved is to use a higher value of r_{critical} than would be used if the values for only two variables had been used (the first column of Table H). If in the example, column 1 had been used, $r_{\text{critical}(.01/2, 80)}$ would have been .283 and not .330.

Example Problem 10.13

A researcher was interested in the correlation between the spatial accuracy in the design of a building and the designer's initial perspective of the problem. Fifty-two architectural students were given the following task: They were asked to draw three different buildings, beginning each drawing from a different perspective. These three initial perspectives were as follows:

1. Picturing the building as a whole.
2. Picturing each part of the building.
3. Picturing each part of the building as it fits into the form of the whole building.

Then each drawing was rated according to its spatial accuracy. The correlations listed in Table 10-4 were obtained from these ratings. Test whether $\rho_{XY} = 0$ for these correlations ($\alpha = .05$). Include the following items in your answer:

a. Null and alternative hypotheses
b. $r_{critical}$
c. Conclusion

TABLE 10-4 Correlations for the architecture study

	Initial Perspective		
Initial Perspective	1	2	3
1	1	.54	.67
2		1	.32
3			1

STATISTICAL INFERENCE ABOUT A DIFFERENCE BETWEEN POPULATION CORRELATION COEFFICIENTS

The purpose of this statistical test is to determine whether or not the observed difference between two correlation coefficients ($r_1 - r_2$), based on independent samples, may be due to chance or represents a difference between population correlation coefficients. Concern for differences between correlations sampled from two independent populations arises from substantive research. For example, we might hypothesize that the effectiveness of, say, structured and unstructured lectures might well depend on the characteristics of students attending them. Students low in anxiety might learn equally well from either type of lecture. In this case, we expect the correlation between anxiety and achievement in structured lectures to be close to zero since students both low and high in anxiety are expected to do well. And we expect a negative correlation between anxiety and achievement in the unstructured lecture since students low in anxiety are expected to do better than students high in anxiety. In other words, we expect that the correlation between anxiety and achievement in structured lectures will be smaller than the correlation between anxiety and achievement in unstructured lectures.

Table 10-5 provides a representation of this design along with the predicted direction of the correlation coefficients. The purpose of the significance test, then, is to determine whether the observed difference between the correlation of anxiety with achievement in structured and unstructured lectures may be due to chance or to a systematic effect of the type of lecture the students received.

TABLE 10-5 Design of a hypothetical aptitude × treatment interaction study: Comparing the difference between two correlations based on independent samples

| | Lecture Type | | | |
| | Structured (1) | | Unstructured (2) | |
Subject	*Anxiety (X_1)*	*Achievement (Y_1)*	*Anxiety (X_2)*	*Achievement (Y_2)*
1	X_{11}	Y_{11}	X_{12}	Y_{12}
2	X_{21}	Y_{21}	X_{22}	Y_{22}
⋮	⋮	⋮	⋮	⋮
n	X_{n1}	Y_{n1}	X_{n2}	Y_{n2}
	$r_{xy}=0$		$r_{xy}<0$	

The sampling distribution of the differences between sample correlations ($r_{X_1Y_1} - r_{X_2Y_2}$) based on independent samples can be modeled by the normal distribution if the observed correlations are transformed to Fisher's **Z**'s. See Formulas 10-11 and 10-12.

$$z_{r_1-r_2 \text{ observed}} = \frac{Z_{r_1} - Z_{r_2}}{s_{r_1-r_2}} \quad \textbf{(10-11)}$$

where:

$s_{r_1-r_2}$ = standard error of the difference between correlations

$$s_{r_1-r_2} = \sqrt{\frac{1}{n_1-3} + \frac{1}{n_2-3}} \quad \textbf{(10-12)}$$

In the test for differences between two correlations based on independent samples, the following design requirements should be met:

1. Subjects are randomly and independently sampled.
2. A subject appears in one and only one cell of the design. Subjects may be randomly assigned to one of the two cells (e.g., control or experimental group in a true experimental design). Or they may be drawn from two distinct populations such as males and females in a criterion group design.
3. For each subject, two measures are available, X and Y. Often, X is an aptitude variable and Y is a posttest variable.

The null and alternative hypotheses for a nondirectional alternative hypothesis are:

$H_0: \rho_1 - \rho_2 = 0$ or $H_0: \rho_1 = \rho_2$
$H_1: \rho_1 - \rho_2 \neq 0$ $H_1: \rho_1 \neq \rho_2$

For a directional alternative hypothesis, the null and alternative hypotheses are:

$$H_0: \rho_1 - \rho_2 = 0 \quad \text{or} \quad H_0: \rho_1 = \rho_2$$
$$H_1: \rho_1 - \rho_2 < 0 \qquad\qquad H_1: \rho_1 < \rho_2$$

or

$$H_0: \rho_1 - \rho_2 = 0 \quad \text{or} \quad H_0: \rho_1 = \rho_2$$
$$H_1: \rho_1 - \rho_2 > 0 \qquad\qquad H_1: \rho_1 > \rho_2$$

Three assumptions are made in testing the null hypothesis:

1. Independence of samples (see the design requirements)
2. Bivariate normality for each population
3. Sample sizes n_1 and n_2 both greater than 20

Since each of the assumptions was discussed earlier in this chapter, additional comments are unnecessary here.

Computational Formula for the Statistical Test.   The computational form of the formula for calculating $z_{(r_1 - r_2)}$ is given in Formula 10-11a.

$$z_{r_1 - r_2 \text{ observed}} = \frac{\mathbf{Z}_{r_1} - \mathbf{Z}_{r_2}}{\sqrt{\dfrac{1}{n_1 - 3} + \dfrac{1}{n_2 - 3}}} \qquad\qquad \textbf{(10-11a)}$$

In the use of this formula, the correlation coefficients from the two independent samples, r_1 and r_2, have to be transformed to Fisher's $\mathbf{Z}$'s, using Table I in Appendix II.

As an example, suppose the study of the interaction between anxiety and type of lecture had been carried out on a sample of 46 subjects assigned randomly to the structured lecture or unstructured lecture ($n_1 = n_2 = 23$). For subjects receiving the structured lecture, the correlation between anxiety and achievement was $r_1 = -.12$; the correlation between anxiety and achievement was $r_2 = -.63$ for the unstructured lecture.

Before Formula 10-11a can be used, the observed correlations must be transformed to $\mathbf{Z}$'s. Since both correlations are negative, the r and $\mathbf{Z}$ values in Table I are read as if they were negative:

$$\mathbf{Z}_{r_1 = -.120} = -.121 \quad \text{and} \quad \mathbf{Z}_{r_2 = -.630} = -.741$$

If these values and the sample sizes are placed in Formula 10-11a, we have:

$$z_{r_1 - r_2 \text{ observed}} = \frac{\mathbf{Z}_{r_1} - \mathbf{Z}_{r_2}}{\sqrt{\dfrac{1}{n_1 - 3} + \dfrac{1}{n_2 - 3}}} = \frac{(-.121) - (-.741)}{\sqrt{\dfrac{1}{23 - 3} + \dfrac{1}{23 - 3}}}$$

$$= \frac{.620}{\sqrt{.10}} = \frac{.620}{.31623} = 1.96$$

TABLE 10-6 Decision rules for the anxiety vs. type of lecture study

Test	α	Do Not Reject H_0 If	Reject H_0 If
Nondirectional	.05	$|z_{r_1-r_2\text{obs.}}| < 1.96$	$|z_{r_1-r_2\text{obs.}}| \geq 1.96$
	.01	$|z_{r_1-r_2\text{obs.}}| < 2.58$	$|z_{r_1-r_2\text{obs.}}| \geq 2.58$
Directional	.05	$|z_{r_1-r_2\text{obs.}}| < 1.65$	$|z_{r_1-r_2\text{obs.}}| \geq 1.65$
(in predicted	.01	$|z_{r_1-r_2\text{obs.}}| < 2.33$	$|z_{r_1-r_2\text{obs.}}| \geq 2.33$
direction)			

Decision Rules for the Statistical Test.   Since this test uses the normal distribution as a model of the sampling distribution of $z_{r_1-r_2}$, the critical values are stated specifically in Table 10-6.

In our example, the correlation between anxiety and achievement under the structured lesson (r_1) was expected to be close to zero; this correlation under the unstructured lesson (r_2) was expected to be negative. This expectation leads to the following hypotheses:

H_0: $\rho_1 = \rho_2$

H_1: $\rho_1 > \rho_2$ (since ρ_2 is expected to be negative)

If α is set at .05, we have the following decision rule:

1. If $|z_{r_1-r_2\text{ observed}}| < 1.65$, do not reject H_0.
2. If $|z_{r_1-r_2\text{ observed}}| \geq 1.65$, reject H_0.

Since $z_{r_1-r_2\text{ observed}} = 1.96$, which is greater than 1.65, the null hypothesis should be rejected. The correlation between anxiety and achievement is lower (negative) in the unstructured lecture than in the structured lecture.

Numerical Example.   A study was conducted to determine the effect on final exam scores of college instructors encouraging their introductory psychology students to conform or to be independent on their assignments and in class discussions. Specifically, the researcher predicted that students who were high in need for independence would benefit most from the independence treatment; students low in need for independence would benefit most from the conformity treatment.

Prior to instruction, a random sample of 106 college sophomores who were among those enrolled in introductory psychology received a measure of need for independence. Then they were randomly assigned to either the independence treatment ($n_I = 53$) or the conformity treatment ($n_C = 53$). At the end of the semester of instruction, all students received the final examination. The results of the study are summarized in Table 10-7.

The data in this table can be used to determine whether the correlation between scores on need for independence and final-exam scores in the independence treatment differs from this correlation in the conformity treatment. The steps in conducting this test are summarized in Procedure 10-7.

TABLE 10-7 Descriptive statistics for the study of the effect of instructional treatment (independence or conformity) on final-exam scores of students differing on need for independence

| | Teaching Style | | | |
| | Independence (I) | | Conformity (C) | |
Descriptive Statistic	*Need (X_1)*	*Final Exam (Y_1)*	*Need (X_2)*	*Final Exam (Y_2)*
Mean	24	93.87	25	79.50
Standard Deviation	2	7.18	2	15.90
r_{XY}		.45		−.39
n		53		53

PROCEDURE 10-7 Steps in testing H_0: $\rho_1 = \rho_2$ (example data from Table 10-7)

Operation

1. Specify the hypotheses:

H_0: $\rho_1 = \rho_2$

H_1: $\rho_1 \neq \rho_2$ (nondirectional)

or

H_1: $\rho_1 > \rho_2$ (directional)

or

H_1: $\rho_1 < \rho_2$

2. Specify the level of significance.

3. Specify the decision rule.

4. Verify that assumptions and design requirements have been met.

   a. Subjects are randomly and independently sampled.

   b. A subject appears in one and only one cell of the design.

   c. For each subject, two measures are available.

   d. The samples are independent.

   e. The distribution is bivariate normal.

   f. Sample sizes n_1 and n_2 are both greater than 20.

5. Locate values of Z_{r_1} and Z_{r_2} from Table I.

Example

H_0: $\rho_I = \rho_C$

H_1: $\rho_I > \rho_C$

(i.e., ρ_I is positive and ρ_C is negative.)

Let $\alpha = .01$.

With $\alpha = .01$ (one-tail):

   a. Do not reject H_0 if $|z_{r_1 - r_2 \text{ observed}}| < 2.33$.

   b. Reject H_0 if $|z_{r_1 - r_2 \text{ observed}}| \geq 2.33$.

Assume all assumptions and requirements have been met for the purposes of this computational model.

$$Z_{r_1 = .45} = .485$$

$$Z_{r_2 = -.39} = -.412$$

Operation	Example

6. Insert the appropriate values into Formula 10–11a and solve:

$$z_{r_1 - r_2 \text{ obs.}} = \frac{\mathbf{Z}_{r_1} - \mathbf{Z}_{r_2}}{\sqrt{\dfrac{1}{n_1 - 3} + \dfrac{1}{n_2 - 3}}}$$

$$z_{r_1 - r_2 \text{ obs.}} = \frac{(.485) - (-.412)}{\sqrt{\dfrac{1}{53 - 3} + \dfrac{1}{53 - 3}}} = 4.49$$

7. State the conclusions.

Since $|z_{r_1 - r_2 \text{ observed}}| > 2.33$, we reject H_0. We conclude that the correlation between need for independence and final exam scores differed significantly in the two treatment populations. Notice that this finding leads to the following rule for deciding how to assign students to introductory psychology classes: Students high in need for independence should be assigned to the independence treatment; students low in need for independence should be assigned to the conformity treatment.

Example Problem 10.14

A study was conducted to determine the effects of introversion/extroversion on performance in a clinical psychology course. In particular, the researcher predicted that introverted students would learn most in a course in which discussion was emphasized; extroverted students would learn most in a course that used role playing to illustrate important concepts. Prior to instruction, a random sample of 96 clinical psychology students was administered a measure of introversion/extroversion. A high score on the measure indicates extroversion, and a low score indicates introversion. Subjects were then randomly assigned to the discussion ($n_1 = 48$) or role-playing ($n_2 = 48$) treatments. At the end of the course, all subjects took the same examination. The results are given in Table 10-8. Determine whether the correlation between introversion/extroversion and examination scores differs in the two instructional treatments. (Let $\alpha = .05$.) Include the following items in your answer:

a. Null and alternative hypotheses
b. Values of $\mathbf{Z}_{r_1}$ and $\mathbf{Z}_{r_2}$
c. Calculation of $z_{r_1 - r_2 \text{ observed}}$
d. Decision rule
e. Conclusions

TABLE 10-8 Results of the introversion/extroversion study

	Instructional Treatment			
	Discussion		Role Playing	
Descriptive Statistic	I/E (X_1)	Exam Score (Y_1)	I/E (X_2)	Exam Score (Y_2)
Mean	20	57	22	59
Standard Deviation	3	7	4	8
r_{XY}		−.25		.40
n		48		48

The statistical analysis leads us to reject the null hypothesis. In the populations, the two correlations differed. If the null hypothesis were not rejected, the conclusion would be that the observed difference was not reliable and could have arisen by chance.

SUMMARY

This chapter presents hypothesis-testing procedures using the normal distribution. More specifically, it presents these procedures for testing for case I and II research questions: (I) "Does a particular sample belong to a specified population?" and (II) "Might the observed difference between two sample means (e.g., from an experimental and control group) arise by chance or from differences in populations?" The "z test" is presented for dealing with means ($z_{\bar{X}}$) and correlations (z_r) in case I research studies, and difference between means ($z_{\bar{X}_1 - \bar{X}_2}$) and correlations ($z_{r_1 - r_2}$) in case II research.

Two basic ideas in hypothesis testing are elaborated. First, the null hypothesis is assumed to be true until falsified. Second, since just one sample out of an indefinitely large number of samples is taken from the population, sample means (or correlations) will differ from the population mean (or correlation) by chance alone (i.e., sampling error).

Six fundamental statistical concepts follow from these ideas. First, the notion of a *sampling distribution* was introduced as a model of the variability to be expected when repeatedly sampling from a population under the null hypothesis. Second, the characteristics of the sampling distribution—the shape (normal; cf. central limit theorem), central tendency, and variability—were demonstrated. Third, the sampling distribution was shown to be a *probability* distribution that could be used for answering "how likely" questions about sample findings. Fourth, this probability distribution was used to describe the *level of significance* and how it is used for deciding whether or not to reject the null hypothesis. Fifth, *one-* (directional) and *two-tail* (nondirectional) significance tests were distinguished. Finally, *confidence intervals* and their relation to hypothesis testing were presented.

ANSWERS TO EXAMPLE PROBLEMS

1. **a.** Approximately normal
   b. The population mean (50)
   c. $\sigma_{\bar{X}} = \dfrac{\sigma}{\sqrt{N}} = \dfrac{14}{\sqrt{14}} = 2.00$

2. **a.** $z_{\bar{X}} = \dfrac{26 - 20}{2} = 3.00$

   $p(\bar{X} \geq 26) = .0013$

   b. $z_{\bar{X}} = \dfrac{16 - 20}{2} = -2.00$

   $p(\bar{X} \leq 16) = .0228$

   c. $z_{\bar{X}=16} = -2.00$ (from Example Problem 10.2b)

   $p(\bar{X} \leq 16) = .0228$ (from Example Problem 10.2b)

$$z_{\bar{X}=24} = \frac{24 - 20}{2} = 2.00$$

$$p(\bar{X} \geq 24) = .0228$$

$$p(\bar{X} \leq 16 \text{ or } \bar{X} \geq 24) = .0228 + .0228 = .0456$$

3. **a.** Reject H_0.
   b. Do not reject H_0.

4. **a.** $z_{\bar{X} \text{ critical}} = 1.96$ and -1.96
   b. $z_{\bar{X} \text{ critical}} = -1.65$

5. **a.** *Step 1.* Hypotheses:
   (a) $H_0: \mu = 50$
   (b) $H_1: \mu > 50$
   Step 2. Decision rule with $\alpha = .05$:
   (a) Reject H_0 if $z_{\bar{X} \text{ observed}} \geq 1.65$.
   (b) Do not reject H_0 if $z_{\bar{X} \text{ observed}} < 1.65$.
   Step 3. Computation of $z_{\bar{X} \text{ observed}}$:

   $$z_{\bar{X} \text{ observed}} = \frac{\bar{X} - \mu}{\sigma_{\bar{X}}} \quad \text{where} \quad \sigma_{\bar{X}} = \frac{\sigma}{\sqrt{N}}$$

   $$z_{\bar{X} \text{ observed}} = \frac{53.4 - 50}{2} = 1.7 \quad \text{since} \quad \sigma_{\bar{X}} = \frac{14}{\sqrt{49}} = 2.0$$

   Step 4. Decision $z_{\bar{X} \text{ critical}} = 1.65$; $z_{\bar{X} \text{ observed}} > z_{\bar{X} \text{ critical}}$; so reject H_0.
   Step 5. Conclusion: The mean mechanical ability of seniors in the vocational program is greater than that of seniors statewide.

   b. *Step 1.* Hypotheses:
   (a) $H_0: \mu = 50$
   (b) $H_1: \mu \neq 50$
   Step 2. Decision rule with $\alpha = .05$:
   (a) Reject H_0 if $|z_{\bar{X} \text{ observed}}| \geq 1.96$.
   (b) Do not reject H_0 if $|z_{\bar{X} \text{ observed}}| < 1.96$.
   Step 3. Computation of $z_{\bar{X} \text{ observed}}$: Same as for 5a; $z_{\bar{X} \text{ observed}} = 1.7$
   Step 4. Decision: $|z_{\bar{X} \text{ observed}}| < z_{\bar{X} \text{ critical}}$, so do not reject H_0.
   Step 5. Conclusion: There is insufficient evidence to conclude that the mean mechanical ability of seniors in the vocational program is different from that of seniors statewide. The observed difference may have been due to chance.

   c. Conclusions based on the two tests differ. This occurs because the value of $z_{\bar{X}}$ corresponding to the sample mean is greater than $z_{\bar{X} \text{ critical}}$ (one-tailed) but less than $z_{\bar{X} \text{critical}}$ (two-tailed). Since the value of $z_{\bar{X} \text{critical}}$ marks off 5 percent of the area in *both* tails, the value of $z_{\bar{X} \text{ critical}}$ at each tail marks off 2.5 percent of the distribution. This accounts for the larger value of $z_{\bar{X}}$ in the upper tail compared with the value of $z_{\bar{X} \text{ critical}}$ for a one-tailed test.

6. $\text{CI}_{.95}$:

   $$\bar{X} - 1.96\sigma_{\bar{X}} \leq \mu \leq \bar{X} + 1.96\sigma_{\bar{X}}$$

   $$30 - (1.96)(4) \leq \mu \leq 30 + (1.96)(4)$$

   $$22.16 \leq \mu \leq 37.84$$

$$\text{CI}_{.99}: \qquad \bar{X} - 2.58\sigma_{\bar{X}} \leq \mu \leq \bar{X} + 2.58\sigma_{\bar{X}}$$
$$30 - (2.58)(4) \leq \mu \leq 30 + (2.58)(4)$$
$$19.68 \leq \mu \leq 40.32$$

7. a. $\text{CI}_{.95}:$ $\qquad \bar{X} - 1.96\sigma_{\bar{X}} \leq \mu \leq \bar{X} + 1.96\sigma_{\bar{X}}$
$$53.4 - (1.96)(2) \leq \mu \leq 53.4 + (1.96)(2)$$
$$49.48 \leq \mu \leq 57.32$$

b. Do not reject H_0, since the 95 percent confidence intervals such as this one includes μ.

c. Same decision about H_0, with a two-tailed hypothesis test at $\alpha = .05$ and with a 95 percent confidence interval.

8. $\sigma_{\bar{X}_E} = \dfrac{8}{\sqrt{64}} = 1.0 \qquad \sigma_{\bar{X}_C} = \dfrac{8}{\sqrt{64}} = 1.0$

$\sigma_{\bar{X}_E - \bar{X}_C} = \sqrt{(1.0)^2 + (1.0)^2} = \sqrt{1.00 + 1.00} = \sqrt{2.00} = 1.41$

9. a. $z_{\bar{X}_1 - \bar{X}_2} = \dfrac{(\bar{X}_1 - \bar{X}_2) - (\mu_1 - \mu_2)}{\sigma_{\bar{X}_1 - \bar{X}_2}} = \dfrac{2.50 - 0}{1.20} = 2.08,$ from Table B

$p(z_{\bar{X}_1 - \bar{X}_2} \geq 2.08) = .0188$

b. From Table B, the value of z_{critical} corresponding to .01 of the area under the normal curve in the upper tail of the distribution is 2.33.

10. *Step 1.* Hypotheses:
$\qquad$ (a) H_0: $\mu_{SC} - \mu_{RC} = 0$
$\qquad$ (b) H_1: $\mu_{SC} - \mu_{RC} \neq 0$
$\quad$ *Step 2.* Decision rule with $\alpha = .01$ (*two-tailed*):
$\qquad$ (a) *Reject* H_0 if $|z_{\bar{X}_{SC} - \bar{X}_{RC} \text{ observed}}| \geq z_{\bar{X}_{SC} - \bar{X}_{RC} \text{ critical}} = 2.58.$
$\qquad$ (b) *Do not reject* H_0 if $|z_{\bar{X}_{SC} - \bar{X}_{RC} \text{ observed}}| < z_{\bar{X}_{SC} - \bar{X}_{RC} \text{ critical}} = 2.58.$
$\quad$ *Step 3.* Computation of $z_{\bar{X}_{SC} - \bar{X}_{RC} \text{ observed}}$:

$$z_{\bar{X}_{SC} - \bar{X}_{RC} \text{ observed}} = \frac{(\bar{X}_{SC} - \bar{X}_{RC}) - (\mu_{SC} - \mu_{RC})}{\sigma_{\bar{X}_{SC} - \bar{X}_{RC}}} = \frac{\bar{X}_{SC} - \bar{X}_{RC}}{\sigma_{\bar{X}_{SC} - \bar{X}_{RC}}}$$

$$\sigma_{\bar{X}_{SC} - \bar{X}_{RC}} = \sqrt{\sigma_{\bar{X}_{SC}}^2 + \sigma_{\bar{X}_{RC}}^2}$$

$$\sigma_{\bar{X}_{SC}} = \frac{\sigma_{SC}}{\sqrt{n_{SC}}} = \frac{5}{\sqrt{36}} = .83$$

$$\sigma_{\bar{X}_{RC}} = \frac{\sigma_{RC}}{\sqrt{n_{RC}}} = \frac{5}{\sqrt{36}} = .83$$

$$\sigma_{\bar{X}_{SC} - \bar{X}_{RC}} = \sqrt{(.83)^2 + (.83)^2} = \sqrt{.69 + .69} = 1.17$$

$$z_{\bar{X}_{SC} - \bar{X}_{RC}} = \frac{50 - 48}{1.17} = 1.71$$

$\quad$ *Step 4.* Decision: Since $|z_{\bar{X}_{SC} - \bar{X}_{RC} \text{ observed}}| < z_{\bar{X}_{SC} - \bar{X}_{RC} \text{ critical}}$, do not reject H_0.
$\quad$ *Step 5.* Conclusion: The achievement of EMR children in special classes does not differ significantly from that of EMR children in regular classes.

11. **a.** $CI_{.95}$: $(\bar{X}_E - \bar{X}_C) \pm 1.96\sigma_{\bar{X}_E - \bar{X}_C}$

$(56 - 53) \pm 1.96(1.50)$

3 ± 2.94

Thus,

$CI_{.95}$: $.06 \leq \mu_E - \mu_C \leq 5.94$

b. $CI_{.99}$: $(\bar{X}_E - \bar{X}_C) \pm 2.58\sigma_{\bar{X}_E - \bar{X}_C}$

$(56 - 53) \pm 2.58(1.50)$

3 ± 3.87

Thus

$CI_{.95}$: $-.87 \leq \mu_E - \mu_C \leq 6.87$

12. **a.** H_0: $\rho_{XY} = 0$ (X and Y are linearly independent), H_1: $\rho_{XY} \neq 0$
    b. $Z_r = .549$, $Z_\rho = .000$
    c. $z_{r\,observed} = (Z_r - Z_\rho)\sqrt{N-3} = .549\sqrt{52-3} = (.549)(7) = 3.843$
    d. If $|z_{r\,observed}| < 1.96$, do not reject H_0. If $|z_{r\,observed}| \geq 1.96$, reject H_0.
    e. Since $|z_{r\,observed}| = 3.843$, $|z_{r\,observed}| > 1.96$. Reject H_0.
    f. Conclude that attitudes and achievement are not independent.

13. **a.** H_0: $\rho_{XY} = 0$, H_1: $\rho_{XY} \neq 0$
    b. $r_{crit.(.05/2,50)} = .336$
    c. The null hypothesis is rejected for the correlation between perspective 1 with that of 2 and 3; the null hypothesis is not rejected for the correlation between perspectives 2 and 3.

14. **a.** H_0: $\rho_D = \rho_{RP}$, H_1: $\rho_D < \rho_{RP}$ (i.e., ρ_D will be negative and ρ_{RP} will be positive)
    b. $Z_{r_1} = -.255$, $Z_{r_2} = .424$

c.
$$z_{r_1-r_2\,obs.} = \frac{-.255 - .424}{\sqrt{\dfrac{1}{48-3} + \dfrac{1}{48-3}}} = \frac{-.679}{\sqrt{.04}} = \frac{-.679}{.2} = -3.4$$

d. If $|z_{r_1-r_2\,obs.}| < 1.65$, do not reject H_0. If $|z_{r_1-r_2\,obs.}| \geq 1.65$, reject H_0.
e. Since $|z_{r_1-r_2}| > 1.65$, reject H_0. Conclude that correlations differ significantly in the two instructional treatments.

EXERCISES

1. What are some of the important (a) similarities and (b) differences between a frequency distribution and a sampling distribution?

2. The assertion is made that, by setting forth the null hypothesis such as H_0: $\mu = 100$, the sampling distribution can be specified and its shape, central tendency, and spread are known. Show how this is so. (If it helps to be concrete, assume that $\sigma = 16$ and $N = 64$.)

3. In the study of the disparity between men's and women's college grades, one hypothesis was that women earned higher grades than men for a variety of "feminine" reasons (see Chapter 5 for a description and Table 5-1 for data). The mean grade point average (GPA) for the 20 men in the sample was 2.905 and for the 20 women was 2.955. The standard deviation in the population is known to be .34.

   a. State a null and alternative hypothesis for this study.
   b. Draw a picture of the sampling distribution under the null hypothesis (what do you assume, if anything?).
   c. Do a statistical test of the null hypothesis.
   d. What do you conclude?
   e. Construct the 95 percent confidence interval. Does this jibe with what you found and concluded in c and d?

4. In the sex disparity study, the correlation between SAT scores and GPAs was .0214 for the sample of 40 subjects (ignoring gender). In contrast, the correlation between these two variables for males was −.2369 and for females was +.3760(!).

   a. State a null and alternative hypothesis for this study.
   b. Do a statistical test of the null hypothesis for the total group and by each sex (α = .05).
   c. What do you assume, if anything?
   d. What do you conclude?

5. Test for the difference between the SAT/GPA correlations for males (−.2369) and females (.3760).

   a. State a null and alternative hypothesis for this study.
   b. Do a statistical test of the null hypothesis of no gender difference (α = .05).
   c. What do you assume, if anything?
   d. What do you conclude?

ANSWERS TO EXERCISES

1. a. Similarities: The sampling distribution can be thought of as a frequency distribution or, more specifically, as a relative frequency distribution.

   b. Differences: Frequency distributions describe scores and sampling distributions describe estimators such as means or correlations. The sampling distribution is normal for sample sizes over 30 even if the distribution of scores in the population is nonnormal. The sampling distribution has a mean equal to the population mean under the null hypothesis and the mean of the frequency distribution is the sample mean. Finally, the spread of the sampling distribution is smaller than that of the frequency distribution by a factor of $\sqrt{N}$.

2. Once the null hypothesis is specified, and for samples of 30 or more, we know that the sampling distribution will be normally distributed with a mean equal to the mean under the null hypothesis, and a spread equal to $\sigma/\sqrt{N}$. Using the concrete information in the

example, the sampling distribution will be normal since $N = 64$, its mean will be 100 under the null hypothesis, and its spread will be $16/\sqrt{64} = 16/8 = 2$.

3. a. $H_0: \mu_F - \mu_M = 0$
$H_1: \mu_F - \mu_M > 0$
(based on prior research; a nondirectional hypothesis is acceptable as well)

   b. Because $N < 30$, normality of GPAs must be assumed. However, GPAs may not be normal (e.g., with grade inflation, the population distribution may be negatively skewed) and the normal distribution may not be a good model for the probability distribution.

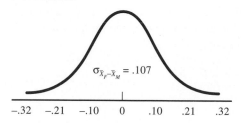

$$\sigma_{\bar{X}_F - \bar{X}_M} = .107$$

| $-.32$ | $-.21$ | $-.10$ | 0 | .10 | .21 | .32 |

   c. $z_{\bar{X}_F - \bar{X}_M} = \dfrac{2.955 - 2.905}{\sqrt{(.076)^2 + (.076)^2}} = \dfrac{.050}{.107} = .465$

   d. Do not reject the null hypothesis. Contrary to past research, the data do not support a conclusion that women have higher GPAs, on average, than men.

   e. $CI_{.95} = -.16 \le \mu_F - \mu_M \le .26$. (Just in case you didn't round off, the exact calculation shows the lower bound of the interval to be $-.15972$ and the upper bound to be $.25972$.). The interval contains 0 as a plausible mean population difference confirming the conclusion drawn from the hypothesis-testing framework.

4. a. H_0

   $H_0: \rho = 0$

   $H_1: \rho > 0$

   Note: A directional alternative hypothesis was specified because aptitude and GPA are known to be positively correlated. Note also that there's no reason to do anything more with the correlation for males since it falls within the fully stated null hypothesis region: $H_0: \rho \le 0$.

   b. Using Table G in Appendix II, $N - 2 = 38$ for the total group and 18 for the girls, we find for a one-tail test:

   $r_{critical(.05, df = 38)} = .2646$ (interpolating) and $r_{critical(.05, df = 18)} = .3783$.

   c. We assume independence, normality, and N of 30 or over. The critical value for women, then, may not be accurate.

   d. Do not reject the null hypothesis for either the total correlation or the women's correlation. There is insufficient evidence for us to conclude that, in the population, the correlation is not 0.

5. a. H_0: $\rho_{men} = \rho_{women}$; H_1: $\rho_{men} \neq \rho_{women}$. A nondirectional alternative hypothesis was used because there is no reason to expect differences in correlations based on gender.

  b. $z_{r_1 - r_2 \, obs.} = \dfrac{-.239 - .394}{\sqrt{\dfrac{1}{20-3} + \dfrac{1}{20-3}}} = \dfrac{-.633}{\sqrt{.118}} = \dfrac{-.633}{.34} = -1.86$

  c. We assume that the subjects are independent and each is in one and only one cell of the design, that the cells are independent, that the distribution is bivariate normal, and that n_1 and n_2 are both greater than 20. Note that $n_1 = n_2 = 20$. The test lacks power and the use of the normal distribution may be suspect.

  d. Do not reject the null hypothesis. Although the sample correlations are in opposite directions and the difference large, the sample sizes are too small to detect the differences statistically.

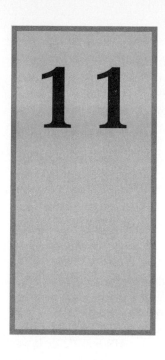

11

Decisions, Error, and Power

In making statistical inferences, the researcher is cast in the role of decision maker: "To reject or not to reject the null hypothesis? That is the decision!" To be *absolutely* certain about making a correct decision, the researcher would have to observe the entire population. But since, in the behavioral sciences, populations are often infinite or at least indefinitely large, observing the entire population is impossible.

Thus, the decision maker usually operates under conditions of *uncertainty*. To make decisions about what is true in the population, she must draw a random sample from the population and, from this random sample, *infer* what is true of the population. From this inference, the researcher decides whether or not to reject the null hypothesis.

One example used in Chapter 10 to illustrate this problem in decision making was the study of determining whether the resting heart rates (HRs) of long-distance runners differed from the HRs of the general population. The researcher suspected that runners, on average, would have lower HRs than people in the general population. In a test of this supposition, a random sample of runners ($N = 36$) was drawn from the population and their HRs measured. Their average HR was 65 beats per minute (bpm). Since the mean HR in the population is known to be 72 bpm with a standard deviation of 9 bpm, should the researcher decide that runners have lower HRs, on average, than do people in general?

In order to answer this question, we must recognize that since the entire runner population was not observed, the sample mean of 65 might not be the true value for this population. Thus, there is some degree of uncertainty about whether the value of the sample mean accurately estimates the population mean. This uncertainty makes our decision less than absolutely certain. And it leads to a second question: "What is the probability of observing a sample mean of 65 when, in fact, the true mean of the population is 72?" Chapter 10 provided the information needed to answer questions like this one. If the probability were less than .05, we agreed to conclude that runners' mean HR is below 72. If the probability was greater than .05, we agreed that there was insufficient evidence to conclude that the population mean differed from 100.

This chapter formalizes this decision-making process. It deals with three topics. The first topic is the type of errors in inference that can arise from hypothesis-testing procedures. The second topic is the *power* of a statistical test, the probability of rejecting a false null hypothesis. You will learn procedures for determining the power of one-sample (case I) and two-sample (case II) tests of means. The third topic is methods for estimating sample size for research studies comparing means.

DECISIONS IN STATISTICAL INFERENCE

In the HR study, the researcher was interested in determining whether the average HR in a population of runners was less than the mean of 72 bpm in the general population. If he were omniscient, he would know the answer: either the runners' average HR was 72 or it was less than 72. These two alternative answers to the researcher's question are shown in Figure 11-1. Thus, there are two possible states of affairs in the population: Either the mean HR in the runner population is 72 bpm ($\mu = 72$) or it is less than 72 ($\mu < 72$).

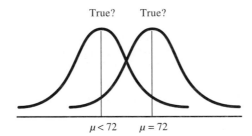

FIGURE 11-1
Alternative inferences in the long-distance runner study

However, the researcher does not in fact know the true state of affairs in the population. Hence he must infer from sample data to decide whether 72 bpm can be rejected.

This decision problem has two features. First, there is a true state of affairs that the researcher would like to know about—in this case, the mean HR in the runner population. Second, he must infer the true state of affairs from sample data with some chance of error.

Probabilities of Type I and II Errors

This decision problem can be cast into the familiar hypothesis-testing framework. For our example, we have:

H_0: $\mu = 72$

H_1: $\mu < 72$

In the population, the *null hypothesis is either true or false.* The sample data may lead the researcher to *decide to reject or not reject the null hypothesis,* and he may be *correct or incorrect.* Table 11-1 shows this decision problem. The researcher makes a correct decision when he decides the following:

1. Not to reject a true null hypothesis
    In our example study, if the null hypothesis is true (column 1 of Table 11-1) and runners' HRs do not differ, on average, from the general population, the researcher makes a correct decision by not rejecting the null hypothesis (row 1).

TABLE 11-1 The decision problem in making inferences from sample
data within the hypothesis-testing framework

Decision Alternatives	True Situation in the Population	
	H_0 Is *True*	H_0 Is *False*
Do Not Reject H_0	Correct Decision $(1 - \alpha)$	Type II Error (β)
Reject H_0	Type I Error (α)	Correct Decision (Power $= 1 - \beta$)

2. Reject a false null hypothesis
    If runners' HRs do, in fact, differ from the general population, on average (column 2), the researcher should decide to reject the null hypothesis (row 2).

However, the researcher can also make *two types of errors:*

1. Type I: Reject a true null hypothesis
    The researcher might conclude that runners' average HR is lower than that in the general population when, in fact, it is not (row 2, column 1 of Table 11-1).
2. Type II: Not to reject a false null hypothesis
    The researcher may conclude that runners' average HR is 72 when, in fact, it is less than 72 (row 1, column 2).

In Chapter 10, we focused on the first column of Table 11-1: The null hypothesis was assumed to be *true* and we were concerned with the error of rejecting a true null hypothesis. To avoid making this **Type I error,** we conservatively set the statistical significance level, α—the probability of rejecting a true null hypothesis—at .05 or .01. In the runner study, $\alpha = .05$. By making a small, we had a high probability of making a correct decision *if H_0 were true*: $1 - \alpha = 1 - .05 = .95$.

However, Table 11-1 points out that in the population, *the null hypothesis can be false,* and this leads to a different set of considerations. To give this situation some reality, let's step back for a moment and consider what research is all about. A study is conducted because there is good reason to believe that the null hypothesis is false—otherwise, why do the study? Thus, the long-distance runner study was conducted because there was good reason to suspect lower HRs. Rosenthal and Jacobson conducted their study of teacher expectancy because theory and research suggested an expectancy effect. Majasan conducted his study because he had evidence that the congruence between teachers' and students' beliefs influenced students' achievement. In all cases, researchers set up the null hypothesis and attempt to knock it down (reject it). If they succeed, they indirectly receive support for their alternative hypothesis. It is the alternative hypothesis that led to the study in the first place. This short sermon should have convinced you that the second column in Table 11-1 has great relevance to research.

When the null hypothesis is false, the researcher—the decision maker—commits an error by not rejecting the null hypothesis. In the runner study, if H_0 is, in fact, false, the researcher commits an error by not rejecting H_0: $\mu = 72$. The probability of making this **Type II error** is labeled β (beta):

$$p(\text{not rejecting a false } H_0) = p(\text{Type II error}) = \beta$$

When the null hypothesis is false and the researcher decides to reject it—something he set out to do—the researcher makes a correct decision. Appropriately, *the probability of correctly rejecting a false null hypothesis is called the* **power** *of the statistical test.* If, in fact, runners have lower HRs, on average, the researcher should correctly reject H_0: $\mu = 72$. The power of a statistical test gives the probability of detecting a true difference between runners' HRs, on average, and HRs in the general population if the difference truly exists. Researchers, then, should take a power trip. They should strive to design the most powerful experiments possible. There seems little reason to spend time and money on an experiment that has little chance of detecting a difference when the difference is actually there.

Notice that probabilities in both columns of Table 11-1 sum to 1. Since the probability of a Type II error—not rejecting a false null hypothesis—is β, the *power*—the probability of rejecting a false null hypothesis—must be $1 - \beta$:

$$\text{power} = p(\text{rejecting a false } H_0) = 1 - \beta$$

A method for determining the power of a statistical test will be presented. From this method, you can estimate power either before or after conducting an experiment.

In designing research, then, the researcher should strive for power and minimize the probability of a Type I error. Although this is an admirable goal, like most admirable goals, it is easier said than done.

Trade-Off Between Level of Significance and Power of the Statistical Test

In trying to decrease both α (the probability of rejecting a true null hypothesis—Type I error) and β (the probability of not rejecting a false null hypothesis—Type II error), we meet a problem. As one type of error (e.g., α) decreases, the other (e.g., β) tends to increase. (This inverse relationship is not a simple one, as will be shown later on in the chapter.)

In order to deal with this trade-off, researchers follow established conventions for setting the level of significance α. Since α, or the probability of a Type I error, is directly under the researcher's control, it is, by convention set at .05 or .01 (prior to collecting data, of course). This convention is conservative; researchers tend to consider rejecting a true null hypothesis a serious error. By committing such an error, for example, the researcher could be led up a blind alley and not realize it until several additional studies had been conducted. Or the substance of the research might involve potential harm to people such that the probability of a Type I error should be minimized. For example, medical studies seek to determine safe drug dosages. If the null hypothesis is that the drug is harmful at a certain level, the researcher does not want to reject this hypothesis until he is virtually certain that no harm will come to the potential patient. Thus, in this case, α might be set extremely conservatively (at, say, .0001).

However, there are situations in which the risk of a Type II error is of greater concern than the risk of a Type I error. In many educational studies, for example, two or more instructional methods may cost about the same and have no adverse effects on students. In this case, a Type I error—concluding that one treatment is better than the others when, in fact, it is not—seems not to be too costly in dollars or risks to students. However, a Type II error—concluding that there is no difference between treatments when, in fact, there is a true difference—seems costly in the sense that students may be denied an instruction that would truly help them learn. The decision about the appropriate level of significance (α), then, should not be made on the basis of statistical convention alone; common sense should also be used in considering the risk involved in making a Type I or a Type II error.

POWER OF A STATISTICAL TEST

To present the statistical concept of power, we use case I research because it provides a framework in which this concept is easiest to understand. Recall that this research is designed to answer the question "Does a particular sample belong to a hypothesized population?" (See Chapters 8 and 10 for detailed discussions.) Also recall that a statistical test may be one- or two-tailed. We further restrict the presentation to one-tail significance tests because it is easier to understand than a presentation of two-tail tests.

To begin, a review of the hypothesis-testing framework is helpful. In this review, the example of the HR study will be used. The hypothesis-testing perspective works with the first column in Table 11-1—the case where H_0 is true. The following steps are taken in hypothesis testing:

1. An exact hypothesis about the population parameter μ is stated:

   H_0: $\mu = 72$

2. An inexact, alternative hypothesis is stated:

   H_1: $\mu < 72$

   Note that this alternative is a *directional* alternative hypothesis: μ is *less than* 72. It is tested indirectly by testing H_0 directly. This alternative hypothesis is *inexact,* since it is not stated as one value. We should be equally ready to reject H_0 if, in fact, $\mu = 71.1$, 70.0, or 61.

3. The level of significance (α) is set at .05 by convention.
4. Runners ($N = 36$) are randomly sampled from the population. The sample mean $\bar{X}$ is used as an estimate of μ.
5. Given the sample data, a decision is made on whether or not to reject the null hypothesis. For a one-tail test, the decision rule is as follows:

   a. If $z_{\bar{X} \text{ observed}}$ equals or is less than -1.65, reject the null hypothesis.
   b. If $z_{\bar{X} \text{ observed}}$ is greater than -1.65, do not reject the null hypothesis, where:

$$z_{\bar{X} \text{ observed}} = \frac{\bar{X} - \mu}{\sigma_{\bar{X}}}$$

(See Figure 11-2.)

Several features of this hypothesis-testing framework are important for understanding power. First, the distribution shown in Figure 11-2 is a sampling distribution of means. It is also a probability distribution. It indicates that assuming H_0 is true, an extremely high sample mean will be drawn from that population 5 times in 100. That is, the probability of Type I error is .05. Second, by using this distribution for testing the null hypothesis, we have *assumed that the null hypothesis is true*. Remember, the null hypothesis is always assumed to be true until shown to be unlikely. Thus, Figure 11-2 shows the sampling distribution under the null hypothesis with a mean of 72. Third, the hypothesis-testing framework focuses on the first column of Table 11-1: the probability of a correct or incorrect decision when the null hypothesis is true.

Now, let's move slowly into the power trip. In order to do so, Table 11-1 suggests that we must consider the case in which the null hypothesis is, in fact, false. If the null hypothesis is false, *Figure 11-2 is not the sampling distribution from which the researcher sampled.* Rather, *some alternative sampling distribution would provide the correct picture.* Using the value of $z_{\bar{X} \text{ critical}} = -1.65$, which is always determined with the assumption that H_0 is true, what would we decide to do about our sample mean, which in fact was sampled from a *different* sampling distribution? If we decide to reject the null hypothesis, the decision is a correct one. But if we decide not to reject the null hypothesis when we should have, we have committed a Type II error.

Since the case of a false null hypothesis corresponds to the alternative hypothesis, the problem is as follows: The alternative hypothesis is not an exact hypothesis. All it says is that the true population mean is less than 72. There are an infinite number of means less than 72. Which one is true? At first glance, it may seem an impossible problem has been identified. However, there is a heuristic solution. The solution is to select one of the infinity of alternative means and assume that it is the "true" mean. We can determine the power by assuming that a specific value of μ is correct—a value different from μ under the null hypothesis—and then determine whether we would have correctly rejected the null hypothesis.

One way to make this selection is to decide how much of a deviation from a mean of 72 would be important to know about. Suppose health physiologists are interested only in a difference of 3 bpm or more. They would not mind making a Type II error on the basis of less than 3 bpm. That is, they would not be concerned by falsely concluding that the runners' mean HR is 72 when, in fact, it is 71 or even 70. In this case, let's choose a mean

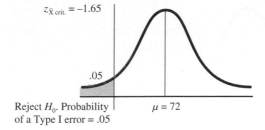

FIGURE 11-2

Distribution of scores under H_0 in the hypothetical runner study

of 69 as the true value of μ for runners. In so doing, we have an *exact* alternative hypothesis to work with.

At this point, we know that H_0 is false and that the true population mean is 69. The question remains whether our statistical test would be powerful enough to detect this 3-point difference.

This reasoning is presented pictorially in Figure 11-3. The critical region for rejecting H_0 is shown in Figure 11-3a, the theoretical sampling distribution under H_0 with $\mu = 72$ and $\sigma_{\bar{X}} = \sigma/\sqrt{N} = 9/\sqrt{36} = 1.5$. (*Note:* The mean that corresponds to $z_{\bar{X} \text{ critical}}$ is 69.52; that is, this mean falls 1.65 standard errors below 72: $72 - (1.65)(1.5) = 69.52$.) The critical region is established in the usual way and does not depend on the particular value of μ chosen for the exact alternative hypothesis. Figure 11-3b shows the true sampling distribution with mean 69 and a standard error of 1.5. When the critical region is projected into the true alternative sampling distribution, it cuts through the distribution just above the mean at $\bar{X}_{\text{critical}} = 69.52$ (Figure 11-3b). Notice that more than half of the alternative sampling distribution falls below the rejection region. Thus, if repeated samples were drawn from the sampling distribution under the true alternative hypothesis, over 50 percent of the sample means would lead us to correctly reject the H_0. In other words, the power of this statistical test is greater than .50. Conversely, the probability of a Type II (β) is less than .50.

METHOD FOR DETERMINING POWER

The method just used to illustrate, conceptually, how the power of a statistical test can be determined is too cumbersome for practical use. Fortunately, a quick approximation is available for determining the power of case I and II, one- and two-tail statistical tests (cf. Friedman, 1982; see also Cohen, 1988, 1992b). With three pieces of information—α, N, and effect size—Table M in Appendix II can be used to determine power.

Before we use Table M, the effect size needs explanation. *Effect size* is the discrepancy between the null hypothesis and the alternative hypothesis of interest. For case I research focused on the population mean, as is the HR study, effect size is the difference between μ_0 and μ_1 (the population means under H_0 and H_1, respectively) that you want your statistical test to detect (cf. Cohen, 1992a, b). We define Δ_I as the standardized difference between μ_0 and μ_1:

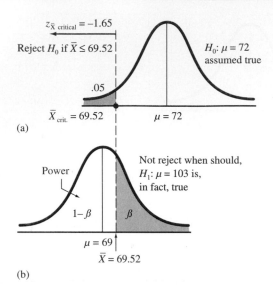

(a)

(b)

FIGURE 11-3

Sampling distributions of means in the long-distance runner study: (a) under H_0: $\mu = 72$; (b) under H_1: $\mu = 69$ (one-tail test)

$$\Delta_I = \frac{|\mu_1 - \mu_0|}{\sigma} \qquad\qquad\qquad (11\text{-}1)$$

where:

μ_1 = population mean under H_1
μ_0 = population mean under H_0
σ = population standard deviation

In words, Δ_I tells how large a difference you want to detect in your study—not in terms of an actual score but in terms of a z score. If Δ_I were .33, this value would mean that the researcher wanted to detect a difference of 1/3 of a standard deviation between μ_1 and μ_0. As a rule of thumb, Cohen (1992a, p. 154) defines a "small effect" as $\Delta_I = .20$; the researcher wishes to detect a difference of 1/5 of a standard deviation between μ_1 and μ_0. A "medium effect" is defined as $\Delta_I = .50$; and a "large effect" is defined as $\Delta_I = .80$. As you become comfortable with "Δ," you will be able to express the difference of theoretical or practical importance in your own research without reference to this rule of thumb.[1]

---

[1]Cohen (1992a) defines effect sizes for other statistical tests such as the tests for correlations presented in Chapter 10. For a statistical test of a correlation, the correlation itself, r_{XY}, is the measure of the effect size and $r = .10$ is a small effect, $r = .30$ is a medium effect, and $r = .50$ is a large effect. For differences between correlations, the effect size index is $q = Z_{r_1} - Z_{r_2}$ (Fisher's Z) and $q = .10$ is a small effect, $q = .30$ is medium, and $q = .50$ is large.

When we have information about effect size, sample size, and significance level (one- or two-tail), Table M provides a rough approximation of the power of a statistical test. In the HR study (see Figure 11-3), we reasoned that the power of the one-tail test for determining a 3-bpm difference in HR was greater than .50 when $\mu_0 = 72$ and $\mu_1 = 69$, $N = 36$, $\sigma = 9$, and $\alpha = .05$. Information from this hypothetical study can be used to determine effect size, the only missing piece of information for Table M. From Formula 11-1, we have

$$\Delta_I = \frac{|69 - 72|}{9} = \frac{3}{9} = .33$$

Referring to Table M, find the part of the table corresponding to one-tail, case I research, part a. Next, locate that part of the table corresponding to $\alpha = .05$. Then locate the closest column corresponding to $\Delta_I = .33$. Now find the table entry—the sample size—that comes closest to 36. That number is 38. Finally, read the power of the statistical test for that row: .70. (For a summary of these steps, see Procedure 11-1.)

PROCEDURE 11-1 Practical method for determining power

Operation	Example
1. Determine the following values: **a.** Sample size **b.** Level of significance **c.** One- or two-tail test **d.** Standardized difference to be detected by the statistical test For case I, use Formula 11-1: $$\Delta_I = \frac{|\mu_1 - \mu_0|}{\sigma}$$ For case II, use Formula 11-2 (see discussion in text below): $$\Delta_{II} = \frac{|\mu_1 - \mu_2|}{\sigma}$$ Alternatively, for either design, state the difference in standard deviation units.	Using information from Figure 11-3, we have a case I design, with: $n = 36$ $\alpha = .05$ one-tail test: $$\Delta_I = \frac{|69 - 72|}{9} = \frac{3}{9} = .33$$ The researcher wishes to detect a difference of 1/3 standard deviation.
2. Enter Table M and identify the appropriate part of the table for your test: **a.** Case I, one-tail **b.** Case I, two-tail **c.** Case II, one tail **d.** Case II, two-tail	 Part a is the appropriate part of Table M.
3. Locate the column of Table M corresponding to Δ.	$\Delta_I = .33$

Operation	Example
4. Locate the part of the table corresponding to $\alpha = .05$.	For $\alpha = .05$, we use the left-hand column of the table.
5. Find the table entry—*sample size*—that is closest to your sample size in the appropriate effect size column.	*Note: Sample size* is given for the only group in case I research and for *one group* in case II research. $$n = 36$$
6. Read the power corresponding to a sample size n for α and Δ.	The power is .70 for $\alpha = .05$ (one-tail), $\Delta_I = .33$, and $n = 36$.

Example Problem 11.1

In the study of college achievement (Chapter 5), researchers asked whether the average SAT score of the University of California students was higher than the national average SAT score (1000), as they had reason to believe. Suppose that, first, the researchers are interested in detecting a 100-point difference or more; second, the sample consisted of 40 students; and third, the standard deviation in the population is known to be 200.
(a) What is the power of the statistical test at $\alpha = .05$?
(b) What is β?

As an example of the use of Table M for two-tail case I research, suppose that the researcher did not have good reason to expect runners' HRs to be, on average, lower than those in the general population (72 bpm). We should then determine power for a two-tail case I statistical test. Part b of Table M provides the relevant information with $\alpha = .05$, $N = 36$, and $\Delta_I = .33$. The power is .60, approximately.

In a similar manner, Table M can be used for case II research. To do so, the effect size for case II designs has to be defined. For mean comparisons, effect size is the size of the difference between population means in standard deviation units:

$$\Delta_{II} = \frac{|\mu_1 - \mu_2|}{\sigma} \tag{11-2}$$

where:

μ_1 = population mean of group 1
μ_2 = population mean of group 2
σ = population standard deviation (assumed to be equal in two populations)

Now, let's return to determining power for case II research (see Procedure 11-1). Suppose a researcher is *planning a study* to test a theory of spatial cognition. He plans to use 150 subjects in each of two groups (i.e., $n_1 = n_2 = 150$, $N = 300$). Since he has not run a pilot study, he expresses the effect size in standard deviation units. He would like to detect a population difference between the two groups of .35 standard deviation (i.e., $\Delta_{II} = .35$). To be conservative, he will conduct a two-tail statistical test at $\alpha = .01$. Before doing so, however, he checks Table M to make sure the proposed experiment has sufficient power to make it worthwhile to run. Part d of Table M provides the relevant information when entered with $\alpha = .01$ (two-tail), $\Delta_{II} = .35$, and the size of the sample in one group, 150. The power of the proposed statistical test, then, is roughly .70. He notes from the table that by increasing each group by 40 subjects ($n = 190$), power increases to .80, a more acceptable level, and plans to do so.

Several characteristics of Table M are noteworthy in understanding the concept of power. First, because the table is based on the normal distribution, the smallest sample size in the table is 30. Second, all other things being equal, as sample size increases, so does power. Run your finger down the first column of numbers in part a for $\alpha = .10$, and you will find that power increases from .60 to .90 as sample size increases from 104 to 291. Third, all else being equal, as the level of significance becomes more conservative, going from .10 to .01, power decreases. Reading from the same section of Table M, we find that with a sample size of 291 ($\Delta_I = .15$), power is .90. Now, how much power does a sample of 291 buy you if $\alpha = .05$ and .01? At .05, the power is roughly .70; and at .01, power is about .60. Fourth, all other things being equal, as the magnitude of the treatment effect increases (i.e., Δ increases), so does power. For example, a sample of 104 observations buys you power of .60 if $\Delta_I = .15$, power of roughly .80 if $\Delta_I = .20$, and power of .90 if $\Delta_I = .25$.

We now turn to a more detailed consideration of the factors that affect power.

Example Problem 11.2

a. Suppose that the researchers in the study of college achievement had no reason to believe that the SAT scores of University of California students were above the national average. What is the power of a two-tail statistical test at $\alpha = .05$? What is β?

b. A researcher, interested in strategies for learning from prose, plans to randomly assign 30 subjects to each of two groups: (a) *subject-generated* (SG) underlining condition, in which subjects were instructed to underline the most important sentence in each paragraph; and (b) *experimenter-provided* (EP) condition, in which subjects were provided with a sentence in each paragraph already underlined. All subjects will be given a comprehension test after reading the passage. Suppose also that, first, the experimenter is interested in detecting a two-point difference between the groups; second, he has a theory and pilot data to suggest that the SG group would show significantly greater comprehension than the EP group; and third, $\sigma_{SG} = \sigma_{EP} = 3$. What is the power of this statistical test at $\alpha = .01$ (one-tail)? What is the value of β?

FACTORS INFLUENCING POWER

At this point, you know how to determine the power of a statistical test, but that does not necessarily help unless you can do something to improve the power if your statistics suggest that you should. A number of factors influence the power of a statistical test and some are under your control. By systematically manipulating such factors as sample size, you can manipulate the power of your statistical test.

There are four factors that influence the power of statistical tests, and three of them you can control. Each factor is discussed in the following paragraphs.

Level of Significance

One factor under your control is the level of significance, α. *The power of a statistical test increases as α increases.* Thus, if all other factors influencing power are held constant, as α increases from .01 to .05 to .10, and so on, power increases. This relationship between power and α is shown in Figure 11-4. As α increases, so does the power of the statistical test (unshaded area under the sampling distribution for the alternative, "true," hypothesis).

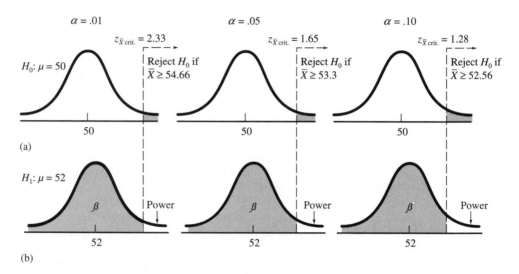

FIGURE 11-4

Illustration of the relationship between α and power: (a) sampling distributions under H_0; sampling distributions under H_1 (assume true $\mu = 54$; $\sigma_{\bar{X}} = 2$)

Magnitude of the Treatment Effect

The magnitude of the treatment effect—the size of the difference between μ_1 and μ_2—also affects the power: *the greater the treatment effect, the greater the power,* all other things equal. If the treatment effect is small, the sampling distributions under H_0 and H_1 will overlap greatly, reducing the probability of detecting a true difference. If the effect is large, the sampling distributions under H_0 and H_1 will scarcely overlap, the difference will be easy to detect, and power will be high.

Although the magnitude of the treatment effect is not directly under the researcher's control, researchers should carefully develop a treatment by pilot testing and revising it. In this way, noise or error in estimating the treatment effect can be reduced.

Variability in the Population

A third factor affecting power is the variability in the population. All other factors equal (α, N, and Δ), *the smaller the standard deviation of the population, the greater the power.* The reasoning is as follows. As the overlap between the sampling distribution under the null and the specific alternative hypotheses decreases, power increases, since all sample means from the "true" alternative distribution fall in the rejection region. The overlap of these sampling distributions depends, in part, on the population standard deviation σ in the formula for the standard error: $\sigma_{\bar{X}} = \sigma/\sqrt{N}$. Thus, for constant N, the spread or potential overlap of the sampling distributions under the null and specific alternative hypotheses increases as σ increases. This relationship is shown in Figure 11-5.

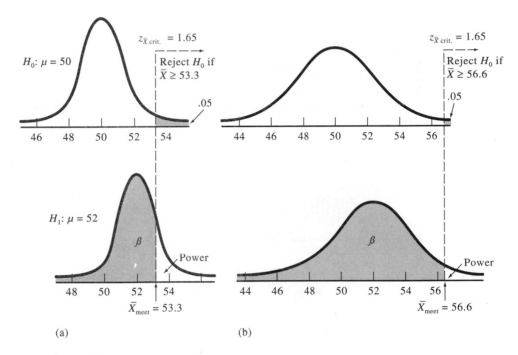

FIGURE 11-5
Illustration of the relationship between power and variability ($N = 64$): (a) sampling distributions under H_0 and H_1 with $\sigma = 16$, so $\sigma_{\bar{X}} = 2$; (b) sampling distribution under H_0 and H_1 with $\sigma = 32$ and $\sigma_{\bar{X}} = 4$

The researcher can control the magnitude of the population standard deviation in a number of ways. One way to control σ is to sample subjects from a homogeneous population. Instead of sampling subjects from all ranges of socioeconomic status, for example, only middle-class students might be sampled. A second way to control σ is to make sure that the dependent variable is reliable, since unreliability increases σ by introducing unnecessary error. A third way to control σ is to use statistical techniques such as the analysis of covariance or a randomized-blocks design since they provide the most efficient estimates of variance if their assumptions are met (see Chapters 15 and 17).

Sample Size

Sample size influences power by influencing the spread of the sampling distributions under H_0 and H_1. By increasing the sample size and holding all other factors constant, the variability of the sampling distribution decreases. Reducing $\sigma_{\bar{X}}$ decreases the overlap between the distribution under the null hypothesis and the distribution under the alternative hypothesis. Thus more and more of the sample means drawn from the distribution under the "true" alternative hypothesis fall in the rejection region of the null hypothesis. Hence, power is increased. The effect of sample size on power is shown in Figure 11-6.

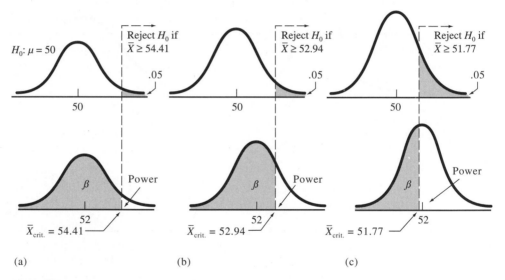

FIGURE 11-6

Illustration of the relationship between power and sample size ($\sigma = 16$): (a) sampling distributions under H_0 and H_1 with $N = 36$, so $\sigma_{\bar{X}} = 2.67$; (b) sampling distribution under H_0 and H_1 with $N = 81$ so $\sigma_{\bar{X}} = 1.78$; (c) sampling distribution under H_0 and H_1 with $N = 225$, so $\sigma_{\bar{X}} = 1.07$

Some Wisdom

Sample size influences power indirectly by affecting the variability of the sampling distribution. You can design an experiment that is extremely powerful just by increasing sample size. From a practical standpoint, trivial differences may be statistically significant. Also even poor experimental treatments may be found to differ significantly from control treatments. Wisdom must come into play when the researcher balances the factors influencing the power of a statistical test by designing a study with the following features:

1. The best treatments possible, so that the treatment effect is as strong as possible
2. An α set at a conservative level (e.g., .05 or .01) so that the probability of a Type I error is minimized
3. Sample sizes large enough so that theoretically and/or practically significant differences are detected

Since the sample size is such an important factor influencing power, a method for estimating the needed sample size for an experiment is given next.

METHOD FOR ESTIMATING SAMPLE SIZE

In estimating the size of a sample needed for a study, there are a number of factors to be taken into consideration: the probability of a Type I error (α), the probability of a Type II error (β or, alternatively, power, which is $1 - \beta$), and the size of the difference between means to be detected in the study, expressed in standard deviation (σ) units. Prior to a study, a researcher should be able to state desired levels of the three factors influencing the sample size. For example, α might be set at .05 by convention, and β might be set at .10, giving a power of $1 - \beta = .90$. While the conventions for setting β are not as well established as those for setting α, often β is set at .20 or lower (power $\geq .80$). With $\beta \leq .20$, the researcher assures a reasonable probability of detecting a difference if the difference exists. Notice also that, as is almost always the case, α is more conservative than β. This conservatism reflects most researchers' greater concern for a Type I than a Type II error. However, as pointed out earlier, there may be situations in which a Type II error is more costly than a Type I error, and you may want to make corresponding adjustments in α and β.

The researcher should also have some notion of how big a difference the study must detect. This factor can be approached in several ways. In applied research, a statistically significant difference should also have practical importance. For example, in an evaluation of two reading curricula, the difference might have to be reasonably large to have practical value, especially when differential costs of implementing the curricula are considered. In basic research, theory might indicate the size of a difference between experimental and control treatments. Sometimes it may be important to detect a very small difference in testing theory.

Sometimes the researcher has a notion of the magnitude of difference to be detected but cannot translate the size of the difference into a number because she is not sure of the measurement scale: Should the difference be 1 point? 5 points? Nevertheless the researcher might state that she would like to detect a difference of, say, a half a standard deviation between the experimental and control groups (i.e., $\Delta_{II} = .50$).

Conceptual Underpinnings

In examining methods for determining sample size, let's begin conceptually with case I research. A one-tail test is used, not because the conclusion for determining sample size will differ in important ways for a two-tail test or for case II studies, but because the one-tail test is easiest to understand.

In developing ideas about determining sample size, we will use the heart-rate study as an example. A researcher hypothesized that the mean HR of runners was lower than that in the general population ($\mu = 72$, $\sigma = 9$). He tested this hypothesis at $\alpha = .05$. Let's assume that for this study, the desired power was .90, so $\beta = .10$. Finally, the ability to detect a difference of 3 bpm or more below 72 was considered important. With these three pieces of information, we can set up two sampling distributions: one representing the null hypothesis, H_0: $\mu = 72$, and one representing the specific alternative hypothesis, H_1: $\mu = 69$. When we draw a picture of these two sampling distributions, *the two distributions must be scaled to represent the situation in which $\beta = .10$*—that is, 10 percent of the distribution under the alternative hypothesis falls in the nonrejection region of the distribution under the null hypothesis. Thus 10 percent of the sample means would lead the researcher not to reject a false hypothesis—that is, to commit a Type II error. Figure 11-7 provides a picture of this situation.

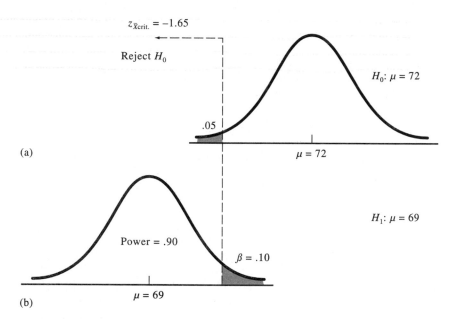

FIGURE 11-7
Hypothetical sampling distributions when $\alpha = .05$, $\beta = .10$, and a difference (D) of 3 points is important (one-tail test): (a) sampling distribution under H_0; (b) sampling distribution under H_1

The key point to notice is that when we draw the figures to the appropriate scale, there is only one value of the standard error of the mean—the index of the spread or variability of each sampling distribution—that allows the two distributions to overlap exactly so $\beta = .10$. As mentioned earlier, the variability of the sampling distribution—that is, the standard error, $\sigma_{\bar{X}}$—depends on the population standard deviation and the sample size. As $\sigma_{\bar{X}}$ decreases, the likelihood of detecting true differences between the sample and population—power—increases, since the overlap between the distributions under H_0 and H_1 is decreased. Mathematically, the figure can be drawn to scale by finding the exact value of N, the sample size, which adjusts the standard error so that the overlap of the two distributions produces $\beta = .10$.

Practical Method

Fortunately, there is a practical method for determining sample size. Sample size can be determined, approximately, using Table M, armed with α, power, and effect size (Δ).

Sample Size for Case I Research: One-Tail Tests

With α, power, and Δ_I, part a of Table M provides approximate sample sizes for one-tail, case I research. (Sample sizes are approximate because N's are given only for certain values of α, power, and Δ_I.) Consider the runners' HR study. The null hypothesis was that the mean HR in the population was 72. Suppose the researcher does not know σ and is interested in detecting a "small effect," say, 1/5 of a standard deviation, so that $\Delta_I = .20$. Furthermore, he sets α at .05 (one tail) and wants the power to be .90 ($\beta = .10$). From part a of Table M, the sample size needed is 215. That's all there is to it! In the hypothetical HR study, the effect size was much larger than .20. The difference between the sample mean (65) and the population mean under the null hypothesis (72) was 7 bpm. With $\sigma = 9$, $\Delta_I = 7/9 = .78$, a large effect. From Table M, the sample size needed to detect this effect at .05 one tail with power .90 (assuming $\Delta_I = .80$) is under 30. This is consistent with the finding reported before that the power of the statistical test with N = 36 was > .90.

Example Problem 11.3 ▬▬▬▬▬▬▬▬▬▬▬▬▬▬▬▬▬▬▬▬▬▬▬▬▬▬▬▬▬▬▬▬▬▬▬▬▬▬

Suppose that the researchers in the study of college achievement decided to replicate their study with another sample of University of California students. They decided that they wanted to detect a 100-point difference or more above the national average of 1000 on the Graduate Record Examination (GRE), and they wanted to set $\alpha = .05$ (one tail) and $\beta = .10$. Assuming that $\sigma = 200$, what sample size should they use?

Sample Size for Case I Research: Two-Tail Tests

To determine sample size for two-tail tests, use part b of Table M. Suppose a two-tail test was to be used in the HR study. With $\alpha = .05$, $1 - \beta = .90$, and $\Delta_I = .20$, we find $N = 262$ from Table M. Not surprisingly, a larger N is needed for a two-tail than a one-tail test to achieve the same power, holding α and Δ_I constant.

Example Problem 11.4 ▬▬▬▬▬▬▬▬▬▬▬▬▬▬▬▬▬▬▬▬▬▬▬▬▬▬▬▬▬▬▬▬▬▬▬▬▬▬

Suppose that the researchers in Example Problem 11.3 wished to conduct a two-tail test. What sample size should they use?

Sample Size for Case II Research: One- and Two-Tail Tests

The same procedure for determining sample size with Table M is used for case II research. With α, $1 - \beta$, Δ_{II} in hand, approximate sample sizes can be determined. As an example, consider the hypothetical teacher expectancy study. The observed difference between the means of the control and experimental groups was .66 score point (!). Although this difference certainly has little practical importance, it may be theoretically important, since expectancy theory predicts a difference but does not indicate the magnitude. Suppose that the data showing the difference of .66 point were taken from a pilot study. The researchers then wished to determine the sample size needed to detect this difference in their major study, in which a one-tail test is planned at $\alpha = .05$ and $\sigma = 9.2$, and power of that test is to be .80 ($\beta = .20$). $\Delta_{II} = .66/9.20 = .07$. This is, indeed, a very small effect. A very large sample size will be needed. From part c of Table M, we cannot find $\Delta_{II} = .07$. The best we can do is to use $\Delta_{II} = .15$ and find $n = 551$. Clearly, more than 551 subjects will be needed *in each group*. Here you see why Table M provides only approximate sample sizes.

Example Problem 11.5

Suppose that researchers in the prose-learning study in Example Problem 2b wished to determine the sample size needed to detect a 1.2-point difference between the groups when $\alpha = .01$ (one-tail) and $\beta = .20$. Assuming that $\sigma = 3$, what sample size is needed?

For a two-tail test with $\alpha = .05$, $1 - \beta = .80$, and $\Delta_{II} = .07$, we find N from part d of Table M: $n = 697$. Certainly more than 700 subjects *per group* will be needed to detect such a small effect.

Example Problem 11.6

Suppose that the researchers in the prose-learning study in Example Problem 11.2b did not know σ and were interested in detecting a large effect. What sample size would be required if $\alpha = .05$ (two tail), $\beta = .10$?

SUMMARY

This chapter discusses *errors* associated with making statistical inferences. *Type I errors* and *Type II errors* are defined and their relationship discussed. *Power* of a statistical test is defined, procedures for estimating it with case I and case II research are presented, and factors influencing power are described. Finally, a method for determining approximate *sample size* is presented.

ANSWERS TO EXAMPLE PROBLEMS

1. **a.** Difference = 100, N = 40, $\sigma = 200$, and $\alpha = .05$ (one tail)

    $\Delta_I = 100/200 = .50$

    From Table M (part a), power is greater than .90
   b. $\beta = .10$

2. **a.** Using information in 1, from Table M (part b), power is just under .90.
   b. Difference = 2, n = 30, σ = 3, and α = .01 (one tail)

   $\Delta_{II} = 2/3 = .67$.

   From Table M (part a), power is just under .60. β is just over .40
3. Difference = 100, β = .10 so power = .90, σ = 200, and α = .05 (one tail)

   $\Delta_I = 100/200 = /50$

   From Table M (part a), $N = 34$
4. From Table M (part b), $N = 42$
5. Difference = 2, power = .80 (i.e., $1 - .20$), σ = 3, and α = .01 (one tail)

   $\Delta_{II} = 1.2/3 = .40$

   From Table M (part c), $n = 126$ in each group
6. Δ_{II} = .80, a large effect. α = .05 (two tail) and power = .90. From Table M (part d), $n = 33$ in each group.

EXERCISES

In the teacher expectancy study (Chapter 2), the mean posttest IQ scores of control- and experimental-group students are given Table 11-2. The following questions refer to these data.

TABLE 11-2 Posttest ability scores from the hypothetical teacher expectancy study: Mean, standard deviation (SD), and sample size (N): Descriptive statistics based on data in Table 2-1

	Control	Experimental	Combined
		Group	
Mean	109.57	110.23	109.90
SD	9.17	9.38	9.20
N	30	30	60

1. What is the power of a test of the null hypothesis that the mean IQ of all subjects combined is 100 (assume σ = 9.2) when the true mean is 109.90 (σ = .01, one tail)?
2. Draw a picture of the sampling distribution of means under the null and specific alternative hypothesis in 1 above.
3. What is the power of a statistical test of the difference between the control and experimental groups in mean IQ when the true difference is as observed in the sample (α = .05, one tail) and σ = 9.2?
4. How large a sample would be needed to detect a difference (at α = .05, two tail) between the null hypothesis of mean ability = 100 (σ = 9.2) and the alternative that the true mean ability is as observed in the control group at *pretest,* 96.90, with power .90?
5. Assuming the data in Table 11-2 were generated by a pilot study, how large a sample would be needed in the main study to detect a very small effect (say, .15) with α = .05 (one tail) and power = .90?

6. The following statement is often heard about research with large sample sizes: "The difference was statistically significant but of little practical import."

   a. What is meant by this statement?

   b. In addition to the statistical test, what other statistic might be presented to show the practical impact of the difference?

ANSWERS TO EXERCISES

1. From part a of Table M, power > .90. (*Note:* $\Delta_I = (109.9 - 100.00)/9.20 = 1.08$.)
2. First, to scale the distributions, calculate the standard error of the mean: $\sigma_{\bar{X}} = \sigma/\sqrt{N} = 9.20/\sqrt{60} = 9.20/7.75 = 1.19$. The true mean, 109.90, falls 8.32 standard errors above 100 ($109.90 - 100/1.19 = 8.32$). Scale the distributions accordingly.

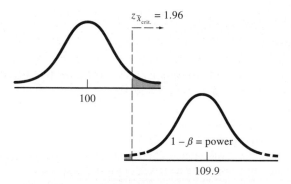

3. From part c of Table M, power is far below .60. (*Note:* $\Delta_{II} = (110.23 - 109.57)/(9.2) = .07!$)
4. From part b of Table M, N is (approximately) 86.
5. From part c of Table M, $n_1 = n_2 = 763$, so $N = 1526$.
6. a. With large sample sizes, the power of statistical tests to detect even very small differences is quite high.
   b. To provide a practical index of the magnitude of the difference, report effect size (Δ) where $\Delta = .20$ is small, $\Delta = .50$ is moderate, and $\Delta = .80$ is large.

V Statistical Tests For Between- Subjects Designs

n behavioral research, subjects may be randomly sampled from some population—often sophomores enrolled in introductory courses in psychology, sociology, or statistics—and then randomly assigned to one or two or more groups constituting control and experimental groups. A comparison of the groups tells something about the effect of the treatments. Or subjects may be randomly sampled from each of two or more populations—"normals" and "schizophrenics," or low, middle, and high socioeconomic status—and differences between these samples examined. In either type of study, each group of subjects receives or has received a different treatment. And in either study, a comparison that reveals something about the differences between groups involves a comparison between different groups of subjects.

Research designs from which inferences are drawn about treatment effects on several populations of subjects are called **between-subjects designs**. Between-subjects designs may qualify as true experiments, or they may represent ex post facto designs. In the prototypical between-samples experimental design, subjects are randomly sampled from some population and then randomly assigned to a control or experimental group. This true experiment can be extended to include more than one experimental group and more than one control group, so that subjects are randomly assigned to one and only one control or experimental group. This true experiment can also be extended to factorial experiments in which two or more independent variables are examined simultaneously. Subjects are randomly assigned to one and only one cell of the design representing a unique combination of two or more variables. As with all true experimental designs, statements can be made about the cause-and-effect relationship between the independent variable or variables and the dependent variable.

Criterion group designs—a type of ex post facto design— are also between-subjects designs. The prototypical criterion group design is the comparison of subjects from a "normal" population and a "deviant" population. The study comparing normals and schizophrenics is a criterion group design. The criterion group design can be extended to include more than two groups and not necessarily a comparison of normals and deviates. The study comparing samples of subjects from the three levels of socioeconomic status is an example. Finally, two or more individual-difference variables can be combined in factorial fashion for a factorial criterion group design. For the sake of an example, consider the comparison of normals and schizophrenics drawn from three socioeconomic levels. As with all ex post facto designs, statements *cannot* be made about the cause-and-effect relationship between the independent variable or variables and the dependent variable. Rather, these designs test hypotheses about the association (correlation) between variables.

A third type of between-subjects design is a factorial design that combines a true experimental design with a criterion group design. For example, an experimenter might randomly assign subjects who are either high or low on some variable (such as anxiety) to a control group or an experimental group. This assignment provides a 2×2 factorial design with two levels of anxiety (low, high) and two levels of treatment (control, experimental). The design contains four cells corresponding to the combinations of the two independent variables: low anxiety–control, low anxiety–experimental, high anxiety–control, and high anxiety–experimental. A comparison of the mean performance of the low- and high-anxiety groups constitutes a criterion group design. Causal interpretations of the effect of anxiety on the dependent variable are not warranted. However, the comparison of the difference between the means of control and experimental groups represents a true experimental design, and so a causal interpretation of this difference is warranted. Finally, a comparison of the four means corresponding to each cell of the design provides information about the unique effects of anxiety and treatment combined. If the means of the control and experimental groups are compared at each of the two levels of the anxiety variable, causal interpretations of the differences are warranted.

A number of well-known statistical tests are available for examining the data from between-subjects designs. In this section, two such tests are covered: (1) the *t* test, and (2) the analysis of variance. The *t test* is used to compare means from case I and case II research designs. It is used instead of the *z* test (Chapter 10) because it does not require knowledge of the population variance. Chapter 12 in this section describes *t* tests for between-subjects designs. For continuity, and conceptual relatedness, a *t* test is presented for designs in which the same person is measured under different conditions (e.g., pretest and posttest) or matched pairs of subjects are measured in their respective control and experimental conditions (i.e., the *t* test for "within-subjects" designs—see Section VI).

The *analysis of variance* is used to compare the means of two or more groups. Furthermore, it can be used to compare means from factorial designs. So, it can test the effects of each of two or more independent variables *and* their unique combinations. Chapters 13 and 14 present the analysis of variance.

12

t Tests for Case I and Case II Research

This chapter presents statistical tests for examining data from case I and case II research designs. Case I research designs were characterized by the question, "Does a particular sample belong to a hypothesized population?" In order to answer this question, we draw a single random sample of subjects from some population. A sample statistic such as a mean is calculated. Then a null hypothesis of no difference between the sample mean and the hypothesized population mean is tested. For example, "Does the *mean* heart rate of a sample of runners differ from that of the general population with $\alpha = 72$ bpm?"

Case II research provides data on whether two means are drawn from identical populations or from different populations. For example, in the teacher expectancy study, a random sample of N subjects was drawn from an elementary school population; n_1 subjects are randomly assigned to a control group and n_2 subjects to a "bloomers" group. After the treatment, the mean performance of the two groups was compared to test the null hypothesis of no difference in population means. This test is tantamount to testing the null hypothesis of no treatment effect.

A second type of case II research draws subjects randomly from some population and measures their behavior under two conditions such as two occasions—for example, before and after a treatment (pretest and posttest). Alternatively, the subjects may be *matched* on some variable (e.g., mathematical ability) and then randomly assigned to an experimental and control group. In either design—repeated measures or matched—a dependency is created between the first measure and the second because the same subjects (or "clones") are measured twice. This dependency must be accounted for by the *t* test.

Chapter 10 presented the $z_{\bar{X}}$ test for deciding whether a sample with a particular *mean* was drawn from the hypothesized population under the null hypothesis. The decision whether to reject the null hypothesis rested on the *probability* of observing the sample mean under the assumption that the null hypothesis is true. The normal distribution was used as the model of the sampling distribution for determining the probability assuming σ and $\sigma_{\bar{X}}$ are known and sample size is at least 30. The $z_{\bar{X}_1-\bar{X}_2}$ test was presented for deciding whether two samples were drawn from populations with identical means, assuming a normal sampling distribution and the availability of the population value for and standard error ($\sigma_{\bar{X}_1-\bar{X}_2}$).

The purpose of this chapter is to provide a statistical test for handling data from case I and case II research when, as is the usual case, the population standard deviation and standard error are *unknown* and have to be estimated from sample data. This statistical test is the **t test**. In case II research, a distinction is made between the independent-sample *t* test where different subjects are assigned to the two groups, and the dependent-sample *t* test where the same or matched subjects are measured under two conditions.

CASE I *t* TEST

Purpose and Underlying Logic

The purpose of the *t* test, like that of the $z_{\bar{X}}$ test, is to help us decide whether the sample mean was drawn from a hypothesized population with a specified mean μ or whether it was drawn from some other population with a different mean. The *t* test, unlike the $z_{\bar{X}}$ test, can be used when the standard error of the mean, $\sigma_{\bar{X}}$, is unknown and has to be estimated from sample data. In practice, then, the *t* test is used much more frequently than the $z_{\bar{X}}$ test since we seldom know $\sigma_{\bar{X}}$.

The logic behind the *t* test is quite similar to that underlying the $z_{\bar{X}}$ test, even though its technical development is a bit more complicated. What's problematic is that neither the population mean nor standard error is known and must be estimated from the sample data. So, the first step in solving the problem is to provide sample estimates of the *two* unknown parameters—the mean (μ) and the standard error of the mean ($\sigma_{\bar{X}} = \sigma/\sqrt{N}$). $\bar{X}$ is, of course, the sample estimate of μ. An estimate of the standard error can be provided by using the sample standard deviation (*s*) as an estimate of the population standard deviation (σ). Then an estimate of $\sigma_{\bar{X}}$ is given by:

$$s_{\bar{X}} = \frac{s}{\sqrt{N}} \qquad\qquad \textbf{(12-1)}$$

The next step is to find the distance between a sample mean and the population mean in terms of $s_{\bar{X}}$, and not in terms of $\sigma_{\bar{X}}$, as is done to get $z_{\bar{X}}$ from Formula 10-2:

$$z_{\bar{X}\,observed} = \frac{\bar{X} - \mu}{\sigma_{\bar{X}}}$$

This distance can be determined by replacing $\sigma_{\bar{X}}$ in Formula 10-2 with its estimator, $s_{\bar{X}}$. When this replacement is made, *t* is defined as in Formula 12-2.

$$t_{\text{observed}} = \frac{\bar{X} - \mu}{s_{\bar{X}}} \tag{12-2}$$

Thus t is a measure of the distance between $\bar{X}$ and μ in standard error units ($s_{\bar{X}}$), estimated from the sample data.

The next step is to compare the observed test value with a critical value. For the $z_{\bar{X}}$ test, we know, by the central limit theorem, that the sampling distribution will be normal for $N \geq 30$ since only $\bar{X}$ varies from sample to sample. So we find the critical value in the table for the normal distribution.

To specify the sampling distribution of t, we must recognize that there is a very important difference between $z_{\bar{X}}$ and t. In the t test, both $\bar{X}$ and $s_{\bar{X}}$ vary from sample to sample. $s_{\bar{X}}$ varies because it depends on the sample standard deviation, s, which varies like any other sample estimate of a population parameter. So, for repeated samples, t will vary due to random fluctuations in $\bar{X}$ and s.

Now suppose we randomly draw repeated samples from a normal population, calculate the value of $t = (\bar{X} - \mu)/s_{\bar{X}}$ for each sample, and plot the frequency of the values of t in a frequency distribution. This graph will show a bell-shaped distribution not unlike the normal distribution. This frequency distribution can be modeled by a theoretical (mathematical) distribution. It can be used as a probability distribution under the null hypothesis for determining the probability of observing a sample mean at or beyond some value when $\sigma_{\bar{X}}$ is unknown.

Like the normal sampling distribution, the sampling distribution of t is symmetric in shape (Figure 12-1). Also like the normal distribution, the t distribution can be interpreted as a probability distribution and therefore can be used to determine the probability of observing a sample mean at or beyond some value, assuming that the null hypothesis is true.

There are, however, several important differences between the t and the normal distributions. One difference is that there is a different t distribution for each possible sample size from 2 to infinity, whereas there is only 1 standard normal distribution regardless of sample size. Thus, the sampling distribution of t is actually a family of distributions with a different member for each sample size.

Another difference is that the tails of the t distribution are higher than those of the normal distribution—that is, there is a greater area under the tails of the t distributions (compare Figures 12-1a, b). This difference arises because t is influenced by the variability of $\bar{X}$ and s from samples, but $z_{\bar{X}}$ is influenced only by the variability of $\bar{X}$, since $\sigma_{\bar{X}}$ is constant. One implication is that the critical values of t for rejecting a null hypothesis are higher than the critical values of z, since you have to go farther out in the tails of the t distribution to mark off the 5 percent or 1 percent region (see Figure 12-1).

Finally, as sample size increases, the t distributions become increasingly normal in form. With sample sizes of 30 or more, there is a close fit between the t distribution and the normal distribution (compare Figures 12-1a, d). With an infinite sample size, the t distribution and the normal distribution are identical. Intuitively, this result occurs because as the sample size increases, the sample estimate of $\sigma_{\bar{X}}$ becomes more and more like the parameter itself (i.e., s is a consistent estimator of σ).

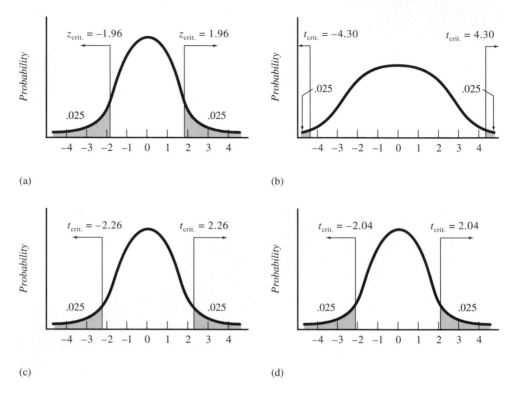

FIGURE 12-1

The normal sampling distribution and members of the family of the sampling distribution of t (critical regions with $\alpha = .05$, two-tail): (a) normal sampling distribution; (b) sampling distribution of t ($df = 2$); (c) sampling distribution of t ($df = 9$); (d) sampling distribution of t ($df = 30$)

Degrees of Freedom

Formally, members of the t distribution family differ according to their *degrees of freedom* (*df;* from 1 to ∞) rather than sample size. Nevertheless, there is a close connection between *df* and *N,* especially for the single-sample case. As a consequence, this seems like an appropriate place to discuss the concept of degrees of freedom in some depth.

The term **degrees of freedom** refers to the independent pieces of information on which a sample statistic is based. For brevity, it is often used for the *number* of such pieces of information. For example, a mean based on a sample of 30 scores is determined from all 30 scores. That is, each score provides an independent piece of information in the calculation of the mean. Or to put it another way, until the mean of the 30 scores is known, we know nothing about the values of each of the scores. However, once the mean of the 30 scores is known, we know something about the 30 scores.

To see how degrees of freedom work, let's consider a numerical example. Suppose a random sample of four scores that range from 0 to 20 is drawn from a population, and three of the scores are 5, 8, and 11. Can you determine the value for the last score without any further information? No, unless you make a lucky guess. Each score provides an independent piece of information for calculating the mean; the mean is based on N degrees of freedom. Suppose now you are told that the mean of the scores is 7. Can you determine the value of the fourth score? The answer is yes. Since the sum of the deviation scores, $\Sigma(X - \bar{X})$, is zero, the fourth score will be that score that makes the sum of the four scores in deviation form equal zero: $(5 - 7) = -2$, $(8 - 7) = 1$, and $(11 - 7) = 4$. The algebraic sum of these three deviation scores is 3. Thus, the fourth score must be, in deviation form, -3. In raw score form, it is the score value 3 points below the mean: $7 - 3 = 4$. Thus, given a random sample of N scores *and* the mean, there are $N - 1$ independent pieces of information, or $N - 1$ degrees of freedom.

Any sample statistic that uses the sample mean in its calculation must be based on no more than $N - 1$ degrees of freedom. For example, a sample variance is calculated by subtracting the mean from each score in the sample. In the calculation of the variance, then, how many independent pieces of information are used to estimate the statistic? Since there are only $N - 1$ independent pieces of information in a set of deviation scores, the variance is estimated with $N - 1$ degrees of freedom.

Furthermore, different sample statistics are based on different numbers of degrees of freedom. As noted before, the mean is based on N degrees of freedom, and the sample variance and standard deviation are based on $N - 1$ degrees of freedom. Recall that the correlation coefficient uses the mean of X and the mean of Y in its calculation. Thus, the correlation coefficient is based on $N - 2$ degrees of freedom. In general, the number of degrees of freedom on which a sample statistic is based depends on the sample size (N) and on the number of sample statistics used in its calculation.

The reason that the *t* distribution is based on degrees of freedom and not sample size is easy to explain now. In the estimation of the standard error of the *t* distribution (a sample statistic), the standard deviation *s* is used (Formula 12-1):

$$s_{\bar{X}} = \frac{s}{\sqrt{N}}$$

So, for the single-sample case, the *t* distribution is based on $N - 1$ degrees of freedom rather than on the sample size, N.

From here on out, you can coast. When the *t* test is carried out on a single mean, the procedures are the same as the procedures for a single-sample $z_{\bar{X}}$ test (see Chapter 10). The only exception is that the sampling distribution of *t* is used instead of the normal distribution. The procedures for carrying out the *t* test are outlined in the following sections.

Hypotheses

The hypotheses tested with the *t* distribution are the same as those tested with the normal sampling distribution. In the case of a two-tail alternative hypothesis, the null and alternative hypotheses are:

H_0: μ = specified value
H_1: $\mu \neq$ specified value

In the case of directional (i.e., one-tail) alternative hypotheses, the null and alternative hypotheses are:

H_0: μ = specified value

H_1: μ > specified value

or

H_0: μ = specified value

H_1: μ < specified value

Assumptions

When we use the sampling distribution of t to test hypotheses about means, the following assumptions are made:

1. The scores are randomly sampled from some population.
2. The scores in the population are normally distributed.

These assumptions should be examined before the t test is performed. Assumption 1 is examined logically. Did the sampling procedures meet the criteria for sampling at random? In order to examine assumption 2, you should visually inspect a frequency distribution of scores in the sample. Look for a symmetric, bell-shaped distribution of scores. Any radical departure of these scores from the expected distribution—such as a couple of very extreme scores—suggests that the assumption of normality does not hold.

This procedure for examining the assumption of normality, however, immediately suggests a paradox. One important feature of the t test is its ability to handle small samples—as small as $N = 2$. But frequency distributions based on small samples seldom tell you much about the distribution of scores in the population; there are just too few scores to get a good idea of the shape of the distribution. How, then, can this assumption be examined? The answer is that for very small samples, the assumption of a normal population cannot be examined. Nevertheless, prior information from larger, similar samples can be used to check this assumption. For example, a sample of four SAT scores will probably not tell you anything about this distribution of scores in the general population of students applying to college. But other data sources with quite large sample sizes show the distribution of SAT scores to be approximately normal. For samples of $N \geq 15$, a frequency distribution of sample data can be used to examine this assumption.

The assumption of a normal distribution of scores in the population, however, does not pose a problem for the t test if N is large (above 30). The t test can be used even if the distribution of scores in the parent population is somewhat nonnormal.[1] However, if N is small, nonnormality may give rise to errors. In this case, tests described in Chapter 20 might be used.

---

[1]There is obviously something of a logical contradiction in stating that a normal distribution is an assumption underlying the t test, and then later saying that violation of this assumption usually is not problematic. In *deriving* any statistical test, certain assumptions are made, such as normality. The assumptions are formal requirements, and it is best not to violate them. However, in practice, statisticians have found that certain violations of these assumptions do not appreciably affect the outcome of the statistical test. This is one such case.

Formula for the *t* Test

The formula for the *t* test has already been given (Formula 12-2):

$$t_{observed} = \frac{\bar{X} - \mu}{s_{\bar{X}}}$$

As an example of the use of the *t* test, suppose that a random sample of nine subjects was drawn from a population of freshmen in a university. The mean score of the sample on the verbal section of the Scholastic Aptitude Test (SAT-V) was 625 with a standard deviation of 90 points. Since the SAT-V was developed so that the mean equals 500 in the general population of high school graduates applying to college, the question arises whether freshmen in this university have, on the average, higher SAT-V scores than the population of high school students who apply to college.

The *t* test can be used in order to decide whether the freshmen in this sample are drawn from a population with a mean of 500 or are drawn from some alternative population. First, the null and alternative hypotheses need to be stated, along with the level of significance:

H_0: $\mu = 500$

H_1: $\mu \neq 500$

$\alpha = .05$

Next, the value of $t_{observed}$ is calculated (Formula 12-2):

$$t_{observed} = \frac{\bar{X} - \mu}{s_{\bar{X}}}$$

$$= \frac{\bar{X} - \mu}{s/\sqrt{N}}$$

$$= \frac{625 - 500}{90/\sqrt{9}} = 4.17$$

The observed value of *t* is 4.17. The next step is to decide whether to reject the null hypothesis on the basis of $t_{observed}$.

Decision Rules for Rejecting the Null Hypothesis

In order to decide whether to reject the null hypothesis, we must use the critical value of *t*. The critical value is the value at or beyond which less than 5 (or 1) percent of the sample *t*'s lie in the sampling distribution of *t*. Since the critical value of *t* depends on the sample size (degrees of freedom), the first step is to determine the number of degrees of freedom for the statistical test. There are $N - 1$ degrees of freedom for the single-sample *t* test. For our example, there are $9 - 1 = 8$ *df*.

The next step is to find the critical value of *t* at $\alpha = .05$. Table C in Appendix II provides these values. The numbers of degrees of freedom are listed in the left-hand column of the table. The body of the table lists the critical values of t. For one-tail tests, use the upper set of column headings with the appropriate level of significance, α; and for two-tail tests, use the lower set of column headings with the appropriate level of significance. For the example with $\alpha = .05$, one tail, and 8 df, first locate .05 under the heading for the two-tail test—the third column of the table—and read down that column to the value that corresponds to 8 df. The value of $t_{critical(.05/2,8)}$ is 2.306. Since $t_{observed}$ (4.17) exceeds $t_{critical}$ (2.306), the null hypothesis should be rejected. The mean score of freshmen at the university is greater than the mean score for the population of high school graduates taking the SAT-V.

More generally, the following set of criteria can be established for deciding whether to reject the null hypothesis.

1. For a two-tail test:

    a. Reject H_0 if $|t_{observed}| \geq t_{critical(\alpha/2,df)}$.
    b. Do not reject H_0 if $|t_{observed}| < t_{critical(\alpha/2,df)}$.

2. For a one-tail test:

    a. Reject H_0 if $|t_{observed}| \geq t_{critical(\alpha,df)}$.
    b. Do not reject H_0 if $|t_{observed}| < t_{critical(\alpha,df)}$.

The notation $t_{critical(\alpha/2,df)}$ can be read as the critical value of t at $\alpha/2$ for a specified number of degrees of freedom.

The data from the example can be used to illustrate how these criteria for deciding about the null hypothesis are applied. To begin, $t_{observed}$ equals 4.17. For a nondirectional test at $\alpha = .05$, $\alpha/2 = .05/2 = .025$. With $df = 8$, Table C provides $t_{critical(.05/2,8)} = 2.306$. Since $|t_{observed}| > t_{critical}$, the null hypothesis should be rejected. For a nondirectional test at $\alpha = .01$, $\alpha/2 = .01/2 = .005$. Again, with $df = 8$, Table C provides $t_{critical(.01/2,8)} = 3.355$. The null hypothesis should be rejected. Finally, for a one-tail test at $\alpha = .01$, $t_{critical(.01,8)} = 2.896$; again, the null hypothesis should be rejected.

Numerical Example

In the hypothetical study of men's and women's college achievement described in Chapter 5, SAT scores were collected on a sample of students from four campuses of the University of California. Table 12-1 presents hypothetical data on the SAT total scores (verbal plus quantitative) for a sample of students at UCLA. From these sample data, are UCLA students representative of the entire population taking the SAT or do these students represent, as expected, a group of students who score above the mean?

To answer this question, we need to know the mean SAT score for all students taking the examination. Since both the SAT verbal and quantitative subscales are constructed to have means of 500, the mean score on the total test is 1000. With this information in hand, a t test can be conducted. Procedure 12-1 summarizes the steps for conducting this test, using data from Table 12-1.

TABLE 12-1 Hypothetical SAT data on a random sample of 10 students from UCLA

Student ID	Score	Student ID	Score
1	1050	6	1075
2	1200	7	1100
3	1100	8	1025
4	1130	9	1000
5	1160	10	1000

$\bar{X} = 1084$ $s = 67.24$

PROCEDURE 12-1 Steps in conducting a *t* test for single-sample designs (example data from Table 12-1)

Operation

1. Specify the null and alternative hypothesis and the level of significance.
   The level of significance is generally set at .05 or .01.

2. Compute $t_{observed}$ by using Formula 12-2:

$$t_{observed} = \frac{\bar{X} - \mu}{s_{\bar{X}}}$$

where:

$$s_{\bar{X}} = \frac{s}{\sqrt{N}} \quad \text{(Formula 12-1)}$$

3. Locate $t_{critical}$ at the specified level of significance with $N - 1$ *df*, using Table C.

4. Decide whether or not to reject the null hypothesis.
   a. Reject H_0 if $|t_{observed}| \geq t_{critical}$.
   b. Do not reject H_0 if $|t_{observed}| < t_{critical}$.

Example

$H_0: \mu = 1000$
$H_1: \mu > 1000$

$\alpha = .01$

$$t_{observed} = \frac{1084 - 1000}{67.24/\sqrt{10}} = \frac{84}{21.26} = 3.95$$

$t_{critical(.01,9)} = 2.821$

Since $|t_{observed}| > t_{critical}$ (3.95 > 2.821), reject H_0. Conclude that students at UCLA have a higher mean SAT score than the general population of students taking the test.

The results of the *t* test indicate that the null hypothesis should be rejected. Students at UCLA have a higher mean SAT score than do high school graduates who take the SAT.

Confidence Intervals for Case I Research

Confidence intervals can also be established by using the *t* distribution with $N - 1$ degrees of freedom. In general, the 95 percent confidence interval is constructed when $\alpha = .05$, and the 99 percent confidence interval is constructed when $\alpha = .01$. These intervals, then, will be referred to as the $100 \times (1 - \alpha)$ percent confidence intervals. The general form of the confidence interval can be expressed as in Formula 12-3.

$$\bar{X} \pm t_{\text{critical}(\alpha/2,df)}(s_{\bar{X}}) \hspace{3cm} \text{(12-3)}$$

or

$$\bar{X} - t_{\text{critical}(\alpha/2,df)}(s_{\bar{X}}) \leq \mu \leq \bar{X} + t_{\text{critical}(\alpha/2,df)}(s_{\bar{X}})$$

The major differences between this confidence interval and the one developed in Chapter 10 are that the t distribution $t_{\text{critical}(\alpha/2,df)}$ is used instead of the normal distribution $z_{\bar{X}(\text{critical},\alpha/2)}$, and $s_{\bar{X}}$ is used instead of $\sigma_{\bar{X}}$.

The 95 percent confidence interval for the data in the example study of SAT-V scores (see the discussion on page 340) can be written as follows:

$$CI_{.95}: \hspace{1cm} \bar{X} - t_{\text{critical}(.05/2,8)}(s_{\bar{X}}) \leq \mu \leq \bar{X} + t_{\text{critical}(.05,8)}(s_{\bar{X}})$$
$$625 - (2.306)(30) \leq \mu \leq 625 + (2.306)(30)$$
$$625 - 69.18 \leq \mu \leq 625 + 69.18$$
$$555.82 \leq \mu \leq 694.18$$

The probability is .95 that an interval formed in this manner will include the population mean μ.[2]

The 99 percent confidence interval can be written as follows:

$$CI_{.99}: \hspace{1cm} \bar{X} - t_{\text{critical}(.01/2,8)}(s_{\bar{X}}) \leq \mu \leq \bar{X} + t_{\text{critical}(.01/2,8)}(s_{\bar{X}})$$
$$625 - (3.355)(30) \leq \mu \leq 625 + (3.355)(30)$$
$$625 - 100.65 \leq \mu \leq 625 + 100.65$$
$$524.35 \leq \mu \leq 725.65$$

The results of our hypothesis-testing procedures indicated that UCLA freshmen have, on the average, higher SAT-V scores than the population of high school graduates taking the SAT. However, notice that the confidence intervals are quite large. These confidence intervals make it abundantly clear that the value of the true population mean for freshmen at the university is in some doubt because of the small sample size.

Example Problem 12.1 ▬▬▬▬▬▬▬▬▬▬▬▬▬▬▬▬▬▬▬▬▬▬▬▬▬▬▬▬▬▬▬▬▬▬▬▬▬▬

Hypothetical SAT total scores for a sample of students at UCSD are shown in Table 12-2. From these sample data, test whether UCSD students are representative of the general population of students taking the SAT or whether they represent an alternative population. Include the following items in your answer.
a. Null and alternative hypotheses
b. t_{observed}

---

[2]Note that the probability statement is about confidence intervals formed in this manner and not the particular interval constructed. Once the sample values are placed in the formula, the probability statement does not hold for that particular instance. (See Chapter 10 for details.)

    c. t_{critical} at $\alpha = .01$ (two-tail)
    d. Conclusions
    e. 99 percent confidence interval
    f. Would you expect the 99 percent confidence interval to include μ under H_0? (Why or why not?)

TABLE 12-2 Hypothetical SAT data on a random sample of 10 students from UCSD

Student ID Number	SAT Total Score	Student ID Number	SAT Total Score
31	1150	36	1150
32	1185	37	1100
33	1200	38	1120
34	1160	39	1080
35	1200	40	1150

$\bar{X} = 1149.5$ $s = 40.31$

CASE II *t* TEST: INDEPENDENT MEANS

The *t* test can be used to test hypotheses with data from two basic between-subjects designs. The first type of design is a true experimental design in which subjects are randomly assigned either to a control group or to an experimental group (see Chapter 1 and the *Student Guide*). The researcher may make causal interpretations of the results. That is, the researcher is able to conclude that the independent variable caused the observed differences between the control group and the experimental group on the dependent variable.

    The second type of design is a criterion-group design. Subjects are selected because they represent one or another population of interest. For example, one group of subjects might be drawn randomly from a population of "neurotics," the other from a population of "normals." Notice that the experimenter does *not* randomly assign subjects to the two groups. The treatment—whatever it was—has been provided by nature (see Chapter 1 and *Student Guide* on ex post facto designs). In general, the criterion-group design sorts subjects into two discrete groups on some individual difference variable (e.g., sex, personality, ability, interest) and compares these two groups on some measure (dependent variable) thought to be related to group membership. The results of such a study *cannot* support an interpretation that the independent variable (e.g., type of subject population) caused the mean difference between the two groups. Rather, a significant difference between the two groups can only be interpreted as demonstrating a relationship between the independent and dependent variables. Thus, the mean difference in reading test scores for girls and boys indicates a relationship between sex and reading ability. However, it does not imply that being a girl, for example, causes higher reading ability. Many variables may underlie the relationship between sex and reading ability, such as social reinforcement for practicing reading or exposure to appropriate models (e.g., primarily female teachers of reading in elementary schools).

Purpose and Underlying Logic

The purpose of the *t* test for two independent means is to help the researcher decide whether the observed difference between two sample means arose by chance or represents a true difference between populations. In the language of hypothesis testing, the purpose of the *t* test is to help us decide whether or not to reject the null hypothesis of no difference between the means of the two populations.

Since this decision cannot be made with certainty, it is probabilistic. The problem, then, is to determine the probability of observing the difference between the sample means of the two groups under the assumption that the null hypothesis is true (i.e., there is no difference between the two groups).

In solving this problem, we must take several steps. The first step is to provide an estimate of the unknown standard error of the differences between means, given by Formula 10-4:

$$\sigma_{\bar{X}_1 - \bar{X}_2} = \sqrt{\sigma_{\bar{X}_1}^2 + \sigma_{\bar{X}_2}^2} = \sqrt{\frac{\sigma^2}{n_1} + \frac{\sigma^2}{n_2}}$$

This estimate can be obtained by using the standard deviation from each sample as an estimate of σ. For samples of equal size ($n_1 = n_2 \geq 2$), the estimate of the standard error of the difference between means is as given in Formula 12-4.

$$s_{\bar{X}_1 - \bar{X}_2} = \sqrt{s_{\bar{X}_1}^2 + s_{\bar{X}_2}^2} = \sqrt{\frac{s^2}{n_1} + \frac{s^2}{n_2}} \tag{12-4}$$

The next step is to provide a measure of the distance between the difference of the sample means ($\bar{X}_1 - \bar{X}_2$) and the difference of their corresponding population means ($\mu_1 - \mu_2$). If the standard error of the differences between means ($\sigma_{\bar{X}_1 - \bar{X}_2}$) were known, then $z_{\bar{X}_1 - \bar{X}_2}$ could be used as the measure (Formula 10-5):

$$z_{\bar{X}_1 - \bar{X}_2} = \frac{(\bar{X}_1 - \bar{X}_2) - (\mu_1 - \mu_2)}{\sigma_{\bar{X}_1 - \bar{X}_2}}$$

In fact, $\sigma_{\bar{X}_1 - \bar{X}_2}$ is not known. But this parameter can be estimated by $s_{\bar{X}_1 - \bar{X}_2}$. When this substitution is made, *t* for differences between means is defined as given in Formula 12-5.

$$t_{\bar{X}_1 - \bar{X}_2 \text{ observed}} = \frac{(\bar{X}_1 - \bar{X}_2) - (\mu_1 - \mu_2)}{s_{\bar{X}_1 - \bar{X}_2}} \tag{12-5}$$

In this case, *t* is a measure of the distance between the difference of the sample means ($\bar{X}_1 - \bar{X}_2$) and the difference of their corresponding population means ($\mu_1 - \mu_2$). Notice that since we sample from populations with identical means in setting up the sampling distribution under H_0, $\mu_1 = \mu_2$, and so $\mu_1 - \mu_2 = 0$. Thus, *t* can be simplified as shown in Formula 12-5a.

$$t_{\bar{X}_1 - \bar{X}_2 \text{ observed}} = \frac{\bar{X}_1 - \bar{X}_2}{s_{\bar{X}_1 - \bar{X}_2}} \tag{12-5a}$$

The final step is to specify the sampling distribution of *t*. Clearly the observed value of *t* will vary from one sample to the next due to random fluctuation in *both* $\bar{X}$ and *s*. If the value of *t* [which is $(\bar{X}_1 - \bar{X}_2)/(s_{\bar{X}_1 - \bar{X}_2})$] is calculated for each of a very large number of samples from a normal population, a frequency distribution for *t* can be graphed, with the values of *t* on the abscissa and the frequencies on the ordinate. This frequency distribution can be modeled by the theoretical (mathematical) distribution of *t*. The theoretical model is called the *sampling distribution of t for differences between independent means*. It can be used as a probability distribution for deciding whether or not to reject the null hypothesis when $\sigma_{\bar{X}_1 - \bar{X}_2}$ is unknown.

Actually, the sampling distribution of *t* for differences between means is a family of distributions. Each particular member of the family depends on degrees of freedom. Specifically, the *t* distribution for differences depends on the number of degrees of freedom in the first sample ($n_1 - 1$) and in the second sample ($n_2 - 1$) of the pair. So the *t* distribution used to model the sampling procedure described before is based on $(n_1 - 1) + (n_2 - 1)$ degrees of freedom, or on $N - 2$ degrees of freedom, where $N = n_1 + n_2$. In the example with $n_1 = n_2 = 10$, a *t* distribution with 18 *df* would be used to model the sampling distribution $[(10 - 1) + (10 - 1) - 9 + 9 = 18$; see Figure 12-2].

The *t* distribution of differences has the following characteristics: First, its mean is equal to zero ($\mu_1 - \mu_2 = 0$) because some differences between sample means are positive ($\bar{X}_1 - \bar{X}_2 > 0$), some are zero ($\bar{X}_1 - \bar{X}_2 = 0$), and some are negative ($\bar{X} - \bar{X}_2 < 0$). Over all differences between pairs, the positive differences cancel the negative differences; so the average difference is zero. Second, the distribution is symmetric in shape and looks like a bell-shaped curve. However, the mathematical rule specifying the *t* distribution is not the same as the rule for the normal distribution, so the *t* and the normal distributions are not the same. Nevertheless, as the sample size increases, the *t* distribution becomes increasingly normal in shape. With an infinite sample size, the *t* distribution and the normal distribution are identical.

Hypotheses

The hypotheses about differences between population means using the sampling distribution of *t* are the same as those tested with the normal sampling distribution described in Chapter 10. In the case of a two-tail alternative hypothesis, the null and alternative hypotheses are:

$$\left\{ \begin{array}{l} H_0: \mu_1 - \mu_2 = 0 \\ H_1: \mu_1 - \mu_2 \neq 0 \end{array} \right\}, \quad \text{i.e.,} \quad \left\{ \begin{array}{l} H_0: \mu_1 = \mu_2 \\ H_1: \mu_1 \neq \mu_2 \end{array} \right\}$$

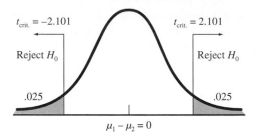

FIGURE 12-2
Sampling distribution of t for differences between means ($df = 18$)

In the case of a directional alternative hypothesis, the null and alternative hypotheses are either:

$$\left\{ \begin{array}{l} H_0\colon \mu_1 - \mu_2 = 0 \\ H_1\colon \mu_1 - \mu_2 > 0 \end{array} \right\}, \quad \text{i.e.,} \quad \left\{ \begin{array}{l} H_0\colon \mu_1 = \mu_2 \\ H_1\colon \mu_1 > \mu_2 \end{array} \right\}$$

or

$$\left\{ \begin{array}{l} H_0\colon \mu_1 - \mu_2 = 0 \\ H_1\colon \mu_1 - \mu_2 < 0 \end{array} \right\}, \quad \text{i.e.,} \quad \left\{ \begin{array}{l} H_0\colon \mu_1 = \mu_2 \\ H_1\colon \mu_1 < \mu_2 \end{array} \right\}$$

Design Requirements for the Use of the t Test

The use of the t test imposes a number of data collection requirements:

1. There is one independent variable with two levels (i.e., groups).
2. A subject appears in one and only one of the two groups.
3. The levels of the independent variable may differ from one and another either qualitatively or quantitatively. Qualitative differences are, for example, differences between scrambled versus organized word lists or differences of sex (male versus female). Quantitative variables are, for example, the amount of time studying or the number of reinforcements.

Assumptions

In using the sampling distribution of t to test for differences between independent means, we make the following assumptions:

1. The scores in the two groups are randomly sampled from their respective populations and are independent of one another.
2. The scores in the respective populations are normally distributed.
3. The variances of scores in the two populations are equal (i.e., $\sigma_1^2 = \sigma_2^2$). This assumption is often called the assumption of **homogeneity of variance.**

The assumption of independence deserves some discussion. It actually has two parts. First, the scores of subjects in one group must be unrelated to the scores of subjects in the other group, a feature called **independence of groups.** Second, scores must be independent of the basis for the administration of the treatments: The application of the treatment to one subject in a group must not influence the way in which the treatment is applied to any other subject in the group. This feature is called **independence of treatments.**

In order to clarify these two parts of the independence assumption, let's consider some examples. The assumption of independence of groups will be violated if (1) Harry and Charlie are both assigned to group 1 because Charlie refused to participate in the study unless he could be with Harry or (2) both Harry and Charlie were given their choice of group and chose group 1. Some examples of a violation of the assumption of independence of treatments are the following:

1. Subjects are assigned to small groups to solve a problem. What each subject does depends, in part, upon what each of them contributes in the group discussion.
2. A group of subjects is listening to a lecture when a gardener distracts them at a critical part by mowing the lawn nearby. Since many subjects were distracted at the same time, what one subject did not learn is related to what some other subject did not learn.
3. During the course of a 4-day study, subjects in one group describe what they are learning to subjects in another group. In effect, all of the subjects receive bits and pieces of all the treatments.

The assumption of independence is tested logically. Close inspection of the sampling procedures should reveal, in a true experiment, that subjects were assigned to one or the other group randomly and received their treatments independently. In a criterion group study, subjects in each group should be randomly sampled from their respective populations.

The assumption of normality can be examined empirically if the sizes of the two groups are about 15 or more. For each group, the scores should be arranged in a frequency distribution. The shape of this distribution can be examined visually to see whether the distribution of scores is *roughly* normal. If sample sizes are too small to inspect the distributions visually, prior information about the distribution of scores from similar subjects can be used.

Assumption 3, homogeneity of variance, can be tested empirically with a number of different statistical tests (e.g., Kirk, 1982; Winer et al., 1991; Wilcox, 1987). If there is any doubt about the equality of variances, Levine's test, a statistical test that does not assume homogeneity of variance, can be used and is available on most statistical packages for personal computers (e.g., SPSS).

Even though the development and interpretation of the *t* test rests on assumptions of independence, normality, and homogeneity of variance, statisticians can check to see just how important some of these assumptions are. Using computer simulations, sometimes called "Monte Carlo" studies, they can draw a large number of random samples from normal and nonnormal populations *assuming the null hypothesis is true,* calculate the *t* statistic for each sample, and decide whether or not to reject the null hypothesis. With, say, 2000 such samples, they can compare the nominal level of significance used to decide whether to reject the null hypothesis (e.g., $\alpha = .05$) with the *actual* number of times out of 2000 that the null hypothesis is rejected. Under the null hypothesis ($\alpha = .05$), about 100 of the 2000 sample *t* tests should lead to a decision to reject the null hypothesis

(100/2000 = .05). If the actual number of times is about what would be expected, statisticians say that the statistical test is **robust** to a violation of the assumption. So, if the nominal and actual rejection rates are roughly the same when sampling from normal and non-normal populations, we say that the t test is robust to the normality assumption. Likewise, Monte Carlo studies can be carried out by simulating sampling from populations with different variances, *assuming the null hypothesis is true.* In this way, the robustness of the statistical test to the homogeneity of variance assumption can be determined.

In general, the t test is robust to the violation of the normality assumption. However, this is no excuse for not inspecting the frequency distribution of scores in your study. If one or both of the two distributions (e.g., distributions of scores in the experimental and control groups) are extremely skewed, a nonparametric statistical test such as the Mann-Whitney U, described in a subsequent chapter, might be considered (see also Wilcox, 1987).

Through Monte Carlo studies, we know that the effect of violating the homogeneity of variance assumption depends on n_1 and n_2. If the number of subjects in both groups is the same ($n_1 = n_2$), the t test is robust. If, however, the sample sizes are quite different, the t test is sensitive to the assumption. In this case, an alternative statistical test can be used (e.g., Levine's). However, the difference between the variance of the two groups may have substantive meaning and may deserve interpretation in its own right. In this case, the differences in variances might become part of the focus of the study.

Formulas for the t Test

The formula for the t test when the sample sizes are equal ($n_1 = n_2$) is given by Formula 12-5a:

$$t_{\bar{X}_1 - \bar{X}_2 \text{ observed}} = \frac{\bar{X}_1 - \bar{X}_2}{s_{\bar{X}_1 - \bar{X}_2}}$$

However, in order to use the t test where sample sizes may be either equal or unequal, we must define $s_{\bar{X}_1 - \bar{X}_2}$ more generally than it was in Formula 12-4. The goal in defining $s_{\bar{X}_1 - \bar{X}_2}$ is to find the best estimate of the population variance by using sample variances. This can be done as follows: Under the assumption of equal population variances ($\sigma_1^2 = \sigma_2^2 = \sigma^2$), s_1^2 and s_2^2 each estimate σ^2. The best estimate of the value of σ^2, then, is the average of s_1^2 and s_2^2. This average is called a **pooled estimate.**[3] So the formula for the t test can be written to reflect this pooling, as shown in Formula 12-5b.

$$t_{\bar{X}_1 - \bar{X}_2 \text{ observed}} = \frac{\bar{X}_1 - \bar{X}_2}{\sqrt{\dfrac{s_{\text{pooled}}^2}{n_1} + \dfrac{s_{\text{pooled}}^2}{n_2}}} = \frac{\bar{X}_1 - \bar{X}_2}{\sqrt{s_{\text{pooled}}^2 \left(\dfrac{1}{n_1} + \dfrac{1}{n_2} \right)}} \qquad \text{(12-5b)}$$

---

[3]The pooled variance is the best estimate in that the standard error of the pooled estimate will be less than the standard error of the pooled estimate of either of the sample statistics taken singly.

The pooled variance estimate s^2_{pooled} is found by computing a weighted average of s^2_1 and s^2_2:

$$s^2_{pooled} = \frac{(n_1 - 1)s^2_1 + (n_2 - 1)s^2_2}{(n_1 - 1) + (n_2 - 1)} = \frac{(n_1 - 1)s^2_1 + (n_2 - 1)s^2_2}{n_1 + n_2 - 2}$$

Note that the pooled estimate weights the sample variances by $n - 1$. The larger the sample size, the more weight given to the sample variance in the pooled estimate.

Incorporating the pooled estimate of the population variance into Formula 12-5b, we obtain Formula 12-5c.

$$t_{\bar{X}_1 - \bar{X}_2 \text{observed}} = \frac{\bar{X}_1 - \bar{X}_2}{\sqrt{\left[\dfrac{(n_1 - 1)s^2_1 + (n_2 - 1)s^2_2}{n_1 + n_2 - 2}\right]\left(\dfrac{1}{n_1} + \dfrac{1}{n_2}\right)}} \qquad \text{(12-5c)}$$

This formula can be used for samples of equal or different sizes.

If the sample sizes are equal ($n_1 = n_2 = n$), the cumbersome denominator in Formula 12-5c reduces to $\sqrt{(s^2_1 + s^2_2)/n}$, and the *t* test can be written as in Formula 12-5d.

$$t_{\bar{X}_1 - \bar{X}_2 \text{observed}} = \frac{\bar{X}_1 - \bar{X}_2}{\sqrt{\dfrac{s^2_1 + s^2_2}{n}}} \qquad \text{(12-5d)}$$

TABLE 12-3 Descriptive statistics for the hypothetical posttest data from the teacher expectancy study: first graders

Control Group					Experimental Group			
X	$\bar{X}$	$X - \bar{X}$	x^2		X	$\bar{X}$	$X - \bar{X}$	x^2
90	105.2	−15.2	231.04		107	116.4	−9.4	88.36
99	105.2	−6.2	38.44		111	116.4	−5.4	29.16
102	105.2	−3.2	10.24		117	116.4	.6	.36
114	105.2	8.8	77.44		125	116.4	8.6	73.96
121	105.2	15.8	249.64		122	116.4	5.6	31.36
Σ 526	526	0	606.80	Σ	582	582	0	223.20

$$s^2 = \frac{606.80}{5 - 1} = 151.70 \qquad\qquad s^2 = \frac{223.30}{5 - 1} = 55.8$$

$$s = \sqrt{151.70} = 12.32 \qquad\qquad s = \sqrt{55.8} = 7.47$$

As an example of how to apply Formulas 12-5c and 12-5d, consider the hypothetical posttest scores for first graders in the teacher expectancy study. (See Table 12-3 for the data and Chapter 2 for a complete description of the study.) In this study, the experimental group (students designated at random to be intellectual bloomers) was expected to score higher than the control group (students not designated as bloomers) on a measure of intellectual ability that was given at the end of the school year. To test whether there was a significant difference between the two groups, calculate t by inserting the appropriate values from Table 12-3 into Formula 12-5c:

$$t_{\bar{X}_1 - \bar{X}_2 \text{observed}} = \frac{\bar{X}_1 - \bar{X}_2}{\sqrt{\left[\dfrac{(n_1 - 1)s_1^2 + (n_2 - 1)s_2^2}{n_1 + n_2 - 2}\right]\left(\dfrac{1}{n_1} + \dfrac{1}{n_2}\right)}}$$

$$= \frac{105.2 - 116.4}{\sqrt{\left[\dfrac{(5 - 1)151.70 + (5 - 1)55.8}{5 + 5 - 2}\right]\left(\dfrac{1}{5} + \dfrac{1}{5}\right)}}$$

$$= \frac{-11.20}{\sqrt{\left(\dfrac{606.8 + 223.2}{8}\right)\left(\dfrac{2}{5}\right)}} = \frac{-11.20}{\sqrt{(103.75)(.4)}}$$

$$= \frac{-11.20}{\sqrt{41.5}} = \frac{-11.20}{6.44} = -1.74$$

Since the sample sizes are equal, Formula 12-5d can also be used to obtain t. These computations are shown in Procedure 12-2, which follows.

Decision Rules for Rejecting the Null Hypothesis

In order to decide whether or not to reject the null hypothesis, compare the observed t value (-1.74 in the example) with a critical value. The symbol t_{critical} designates the points in the t distribution beyond which differences between sample means are unlikely to arise under the null hypothesis. Since there is a different critical value of t for each degree of freedom, the first step is to determine the number of degrees of freedom. For the example data from the teacher expectancy study, there were 5 subjects in the control group (n_1) and 5 subjects in the experimental group (n_2). The degrees of freedom, then, for the critical value of t are:

$$df = (5 - 1) + (5 - 1) = 4 + 4 = 8$$

The next step is to find the critical value of t for 8 degrees of freedom at a specified level of significance α. In the example study, assume that a two-tail test at $\alpha = .01$ was planned before the study was conducted. From Table C,

$$t_{\text{critical}(.01/2,8)} = 3.355$$

Since t_{observed} (1.74) does not exceed the critical value of t (3.355), the null hypothesis should not be rejected. Although the difference between the means was in the expected

TABLE 12-4 Criteria for decision making with the *t* test

Test	Reject H_0 If	Do Not Reject H_0 If
Nondirectional (two-tail)	$|t_{obs.}| \geq t_{crit.(\alpha/2, df)}$	$|t_{obs.}| < t_{crit.(\alpha/2, df)}$
Directional (one-tail)	$|t_{obs.}| \geq t_{crit.(\alpha, df)}$	$|t_{obs.}| < t_{crit.(\alpha, df)}$

direction, the evidence leads us to the conclusion that this difference probably represents a chance occurrence.

In general, the criteria given in Table 12-4 can be established for deciding whether or not to reject the null hypothesis.[4]

The steps in conducting the *t* test for two independent groups are summarized in Procedure 12-2, using data from Table 12-3.

PROCEDURE 12-2 Steps in conducting a *t* test for two independent means (example data from the hypothetical study of teacher expectancy shown in Table 12-3)

Operation	Example
1. Specify the null and alternative hypotheses and the level of significance.	H_0: $\mu_C - \mu_E = 0$ H_1: $\mu_C - \mu_E < 0$ *where:* $C =$ control group $E -$ experimental group $\alpha = .01$
2. Examine the assumptions of the *t* test:	
a. Independent and random sampling	**a.** A description of the sampling procedures for the study given in Chapter 2 suggests that subjects were independently sampled from each age group. (It is unlikely that subjects were actually randomly selected from their respective populations. They were selected from a convenient sample representing each population.)
b. Normality within each population	**b.** The assumption of normality within each population cannot be tested directly here by constructing a frequency distribution, since the number of scores in each group is so small. However, since the *t* test is not sensitive to violations of this assumption, we can proceed.
c. Homogeneity of variances (equal variances in two populations)	**c.** When cell sizes are equal, the *t* test is not sensitive to violations of this assumption. Since cell sizes are equal here ($n_1 = n_2 = 5$), we need not be concerned with testing this assumption.

[4]For ease, we write the absolute value of *t*: $|t_{observed}|$. However, be careful. The one-tail difference between $t_{observed}$ and $t_{critical}$ *must* be in the predicted direction.

Operation	Example

Operation

3. Compute $t_{\bar{X}_1 - \bar{X}_2 \text{ observed}}$ by inserting appropriate values into Formula 12-5c or 12-5d (if $n_1 = n_2$) and solving:

If $n_1 \neq n_2$:

$t_{\bar{X}_1 - \bar{X}_2 \text{ observed}}$

$$= \frac{\bar{X}_1 - \bar{X}_2}{\sqrt{\left[\dfrac{(n_1 - 1)s_1^2 + (n_2 - 1)s_2^2}{n_1 + n_2 - 2}\right]\left(\dfrac{1}{n_1} + \dfrac{1}{n_2}\right)}}$$

or if $n_1 = n_2$:

$$t_{\bar{X}_1 - \bar{X}_2 \text{ observed}} = \frac{\bar{X}_1 - \bar{X}_2}{\sqrt{\dfrac{s_1^2 + s_2^2}{n}}}$$

4. Identify t_{critical} with $n_E + n_C - 2$ degrees of freedom, using Table C.

5. Decide whether or not to reject the null hypothesis.
  a. Reject H_0 if $|t_{\text{observed}}| \geq t_{\text{critical}}$.
  b. Do not reject H_0 if $|t_{\text{observed}}| \leq t_{\text{critical}}$.

Example

From Table 12-3, we have

$$\bar{X}_C = 105.2 \qquad \bar{X}_E = 116.4$$

$$s_C^2 = 151.70 \qquad s_E^2 = 55.8$$

$$n_C = 5 \qquad n_E = 5$$

Since cell sizes are equal, Formula 12-5d can be used:

$$t_{\bar{X}_1 - \bar{X}_2 \text{ observed}} = \frac{105.2 - 116.4}{\sqrt{\dfrac{151.70 + 55.80}{5}}}$$

$$= \frac{-11.2}{\sqrt{\dfrac{207.5}{5}}}$$

$$= \frac{-11.2}{\sqrt{41.5}} = \frac{-11.2}{6.44} = -1.74$$

$$df = 5 + 5 - 2 = 8$$

$$t_{\text{critical}(.01,8)} = 2.896$$

Since $|t_{\text{observed}}| < t_{\text{critical}}$ ($|-1.74| < 2.896$), we cannot reject H_0. We conclude that although the difference between means was in the expected direction, there is insufficient evidence to lead us to believe that this difference represents anything but a chance occurrence.

Confidence Intervals for Case II Research: Independent Means

The $100(1 - \alpha)$ percent confidence interval can be established around the observed differences between means using the t distribution. This procedure is similar to that described in Chapter 10 for constructing confidence intervals using the normal distribution. The major difference is that since the standard error is estimated from sample data, t_{critical} with $df = n_1 + n_2 - 2$ is used rather than z_{critical} in constructing the interval. The general form of the confidence interval is given in Formula 12-6.

$$(\bar{X}_1 - \bar{X}_2) - t_{\text{critical}(\alpha/2, df)} s_{\bar{X}_1 - \bar{X}_2} \leq \mu_1 - \mu_2 \leq (\bar{X}_1 - \bar{X}_2) + t_{\text{critical}(\alpha/2, df)} s_{\bar{X}_1 - \bar{X}_2}$$

$$(12\text{-}6)$$

As an example of constructing confidence intervals, let's set up the 95 percent confidence interval $[95 = 100(1 - .05)]$ for the data from the example study. Three pieces of information are needed: $\bar{X}_1 - \bar{X}_2$, $s_{\bar{X}_1-\bar{X}_2}$, and $t_{critical}$. All three pieces of information are already available. From Procedure 12-2:

$$\bar{X}_1 - \bar{X}_2 = -11.2$$
$$s_{\bar{X}_1-\bar{X}_2} = 6.44$$

The value of $t_{critical}$ for $\alpha/2 = .05/2$ and 8 degrees of freedom can be found in Table C: 2.306.

The 95 percent confidence interval is found as follows (pay attention to negative numbers):

$$CI_{.95}:\quad -11.2 - (2.306)(6.44) \leq \mu_1 - \mu_2 \leq -11.2 + (2.306)(6.44)$$
$$-11.2 - 14.85 \leq \mu_1 - \mu_2 \leq -11.2 + 14.85$$
$$-26.05 \leq \mu_1 - \mu_2 \leq 3.65$$

The interval tells us that over all random samples of differences between means, the true value of $\mu_1 - \mu_2$ lies within the rather large interval such as that bounded by -26.05 to $+3.65$ IQ points, with a probability of .95.

The 99 percent confidence interval can be constructed in a similar way. Only one piece of information is missing: $t_{critical}$ at .01/2. With 8 degrees of freedom, the value of $t_{critical}$ can be found from Table C: 3.355. With this information, the 99 percent confidence interval can be written:

$$CI_{.99}:\quad -11.2 - (3.355)(6.44) \leq \mu_1 - \mu_2 \leq -11.2 + (3.355)(6.44)$$
$$-11.2 - 21.61 \leq \mu_1 - \mu_2 \leq -11.2 + 21.61$$
$$-32.81 \leq \mu_1 - \mu_2 \leq 10.41$$

The 99 percent confidence interval tells us that over all possible samples, one must allow an enormous range of values (e.g., -32.81 to $+10.41$) in order to include the true difference between means with probability .99.

Example Problem 12.2

Table 12-5 presents moral judgments, along with descriptive statistics, for subjects 4–6 years old and 16–18 years old for an event in which the *outcome* was positive , whereas the actor's *intent* was negative. In this situation, Piaget's theory predicts that young children will give positive ratings (since the outcome was positive) and adults will give negative ratings (since the intent was negative). Test this hypothesis at $\alpha = .05$. Include the following items in your answer:

a. Null and alternative hypotheses
b. Test of each assumption or explanation for not conducting the test
c. $t_{observed}$
d. $t_{critical}$
e. Conclusions
f. 95 percent confidence interval

TABLE 12-5 Hypothetical moral judgments and descriptive statistics for a moral act: The outcome was positive but the actor's intent was negative

Subject	Young Children (Group 1)	Young Adults (Group 5)
1	1	−5
2	−1	−2
3	−1	−2
4	1	−2
5	2	−3
Σ	2	−14
$\bar{X}$	.40	−2.80
s^2	1.80	1.70
s	1.34	1.30

CASE II t TEST: DEPENDENT MEANS

The *t* **test for dependent means** can be used to examine data from designs when two observations are made on each subject or when one observation is made on each of the two members of a matched pair. As an example, consider a study of the effects of training on listening skills. In a study with repeated observations on the same group of subjects, subjects would be given a pretest on listening skills, a treatment to improve these skills, and then a posttest on listening skills. [This study is a preexperimental design and is not recommended for drawing causal interpretations about the effect of listening training (see Chapter 1, "Designs for Behavioral Research").] In a study with matching, pairs of subjects would be matched on their scores from a pretest of listening skills. Then one member of each pair would be randomly assigned to, say, a control group, and the other member would be assigned to the group receiving the listening treatment. Afterward, all subjects would be tested again for listening skills. More complicated designs can be conceived, such as one-way designs with more than two observations (levels) or factorial designs. For them, the *randomized-block* ANOVA is an appropriate statistical test and is covered in later chapters in Section VI.

Purpose and Underlying Logic

The *t* test for dependent means helps us decide whether the difference between two sample means may be due to chance or to a true difference between population means. Even though the data come from the same sample or matched pairs of subjects, we speak of the difference between two sample means because the subjects received two different treatments. Nevertheless, since the scores in the two treatment or observation conditions are based on the same or matched subjects, they are correlated. The *t* test for dependent samples takes this correlation into account.

The sampling distribution of *t* can be used to determine the probability of observing a difference between means as large as or larger than the difference in the sample data. The logic behind using the sampling distribution of *t* for examining differences between means with the dependent-mean *t* test is similar to that for the independent-mean *t* test. The major difference is in the standard error of the differences between means. The standard error is usually larger for independent samples than for dependent samples. This result can be seen by comparing the two formulas for the standard errors. The standard error of the difference between means for the independent *t* test with equal cell sizes is given by Formula 12-4:

$$s_{\bar{X}_1 - \bar{X}_2} = \sqrt{s_{\bar{X}_1}^2 + s_{\bar{X}_2}^2}$$

For the dependent *t* test, the standard error of the difference between means, $s_{\bar{X}_1 - \bar{X}_2}^*$, is given by Formula 12-7:

$$s_{\bar{X}_1 - \bar{X}_2}^* = \sqrt{s_{\bar{X}_1}^2 + s_{\bar{X}_2}^2 - 2r_{12}s_{\bar{X}_1}s_{\bar{X}_2}} \qquad\qquad \text{(12-7)}$$

where:

$*$ = indicates dependent samples

$s_{\bar{X}}$ = standard error of the mean $(s/\sqrt{N})$

r_{12} = correlation between subjects' scores in treatment 1 and treatment 2

Formula 12-7 looks worse than it is. The standard error of the difference between means based on dependent samples depends on the standard error (squared) of the mean of sample 1, and the standard error (squared) for sample 2, just as in the formula for independent samples. Furthermore, $s_{\bar{X}_1 - \bar{X}_2}^*$ takes into account the fact that there is a correlation between subjects' scores in treatments 1 and 2, since the same subjects or matched pairs of subjects are observed in both treatments: $2r_{12}s_{\bar{X}_1}s_{\bar{X}_2}$. If subjects' scores are positively correlated—something we almost always expect—then some number will be subtracted from $s_{\bar{X}_1}^2 + s_{\bar{X}_2}^2$ in arriving at $s_{\bar{X}_1 - \bar{X}_2}^*$. Thus, usually, $s_{\bar{X}_1 - \bar{X}_2}^*$ will be smaller than $s_{\bar{X}_1 - \bar{X}_2}$.[5] This result occurs because by subtracting the correlation between subjects' scores in the two treatment conditions, we removed the variability within a group (error) due to individual differences between subjects. Hence, the error term for designs with repeated measures on the same subjects or with matched subjects is usually smaller than the error term for a between-subjects design.

Although $s_{\bar{X}_1 - \bar{X}_2}^*$ and $s_{\bar{X}_1 - \bar{X}_2}$ refer to apparently different formulas, actually both come from the same general formula. In order to see why the apparent difference vanishes, think about an independent *t* test with subjects randomly assigned to one or the other group. What do you expect the correlation *r* between the scores of subjects in treatment 1 and treatment

---

[5]In rare cases, the correlation may be negative. In this case, $s_{\bar{X}_1 - \bar{X}_2}^*$ will be larger than $s_{\bar{X}_1 - \bar{X}_2}$. (However, the finding of a negative correlation may be substantively important—more so than the comparison of means.)

2 to be? Well, since subjects were randomly assigned, the correlation should be zero. If $r = 0$ in Formula 12-7, then:

$$s^*_{\bar{X}_1 - \bar{X}_2} = \sqrt{s^2_{\bar{X}_1} + s^2_{\bar{X}_2} - (2)(0)s_{\bar{X}_1}s_{\bar{X}_2}}$$

$$= \sqrt{s^2_{\bar{X}_1} + s^2_{\bar{X}_2}}$$

$$= s_{\bar{X}_1 - \bar{X}_2}$$

which is Formula 12-4. So the formula for the standard error of the differences between means with independent samples has already taken into account the fact that r_{12} is expected to be zero.

The formula for the dependent t test is similar to the formula for the independent t test. It is given in Formula 12-8.

$$t^* = \frac{(\bar{X}_1 - \bar{X}_2) - (\mu_1 - \mu_2)}{\sqrt{s^2_{\bar{X}_1} + s^2_{\bar{X}_2} - 2r_{12}s_{\bar{X}_1}s_{\bar{X}_2}}} \qquad (12\text{-}8)$$

with $df = n - 1$ and
where:

t^* = dependent-sample t test

n = number of subjects in *one* of the two cells

(Notice that $n_1 = n_2 = n$, since the same subjects or matched pairs of subjects are observed in each of the two cells.)

One difference between the independent t test and the dependent t test is that $s^*_{\bar{X}_1 - \bar{X}_2}$ is used for the standard error rather than $s_{\bar{X}_1 - \bar{X}_2}$. A second difference is that the t test for independent samples (t) is based on $n_1 + n_2 - 2$ degrees of freedom, whereas the dependent t test (t^*) is based on $n - 1$ degrees of freedom. We have fewer degrees of freedom for the dependent t test because the scores of subjects in treatment 1 are correlated with—not independent of—the scores in treatment 2. There are only n different subjects and so only n independent observations. Thus, there are $n - 1$ degrees of freedom for the dependent t test.

Hypotheses

The hypotheses about differences between population means using the sampling distribution of t for dependent samples are exactly the same as the hypotheses for the independent t test (see pp. 345–346).

Design Requirements for the Use of the t^* Test

The use of the t^* test imposes a number of requirements on data collection:

1. There is one independent variable with two levels (i.e., two cells in the design).

2. The same group of subjects is observed under both treatment conditions, or matched pairs of subjects are observed so that one member of the pair is observed under treatment 1 and the other member of the pair is observed under treatment 2.

3. The levels of the independent variable may differ from one another either quantitatively or qualitatively. Qualitative differences are, for example, driving performance in cars with manual and automatic transmissions or strength before and after "pumping iron" (working with weights). Quantitative differences are, for example, a person's ability to recognize familiar objects at different distances, the amount of drug dosage given to rats, or the number of reinforcements.

Assumptions

In the use of the sampling distribution of *t* to test for differences between dependent means, the following assumptions are made:

1. The scores of the *n* subjects are independently and randomly sampled from the two respective populations.
2. The scores in the respective populations are normally distributed.
3. The variance of scores in the respective populations are equal (homogeneity of variances: $\sigma_1^2 = \sigma_2^2$).

These assumptions and the (lack of) sensitivity of the *t* test to them were discussed extensively in this chapter and will not be discussed again here.

Conceptual Formula for the t^* Test

Since under the null hypothesis $\mu_1 - \mu_2 = 0$, the conceptual formula for the t^* test can be written as shown in Formula 12-8a.

$$t^*_{observed} = \frac{\bar{X}_1 - \bar{X}_2}{\sqrt{s_{\bar{X}_1}^2 + s_{\bar{X}_2}^2 - 2r_{12}s_{\bar{X}_1}s_{\bar{X}_2}}} \tag{12-8a}$$

with $df = n - 1$.

As an example of how this conceptual formula can be applied, data from the hypothetical study of teacher expectancy will be used. Specifically, the pre- and posttest scores of the first graders in the experimental group will be examined (see Table 12-6). Recall that these subjects were labeled "bloomers" and teachers expected them to "spurt" in intellectual development over the academic year.

The purpose of this analysis is to determine whether the mean difference of −24.4 points between pre- and posttest scores (92.00 − 116.40 = −24.40) may have arisen by chance or represents a true difference between population means (i.e., the population before the treatment and the population after the treatment). Since the same subjects were observed at pretest and posttest, the t^* test is an appropriate statistic. One word of caution before proceeding: Although we are testing differences between means before and after treatment, a

TABLE 12-6 Hypothetical pre- and posttest scores for first
graders in the experimental group
(see Table 2-1)

	Scores	
Subject	*Pretest*	*Posttest*
1	60	107
2	85	111
3	90	117
4	110	125
5	115	122
$\bar{X}$	92.00	116.40
s	21.97	7.47
r	.946	

significant difference does *not* imply that the treatment caused the change. Remember that
this study is a preexperimental design (see Chapter 1).

In order to conduct the statistical test, we begin by stating the null and alternative
hypotheses and the level of significance:

$$H_0: \mu_1 - \mu_2 = 0$$
$$H_1: \mu_1 - \mu_2 \neq 0$$
$$\alpha = .01$$

Next, we check the assumptions of independent random sampling, normality, and homogeneity of variance. Subjects were randomly sampled and ability scores are known to be
normally distributed; so that takes care of the first two assumptions. However, the variances
at pretest $[(21.97)^2]$ and posttest $[(7.47)^2]$ are not homogeneous. Nevertheless, the t test is
not sensitive to a violation of this assumption, and so we can proceed.[6]

The next step is to insert the data from Table 12-6 into the formula for $t^*_{observed}$. Before
doing so, we have to make two preliminary calculations:

$$s_{\bar{X}_{pre}} = \frac{s_{pre}}{\sqrt{n}} = \frac{21.97}{\sqrt{5}} = 9.83$$

and

$$s_{\bar{X}_{post}} = \frac{s_{post}}{\sqrt{n}} = \frac{7.47}{\sqrt{5}} = 3.34$$

---

[6]A difference between variances in a dependent-means design suggests that there may be an interaction
between subjects and treatments. In this case, the t test represents a conservative test of the null hypothesis (see,
for example, Kirk, 1982). This appears to have happened with this study.

Now all values can be inserted into Formula 12-8a, with the following result:

$$t^*_{observed} = \frac{92.00 - 116.40}{\sqrt{9.38^2 + 3.34^2 - 2(.946)(3.34)(9.83)}}$$

$$= \frac{-24.40}{\sqrt{96.629 + 11.156 - 62.119}}$$

$$= \frac{-24.40}{\sqrt{45.666}} = \frac{-24.40}{6.758} = -3.61$$

Decision Rules for Rejecting the Null Hypothesis

To decide whether to reject the null hypothesis, we must compare $t^*_{observed}$ (-3.61 in the example) with the critical value of *t* designating the regions of the *t* distribution beyond which differences between sample means are unlikely to arise under the null hypothesis. Since there is a different critical value of *t* for each degree of freedom, the first step is to determine the number of degrees of freedom. With one group of subjects, there are $n - 1$ degrees of freedom:

$$df = n - 1$$

For the example data from the teacher expectancy study, there were five subjects, so the degrees of freedom for the critical value of *t* are:

$$df = 5 - 1 = 4$$

The next step is to find the critical value of *t* for 4 degrees of freedom at a specified level of significance (α). Table C at the end of the book provides these values. For $\alpha = .01$, two-tail,

$$t_{critical(.01/2,4)} = 4.604$$

Since $|t^*_{observed}|$ does not exceed $t_{critical}$, the null hypothesis should not be rejected. There is insufficient evidence to conclude that the difference between the pre- and posttest means represented a true difference.

In the example study, suppose the mean score at posttest was expected to exceed the mean score at pretest. For this revision, then, the hypotheses would be:

$$H_0: \mu_{pre} - \mu_{post} = 0$$
$$H_1: \mu_{pre} - \mu_{post} < 0$$
$$\alpha = .01$$

For a one-tail test at $\alpha = .01$ with 4 *df*, $t_{critical}$ can be found in Table C:

$$t_{critical(.01,4)} = -3.747$$

Since the *absolute value* of $t^*_{observed}$ (3.61) does not exceed the critical value of *t* (3.747), the null hypothesis should not be rejected. Although the difference between means was in the expected direction, there is insufficient evidence to conclude that this difference represents anything but a chance occurrence.

In general, the criteria listed in Table 12-4 can be established for deciding whether or not to reject the null hypothesis. Just substitute $|t^*_{obs.}|$ for $|t_{obs.}|$.

Computational Formula for the t^* Test

Whereas the conceptual formula for the dependent t test is reasonably straightforward to use, the correlation between the observations under the two treatment conditions must be calculated. This calculation can be somewhat tedious for large samples, especially in the absence of a calculator or computer. Fortunately, there is a computationally easy formula for the t^* test that does not require calculation of the correlation or calculation of as many sample statistics as does the conceptual formula. The computational formula for the dependent t test is given in Formula 12-9.

$$t^*_{observed} = \frac{\bar{D} - \mu_D}{s_{\bar{D}}} = \frac{\bar{D}}{s_{\bar{D}}} \tag{12-9}$$

In this formula, $\bar{D}$ is the average of the difference between subjects' scores in one treatment condition (or at pretest) and their scores in the other treatment condition (or at posttest). More formally, if X_{p_1} represents subject p's score under treatment 1 (or pretest), and X_{p_2} represents this subject's score under treatment 2 (or posttest), then a difference score for this person is defined as in Formula 12-10.

$$D_p = X_{p_1} - X_{p_2} \tag{12-10}$$

The average difference score, $\bar{D}$, is simply $\bar{X}_1 - \bar{X}_2$:

$$\bar{D} = \frac{\sum_p D_p}{n} = \frac{\sum_p (X_{p_1} - X_{p_2})}{n}$$

$$= \frac{\sum_p X_{p_1}}{n} - \frac{\sum_p X_{p_2}}{n} = \bar{X}_1 - \bar{X}_2$$

Furthermore, μ_D is the mean difference in the population, assumed to be zero under the null hypothesis.

Finally, the standard error of the mean of differences is defined as in Formula 12-11.

$$S_{\bar{D}} = \frac{s_D}{\sqrt{n}} \tag{12-11}$$

And the standard deviation of the difference scores, s_D, is defined as in Formula 12-12.

$$s_D = \sqrt{\frac{\sum\limits_{p}(D_p - \bar{D})^2}{n-1}} \qquad \textbf{(12-12)}$$

Although in presenting the formula, we had to define several new statistics, they are easily and quickly calculated. Procedure 12-3 shows the application of the computational formula for the t^* test, using, as an example, the data on first graders in the hypothetical study on teacher expectancy (Table 12-6).

PROCEDURE 12-3 Steps in testing the difference between means based on dependent samples (data from Table 12-6)

Operation

1. Specify the null and alternative hypotheses and the level of statistical significance.
   If a directional alternative hypothesis is to be stated, it can be expressed as H_1: $D > 0$ or H_1: $D < 0$, depending on the direction of the alternative hypothesis.

2. Examine the assumptions of the t^* test:

3. Set up a computational table with seven columns:

   (1) Subject ID number

   (2) Score in treatment condition 1 (X_1)

   (3) Score in treatment condition 2 (X_2)

   (4) Difference score (D)

   (5) The mean of the difference scores ($\bar{D}$)

   (6) The deviation score ($D - \bar{D}$)

   (7) The square of the deviation scores [$(D - \bar{D})^2$]

Example

H_0: $\mu_D = 0$

H_1: $\mu_D \neq 0$

$\alpha = .01$

See Procedure 12-2, step 2.

(1) Subject	(2) X_1	(3) X_2	(4) $D = X_1 - X_2$	(5) $\bar{D}$	(6) $D - \bar{D}$	(7) $(D - \bar{D})^2$
1	60	107	−47	−24.40	−22.60	510.76
2	85	111	−26	−24.40	−1.60	2.56
3	90	117	−27	−24.40	−2.60	6.76
4	110	125	−15	−24.40	9.40	88.36
5	115	122	−7	−24.40	17.40	302.76
Σ	460	582	(−122)	(−122)	0	911.20

4. Insert the subject's identification number in column 1.

Operation	**Example**

5. Insert the subject's score under treatment 1 in column 2.

6. Insert the subject's score under treatment 2 in column 3.

7. Subtract each subject's score in column 3 from his or her score in column 2 to get the difference score D for each subject in column 4.

8. Sum the difference scores, and divide the sum by n in order to get the mean of the difference scores to enter in column 5:

$$\bar{D} = \frac{\sum_p (D_p)}{n}$$

$$\bar{D} = \frac{(-47) + (-26) + (-27) + (-15) + (-7)}{5}$$

$$= \frac{-122}{5} = -24.40$$

9. Subtract the mean of the difference scores $(\bar{D})$ from each subject's difference score (D) for column 6. *Note: In order to subtract a negative mean from a negative difference score, change the sign of the mean to + and take the sum. See the example. As a computational check, the sum of all $D - \bar{D}$ should equal 0.*

$(-47.00) - (-24.40) = -47.00 + 24.40 = -22.60$, etc., for each subject.

10. Square the values in column 6, and place the results in column 7.

$(-22.60)^2 = 510.76$, etc., for each subject.

11. Sum $(D - \bar{D})^2$, and enter the sum at the bottom of column 7.

$510.76 + 2.56 + 6.76 + 88.36 + 302.76 = 911.20$

12. Calculate the standard deviation of the difference scores by dividing the sum of column 7 (obtained in step 10) by $n - 1$, and then taking the square root (Formula 12-12):

$$s_D = \sqrt{\frac{\sum (D_p - \bar{D})^2}{n - 1}}$$

$$s_D = \sqrt{\frac{911.20}{5 - 1}} = \sqrt{227.8} = 15.093$$

13. Calculate the standard error of the mean differences by dividing the value in step 12 by the square root of n (Formula 12-11):

$$s_{\bar{D}} = \frac{s_D}{\sqrt{n}}$$

$$s_{\bar{D}} = \frac{15.093}{\sqrt{5}} = 6.750$$

You may notice a difference of .008 between $s_{\bar{D}}$ as it is calculated here and $s^*_{\bar{X}_1 - \bar{X}_2}$ as it appears in the denominator of the equation for $t^*_{observed}$ given in the "Conceptual Formula" section. This difference is due to rounding error.

Operation	Example
14. Insert the values from steps 8 and 13 into Formula 12-9 and calculate: $$t^*_{observed} = \frac{\bar{D}}{s_{\bar{D}}}$$	$$t^*_{observed} = \frac{-24.40}{6.750} = -3.61$$
15. From Table C, determine $t_{critical}$ for α, using $n - 1$ degrees of freedom. *Use $t_{critical(\alpha/2,n-1)}$ for two-tail test; $t_{critical(\alpha,n-1)}$ for one-tail test.*	$df = n - 1 = 5 - 1 = 4$ $t_{crit.(.01/2,4)} = 4.604$

16. Establish decision rules for rejecting the null hypothesis.
 	
  a. Do not reject H_0 if $\|t^*_{observed}\| < t_{critical}$.
 	
  b. Reject H_0 if $\|t^*_{observed}\| \geq t_{critical}$.
	a. If $\|t^*_{observed}\| < 4.604$, do not reject H_0.
	
	b. If $\|t^*_{observed}\| \geq 4.604$, reject H_0.

17. Compare $\|t^*_{observed}\|$ (step 14) with $t_{critical}$ (step 16), and decide whether or not to reject H_0.	Since $\|t^*_{observed}\| < t_{critical}$ (3.61 < 4.604), we do not reject H_0. There is insufficient evidence to conclude that there is a significant difference between the two groups.

Numerical Example with Matched Pairs

As an example of a design with matching, consider a study on the effect of the organization of a list of words, all related to minerals, on subjects' recall of the words. In this study, subjects received a list of 50 words, either arranged in a conceptual hierarchy (experimental group) or arranged in a random order (control group). After studying the list for 4 minutes, all subjects worked on a filler task for 1 minute in order to prevent them from rehearsing the words in the list. Then all subjects recalled as many words from the list as possible.

Since there is a positive correlation between verbal ability and recall of conceptually related words, the researcher decided to match subjects on verbal ability in order to remove individual differences in verbal ability from the variability of scores within groups (error). From a random sample of 20 subjects, 10 pairs of subjects were matched on the basis of their vocabulary test scores (blocks A–J; see Table 12-7). Then one member of the pair was randomly assigned to the experimental group, and the other member to the control group (see Table 12-8). Finally, the subjects participated in the experiment as described before. The results are summarized in Table 12-8. The mean number of words recalled in the experimental group was 35.30; the mean number recalled in the control group was 30.50.

Before proceeding to an analysis of the data, consider more closely the data on matching in Table 12-7. Notice that only for subject pairs D, F, and I is the match on vocabulary scores perfect. Furthermore, notice that the vocabulary score of subject 4 is closer to the vocabulary score of subject 5 than to the score of subject 3. Nevertheless, so that a match for subject 3 could be found, subject 4 had to be used. For block B, two points separate the subjects' scores. Finally, note that there is a four-point difference in block J. Although matching is fine in theory, it is sometimes difficult to carry out in practice. The matching in Table 12-7 is reasonably good. Sometimes, there are wide gaps between the scores of matched pairs. And if more than one variable is used for matching, matching may become quite difficult.

TABLE 12-7 Matching on vocabulary scores in the study of the effects of organization on recall

Subject	Score	Pairing	Block	Subject	Score	Pairing	Block
1	30			11	19		
2	29	1, 2	A	12	19	11, 12	F
3	27			13	18		
4	25	3, 4	B	14	17	13, 14	G
5	24			15	15		
6	23	5, 6	C	16	14	15, 16	H
7	22			17	13		
8	22	7, 8	D	18	13	17, 18	I
9	20			19	9		
10	19	9, 10	E	20	5	19, 20	J

TABLE 12-8 Group assignment in the study of the effects of organization on recall

Block	Experimental Group (1)			Control Group (2)		
	Subject ID	Vocabulary	Recall	Subject ID	Vocabulary	Recall
A	2	29	45	1	30	40
B	3	27	42	4	25	36
C	5	24	39	6	23	30
D	7	22	34	8	22	30
E	10	19	32	9	20	33
F	11	19	35	12	19	30
G	13	18	36	14	17	33
H	15	15	34	16	14	28
I	17	13	30	18	13	25
J	19	9	26	20	5	20
Mean		19.50	35.30		18.80	30.50
SD		6.22	5.60		7.02	5.58

$r_{recall} = .894$

To conduct a statistical test, let's set forth the following hypotheses, level of significance, and decision rules:

H_0: $\mu_D = 0$

H_1: $\mu_D > 0$

$\alpha = .05$

$df = n - 1 = 10 - 1 = 9$

$t_{critical(.05,9)} = 1.883$

1. Do not reject H_0 if $|t^*_{observed}| < 1.883$.
2. Reject H_0 if $|t^*_{observed}| \geq 1.883$.

Table 12-9 shows the calculation of $t^*_{observed}$ using the computational formula (Procedure 12-3). Since $|t^*_{observed}|$ (5.90) is greater than $t_{critical}$ (1.883), the null hypothesis should be rejected. We conclude that organization caused the increase in recall.

TABLE 12-9 Calculation of $t^*_{observed}$, using the data from the study of the effects of organization on recall

Block	Experimental X_1	Control X_2	$D = X_1 - X_2$	$\bar{D}$	$D - \bar{D}$	$(D - \bar{D})^2$
A	45	40	5	4.8	.20	.04
B	42	36	6	4.8	1.20	1.44
C	39	30	9	4.8	4.20	17.64
D	34	30	4	4.8	−.80	.64
E	32	33	−1	4.8	−5.80	33.64
F	35	30	5	4.8	.20	.04
G	36	33	3	4.8	−1.80	3.24
H	34	28	6	4.8	1.20	1.44
I	30	25	5	4.8	.20	.04
J	26	20	6	4.8	1.20	1.44
Σ	353	305	48	48	0	59.60

$$s_D = \sqrt{\frac{59.60}{10-1}} = 2.57 \qquad s_{\bar{D}} = \frac{2.57}{\sqrt{10}} = .814 \qquad t^*_{observed} = \frac{35.30 - 30.50}{.814} = \frac{4.8}{.814} = 5.90$$

Example Problem 12.3

A researcher wanted to determine whether army technicians' ability to track targets on a cathode-ray tube (CRT) differed under two conditions of visual display: white foreground on black background and yellow foreground on green background. In a pilot study, a random sample of eight technicians was selected; all eight were observed under both conditions. (So that practice effects were avoided, the order of presenting the two conditions was randomized so that half the subjects received the white-on-black condition first.) The number of targets accurately tracked (out of five possible) is shown in Table 12-10. Conduct a t^* test to determine whether there was a significant difference in the number of targets accurately tracked under the two CRT conditions. (Let $\alpha = .05$.) Include the following items in your answer.

a. An explanation of why the dependent *t* test rather than the independent *t* test is appropriate
b. Null and alternative hypotheses
c. $t_{critical}$
d. Decision rules
e. Computational table (see Procedure 12-3)
f. $t^*_{observed}$
g. Conclusions

TABLE 12-10 Number of targets accurately tracked

Technician	White on Black	Yellow on Green
1	0	2
2	1	1
3	0	3
4	1	2
5	0	0
6	1	4
7	2	3
8	3	4

Confidence Intervals for Case II Research: Dependent Means

The $100(1 - \alpha)$ percent confidence interval can be constructed about the observed difference between means by using the t distribution. The procedure and the interpretation of the confidence interval for correlated data are exactly the same as for independent data. However, where $s^*_{\bar{X}_1-\bar{X}_2}$ was used for independent samples, $s^*_{\bar{X}_1-\bar{X}_2}$ is used with dependent samples. And where t_{critical} was based on $n_1 + n_2 - 2$ degrees of freedom with independent samples, t_{critical} is based on $n - 1$ degrees of freedom with dependent samples. The general form of the confidence interval is given in Formula 12-13:

$$(\bar{X}_1 - \bar{X}_2) - t_{\text{crit.}(\alpha/2,n-1)}s^*_{\bar{X}_1-\bar{X}_2} \leq \mu_1 - \mu_2 \leq (\bar{X}_1 - \bar{X}_2) + t_{\text{crit.}(\alpha/2,n-1)}s^*_{\bar{X}_1-\bar{X}_2}$$

$$(12\text{-}13)$$

If the standard error has been calculated by using difference scores, the general form of the confidence interval can be written as shown in Formula 12-13a.

$$(\bar{X}_1 - \bar{X}_2) - t_{\text{crit.}(\alpha/2,n-1)}s_{\bar{D}} \leq \mu_1 - \mu_2 \leq (\bar{X}_1 - \bar{X}_2) + t_{\text{crit.}(\alpha/2,n-1)}s_{\bar{D}} \quad \textbf{(12-13a)}$$

As an example of constructing a confidence interval with correlated data, let's set up a 99 percent confidence interval for the data from the teacher expectancy study (see Table 12-6 and Procedure 12-3). Three pieces of information are needed:

1. $\bar{X}_1 - \bar{X}_2 = D = -24.40$.
2. $s^*_{\bar{X}_1-\bar{X}_2} = s_{\bar{D}} = 6.758$.
3. $t_{\text{critical}(.01/2,4)} = 4.604$.

The 99 percent confidence interval can be found by inserting these values into Formula 12-13:

$$\text{CI}_{.99}: \quad -24.40 - (4.604)(6.758) \leq \mu_1 - \mu_2 \leq -24.40 + (4.604)(6.758)$$

$$-24.40 - 31.11 \leq \mu_1 - \mu_2 \leq -24.40 + 31.11$$

$$-55.51 \leq \mu_1 - \mu_2 \leq 6.71$$

Over all possible samples of $\bar{X}_1 - \bar{X}_2$, the probability is .99 that a confidence interval constructed like the one before will include the true difference between population means. (Notice that the probability statement is about all possible random samples of $\bar{X}_1 - \bar{X}_2$ or about intervals constructed like the one before, not about the particular interval itself.)

SUMMARY

This chapter presents *t* tests for case I and II research. Case I research addresses the question, "Was a particular sample drawn from a population with a mean specified by the null hypothesis or some alternative population?" Case II research addresses the question, "Are two samples drawn from populations with identical or different means?" *t* tests are more widely used than $z_{\bar{X}}$ or $z_{\bar{X}_1 - \bar{X}_2}$ tests because they can be used when, as is the usual case, the population standard deviation is unknown. Three *t* tests are presented, one for case I research and two for case II research. The case II *t* tests vary depending on whether the two groups are sampled independently or there is a dependence between them (e.g., when the same subject is observed in both groups or when subjects are matched). The *t* distribution is also used to construct 95 and 99 percent confidence intervals for case I research and both types of case II research.

ANSWERS TO EXAMPLE PROBLEMS

1. **a.** H_0: $\mu = 100$

    H_1: $\mu \neq 100$

    b. $t = \dfrac{1149.5 - 1000}{\dfrac{40.31}{\sqrt{10}}} = \dfrac{149.5}{12.75} = 11.73$

    c. $t_{\text{critical}(\alpha=.01/2, df=9)} = 3.25$

    d. Conclusion: Reject the null hypothesis and conclude the population mean at UCSD is greater than 1000.

    e. $1081.94 \leq \mu \leq 1217.06$

    f. No. The *t* test showed that the observed mean was just too unlikely to occur under the null hypothesis, so 1000 would not be included in the interval.

2. **a.** H_0: $\mu_{\text{children}} - \mu_{\text{adults}} = 0$

    H_1: $\mu_{\text{children}} - \mu_{\text{adults}} > 0$

    b. *Independence:* Assume subjects randomly sampled from their respective age groups.
    Normality: Too few subjects per group to check empirically. But the *t* test is robust to violation of this assumption.
    Homogeneity: The variances are very similar.

    c. $t_{\text{observed}} = \dfrac{.40 - (-2.80)}{\sqrt{\dfrac{1.80 + 1.70}{5}}} = \dfrac{3.2}{.84} = 3.81$

    d. $t_{\text{critical}(\alpha=.05, df=8)} = 1.86$

    e. Reject the null hypothesis and conclude findings support Piaget's theory.

    f. $1.64 \leq \mu_{\text{children}} - \mu_{\text{adults}} \leq 4.76$

3. **a.** Same subjects observed under both treatment conditions

    b. H_0: $\mu_D = 0$

    H_1: $\mu_D \neq 0$

    c. $t_{\text{critical}(\alpha=.05/2, df=7)} = 2.365$

    d. Reject the null hypothesis if $t_{\text{observed}} \geq |2.365|$

    e. See Procedure 12-3

    f. $t^*_{\text{observed}} = \dfrac{-1.38}{1.19/\sqrt{8}} = \dfrac{-1.38}{.42} = -3.28$

    g. Reject the null hypothesis. Conclude the yellow-on-green display leads to greater accuracy, on average, than the white-on-black display.

EXERCISES

Data from the study of aggressive males (Chapter 4) are presented in Table 12-11. The following questions refer to these data.

TABLE 12-11   Mean, standard deviation (SD), and sample size (N): Negative intent rating from the hypothetical aggression reduction study

	Pretest	*Posttest*
Aggressive		
Mean	4.72	3.89
SD	1.18	1.81
N	18	18
Nonaggressive		
Mean	3.61	3.50
SD	1.15	1.25
N	18	18

1. Test the null hypothesis ($\alpha = .05$, two-tail) that the mean pretest rating of the aggressive boys is equal to 3.93 (known to be the mean rating of boys in the population with a standard deviation of 1.25). Include:

    a. Null and alternative hypotheses.

    b. t_{observed}

    c. $t_{\text{critical}(\alpha = .05, \text{one-tail})}$

    d. Conclusions

    e. 95 percent confidence interval

    f. Would you expect the 95 percent confidence interval to include 3.93 (why or why not)?

2. Test the null hypothesis ($\alpha = .05$, one-tail) that the difference between the pretest means of the aggressive and nonaggressive boys is 0. Include:

    a. Null and alternative hypotheses.

    b. State the assumptions underlying the *t* test

    c. t_{observed}

    d. $t_{\text{critical}(\alpha = .05, \text{one-tail})}$

    e. Conclusions

3. Using data from Table 4-1, test the null hypothesis of no change in mean aggression rating of aggressive boys from pre- to posttest ($\alpha = .05$, two-tail). Include:

   a. Null and alternative hypotheses.
   b. Assumptions underlying the *t* test
   c. $t_{observed}$
   d. $t_{critical(\alpha = .05, two-tail)}$
   e. Conclusions
   f. 95 percent confidence interval
   g. Would you expect the 95 percent confidence interval to include 0 (why or why not)?

ANSWERS TO EXERCISES

1. a. H_0: $\mu = 3.93$

      H_1: $\mu \neq 3.93$
   b. $t_{observed} = (4.72 - 3.93)/(1.25/\sqrt{18}) = .79/.29 = 2.68$
   c. $t_{critical(\alpha=.05, two-tail, df=17)} = 2.11$ ($df = 18 - 1 = 17$)
   d. Conclusions: Reject the null hypothesis. Conclude that, as expected, aggressive boys receive higher aggression ratings than do boys in the population.
   e. 95 percent confidence interval: $4.29 \leq \mu \leq 5.22$
   f. Would you expect the 95 percent confidence interval to include 3.93 (why or why not)? No, because the null hypothesis was rejected. 3.93 is simply too unlikely to be included in the interval.

2. a. Null and alternative hypotheses.

      H_0: $\mu_{aggressive} - \mu_{nonaggressive} = 0$

      H_1: $\mu_{aggressive} - \mu_{nonaggressive} > 0$
   b. *Independence:* See description of sampling and assignment procedures.
      Normality: Sample sizes are small but nevertheless show a roughly symmetric distribution.
      Homogeneity: The standard deviations (variances) are very close to one another.
   c. $t_{observed} = (4.72 - 3.61)/\sqrt{(1.18^2 + 1.15^2)/18} = 1.11/.39 = 2.85$
   d. $t_{critical(\alpha=.05, one-tail, df=34)} = $ (approx.) 1.69 ($df = 18 + 18 - 2 = 34$)
   e. Conclusions: Reject the null hypothesis. The aggressive boys are rated, on average, higher than the nonaggressive boys at pretest, as expected.

3. a. H_0: $\mu_{pre} - \mu_{post} = 0$

      H_1: $\mu_{pre} - \mu_{post} \neq 0$
   b. Independence, normality, homogeneity of variance.
   c. $t_{observed} = -.83/.42 = -1.98$
   d. $t_{critical(\alpha = .05, two-tail, df=17)} = 2.11$ ($df = 18 - 1 = 17$)
   e. Conclusions: Do not reject the null hypothesis. Although the change is in the expected direction, there is insufficient power to detect the change reliability.
   f. 95 percent confidence interval: $-.06 \leq \mu_{pre} - \mu_{post} \leq 1.72$
   g. Would you expect the 95 percent confidence interval to include 0 (why or why not)? Yes, because 0 is a likely value assuming the null hypothesis is true.

13 One-Way Analysis of Variance

This chapter presents a statistical method for testing hypotheses about differences between two or more population means called the **one-way analysis of variance (ANOVA).** The one-way ANOVA is used to analyze data from designs with one independent variable that produces *two* or *more* groups of subjects. Incidentally, the one-way ANOVA is also known as the one-factor ANOVA, where, in ANOVA jargon, factor means independent variable.

By "one-way" or "one-factor," I mean that subjects are placed into groups in only one way, according to a single independent variable. Subjects are usually placed into levels of the independent variable (groups) by: (1) randomly sampling subjects from populations defined by these levels (e.g., low, middle, high socioeconomic status; a criterion-group design), (2) systematically selecting subjects in existing groupings (e.g., different organizational settings such as one with a traditional hierarchical structure and the other with a horizontal (distributed) structure; a nonequivalent control-group design), or (3) randomly assigning subjects to one of two or more groups (e.g., control, aggression-reduction treatment, attribution retraining; a true experimental design).

As an example of a true experiment with more than two groups, suppose a researcher examined the effectiveness of different counseling practices for helping clients reduce their fear of heights (acrophobia). She might compare the effectiveness of behavior modification and client-centered (Rogerian) therapy with each other and with a control group in which subjects talked informally to a therapist. In this study, then, subjects would be randomly assigned to one of three groups: (1) behavior modification, (2) client-centered therapy, or (3) control. They would receive their treatments and then be flown to Pisa, Italy. There they would be placed at the top of the Leaning Tower and asked to walk to the edge. The dependent variable would be the distance between the subject and the edge after the subject fell to all fours. The differences between the mean distances for each group can be compared by using a one-way analysis of variance.

As an example of the application of the one-way ANOVA to data collected by using a criterion-group design, suppose a researcher was interested in determining the relationship between socioeconomic status (SES) and achievement. In this study, children 10 years of age would be randomly sampled from each of three groups—low, middle, and high SES—and given an achievement test. Differences in the mean achievement of subjects in the three groups could be examined by using a one-way ANOVA.

DESCRIPTION OF THE ANOVA
Purpose and Underlying Logic

Purpose.   The purpose of the one-way ANOVA is to compare the means of two or more groups[1] in order to decide whether the observed differences between them represent a chance occurrence or a systematic effect. The test is called a one-way ANOVA because it compares groups that differ on *one* independent variable (or factor) with two or more levels. For example, in the study of acrophobia, one variable was systematically manipulated—type of counseling technique. This variable had three levels: behavior modification, client-centered therapy, and a control treatment.

In order to get an intuitive idea of how the ANOVA works, we will use the acrophobia example. From the hypothetical data for the counseling study shown in Table 13-1, would you conclude that there is a treatment effect? Or did the difference between the three means (6.33, 2.00, 3.33) arise by chance?

TABLE 13-1 Subjects' scores and descriptive statistics from the hypothetical study of counseling methods (scores represent distances from the edge of the tower)

	Control	Behavior Modification	Rogerian
	5	1	3
	6	2	3
	8	3	4
$\bar{X}$	6.33	2.00	3.33
s	1.53	1.00	.57
s^2	2.34	1.00	.33

---

[1]In a comparison of the means of *two* independent groups, either the *t* test described in Chapter 12 or the one-way analysis of variance presented here may be used.

In providing an answer to this question, the ANOVA compares the variability of scores within a group—variability due to sampling error alone—with the variability between the group means—variability due to sampling error and possible treatment effects. If the variability between groups is considerably greater than the variability within groups, this result is evidence of a treatment effect.

Now consider this approach in more detail. Since all subjects within a group receive the same treatment, the variability of scores within a group is considered error; it represents unsystematic variation. For example, all subjects in the behavior modification group received this type of therapy. The variation of the subjects' scores about the mean ($\bar{X} = 2.00$) represents error variation. Unsystematic error variation may be due to measurement error, random events that occur during the conduct of this study, or both.[2] Within-group variability, then, introduces "noise" in obtaining an estimate of the population mean (μ) for each group.

The variability, or differences between the group means, is viewed as a combination of error variability *and* variability due to treatment effects. Treatment effects represent systematic variations in the scores that can be attributed to the independent variable. These effects represent the "signal" that the researcher is attempting to isolate from the "noise" or error in the data. For example, the differences between the means of the behavior modification, Rogerian, and control groups—2.00, 3.33, and 6.33, respectively—reflect error variation and possibly treatment effects as well.

These two sources of variability, within-group and between-group variability, can be written symbolically as:

$$s^2_{\text{within}} = \text{error variability}$$
$$s^2_{\text{between}} = \text{error variability} + \text{treatment effects}$$

If the variability between group means is much greater than the variability within groups, the ANOVA will lead to a decision to reject the null hypothesis of no difference between population means. That is, there is a treatment effect. If, however, the difference between the sources of variability—within groups and between groups—falls within the range expected from sampling error, the ANOVA will lead to a decision not to reject the null hypothesis. In this case, we conclude that there was not a treatment effect and that differences between group means were due to chance.

The decision of whether or not to reject the null hypothesis is never made with certainty; it is a probabilistic decision. As with the statistical tests discussed previously, the basic problem is to determine the probability of observing chance differences between two or more sample means when the null hypothesis is true. In order to do so, we need a sampling distribution. This theoretical distribution should provide a model of what happens when repeated samples of two or more means are drawn from the same population and compared with one another.

---

[2]Variability between scores within a group also may be due to systematic differences between subjects. For example, subjects may differ in ability. The ANOVA, however, assumes that variability within a group is unsystematic or not worth accounting for or both. If there is important, systematic variation within a group, the ANOVA directs us to remove it by adding a second variable—ability in this example—to the design. This second variable would create a two-way design, ability × treatment. In this way, the effect of ability on the scores can be estimated.

Underlying Logic: The *F* Distribution.   The *F* distribution, a mathematical distribution, provides a model of what happens when repeated random samples of two or more means are drawn from the same population and compared with one another. Intuitively, it works like this: Suppose a researcher draws a random sample of three groups, each of size 10, from the same population. This situation is equivalent to sampling under the null hypothesis of no difference between population means. For each sample, a mean and a variance are calculated. The sample means will probably differ from one another due only to sampling error. (Recall that the standard error of the mean is $\sigma/\sqrt{N}$.) Likewise, the scores within each group will probably differ from each other according to the variation of scores in the population, σ. In this case, then, the variation within groups provides one estimate of **error variability.** And since the sample means are drawn from the same population, so that there is no difference in the population mean, the variation between groups provides a second, independent estimate of error variability:[3]

$$s^2_{within} \approx \text{error variability}$$
$$s^2_{between} \approx \text{error variability} + (\text{treatment effect} = 0 \text{ under } H_0)$$

Since s^2_{within} and $s^2_{between}$ are independent sample estimates of the sampling error, they will not be exactly the same. The degree to which they fluctuate can be measured by dividing one by the other, as shown in Formula 13-1.

$$F_{observed} = \frac{s^2_{between}}{s^2_{within}} \tag{13-1}$$

Now, suppose this sampling procedure under the null hypothesis was carried out many times and each time the ratio of $s^2_{between}$ and s^2_{within} was formed. For each sample, different values of $F_{observed}$ would be obtained. If a frequency distribution were formed by placing values of $F_{observed}$ on the abscissa and the relative frequency on the ordinate, the result would be the sampling distribution of *F* shown in Figure 13-1. It enables us to state the probability of obtaining $F_{observed}$ at or beyond some value, assuming that the null hypothesis is true. If $F_{observed}$ is quite improbable, the null hypothesis should be rejected, the conclusion being that the population means differ—indicating a treatment effect.

The sampling distribution of *F* has several important characteristics. First, the mean of the distribution approaches 1 as the sample size increases. Second, the *F* distribution is unimodal. Third, since the *F* distribution has a lower limit of zero, the sampling distribution is positively skewed. Extremely high values of $F_{observed}$ are more likely to occur than are extremely low values. Or put another way, $s^2_{between}$ tends to take on more extreme values than does s^2_{within}. Fourth, the *F* distribution, like the *t* distribution, is actually a family of distributions, each member of the family differing from the others according to its degrees of freedom. Unlike the shape of the *t* distribution, the shape of the *F* distribution depends on *two* different numbers of degrees of freedom. One set of degrees of freedom depends on

---

[3]For a proof of the independence of the within and between sources of variability, see the Technical Appendix at the end of this chapter.

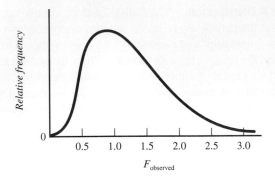

FIGURE 13-1
Sampling distribution of F ($df = 2, 27$)

the number of sample means (groups) being compared, and the other set depends on the number of subjects in each group. Each is now discussed in turn.

Degrees of Freedom between Groups (df_B).   In the example of sampling three groups from the same population, there were three groups. The degrees of freedom for the between-group comparison ($s_{between}^2$) is equal to the number of groups (k) minus 1:

$$df_B = \text{number of groups} - 1 = k - 1$$

In the sampling example with three groups, then, $df_B = 3 - 1 = 2$.

Degrees of Freedom within Groups (df_W).   The second type of degrees of freedom is *within* each group of the design. Again, consider the sampling example with three groups and 10 subjects in each group. Once the mean of a group is known along with nine of the scores in the group, the last score is also known. Thus, with n subjects in a group, there are $n - 1$ degrees of freedom within a group. For example, if $n = 10$, $df = 10 - 1 = 9$. The total number of degrees of freedom within all groups, then, is equal to the sum of the numbers of degrees of freedom within each group across all groups:

$$df_W = df \text{ within group } 1 + df \text{ within group } 2 + \cdots + df \text{ within group } k$$

In the example experiment, with three groups and 10 subjects in each group, we have $df_W = 9 + 9 + 9 = 27$. In general, $df_W = k(n - 1) = kn - k = N - k$.

The fifth characteristic of the F distribution is its relation to the t distribution. Since both the F test and the t test can be used to compare two means (i.e., 1 df between two groups), there must be some relation between the F distribution and the t distribution. As expected, for a two-tail t test, the relationship is:

$$F_{(1, df_W)} = t_{(df_W)}^2$$

Thus the one-way ANOVA and the two-tail t test can be used interchangeably in comparing the differences between two means.

Overview of the ANOVA

The ANOVA divides (partitions) the total variation in scores into variation within groups (s^2_{within}) and variation between groups ($s^2_{between}$). For example, it partitions the variability of all the scores in Table 13-1 (5, 6, . . . , 4) into variability within groups (e.g., variability within the control group: 3, 3, 4) and variability between groups (6.33, 3.33, 2.00). Then it divides $s^2_{between}$ by s^2_{within} to obtain $F_{observed}$. Finally, $F_{observed}$ can be located in the sampling distribution of F in order to decide whether to reject the null hypothesis.

In a presentation of the results of the ANOVA, typically an **ANOVA source table** is used (see Table 13-2). In its simplest form, it represents the following items:

1. The two sources of variation in the dependent variable—between groups and within groups
2. The degrees of freedom for estimating variability from each of the two sources of variation
3. The numerical values representing the variability due to the between-group and within-in-group sources of variation[4]
4. The value of $F_{observed}$

Table 13-2 presents an ANOVA source table for the data from Table 13-1. Notice that $F_{observed}$ is 12.11. Thus $s^2_{between}$ is 12 times greater than s^2_{within}.

TABLE 13-2 ANOVA source table (data from Table 13-1)

Source of Variation	df^a	Mean Square (Variance)	$F_{observed}$
Between groups	$k - 1 = 2$	14.78	$\dfrac{s^2_{between}}{s^2_{within}} = \dfrac{14.78}{1.22} = 12.11^b$
Within groups (error)	$N - k = 6$	1.22	

[a]k = the number of levels of the independent variable; i.e., the number of groups; N = the total number of subjects in the study
[b]Significant at $\alpha = .05$; $p < .05$ in this case

Finally, the value of $F_{observed}$ can be compared with the value of $F_{critical}$ in order to decide whether to reject the null hypothesis of no treatment effects. The $F_{critical}$ value depends on the degrees of freedom for each source of variation and on the level of significance (α). If $F_{observed}$ exceeds $F_{critical}$, we conclude that the difference between $s^2_{between}$ and s^2_{within} did not arise from sampling error. Rather, the population means differ due to a treatment effect. Of

---

[4]Procedures for making these calculations will be presented in later parts of this chapter.

course, we could be wrong, as indicated by the probability of a Type I error, α. In the counseling study with $\alpha = .05$, $F_{critical}$ with 2 and 6 degrees of freedom can be found in Table E at the end of the book: $F_{critical(.05/2, 6)} = 5.14$. Since $F_{observed}$ exceeds $F_{critical}$, the null hypothesis of no treatment effects should be rejected. We conclude that the counseling method (or absence of it) influenced how closely subjects would approach the edge of the Leaning Tower of Pisa.[5]

Why Not Multiple t Tests?   A frequently asked question is, "What's wrong with doing a series of t tests to compare pairs of means?" In the counseling study, for example, a t test might be used to test the following differences: control (C) versus behavior modification (B), C versus Rogerian (R), and B versus R.

The major problem with this procedure is that the three statistical tests are *not independent of one another;* if B is significantly more effective than R, and R more effective than C, we already know that B is more effective than C.

The problem of the lack of independence with multiple t tests is reflected in the probability of a Type I error. If three t tests are conducted independently of each other, each at $\alpha = .05$, the probability of obtaining a significant result by chance from any one of the three statistical tests is *not* .05. The probability is given by Formula 13-2.

$$p(\text{Type I error}) = 1 - (1 - \alpha)^c \tag{13-2}$$

where:
$c = $ number of independent t tests

For the example of three independent t tests,

$$p(\text{Type I error}) = 1 - (1 - .05)^3 = 1 - (.95)^3 = 1 - .86 = .14$$

When t tests are not independent, a complicated pattern of dependence emerges, and it is extremely difficult to specify the probability of a Type I error.

The moral of the story, then, is that the ANOVA should be used to compare the means of three or more independent groups. For two independent groups, only one t test is needed, so either the t test *or* the ANOVA can be used. Both tests will yield equivalent results, since for a two-tail t test, the following relation holds:

$$F_{(1, dfw)} = t^2{}_{(dfw)}$$

---

[5]On the basis of this test, we can only conclude that there was a treatment effect. We cannot conclude that the behavior modification alleviated subjects' fears more effectively than the procedures used in the other two groups. If one is to define the exact nature of this overall effect, comparisons between means (discussed later in this chapter) must be conducted.

Design Requirements

The use of the one-way analysis of variance presupposes that the data have been collected as follows:

1. There is one independent variable with two or more levels, and the levels of the independent variable exhaust the possible levels of interest to the researcher.
2. The levels of the independent variable may differ either qualitatively or quantitatively. For example, the levels of the counseling variable differed qualitatively. If the independent variable were number of hours of homework per week (2, 4, 6, or 8), the levels would differ quantitatively.
3. A subject may appear in one and only one group (level of the independent variable), and the subject represents a random sample from some population.

Hypotheses

The analysis of variance is used to test hypotheses about population means. The null and alternative hypotheses are similar to those tested by the t test, with the exception that additional notation is needed to represent population means for two or more groups. The null hypothesis is:

$$H_0: \mu_1 = \mu_2 = \cdot \cdot \cdot = \mu_i = \cdot \cdot \cdot = \mu_k$$

In the null hypothesis, μ_i represents the population mean of the ith group, and μ_k represents the mean of the population for the kth, or last, group. If all group means are equal in the population, each group mean will equal the grand mean, μ_G.[6] So, the null hypothesis can be written compactly as:

$$H_0: \mu_i - \mu_G = 0 \text{ for all } i$$

The null hypothesis in the counseling study, for example, could be written either:

$$H_0: \mu_C = \mu_B = \mu_R$$

or

$$H_0: \mu_i - \mu_G = 0 \text{ for all } i$$

The alternative hypothesis is that at least some pair of population means differ from one another. Consequently, the alternative hypothesis states that, in the population, not all group means equal the grand mean. In symbols, we can write

$$H_1: \mu_i - \mu_G \neq 0 \text{ for some } i$$

---

[6]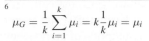
$$\mu_G = \frac{1}{k} \sum_{i=1}^{k} \mu_i = k\frac{1}{k}\mu_i = \mu_i$$

The alternative hypothesis, then, states that of the k means, two or more in the population differ from one another, and, consequently, from the grand mean. The alternative hypothesis in the counseling study would be written the same way:

H_1: $\mu_i - \mu_G \neq 0$ for some i

Directional hypotheses are not tested with the analysis of variance. As noted before, the alternative hypothesis states merely that two or more means differ from one another. To see why the alternative hypothesis in the ANOVA is nondirectional, suppose, for example, you expected the following alternative hypothesis:

H_1: $\mu_1 < \mu_2 > \mu_3 < \mu_4$

What tail are you talking about now?

The results of the analysis of variance, then, enable us to decide whether there was a significant treatment effect. That is, the ANOVA indicates whether any combination of the treatment group means is significantly different from any other combination. However, it does not indicate which particular treatment means are significantly different from each other. If the analysis of variance suggests a significant treatment effect, comparisons between means, discussed later, must be conducted in order to determine which means are significantly different from each other.

Assumptions

When the sampling distribution of F is used to test hypotheses about two or more means, three familiar assumptions are made.

Independence.   The score for any particular subject is independent of the scores of all other subjects. That is, it provides a unique piece of information about the treatment effect.

Normality.   The scores within each treatment population are normally distributed. Put another way, the scores in a particular treatment group are assumed to be sampled from a population of scores that is normal in form.

Homogeneity of Variances.   The variance of scores in each treatment population are equal (i.e., $\sigma_1^2 = \sigma_2^2 = \cdots = \sigma_i^2 = \cdots = \sigma_k^2$). For a discussion of statistical tests of this assumption, see Ramsey (1994).

These assumptions are the same as those underlying the t test for two independent means. They are discussed in some detail in Chapter 12, as are methods for examining them. The ANOVA is robust to violations of the assumption of normality for an independent variable with a fixed number of levels.

When cell sizes are equal, the ANOVA is also robust to violations of the assumption of homogeneity of variances. In the example study of counseling methods, we need not be concerned with testing either of these assumptions, since the cell sizes were equal in all groups (see Table 13-1). For unequal cell sizes, Kirk (1982) and Winer et al. (1991) present some methods for statistically testing the assumption of homogeneity of variances. As long as the assumption of normality is tenable, the use of tests for the homogeneity assumption is reasonable.

Computation of the ANOVA

As noted earlier, the ANOVA focuses on a comparison of the variability within groups (variability due to error) and the variability between groups (variability due to error plus treatment effects, if they exist). In arriving at estimates of these two sources of variation in scores, the ANOVA divides the total variability between scores (regardless of group) into variability within groups and variability between groups, as indicated in Formula 13-3.

$$\text{total variability} = \text{within-group variability} + \text{between-group variability} \qquad \textbf{(13–3)}$$

The total variance over all scores, regardless of group, is defined as the square of the deviation of each individual's (p) score from the mean of all the scores, called the **grand mean** ($\bar{X}_G$), divided by $N - 1$.[7] See Formula 13-4.

$$s^2_{\text{total}} = \frac{\sum_i \sum_p (X_{pi} - \bar{X}_G)^2}{N - 1} \qquad \textbf{(13-4)}$$

(For an explanation of $\sum$, see the review of summation notation in Appendix I.)

When we calculate variances such as the total variance, it is cumbersome to worry about dividing by $N - 1$ until all other calculations are carried out. So in order to get rid of the $N - 1$ for the time being, we multiply it into both sides of the equation to obtain Formula 13-4a.

$$(N - 1)s^2_{\text{total}} = \sum_i \sum_p (X_{pi} - \bar{X}_G)^2 \qquad \textbf{(13-4a)}$$

Formula 13-4a is the formula for the sum of squared deviations of scores from the grand mean. It is most often called the **sum of squares total** and written as in Formula 13-4b.

---

[7]The total variance over all subjects and groups is analogous to the variance for a single set of scores presented in Chapter 4:

$$s^2 = \frac{\sum (X - \bar{X})^2}{n - 1}$$

The variance for a single set of scores is defined as the sum of squared deviations of scores from the mean of the group divided by the appropriate degrees of freedom. Notice that the total variance is defined as the sum over persons and groups (hence the double summation signs) of the squared deviations of scores from the grand mean—the mean over all persons and groups—divided by the appropriate degrees of freedom.

$$\text{sum of squares total} = SS_T = \sum_i \sum_p (X_{pi} - \bar{X}_G)^2 \qquad \textbf{(13-4b)}$$

(This formula is not generally used in computation; an equivalent computational formula is given in Procedure 13-1.)

Likewise, the **sum of squares within groups** (SS_W) can be calculated by squaring the difference between each score in a group and the group mean, and then summing these squared differences over groups. See Formula 13-5.

$$\text{sum of squares within} = SS_W = \sum_i \sum_p (X_{pi} - \bar{X}_i)^2 \qquad \textbf{(13-5)}$$

The **sum of squares between groups** (SS_B) can be found by squaring the difference between each group mean and the grand mean and then summing these squared differences. See Formula 13-6.

$$\text{sum of squares between} = SS_B = \sum_i n_i (\bar{X}_i - \bar{X}_G)^2 \qquad \textbf{(13-6)}$$

In Formula 13-6, n_i appears because we are, in effect, counting the between-group variability once for every subject in a group. Since these are deviation-score formulas for the sums of squares, and raw-score formulas are commonly used in calculating the sums of squares, numerical examples are not given.

All sums of squares, then, are variances that have not yet been divided by their respective degrees of freedom. In calculating the ANOVA, we work with sums of squares. And after the major work in calculation is completed, the sums of squares are divided by their appropriate degrees of freedom to get estimates of the within- and between-group variability. These estimates are called **mean squares.** Note that in Table 13-2, the sums of squares were omitted. But the degrees of freedom and the mean squares (variances) were included.

The formulas for computing the sums of squares are given in Table 13-3 and summarized in Procedure 13-1. These raw-score formulas are equivalent to the deviation-score formulas but are easier to use in computations.[8] As a way of presenting the ANOVA computations, the data from the counseling study are used in Procedure 13-1. For simplification of the calculations, certain preliminary computations and intermediate quantities are used in computing the sums of squares.

---

[8]See the Technical Appendix at the end of this chapter for a proof of the equivalence of deviation- and raw-score formulas.

TABLE 13-3 Computational formulas used in Procedure 13-1 for the one-way ANOVA

Source of Variation	Sum of Squares Formula		df Formula	Mean Square Formula	F
Between groups	$SS_B = \sum\limits_{i=1}^{k} \dfrac{\left(\sum\limits_{p=1}^{n} X_{pi}\right)^2}{n_i} - \dfrac{\left(\sum\limits_{p=1}^{N} X_p\right)^2}{N}$	**(13-8)**	$df_B = k - 1$	$\dfrac{SS_B}{df_B}$	$\dfrac{MS_B}{MS_W}$
Within groups	$SS_W = \sum\limits_{p=1}^{N}(X_p)^2 - \sum\limits_{i=1}^{k} \dfrac{\left(\sum\limits_{p=1}^{n} X_{pi}\right)^2}{n_i}$	**(13-9)**	$df_W = N - k$	$\dfrac{SS_W}{df_W}$	
Total	$SS_T = \sum\limits_{p=1}^{N}(X_p)^2 - \dfrac{\left(\sum\limits_{p=1}^{N} X_p\right)^2}{N}$	**(13-7)**	$df_T = N - 1$		

PROCEDURE 13-1 Steps in calculating sums of squares for the one-way ANOVA

Operation

Example

1. Set up the data summary table.
   Note that N = the total number of subjects; n_i = the number of subjects in group i; $\sum_{1}^{N} X_p$ = the sum of scores over all persons in the study = $\sum_{i}\sum_{p} X_{pi}$. All other notation is standard; see the review of summation notation in Appendix I.

2. Make the following *preliminary computations.*

   a. Sum the scores in each group: See Table 13-3.

   $$\sum_{p=1}^{n} X_{pi}$$

   b. Square the sum of the scores in each group (step 2a) and divide each sum by the number of subjects (n) in the group:

   $$\dfrac{\left(\sum\limits_{p-1}^{n} X_{pi}\right)^2}{n_i}$$

   $$\dfrac{\left(\sum\limits_{p=1}^{n} X_{p1}\right)^2}{n_1} = \dfrac{(19)^2}{3} = 120.33$$

Operation	Example

$$\frac{\left(\sum\limits_{p=1}^{n} X_{p2}\right)^2}{n_2} = \frac{6^2}{3} = 12$$

$$\frac{\left(\sum\limits_{p=1}^{n} X_{p3}\right)}{n_3} = \frac{10^2}{3} = 33.33$$

c. Sum all scores in the summary table, regardless of group, to obtain a total sum:

$$\sum_{1}^{N} X_p$$

$$\sum_{1}^{N} X_p = 5 + 6 + 8 + 1 + 2 + 3 + 3 + 3 + 4 = 35$$

3. Compute the following *intermediate quantities*. Note that these quantities are labeled with symbols in braces { }, to simplify matters later on.

a. Sum the values computed in step 2b to obtain:

$$\{1\} = \frac{\sum\limits_{i=1}^{k}\left(\sum\limits_{p=1}^{n} X_{pi}\right)^2}{n_i}$$

$$\{1\} = \sum_{i=1}^{k} \frac{\left(\sum\limits_{p=1}^{n} X_{pi}\right)^2}{n_i} = 120.33 + 12 + 33.33$$
$$= 165.66$$

b. Square the total sum (step 2c) and divide by N to obtain:

$$\{2\} = \frac{\left(\sum\limits_{p=1}^{N} X_p\right)^2}{N}$$

$$\{2\} = \frac{\left(\sum\limits_{p=1}^{N} X_p\right)^2}{N} = \frac{(35)^2}{9} = 136.11$$

c. Square each score in the summary table and sum these squared scores to obtain:

$$\{3\} = \sum_{p=1}^{N} X_p^2$$

$$\{3\} = \sum_{p=1}^{N} X_p^2 = (5)^2 + (6)^2 + \cdots + (4)^2 = 173$$

4. Compute the sums of squares, using the following computational formulas.

a. Sum of squares total, Formula 13-7.

$$SS_T = \sum_{p=1}^{N} X_p^2 - \frac{\left(\sum\limits_{p=1}^{N} X_p\right)^2}{N} \qquad \textbf{(13-7)}$$

$$SS_T = \{3\} - \{2\} = 173 - 136.11 = 36.89$$

Or:
$$SS_T = \{3\} - \{2\}$$

Operation _____   **Example** _____

b. Sum of squares between groups, Formula 13-8.

$$SS_B = \sum_{i=1}^{k} \frac{\left(\sum_{p=1}^{n} X_{pi}\right)^2}{n_i} - \frac{\left(\sum_{p=1}^{N} X_p\right)^2}{N} \tag{13-8}$$

$$SS_B = \{1\} - \{2\} = 165.66 - 136.11 = 29.55$$

Or:
$$SS_B = \{1\} - \{2\}$$

c. Sum of squares within groups, Formula 13-9.

$$SS_W = \sum_{p=1}^{N} X_p^2 - \sum_{i=1}^{k} \frac{\left(\sum_{p=1}^{n} X_{pi}\right)^2}{n_i} \tag{13-9}$$

$$SS_W = \{3\} - \{1\} = 173 - 165.66 = 7.34$$

Or:
$$SS_W = \{3\} - \{1\}$$

Once the sums of squares have been calculated, they are entered in the summary table in which the final set of computations is carried out to obtain $F_{observed}$. Table 13-4 is an ANOVA summary table for the analysis of the data from the counseling study (see Procedure 13-1). Two sources of variation in scores are shown in the first column—between groups and within groups. The third row, labeled "total," serves here as a computational check, since $SS_T = SS_B + SS_W$ (see Formula 13-3).

The second column of Table 13-4 gives the values of the sums of squares. These values are taken from the computations shown in Procedure 13-1. [Notice that the value of the total sum of squares (36.89) equals the sum of SS_B and SS_W (29.55 + 7.34).]

The third column of Table 13-4 gives the values of between-group and within-group degrees of freedom, using formulas from Table 13-3. The degrees of freedom for estimating the between-group variance is the number of groups (k) minus 1: $df_B = 3 - 1 = 2$. These $k - 1$ degrees of freedom reflect the fact that the variability between groups is estimated from the variability of the k group means about the grand mean. (One degree of freedom is lost by calculating and thus knowing $\bar{X}_G$.)

The within-group degrees of freedom are simply $N - k$: $df_W = 9 - 3 = 6$. The formula for df_W follows from this reasoning: The within-group variance is simply the average of the variances within each group. Since the variances within each population are assumed to be equal (this is the assumption of homogeneity of variance), this average represents a pooled estimate of the common population variance. Each estimate of the population variance is based on $n - 1$ degrees of freedom. If there are k groups, there are k estimates of the common population variance, each based on $n - 1$ degrees of freedom. So $df_W = (n_1 - 1) + (n_2 - 1) + \cdots + (n_k - 1) = N - k$.

The fourth column in Table 13-4, labeled "mean square," gives the result of dividing each sum of squares by its respective degrees of freedom ($MS = SS/df$). The mean squares provide measures of the variability between and within groups. Under the null hypothesis of no difference between means, MS_B and MS_W provide two independent estimates of error variance. Under the alternative hypothesis of a difference between means,

MS_B = variability due to error + variability due to treatment effects

(*Note:* Mean squares are not additive, so there is no entry in the total row of the table.)

TABLE 13-4 Analysis of variance summary table (data from Table 13-1)

Source of Variation	Sum of Squares[a] SS	df	Mean Square MS	F
Between groups	29.55 df_2	$3 - 1 = 2$	$\frac{29.55}{2} = 14.78$	$\frac{14.78}{1.22} = 12.11^b$
Within groups	7.34 df_1	$9 - 3 = 6$	$\frac{7.34}{6} = 1.22$	
Total	36.89	$9 - 1 = 8$		

[a] From Procedure 13-1
[b] $p < .05$; reject the null hypothesis   └ dans table E

The last column of Table 13-3 gives the formula for $F_{observed}$, which is Formula 13-10.

$$F_{observed} = \frac{MS_B}{MS_W}$$ **(13-10)**

From Table 13-4, this F value is 12.11 for the data from the counseling study.

Decision Rules for Rejecting the Null Hypothesis

In order to determine whether to reject the null hypothesis and conclude that there is a significant treatment effect, we must compare $F_{observed}$ with $F_{critical}$, using df_B, df_W, and α. For $\alpha = .05$, $F_{critical}$ can be found in Table E:

$F_{critical(.05,2,6)} = 5.14$

Since $F_{observed}$ exceeds $F_{critical}$, the null hypothesis should be rejected. This decision is noted in Table 13-4 (footnote b). We can conclude that the counseling method produced a significant treatment effect. The observed differences between the three means are not likely to have arisen by chance.

Example Problem 13.1 ▬▬▬▬▬▬▬▬▬▬▬▬▬▬▬▬▬▬▬▬▬▬▬▬▬▬▬▬

In a study of the relationship between study time and learning, high school students were randomly assigned to one of four study time conditions: 10, 20, 45, 75 minutes. Students were given written material on international relations to study and were given an achievement test at the end of the study session. From the data shown in Table 13-5, test whether there was a significant treatment effect at $\alpha = .05$. Include the following items in your answer:

a. Null and alternative hypotheses
b. Tests of assumptions or explanation for not testing
c. Computation of sums of squares (see Procedure 13-1 for format)
d. ANOVA summary table (see Table 13-3 for format)
e. $F_{critical}$
f. Conclusions

TABLE 13-5 Hypothetical data from the study on study time and learning

Person	Study Time (Minutes)			
	10	*20*	*45*	*75*
1	7	9	20	10
2	10	14	18	11
3	6	12	19	13
4	7	11	16	12
5	8	13	18	11
$\bar{X}$	7.6	11.8	18.2	11.4
s	1.52	1.92	1.48	1.14
s^2	2.30	3.70	2.20	1.30

Fixed- and Random-Effects ANOVA

Fixed-Effects ANOVA.   Up to this point, the analysis of variance has been developed for studies meeting the design requirement that the levels of the independent variable exhaust the possible levels of interest to the researcher. The hypothetical counseling study met this requirement. We were interested in the effects of three levels of a counseling variable: control, behavior modification, and Rogerian. The only inference drawn about the treatment effects were inferences about these three counseling methods. If the experiment were replicated, these three groups would comprise the levels of the independent variable in the replication. Because the levels of the independent variable are *fixed*—the same—from one application of the experiment to the next, we call the ANOVA developed so far the *fixed-effects* analysis of variance.

There are a number of conceptual and statistical consequences of fixing the levels of the independent variable. Presented intuitively at the beginning of the chapter, they are as follows: First, the variability of scores within a group is defined as error variance, σ^2. The mean square within groups is the average of the within-group variances; this pooling of sample variances provides the best estimate of σ_2. Second, the variability between groups represents an independent estimate of error variance if H_0 is true. If H_0 is false, MS_B contains both error variability and a treatment effect. Finally, the sampling distribution of F, $F = MS_B/MS_W$, was used to determine whether MS_B was sufficiently greater than MS_W to conclude that H_0 is false and there is a treatment effect.

Random-Effects ANOVA.   Consider, now, a study somewhat different from the counseling study. Suppose a researcher studying mother-infant interactions is concerned that some characteristic of an observer affects the nature of the interaction. Might the rapport established by an observer influence the interaction process?

In principle, there are many possible observers (say, graduate students) that the researcher might employ to collect data on the interaction. Trying out all possible observers would be impractical and, as we shall see, unnecessary. Instead, the researcher draws a random sample of five graduate students. Each is assigned, at random, 10 mother-infant pairs and codes the interaction of each pair by using an observation schedule. Each observer, then, constitutes a "treatment" given to a different sample of $n = 10$ pairs; in all other respects, the pairs are treated the same. From the outcome of the study, the researcher plans to draw inferences about observer effects, not just to the five graduate students participating in the study, but to *all* graduate students in the population.

The design of the mother-infant interaction study differs from the counseling study in one important way. The treatments (in our example, observers) are randomly sampled from a population of treatments; they are not fixed. If the study were replicated, a different set of randomly selected observers would probably participate. By randomly selecting treatments from a population, the researcher is able to generalize from the treatments in the study to treatments in the population that might be used. That is, the researcher is able to infer from the five observers in the interaction study to the entire population of observers that might be used.

The interaction study fits what is called the *random-effects* ANOVA because treatment conditions are randomly sampled with the intent of inferring from the study's treatment effects to the effects in the population. Computationally, the random-effects ANOVA is the same as the fixed-effects ANOVA. Sums of squares, degrees of freedom, and mean squares for the random-effects ANOVA are computed in the same way they are for the fixed-effects ANOVA. But the inferences drawn from the former—to the population of treatments—differ from the inferences drawn from the latter—to the treatments in the study.

This difference in inference is reflected in the null and alternative hypotheses tested in the random-effects ANOVA:

random effects: H_0: $\sigma_i^2 = 0$

$\qquad\qquad\qquad\quad$ H_1: $\sigma_i^2 \neq 0$

fixed effects: $\quad$ H_0: $\mu_i - \mu_G = 0$ for all i

$\qquad\qquad\qquad\quad$ H_1: $\mu_i - \mu_G \neq 0$ for some i

The null hypothesis for the random-effects ANOVA states that in the treatment population (not just for those treatments used in the study), the variance of treatment means is zero—

that is, $\sigma^2_{\mu_i-\mu_G} = \sigma^2_i = 0$. The alternative hypothesis states that the treatment means differ in the population of treatments.

The F test for the one-way, random-effects ANOVA turns out to be the same as the F test for the one-way, fixed-effects ANOVA: MS_B/MS_W. But this will not always be the case. The F rations may vary in designs that contain two or more independent variables, such as factorial designs (see Chapter 14).

Design Requirements.   The design requirements for the random-effects ANOVA are similar to those for the fixed-effects ANOVA, except that the levels of the independent variable represent a random sample from a large population of levels of the independent variable.

Assumptions.   In addition to the assumptions of independence, normality, and homogeneity of errors (which in the fixed-effects ANOVA translated into assumptions of independence, normality, and homogeneity of scores), the random-effects ANOVA assumes the following:

1. The random treatment effects ($a_i = \mu_i - \mu_G$) are *normally* distributed.
2. The random treatment effects (a_i) are independent of the errors.

If the assumptions of normality of treatment effects and independence of treatment effects and errors are violated, the test of the null hypothesis—H_0: $\sigma^2_a = 0$—may be open to question.

STRENGTH OF ASSOCIATION

The overall F test with the one-way ANOVA indicates whether or not the observed differences between treatment means were likely to arise by chance. However, the F test does not give information about the *strength* of the treatment effect, because the probability associated with F depends on sample size as well as the magnitude of the treatment effect. One measure of the strength of the treatment effect for the fixed-effect ANOVA is the proportion of the total variability in a set of scores that can be accounted for by the levels of the independent variable. This proportion of variance is analogous to the proportion of variance discussed in the chapter on correlation (Chapter 6). Recall that r^2_{XY} could be interpreted as the proportion of variance in Y that can be accounted for by knowing X. In the case of the ANOVA, the measure of the strength of a treatment effect indicates how much variance in scores can be accounted for by knowing about differences in treatment groups. This statistic is called **omega-square** ($\hat{\omega}^2$).

Omega-square can be used with data from the study of counseling methods to obtain a measure of the **strength of association** between counseling method (the independent variable) and distance from the edge of the Tower of Pisa (the dependent variable). The formula for estimating omega-square is given by Formula 13-11.

$$\hat{\omega}^2 = \frac{SS_B - (k-1)MS_W}{SS_T + MS_W} \qquad \textbf{(13-11)}$$

The steps in calculating $\hat{\omega}^2$ are summarized in Procedure 13-2, Part A, using the counseling study as an example. Note that $\hat{\omega}^2 = .71$. This result suggests that variations in the independent variable (counseling method) account for a large portion—71 percent—of the variability of the distance measure. In other words, there is a strong relationship between counseling method and reduction of fear of heights as measured by the distance from the edge of the tower.

PROCEDURE 13-2 Steps in computing measures of strength of association

---

Operation	Example

Part A—fixed effects, $\hat{\omega}^2$:

1. Use Formula 13-11:

$$\hat{\omega}^2 = \frac{SS_B - (k-1)MS_W}{SS_T + MS_W}$$

2. Insert the appropriate values from the ANOVA source table into Formula 13-11 and solve.

$SS_B = 29.55$

$MS_W = 1.22$

$SS_T = 36.89$

$$\hat{\omega}^2 = \frac{29.55 - (3-1)(1.22)}{36.89 + 1.22}$$

$$= \frac{27.11}{38.11} = .71$$

Thus 71% of the variance in the dependent variable is accounted for by the differences in counseling treatments.

Part B—random effects, $\hat{\rho}_I$:

1. Use Formula 13-12:

$$\hat{\rho}_I = \frac{MS_B - MS_W}{MS_B + (n-1)MS_W}$$

The following ANOVA table was reported for the mother-infant interaction study:

Source	SS	df	MS	F
Between	100	5	20	2.86[a]
Within	315	45	7	

[a]$p < .05.$

2. Insert the appropriate values from the ANOVA source table into Formula 13-12 and solve.

$$\hat{\rho}_I = \frac{20 - 7}{20 + (10-1)(7)} = .16$$

Thus 16% of the variance in the dependent variable is accounted for by observer differences.

For the random-effects ANOVA, the **intraclass correlation, ρ_I,** provides a measure of the proportion of variance in the dependent variable accounted for by the independent variable. Its estimator is defined in Formula 13-12.

$$\hat{\rho}_I = \frac{MS_B - MS_W}{MS_B + (n-1)MS_W} \qquad\qquad \textbf{(13-12)}$$

The intraclass correlation measures the extent to which within-group variability is small relative to between-group variability. The $\hat{\rho}_I$ is at its maximum when scores within groups are identical and the group means differ among one another. The steps in calculating $\hat{\rho}_I$ are summarized in Procedure 13-2, Part B. In the mother-infant interaction study, approximately 16 percent of the variance in the dependent variable is accounted for by differences in observers.

Example Problem 13.2

Compute the strength of association for the study time experiment described in Example Problem 13.1. Include the following items in your answer.
   a. Computation
   b. Interpretation
Suppose the four study conditions were a random sample from a population of all possible study times. Compute the strength of association. Include the following items in your answer.
   c. Computation
   d. Interpretation

POST HOC COMPARISONS OF MEANS

To summarize briefly, the overall F test in the analysis of variance indicates whether or not there are significant differences between means. Omega-square (ω^2), for example, indicates the strength of the treatment effect. However, when the study includes *more than two groups*, neither statistic indicates which means differ statistically from the others. In the counseling study, the overall F indicated a significant effect for the method but several questions still remain. Is the mean of the behavior modification (B) group significantly less than the mean of the Rogerian (R) group? Or is the mean of the R group significantly less than the mean of the control (C) group? Does the mean of the B group differ from the average of the other two means (R and C)? For one to determine just where the differences between means lie, additional statistical tests are needed.

When a researcher conducts tests for differences between means, typically, a wide variety of comparisons are of interest. The researcher wants to ferret out, in an "after-the-fact," or *post hoc*, fashion, which mean differences gave rise to the significant F test. Admittedly, then, the study is exploratory and the researcher seeks to determine mean differences through **post hoc comparisons.** The good news is that there is a wide variety of methods available for conducting post hoc comparisons; the bad news is that you have to choose one to use. For example, Dunnett's post hoc comparison method is designed specifically for comparing experimental groups against a control group. Newman-Keuls' method takes into account the ordering of the magnitude of differences in sample means to provide a powerful test of differences between means, but some statisticians question the use of sample mean in order to conduct post hoc tests. The Bonferroni procedure is simple to use but lacks power when a large number of post hoc comparisons are made, which is usually the case with post hoc comparisons. Scheffé's method is considered by many the benchmark post hoc comparison method following on a significant F test. It provides the greatest flexibility in making mean comparisons, but at a cost of power. And Tukey's method is limited to pairwise comparisons. Since the smorgasbord of post hoc comparisons is so full, only the most frequently used tests are presented here: Scheffé's method and Tukey's method. Texts such as Winer, Brown, & Michels (1991) or Kirk (1982) contain most of the smorgasbord if you still have an appetite for post hoc comparisons after this presentation.

Post Hoc Comparisons

Post hoc comparisons refer to statistical comparisons of means that have not been planned but that look interesting to the researcher on the basis of the sample data. They allow the researcher to snoop through the data to find out where the differences occurred which gave rise to the significant, overall F. Put another way, if the overall F is significant, at least one out of all possible comparisons between pairs of means or complex combinations of means will be significant. Post hoc comparisons are methods for discovering where the difference or differences lie.

The first step is to identify the means to be compared. After inspecting the counseling-study data, suppose we decide to test the difference between the control group ($\bar{X}_C = 6.33$) and the average of the two treatment groups ($\bar{X}_B = 2.00$ and $\bar{X}_R = 3.33$). The null hypothesis to be tested is:

$$H_0: \mu_C = \frac{\mu_B - \mu_R}{2}$$

The null hypothesis states that in the population, the mean of the control group equals the average of the means of the behavior modification and Rogerian groups. The control group is compared with the average of the two treatment groups because we are interested in whether there is a treatment effect, and we will take the mean of the two treatment groups as the best estimate of the effect. (Practically speaking, we take the mean of the two treatment groups so that the treatment effect is not given twice the weight of the control group.)

The alternative hypothesis is:

$$H_1: \mu_C \neq \frac{\mu_B + \mu_C}{2}$$

Post hoc comparisons are always nondirectional tests because the alternative hypothesis is formulated *after* the researcher has eyeballed the data.

In addition, suppose you decide to test the difference in population means between the behavior modification and Rogerian treatments. In this case, the null and alternative hypothesis are:

$$H_0: \mu_B = \mu_R$$
$$H_1: \mu_B \neq \mu_R$$

The next step is to write the comparisons specified by the hypotheses as a set of weighted means, where the sum of the weights is equal to zero. A comparison, then, is defined formally as the weighted sum of k population means. If w_i represents the weight (a number) assigned to the mean of treatment i, a comparison can be defined formally as in Formula 13-13.

$$C = w_1\mu_1 + w_2\mu_2 + \cdots + w_k\mu_k = \sum_1^k w_i\mu_i \qquad \text{(13-13)}$$

A **sample comparison** is defined in exactly the same way as the population comparison, except that sample means are used. See Formula 13-13a.

$$\hat{C} = w_1\bar{X}_1 + w_2\bar{X}_2 + \cdots + w_k\bar{X}_k = \sum_1^k w_i\bar{X}_i \qquad \text{(13-13a)}$$

Since this sample comparison is used to estimate the population comparison of interest, a caret (^) is placed over the C.

The weights assigned to each mean may consist of any set of real numbers not all equal to zero. They are determined by the comparison the researcher wishes to make. For example, two alternative hypotheses were identified for the counseling study:

$$H_1\text{: } \mu_C \neq \frac{\mu_B + \mu_R}{2}$$

and:

$$H_2\text{: } \mu_B \neq \mu_R$$

These hypotheses can be translated into comparisons. Hypothesis H_2 specifies a comparison between the means of the behavior modification and the Rogerian groups. A set of k weights, then, should be constructed to compare $\bar{X}_B$ with $\bar{X}_R$ and to ignore $\bar{X}_C$ for the purposes of this comparison. Thus we assign the following set of weights to $\bar{X}_C$, $\bar{X}_B$, and $\bar{X}_R$, respectively: 0, +1, and −1. More formally, this comparison can be defined as the weighted sum of $k = 3$ means:

$$\hat{C}_2 = (0)\bar{X}_C + (1)\bar{X}_B + (-1)\bar{X}_R = \bar{X}_B - \bar{X}_R$$

Notice that when we use zero, the control group drops out of this comparison. Finally, there is nothing magic about this set of weights. A different set of weights could have been assigned (e.g., 0, +2, −2; or 0, −2, +2; or 0, +½, −½; or 0, −½, +½).

The procedure for assigning a set of weights to the first alternative hypothesis is somewhat more complex:

$$H_1\text{: } \mu_C \neq \frac{\mu_B + \mu_R}{2}$$

The trick is to recognize that this hypothesis identifies a comparison between the mean for the control group against the average of the means for the B and R groups. This comparison can be accomplished by the following sets of weights: +1, −½, −½, or +2, −1, −1:

$$\hat{C}_1 = (1)\bar{X}_C + (-\tfrac{1}{2})\bar{X}_B + (-\tfrac{1}{2})\bar{X}_R = \bar{X}_C - \frac{\bar{X}_B + \bar{X}_R}{2}$$

or

$$\hat{C}_1 = (2)\bar{X}_C + (-1)\bar{X}_B + (-1)\bar{X}_R = 2\bar{X}_C - (\bar{X}_B + \bar{X}_R)$$

In writing weights for planned comparison, then, we can use any set of real numbers, not all equal to zero. *The only restriction is that the sum of the weights equals zero.* More formally, the requirement is as stated in Formula 13-14.

$$w_1 + w_2 + \cdots + w_k = 0$$

$$\sum_{1}^{k} w_i = 0 \qquad\qquad (13\text{-}14)$$

In order to check this requirement, we can obtain the algebraic sum of the weights. For the weights representing the comparison suggested by H_1, the algebraic sum of the weights is:

$$+1 - \tfrac{1}{2} - \tfrac{1}{2} = 0$$

or

$$2 - 1 - 2 = 0$$

Either set of weights satisfies the requirement of summing to zero, as do all sets of weights given in this section. (See step 2 in Procedure 13-3.)

PROCEDURE 13-3 Steps in specifying weights for Scheffé's comparisons (data from Table 13-1)

Operation	Example		
1. Identify the hypotheses from inspection of the means.	$H_1: \mu_C \neq \dfrac{\mu_B + \mu_R}{2}$ $H_2: \mu_C \neq \mu_R$		
2. Assign weights to means so that the comparisons identified by the hypotheses in step 1 are specified. *The sum of the weights for each comparison must equal zero (Formula 13-14):* $\displaystyle\sum_{1}^{k} w_i = 0$	$\bar{X}_C = 6.33$ $\bar{X}_B = 2.00$ $\bar{X}_R = 3.33$		
	$\hat{C}_1[\bar{X}_C$ vs. $(\bar{X}_B + \bar{X}_R)/2]$ $\quad 1$	$-\tfrac{1}{2}$	$-\tfrac{1}{2}$
	$\hat{C}_2(\bar{X}_B$ vs. $\bar{X}_R)$ $\quad 0$	$+1$	-1

Operation	Example
3. Add the weights for each comparison in order to verify the accuracy of step 2.	$\hat{C}_1 : (+1) + (-\frac{1}{2}) + (-\frac{1}{2}) = 0$ $\hat{C}_2 : 0 + (+1) + (-1) = 0$
4. Write the comparisons in the form of a weighted sum of means (Formula 13-13a): $$\hat{C} = \sum_1^k w_i \bar{X}_i$$	$\hat{C}_1 = (+1)\bar{X}_C + (-\frac{1}{2})\bar{X}_B + (-\frac{1}{2})\bar{X}_R$ $\hat{C}_2 = (0)\bar{X}_C + (+1)\bar{X}_B + (-1)\bar{X}_R$

Once the comparison between means has been written, the value of the comparison ($\hat{C}$) can be found by simply inserting the appropriate values and carrying out the arithmetic operations, as shown in Procedure 13-4.

PROCEDURE 13-4 Steps in computing a comparison ($\hat{C}$) between means (data from Table 13-1)

Operation	Example
1. Begin with a comparison written in the form of a weighted sum of means (Formula 13-13a): $$\hat{C} = \sum_1^k w_i \bar{X}_i$$	$\hat{C}_1 = (+1)\bar{X}_C + (-\frac{1}{2})\bar{X}_B + (-\frac{1}{2})\bar{X}_R$ $\hat{C}_2 = (0)\bar{X}_C + (+1)\bar{X}_B + (-1)\bar{X}_R$
2. Insert appropriate values for each mean and solve.	$\hat{C}_1 = (+1)(6.33) + (-\frac{1}{2})(2) + (-\frac{1}{2})(3.33)$ $\quad = 6.33 - 1 - 1.67 = 3.66$ $\hat{C}_2 = (0)(6.33) + (+1)(2) + (-1)(3.33)$ $\quad = 0 + 2 - 3.33 = -1.33$

Notice that the value of the comparison (contrast) will depend on the particular set of weights chosen. For example, suppose the following weights were used for contrast 1: 2, − 1, −1. Then:

$$\hat{C}_1 = (2)\bar{X}_C + (-1)\bar{X}_B + (-1)\bar{X}_R = (2)6.33 + (-1)(2) + (-1)(3.33)$$
$$= 12.66 - 2 - 3.33 = 7.33$$

In this case, the value 7.33 represents the difference between two times the mean of the control group and the sum of the two means for the counseling groups. Although differences in weights influence the magnitude of $\hat{C}$, they are taken into account in conducting a statistical test—this is the next topic.

The only requirement for using post hoc comparisons as a statistical test of differences between means is that the *overall F in the ANOVA must be significant.* If the overall F is significant, post hoc comparisons permit you to make a large number of statistical tests, all of them at a preset level of significance. For example, in the counseling study with three groups (means), six comparisons can be examined: B versus R, B versus C, R versus C, BR versus C, BC versus R, and RC versus B. Using Scheffé's method of post hoc comparison, for example, all six statistical tests can be so conducted that the level of significance (α) for all six tests taken together does not exceed a preset value of α such as .05 or .01.

If the overall F is *not* significant, post hoc comparisons can still be conducted, but *the statement about the probability of a Type I error (α) is not necessarily true.* In this case, the comparisons simply flag differences between means that might be interesting to explore in future studies.

Scheffé's Test

The most widely applicable of all the methods of post hoc comparison is **Scheffé's test.** It permits comparisons of pairs of means and of complex combinations of means. Furthermore, it is the most widely accepted test for making post hoc comparisons.

For each post hoc comparison, the t distribution can be used to determine whether the differences between two sample means or between combinations of means arose by chance. For each comparison, the null and alternative hypotheses are written in terms of the population contrast C: H_0: $C = 0$ and H_1: $C \neq 0$. Note that H_0: $C = 0$ is the same as the hypothesis H_0: $\mu_B = \mu_R$ or H_0: $\mu_C = (\mu_B + \mu_R)/2$, depending on how you define the contrast. In addition, α is set at $\alpha = .05$ or $\alpha = .01$, consistent with the overall F test.

In order to test each comparison statistically, we use a t test. Specifically, we use Formula 13-15 to obtain the *observed value* of t.

$$t_{observed} = \frac{\hat{C}}{\sqrt{MS_W \left(\frac{w_1^2}{n_1} + \frac{w_2^2}{n_2} + \cdots + \frac{w_k^2}{n_k} \right)}} \qquad \text{(13-15)}$$

where:
$\hat{C}$ = value of the contrast
MS_W = mean square within groups (error) from the ANOVA table
w = weight
k = number of groups

If, as in this case and throughout this text, the number of subjects in each of the groups is the same (i.e., $n_1 = n_2 = \cdots = n_k$), then Formula 13-15 can be simplified as shown in Formula 13-15a.

$$t_{observed} = \frac{\hat{C}}{\sqrt{\frac{MS_W}{n}(w_1^2 + w_2^2 + \cdots + w_k^2)}} \qquad \text{(13-15a)}$$

Finally, if the comparison is between only two of the k means with equal cell size, the formula can be simplified even further, as in Formula 13-15b.

$$t_{observed} = \frac{\hat{C}}{\sqrt{\dfrac{2MS_W}{n}}} \qquad \text{(13-15b)}$$

Formula 13-15b is equivalent to the formula given for the t test in Chapter 12 when $n_1 = n_2$. Notice that $\hat{C}$ amounts to $\bar{X}_1 - \bar{X}_2$ and the denominator involves the pooled sample variance divided by n:

$$\sqrt{\frac{2s_{pooled}^2}{n}} = \sqrt{\frac{s_1^2 + s_2^2}{n}}$$

The steps involved in calculating $t_{observed}$ are summarized in steps 5a and 5b of Procedure 13-5, which follows.

Scheffé's test uses the t test given in Formulas 13-15a, b. This seems too good to be true; there must be a catch. Well, there is. The catch comes in when the value of $t_{critical}$ is calculated. The value of $t_{critical}$ for Scheffé's test, labeled $t'_{critical}$, is given in Formula 13-16.

$$t'_{critical} = \sqrt{(k-1)F_{critical(\alpha, k-1, df_W)}} \qquad \text{(13-16)}$$

where:
  k = number of groups
  $F_{critical}$ = critical value of the F distribution with $k - 1$ degrees of freedom
  in the numerator and df_W in the denominator

The steps in conducting post hoc comparisons using Scheffé's test are summarized in Procedure 13-5. When the value of $t'_{critical}$ (3.21 in our example) is compared with the value of $t_{critical}$ ($\alpha = .05$, 6 df) that would be used in a regular t test (2.447), the price for making all possible comparisons becomes apparent. In order to control for the probability of a Type I error, the Scheffé method increases the critical value for determining significance.

PROCEDURE 13-5 Steps in conducting Scheffé's test for making post hoc comparisons between means (data from Table 13-1)

Operation	Example
1. Identify the hypotheses between the means to be tested. *These hypotheses may be based on the researcher's hunches about the results, snooping through the*	Suppose we wished to test: $\bar{X}_C$ vs. $\bar{X}_R$ H_1: $\mu_C \neq \mu_R$

Operation	Example

Operation

data, or both. *Alternative hypotheses are nondirectional, since the direction of differences between means is not specified prior to the conduct of the study.*

2. Assign weights to the means so that the comparisons identified by the hypotheses in step 1 are specified. *Comparisons need not be independent, but the sum of the weights must equal zero (Formula 13-14):*

$$\sum_{1}^{k} w_i = 0$$

3. Write the comparison(s) in the form of a weighted sum of means (Formula 13-13a):

$$\hat{C} = \sum_{1}^{k} w_i \bar{X}_i$$

4. Insert appropriate values for each mean and solve.

5. Conduct Scheffé's test.

   a. Specify the null and alternative hypotheses for each contrast.
   Alternative hypotheses are always nondirectional (see step 1).

   b. Compute $t_{observed}$, using Formulas 13-15, 13-15a, or 13-15b.

   c. Compute $t'_{critical}$, by inserting the appropriate values into Formula 13-16 and solving:

   $$t'_{crit.} = \sqrt{(k-1)F_{crit.(\alpha, k-1, df_W)}}$$

   where:

   k = number of groups
   $F_{crit.}$ = F distribution at the specified α level with $k-1$ degrees of freedom in the numerator and df_W in the denominator

   d. If $|t_{observed}| \geq t'_{critical}$, reject H_0.
   If $|t_{observed}| < t'_{critical}$, do not reject H_0.

Example

$$\bar{X}_C = 6.33 \quad \bar{X}_B = 2.00 \quad \bar{X}_R = 3.33$$
$$+1 \qquad\qquad 0 \qquad\qquad -1$$

$$\hat{C} = (+1)(\bar{X}_C) + (0)(\bar{X}_B) + (-1)(\bar{X}_R)$$

$$\hat{C} = (+1)(6.33) + (0)(2.00) + (-1)(3.33)$$
$$= 6.33 + 0 - 3.33 = 3.00$$

H_0: $C = 0$
H_1: $C \neq 0$

Using Formula 13-15b, we have

$$t_{obs.} = \frac{3.00}{\sqrt{\dfrac{2(1.22)}{3}}} = \frac{3.00}{\sqrt{\dfrac{2.44}{3}}} = \frac{3.00}{\sqrt{.81}} = \frac{3.00}{.9}$$
$$= 3.33$$

Let $\alpha = .05$. Since there were 3 groups, $k = 3$. And $F_{critical}$ with $k - 1 = 2$ df in the numerator and 6 df in the denominator (see df in Table 13-2) equals 5.14 (see Table E). Thus,

$$t'_{crit.} = \sqrt{2(5.14)} = \sqrt{10.28} = 3.21$$

Since $|3.33| > 3.21$, we reject H_0. We conclude that μ_C is significantly higher than μ_R.

Example Problem 13.3

The following results were obtained in a replication of the experiment on study time (described in Example Problem 13.1) with 20 subjects in each group:

Study Time (Minutes)	10	20	45	75
$\bar{X}$	6	10	18	11

The summary table for the one-way ANOVA for these data is shown in Table 13-6.

TABLE 13-6 ANOVA for Example Problem 13.3

Source of Variation	SS	df	MS	F
Between groups	345	3	115.00	10.66
Within groups	820	76	10.79	
Total	1165			

From these data, make the following post hoc comparison, using Scheffé's method ($\alpha = .05$):

$$\mu_{20\ min}\ \text{versus}\ \mu_{45\ min}$$

Include the following items in your answer:
  a. Null and alternative hypotheses
  b. Set of weights for the comparison
  c. Computation of $\hat{C}$
  d. t test
  e. $t'_{critical}$
  f. Conclusions

Tukey's HSD Test

Tukey's HSD (honestly significant difference) test is designed for making all possible pairwise comparisons between means at an overall level of significance α. This test is more powerful than Scheffé's all-purpose test for comparing *pairs* of means; it should not be used for testing complex comparisons (i.e., a comparison involving more than two means).

Tukey's HSD test is conducted by comparing the difference between each pair of means with the value of *HSD*. The value of *HSD* is given by Formula 13-17.

$$HSD = q_{(\alpha, df_W, k)} \sqrt{\frac{MS_W}{n}} \qquad \qquad \textbf{(13-17)}$$

where:
  q = value of studentized range statistic from Table F
  α = probability of a Type 1 error
  df_W = degrees of freedom for MS_W
  k = number of groups
  n = number of subjects within a group [if n differs greatly from group to group, see Kirk (1982)]

The value of *HSD* is based on a sampling distribution called the *studentized range statistic*. The sampling distribution of q builds on the fact that for random samples from the same population (i.e., groups with no systematic differences), the range of sample differences tends to increase as the sample size increases. This distribution is given in Table F.

Three pieces of information are needed to locate the value of q in Table F in the Appendix: α, df_W, and k. The value of q is found by locating the number of degrees of freedom for $MS_W (df_W)$ and the specified α level in the rows of the table and the number of groups in the columns of the table. The intersection of this row and column gives the value of q.

The differences between all pairs of means are then compared with the value of *HSD*. If the difference between a pair of means is greater than or equal to *HSD*, the two means are (honestly) significantly different at the specified level of α.

The steps in conducting all pairwise comparisons between means by using Tukey's HSD test are summarized in Procedure 13-6, using an example from the hypothetical counseling study. Notice that Tukey's test indicates that the mean of the control group is significantly different from the mean of both counseling groups. These results suggest that the counseling groups produced greater effects than did the control group.

PROCEDURE 13-6 Steps in conducting Tukey's HSD test: post hoc comparisons between all pairs of means (data from the hypothetical counseling study)

Operation	Example

1. Specify the null and alternative hypotheses:

H_0: $C = 0$

H_1: $C \neq 0$

Hypotheses are specified for all pairs of means, since Tukey's HSD test is designed for making all pairwise comparisons among means. The alternative hypothesis is nondirectional, since the direction of differences between means is not specified prior to the study.

Example

H_0: $C = 0$

H_1: $C \neq 0$

where:

$C = \mu_i - \mu_{i'}$ for all pairs

2. Do the following:

a. Set up a table with the mean of each group listed along the rows and columns of the table. Means are listed in *order of size* from smallest to largest. *The table should have k rows and k columns, where k is the number of groups.*

	$\bar{X}_B = 2.00$	$\bar{X}_R = 3.33$	$\bar{X}_C = 6.33$
$\bar{X}_B = 2.00$	—	1.33	4.33
$\bar{X}_R = 3.33$		—	3.00
$\bar{X}_C = 6.33$			—

b. Compute the difference between each pair of means by subtracting the mean listed in each row from the mean listed in each column. Enter this value into the appropriate cell of the table. *Only the differences above the diagonal must be calculated, since the values below the diagonal will be the same except for sign.*

Operation	Example

Operation

3. Compute *HSD*, using Formula 13-17:

$$HSD = q_{(\alpha, df_W, k)} \sqrt{\frac{MS_W}{n}}$$

where:

q = value of studentized range statistic from Table F

α = probability of a Type I error

df_W = degrees of freedom for MS_W

k = number of groups

n = number of subjects within groups

4. Compare the differences between means listed in the table (step 2) with the value of *HSD*. If any difference is greater than or equal to the value of *HSD*, reject H_0. For differences which are greater than *HSD*, conclude that the means are significantly different at the specified α level.

Example

Let:

$$\alpha = .05$$
$$df_W = 6$$
$$k = 3$$

$$HSD = q_{(.05, 6, 3)} \sqrt{\frac{1.22}{3}} = 4.34 \sqrt{\frac{1.22}{3}}$$
$$= 4.34(0.64) = 2.78$$

	$\bar{X}_B = 2.00$	$\bar{X}_R = 3.33$	$\bar{X}_C = 6.33$
$\bar{X}_B = 2.00$	—	1.33	4.33[a]
$\bar{X}_R = 3.33$		—	3.00[a]
$\bar{X}_C = 6.33$			—

[a] $p < .05$.

Reject H_0. Draw the following conclusions for the population:

a. The means of the behavior modification and control groups are significantly different.

b. The means of the Rogerian and control groups are significantly different.

c. The means of the behavior modification and Rogerian groups are not significantly different.

Example Problem 13.4

Using the data from the experiment on study time in Example Problem 13.3, compare all pairs of means by using Tukey's HSD test. (Let $\alpha = .05$.) Include the following items in your answer:

a. Null and alternative hypotheses

b. Table of differences between means

c. Computation of *HSD*

d. Conclusions

PLANNED COMPARISONS OF MEANS

An alternative to the analysis of variance for comparing differences among two or more means is the method of **planned comparisons.** With planned comparisons, hypotheses about differences among *specific* means must be set forth *before* the research is conducted. In order to state hypotheses a priori, the researcher must have a strong theory and prior research on which to base and justify the hypotheses. The researcher's reward for using this method is *power.* Planned comparisons are more powerful than the ANOVA for testing hypotheses. The price paid for this power is that planned comparisons are restrictive. The researcher must know a lot about the phenomenon under study and cannot use this method to snoop through the data to explore interesting results that were not predicted prior to the study. As with most things in life, however, there is a middle ground. Planned comparisons can be combined with post hoc comparisons to enable the researcher to have the best of both worlds.

Figure 13-2 provides a schematic of the decisions a researcher makes in statistically testing differences among means. Before the study is conducted, the researcher decides whether to use planned comparisons. If the study is exploratory with the intent of snooping through the data, the decision is no. The study is conducted and the ANOVA is used with post hoc comparisons following a significant overall F (right side of Figure 13-2).

If the researcher decides to conduct planned comparisons, she must determine whether the hypotheses are orthogonal—that is, whether they provide independent, nonoverlapping information (left side of Figure 13-2). If the hypotheses are orthogonal, the statistical tests presented in this chapter can be used. If the comparisons are nonorthogonal—for example, the control group mean is compared with the mean of each experimental group; such comparisons provide overlapping information—statistical tests presented in, for example, Kirk (1982) can be used.

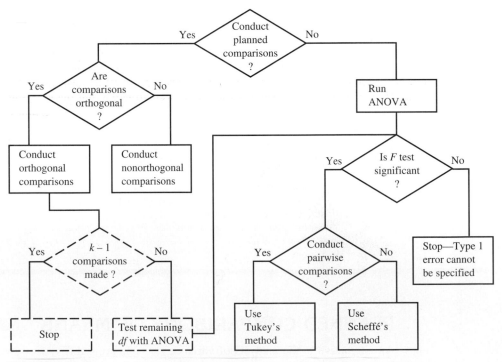

FIGURE 13-2

Relation between planned comparisons and ANOVA with post hoc comparisons [broken lines indicate topics not covered in this textbook; see, for example, Kirk (1982)]

Finally, if fewer than all possible orthogonal comparisons are made,[9] the sum of squares associated with the orthogonal comparisons can be removed from the total sum of squares, and the remainder can be tested with the ANOVA. If the overall F is significant, data snooping with post hoc comparisons can be carried out.

OVERVIEW

In planned comparisons, hypotheses about differences between means must be set forth before the study is conducted. In doing so, the researcher should have strong theoretical reasons, strong empirical evidence, or preferably both. Once the hypotheses have been set forth, comparisons between means for each hypothesis can be identified. These comparisons are written as a set of weighted means with the sum of the weights equal to zero (see what follows). Finally, for the statistical test presented here, each comparison must be independent of every other comparison. These comparisons are often referred to as "orthogonal contrasts" because they contain independent or nonoverlapping pieces of information. Each of these points is discussed in detail here.

Comparisons Planned Prior to the Conduct of the Study

Comparisons between the k treatment means must be planned prior to the conduct of the study. As an example, consider the counseling study. Contrary to popular belief, the results of prior research suggest that psychotherapy is more effective than control treatments (Smith & Glass, 1977). However, the results of research are equivocal with respect to whether behavior modification or Rogerian therapy is more effective with phobias like acrophobia. (Some evidence suggests the former is more effective, but the research has methodological problems.) Thus, on the basis of theory and prior research, it seems safe to hypothesize that subjects in the control group will not come as close to the edge of the Pisa tower as will subjects in the two counseling groups. The mean of the control group, then, will be greater than the average of the means for the two therapy groups:

$$H_1: \mu_C > \frac{\mu_B + \mu_R}{2}$$

With the alternative hypothesis specified, we assign a set of weights to form a planned comparison, as was done for the post hoc comparison (see Procedure 13-3). That is, weights are assigned to planned comparisons in the same way they are assigned to post hoc comparisons. Nothing new here.

---

[9]The maximum number of orthogonal comparisons is equal to the degrees of freedom for all between-group comparisons. If k is the number of groups (or cells in a two-way design), a maximum of $k - 1$ orthogonal comparisons can be made.

Independence of Pairs of Comparisons

The new requirement is that each comparison be independent of every other comparison. The independence of a set of comparisons depends only on the set of weights assigned to each mean and in no way depends on the values of the means observed. Assuming equal cell sizes, *two comparisons are independent if the sum of the cross products of their corresponding weights is zero.*[10] If w_{1i} represents the weight assigned to the mean from treatment i in the first comparison and w_{2i} the weight assigned to the mean from treatment i in the second comparison, the requirement for independence can be written formally as shown in Formula 13-18.

$$w_{11}w_{21} + w_{12}w_{22} + \cdots + w_{1k}w_{2k} = 0$$

$$\sum_{1}^{k} w_{1i}w_{2i} = 0 \qquad\qquad (13\text{-}18)$$

(See step 5 of Procedure 13-7 for verifying the independence of comparisons.)

PROCEDURE 13-7 Steps in specifying weights for planned comparisons (data from Table 13-1)

Operation	Example
1. Identify hypotheses from prior theory, research, or both. *Strong evidence must exist for these predictions.*	$H_1: \mu_C > \dfrac{\mu_B + \mu_R}{2}$ $H_2: \mu_B \neq \mu_R$

---

[10] We assume equal sample sizes. This assumption is not a requirement for planned comparisons. But if we make this assumption, the identification of independent comparisons is simplified. If sample sizes are unequal, the requirement in Formula 13-18,

$$\sum_{1}^{k} w_{1i}w_{2i} = 0$$

can be modified as follows:

$$\sum_{1}^{k} \frac{w_{1i}w_{2i}}{n_i} = 0$$

Here the cross product of the comparison weights for each sample is weighed inversely by n_i before the sum is taken. If this weighted sum of weights equals zero, the comparisons may be regarded as independent.

Operation_____

2. Assign weights to the means so that the comparisons identified by the hypotheses in step 1 are specified. *The sum of the weights for each comparison must equal zero (Formula 13-14):*

$$\sum_{1}^{k} w_i = 0$$

3. Add the weights for each comparison in order to verify the accuracy of step 2.

4. Write the comparisons in the form of a weighted sum of means (Formula 13-13a):

$$\hat{C} = \sum_{1}^{k} w_i \bar{X}_i$$

5. For each pair of comparisons, cross multiply the weights corresponding to each mean, using Formula 13-18:

$$\sum_{1}^{k} w_{1i} w_{2i} = 0$$

For each pair of comparisons, the sum of the cross products of corresponding weights must equal zero.

6. Only $k - 1$ independent comparisons may be defined.

Example_____

	$\bar{X}_C =$ 6.33	$\bar{X}_B =$ 2.00	$\bar{X}_R =$ 3.33
$\hat{C}_1[\bar{X}_C$ vs. $(\bar{X}_B + \bar{X}_R)/2]$	1	$-\frac{1}{2}$	$-\frac{1}{2}$
$\hat{C}_2(\bar{X}_B$ vs. $\bar{X}_R)$	0	$+1$	-1

$\hat{C}_1 : (+1) + (-\frac{1}{2}) + (-\frac{1}{2}) = 0$

$\hat{C}_2 : 0 + (+1) + (-1) = 0$

$\hat{C}_1 = (+1)\bar{X}_C + (-\frac{1}{2})\bar{X}_B + (-\frac{1}{2})\bar{X}_R$

$\hat{C}_2 = (0)\bar{X}_C + (+1)\bar{X}_B + (-1)\bar{X}_R$

$\hat{C}_1$ vs. $\hat{C}_2$:

$(+1)(0) + (-\frac{1}{2})(+1) + (-\frac{1}{2})(-1) = 0$

Since $k = 3$, only two independent comparisons can be specified. Suppose a third hypothesis was specified:

$$H_3: \bar{X}_C \neq \bar{X}_R$$

Then:

$$\hat{C}_3 = (1)\bar{X}_C + (0)\bar{X}_B + (-1)\bar{X}_R$$

Comparison $\hat{C}_3$ is not independent of $\hat{C}_1$ or $\hat{C}_2$.

$\hat{C}_1$ vs. $\hat{C}_3$:

$(1)(1) + (-\frac{1}{2})(0) + (-\frac{1}{2})(-1) \neq 0$

$\hat{C}_2$ vs. $\hat{C}_3$:

$(0)(1) + (+1)(0) + (-1)(-1) \neq 0$

For k treatment groups, $k - 1$ independent comparisons can be defined. Thus, in any study, one set of $k - 1$ planned orthogonal comparisons may be conducted. However, for k means, one can write more than one set of $k - 1$ comparisons.

In the counseling study with $k = 3$ groups, $3 - 1 = 2$ independent comparisons can be defined. Once the two comparisons have been identified, a third comparison cannot be specified that will be independent—that is, it will not satisfy the requirement that the sum of the cross products of the weights equals zero. For example, suppose that prior empirical evidence suggested a third comparison—the control group versus the Rogerian group:

$$\hat{C}_3 = (1)\bar{X}_C + (0)\bar{X}_B + (-1)\bar{X}_R$$

This comparison will not be independent of $\hat{C}_1$ or $\hat{C}_2$ (see step 6 of Procedure 13-7). Furthermore, no set of weights can be identified such that $\hat{C}_3$ will be independent of both $\hat{C}_1$ and $\hat{C}_2$.

Computation of the Value of a Comparison

Once the comparison between means has been written, the value of the comparison $(\hat{C})$ can be found by simply inserting the appropriate values and carrying out the arithmetic operations. For example,

$$\hat{C}_1 = (1)\bar{X}_C + (-\tfrac{1}{2})\bar{X}_B + (-\tfrac{1}{2})\bar{X}_R$$
$$= (1)(6.33) + (-\tfrac{1}{2})(2) + (-\tfrac{1}{2})(3.33)$$
$$= 6.33 - 1 - 1.67 = 3.66$$

The difference between the mean of the control group and the average of the means of the other two groups is 3.66.

Statistical Test for Planned Comparisons

For each planned orthogonal comparison, the t distribution can be used to determine whether or not the difference between two means or between combinations of means arose by chance. For each comparison, the null and alternative hypotheses are H_0: $C = 0$ and H_1: $C \neq 0$ for a nondirectional alternative hypothesis; or H_1: $C > 0$ or H_1: $C < 0$ for directional alternative hypotheses.

In addition, α is also set before the data are collected. Typically, each t test is performed at $\alpha = .05$ or $\alpha = .01$. However, if each orthogonal comparison is conducted at $\alpha = .05$, we know that the probability of a Type I error for the *two planned comparisons* in the counseling study will be .0975, using Formula 13-2:

$$p(\text{Type I error}) = 1 - (1 - .05)^2 = .0975$$

For this reason, the level of significance for each orthogonal comparison is often set at α/c, where c is the number of orthogonal comparisons to be carried out. In our example with $\alpha/2$, $p(\text{Type I error}) = .0437$, close to the .05 level.

Each orthogonal comparison is tested statistically with a t test. Formula 13-15a can be used when, as we assume throughout, sample sizes are equal.

$$t_{\text{observed}} = \frac{\hat{C}}{\sqrt{\dfrac{MS_W}{n}(w_1^2 + w_2^2 + \cdots + w_k^2)}}$$

where:

$\hat{C}$ = value of the contrast

MS_W = mean square within groups (error) that can be obtained from an ANOVA table

k = number of groups

If the comparison is between only two means with equal cell size, Formula 13-15b can be used:

$$t_{observed} = \frac{\hat{C}}{\sqrt{\dfrac{2MS_W}{n}}}$$

The critical value of t can be found in Table C. The number of degrees of freedom for the critical value equals $N - k$ or the df_W from the ANOVA table. If $|t_{observed}|$ is greater than or equal to $t_{critical}$, reject H_0. If $|t_{observed}|$ is less than $t_{critical}$, do not reject H_0. The steps in conducting a statistical test for planned comparisons are the same as those for Scheffé's method, except that $t'_{critical}$ need not be calculated. The steps are summarized in Procedure 13-5, steps 1–5b.

Planned (a priori) comparisons represent the most powerful method for statistically testing for differences between three or more means. With planned comparisons, the ANOVA is used to calculate the mean square within groups (error); *the F value need not be computed.* Thus, planned comparisons are more powerful than the overall ANOVA.

However, as history tells us, one always pays a price for power. Planned comparisons are no exception. If we are to conduct these comparisons, two requirements must be met:

1. Comparisons must be planned and justified prior to conducting the study.
2. The comparisons must be independent of one another, so that $k - 1$ comparisons can be conducted, at most.

Example Problem 13.5

Suppose that, in a replication of the experiment on study time, researchers set forth the following hypotheses to be tested prior to the study:

1. $\mu_{45\,min}$ is greater than $\mu_{75\,min}$.
2. $\mu_{10\,min}$ is less than the average for the other three groups.

Test both comparisons between means at $\alpha = .05$. Include the following items in your answer.

a. A table showing weights for each comparison (contrast) with verification that $\sum w_i = 0$ and that the contrasts are independent (see Procedure 13-7)

b. Null and alternative hypotheses for $\hat{C}_1$

c. Computation of $\hat{C}_1$

d. The t test for contrast 1

e. $t_{critical}$ for contrast 1

f. Conclusion

g. Steps b–f for contrast 2

h. Maximum number of independent comparisons that could be conducted

SUMMARY

This chapter presents the *one-way analysis of variance* (ANOVA), a statistical method for determining whether observed differences between the means of two or more independent samples of subjects are likely to have arisen by chance. The purposes, underlying logic, and procedures for computing and interpreting the ANOVA are discussed for fixed-effects designs and then for random-effects designs. *Omega-square* (ω^2), a measure of strength of association or the strength of the treatment effect for fixed-effects ANOVA, and the *intraclass correlation,* a measure for random-effects ANOVA, are presented. Finally, methods for making *comparisons between means* to determine which means differ statistically from the others are discussed. *Post hoc comparisons* are used when the overall F in the ANOVA is significant and comparisons have not been planned prior to the study but look interesting on the basis of the sample data. The most widely applicable methods for making post hoc comparisons, *Scheffé's test* and *Tukey's HSD test,* are presented. *Planned comparisons* provide an alternative to the analysis of variance and post hoc comparisons (a significant overall F test is not required). When theory and prior research enable the researcher to set forth hypotheses to be tested prior to the study, planned comparisons can be used. This chapter concluded with a presentation of a method for making planned, orthogonal comparisons.

TECHNICAL APPENDIX
Independence of Variability within- and between Groups

The following presentation will be more meaningful if you read the section "Computation of the ANOVA" first. The proof works with sums of squares—variances multiplied by their degrees of freedom. The goal is to show that the total variability in scores—$\sum_i \sum_p (X_{pi} - \bar{X}_G)^2$—can be partitioned into two independent components: within group variability—$\sum_i \sum_p (X_{pi} - \bar{X}_i)^2$—and between-group variability—$\sum_i n_i (\bar{X}_i - \bar{X}_G)^2$:

$$(X_{pi} - \bar{X}_G) = (X_{pi} - \bar{X}_i) + (\bar{X}_i - \bar{X}_G)$$

The deviation of a score from the grand mean can be written as the deviation of the score from its group mean plus the deviation of its group mean from the grand mean.

$$(X_{pi} - \bar{X}_G)^2 = [(X_{pi} - \bar{X}_i) + (\bar{X}_i - \bar{X}_G)]^2$$

Squaring both sides.

$$\sum_i \sum_p (X_{pi} - \bar{X}_G)^2 = \sum_i \sum_p [(X_{pi} - \bar{X}_i) + (\bar{X}_i - \bar{X}_G)]^2$$

Summing over persons and groups.

$$\sum_i \sum_p (X_{pi} - \bar{X}_G)^2 = \sum_i \sum_p (X_{pi} - \bar{X}_i)^2$$
$$+ \sum_i \sum_p (\bar{X}_i - \bar{X}_G)^2$$
$$+ \sum_i \sum_p (X_{pi} - \bar{X}_i)(\bar{X}_i - \bar{X}_G)$$

Expanding the right side.

$$\sum_i \sum_p (X_{pi} - \bar{X}_G)^2 = \sum_i \sum_p (X_{pi} - \bar{X}_i)^2$$

Distributing the summation.

$$+ \sum_i \sum_p (\bar{X}_i - \bar{X}_G)^2$$

$$+ \sum_i (\bar{X}_i - \bar{X}_G) \sum_p (X_{pi} - \bar{X}_i)$$

$$\sum_i \sum_p (X_{pi} - \bar{X}_G)^2 = \sum_i \sum_p (X_{pi} - \bar{X}_i)^2$$

The sum of deviation scores is zero:

$$\sum_p (X_{pi} - \bar{X}_i) = 0$$

$$+ \sum_i \sum_p (\bar{X}_i - \bar{X}_G)^2 + 0$$

$$\sum_i \sum_p (X_{pi} - \bar{X}_G)^2 = \sum_i \sum_p (X_{pi} - \bar{X}_i)^2$$

The effect, $(\bar{X}_i - \bar{X}_G)$, is constant for all (n_i) persons within a group.

$$+ \sum_i n_i (\bar{X}_i - \bar{X}_G)^2$$

Equivalence of Deviation- and Raw-Score Formulas

As an example of the equivalence of the deviation- and raw-score formulas, consider the equivalence for the total sum of squares. The deviation score formula is

$$SS_T = \sum_i \sum_p (X_{pi} - \bar{X}_G)^2$$

Formula 13–4b.

$$= \sum_i \sum_p (X_{pi}^2 - 2X_{pi}\bar{X}_G + \bar{X}_G^2)$$

Squaring.

$$= \sum_i \sum_p X_{pi}^2 - 2\bar{X}_G \sum_i \sum_p X_{pi} + \sum_i \sum_p \bar{X}_G^2$$

Distributing summation and rule for summation of a constant.

$$= \sum_i \sum_p X_{pi}^2 - 2\bar{X}_G(N\bar{X}_G) + N\bar{X}_G^2$$

$$\bar{X} = \frac{\sum X}{N}; \sum X = N\bar{X}$$

$$= \sum_i \sum_p X_{pi}^2 - 2N\bar{X}_G^2 + N\bar{X}_G^2$$

Combining terms.

$$= \sum_i \sum_p X_{pi}^2 - N\bar{X}_G^2$$

Combining terms.

$$= \sum_i \sum_p X_{pi}^2 - N\frac{\left(\sum_i \sum_p X_{pi}\right)^2}{N^2}$$

$$N\bar{X}_G = \sum_i \sum_p X_{pi}; \text{ thus,}$$

$$= \sum_i \sum_p X_{pi}^2 - \frac{\left(\sum_i \sum_p X_{pi}\right)^2}{N}$$

$$\bar{X}_G = \frac{\sum_i \sum_p X_{pi}}{N}$$

Thus we have Formula 13-7 (in Procedure 13-1), which is the raw-score formula. The raw-score formulas corresponding to the deviation score formulas for SS_B and SS_W (Formulas 13-5 and 13-6) are given in Table 13-3 and Procedure 13-1.

ANSWERS TO EXAMPLE PROBLEMS

1. The ANOVA reported here was carried out with SPSS software.[11]
   a. H_0: $\mu_i - \mu_G = 0$ for all i or H_0: $\mu_{10} = \mu_{20} = \mu_{45} = \mu_{75}$

      H_1: $\mu_i - \mu_G = 0$ for some i
   b. *Independence:* By random assignment we assume independence. However, the researcher should ensure that the study times were adhered to, and students studied independently.

   Normality: The sample sizes are too small to inspect frequency distributions. The ANOVA is robust to violation of this assumption.

   Homogeneity. SPSS provides a statistical test, Levene's test, of the following null and alternative hypotheses:

   H_0: $\sigma_i^2 = \sigma_{i'}^2$ for all i and i'

   H_1: $\sigma_i^2 \neq \sigma_{i'}^2$ for some i and i':

   Levene Test for Homogeneity of Variances
   Statistic   df1   df2   2-tail Sig.
   .3673   3   16   .778

   Do not reject the null hypothesis. Moreover, the ANOVA is robust to violation of this assumption, especially with equal cell sizes.
   c. See Sum of Squares in Source Table below.
   d. SPSS Source Table.

| | | *Analysis of Variance* | | | |
Source	*D.F.*	*Sum of Squares*	*Mean Squares*	*F Ratio*	*F Prob.*
Between Groups	3	289.7500	96.5833	40.6667	.0000
Within Groups	16	38.0000	2.3750		
Total	19	327.7500			

Note: SPSS does not follow convention and places D.F. before Sum of Squares.

[11]SPSS Program Setup:
ONEWAY
achieve BY stdtime(10 75)
/RANGES = TUKEY
/RANGES = SCHEFFE
/HARMONIC NONE
/STATISTICS HOMOGENEITY
/FORMAT NOLABELS
/MISSING ANALYSIS.

e. $F_{\text{critical } (\alpha = .05, df = 3,16)} = 3.24$

f. Reject the null hypothesis. Conclude that there is a learning effect due to study time.

2. a. $\hat{\omega}^2 = \dfrac{SS_B - (k-1)MS_W}{SS_T + MS_W} = \dfrac{289.75 - (4-1)2.38}{327.75 + 2.38} = .86$

b. Study time accounted for 86 percent of the variance in achievement.

c. $\hat{\rho}_I = \dfrac{MS_B - MS_W}{MS_B + (n-1)MS_W} = \dfrac{96.58 - 2.38}{327.75 + (5-1)2.38} = .89$

d. Study time accounted for 89 percent of the variance in achievement.

3. a. $H_0: C = 0, H_1: C \neq 0$

b.

Comparison	Set of Weights			
	$\bar{X}_{10\,min} = 6$	$\bar{X}_{20\,min} = 10$	$\bar{X}_{45\,min} = 18$	$\bar{X}_{75\,min} = 11$
$\bar{X}_{20\,min}$ vs. $\bar{X}_{45\,min}$	0	1	−1	0

c. $\hat{C} = (0)(6) + (1)(10) + (-1)(18) + (0)(11) = -8$

d. $t = \dfrac{\hat{C}}{\sqrt{\dfrac{2MS_W}{n}}} = \dfrac{-8}{\sqrt{\dfrac{2(10.79)}{20}}} = -7.70$

e. $t'_{\text{critical}} = \sqrt{(k-1)F_{\text{critical}}} = \sqrt{(4-1)2.74} = 2.87$

f. Since $|t_{\text{observed}}| > t_{\text{critical}}$, reject H_0. Conclude that there is a significant difference between the means of the group given 20 minutes of study time and the group given 45 minutes of study time.

4. a. $H_0: C = 0, H_1: C \neq 0$, for each pairwise comparison.

b.

	$\bar{X}_{10\,min} = 6$	$\bar{X}_{20\,min} = 10$	$\bar{X}_{75\,min} = 11$	$\bar{X}_{45\,min} = 18$
$\bar{X}_{10\,min} = 6$	—	4[a]	5[a]	12[a]
$\bar{X}_{20\,min} = 10$		—	1	8[a]
$\bar{X}_{75\,min} = 11$			—	7[a]
$\bar{X}_{45\,min} = 18$				—

[a]$p < .05$.

c. $HSD = q_{(.05,76,4)} \sqrt{\dfrac{10.79}{20}} = 3.74(.73) = 2.73$

d. Reject H_0. The differences between means marked by footnote a in the table shown in part b are significant at $\alpha = .05$. Note that the largest differences are found between the 45-minute group and the other three groups. This pattern of results suggests that 45 minutes is the optimal study time (i.e., produces the highest achievement).

5. **a.** Set of weights:

Comparison	$\bar{X}_{10\ min}$	$\bar{X}_{20\ min}$	$\bar{X}_{45\ min}$	$\bar{X}_{75\ min}$	Sum of Weights
$\hat{C}_1 : \bar{X}_{45\ min}$ vs. $\bar{X}_{75\ min}$	0	0	1	-1	0
$\hat{C}_2 : \bar{X}_{10\ min}$ vs. $\dfrac{\bar{X}_{20} + \bar{X}_{45} + \bar{X}_{75}}{3}$	3	-1	-1	-1	0

Check on independence:

$$\hat{C}_1 \text{ vs. } \hat{C}_2 :\qquad (0)(3) + (0)(-1) + (1)(-1) + (-1)(-1) = 0$$

b. $H_0: C_1 = 0, H_1: C_1 > 0$

c. $\hat{C}_1 = \sum_{1}^{k} w_i \bar{X}_i = 1(18) + (-1)(11) = 7$

d. $t = \dfrac{\hat{C}}{\sqrt{\dfrac{2MS_W}{n}}} = \dfrac{7}{\sqrt{\dfrac{2(10.79)}{20}}} = 6.74$

e. Since α was set at .05, $t_{critical(.05,.76)} = 1.671$.

f. Since $t_{observed} > t_{critical}$, reject H_0. Conclude that the mean of the study group given 45 minutes is significantly greater than the mean of the study group given 75 minutes.

g. *Step b.* $H_0: C_2 = 0, H_1: C_2 < 0$
Step c. $\hat{C}_2 = (3)(6) + (-1)(10) + (-1)(18) + (-1)(11) = -21$
Step d. $\hat{C}_2$:

$$t = \frac{\hat{C}}{\sqrt{\dfrac{MS_W}{n}(w_1^2 + w_2^2 + \cdots + w_k^2)}}$$

$$= \frac{-21}{\sqrt{\dfrac{10.79}{20}[(3)^2 + (-1)^2 + (-1)^2 + (-1)^2]}} = -8.25$$

Step e. $t_{critical(.05,.76)} = 1.671$
Step f.   Since $|t_{observed}| > t_{critical}$, reject H_0. Conclude that the mean of the study group given 10 minutes is significantly lower than the average of the other three groups.

h. $k - 1 = 4 - 1 = 3$ independent comparisons could be conducted.

EXERCISES

Hudley & Graham (1993) hypothesized that boys' aggressive behavior might be the consequence of their misattributing the intent of others ("actors") in ambiguous situations (see Chapter 4 for details). If Hudley and Graham were right, teaching these boys to interpret actors' intent as something other than negative in ambiguous situations should ultimately lessen their aggressive behavior. To test this hypothesis, Hudley and Graham randomly assigned boys to one of three groups: (1) experimental (attribution retraining), (2) attention (simply paying attention to boys with no special training), and (3) control (no special attention given). After treatment, the boys were asked to rate actors' intents in ambiguous situations. The hypothesis, stated specifically, was that the average negative intent rating would be lower in the experimental group than in the other two groups. Data bearing on this hypothesis are presented in Table 13-7. You might want to use a statistical package to run these data; I did.

TABLE 13-7 Hypothetical data on boys' perceptions of negative intent after treatment: Ambiguous situations

Group[a]	Negative Intent Rating	Group	Negative Intent Rating
1	3	2	4
1	1	2	2
1	2	2	3
1	2	2	6
1	2	2	3
1	1	2	5
1	2	3	4
1	4	3	4
1	3	3	5
1	1	3	5
1	4	3	4
1	4	3	7
2	6	3	5
2	6	3	2
2	5	3	4
2	3	3	3
2	4	3	4
2	6	3	4

[a] 1 = Attribution retraining, 2 = attention control, 3 = control.

1. Present sample statistics that bear on the hypothesis. Do these statistics support the hypothesis?
2. Do a statistical test (ANOVA) to determine whether the observed sample mean differences arose by chance.

a. State the assumptions underlying this statistical test and present either empirical evidence or a justification for the use of the test.

b. State the null and alternative hypotheses tested

c. Report the results of the ANOVA in a summary table

d. Interpret the findings; what do you conclude?

e. Report the results of mean comparisons to explore the Hudley-Graham hypothesis. Explain your choice of comparison method.

f. With the comparisons in hand, what do you conclude now about the Hudley-Graham hypothesis?

ANSWERS TO EXERCISES

Note: The data-based answers to the exercises are taken from edited SPSS runs with Negative Intent Rating as the dependent variable.

1. Sample Statistics[12]

GROUP:	Label	Mean	Std Dev	Minimum	Maximum	N
1	Retraining	2.42	1.16	1.00	4.00	12
2	Attention	4.42	1.44	2.00	6.00	12
3	Control	4.25	1.22	2.00	7.00	12
Total		3.69	1.55	1.00	7.00	36

---

[12]SPSS Program Setup:
SORT CASES BY group (A).
Report
/FORMAT = CHALIGN(BOTTOM) BRKSPACE(0) SUMSPACE(0) AUTOMATIC NOLIST
PAGE(1) MISSING'.' LENGTH(1, 59)ALIGN(LEFT) TSPACE(1) FTSPACE(1)
MARGINS(1,20)
/TITLE RIGHT 'Page)PAGE'
/VARIABLES
intent (VALUES) (RIGHT) (OFFSET(0))
/BREAK (TOTAL) 'Grand Total' (SKIP(1))/SUMMARY
MEAN(intent) SKIP(1) 'Mean'
/SUMMARY MIN(intent) 'Minimum'
/SUMMARY MAX(intent) 'Maximum'
/SUMMARY VALIDN(intent) 'N'
/SUMMARY STDDEV(intent) 'StdDev'
/BREAK group (LABELS) (LEFT) (OFFSET(0))(SKIP(1))
/SUMMARY MEAN(intent) SKIP(0) 'Mean'
/SUMMARY MIN(intent) 'Minimum'
/SUMMARY MAX(intent) 'Maximum'
/SUMMARY VALIDN(intent) 'N'
/SUMMARY STDDEV(intent) 'StdDev'.

The sample data are consistent with the hypothesis that attribution retraining will reduce aggressive boys' perception of negative intent in ambiguous situations; the two control groups appear to be about the same: aggressive boys perceive negative intent in ambiguous situations.

2. a. *Independence:* By random assignment, we assume independence. However, the conduct of the experiment should be carefully monitored to ensure independence was maintained.

   Normality: An inspection of the frequency distributions in each group suggests that the normality assumption may be justified (i.e., somewhat symmetrical) but there are just too few data to get a good handle on the shapes of the distributions. Nevertheless, the ANOVA is robust to violation of this assumption.

   Homogeneity: SPSS provides a statistical test, Levene's test, of this assumption along with the ANOVA run (see below).

   Levene Test for Homogeneity of Variances

Statistic	df1	df2	2-tail Sig.
1.1477	2	33	.330

   Do not reject the null hypothesis of equal population variances. Moreover, the ANOVA is robust to violation of this assumption, especially with equal cell sizes.

   b. H_0: $\mu_i - \mu_G = 0$ for all i or H_0: $\mu_{10} = \mu_{20} = \mu_{45} = \mu_{75}$
      H_1: $\mu_i - \mu_G = 0$ for some i

   c. Analysis of Variance[13]

   | | | Analysis of Variance | | | |
Source	D.F.	Sum of Squares	Mean Squares	F Ratio	F Prob.
Between Groups	2	29.5556	14.7778	9.0169	.0008
Within Groups	33	54.0833	1.6389		
Total	35	83.6389			

   d. Reject the null hypothesis. Conclude that there is a significant effect. The next step is to determine just what that effect is.

   e. In what follows, both Tukey's and Scheffé's post hoc comparisons are presented from the SPSS output. There was insufficient empirical evidence to support planned comparisons in this study.

---

[13]SPSS Program Setup:
ONEWAY
intent BY group(1 3)
/RANGES = TUKEY
/RANGES = SCHEFFE
/HARMONIC NONE
/STATISTICS HOMOGENEITY
/FORMAT NOLABELS
/MISSING ANALYSIS.

Variable INTENT
By Variable GROUP

Multiple Range Tests: Tukey-HSD test with significance level .05

The difference between two means is significant if
MEAN(J)–MEAN(I) >= .9052 * RANGE * SQRT(1/N(I) + 1/N(J))
with the following value(s) for RANGE: 3.46

(*) Indicates significant differences, which are shown in the lower triangle

		G	G	G
		r	r	r
		p	p	p
		1	3	2
Mean	*GROUP*			
2.4167	Grp 1			
4.2500	Grp 3	*		
4.4167	Grp 2	*		

Homogeneous Subsets (highest and lowest means [within a subset] are not significantly different)

Subset 1

Group	*Grp 1*
Mean	2.4167

Subset 2

Group	*Grp 3*	*Grp 2*
Mean	4.2500	4.4167

Note: Subgroup 1 differs significantly from subgroup 2, supporting the Hudley-Graham hypothesis.

Variable   INTENT
By Variable   GROUP

Multiple Range Tests: Scheffé test with significance level .05

The difference between two means is significant if
MEAN(J)–MEAN(I) >= .9052 * RANGE * SQRT(1/N(I) + 1/N(J))
with the following value(s) for RANGE: 3.62

(*) Indicates significant differences, which are shown in the lower triangle

		G	G	G
		r	r	r
		p	p	p
		1	**3**	**2**
Mean	*GROUP*			
2.4167	Grp 1			
4.2500	Grp 3	*		
4.4167	Grp 2	*		

Homogeneous Subsets (highest and lowest means are not significantly different)

Subset 1

Group	*Grp 1*
Mean	2.4167

Subset 2

Group	*Grp 3*	*Grp 2*
Mean	4.2500	4.4167

Note: Subgroup 1 differs significantly from subgroup 2, supporting the Hudley-Graham hypothesis.

    f. Conclude that the data support the Hudley-Graham hypothesis as described in 1 above.

14

Factorial Analysis of Variance

- Description of the Two-Way ANOVA
- Fixed, Random, and Mixed Models
- Strength of Association
- Post Hoc Methods for Comparing Means
- Planned Comparisons of Means
- Summary
- Answers to Example Problems
- Exercises
- Answers to Exercises

The **factorial analysis of variance** is a statistical method for examining data from factorial designs (see Section V for alternative between-subjects factorial designs). It is used to test several hypotheses about differences between means in the factorial design. In this chapter, the conceptual underpinnings and the techniques for using the factorial analysis of variance are presented along with two general methods for interpreting the results. One method is to measure the strength of association between each independent variable (and combination of independent variables) and the dependent variable. *Omega-square* and the *intraclass correlation* provide a measure of the strength of association for fixed- and random-effects ANOVA, respectively (see Chapter 13). The second method for interpreting the results of the factorial ANOVA is *post hoc comparisons*. These comparisons test for differences between specific pairs or combinations of means. *Scheffé's* and *Tukey's* methods of post hoc comparison, presented in Chapter 13, are extended to test differences between means in factorial designs. An alternative to the ANOVA, *planned comparisons,* is also presented.

Sample data for the factorial ANOVA may be obtained in true experiments, from factorial criterion group designs, or from combinations of the two. For example, the ANOVA may be used to examine data from the teacher expectancy study (Chapter 2), a 2×6 factorial design with two levels of treatment ("bloomers" and control) and six grade levels; from the attributional intervention study (Chapter 4), a $2 \times 3 \times 2$ factorial design with two levels of aggressiveness (aggressive, nonaggressive), three levels of treatment (experimental, attention, control), and two test occasions (pretest, posttest); and from the study of men's and women's achievement in college (Chapter 5), a $2 \times 4 \times 4$ factorial design with two levels of gender (male, female), three levels of subject matter major (physical sciences, social sciences, and humanities), and four levels of a campus variable (UCLA, UCSD, UCI, and UCD).

Although factorial designs with many factors can be (and have been) conceptualized and conducted, this chapter is restricted to factorial designs with two independent variables. The analysis of variance applied to factorial designs with two factors is often called the two-way ANOVA. Restricting the focus to the two-way ANOVA is not a major limitation, since the presentation can be extended directly to factorial designs with any number of factors. A second restriction is that the presentation will be limited to designs with equal numbers of subjects in each cell. This restriction simplifies the presentation and interpretation of the results of the factorial ANOVA. Finally, the presentation will be limited to **completely crossed designs**—that is, designs in which each level of one factor occurs with (i.e., is "crossed with") each level of the other factor. In the study of teacher expectancy, treatment is crossed with grade level, so that both levels of the treatment factor (control and experimental) are observed with each level of the grade factor (see Figure 14-1a). That is, subjects were randomly selected from each grade level and randomly assigned to one of the two treatment groups (i.e., cells of the design). If all levels of one factor do not occur with all levels of the other factor, the design is not crossed. For example, suppose that in the hypothetical study of teacher expectancy, "bloomers" were randomly selected from grades 1 through 3 and control group subjects were randomly selected from grades 4 through 6. In this case, some cells of the design are empty. Every level of one variable (grade level) does not occur with every level of the other variable (treatment group) (see Figure 14-1b). The material presented in this chapter does not bear directly on such designs.

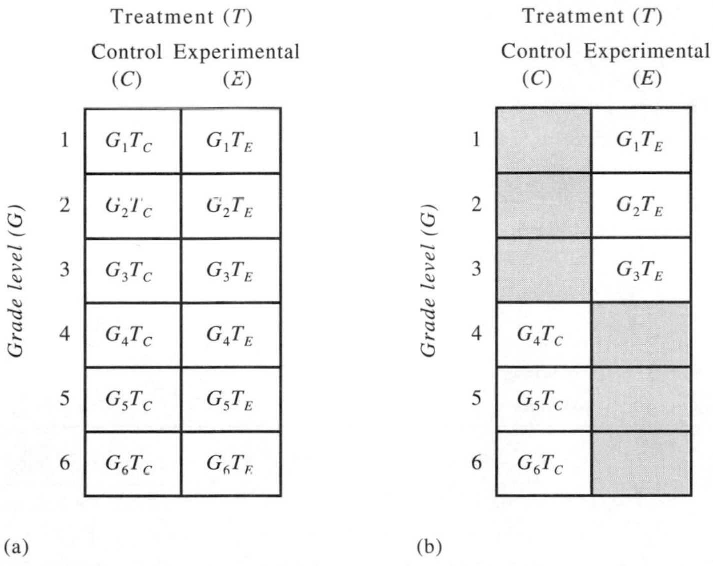

(a)   (b)

FIGURE 14-1
Examples of crossed and not crossed factorial designs: (a) 2×6 crossed factorial design; (b) 2×6 factorial design that is not crossed

DESCRIPTION OF THE TWO-WAY ANOVA
Purpose and Underlying Logic

Purpose. The purpose of the two-way ANOVA is to compare the mean scores from four or more groups[1] in a factorial design in order to decide whether the differences between means may be due to chance or to the effect of the first factor (called the **main effect** for factor A), the second factor (main effect for factor B), or a combination of certain levels of the first factor with certain levels of the second factor (called the **interaction effect**). As a concrete example of the possible effects in a two-way design, consider the data from the expectancy study shown in Table 14-1. Information about the effect of the expectancy treatment on ability scores can be obtained by comparing the mean scores of the control group and experimental group at the bottom of Table 14-1. These mean scores are calculated by ignoring the grade-level factor; they are based on 6 (grade levels) × 5 (subjects within a cell) = 30 scores. Notice that the means can be compared without bias because both are based on scores from the same number of subjects in each of the six grades, who were randomly assigned to the experimental or control group. Finally, the difference between the two means is quite small—.66 point. A t test or one-way ANOVA probably would not show the difference to be statistically significant.[2]

Information about the effect of grade level on the ability scores can be obtained by comparing the means for each grade level in the right-hand column of Table 14-1. These means

TABLE 14-1 Mean posttest scores from the study of teacher expectancy ($n = 5$; raw data in Table 1-1)

Grade Level	Treatment Control	Experimental	Mean Scores Representing the Effect for Grade Level
1	105.20	116.40	110.80
2	105.80	117.20	111.50
3	109.00	106.60	107.80
4	109.40	106.20	107.80
5	116.20	109.20	112.70
6	111.80	105.80	108.80
Mean Scores Representing the Effect for Treatment	109.57	110.23	

[1] In a crossed factorial design, the smallest number of groups, 4, arises from a 2 × 2 design (2 × 2 = 4 groups).

[2] The main effect in a two-way ANOVA is not the same as the between-group effect in a one-way ANOVA, ignoring the other independent variable. The within-group error term for the one-way ANOVA will include variation due to the main effect of the ignored second variable and the interaction effect of the two independent variables. One of the values of the two-way ANOVA is that the systematic variation of scores between subjects due to a second independent variable can be isolated and so removed from the error term.

are calculated by ignoring the treatment factor; they are based on 2 (treatment groups) × 5 (subjects within a cell) = 10 scores. Again, they can be compared without bias because in each case, the same number of scores from both the experimental and control groups enters into the calculation. Finally, the differences between the means are reasonably small (range = 4.9 points). A one-way ANOVA could be run to test the differences between these six means statistically.

Finally, the main body of the table contains information about the effects of combinations of grade level and treatment. Notice that the highest mean scores occur in only 3 of the 12 cells of the design. The greatest expectancy advantage occurs with first and second graders, and the reverse occurs with fifth graders in the control group. The data in the cells of the design, then, suggest that the expectancy effect may occur at certain grade levels (1 and 2), does not occur at other grade levels (3 and 4), and reverses itself at other grade levels (5 and 6).

Often the question is asked, "Why not run two separate one-way research studies testing each factor separately instead of using a factorial design?" There are three good reasons. The first reason is economy of time and resources. The second, more important reason is that more information is gained from the factorial design than from the combination of two one-way designs. For example, if the expectancy study had been conducted as two separate one-way designs, information about the effects of treatment and grade level would be obtained, but information would not have been obtained about certain combinations where the largest differences between means arose. A major benefit of the factorial design over several one-way designs, then, is that factorial designs test three hypotheses—one for each of the two independent variables and one for the combination of the two independent variables—whereas separate one-way designs only test hypotheses about the main effect of each independent variable. The third, equally important reason is that the error variance will be more precisely estimated in a factorial design than in a one-way design. For example, systematic variation of subjects' scores within a cell of a one-way design might be due to, say, differences in subjects' knowledge, in addition to other, unidentified sources of variations. If we treat "level of knowledge" as a second factor in a factorial design, this systematic variation can be removed from the variation within groups. In this way, a more precise estimate of unsystematic variation—error—can be obtained in the factorial design.

In summary, the two-way ANOVA tests three hypotheses statistically. One hypothesis refers to the main effect for the first variable, another to the main effect for the second variable, and the third to the unique effect of certain levels of one variable paired with certain levels of the other variable.

This last hypothesis is called an interaction hypothesis. It is viewed as a *unique* effect because it cannot be predicted from knowedge of the main effect for factor 1 or for factor 2. Perhaps an analogy will help explain this concept. Knowing the properties of hydrogen and oxygen allows us to predict that they will combine (can be "crossed" in factorial fashion), but it does not permit us to predict all of the properties that, when they are combined, we will get with water. Knowing the properties of sodium and chlorine allows us to predict that they will combine, but it does not allow us to predict all of the properties that, when they are combined, we will get with salt. Finally, knowing that there is no effect due to treatment in the study of teacher expectancy and, at best, there is a weak effect due to grade level does not allow us to predict that the expectancy effect will operate as hypothesized at certain grade levels (1 and 2) and not at others (5 and 6).

Often, in order to examine the interaction hypothesis, we present the data from a study in a graph. The mean values on the dependent variable are identified on the ordinate of the graph, and one of the two independent variables is identified on the abscissa. If one of the two independent variables is an individual-difference variable, it is identified on the abscissa. If both are individual-difference variables, either may be placed on the abscissa. Finally, the remaining independent variable is represented as two or more lines on the graph (depending on the number of levels of that variable).

Figure 14-2 presents a graph of the data from the expectancy study. The means from the main body (cells) of Table 14-1 are plotted, with one line representing the control group and the other line representing the experimental group. From this figure, it is clear that there is an interaction effect:

1. A large difference between means in favor of the experimental group occurs at grades 1 and 2.
2. A very small difference occurs at grades 3 and 4.
3. A moderate difference in favor of the control group occurs at grades 5 and 6.

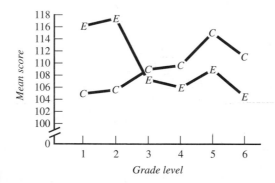

FIGURE 14-2

Interaction between treatment and grade level in the study on teacher expectancy (data from Table 14-1)

In general, interactions can take on several visual representations when graphed. Some examples are shown in Figure 14-3. A **disordinal interaction** occurs when the lines in a graph cross (see Figures 14-2 and 14-3a). A disordinal interaction indicates that the effects of the levels of one factor (e.g., factor B) reverse themselves as the levels of the other factor (e.g., factor A) change. For example, at level a_1 in Figure 14-3a, the mean of the group receiving level b_2 is considerably higher than the mean of the group receiving level b_1. However, this pattern is reversed at level a_2. At a_2, the mean of the group receiving level b_1 is higher than the mean of the group receiving level b_2.

An **ordinal interaction** occurs when the lines on the graph are not parallel and they do not cross (Figures 14-3b, c). This pattern suggests a greater difference between groups at one level of a factor than at the other level of the same factor. For example, in Figure

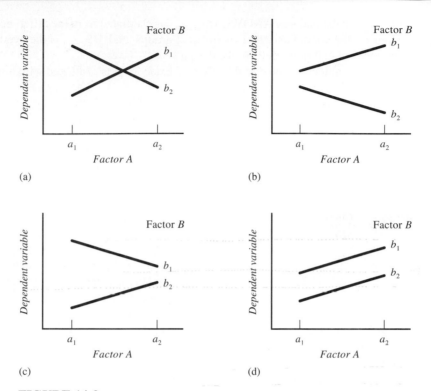

FIGURE 14-3
Some examples of graphs displaying disordinal, ordinal, and no interactions: (a) disordinal interaction; (b) ordinal interaction; (c) ordinal interaction; (d) no interaction

14-3b, the difference between means at level a_1 (group a_1b_1 versus a_1b_2) is quite small. However, at level a_2, the difference between the means (group a_2b_1 versus a_2b_2) is quite large.

Finally, parallel lines on such a graph (Figure 14-3d) indicate the absence of an interaction. This pattern suggests a similar pattern of means on one factor at each level of the other factor. For example, in Figure 14-3d, the means for levels b_1 and b_2 show a similar pattern at a_1 and a_2. In both cases, the means of groups receiving level b_1 are higher than the means of groups receiving b_2.

Underlying Logic.   The statistical rationale underlying the two-way ANOVA is similar to that of the one-way ANOVA (see Chapter 13 for a full discussion). The two main-effect hypotheses and the interaction hypothesis in a two-way design are independent of one another, and so a separate F test is conducted for each of them. Thus, in the study of teacher expectancy, one hypothesis refers to the effect of the treatment (i.e., experimental versus control) and an F test would be conducted as follows:

$$F = \frac{MS_{\text{treatment}}}{MS_{\text{within}}}$$

Just as with the one-way ANOVA, $MS_{\text{treatment}}$ is estimated from the differences between the means of the control and the experimental groups, and MS_{within} is the average within-cell variance over all of the cells in the design.

The hypothesis related to the effect of grade level is evaluated with a second F test:

$$F = \frac{MS_{\text{grade level}}}{MS_{\text{within}}}$$

The $MS_{\text{grade level}}$ is estimated from the differences between the six row means in Table 14-1, and MS_{within} is the same as defined before.

Finally, the interaction hypothesis is tested with a third F test:

$$F = \frac{MS_{\text{interaction}}}{MS_{\text{within}}}$$

The $MS_{\text{interaction}}$ is estimated from the pattern of the differences between the 12 means in the main body of Table 14-1, and MS_{within} is again the same as defined before.

Each of the three F tests test the null hypothesis that there are no effects. For example, under the null hypothesis of no expectancy effect, the difference between the means of the experimental and control groups is hypothesized to arise by chance. In this case, the variance due to treatment ($MS_{\text{treatment}}$) is assumed to represent an independent sample of error variability.

In presenting the results of the two-way ANOVA, we use an ANOVA source table (see Table 14-2). As with the one-way ANOVA, the sources of variation in the dependent variable are identified. However, in the case of the two-way ANOVA, there are three sources of between-group variation, not just one source, as in the one-way ANOVA. These three sources correspond to each of the three independent hypotheses tested: main effect for A, main effect for B, and interaction of A and B. Finally, the fourth source of variability is within-group (error) variability.

For each of the four sources of variation, the corresponding sums of squares, degrees of freedom, and mean squares are presented. And a separate F test is conducted for each of the three independent hypotheses.

Finally, the value of F_{observed} for each hypothesis can be compared with its corresponding value of F_{critical} in order to decide whether to reject the null hypothesis. The value

TABLE 14-2 Source table for the two-way ANOVA (data taken from the study of teacher expectancy)

Source of Variation	Sum of Squares	df	MS	F_{observed}
Treatment (A)	6.67	1	6.67	.082
Grade level (B)	212.40	5	42.48	.525
Treatment × grade level ($A \times B$)	884.32	5	176.86	2.185
Within-group (error)	3885.97	48	80.96	

of $F_{critical}$ depends on the degrees of freedom for each source of variation in the F test and the level of significance (α). If $F_{observed}$ exceeds $F_{critical}$, we conclude that the difference between means did not arise from sampling error but, rather, from a treatment effect. Of course, we could be wrong, as indicated by the probability of a Type I error, α. In Table 14-2, three hypotheses are tested, one with 1 and 48 df and two with 5 and 48 df. The value of $F_{critical}$ for 1 and 48 df is (approximately) 4.04, and for 5 and 48 df, it is (approximately) 2.41. By comparing $F_{observed}$ with $F_{critical,}$ we conclude that there is no main effect due to treatment or grade level and no effect due to the interaction of treatment and grade level. However, the results in Table 14-2 suggest the possibility of an interaction, which might be examined in future research with a larger sample of subjects.

Design Requirements

The use of the two-way ANOVA presupposes that the data have been collected as follows:

1. There are two independent variables, each with two or more levels. In this chapter, the two variables are assumed to be completely crossed. For now, assume that the levels of the two independent variables exhaust the possible levels of interest to the researcher (fixed-effect ANOVA).
2. The levels of the independent variables may differ either qualitatively or quantitatively. The distinction between "bloomers" and controls in the teacher expectancy study is an example of a qualitative difference. The distinction between grade levels is an example of a quantitative difference.
3. A subject may appear in one and only one cell of the design, and the subject represents a random sample from the population defined by that cell (e.g., fourth-grade "bloomers").

Hypotheses

The two-way ANOVA is used to test three hypotheses. Two of these hypotheses refer to the main effects of factor A and factor B, and the third refers to the interaction effect of factors A and B. For factor A with q levels, the null hypothesis is:

$$H_0: \mu_1 = \mu_2 = \cdots = \mu_i = \cdots = \mu_q \quad \text{or} \quad H_0: \mu_i = \mu_G \quad \text{for all } i$$

The null hypothesis states that in the population, the means for all of the levels of factor A are equal. The notation μ_i refers to the mean at any unidentified level of factor A, and μ_G refers to the grand mean. The alternative hypothesis is:

$$H_1: \mu_i \neq \mu_{i'} \quad \text{for some } i \text{ and } i'$$

This hypothesis states that at least some distinct pair of means (μ_i and $\mu_{i'}$) differ from one another in the population.

A similar interpretation can be given to the null and alternative hypotheses for factor B with r levels:

$$H_0: \mu_1 = \mu_2 = \cdots = \mu_j = \cdots = \mu_r \quad \text{or} \quad H_0: \mu_j = \mu_G \quad \text{for all } j$$
$$H_1: \mu_j \neq \mu_{j'} \quad \text{for some } j \text{ and } j'$$

In this case, j refers to any unidentified level of the B factor, and μ_j and $\mu_{j'}$ represent a distinct pair of means.

Intuitively, it would seem as if the null and alternative hypotheses for the interaction should be written in a manner similar to the hypotheses for main effects using the cell means. However, they are not, because the cell means reflect not only the interaction effect, but also the effects of factors A and B if one or both exist. Since the interaction provides information about the unique effect of the combination of the levels of factor A with the levels of factor B, the main effects of A and B have to be removed from the cell means. In order to avoid the cumbersome notation showing the effects of A and B removed from the cell means, we will write the interaction hypotheses as:

H_0: interaction effect $= 0$

H_1: interaction effect $\neq 0$

By testing each of these hypotheses, we can make a decision about the null hypothesis for each effect. That is, the two-way ANOVA indicates whether there is an effect due to factor A, factor B, and the interaction of A and B. However, if there are, for example, more than two levels of factor A, it will not indicate which treatment means are significantly different from each other. Likewise, if there is a significant interaction effect, the overall F test of the interaction will not indicate where it lies. In order to determine specific differences, we must make comparisons between means, using procedures such as Scheffé's or Tukey's method, just as we did with the one-way ANOVA.

Assumptions

Three assumptions are made in using the sampling distribution of F to test each of the three hypotheses in the two-way, fixed-effect ANOVA:

1. *Independence:* The score for any particular subject is independent of the scores of all other subjects—that is, it provides a unique piece of information about the effect.
2. *Normality:* The scores within each cell of the design are drawn from a population in which scores are normally distributed. Put another way, the scores in a particular cell of the design are assumed to be sampled from a population of scores that is normal in form.
3. *Homogeneity of variances:* The variances of scores in the populations underlying all the cells of the design are equal.

These assumptions are the same as those underlying the t test with two independent groups. Methods for examining these assumptions are given in Chapter 12.

The two-way ANOVA is not sensitive to the violation of the assumption of normality. When cell sizes are equal, the ANOVA is also not sensitive to violations of the assumption of homogeneity of variances.

Computation of the Two-Way ANOVA

In the one-way ANOVA, the total variability between scores was partitioned into two independent sources of variability, within-group variability and between-group variability (Formula 13-3):

total variability = variability between groups + variability within groups (error)

In a similar manner, the total variability between scores in the two-way ANOVA is partitioned into four sources of variability—the effects of factor A, of factor B, of the interaction of A and B, and the variability within groups or error:

total variability = variability due to factor A

+ variability due to factor B

+ variability due to interaction $(A \times B)$

+ variability within groups (error)   **(14-1)**

As with the one-way ANOVA, in the two-way ANOVA, we work with sums of squares instead of variances (mean squares) when the computations are carried out. Then, once the computations are completed, the sums of squares are divided by their respective degrees of freedom in order to get mean squares or variances. Finally, $F_{observed}$ is calculated for each of the three effects by dividing the variability for each effect by the within-group variance.

Table 14-3a gives the deviation score formulas for calculating the sums of squares in the two-way ANOVA. The procedure for computing the two-way ANOVA with raw-score formulas is presented in the *Study Guide*. From now on, due to the complexity of the computational procedures, the textbook will focus on conceptual formulas and interpretations and the computational procedures may be found in the *Guide*.

In describing the formulas in Table 14-3a, let's use the design and data shown in Table 14-3b. Suppose that the hypothetical data are taken from a study of the effects of certain instructional treatments on the reading comprehension of subjects classified as low or high in verbal ability. Specifically, the experimenter provided three different versions of text material to the subjects. In one version, factual questions were inserted after every four paragraphs, and subjects were asked to answer the questions as they read. A second version of the text contained questions after every four paragraphs that tested comprehension of the material. The third version did not contain questions (control group). Twelve college sophomores were divided into groups of low and high verbal ability and then randomly assigned to one of the three text groups so that there were two subjects per cell (to keep the example simple). This experiment, then, is a 2×3 (verbal ability × question type) design. After reading the text material, subjects took an achievement test. (See Table 14-3b for the results of this test.)

Now let's look at the formulas in Table 14-3a. First, notation. A person's score is denoted by X_{pij}, with p representing a particular person $(p = 1, \ldots, n)$, i a particular level of factor A $(i = 1, \ldots, q)$, and j a particular level of factor B $(j = 1, \ldots, r)$. A cell mean—scores averaged over persons in a cell—is $\bar{X}_{ij}$, where the dot (.) shows the average is over all (n) persons in the cell. Similarly, a row mean representing the effect of factor A is averaged over persons and levels of factor B: $\bar{X}_{i.}$, where the dots show that the average is over persons within a cell and over levels of factor B. And $\bar{X}_{.j}$—a column mean—is the mean over persons and levels of factor A.

As can be seen from Table 14-3a, the sum of squares for factor A is simply the sum of the squared deviations of each row mean from the grand mean. The term, $n_j [(n)(r)]$, multiplying the sum is the number of scores averaged to obtain $\bar{X}_{i.}$. Sum of squares B is the sum

TABLE 14-3 Sums of squares deviation-score formulas for the two-way ANOVA with a hypothetical 2×3 reading comprehension design

(a)

Source	Sums of Squares Formula	
Factor A	$n_j \sum_{i=1}^{q} (\bar{X}_{.i.} - \bar{X}_G)^2$	**(14-2)**
Factor B	$n_i \sum_{j=1}^{r} (\bar{X}_{..j} - \bar{X}_G)^2$	**(14-3)**
Interaction (A $\times$ B)	$n \sum_{i=1}^{q} \sum_{j=1}^{r} (\bar{X}_{.ij} - \bar{X}_{.i.} - \bar{X}_{..j} + \bar{X}_G)^2$	**(14-4)**
Within Group (error)	$\sum_{i=1}^{q} \sum_{j=1}^{r} \sum_{p=1}^{n} (\bar{X}_{pij} - \bar{X}_{.ij})^2$	**(14-5)**

(b)

Verbal Ability (A)	Question Type (B)			Row Mean
	b_1 Control	b_2 Factual	b_3 Comprehension	
a_1 **Low**	1	1	7	
	2	2	8	
	$\bar{X} = 1.5$	$\bar{X} = 1.5$	$\bar{X} = 7.5$	3.50
a_2 **High**	8	3	3	
	9	4	4	
	$\bar{X} = 8.5$	$\bar{X} = 3.5$	$\bar{X} = 3.5$	5.17
Column Mean	5.00	2.50	5.50	

of the squared deviations of each column mean from the grand mean. Again, n_i is the number of scores averaged to obtain $\bar{X}_{.j}$. The sum of squares interaction shows that the effects of factors A and B are removed.[3] Finally, the error term is the sum of the squared deviations of each score from its respective cell mean, summed over all cells.

Now let's take a look at Table 14-3b to get some idea of what the effects were in the hypothetical reading comprehension study. First, factor A: Verbal Ability. As expected, subjects high in verbal ability scored higher than subjects low in verbal ability, on average (5.17

---

[3]To see this, some additional information is needed. The interaction effect is the unique effect of factors A and B together, after the effect of each factor is removed. An effect is defined as a deviation between a mean and the grand mean. The effect of factor A is defined as $\bar{X}_i - \bar{X}_G$ and the effect of factor B is defined as $\bar{X}_j - \bar{X}_G$. The interaction effect is defined as

$$\bar{X}_{.ij} - (\bar{X}_{.i.} - \bar{X}_G) - (\bar{X}_{..j} - \bar{X}_G) - \bar{X}_G = \bar{X}_{.ij} - \bar{X}_{.i.} + \bar{X}_G - \bar{X}_{..j} + \bar{X}_G - \bar{X}_G$$
$$= \bar{X}_{.ij} - \bar{X}_{.i.} - \bar{X}_{..j} + \bar{X}_G + \bar{X}_G - \bar{X}_G$$
$$= \bar{X}_{.ij} - \bar{X}_{.i.} - \bar{X}_{..j} + \bar{X}_G$$

versus 3.50, respectively). Second, factor B: Question Type. Subjects in the control group and comprehension group tended to earn higher scores, on average, than did subjects in the factual group (5.00 and 5.50 versus 2.50). Third, the interaction: Ability × Question Type. Low-ability subjects profited most from the comprehension questions and high-ability subjects profited most from the test without questions. (Compare the pattern of cell means to get a sense of the interaction.) Finally, the variability of scores within each cell is the same, and this variability is quite small.

The pattern of results in the two-way ANOVA should reflect these descriptive data. For verification of these results, the sums of squares calculated with the formulas in Table 14-3a can be entered into an ANOVA summary table and the three F ratios can be calculated with the formulas in Table 14-4. The first column of this source table enumerates the sources of variation in the experiment. The second column contains the sums of squares. Note that the sums of squares total (SS_T) can be used as a computational check, according to Formula 14-6.

TABLE 14-4 Formulas used in completing the source table for the two-way ANOVA

Source of Variation	Sums of Squares[a]	df[b]	Mean Square	$F_{observed}$
Factor A	SS_A (Formula 14-2)	$df_A = q - 1$	$\dfrac{SS_A}{df_A}$	$F_A = \dfrac{MS_A}{MS_W}$
Factor B	SS_B (Formula 14-3)	$df_B = r - 1$	$\dfrac{SS_B}{df_B}$	$F_B = \dfrac{MS_B}{MS_W}$
Interaction of factors A and B	SS_{AB} (Formula 14-4)	$df_{AB} = (q-1)(r-1)$	$\dfrac{SS_{AB}}{df_{AB}}$	$F_{AB} = \dfrac{MS_{AB}}{MS_W}$
Within group (error)	SS_W (Formula 14-5)	$df_W = qr(n-1)$	$\dfrac{SS_W}{df_W}$	
Total	SS_T (Formula 14-6)	$df_T = qrn - 1$		

[a] Formulas are in Table 14-3a.
[b] n is the number of subjects in a cell; q is the number of levels of factor A; r is the number of levels of factor B.

$$SS_T = SS_A + SS_B + SS_{AB} + SS_W \qquad\qquad (14\text{-}6)$$

The third column of the table gives the formulas for finding the degrees of freedom associated with each source of variation. Note that, like the sums of squares, the degrees of freedom for each source of variation are additive, so df_T can be used as a computational check (see Formula 14-7).

$$df_T = df_A + df_B + df_{AB} + df_W \qquad\qquad\qquad \textbf{(14-7)}$$

The fourth column gives the formulas for calculating mean squares, and the fifth column gives the formulas for calculating F_{observed}.

The results of the two-way ANOVA for the data from the comprehension study are presented in Table 14-5. These results are consistent with our eyeball analysis of the descriptive data.

TABLE 14-5 ANOVA summary table: Results of the study of comprehension from prose material

Source of Variation	Sum of Squares	df	Mean Squares	$F_{observed}$[a]
Verbal ability (A)	8.34	1	8.34	16.68
Question type (B)	20.67	2	10.34	20.67
$A \times B$	60.66	2	30.33	60.66
Within group (error)	3.00	6	.50	
Total	92.67	11		

[a] $F_{\text{crit.}(\alpha=.05, df=1,6)} = 5.99$, $F_{\text{crit.}(\alpha=.05, df=2,6)} = 5.14$; $p < .05$.

Decision Rules for Rejecting the Null Hypothesis

In order to determine whether to reject the null hypothesis for each of the three hypotheses tested by the two-way ANOVA, we must compare F_{observed} with F_{critical}. Furthermore, since F_{critical} depends on the degrees of freedom associated with each effect and the error term, there will be different values of F_{critical} for different pairs of degrees of freedom. In order to find the value of F_{critical} in Table E, we need to know three pieces of information: α, df_{effect}, and df_{error}. For the data from the hypothetical study of comprehension from prose material (Table 14-5), two critical values of F are needed, since there are two different pairs of degrees of freedom: 1 and 6, and 2 and 6. If α is .05, the values of F_{critical} are:

$$F_{\text{critical}(.05,1,6)} = 5.99$$
$$F_{\text{critical}(.05,2,6)} = 5.14$$

Since F_{observed} in each case exceeds its corresponding value of F_{critical}, the null hypothesis for factors A and B and the interaction should be rejected. There is a significant effect due to A, B, and AB.

Interpretation of the Results of the Two-Way ANOVA

In interpreting the results of the two-way ANOVA, we start with the interaction effect and work upward. The rationale for doing so is as follows: An interaction effect implies that certain combinations of the levels of factors A and B have different effects than do other combinations. Thus the effect of factor *A* may depend on the level of factor *B* with which it is combined. Similarly, the effect of factor *B* may depend on the level of factor *A* with which it is combined. For example, the data from the reading study show that there is *no best* treatment (b_1 vs. b_2 vs. b_3). Rather, the effects of treatments depend on the verbal ability of the subject. Thus the effect of factor *B* (treatment) depends on the level of factor *A* (ability) with which it is combined. In short, the existence of a significant interaction in the data means the main effects of factors *A* and *B* must be qualified. One level of factor *A* does not always produce the "best" results, nor does one particular level of factor *B*. The effects of factors *A* and *B* depend on each other.

When we interpret a significant interaction such as the one shown in Tables 14-3 and 14-5, the first step is to plot the interaction. (The steps in plotting an interaction are given in Procedure 14-2 in the *Student Guide,* using data from the comprehension study.) The completed graph of this interaction is shown in Figure 14-4. This graph shows that subjects low in verbal ability benefited most from the comprehension treatment and least from either the factual or the control treatment. Subjects high in verbal ability benefited most from the control treatment and least from either the factual or the comprehension treatment. The graph shows clearly that both the main effects for factor *A* (ability) and factor *B* (treatment) must be qualified. Subjects high in verbal ability do not always have the highest performance. And one treatment does not always produce the highest performance. The effect of ability depends on what treatment the person received, and the effect of treatment depends on the verbal ability of the subject.

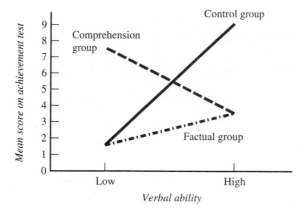

FIGURE 14-4
Graph of verbal ability × question type interaction

Example Problem 14.1

In the hypothetical study of the determinants of emotion (after Schacter & Singer's study, 1962), two theories were compared. The physiological-state theory asserted that emotion is the feeling accompanying a physiological state of arousal and that different physiological states (e.g., heart rate, numbness) led to different emotional states. The two-component theory asserted that emotion was produced by general physiological arousal and by cognitive factors involved in identifying, labeling, and interpreting a stirred-up physiological state. (For an update on this classic experiment, see Sinclair et al., 1994.)

For an examination of these two theories, a hypothetical experiment was conducted, using a 2×4 design. The factor with two levels is the situation in which subjects find themselves (euphoria versus anger). The physiological-state theory does not implicate this variable, but the two-component theory asserts that subjects will interpret (i.e., identify, label, and interpret) heightened physiological arousal with respect to the situation if no other explanation is readily available. The four-level factor combines ingesting a drug such as epinephrine (adrenaline) or a placebo[4] and being given an accurate explanation of what to expect (e.g., increased heart and respiration rates), an inaccurate explanation (numbness and itching), or no explanation (see Table 14-6). Subjects rated their feelings on a scale from 0 (angry) to 8 (happy).

The physiological-state theory asserts that subjects will experience the same emotion in all three drug conditions and that subjects in the placebo condition will not experience emotion. In contrast, the two-component theory predicts differences in emotion in the three drug conditions. In the condition "drug + accurate explanation," the theory asserts that situational factors should play a minor role in determining emotion; but in the other two drug conditions, situational factors should play an important role. Hence, the two-component model posits an interaction between treatment and situation.

TABLE 14-6   Hypothetical data for the study
on the determinants of emotion

	Situation	
Treatment	*Euphoria*	*Angry*
Drug + Accurate	5	2
Explanation	4	3
	6	2
	5	1
Drug + Inaccurate	6	1
Explanation	7	1
	5	0
	6	2
Drug + No	6	2
Explanation	7	3
	5	2
	5	3
Placebo	4	4
	4	4
	4	3
	6	3

Note: Scores refer to subjects' ratings of their feelings on a scale from 0 (angry) to 8 (happy).

---

[4]Clearly, ethical issues arise when drugs are given to human subjects in experiments. We assume that all subjects gave their informed consent prior to the study; that the potential benefits of this study far outweigh the potential harm to a subject; and that subjects were screened by a physician before being permitted to participate. In addition, we assume that subjects are not necessarily aware that this particular study is the one in which, with their informed consent, their state of physiological arousal is being influenced. Again, we assume that the potential benefits of the study outweigh this risk of deception.

Using these data, test whether there were significant main effects for treatment and situation and whether there was a significant interaction effect at $\alpha = .05$. Include the following items in your answer.

a. Null and alternative hypotheses for each effect
b. Tests of assumptions or explanation for not testing
c. Computation of sums of squares
d. ANOVA summary table
e. $F_{critical}$ for each effect
f. Conclusions for each effect
g. A graph of the interaction

In order to be sure that this interpretation of the effects of the interaction in terms of differences between all means is accurate (and does not depend on chance), we should conduct post hoc comparisons of means. The methods for conducting these tests are described in a later section of this chapter.

If, however, there is no interaction effect, then it is appropriate to interpret the main effects. Suppose a study was conducted to determine the effects of motivation level and treatment on performance. The results showed no interaction effect. In this case, statements such as the following can be made: "The experimental treatment produced a significantly greater effect than the control treatment (factor *A*), regardless of the motivation level of the subjects (factor *B*)." Or "Subjects randomly assigned to the high-motivation treatment (*B*) performed significantly better than did subjects assigned to the low-motivation treatment, regardless of whether they were in the experimental or control groups (*A*)."

In the interpretation of the main effects of factors with only two levels, a significant overall *F* for those factors indicates that the difference between the two means corresponding to the two levels is significant. In this case, a post hoc comparison is unnecessary. In the interpretation of the main effects of factors with three or more levels, a significant overall *F* indicates that there is at least one significant difference between the means corresponding to the levels of the factor. In this case, additional post hoc analyses must be conducted.

FIXED, RANDOM, AND MIXED MODELS

To this point, we have developed the factorial ANOVA with fixed effects. The levels of factors *A* and *B* are fixed; they exhaust all possible levels of the two independent variables. The researcher intends to draw inferences only to those levels observed in the experiment.

In contrast, consider an experiment that examines the structural equivalence of science passages in textbooks. Four *randomly* selected science experts judged the structural equivalence of two *randomly* selected passages from each of three *randomly* selected textbooks. The researcher included different experts because of a concern that not all experts would agree on the structural equivalence of textbook passages with a normative model of science passages. Experts were randomly sampled because the researcher intended to generalize the findings to all such experts. Textbooks were selected randomly because the researcher intended to generalize the findings to the entire population of science textbooks. Finally, passages were randomly selected as representative of the population of the text's passages. Passages are the "subjects" in this study; each was rated for its structural equivalence to the normative passage. The result is a 4×3 (expert $\times$ textbook) design. Both experts (factor A) and textbooks (factor B) are random factors. This design is shown schematically in Table 14-7. A *random-effects* ANOVA was used to analyze the experts' ratings of passages.

Suppose, instead, that although experts are sampled randomly, the researcher systematically selects textbooks. (Perhaps those three textbooks were more widely used than any others.) In this case, experts constitute a random factor, but *textbooks* represent a *fixed* factor. Factorial designs with one (or more) random factor(s) and one (or more) fixed factor(s) are analyzed with the *mixed-model ANOVA*. With this mixed model, the researcher intends to draw inferences about the structural equivalence of science passages rated by all possible science experts in just these three textbooks. The experiment will tell the researcher nothing about the structural equivalence of passages in other texts.

TABLE 14-7 Expert $\times$ textbook experiment with two passages (P) per cell[a]

Expert	Textbook		
	1	**2**	**3**
1	P_1	P_3	P_5
	P_2	P_4	P_6
2	P_7	P_9	P_{11}
	P_8	P_{10}	P_{12}
3	P_{13}	P_{15}	P_{17}
	P_{14}	P_{16}	P_{18}
4	P_{19}	P_{21}	P_{23}
	P_{20}	P_{22}	P_{24}

[a]Both experts and textbooks were randomly selected.

It turns out that random- and mixed-effects ANOVAs differ from the fixed-effects ANOVA in the hypotheses tested, the nature of the F test, and the inferences drawn from the test. Here we briefly present the important features of random- and mixed-effects, two-way ANOVAs for hypothesis testing. (Before proceeding, you may find a review of the section "Fixed- and Random-Effects ANOVA" in Chapter 13 helpful.)

The Random-Effects Model

Computationally, the random-effects factorial ANOVA is the same as the fixed-effects factorial ANOVA. Sum of squares, degrees of freedom, and mean squares are computed in the same way. However, for hypothesis-testing purposes, the F ratios are calculated differently. A comparison of the F ratios for the fixed-effects ANOVA and the random-effects ANOVA is given in Table 14-8.

Design Requirements.   The design requirements for the random-effects factorial ANOVA are similar to those for the fixed-effects factorial ANOVA, except that the levels of factors A and B are randomly sampled from their respective populations.

TABLE 14-8 F ratios for the fixed- and random-effects models

F	Fixed Effects	Random Effects
$A =$	$\dfrac{MS_A}{MS_W}$	$\dfrac{MS_A}{MS_{AB}}$
$B =$	$\dfrac{MS_B}{MS_W}$	$\dfrac{MS_B}{MS_{AB}}$
$AB =$	$\dfrac{MS_{AB}}{MS_W}$	$\dfrac{MS_{AB}}{MS_W}$

Hypotheses.   The *hypotheses* tested with the random-effects factorial ANOVA reflect the fact that the researcher wishes to generalize beyond the observed levels of factors A and B to all possible levels of A and B. The hypotheses tested, then, are not directly about means, as in the fixed-effects factorial ANOVA, but about the *variance* among treatment means in the population (see Table 14-9). The rationale for testing hypotheses about variances among population means goes like this. In a random-effects design, the levels of the independent variables that are observed in one application of the design will differ from the levels observed in the next application due to random sampling. Hence, the particular sample means in one application of the design are, in and of themselves, of little interest beyond providing a picture into the variability among population means. Another application of the random-effects design would produce a sample with different levels of the independent variables. The variance among sample means, then, provides an estimate of just how different the population means are (i.e., the variance among population means) and how different we should expect them to be on the next application of the design.

TABLE 14-9 Hypotheses for the fixed- and random-effects models

Effect	Fixed Effects	Random Effects
A	$H_0: \mu_i - \mu_G = 0$ for all i $H_1: \mu_i - \mu_G \neq 0$ for some i	$H_0: \sigma_A^2 = 0$ $H_1: \sigma_A^2 \neq 0$
B	$H_0: \mu_j - \mu_G = 0$ for all j $H_1: \mu_j - \mu_G \neq 0$ for some j	$H_0: \sigma_B^2 = 0$ $H_1: \sigma_B^2 \neq 0$
AB	$H_0:$ interaction effect $= 0$ $H_1:$ interaction effect $\neq 0$	$H_0: \sigma_{AB}^2 = 0$ $H_1: \sigma_{AB}^2 \neq 0$

Assumptions.   The following assumptions are made in carrying out statistical tests with the random-effects factorial ANOVA:

1. The effects of factor A are normally distributed with mean zero and variance σ_A^2.

2. The effects of factor B are normally distributed with mean zero and variance σ_B^2.
3. Each interaction (cell) effect has a normal distribution with mean zero and variance σ_{AB}^2.
4. The errors are normally distributed with mean zero and variance σ_e^2.
5. The effects of factors A and B, their interaction, and errors are pairwise independent.

For reasonably large sample sizes, departures from the assumption of normality among the error distributions have only minor effects on hypothesis testing. As long as assumption 5 holds, theoretically, we need not be concerned about the assumption of homogeneity of errors. Independence, of course, is always important.

TABLE 14-10   Random-effects ANOVA for the expert ×
textbook design

Source	Sum of Squares	df	Mean Square	F
Experts (A)	60	3	20	$\frac{20}{4} = 5.00^a$
Textbook (B)	12	2	6	$\frac{6}{4} = 1.50$
$A \times B$	24	6	4	$\frac{4}{3} = 1.33$
Within (error)	18	6	3	

$^a p < .05.$

Interpretation.   The results of the random-effects expert × textbook ANOVA are presented in Table 14-10. We interpret the findings to indicate that the mean ratings of passages by experts differ in the population. Some experts are more "lenient" than others in judging structural equivalence. In the population, textbooks do not differ in the mean structural equivalence of their passages. And mean ratings of each combination of expert and textbook do not differ significantly in the population after the main effect for experts is accounted for. Put another way, regardless of expert, textbook means are ordered in the same way (i.e., textbook 1 is more similar than 2 to the normative passage structure, and 2 is more similar than 3).

The Mixed-Effects Model

The *mixed-effects* ANOVA is, as its name implies, a combination or mixture of the fixed- and random-effects ANOVA. It has one (or more) fixed factor(s) and one (or more) random factor(s). In the example (expert × textbook) design, if the textbooks were chosen because they are used most widely, textbook would be a fixed factor, and experts would remain a random factor. In this case, the expert × textbook design would constitute a mixed model, and the mixed-effects ANOVA should be used to analyze the data on the structural equivalence of science passages.

TABLE 14-11 *F* ratios for fixed-, random-, and mixed-effects models

F	*Fixed Effects* A Fixed B Fixed	*Random Effects* A Random B Random	*Mixed Effects* A Fixed B Random	A Random B Fixed
A	$\dfrac{MS_A}{MS_W}$	$\dfrac{MS_A}{MS_{AB}}$	$\dfrac{MS_A}{MS_{AB}}$	$\dfrac{MS_A}{MS_W}$
B	$\dfrac{MS_B}{MS_W}$	$\dfrac{MS_B}{MS_{AB}}$	$\dfrac{MS_B}{MS_W}$	$\dfrac{MS_B}{MS_{AB}}$
AB	$\dfrac{MS_{AB}}{MS_W}$	$\dfrac{MS_{AB}}{MS_W}$	$\dfrac{MS_{AB}}{MS_W}$	$\dfrac{MS_{AB}}{MS_W}$

Computationally, the mixed-effects ANOVA is the same as the fixed-effects factorial ANOVA. However, for hypothesis-testing purposes, the *F* ratios are calculated somewhat differently from either the fixed-effects or random-effects ANOVAs. As might be expected, certain *F* ratios are the same as *F* ratios for the fixed-effects ANOVA, and others are the same as *F* ratios for the random-effects ANOVA. The *F* ratio depends on whether factor *A* or *B* is random; see Table 14-11. Additionally, the interpretation of the results of a mixed-model ANOVA differs somewhat from the interpretation of either the fixed- or random-effects ANOVA.

Design Requirements.   The design requirements for the mixed-model ANOVA are similar to those for the fixed-effects, two-way ANOVA, except that the levels of one factor are randomly sampled.

Hypotheses.   The null and alternative hypotheses tested with the mixed-model ANOVA are, not surprisingly, a mixture of the hypotheses tested with the fixed- and random-effects models. These hypotheses are set forth in Table 14-12.

TABLE 14-12 Hypotheses for the mixed model

Effect	*A Fixed (a)* B Random (B)	*A Random (A)* B Fixed (b)
A	$H_0: \mu_i - \mu_G = 0$ for all i $H_1: \mu_i - \mu_G \neq 0$ for some i	$H_0: \sigma_A^2 = 0$ $H_1: \sigma_A^2 \neq 0$
B	$H_0: \sigma_B^2 = 0$ $H_1: \sigma_B^2 \neq 0$	$H_0: \mu_j - \mu_G = 0$ for all j $H_1: \mu_j - \mu_G \neq 0$ for some j
AB	$H_0: \sigma_{aB}^2 = 0$ $H_1: \sigma_{aB}^2 \neq 0$	$H_0: \sigma_{Ab}^2 = 0$ $H_1: \sigma_{Ab}^2 \neq 0$

Assumptions. If factor A is fixed and factor B is random, we make the following assumptions:

1. The effect of factor B and the interaction effect are jointly normal, each with mean zero and variance σ_B^2 and σ_{AB}^2, respectively.
2. The errors are normally distributed, with mean zero and variance σ_e^2.
3. The errors are independent of the effect of B and the interaction effect.
4. The errors are independent.

Interpretation.   The results of the experts (random) × textbook (fixed) design are presented in Table 14-13. We interpret these findings to indicate that the mean ratings of passages differ across experts in the population; some experts are more lenient than others in judging equivalence of passage structure. However, the mean structural-equivalence ratings do not differ significantly among textbooks 1, 2, and 3. Finally, the interaction of experts and texts is not statistically significant.

TABLE 14-13   Mixed-effects ANOVA for the expert × textbook design

Source	Sum of Squares	df	Mean Square	F
Experts (A) (random)	60	3	20	$\frac{20}{4} = 5.00^a$
Textbook (B) (fixed)	12	2	6	$\frac{6}{3} = 2.00$
$A \times B$ (random)	24	6	4	$\frac{4}{3} = 1.33$
Within (random error)	18	6	3	

[a] $p < .05.$

STRENGTH OF ASSOCIATION

The overall F test for each hypothesis in the two-way ANOVA indicates whether the observed differences between cell means, column means, and row means were likely to arise by chance. However, the F test does not give information about the *strength* of each effect. As with the one-way ANOVA (Chapter 13), the statistic omega-square ($\hat{\omega}^2$) can be used with fixed-effects designs as an index of the strength of association between the levels of each effect (A, B, and AB) and the dependent variable. For each of the three effects, the numerator of the formula for omega-square is slightly different. See Formulas 14-8a–c.

$$\hat{\omega}_A^2 = \frac{SS_A - (df_A)MS_W}{SS_T + MS_W} \tag{14-8a}$$

$$\hat{\omega}_B^2 = \frac{SS_B - (df_B)MS_W}{SS_T + MS_W} \tag{14-8b}$$

$$\hat{\omega}_{AB}^2 = \frac{SS_{AB} - (df_{AB})MS_W}{SS_T + MS_W} \tag{14-8c}$$

Procedure 13-2 shows the steps in calculating omega-square. Typically, omega-square is calculated only for significant effects in the two-way ANOVA. In the hypothetical study of reading comprehension, all three effects were significant, and the omega-square statistic for each effect can be calculated by using data from Table 14-5:

$$\hat{\omega}_A^2 = \frac{8.34 - (1)(.50)}{92.67 + .50} = \frac{7.84}{93.17} = .08$$

$$\hat{\omega}_B^2 = \frac{20.67 - (2)(.50)}{92.67 + .50} = \frac{19.67}{93.17} = .21$$

$$\hat{\omega}_{AB} = \frac{60.66 - (2)(.50)}{92.67 + .50} = \frac{59.66}{93.17} = .64$$

Clearly, the strongest effect in the data is due to the interaction. The unique interaction effect accounts for 64 percent of the variance in achievement test scores. The treatment effect accounts for 21 percent, and the effect of verbal ability accounts for only 8 percent.

For the *random-effects model,* the **intraclass correlation** ($\hat{\rho}_I$) indexes the strength of association. In a two-factor ANOVA, $\hat{\rho}_I$ can be calculated for the two main effects and their interaction by using Formulas 14-9a–c.

$$\hat{\rho}_{I(A)} = \frac{\hat{\sigma}_A^2}{\hat{\sigma}_A^2 + \hat{\sigma}_B^2 + \hat{\sigma}_{AB}^2 + \hat{\sigma}_e^2} \tag{14-9a}$$

$$\hat{\rho}_{I(B)} = \frac{\hat{\sigma}_B^2}{\hat{\sigma}_A^2 + \hat{\sigma}_B^2 + \hat{\sigma}_{AB}^2 + \hat{\sigma}_e^2} \tag{14-9b}$$

$$\hat{\rho}_{I(AB)} = \frac{\hat{\sigma}_{AB}^2}{\hat{\sigma}_A^2 + \hat{\sigma}_B^2 + \hat{\sigma}_{AB}^2 + \hat{\sigma}_e^2} \tag{14-9c}$$

To use Formulas 14-9a–c, we need estimates of the variance components—σ_A^2, σ_B^2, σ_{AB}^2, and σ_e^2. These estimates can be obtained from Formulas 14-10a–d.

$$\hat{\sigma}_A^2 = \frac{MS_A - MS_{AB}}{nr} \tag{14-10a}$$

$$\hat{\sigma}_B^2 = \frac{MS_B - MS_{AB}}{nq} \qquad\qquad \textbf{(14-10b)}$$

$$\hat{\sigma}_{AB}^2 = \frac{MS_{AB} - MS_W}{n} \qquad\qquad \textbf{(14-10c)}$$

$$\hat{\sigma}_e^2 = MS_W \qquad\qquad \textbf{(14-10d)}$$

To show how Formulas 14-9 and 14-10 are used, let's take the results of the random-effects, expert × textbook experiment in Table 14-10. From the mean squares in this table, the variance components can be calculated as follows:

$$\hat{\sigma}_A^2 = \frac{20 - 4}{2 \times 3} = \frac{16}{6} = 2.67$$

$$\hat{\sigma}_B^2 = \frac{6 - 4}{2 \times 4} = \frac{2}{8} = .25$$

$$\hat{\sigma}_{AB}^2 = \frac{4 - 3}{2} = \frac{1}{2} = .50$$

$$\hat{\sigma}_e^2 = 3.00$$

Since the expert main effect is statistically significant, we calculate the proportion of variance in judgments accounted for by variation among experts:

$$\hat{\rho}_{I(A)} = \frac{2.67}{2.67 + .25 + .50 + 3.00} = \frac{2.67}{6.42} = .42$$

Forty-two percent of the variation in judgments is associated with disagreements among experts in their average ratings. That is, experts vary considerably in their average ratings of the structural equivalence of science passages. Since neither the textbook main effect nor the interaction of experts and textbooks is statistically significant, the intraclass correlation is not calculated for either.

Measures of the strength of association for main and interaction effects in the *mixed-model ANOVA* are more tedious to calculate. A modified version of omega-square is used to calculate the strength of association for the fixed factor. And a modified version of the intraclass correlation is used to calculate the strength of association for the random factor and interaction. Kirk (1982, p. 389) provides these modified formulas.

Example Problem 14.2 ▬▬▬▬▬▬▬▬▬▬▬▬▬▬▬▬▬▬▬▬▬▬▬▬▬▬▬▬

Using the data from Example Problem 14.1, compute the strength of association for the main effects of factor A and factor B and their interaction. Include the following items in your answer.
a. Computation
b. Interpretation

Using the information in Table 14-14, compute the strength of association for a study with factors *A* and *B* random. Include the following items in your answer.

c. Computation
d. Interpretation

TABLE 14-14 ANOVA results for parts c and d

Source	SS	df	MS	F
A	72.00	4	18.00	2.00
B	48.00	2	24.00	2.67
AB	72.00	8	9.00	2.25[a]
Within	540.00	135	4.00	

[a]$p < .05$.

POST HOC METHODS FOR COMPARING MEANS

The overall F tests in the two-way ANOVA indicate whether there are significant differences between means, and measures of the strength of association (omega-square, intraclass correlation) provide information about the proportion of variance in the dependent variable associated with factors *A* and *B* and their interaction. However, if there are more than two levels of a factor, neither statistic indicates which means differ from each other. In this section, Scheffé's and Tukey's methods for making **post hoc comparisons** are presented. For a presentation of a smorgasbord of tests, see Toothaker (1993). Since these methods are analogous to their application in a one-way ANOVA, the details given in Chapter 13 should be reviewed, if necessary, before proceeding.

Scheffé's Method

Scheffé's test for post hoc comparisons in the two-way ANOVA is somewhat analogous to its use in the one-way ANOVA (see Chapter 13). If a significant interaction is found in the data, Scheffé's method is used to examine patterns in cell means. (For a discussion of comparisons for examining the interaction effect, see Toothaker, 1993.) These comparisons are guided by a graph of the interaction effect. The type of comparisons, pairwise or complex, would depend on the observed differences between the cell means as revealed by the graph. In the absence of a significant interaction, the significant main effects (with more than two levels) become the focus of post hoc comparisons. In this case, the row and column means are compared (cf. Tables 14-1 and 14-3). With Scheffé's method, as many comparisons as possible can be carried out, all at a specified level of significance (α). (*Note:* The formulas given throughout the remainder of this section assume a fixed-effects ANOVA.)

Interaction Effects.   In a post hoc examination of a significant interaction, a graph guides the comparison of means. The procedures for calculating $t_{observed}$ for a particular comparison are exactly the same as those described in Chapter 13 for Scheffé's method with a one-way ANOVA. The $q \times r$ cell means are treated as if they were k means in a one-way ANOVA. The null and alternative hypotheses are:

H_0: $C = 0$

H_1: $C \neq 0$

A sample comparison is defined as in Formula 13-13a:

$$\hat{C} = w_1 \bar{X}_i + w_2 \bar{X}_2 + \cdots + w_k \bar{X}_k$$

And $t_{observed}$ is (Formula 13-15a)

$$t_{observed} = \frac{\hat{C}}{\sqrt{\dfrac{MS_W}{n}(w_1^2 + w_2^2 + \cdots + w_k^2)}}$$

In order to decide whether to reject the null hypothesis, we need a critical value. Just as with the one-way ANOVA, the critical value for the Scheffé test takes into account the fact that all possible comparisons could be made at a particular level of significance (e.g., $\alpha = .05$). The critical value can be obtained from Formula 13-16:

$$t'_{critical} = \sqrt{(k-1)F_{critical(\alpha, k-1, df_W)}}$$

TABLE 14-15   Some comparisons examining the interactions shown in Figure 14-4

Ability:	Low			High		
Treatment:	*Control*	*Factual*	*Comprehension*	*Control*	*Factual*	*Comprehension*
Means:	1.5	1.5	7.5	8.5	3.5	3.5
$\hat{C}_1$	−1	−1	2	0	0	0
$\hat{C}_2$	0	0	0	2	−1	−1
$\hat{C}_1 = (-1)(1.5)$		+(−1)(1.5)	+(2)(7.5)	+0	+0	+0 = 12
$\hat{C}_2 =$	0	+0	+0	+(2)(8.5)	+(−1)(3.5)	+(−1)(3.5) = 10

Since the procedures for comparing cell means in a two-way ANOVA using Scheffé's method are virtually the same as the procedures for a one-way ANOVA, Procedure 13-5 can be used. As an example of how an interaction might be explored, consider the data from the prose-learning study (Tables 14-3 and 14-5). Since a significant interaction between verbal ability and treatment was found, post hoc comparisons are in order. Figure 14-4 on p. 429 provides a visual representation of the interaction. From this figure, a number of comparisons can be identified to examine the interaction. For subjects low in verbal ability, the mean of the comprehension group should be compared with the means of the other two groups. For subjects high in verbal ability, the mean of the control group should be compared with the means of the two treatment groups (see Table 14-15). The value of $t_{observed}$ for each comparison can be found with Formula 13-15a:

$\hat{C}_1$: $t_{observed} = \dfrac{12}{\sqrt{\dfrac{.50}{2}[(-1)^2 + (-1)^2 + 2^2 + 0^2 + 0^2 + 0^2]}} = 9.80$

$\hat{C}_2$: $t_{observed} = \dfrac{10}{\sqrt{\dfrac{.50}{2}[0^2 + 0^2 + 0^2 + 2^2 + (-1)^2 + (-1)^2]}} = 8.16$

In order to decide whether to reject the null hypothesis, we must calculate $t'_{critical}$ with Formula 13-16:

$$t'_{critical} = \sqrt{(5)F_{critical(.05,5,6)}} = \sqrt{(5)(4.39)} = 4.69$$

Since in both cases $t_{observed}$ exceeds $t'_{critical}$, the null hypothesis should be rejected, with the conclusion that the observed differences are reliable. Low-ability students perform best in the comprehension group; high-ability students perform best in the control group.

One last comment: The comparisons made so far certainly are important in examining the interaction. However, other comparisons are also of interest, such as the comparison of means for subjects low and high in verbal ability for each of the treatment groups.

Main Effects for A and B.   In the absence of a significant interaction, comparisons between row means (main effect of A) and column means (main effect of B) become the focus of post hoc comparisons. For clarity, a row mean that reflects the effect of factor A will be denoted by $\bar{A}_i$, and a column mean that reflects the effect of factor B will be denoted by $\bar{B}_j$. The marginal means in Table 14-3 can be used to illustrate this new notation: $\bar{A}_1 = 3.50$, $\bar{A}_2 = 5.17$; $\bar{B}_1 = 5.00$, $\bar{B}_2 = 2.50$, $\bar{B}_3 = 5.50$.

For the comparison of the means representing the main effect of A, a comparison $\hat{C}_A$ is defined as in Formula 14-11.

$$\hat{C}_A = w_1\bar{A}_1 + w_2\bar{A}_2 + \cdots + w_q\bar{A}_q = \sum_{i=1}^{q} w_i\bar{A}_i \qquad \textbf{(14-11)}$$

The formula for testing the usual hypotheses is given in Formula 14-12.

$$t_{observed(A)} = \dfrac{\hat{C}_A}{\sqrt{\dfrac{MS_W}{nr}(w_1^2 + w_2^2 + \cdots + w_q^2)}} \qquad \textbf{(14-12)}$$

In order to decide whether to reject the null hypothesis, we must compare $F_{observed}$ with $F'_{critical}$ corresponding to the test of the A main effect. This statistic is defined in Formula 14-13.

$$t'_{\text{critical}(A)} = \sqrt{(df_A)F_{\text{critical}(\alpha, df_A, df_W)}} \qquad \textbf{(14-13)}$$

As an illustration of how the formula operates, the data from the prose-learning study will be used. However, in this example, normally the main effect of A would not be tested, for two reasons. First, there are only two levels of A, so the overall significant F test indicates that they differ. Second, there is an AB interaction, so an examination of cell means is in order. With these caveats, the use of the formulas can be illustrated:

$$\hat{C}_A = (-1)(3.50) + (1)(5.17) = 1.67$$

$$t_{\text{observed}(A)} = \frac{1.67}{\sqrt{\frac{.5}{(2)(3)}[(-1)^2 + 1^2]}} = \frac{1.67}{.4} = 4.18$$

If the test is conducted at $\alpha = .05$, then $F_{\text{critical}(.05, 1, 6)}$ is equal to 5.99, and:

$$t'_{\text{critical}(A)} = \sqrt{(1)(5.99)} = 2.45$$

Since $t_{\text{observed}(A)}$ exceeds t'_{critical}, the null hypothesis should be rejected and the conclusion drawn that subjects high in verbal ability scored, on the average, higher than subjects low in verbal ability on the achievement test.

For a comparison of the means representing the *main effect of B*, a comparison $\hat{C}_B$ is defined as in Formula 14-14.

$$\hat{C}_B = w_1\bar{B}_1 + w_2\bar{B}_2 + \cdots + w_r\bar{B}_r = \sum_{j=1}^{r} w_j\bar{B}_j \qquad \textbf{(14-14)}$$

The formula for testing the usual null and alternative hypotheses is given in Formula 14-15.

$$t_{\text{observed}(B_j)} = \frac{\hat{C}_{B_j}}{\sqrt{\frac{MS_W}{nq}(w_1^2 + w_2^2 + \cdots + w_r^2)}} \qquad \textbf{(14-15)}$$

In order to decide whether to reject H_0: $C = 0$, we must compare t_{observed} with t'_{critical} corresponding to the test of the B main effect. This statistic is given in Formula 14-16.

$$t'_{\text{critical}(B)} = \sqrt{(df_B)F_{\text{critical}(\alpha, df_B, df_W)}} \qquad \textbf{(14-16)}$$

As an illustration of how this formula works, the data from the prose-learning study will be used, with the caveat that since the interaction was significant, this main effect probably would not be of particular interest. For the purpose of this comparison, let's compare the two treatment groups ($\bar{B}_2 = 2.50$, $\bar{B}_3 = 5.50$) against the control group ($\bar{B}_1 = 5.00$):

$$\hat{C}_{B_j} = (-2)(5.00) + (1)(2.50) + (1)(5.50) = -10 + 8 = -2$$

$$t_{observed(B)} = \frac{-2}{\sqrt{\frac{.50}{(2)(2)}[(-2)^2 + 1^2 + 1^2]}} = \frac{-2}{.87} = -2.30$$

If the test is conducted at $\alpha = .05$, then $F_{critical(05,2,6)}$ is equal to 5.14, and

$$t_{critical(B)} = \sqrt{(2)(5.14)} = 3.21$$

Since $|t_{observed(B)}|$ does not exceed $t'_{critical(B)}$, the null hypothesis cannot be rejected. The steps in conducting Scheffé's test for examining the main effects of factors A and B are summarized in Procedure 15-3 in the *Student Guide*.

Example Problem 14.3

a. The interaction effect in Example Problem 1 was significant. Using the data from this problem, compare the means of the three treatment groups against the placebo group in the euphoria situation using Scheffé's test. (Let $\alpha = .05$.) Include the following items in your answer.
    1. Null and alternative hypotheses
    2. Set of weights for the comparison
    3. Computation of $\hat{C}$
    4. $t_{observed}$
    5. $t'_{critical}$
    6. Conclusions
b. Examine the main effect of treatment by comparing the three means of the drug groups against the mean of the placebo group, using Scheffé's test. (Let $\alpha = .05$.) Include steps 1–6 of part a in your answer.

Tukey's HSD Test

In some cases, the researcher may be interested in examining differences between all possible pairs of means, given a significant main effect or interaction. This is data snooping at its best and serves to discover what happened in the present study and to formulate hypotheses for subsequent studies. For this purpose, Tukey's HSD (honestly significant difference) test can be used instead of Scheffé's method. For pairwise comparisons, Tukey's test is more powerful than Scheffés.

The use of Tukey's HSD test for comparing all possible pairs of cell means in a factorial design is analogous to its use in a one-way design. The only difference is that the factorial design must be arranged as a one-way design with $q \times r = k$ levels. In this case, each cell of the factorial design is considered a separate level of the treatment variable. In the hypothetical study of prose learning, a 2×3 (verbal learning $\times$ type of questioning treatment) factorial design was used. When it is treated as a one-way design, there are $2 \times 3 = 6$ levels of the treatment variable. Once the two-way factorial design is arranged as a one-way design, the procedure for conducting Tukey's HSD test is exactly the same as that for the one-way design. The procedure for using Tukey's best, then, is given in Procedure 13-6. Tukey's test can also be used with row and column means corresponding to the main effects for factors A and B, respectively. For factor A, devide MS_W by nr instead of n; and for factor B, divide MS_W by nq instead of n (see step 3 in Procedure 13-6).[5]

Example Problem 14.4

Using the data from Example Problem 14.1, compare all pairs of means by using Tukey's HSD test. (Let $\alpha = .05$.) Include the following items in your answer.
  a. Null and alternative hypotheses
  b. Table of differences between means
  c. Computation of *HSD*
  d. Conclusions

PLANNED COMPARISONS OF MEANS

In making planned comparisons with data from a factorial design, the researcher uses the two-way ANOVA to obtain the value of MS_W. There is no need to calculate $F_{observed}$ for each effect (A, B, and AB) since planned comparisons are conducted without regard to a significant overall F.

Planned comparisons with a two-way design are made in the same manner as with a one-way design. The key to the similarity is to recognize that a two-way design with $q \times r$ cells can be treated as a one-way design. Specifically, a $q \times r$, two-way ANOVA is treated as a one-way ANOVA with $q \times r = k$ levels. In this case, the two-way ANOVA is stretched into one long one-way ANOVA. Each cell in the two-way ANOVA is considered to be a separate level—one of the k levels of the treatment variable. In the hypothetical study of prose learning (see Tables 14-3 and 14-5), for example, the 2×3 (ability $\times$ treatment) design would be stretched into a one-way design with $k = 2 \times 3 = 6$ levels (see Table 14-16).

With k levels for a planned comparison, there are $k - 1$ degrees of freedom. A maximum, then, of $k - 1$ orthogonal comparisons can be made. Each comparison accounts for 1 degree of freedom. For the prose-learning study, five orthogonal comparisons are possible ($k - 1 = 6 - 1 = 5$).

---

[5]For some it is counterintuitive to divide MS_W by nr when dealing with factor A which has q levels! Actually, nr is simply the total number of cases that entered into the calculation of a factor A mean. That is, nr is the number of subjects within a cell times the number of levels of factor B. This gives the number of observations entering into the calculation of a factor A means. For example, in Table 14-3b, $n = 2$, $q = 2$, and $r = 3$. For the two means representing the levels of factor A ($a_1 = 3.50$ and $a_2 = 5.17$), it is clear that 6 scores entered into the calculation of each of these means: 2 subjects per cell ($n = 2$) summed across three conditions ($r = 3$—b_1, b_2 and b_3). The same reasoning holds for dividing by nq when dealing with comparisons of the levels of factor B.

A comparison in a two-way design is defined in exactly the same way as for the one-way design with $q \times r = k$ levels:

$$\hat{C} = w_1 \bar{X}_1 + w_2 \bar{X}_2 + \cdots + w_k \bar{X}_k$$

Table 14-17 presents three of five possible orthogonal comparisons for the hypothetical study of prose learning. The first comparison is between the low- and high-ability groups. The mean performance of the low-ability subjects is compared with the mean performance of the high-ability subjects. Notice that when we compare the two ability groups, the means of the three treatment groups are combined. Since there are only two levels of the ability variable, the comparison is equivalent to testing the main effect of A. The second comparison is between the control group and the two treatment groups combined (fact + comprehension). And the third comparison is between the fact and comprehension treatments, using data from the low-ability subjects.

TABLE 14-16 Cell means from a two-way ($q \times r$) ANOVA arranged in a one-way design (see Table 14-3)

	Cells of the Design					
Levels of A:	*Low Ability (a_1)*			*High Ability (a_2)*		
	Control	*Fact*	*Comprehension*	*Control*	*Fact*	*Comprehension*
Levels of B:	*(b_1)*	*(b_2)*	*(b_3)*	*(b_1)*	*(b_2)*	*(b_3)*
	1.5	1.5	7.5	8.5	3.5	3.5

TABLE 14-17 Some planned comparisons for the hypothetical study of prose learning: A 2×3 design

	Levels of A:	*Low Ability (a_1)*			*High Ability (a_2)*		
		Control	*Fact*	*Comprehension*	*Control*	*Fact*	*Comprehension*
	Levels of B:	*(b_1)*	*(b_2)*	*(b_3)*	*(b_1)*	*(b_2)*	*(b_3)*
Comparison	*Mean:*	1.5	1.5	7.5	8.5	3.5	3.5
1		-1	-1	-1	$+1$	$+1$	$+1$
2		-2	$+1$	$+1$	-2	$+1$	$+1$
3		0	-1	$+1$	0	0	0

For a statistical test of each comparison, the null and alternative hypotheses for the two-way design are the same as for the one-way design:

H_0: $C = 0$

H_1: $C \neq 0$ or $C > 0$ or $C < 0$

Finally, the statistical test for planned comparisons in a two-way design is the same as it is in a one-way design. For equal cell sizes, the t test is:

$$t_{observed} = \frac{\hat{C}}{\sqrt{\dfrac{MS_W}{n}(w_1^2 + w_2^2 + \cdots + w_k^2)}}$$

with:

$$df = qr(n - 1)$$
$$= k(n - 1)$$
$$= N - k$$

The data from Table 14-17 can be used as a numerical example of how the planned comparison is carried out. In this example, comparison 1 (the main effect of A) is tested at $\alpha = .05$. On the basis of theory and prior research, the mean score of the high-ability group is expected to be higher than the mean score of the low-ability group. More specifically, the null and alternative hypotheses for this comparison are

$$H_0: C_1 = 0$$
$$H_1: C_1 > 0$$

The value of $\hat{C}_1$ is found, and $t_{observed}$ is calculated:

$$\hat{C}_A = (-1)(1.5) + (-1)(1.5) + (-1)(7.5) + (1)(8.5) + (1)(3.5) + (1)(3.5)$$
$$= -1.5 - 1.5 - 7.5 + 8.5 + 3.5 + 3.5 = 5$$

$$t_{observed} = \frac{5}{\sqrt{\frac{.50}{2}[(-1)^2 + (-1)^2 + (-1)^2 + 1^2 + 1^2]}}$$

$$= \frac{5}{\sqrt{\frac{.50}{2}(6)}} = \frac{5}{\sqrt{1.50}} = 4.08$$

In order to decide whether to reject the null hypothesis, we need the critical value of t with $N - k = 12 - 6 = 6$ df. From Table C, this value for a one-tail test at $\alpha = .05$ is 1.943. Since $t_{observed}$ exceeds $t_{critical}$, the null hypothesis should be rejected. Subjects high in verbal ability scored, on the average, higher than subjects low in verbal ability.

The steps in testing each of the comparisons in a two-way design are identical to the steps in testing a comparison in a one-way design.

Example Problem 14.5

a. Using the data in Example Problem 14.1, write a comparison of the three means in the euphoria situation with the three means in the anger condition. Test the hypothesis at $\alpha = .05$, and include the following items in your answer.
    1. A table of weights for the contrast, with verification that the weights are properly specified
    2. Null and alternative hypotheses
    3. Computation of $\hat{C}$
    4. t test
    5. $t_{critical}$
    6. Conclusion

    b. Both theories predict no difference between the means of the placebo condition in the euphoria and anger situations. Compare the means of the placebo group in the euphoria and anger situations ($\alpha = .05$). Include items 1–6 of part a in your answer as well as a check to see whether this comparison is independent of the first one.

SUMMARY

This chapter presents the *factorial analysis of variance* (ANOVA), a statistical test used to test hypotheses about the difference between means in true factorial experiments or in factorial criterion group designs. The discussion is restricted to the *two-way* ANOVA: the analysis of factorial designs with two factors having equal cell sizes. The purpose, underlying rationale, and procedures for computing and interpreting two-way, fixed-, random-, and mixed-effects model ANOVAs are presented. Procedures for computing the strength of association (omega-square, intraclass correlation) for main effects and the interaction effect are also discussed. Finally, post hoc and planned comparisons between means are presented.

ANSWERS TO EXAMPLE PROBLEMS

1. **a.** Main effect for factor *A* (situation):

   H_0: $\mu_E = \mu_A$

   H_1: $\mu_E \neq \mu_A$

   Main effect for factor *B* (treatment):

   H_0: $\mu_1 = \mu_2 = \mu_3 = \mu_4$

   H_1: $\mu_j \neq \mu_{j'}$ for some j and j'

   Interaction effect (situation $\times$ treatment):

   H_0: interaction effect $= 0$

   H_1: interaction effect $\neq 0$

   b. *Independence:* Random assignment of subjects to cells of the design and "treatment" given to individuals.

   Normality: This assumption is not tested, since ANOVA is not seriously affected by violations of this assumption.

   Homogeneity of variances: This assumption is not tested, since ANOVA is not seriously affected by violations of this assumption when cell sizes are equal.

   c. *Step 1.* The data summary table is given in Example Problem 14.1.

   Step 2. Table of cell sums:

   a_1 = euphoria a_2 = anger
   b_1 = drug + accurate explanation b_2 = drug + inaccurate explanation
   b_3 = drug + no explanation b_4 = placebo

	b_1	b_2	b_3	b_4	*Total Sums* *for Rows*
a_1	20	24	23	18	85
a_2	8	4	10	14	36
Total Sums *for Columns*	28	28	33	32	

Step 3. $\dfrac{(20)^2}{4} = 100 \quad \dfrac{(24)^2}{4} = 144 \quad \dfrac{(23)^2}{4} = 132.25 \quad \dfrac{(18)^2}{4} = 81 \quad \dfrac{8^2}{4} = 16$

$\dfrac{4^2}{4} = 4 \quad \dfrac{(10)^2}{4} = 25 \quad \dfrac{(14)^2}{4} = 49$

Step 4. $\dfrac{(85)^2}{16} = 451.56 \quad \dfrac{(36)^2}{16} = 81$

Step 5. $\dfrac{(28)^2}{8} = 98 \quad \dfrac{(28)^2}{8} = 98 \quad \dfrac{(33)^2}{8} = 136.13 \quad \dfrac{(32)^2}{8} = 128$

Step 6. $\displaystyle\sum_{p=1}^{N} X_p = 5 + 4 + \cdots + 3 + 3 = 121$

Step 7. Intermediate quantities:

$$\{1\} = \frac{\left(\displaystyle\sum_{p=1}^{N} X_p\right)^2}{nqr} = \frac{(121)^2}{(4)(2)(4)} = 457.53$$

$$\{2\} = \sum_{i=1}^{q} \frac{\left(\displaystyle\sum_{j=1}^{r}\sum_{p=1}^{n} X_{pij}\right)^2}{nr} = 451.56 + 81 = 532.56$$

$$\{3\} = \sum_{j=1}^{r} \frac{\left(\displaystyle\sum_{i=1}^{q}\sum_{p=1}^{n} X_{pij}\right)^2}{nq} = 98 + 98 + 136.13 + 128 = 460.13$$

$$\{4\} = \sum_{i=1}^{q}\sum_{j=1}^{r} \frac{\left(\displaystyle\sum_{p=1}^{n} X_{pij}\right)^2}{n} = 100 + 144 + 132.25 + 81 + 16 + 4 + 25 + 49$$
$$= 551.25$$

$$\{5\} = \sum_{p=1}^{N} X_p^2 = 5^2 + 4^2 + \cdots + 3^2 + 3^2 = 567$$

Step 8. Sums of squares:

$SS_T = \{5\} - \{1\} = 567 - 457.53 = 109.47$

$SS_A = \{2\} - \{1\} = 532.36 - 457.53 = 75.03$

$SS_B = \{3\} - \{1\} = 460.13 - 457.53 = 2.6$

$SS_{AB} = \{4\} - \{2\} - \{3\} + \{1\} = 551.25 - 532.56 - 460.13 + 457.53 = 16.09$

$SS_W = \{5\} - \{4\} = 567 - 551.25 = 15.75$

d. ANOVA summary table:

Source	*Sum of Squares*	*df*	*Mean Square*	F_{obs}
Factor *A*	75.03	1	75.03	113.68
Factor *B*	2.60	3	.87	1.32
A × *B*	16.09	3	5.36	8.12
Within groups	15.75	24	.66	
Total	109.47	31		

e. $F_{critical(.05,1,24)} = 4.26$; this critical value applies to the test of *A*. $F_{critical(.05,3,24)} = 3.01$; this critical value applies to *B* and *AB*.

f. Main effect for *A*: Since $F_{observed} > F_{critical}$, reject H_0. There was a significant difference in the mean ratings of students in different situations. Main effect for *B*: Since $F_{observed} < F_{critical}$, do not reject H_0. There was not a significant difference in the mean ratings of subjects in the four treatment conditions. Interaction of *A* and *B*: Since $F_{observed} > F_{critical}$, reject H_0. There was a statistically significant interaction.

g. Graph of interaction:

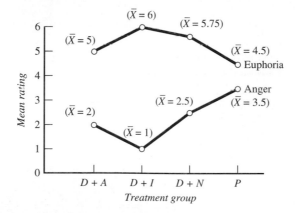

2. a. $\hat{\omega}_A^2 = \dfrac{75.03 - (1)(.66)}{109.47 + .66} \approx .68$

Sixty-eight percent of the variance in ratings is accounted for by differences in situations.

$$\hat{\omega}_B^2 = \frac{2.60 - (3)(.66)}{109.47 + .66} \approx .005$$

Less than 1 percent of the variance in ratings is accounted for by differences in treatment group. (Since this effect was not statistically significant, $\hat{\omega}^2$ typically would not be calculated.)

$$\hat{\omega}_{AB}^2 = \frac{16.09 - (3)(.07)}{109.47 + .07} \approx .13$$

b. Thirteen percent of the variance in ratings was due to the interaction of situation and treatment.

c. $df_W = qr(n-1)$ $n = \dfrac{df_W}{qr} + 1 = \dfrac{135}{15} + 1 = 10$

$$\hat{\sigma}_A^2 = \frac{18.00 - 9.00}{(10)(3)} = \frac{9}{30} = .30$$

$$\hat{\sigma}_B^2 = \frac{24.00 - 9.00}{(10)(5)} = \frac{15}{50} = .30$$

$$\hat{\sigma}_{AB}^2 = \frac{9.00 - 4.00}{10} = \frac{5}{10} = .50$$

$$\hat{\rho}_{AB} = \frac{.50}{.30 + .30 + .50 + 4.00} = \frac{.50}{5.10} = .10$$

d. Since the A and B main effects are not statistically significant, $\hat{\rho}_A^2$ and $\hat{\rho}_B^2$ were not calculated. The AB interaction accounts for 10 percent of the variance in the dependent variable.

3. **a.** 1. $H_0: C = 0$
      $H_1: C \neq 0$

   2. For the euphoria situation (a_1):

		a_1				a_2		
	b_1	b_2	b_3	b_4	b_1	b_2	b_3	b_4
Means	5	6	5.75	4.5	2	1	2.5	3.5
$\hat{C}_1$	1	1	1	-3	0	0	0	0

   3. $\hat{C}_1 = (1)(5) + (1)(6) + (1)(5.75) + (-3)(4.5) = 3.25$

   4. $t_{observed} = \dfrac{3.25}{\sqrt{\dfrac{.66}{4}[1^2 + 1^2 + 1^2 + (-3)^2]}} = \dfrac{3.25}{\sqrt{1.98}} = \dfrac{3.25}{1.41} = 2.30$

   5. $t'_{critical} = \sqrt{(7)F_{critical(.05,7,24)}} = \sqrt{(7)(2.42)} = 4.12$

   6. Since $|t_{observed}| < t'_{critical}$, do not reject H_0. Conclude that the means of the drug groups in the euphoria situation do not differ significantly.

b. 1. $H_0: C = 0$
$H_1: C \neq 0$

2.

	$\bar{B}_1$	$\bar{B}_2$	$\bar{B}_3$	$\bar{B}_4$
Column				
Mean	3.50	3.50	4.13	4.00
$\hat{C}_B$	+1	+1	+1	−3

$^*p < .05$

3. $\hat{C}_B = (1)(3.5) + (1)(3.5) + (1)(4.13) + (-3)(4) = -.87$

4. $t_{observed} = \dfrac{.87}{\sqrt{\dfrac{.66}{(4)(2)}[(1)^2 + (1)^2 + (1)^2 + (-3)^2]}} = \dfrac{.87}{\sqrt{.99}} = \dfrac{.87}{.99} = .88$

5. $t'_{critical(B)} = \sqrt{(3)F_{critical(.05,3,24)}} = \sqrt{(3)(3.01)} = \sqrt{9.03} = 3.00$

6. Since $t_{observed}$ does not exceed $t'_{critical}$, do not reject H_0.

4. a. $H_0: \mu_1 = \mu_2 = \cdots = \mu_8$, $H_1: \mu_1 \neq \mu'_i$
b.

	$\bar{X}_{22} =$ 1.00	$\bar{X}_{21} =$ 2.00	$\bar{X}_{23} =$ 2.50	$\bar{X}_{24} =$ 3.50	$\bar{X}_{14} =$ 4.50	$\bar{X}_{11} =$ 5.00	$\bar{X}_{13} =$ 5.75	$\bar{X}_{12} =$ 6.00
$\bar{X}_{22}= 1.00$	—	1.00	1.50	2.50*	3.50*	4.00*	4.75*	5.00*
$\bar{X}_{21}= 2.00$		—	.50	1.50	2.50*	3.00*	3.75*	4.00*
$\bar{X}_{23}= 2.50$			—	1.00	2.00*	2.50*	3.25*	3.50*
$\bar{X}_{24}= 3.50$				—	1.00	1.50	2.25*	2.50*
$\bar{X}_{14}= 4.50$					—	.50	1.25	1.50
$\bar{X}_{11}= 5.00$						—	.75	1.00
$\bar{X}_{13}= 5.75$							—	.25
$\bar{X}_{12}= 6.00$								—

$^*p < .05$

c. $HSD = q(.05, 24, 8)\sqrt{\dfrac{.66}{4}} = (4.68)(.41) = 1.91$

d. For all starred entries in the table, reject the null hypothesis.

5. a. 1.

	Euphoria (a_1)				Anger (a_2)			
	b_1	b_2	b_3	b_4	b_1	b_2	b_3	b_4
	1	1	1	0	−1	−1	−1	0

$\left[\sum w_i = 1 + 1 + 1 + 0 + (-1) + (-1) + 0 = 0\right]$

2. $H_0: C = 0$
$H_1: C \neq 0$

3. $\hat{C} = (1)(5) + (1)(6) + (1)(5.75) + (0)(4.5) + (-1)(2) + (-1)(1) + (-1)(2.5) + (0)(3.5) = 11.25$

4. $t_{observed} = \dfrac{11.25}{\sqrt{\dfrac{.66}{4}[1^2 + 1^2 + 1^2 + 0^2 + (-1)^2 + (-1)^2 + (-1)^2 + 0^2]}}$

$= \dfrac{11.25}{\sqrt{.99}} = \dfrac{11.25}{.99} = 11.36$

5. $t_{critical(.05/2.24)} = 2.064$

6. Since $t_{observed} > t_{critical}$, reject H_0. Conclude that the mean ratings are higher in the euphoria condition than in the anger condition. This finding lends support to the two-component theory.

b. 1.

	a_1				a_2		
b_1	b_2	b_3	b_4	b_1	b_2	b_3	b_4
0	0	0	1	0	0	0	−1

$\left[\sum w_i = 0 \text{ and} \right.$
$\sum w_{1i}w_{2i} = (1)(0) + (1)(0) + (1)(0) + (0)(1) + (-1)(0) + (-1)(0) + (-1)(0)$
$\left. + (0)(-1) = 0\right]$

2. $H_0: C = 0$
$H_1: C \neq 0$

3. $\hat{C} = (1)(4.5) + (-1)(3.5) = 1$

4. $t_{observed} = \dfrac{1}{\sqrt{\dfrac{2(.66)}{4}}} = \dfrac{1}{\sqrt{.33}} = \dfrac{1}{.57} = 1.74$

5. $t_{critical(.05/2.24)} = 2.064$

6. Since $|t_{observed}| < t_{critical}$, do not reject H_0. Conclude that there is not a statistically significant difference between the means of the placebo groups in the euphoria and anger conditions.

EXERCISES

Hudley & Graham (1993) hypothesized that boys' aggressive behavior might be the consequence of their misattributing the intent of others ("actors") in ambiguous situations (see Chapter 4 for details). If Hudley and Graham were right, teaching these boys, especially aggressive as compared to nonaggressive boys, to interpret actors' intent as something other than negative in ambiguous situations should ultimately lessen their aggressive behavior.

To test this hypothesis, Hudley and Graham randomly assigned aggressive and nonaggressive boys to one of three groups: (1) experimental (attribution retraining), (2) attention control (simply paying attention to boys with no special training), and (3) control (no special attention given). After treatment, the boys were asked to rate actors' intents in ambiguous situations. Data bearing on the hypothesis are presented in Table 14-18.

TABLE 14-18 Hypothetical data on aggressive and nonaggressive boys' perceptions of negative intent after treatment: Ambiguous situations

Group[a]	Aggression[b]	Negative Intent Rating	Group	Aggression	Negative Intent Rating
1	1	3	2	2	4
1	1	1	2	2	2
1	1	2	2	2	3
1	1	2	2	2	6
1	1	2	2	2	3
1	1	1	2	2	5
1	2	2	3	1	4
1	2	4	3	1	4
1	2	3	3	1	5
1	2	1	3	1	5
1	2	4	3	1	4
1	2	4	3	1	7
2	1	6	3	2	5
2	1	6	3	2	2
2	1	5	3	2	4
2	1	3	3	2	3
2	1	4	3	2	4
2	1	6	3	2	4

[a] Group: 1 = experimental, 2 = attention control, 3 = no treatment control.
[b] Aggression: 1 = aggressive, 2 = nonaggressive.

1. Present sample statistics that bear on the hypothesis. Do these statistics support the hypothesis?
2. Do a statistical test (ANOVA) to determine whether the observed sample mean differences arose by chance.

   a. State the assumptions underlying this statistical test and present either empirical evidence or a justification for the use of the test.
   b. State the null and alternative hypotheses tested
   c. Report the results of the ANOVA in a summary table
   d. Interpret the findings; what do you conclude?
   e. Report the results of post hoc mean comparisons ($\alpha = .05$) to explore the Hudley-Graham hypothesis. Explain your choice of comparison method.
   f. Carry out planned comparison(s) ($\alpha = .05$) that most directly map on to the hypothesis that the teaching effect will be greatest for aggressive boys compared to nonaggressive boys. (If more than one is planned, show that they are orthogonal.)

g. With the comparisons in hand, what do you conclude now about the Hudley-Graham hypothesis?

ANSWERS TO EXERCISES

1. SPSS Descriptives on Posttest

Variables[a]	Mean	Std Dev	Minimum	Maximum	N
A1G1	1.83	.75	1.00	3.00	6
A1G2	5.00	1.26	3.00	6.00	6
A1G3	4.83	1.17	4.00	7.00	6
A2G1	3.00	1.26	1.00	4.00	6
A2G2	3.83	1.47	2.00	6.00	6
A2G3	3.67	1.03	2.00	5.00	6
A1	3.89	1.81	1.00	7.00	18
A2	3.50	1.25	1.00	6.00	18
G1	2.42	1.16	1.00	4.00	12
G2	4.42	1.44	2.00	6.00	12
G3	4.25	1.22	2.00	7.00	12

[a]A = Aggression (1 = aggressive, 2 = nonaggressive); G = Group
(1 = experimental, 2 = attention, 3 = control).

The descriptive statistics provide support for the Hudley-Graham hypothesis. The aggressive boys in the experimental group show, on average, the least negative intent—substantially less than aggressive boys in the other two groups, and even less than nonaggressive boys, regardless of group.

2. a. *Independence:* By random assignment, we assume independence. However, the conduct of the experiment should be carefully monitored to ensure independence was maintained.

   Normality: There are too few cases to examine frequency distributions within the six cells of the design. Nevertheless, the ANOVA is robust to violation of this assumption.

   Homogeneity: SPSS provides a statistical test, Levene's test, of this assumption. [To do this test for the two-way ANOVA, create a variable, say, ONEWAY, with 6 levels ($q * r = 2 * 3 = 6$ levels) and use the one-way ANOVA routine in SPSS.

   Levene Test for Homogeneity of Variances

Statistic	df1	df2	2-tail Sig.
.6841	5	30	.639

   Do not reject the null hypothesis. Moreover, the ANOVA is robust to violation of this assumption, especially with equal cell sizes.

   b. $H_0: \mu_i = \mu_G$ for all i; $H_1: \mu_i \neq \mu_{i'}$ for some i and i'

H_0: $\mu_j = \mu_G$ for all j; H_1: $\mu_j \neq \mu_{j'}$ for some j and j'

H_0: interaction effect = 0; H_1: interaction effect $\neq$ 0

c. SPSS ANOVA Models: Simple Factorial

$* * *$ ANALYSIS OF VARIANCE $* * *$
   POSTTEST
by AGGRESS   Aggression
   GROUP   Treatment Group

UNIQUE sums of squares   [Relevant only to designs with unequal
All effects entered simultaneously N's, which is beyond the scope of textbook]

Source of Variation	Sum of Squares	df	Mean Square	F	Sig of F
Main Effects[a]	30.917	3	10.306	7.390	.001
AGGRESS	1.361	1	1.361	.976	.331
GROUP	29.556	2	14.778	10.598	.000
2-Way Interactions	10.889	2	5.444	3.904	.031
AGGRESS GROUP	10.889	2	5.444	3.904	.031
Explained[b]	41.806	5	8.361	5.996	.001
Residual[c]	41.833	30	1.394		
Total	83.639	35	2.390		

[a]Sum of the two main effects (sums of squares and *df* are additive).
[b]Sum of main effects and interaction representing a test of systematic variation in entire design.
[c]Within-group or error variance.

36 cases were processed.
0 cases (.0 pct) were missing.

d. As hypothesized, the group × aggression interaction was statistically significant. We focus, then, on interpreting this interaction. The SPSS graph of the interaction (below) proves helpful in interpreting the results. Attribution retraining has a big effect, a substantially bigger effect than the attention or control conditions, especially for aggressive compared to nonaggressive boys.

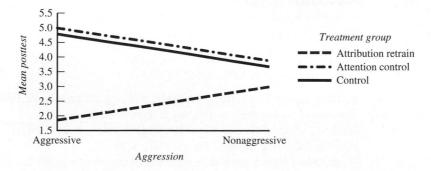

e. Based on the graph of the interaction, one post hoc comparison seems to be most pressing: comparing the difference between attribution retraining and the two control groups for aggressive vs. nonaggressive boys. That is, is the gap between the groups bigger for aggressive than nonaggressive boys? This complex comparison calls for Scheffé's method. (The SPSS One-Way ANOVA program permits the user to define a contrast of interest and test the contrast with a t test.) Nevertheless, Tukey's method would also provide comparisons of interest and so is included here for all pairs of means using SPSS (One-Way ANOVA program).

Group 1 = G1A1   Group 3 = G2A1   Group 5 = G3A1

Group 2 = G1A2   Group 4 = G2A2   Group 6 = G3A2

Scheffé's Test of Gap Contrast:

[(Group 3 + Group 5 – 2 * Group 1) – (Group 4 + Group 6 – 2 * Group 2)]

= Group 3 + Group 5 – 2 * Group1 – Group 4 – Group 6 + 2 * Group2

=   +1   +1   –2   –1   –1   +2

Variable POSTTEST

By Variable ONEWAY

Contrast Coefficient Matrix: Contrast 1

Group	1	2	3	4	5	6
Weight	–2	+ 2	+1	–1	+1	–1

[*Note:* The sum of the weights is 0.]

Pooled Variance Estimate

	Value	S. Error	T Value	D.F	T Prob.
Contrast 1	4.6667	1.6700	2.794	30.0	.009

Note: The T Prob is not the Scheffé critical value, but rather the tabled t critical value (i.e., the value for a planned comparison! This anticipates the findings for 2f). So, the critical value of t for a Scheffé comparison must be calculated to evaluate the results provided by SPSS: $t_{critical} = \sqrt{(k-1)F_{critical(.05,5,30)}} = \sqrt{(5)(2.42)} = 3.48$. We find that although the difference in the observed gap is in the predicted direction, this difference is not statistically significant for the post hoc comparison. Nevertheless, Tukey's test sheds light on where the differences lie.

Variable POSTTEST

By Variable ONEWAY

Multiple Range Tests: Tukey HSD test with significance level .050
The difference between two means is significant if
MEAN(J)–MEAN(I) > = .8350*RANGE*SQRT(1/N(I)+1/N(J))
with the following value(s) for RANGE: 4.30
(*) Indicates significant differences, which are shown in the lower triangle

```
                        G G G G G G
                        r r r r r r
                        p p p p p p
                        1 2 6 4 5 3
          Mean          ONEWAY
          1.8333        Grp 1
          3.0000        Grp 2
          3.6667        Grp 6
          3.8333        Grp 4
          4.8333        Grp 5      *
          5.0000        Grp 3      *
```

Homogeneous Subsets (highest and lowest means are not significantly different):

Subset 1					
Group	Grp 1	Grp 2	Grp 6	Grp 4	
Mean	1.8333	3.0000	3.6667	3.8333	

Subset 2					
Group	Grp 2	Grp 6	Grp 4	Grp 5	Grp 3
Mean	3.0000	3.6667	3.8333	4.8333	5.0000

Tukey's test shows that aggressive boys not receiving attribution retraining express significantly greater negative intent than to the other boys, on average (Subset 1). Moreover, aggressive boys in the attribution retraining group perceive significantly less negative intent than do all others, on average (Subset 2). This pattern of significant mean differences is consistent with the Hudley-Graham hypothesis.

f. The Scheffé contrast described in 2e is consistent with the contrast proposed for the planned contrast. (You might have had another planned comparison in mind that got at the Hudley-Graham hypothesis. That's OK.) Moreover, the t test for the contrast reported in 2e provides the planned comparison t test. $t_{critical(.05,df=30, one tail)} = 1.697$. Based on the planned comparison, the difference in the mean gap for aggressive boys is significantly greater than the mean gap for the nonaggressive boys. This provides strong support for the Hudley-Graham hypothesis and demonstrates the power of planned comparisons.

g. There is strong support for the Hudley-Graham hypothesis.

VI STATISTICAL TESTS FOR WITHIN-SUBJECTS AND MIXED DESIGNS

In a *between-subjects design,* a subject is observed in one and only one cell of the design—both in one-way designs and in factorial designs. Often it is desirable and sometimes it is possible to observe one subject in more than one treatment condition. Designs with repeated observations on the same subject are called **within-subjects designs.** An example may help clarify this distinction. Teachers' estimates of their students' academic performance depend on a number of factors such as the students' abilities, participation in class, work habits, and so on. For an examination of the influence of some of these factors on teachers' expectations, suppose a 3×3 design is constructed with three levels of ability (high, average, low) and three levels of participation (high, average, low). For each of the nine cells of the design, a description of a hypothetical student is written; for example, one student is described as high in academic ability and participation, another is high in ability and average in participation, still another is low in ability and average in participation, etc. A treatment, then, consists of having a subject (teacher) read the description of a particular hypothetical student. The dependent variable is the teacher's rating of how well that student would do in his or her class. Since it is possible to have all subjects (teachers) read and rate each of the nine descriptions (treatments), we have a *within-subjects design.* There are repeated observations on the same subjects, since each teacher reads about and rates each student description (treatment). A factorial ANOVA can be used to examine differences between mean ratings.

If, instead, *n* teachers are randomly assigned to each of the nine cells of the design, we have a *between-subjects design;* again, a two-way ANOVA can be used to examine differences between mean ratings. Whereas the ANOVA can be used to examine data from between-subjects and within-subjects designs, the statistical procedures for the within-subjects design are somewhat different from those for the between-subjects design.

Another example of a within-subjects design is the pretest-posttest preexperimental design (see Chapter 1). With this design, subjects are observed at pretest, then they receive a treatment, and finally they are observed at posttest. For each subject in the study, then, there are two observations. This design can be extended to include not only a pretest and a posttest but also a retention test 1 week after the treatment. In this case, three observations are made on each subject. If a delayed retention test (e.g., 1 month after treatment) is incorporated into the design, four observations are made on the same subjects. You can see why within-subjects designs are often called *repeated-measures designs*.

A final example will complete the description of the major types of within-subjects designs. Pairs of subjects, for example, could be *matched* on one or more individual-difference variables (IDV), such as academic ability, and then randomly assigned to one of two treatment groups. In this design, matched subjects are considered to be more similar to one another than to other subjects in the design. In fact, the idea behind this design is that subjects who are matched with one another are considered to be "images" of each other for the purpose of the study. They are treated as if the same subject were observed in each treatment. For example, 50 pairs of subjects ($N = 100$) might be matched on a measure of verbal ability and then randomly assigned to a control and an experimental group. They would receive an instructional treatment, and then the average performance of the two groups would be compared.

In a within-subjects design using matching, two important requirements can be identified (among many). First, subjects should be matched on one or more individual-difference variables that are correlated with the dependent variable. In the example experiment, verbal ability was known to be correlated with the dependent variable (achievement) in the instructional setting ($r \approx .60$). Second, the number of subjects that have to be matched with one another depends on the number of cells in the design. If, as in the example study, there are two cells in the design, pairs of subjects are matched. One person in the pair is randomly assigned to the first cell, and the second person is assigned to the second cell. If there are six cells in a factorial design, six subjects have to be found who match on the IDV. In this way, *blocks* of six matched subjects are formed. Within each block, subjects are randomly assigned to one of the six cells of the design. You can see why within-subjects designs are sometimes called *randomized-block designs*.

In summary, *within-subjects designs* take three general forms:

1. The same subject is observed under all treatment conditions.
2. The same subject is observed before and after a treatment (e.g., pretest-posttest design).
3. Subjects are *matched* on an IDV and then randomly assigned to the treatments.

All three forms of within-subjects designs are treated as if multiple observations had been made on the same subject.

In within-subjects designs, whatever is uniquely characteristic of a subject under one treatment will also be characteristic of him or her under the other treatments. For example, some subjects will be generally more responsive to treatments than others.

Thus subjects' scores under different treatments will be related or dependent upon each other, and there will be (usually) a positive correlation between subjects' scores under the different treatment conditions. Statistical tests for data from within-subjects designs take this correlation into account.

The major advantage of the within-subjects design over the between-subjects design is that it provides a more powerful test of the null hypothesis. That is, because we observe the same subjects under all treatment conditions, the measure of error variability ("error term") for the within-subjects design is smaller than for the between-subjects design. In the between-subjects design, variability within a group (error) may be due to experimental error *and* individual differences between subjects. In the within-subjects design, we can estimate the variability due to individual differences within a group from the repeated observations on the same subjects and remove this source of variability from the error term. Hence, in within-subjects designs, variability is due primarily to experimental error, so the error variability in this design is less than in the between-subjects design.

The major disadvantage of this design is that it does not always fit the research we wish to do. For example, it does not make sense to teach a group of subjects a social studies lesson by method A and then teach them the same lesson by method B. Likewise, in a study of memory, it does not make sense to have the same subjects study and recall a list of words presented in a random order and then have them study and recall the same list of words in a conceptual order. In these and many other cases, we have *multiple-treatment inference*. In addition, studies with a large number of treatment conditions may fatigue or bore subjects participating in all conditions. Although matching can be used to overcome fatigue or boredom, the greater the number of treatment conditions, the larger the blocks of matched subjects must be. It is extremely difficult to match two subjects adequately, let alone six or more.

The moral of the story is that whenever they are appropriate (and this is an important qualification), within-subjects designs get the job done with fewer subjects than between-subjects designs, if one holds *power* constant. If within-subjects designs cannot be implemented, between-subjects designs should be used. In some cases, it is possible and desirable to combine within-subjects and between-subjects designs. These designs are called, not surprisingly, *mixed designs*.

One familiar example of a mixed design is the pretest-posttest, control-group experimental design (see Chapter 1). Subjects are randomly assigned to a control or an experimental group; this is the between-subjects part of the design. They receive a pretest and then a posttest after the treatment; these repeated observations on all subjects constitute the within-subjects part of the designs. This design is represented schematically in Table VI-1.

Perhaps an analogy will help make sense of a mixed design. Think of the control and experimental groups as two separate plots of land. This is the between-subjects part of the design. Each plot of land is split into sections (pretest and posttest in Table VI-1); this is the within-subjects part of the design. It turns out that this analogy has a history. The mixed design was developed for agricultural research; different fertilizers were applied within each of several plots of land. Hence, a mixed design is often called a *split-plot design*.

TABLE VI-1 Schematic representation of a mixed design: Pretest-posttest control-group design

Between Subjects	Within Subjects	
	Pretest	*Posttest*
Experimental Group	$X_{1E(pre)}$	$X_{1E(post)}$
	$X_{2E(pre)}$	$X_{2E(post)}$
	$\vdots$	$\vdots$
	$X_{nE(pre)}$	$X_{nE(post)}$
Control Group	$X_{1C(pre)}$	$X_{1C(post)}$
	$X_{2C(pre)}$	$X_{2C(post)}$
	$\vdots$	$\vdots$
	$X_{nC(pre)}$	$X_{nC(post)}$

Another example of a mixed design may be helpful. Recall the study of the factors influencing teachers' estimates of how well students will perform academically. This study was a 3×3 (ability $\times$ participation), within-subjects design. All N teachers provided ratings in all nine treatment conditions. Suppose, before the study, teachers were divided into two groups on the basis of their beliefs about teaching: progressives (P) and traditionals (T). Since teachers can be assigned to one and only one of the two groups, P or T, this part of the design is a between-subjects design. Since all teachers, P and T alike, are observed under all nine treatment conditions, this part of the study is a within-subjects design. In all, we have a $2 \times 3 \times 3$ (belief $\times$ ability $\times$ participation), split-plot (mixed) design, with beliefs as the between-subjects factor and information about student ability and participation as the within-subjects factors.

15

Randomized-Blocks Analysis of Variance

- Description of the Randomized-Blocks ANOVA
- Strength-of-Association
- Reliability
- Summary
- Answers to Example Problems
- Exercises
- Answers to Exercises

The **randomized-blocks analysis of variance (RBANOVA)** can be used to examine data from within-subjects designs. The data may come from repeated measures on the same subject. Hence, the RBANOVA is often called *repeated-measures* ANOVA. For example, the behavior of each subject might be measured under each of four treatment conditions where the order of the conditions has, if possible, been randomized. In this case, each subject represents a *block* of four measures—hence the name *randomized-blocks* ANOVA.

Alternatively, the data may come from a design in which subjects are *matched* on a variable known to be related to the dependent variable. Each member of the *block* of matched subjects would be randomly assigned to a different treatment condition—hence the name *randomized-blocks* ANOVA. For example, each of four matched subjects in a block might be randomly assigned to a different treatment condition. This assignment process would be carried out for each of the blocks of four matched subjects until subjects in all blocks had been assigned to a treatment condition.

The RBANOVA, then, extends the *t* test for dependent samples[1] beyond simply two observations on a single subject or one observation on each member of a matched pair. That is, it enables us to treat, statistically, within-subjects research designs with more than two treatments (e.g., control, treatment 1, treatment 2) or more than two observation occasions

---

[1]The *t* test for dependent samples was presented in Chapter 13 (Section V: "Between-Subjects Designs") on *t* tests for the purpose of continuity; *t* tests for single samples, independent samples, and dependent samples tend to be taught together. Conceptually, however, the *t* test for dependent samples should appear in Section VI ("Within-Subjects and Mixed Designs") since it is used to test hypotheses about treatment effects in *within-subjects* designs. In the end, I acquiesced to typical practice and put all the *t* tests together in Chapter 13.

(e.g., pretest, posttest, retention test). Put still another way, the RBANOVA is to the t test for dependent samples what the one-way ANOVA is to the t test for two independent samples.

In this chapter, the RBANOVA's underpinnings are presented along with the techniques for using the statistical test. More specifically, the RBANOVA is presented as a technique for *testing hypotheses* and as a technique for *estimating the reliability* of behavioral measurements.

As an example of a within-subjects design aimed at testing hypotheses, consider Weiner & Peter's (1973) study of moral judgment. They hypothesized that information about an actor's *intent,* more than the *outcome* of the act, would influence the extent to which late adolescents rewarded or punished the actor. In a test of this hypothesis, subjects aged 16–19 years read four (randomly ordered) scenarios and after each scenario punished or rewarded the actor on a scale from −5 (punish) to +5 (reward). In one scenario, the actor intended good and the outcome was positive; in another, the actor intended good and the outcome was negative; in a third, the actor's intentions were bad but the outcome was positive (good); and in the fourth, the actor's intentions were bad and the outcome was negative. In this design, then, each scenario represents a treatment, and a subject is observed in each cell of the design (see Table 15-1). Hence, we have a within-subjects design, with each subject observed under each of four treatment conditions.

TABLE 15-1 Hypothetical data on the determinants of moral judgments in late adolescence

	Treatment				
	Intent		Outcome		
Subject	Positive	Negative	Positive	Negative	Mean
1	2.5	−4.0	−1.0	−.5	−.75
2	4.0	−2.5	1.0	.5	.75
3	2.5	−3.0	.0	−.5	−.25
4	3.0	−2.0	.5	.5	.50
5	3.5	−3.0	.5	.0	.25
Mean	3.1	−2.9	.2	.0	.10

Suppose that instead of observing each subject in all four treatment conditions, we *matched* subjects on a measure of moral maturity. The four highest-scoring subjects would be placed in *block 1,* the next four in *block 2,* etc., until the lowest-scoring four subjects were placed in *block N.* Then, the subjects in each block would be randomly assigned to one of the treatments—hence the name *randomized-blocks* design. In using this design, we assume that for the purpose of the study, subjects within a block are very similar ("clones") and are different from subjects in other blocks; that is, subjects within a block are exchangeable for one another but not exchangeable for subjects in other blocks.

The RBANOVA can also be used to estimate the reliability of a measurement. For example, suppose that 250 college students responded to a 10-item measure of self-concept. For example, one item might be as follows:

I usually have a positive outlook on life.

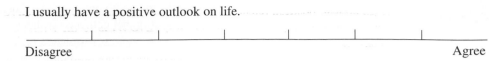

Disagree   Agree

For each subject, then, we have 10 responses on a 7-point, Likert type of rating scale. Hence, we have a within-subjects design with scales corresponding to "treatments." We can use the RBANOVA to estimate reliability, the proportion of total variance attributable to systematic differences among subjects.[2]

DESCRIPTION OF THE RANDOMIZED-BLOCKS ANOVA

Purpose and Underlying Logic

The purpose of the RBANOVA in hypothesis testing (where interest attaches to treatment effects) is to help the researcher decide whether the observed differences between two or more sample means may be due to chance or to systematic differences among population means. The RBANOVA—like its between-subjects counterpart, the one-way ANOVA—partitions the total variability among scores into systematic variability due to treatment differences and to unsystematic variability or error. However, the RBANOVA also takes into account the fact that we have two or more observations on the *same* subject, and it uses that information to provide a more precise estimate of experimental error. The RBANOVA, then, is similar to the *t* test for dependent samples and removes the effects of systematic differences among subjects from the error term.

Consider, for example, the data in Table 15-1. Subjects' ratings can be partitioned into separate sources of variation, much like we did in the factorial ANOVA. One factor is the *treatment* condition—the information about intent and outcome in the four scenarios. Sample means for each scenario are presented in the last row of the table. A second factor is *subjects*—we have ratings for each subject under each treatment condition. If we average each subject's ratings over the four conditions, we have an estimate of each subject's tendency to punish or reward. Some subjects may be more lenient (e.g., subject 2) than others (e.g., subject 1). This *systematic* difference among subjects can be estimated from the variation among the means in the last column of Table 15-1 and *omitted* from our definition of experimental error.

So far, so good. We have a treatment × subjects design; and if the analogy with the two-way ANOVA holds, we should expect to partition the scores into two additional sources of variation: (1) the treatment × subjects interaction and (2) the within-cell error. But look closely at Table 15-1 and the cell with subject 1 as a row and positive intent as the (first) column. We have only *one* score, 2.5, and not a set of scores that would enable us to estimate within-cell variation, or error. More generally, in a RBANOVA, we have *one obser-*

---

[2]In classical theory (Lord & Novick, 1971), this value is the proportion of observed-score variance attributed to true-score variance; in generalizability theory (Cronbach et al., 1972; Shavelson & Webb, 1991), this value is the proportion of expected observed-score variance attributed to universe-score variance.

vation in each and every cell. Consequently, the treatment × subjects' interaction *cannot* be estimated apart from error. With one observation per cell, we say that the interaction effect is confounded with error. The best we can do, then, is estimate a *residual* source of variance that combines the interaction effect and error. In a test of the treatment-effect hypothesis, the focus of our substantive research, this confounding has, as we shall see, important consequences for how we conduct statistical tests.

In the RBANOVA, the levels of the treatment variable typically exhaust all levels of interest, and treatment, therefore, is a fixed effect. Subjects are usually considered to be randomly sampled and so constitute a random factor. A mixed-effects model of the RBANOVA, then, is the most commonly encountered model. We present the results of the mixed-effects RBANOVA in Table 15-2.

TABLE 15-2 Source table for the mixed-effects RBANOVA (data from Table 15-1)

Source	Sum of Squares	df	Mean Squares	F
Treatment (A)	90.1	3	30.03	231.00^a
Subjects (S)	5.8	4	1.45	11.15^b
Residual (AS, e)	1.6	12	.13	
Total	97.3	19		

$^a F_{critical(.01, df=3,12)} = 5.95$
$^b F_{critical(.01, df=4,12)} = 5.41$

The RBANOVA can also be used as a statistical tool for estimating the reliability of a measurement. In reliability analyses, we use the RBANOVA to estimate variance components (see Chapter 14) for subjects (called "true-score variance"), for rating scales or test items (cf. "treatments," the difference in average ratings or the difference in test item difficulty), and for the residual or "measurement error." This information enables us to form a reliability coefficient, r_{XX}: the ratio of true-score to observed-score variance.

The reliability coefficient indicates, for example, how much of the observed variation in self-concept ratings or achievement test scores is due to systematic differences among people.

Design Requirements: Fixed-Effect RBANOVA

The use of the *fixed-effect* (see Chapters 13 and 14) RBANOVA presupposes that the data have been collected as follows:

1. There is one independent variable with two or more levels (i.e., $k \geq 2$).
2. The levels of the independent variable may differ qualitatively (e.g., variation in moral judgment scenarios) or quantitatively (e.g., amount of drug dosage).
3. The same subject is observed under all k levels of the independent variable (each "block" contains one subject with k observations), or k subjects are assigned to each block so that the variability among subjects within a block is less than the variability among blocks (each "block" contains k subjects, each with one observation).

4. Subjects are randomly assigned within a block to levels of the independent variable, unless the same subject is observed in all k conditions, in which case the order of treatments should be randomized if feasible.

Guidelines for forming *blocks* of homogeneous subjects are the same as those given for forming matched pairs. If we match subjects on a variable known to correlate with the dependent variable, the block requirement can be met. In the moral judgment example with matched or blocked subjects, subjects were blocked on a measure of "moral maturity" that, let's say, correlated highly (e.g., $r = .65$) with moral judgments. Hence, variability among subjects' moral judgments within a block should be less than variability in moral judgments among blocks.

Hypotheses

In the RBANOVA, the researcher knows that subjects differ so that attention focuses on the statistical test of the following null and alternative hypotheses regarding k treatments:

H_0: $\mu_1 = \mu_2 = \cdots = \mu_k$

H_1: $\mu_i \neq \mu_{i'}$ for some i and i'

As explained before, there is no statistical test for the treatment × subjects interaction because the interaction is confounded with experimental error.

Assumptions.   The fixed-effects RBANOVA is seldom used because in behavioral research, subjects or blocks are usually considered random effects. For this reason, we present assumptions made in using the mixed-effects model in hypothesis testing.

1. The sum of the treatment effects (factor A) equals zero, and the variation due to the treatment effects is given by $\Sigma(\mu_i - \mu_G)^2/(k - 1)$.
2. The expected values of the random variables—*block* (factor B, subjects), *block × treatment* (AB), and *error*—are zero.
3. The errors are independent and normally distributed with population mean zero and variance σ_e^2.
4. The random variables *blocks* (subjects) are independent and normally distributed, with population mean zero and variance σ_s^2, and they are independent of the *block × treatment* interaction.
5. The random variables *block × treatment* are normally distributed with population mean zero and variance σ_{AS}^2. Note that the random variables *block* (subject) × *treatment* are *not* assumed to be independent.
6. The population variance-covariance matrix, containing a variance for each treatment condition and a covariance for each pair of treatment conditions, is *circular.*[3] This circularity assumption is less restrictive than the compound symmetry assumption in that

---

[3]Rather than assume compound symmetry with equal variance and covariances, circularity only assumes that $(\sigma_1^2 + \sigma_2^2 - \sigma_{12}) = (\sigma_1^2 + \sigma_3^2 - \sigma_{13}) = \ldots$. (See Weiner et al., 1991 or Kirk, 1982, for details.)

a zero block × treatment effect is *not* assumed (see assumption 5 and Weiner et al., 1991). Nevertheless, the circularity assumption is not intuitive and so I focus on compound symmetry to give you a flavor of the assumptions made in RBANOVA hypothesis testing. Compound symmetry implies that the population variances across treatment groups are equal, and the covariances between scores in pairs of treatment groups are equal. The consequence of these two assumptions is that the correlation between the scores for subjects (or blocks) in treatments 1 and 2 is equal to the correlation between scores in treatments 1 and 3, is equal to the correlation between scores in treatments 2 and 3, etc. If we let the Greek letter rho (ρ) represent the population correlation coefficient, we assume that $\rho_{12} = \rho_{13} = \cdots = \rho_{k-1,k}$.

For example, correlations between moral judgment ratings were calculated for all pairs of the four treatment conditions and placed in the matrix shown in Table 15-3. Along the main diagonal of the matrix are the variances of scores in each treatment condition, and off the diagonal are correlations. Since $r_{XY} = r_{YX}$, the matrix is symmetric, and only half the matrix is filled in. The lower triangle is redundant.

The correlations are all positive and range from .49 to .84, a "bounce" in coefficients not unexpected with a *sample* of only five subjects. Moreover, the variances range from .43 to .57, suggesting that the homogeneity-of-variance assumption has been met. [For a formal statistical test of the "symmetry" of this matrix (with covariances, not correlations), see, for example, Kirk (1982).]

TABLE 15-3 Correlation of moral judgment ratings between all pairs of treatment conditions

		Treatment		
Treatment	*1*	*2*	*3*	*4*
1	$(.43)^a$	.49	.83	.77
2		(.55)	.84	.84
3			(.57)	.82
4				(.55)

[a]( ) = variances bearing on the equal-variances assumption of the compound symmetry assumption.

If the correlations are not equal, the *F* test is *positively biased*, that is, the probability of rejecting a true null hypothesis is greater than that set forth at .05 or .01. If the correlations are unequal, the procedures for carrying out the *F* test need to be modified. (For an evaluation of the procedure presented here and others, see Quintana & Maxwell, 1994.) The following steps should be taken in testing the null hypothesis:

1. Use $F_{\text{critical}[\alpha, df(\text{treatment}), df(\text{residual})]}$ to test the null hypothesis.

   a. If the null hypothesis cannot be rejected, stop. No further testing is needed.
   b. If you reject the null hypothesis, continue to step 2.

2. Use $F_{\text{critical}[\alpha, df(\text{treatment})=1, df(\text{residual})=n-1]}$ to test the null hypothesis.

   a. If the null hypothesis is rejected, conclude a treatment effect.
   b. If the null hypothesis cannot be rejected, consult Kirk (1982) for a statistical test of symmetry of the variance-covariance matrix. If the assumptions of equal variances and covariances (i.e., equal correlations if the assumptions hold, since $r_{XY} = \text{Cov}_{XY/s_X s_Y}$) are met, reject the null hypothesis. If the assumptions are violated, do not reject the null hypothesis. In this case, another statistical model such as Hoetellings T^2 might be used (see Kirk, 1982; Scheffé, 1959).

This rule of thumb is meant to save you a lot of statistical gymnastics with the statistical tests involving symmetry. It says that if you cannot reject H_0 when the test is positively biased, you don't have a treatment effect. If you reject the null hypothesis with both the regular degrees of freedom and the *conservative* degrees of freedom $(1, n-1)$, again, there is no problem; you conclude a treatment effect. Only when things fall through the cracks—when you reject H_0 with the regular *df* and not with the conservative *df*—do you need to conduct the test of symmetry to determine which result to trust.

However, if the correlations among treatment conditions are different (e.g., some strongly positive; some close to zero or negative), the substantive interpretation of these findings may be at odds with the RBANOVA; and a different statistical analysis may be needed (cf. Cronbach & Snow, 1977; Rogosa, 1980). Differences in correlations imply that subjects' performances depend upon the nature of the treatment. For certain subjects, treatment A may produce high scores; but for other subjects, treatment B may. If there is strong evidence of a subject $\times$ treatment interaction, interest attaches less to the treatment main effect than to this interaction. Then an attempt should be made to find a measure of student aptitude that accounts for the interaction. In the context of our hypothetical study of moral judgments, where subjects were blocked on a measure of moral maturity, we might focus our attention on the correlations (or regression coefficients) between moral maturity and moral judgments in *each* of the four treatment conditions, looking for differences among the four coefficients.

Computation of the RBANOVA

In the RBANOVA, total variability among scores can be partitioned into three sources:

total variability = variability between treatments
                    + variability between subjects + residual

Computationally, the RBANOVA provides additive sums of squares (*SS*) and degrees of freedom (*df*) corresponding to each source of variation:

$SS_{\text{total}} = SS_{\text{treatments}} + SS_{\text{subjects}} + SS_{\text{residual}}$

$df_{\text{total}} = df_{\text{treatments}} + df_{\text{subjects}} + df_{\text{residual}}$

To compute these sums of squares, use the computational procedure in the *Student Guide* (Procedure 15-1). Data from the hypothetical study of moral judgment (Table 15-1) are used to exemplify the steps in calculation. Alternatively, a statistical package can be used to compute the sums of squares (and the RBANOVA). For instance, the Reliability Program in SPSS provides an RBANOVA and Tukey's test of additivity (see "Answers to Exercises" at the end of this chapter for an example).

Once the sums of squares are obtained, mean squares can be calculated by dividing by the respective degrees of freedom. For the treatment factor, $df_{treatment} = k - 1$; for subjects, $df_{subjects} = n - 1$; and for the residual, $df_{residual} = (k - 1)(n - 1)$ (see Table 15-4). Finally, as a check, these degrees of freedom should sum to the total degrees of freedom, $kn - 1$.

To calculate the mean square for treatments, for example, divide $SS_{treatment}$ by $df_{treatment}$: $90.1/3 = 30.03$. Do likewise to obtain mean squares for subjects and the residual (see Table 15-2). Finally, under the previous assumptions,

$$F_{treatment} = \frac{MS_{treatment}}{MS_{residual}} \quad \text{and} \quad F_{subjects} = \frac{MS_{subjects}}{MS_{residual}}$$

Note that additivity is assumed in fixed-effects model statistical tests, and in the mixed model's statistical test of the subject effect. Subjects are expected to vary and its statistical test is not, typically, of substantive interest. Finally, additivity is not assumed in statistical tests with the random-effects model.

TABLE 15-4 ANOVA summary table

Source	Sum of Squares	df	Mean Squares	Fixed	Random	Mixed
					F	
Treatment (A)	SS_A	$k - 1$	$\dfrac{SS_A}{k - 1}$	$^a\dfrac{MS_A}{MS_{res.}}$	$\dfrac{MS_A}{MS_{res.}}$	$\dfrac{MS_A}{MS_{res.}}$
Subjects (S)	SS_S	$n - 1$	$\dfrac{SS_S}{n - 1}$	$^a\dfrac{MS_S}{MS_{res.}}$	$\dfrac{MS_S}{MS_{res.}}$	$^a\dfrac{MS_S}{MS_{res.}}$
Residual (AS, e)	$SS_{res.}$	$(k - 1)(n - 1)$	$\dfrac{SS_{AS}}{(k - 1)(n - 1)}$			

^{a}Assumes additivity of block $\times$ treatment effect.

Decision Rules for Rejecting the Null Hypothesis

To determine whether to reject the null hypothesis for each of the two hypotheses-tested (treatments and subjects), we must compare $F_{observed}$ (see Table 15-2) with $F_{critical}$. The value of $F_{critical}$ depends on the degrees of freedom associated with each effect and the residual term. To find $F_{critical}$ for the treatment and subjects effect in the moral judgment study, we turn to Table E with three pieces of information in mind: α, df_{effect}, and $df_{residual}$. Let's use $\alpha = .01$ and determine $F_{critical}$ for the treatment and subjects effects, respectively:

$$F_{critical(.01,3,12)} = 5.95$$
$$F_{critical(.01,4,12)} = 5.41$$

Since $F_{observed}$ exceeds $F_{critical}$ in both cases, the null hypothesis for treatments (scenarios) and subjects should be rejected.

Interpretation of the Results of the RBANOVA

The results of the mixed-effects RBANOVA are reported in Table 15-2 for the moral judgment study. Since we concluded before that the assumptions had been met (see the "Assumptions" section), the results in Table 15-2 can be interpreted. We reject the null hypothesis of no difference among the effects of the scenarios and conclude a treatment effect. From Table 15-1, a clear pattern emerges. Adolescents reward positive intent, punish negative intent, and ignore outcome information.

Of course, this observation should be followed by a post hoc test of the differences between means. By replacing MS_{error} with $MS_{residual}$ in the formulas for Scheffé's and Tukey's tests in Chapter 13, we can use these revised formulas with the RBANOVA. Procedures 13-4 and 13-5 provide the steps for carrying out post hoc comparisons. As an example, suppose we decided to test the difference between positive and negative intent ($\bar{X} = 3.1$ vs. $\bar{X} = -2.9$) at $\alpha = .01$. We have the following result for Scheffé's test:

$$t_{obs.} = \frac{\hat{C}}{\sqrt{\frac{MS_{res.}}{n}(w_1^2 + w_2^2 + \cdots + w_k^2)}} = \frac{3.1 - (-2.9)}{\sqrt{\frac{.13}{5}[(1)^2 + (-1)^2 + (0)^2 + (0)^2]}}$$

$$= \frac{6}{.026 \times 2} = \frac{6}{.228} = 26.31$$

The critical value of t is:

$$t'_{crit.} = \sqrt{(k-1)F_{crit.\alpha,k-1,df(res.)}} = (4-1)5.95 = 4.22$$

For Tukey's test, we have:

$$HSD = q_{\alpha,df(res.),k}\sqrt{\frac{MS_{res.}}{n}} = q_{.01,12,4}\sqrt{\frac{1.3}{5}} = 5.5(.16) = .89$$

For Scheffé's test, we decide, since $t_{observed}$ exceeds $t_{critical}$, to reject H_0: $C = 0$. For Tukey's test, since the mean difference (6 points) exceeds HSD (.89), we reject H_0: $C = 0$.

Finally, the main effect for subjects is, as expected, statistically significant. By separately estimating the subject effect, we remove this systematic variation from the measure of error. This test is similar to the dependent t test when the term reflecting systematic differences between subjects was removed from the standard error of the difference between means (Formula 12-7):

$$\sqrt{s_{\bar{X}_1}^2 + s_{\bar{X}_2}^2 - \underbrace{2r_{12}s_{\bar{X}_1}s_{\bar{X}_2}}_{\substack{\text{systematic differences} \\ \text{among subjects}}}}$$

STRENGTH OF ASSOCIATION

A significant F indicates that there is a relation between the independent and dependent variables. For the *fixed-effects* model, $\hat{\omega}^2$ (omega-square) provides a measure of strength of association.

$$\hat{\omega}^2 = \frac{SS_A - (k-1)MS_{\text{res.}}}{SS_T + MS_{\text{res.}}} \qquad \textbf{(15-1)}$$

For the *random-effects* model, the intraclass correlation ($\hat{\rho}_I$) indexes the strength of association. First, we calculate the variance components as in Formula 15-2.

$$\hat{\sigma}_A^2 = \frac{MS_A - MS_{\text{res.}}}{n} \qquad \textbf{(15-2a)}$$

$$\hat{\sigma}_s^2 = \frac{MS_s - MS_{\text{res.}}}{k} \qquad \textbf{(15-2b)}$$

$$\hat{\sigma}_{\text{res.}}^2 = MS_{\text{res.}} \qquad \textbf{(15-2c)}$$

Then we calculate $\hat{\rho}_I$ as in Formula 15-3.

$$\hat{\rho}_I = \frac{\hat{\sigma}_a^2}{\hat{\sigma}_a^2 + \hat{\sigma}_s^2 + \hat{\sigma}_{\text{res.}}^2} \qquad \textbf{(15-3)}$$

The appropriate mean squares can be found in an RBANOVA source table and entered into Formulas 15-2a–c to calculate the variance components that are needed for Formula 15-3.

A modified version of omega-square and the intraclass correlation (Kirk, 1982) can be used to calculate the strength of association for the fixed and random effects in the *mixed-model* RBANOVA. For the fixed and random effects, respectively, we have Formulas 15-4a, b.

$$\hat{\omega}_{\text{mixed}}^2 = \frac{\left[\dfrac{k-1}{nk}(MS_A - MS_{\text{res.}})\right]}{MS_{\text{res.}} + (MS_S - MS_{\text{res.}})/k + \left[\dfrac{k-1}{nk}(MS_A - MS_{\text{res.}})\right]} \qquad \textbf{(15-4a)}$$

$$\hat{\rho}_{\text{mixed}}^2 = \frac{\hat{\sigma}_s^2}{\sigma_e^2 + \sigma_s^2 + (MS_A - MS_{\text{res.}})/n} \qquad \textbf{(15-4b)}$$

Applying Formulas 15-4a, b to the hypothetical data on moral judgments (see Table 15-2), we find for the fixed (treatment) factor:

$$\hat{\omega}^2_{mixed} = \frac{\left[\dfrac{3}{(5)(4)}(30.03 - .13)\right]}{.13 + (1.45 - .13)/4 + \left[\dfrac{3}{(5)(4)}(30.03 - .13)\right]}$$

$$= \frac{4.49}{4.95} = .91$$

For the random (subjects) factor, we find:

$$\hat{\rho}^2_{mixed} = \frac{.33}{.13 + .33 + 5.98}$$

$$= \frac{.33}{6.44} = .05$$

Example Problem 15.1

One important aspect of problem solving is the ability to translate the representation of the problem as given into a representation of the problem that admits to a solution. For example, word problems in physics often have to be translated into some figural representation, and then translated into one or more equations before a solution can be arrived at. This feature suggests that as the number of symbolic translations needed to solve a problem increases, the difficulty of the problem should increase also.

In a test of this hypothesis, a random sample of 41 subjects was given, individually and in random order, four types of problems to solve in which the number of transformations required was 0, 1, 2, or 3. The results indicated that the sum of squares for problem type was 25.0, the sum of squares for subjects was 320.0, and the mean square residual was 1.01. The means for problems with 0, 1, 2, and 3 transformations were 8.0, 6.0, 5.0, and 2.0, respectively, with a total of 10 points possible for any one problem type. The variances for each of the problem types were roughly equivalent; the correlation of scores between any two conditions ranged from .25 to .89.

a. State the null and alternative hypotheses for each effect in this design.
b. State the assumptions required to test the null hypothesis.
c. Construct an ANOVA table from the information given.
d. Give $F_{critical}$ for testing the problem-type effect, and justify the value or values chosen. State your conclusions.
e. If you conclude a significant problem-type effect, compare the 0 and 3 transformation conditions to see whether, in the population, there is a difference.

RELIABILITY

Reliability refers to the consistency or dependability of a behavioral measurement. The notion is that assuming the subject is in a steady state, a measure on that subject should give exactly the same reading upon repeated measures with the same instrument or with equivalent instruments that are used interchangeably to measure the same thing. To the extent that repeated measurements on the same subject disagree, we call this *measurement error*. Measurement error gives rise to inconsistency in measurements and hence makes these measurements less dependable.

To assess reliability, we can take multiple measurements on a sample of subjects. Systematic variation among these subjects (σ_s^2) reflects measurement consistency or dependability. Random fluctuations in the measurement reflect error (σ_e^2). In classical test theory, we define reliability ($r_{XX'}$) as in Formula 15-5.

$$r_{XX'} = \frac{\sigma_s^2}{\sigma_s^2 + \sigma_e^2} \qquad \text{(15-5)}$$

In practice, there are a number of ways to assess reliability. We can take multiple measurements on the same subjects with the same instrument at different times. Assuming subjects are in a steady state, differences in readings on the instrument for a given subject reflect measurement error. This method of assessing reliability is typically called *test-retest* reliability. Table 15-5 provides a general schematic of a reliability design. Variable X might represent test scores based on the sum of correct item responses, reaction times, or self-concept scores based on the sum of a set of ratings.

TABLE 15-5 Schematic of a reliability design

Subjects	Repeated Measurements			
	1	*2*	$\cdots$	*k*
1	X_{11}	X_{12}	$\cdots$	X_{1k}
2	X_{21}	X_{22}	$\cdots$	X_{2k}
$\vdots$	$\vdots$	$\vdots$	$\vdots$	$\vdots$
n	X_{n1}	X_{n2}	$\cdots$	X_{nk}

A second way to assess reliability is to take multiple readings with different versions of the same instrument (e.g., parallel versions of a test). Interchangeable versions of the instrument (e.g., test) might be chosen at random to provide measurements at one point in time. For example, *test items,* purporting to measure the same attribute, might be randomly selected from an item pool and used to provide multiple measurements. Again, assuming the subjects are in a steady state, inconsistencies in readings (e.g., in test or item scores) reflect error. When alternative forms of the instrument are used, we call this method of estimating reliability *alternative-forms* or *parallel-forms* reliability. Variable X in Table 15-5 would represent scores on alternative forms.

Now consider the case where the parallel tests consist of only one item each. If k tests (of one item each) are given to subjects at the same time, we can use these repeated measures to index reliability. Assuming a steady state, variation in a person's item scores (e.g., right/wrong) represents measurement error. Reliability estimated in this way is called *internal-consistency* reliability. Variable *X* in Table 15-5 would represent item scores.

By now I hope it is clear, especially from Table 15-5, that reliability data are collected in a *subjects* × *treatments (test)*, randomized-blocks design with repeated measures on the same subjects. More specifically, the data are collected as a random-effects model, randomized-blocks design. The RBANOVA can be used to estimate the variance components for subjects (σ_s^2)—reflecting systematic variation—and measurement error (σ_{res}^2) using Formulas 15-2a, c. The values of these variance components estimates can be entered into Formula 15-5a to obtain the reliability coefficient.

$$r_{XX'} = \frac{\hat{\sigma}_s^2}{\hat{\sigma}_s^2 + \dfrac{\hat{\sigma}_e^2}{k}} \tag{15-5a}$$

where:
   k = number of repeated measures on a subject

Formula 15-5a differs from the conceptual formula for reliability in that estimated variance components are used and σ_{res}^2 is divided by *k*, the number of repeated measures on a subject with the same instrument in test-retest reliability, with randomly parallel tests in parallel-forms reliability, or with randomly parallel items in internal-consistency reliability. Term *k* simply adjusts the formula to reflect the number of measurement occasions (retest reliability), the number of parallel tests (parallel-forms reliability), or the length of a test (number of items, internal-consistency reliability).[4]

From this formula, we can see that as *k* increases, so does $r_{XX'}$, because the denominator decreases in magnitude. Increasing the number of observations you have on an individual, the number of tests, or the item scores improves the reliability of your measurement—which is consistent with common sense.

Estimating Test-Retest Reliability

Table 15-6 provides hypothetical data on the test reliability of a measure of emotional self-concept (e.g., Marsh & Shavelson, 1985). Each subject's score is the sum of 10 self-ratings on items such as the following:

I usually look on the good side of things.

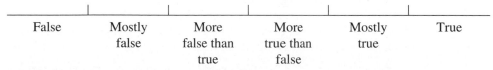

| False | Mostly false | More false than true | More true than false | Mostly true | True |

This facet of self-concept was measured on two occasions, 1 week apart. Since none of the students reported an especially emotionally disturbing event during this period, we

---

[4]In classical theory, *k* provides the Spearman-Brown prophecy formula adjustment for test length.

TABLE 15-6 Test-retest data on emotional self-concept

	Occasion	
Subject	1	2
1	65	64
2	61	65
3	58	55
4	50	45

TABLE 15-7 Estimation of variance components for the self-concept reliability study

Source	SS	df	MS	Variance Component
Subjects (s)	359.37	3	119.79	$\hat{\sigma}_s^2 = 56.167$
Occasions (o)	3.13	1	3.13	$\hat{\sigma}_o^2 = .000$
$s \times o$	22.38	3	7.46	$\hat{\sigma}_{so}^2 = 7.458$

assume that the self-concept of each was in a steady state. The data are given in Table 15-6.

The results of a random-effects model RBANOVA are presented in Table 15-7. Note that an F test is not performed because we are interested only in using the RBANOVA to obtain the variance components shown in the table (see Formula 15-2 to compute variance components). With the variance components, we calculate reliability by using Formula 15-5a:

$$r_{XX'} = \frac{\hat{\sigma}_s^2}{\hat{\sigma}_s^2 + \dfrac{\hat{\sigma}_{res.}^2}{k}} = \frac{56.167}{56.167 + \dfrac{7.458}{2}} = \frac{56.167}{59.896} = .94$$

Note that by using $k = 2$, we have the reliability of the self-concept scores averaged over the two occasions. To determine the reliability of the self-concept scores for one occasion, we let $k = 1$ and recalculate:

$$r_{XX'} = \frac{\hat{\sigma}_s^2}{\hat{\sigma}_s^2 + \hat{\sigma}_{res.}^2} = \frac{56.167}{56.167 + 7.458} = \frac{56.167}{63.626} = .88$$

Estimating Internal-Consistency Reliability

Table 15-8 provides subjects' scores (0 or 1) on each item of a five-item test. The subjects took the test at the conclusion of an experiment, and the researcher would like to estimate the reliability of the measurement. Table 15-9 contains the results of a random-model RBANOVA on the item data and the estimated variance components.

TABLE 15-8 Test-retest data on five-item test

Subject	Test Item				
	1	2	3	4	5
1	1	0	0	0	0
2	0	1	1	0	0
3	1	0	0	1	0
4	1	1	1	1	1

TABLE 15-9 Estimation of variance components for the five-item test

Source	SS	df	MS	Variance Component
Subjects (s)	1.800	3	.600	$\hat{\sigma}_s^2 = .075$
Items (i)	.500	4	.125	$\hat{\sigma}_i^2 = .000$
$s \times i$	2.700	12	.225	$\hat{\sigma}_{si}^2 = .225$

From the data of Table 15-9, the reliability of a test score based on all items ($k = 5$) is

$$r_{XX'} = \frac{\hat{\sigma}_s^2}{\hat{\sigma}_s^2 + \dfrac{\hat{\sigma}_{res.}^2}{k}} = \frac{.075}{.075 + \dfrac{.225}{5}} = \frac{.075}{.120} = .63$$

Example Problem 15.2

In Example Problem 15.1, 41 subjects solved four different problem types varying in the number of transformations required for problem solution. Suppose the researcher decides to use the sum of each subject's scores on all four problem types to get a measure of problem-solving ability. Once this problem-solving score is obtained, it will be used to predict scores on a mathematics achievement test. Use the information provided in Example Problem 15.1 to determine the reliability of this problem-solving score.

SUMMARY

This chapter presents the *randomized-blocks analysis of variance* (RBANOVA), a statistical test used to examine differences between means collected from within-subjects designs. The purpose and underlying rationale and the procedures for computing and interpreting fixed-, random-, and mixed-effects RBANOVA are presented. Special attention is paid to stringent assumptions required for the F test with the RBANOVA. Procedures for computing the strength of association are presented and exemplified, as are Scheffé's and Tukey's methods of post hoc comparison. In addition, the RBANOVA, as a procedure for estimating variance components, is applied to the problem of determining the reliability of a behavioral measurement. More specifically, methods for estimating the reliability of test scores and rating scales are presented.

ANSWERS TO EXAMPLE PROBLEMS

1. **a.** $H_0: \mu_1 = \mu_2 = \mu_3 = \mu_4$, $H_1: \mu_i \neq \mu_i$

   b. 1. *Independence:* Subjects were randomly sampled, received the problems in random order, and were tested individually. Hence we can assume independence of errors and subject effects.
   2. *Normality:* No information on the distribution of scores or subject effects is given. Usually the assumption of normality holds for such data, and there is no indication of a floor or ceiling effect. Finally, the RBANOVA is robust to the normality assumption.
   3. *Compound symmetry* (or *circularity*): The problem states that the variances are roughly equal, implying that in the population this is the case. However, the sample data suggest that this assumption may have been violated; correlations range from .25 to .89. In this case, an $F_{obs.}$ must be compared with a sequence of $F_{crit.}$ values before deciding whether or not to reject the null hypothesis.

   c.

   ### ANOVA TABLE

Source	SS	df	MS	F
Problem type (p)	25.0	3	8.33	8.25
Subjects (s)	360.0	40	9.00	
Residual (ps)	121.2	120	1.01	

   d. Because there is reason to believe that the assumption of compound symmetry has been violated, we proceed with a sequence of F tests. First, we carry out the F test with the usual degrees of freedom. If H_0 is rejected, we carry out an F test with conservative degrees of freedom (1 and $n-1$). If we reject H_0, we conclude a treatment effect. So, in testing the problem-type effect, first $F_{obs.}$ is compared with $F_{crit.(.05,3,120)} \approx 2.68$. Since $8.25 > 2.68$, we continue using the conservative degrees of freedom: $F_{crit.(.05,1,40)} = 4.08$. Since $8.25 > 4.08$, we conclude a significant problem-type effect and become interested in post hoc comparisons.

   e. $HSD = q(.05, 120, 4)\sqrt{\dfrac{1.01}{41}} = 3.68(.16) = .589$

   Since $8 - 2 = 6$ exceeds .58, we conclude that in the population, the means differ and that problems with three transformations are more difficult than problems that do not require a transformation of the information given.

2. The reliability of a measurement with k items is given by Formula 15-5a. To use this formula, we need to know the number of items (problem types in our example here), the variance component for subjects, and the variance component for the residual. Formulas 15-2b, c provide a means for obtaining the variance components:

   $$\hat{\sigma}^2_{res.} = 1.01$$
   $$\hat{\sigma}^2_s = \frac{9.00 - 1.01}{41} = .195$$

Substituting these values in Formula 15-5a, we have:

$$r_{XX'} = \frac{.195}{.195 + (1.01/4)} = \frac{.195}{.448} = .44$$

Clearly, this reliability coefficient is too low for use in prediction, and the researcher should reconsider the proposed study.

EXERCISES

Hudley & Graham (1993) hypothesized that boys' aggressive behavior might be the consequence of their misattributing the intent of others in ambiguous situations, and that these boys could be retrained to more appropriately attribute intent in such situations (see Chapter 4). Consequently, Hudley and Graham would predict that the aggressive boys' perceptions of negative intent would, on average, decrease from pre- to posttest. Use the data in Table 15-10 to test this hypothesis.

TABLE 15-10   Aggressive boys' ratings of negative intent in ambiguous situations

Group[a]	Pretest	Posttest	Group	Pretest	Posttest
1	6.00	3.00	2	4.00	3.00
1	4.00	1.00	2	6.00	4.00
1	4.00	2.00	2	6.00	6.00
1	5.00	2.00	3	3.00	4.00
1	4.00	2.00	3	4.00	4.00
1	5.00	1.00	3	5.00	5.00
2	7.00	6.00	3	5.00	5.00
2	6.00	6.00	3	3.00	4.00
2	3.00	5.00	3	5.00	7.00

[a]1 = experimental, 2 = attention control, 3 = no treatment control.

1. Present sample statistics that bear on the hypothesis. Do these statistics support the hypothesis?
2. Use the RBANOVA to determine whether the observed sample mean differences arose by chance.

   a. Evaluate the assumption of compound symmetry.
   b. State the null and alternative hypotheses tested.
   c. Report the results in a summary table.
   d. Do you need to do post hoc comparisons? Why or why not? If you do, report the findings.
   e. Report a measure of the strength of association between the treatment variable and rating of negative intent.
   f. Interpret the findings; what do you conclude?

3. Do a *t* test to see if the mean pre- to posttest change is statistically significant.

   a. Report the results
   b. Compare the findings with the treatment effect in the RBANOVA. Are they related? Why or why not?

4. Calculate the reliability of scores from randomly parallel forms of a test using data in Table 15-11. Interpret the coefficient.

TABLE 15-11 Scores from randomly parallel tests

| | Test Form | | |
Subject	A	B	C
1	4	4	4
2	6	7	6
3	8	7	7
4	6	8	7
5	2	1	1
6	5	4	4
7	4	5	6
8	7	7	6

ANSWERS TO EXERCISES

1.

SPSS for MS WINDOWS:
REPORT SUMMARIES PROGRAM
AGGRESS: 1.00 Aggressive

	PRETEST	POSTTEST
Mean	4.72	3.89
StdDev	1.18	1.81

As hypothesized, the mean perceived negative intent dropped from pre- to posttest.

2. a. The assumption of compound symmetry states that the population variances are equal as are the correlations. From the descriptive statistics, we can conclude that the assumption of homogeneity of variance holds. Since there is only one correlation, we cannot evaluate this part of the assumption. Indeed, with only two measures on each subject, the compound symmetry assumption becomes an assumption of variance homogeneity.

   b. The hypothesis of interest is the treatment hypothesis:

   H_0: $\mu_1 = \mu_2$
   H_1: $\mu_1 \neq \mu_2$

c. The Reliability Program in SPSS was used to generate the RBANOVA summary table below by requesting an ANOVA table and Tukey's nonadditivity test. The table was edited since SPSS presents more information than is needed (see the table that follows). The important information is: "Between People" (Subjects), "Between Measures" (Occasions), and "Residual." The residual is divided into Tukey's non-additivity test (which was not significant at $\alpha = .05$) and "Balance" (i.e., that residual variation not due to linear nonadditivity).

Source	Sum of Squares	df	Mean Squares	F	Prob.
Occasion	6.25	1	6.25	3.90	.065
Subjects	52.14	17	3.07		
Residual	27.25	17	1.60		

Note: If you used only the subjects who received the experimental treatment (Group 1), you would have found the following (taken directly fron SPSS).

RELIABILITY ANALYSIS–SCALE (ALPHA)
Analysis of Variance

Source of Variation	Sum of Sq.	df	Mean Square	F	Prob.
Between People	4.7500	5	.9500		
Within People	25.5000	6	4.2500		
Between Measures	24.0833	1	24.0833	85.0000	.003
Residual	1.4167	5	.2833		
Nonadditivity	.0132	1	.0132	.0375	.8559
Balance	1.4035	4	.3509		
Total	30.2500	11	2.7500		

The remaining answers refer to the analysis with all three groups.

d. No, there are only two means. Moreover, the mean difference is not statistically significant so post hoc comparisons are not called for.

e. Because the treatment effect was not statistically significant, omega-square, the appropriate measure of strength of association for a fixed factor, would not normally be calculated. For practice, here's the calculation:

$$\hat{\omega}^2 = \frac{\left[\dfrac{1}{18*2}(6.25-1.60)\right]}{1.60 + \dfrac{3.07-1.60}{2} + \left[\dfrac{2-1}{18*2}(6.25-1.60)\right]} = \frac{.1302}{1.60+.735+.1302} = .05$$

Not surprisingly, the proportion of variation in intent ratings based on the pretest-posttest difference was small: 5 percent.

f. Although the mean increase was in the predicted direction, it was not statistically significant. This is due to the small sample size and the fact that the treatment was given to and only effective for, subjects in Group 1: Experimental.

3. a. Results of the t^* test using SPSS's paired t test program were as follows:
$t^*_{observed} = 1.97$, $df = 17$, Prob $= .065$.

    b. The same conclusion is reached: Do not reject the null hypothesis. Moreover, the probability of observing sample mean difference at or beyond what we did was .065 in both cases. That is, the two tests of the treatment effect are identical.

4. SPSS Reliability was run to obtain mean squares with which to calculate variance components and reliability. It also provides descriptive statistics and a reliability estimate that can be used to check our calculations here.

RELIABILITY ANALYSIS–SCALE (ALPHA)

		Mean	StdDev	Cases
1.	A	5.2500	1.9086	8.0
2.	B	5.3750	2.3261	8.0
3.	C	5.1250	2.0310	8.0

Note: The randomly parallel tests are of about equal difficulty —roughly equal means.

Correlation Matrix

	A	B	C
A	1.0000		
B	.8768	1.0000	
C	.8384	.9563	1.0000

Note: The randomly parallel forms correlate highly with each other, as would be expected if they are reliable.

Analysis of Variance

Source of Variation	Sum of Sq.	df	Mean Square	F
Between People	85.1667	7	12.1667	
Within People	7.3333	16	.4583	
Between Measures	.2500	2	.1250	[.2471[a]]
Residual	7.0833	14	.5060	
Total	92.5000	23	4.0217	

[a] Not used in reliability analysis.

Reliability Coefficients   3 items [Scores averaged over 3 forms]
Alpha $= .9584$ Standardized item alpha $= .9606$

    This concludes the SPSS output. Now let's calculate relevant variance components:

$$\hat{\sigma}^2_s = \frac{12.167 - .506}{3} = 3.887$$

$$\hat{\sigma}^2_{res.} = .506$$

Calculate reliability for subjects' scores based on 1 test ($k = 1$) and for 3 tests ($k = 3$). Note that the calculation for 3 tests should be equal to alpha given before.

$$r_1 = \frac{3.887}{3.887 + \dfrac{.506}{1}} = .8848$$

$$r_3 = \frac{3.887}{3.887 + \dfrac{.506}{3}} = .9584$$

The proportion of observed-score variance accounted for by systematic differences in the performance of subjects is .88 with scores from one test and .96 with scores averaged (or summed) across three tests.

16

Split-Plot Analysis of Variance

- Description of the SPANOVA
- Interpretation of the Results of the SPANOVA
- Random and Mixed Models of SPANOVA
- Strength of Association
- Post Hoc Comparisons
- Summary
- Answers to Example Problems
- Exercises
- Answers to Exercises

The **split-plot analysis of variance (SPANOVA)** can be used to analyze data from mixed designs—designs with one or more between-subjects factors and one or more within-subjects factors (see the introduction to Section VI). One of the most common mixed designs is the pretest-posttest, true experimental design. Subjects are randomly assigned to a control or experimental group—a between-subjects factor. They are given a pretest before and a posttest after their respective treatments. Time of measurement is the within-subjects factor.

The teacher expectancy study (see Chapter 2) fits this description. Subjects were randomly assigned to an experimental ("bloomers") or control group, and ability was measured at pretest and posttest. In addition, subjects were drawn from grades 1–6; grade level is a second between-subjects factor. Thus, the design of the teacher expectancy study is a $2 \times 6 \times 2$ mixed design with two between-subjects factors (treatment group and grade level) and one within-subject factor (test occasion). A SPANOVA can be used to analyze the ability data.

The study of moral judgments (see Chapter 15) is another example of a mixed design. Subjects judged an actor on the basis of information about the actor's intent (positive or negative) and the outcome of an event (positive or negative). The same subjects, aged 18–19 years, judged the actor under all four combinations or conditions of intent and outcome. Hence, the experimental variable (the four conditions) was a within-subjects variable, and the age variable was a between-subjects factor. Chapter 15 showed the application of the randomized-blocks analysis of variance to data from a within-subjects variable. A second factor in the moral judgment study, held constant in Chapter 15, was age. Groups of subjects 4–6, 7–9, 10–12, 13–15, and 16–19 years of age judged the actor under the four conditions. Age, then, is a between-subjects variable. So the study of moral judgments is a 5×4 mixed design, with one between-subjects factor (age) and one within-subjects factor (condition). Finally, some of you may have noticed that the within-subjects "treatment condition" variable with four levels is really a factorial combination of two independent variables: intent (positive, negative) and outcome (positive, negative). Consequently, the moral judgment study in its full design is a $5 \times 2 \times 2$ mixed design with one between-subjects variable (age) and two within-subjects variables (intent and outcome). A SPANOVA can be used to analyze the ratings from the full moral judgment study.

In this chapter, the SPANOVA's conceptual underpinnings are presented along with techniques for statistically testing hypotheses. Particular attention will be paid to the SPANOVA's strong assumptions about the data from the within-subjects part of the design. To simplify matters, we will consider only the simplest of within-subjects designs, the design with one between-subjects factor and one within-subjects factor. Once you have a firm grasp of the analysis of data from this, the simplest design, you should be able to understand treatments of more complex models in more advanced texts such as Winer, Brown, & Michels (1991) and Kirk (1982).

DESCRIPTION OF THE SPANOVA

Purpose and Underlying Logic

The purpose of the SPANOVA is to help the researcher decide whether the observed differences between means may be due to chance or to systematic differences among the population means. More specifically, the SPANOVA helps the researcher decide whether differences in the means on the between-subjects variable (e.g., control vs. experimental "bloomers" group) arose by chance, whether the differences in means on the within-subjects variable (e.g., pretest vs. posttest ability) arose by chance, and whether the *interaction* of the between-subjects variable group with the within-subjects variable arose by chance.

The SPANOVA presented in this chapter is a two-way ANOVA. Like the two-way ANOVA in Chapter 14, it partitions the total variability among scores into systematic variability due to factor A (e.g., group), factor B (test occasion), their interaction (AB), and error. Unlike the two-way ANOVA, the SPANOVA distinguishes error associated with the between-subjects factor and the within-subjects factor. Error associated with the between-subjects factor is calculated just as it is in the one-way ANOVA (see Chapter 13). Error associated with the within-subjects factor and the interaction is calculated just as it is in the RBANOVA (Chapter 15). Here we take advantage of the repeated measurements on the same subjects (or blocked clones) to remove systematic differences among subjects in estimating experimental error.

To illustrate the SPANOVA, hypothetical data from the moral judgment study described in Chapter 15 will be used (see Table 16-1). Recall that, in the original study, Weiner & Peter (1973) hypothesized that information about an actor's *intent,* more than the *outcome* of an act in a moral situation, would influence the extent to which late adolescents rewarded or

TABLE 16-1 Listing of hypothetical data from a study of children's and adults' moral judgments

		Moral Situation[a]			
ID	Age[b]	O+ I+	O+ I−	O− I+	O− I−
01	1	2	1	−2	−3
02	1	2	−1	−3	−3
03	1	3	−1	1	−2
04	1	3	1	−1	−4
05	1	4	2	−2	−1
06	2	2	−2	2	−3
07	2	3	−2	−1	−4
08	2	3	−3	2	−4
09	2	4	−4	1	−2
10	2	3	1	3	−5
11	3	3	−2	4	−5
12	3	3	−3	3	−3
13	3	4	1	−1	−4
14	3	2	−3	1	−3
15	3	4	−4	3	−3
16	4	3	−3	2	−3
17	4	4	−2	3	−4
18	4	4	−4	1	−2
19	4	3	−1	4	−3
20	4	4	−5	3	−5
21	5	3	−5	2	−3
22	5	4	−2	4	−3
23	5	2	−2	3	−4
24	5	3	−2	3	−2
25	5	4	−3	3	−3

[a] O = outcome (positive or negative); I = intent (positive or negative).
[b] 1 = 4–6 years, 2 = 7–9 years, 3 = 10–12 years, 4 = 13–15 years, 5 = 16–18 years.

punished the actor. In contrast, young children were expected to depend more on outcome than on intent information in rewarding or punishing the actor. Specifically, then, an age × moral situation interaction was hypothesized. In a test of this hypothesis, subjects aged 4 to 18 years read four (randomly ordered) scenarios that varied *intent* and *outcome*. After each scenario, subjects punished or rewarded the actor on a scale from −5 (punish) to +5 (reward).

The results of a 5 × 4 (age × situation) SPANOVA using the hypothetical data are presented in Table 16-2. This table demonstrates the partitioning of the total variability among

TABLE 16-2 SPANOVA source table[a] (data from Table 16-1)

Source	Sums of Squares	df	Mean Squares	F
Between Subjects				
Age (A)	1.54	4	.39	.27[b]
Subjects w. Groups	28.50	20	1.43	
Within Subjects				
Treatment (B)	667.15	3	222.38	134.77[c]
AB	101.50	12	8.46	5.12[d]
B × Subjects w. Groups	99.10	60	1.65	

[a] SPSS Program Setup:
  manova oposipos oposineg onegipos onegineg by age(1,5)
      /wsfactors=group(4)
      /contrast(group)=difference
      /rename=cons dif2v1 dif3v21 dif4v321 /print=signif(averf) homogeneity(boxm)
      /design age.
[b] $F_{critical(.05,4,20)} = 2.87$
[c] $F_{critical(df_{conservative} = .05,1,20)} = 4.35$; $F_{critical(df_{conventional} = .05,3,60)} = 2.76$
[d] $F_{critical(df_{conservative} = .05,4,20)} = 2.87$; $F_{critical(df_{conventional} = .05,12,60)} = 1.92$

scores into between-subjects and within-subjects variability. It also demonstrates that *two separate error terms* can be isolated—one for the between-subjects variable ("Subjects within Groups") and one for the within-subjects variable and interaction ("*B* × Subjects within Groups").

A significant age × treatment interaction was predicted and found. The age × treatment interaction means are plotted in Figure 16-1. These data are consistent with the hypothesis, but they indicate also that by school age (7–9 years), less credence is given to outcome than intent information. Of course, this interpretation is tentative and must await confirmation with appropriate post hoc comparisons.

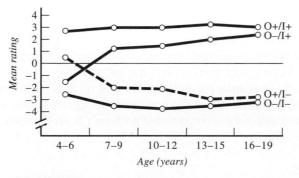

FIGURE 16-1
Interaction between age and type of information in moral judgments

Design Requirements

The use of the fixed-effect SPANOVA presupposes that the data have been collected as follows:

1. There are two independent variables, each with two or more levels. One independent variable is a between-subjects variable with q levels, and the other is a within-subjects variable with r levels, where q and r are greater than or equal to 2.
2. The between-subjects variable can be of two types: manipulated by the researcher or measured by the researcher. In the former case, subjects are randomly selected from a population and randomly assigned to levels of the between subjects variable (e.g., control and experimental groups). In the latter case, subjects are randomly sampled from their respective populations (e.g., age level).
3. For the within-subjects variable, if repeated measures are taken on the same subject, each block contains one subject. If subjects are matched (clones) within each block, the number of matched subjects equals the number of levels of the within-subjects variable (r). In the latter case, subjects within a block would be randomly assigned to the r levels of the within-subjects variable. Thus, each cell would contain a single subject.

   a. For the case where repeated measures are taken on the same subjects, subjects are randomly selected and randomly assigned to one of the q levels of the between-subjects variable or are randomly selected from their respective populations.
   b. For the case of matched (blocked) subjects, blocks (of r subjects) are randomly selected and randomly assigned to one of the q levels of the between-subjects variable or are randomly selected from their respective populations.

4. For the repeated-measures case, the order of the r treatment conditions should be randomized. The exception to this rule is when the treatment precludes randomized order, as with a pretest-posttest, within-subjects variable.

To better understand these design requirements, let's apply them to the moral judgment and teacher expectancy studies. In the moral judgment study, age is a measured between-subjects variable with $q = 5$ levels. Treatment condition (i.e., the scenarios) describing the actor's intent and the event's outcome is a within-subjects variable with $r = 4$ levels. Subjects from each age level are randomly sampled from their respective populations. Since the same subject is observed in all four treatment conditions, the order of the treatments should be randomized.

In the teacher expectancy study, treatment (control vs. "bloomers") is researcher-manipulated; subjects are randomly sampled from a population and randomly assigned to control and experimental groups ($q = 2$). Test occasion (pretest, posttest) is the within-subjects variable with $r = 2$ levels. Test order precludes randomization of presentation order. (If there had been two parallel forms of the ability test, order could and should be randomized. A randomly determined half of the subjects would get form 1 at pretest and form 2 at posttest; the other half, vice versa.)

Hypotheses

In the fixed-effect SPANOVA, the following hypotheses are tested for the between-subjects factor, the within-subjects factor, and their interaction, respectively:

$H_0: \mu_1 = \mu_2 = \cdots = \mu_i = \cdots = \mu_q$

$H_1: \mu_i \neq \mu_{i'}$ for some i and i'

$H_0: \mu_1 = \mu_2 = \cdots = \mu_j = \cdots = \mu_r$

$H_1: \mu_j \neq \mu_{j'}$ for some j and j'

H_0: interaction effect $= 0$

H_1: interaction effect $\neq 0$

Research hypotheses leading to the design of this study can be evaluated by means of statistical tests of the null hypotheses. If one or more of the null hypotheses are rejected, post hoc comparisons should be carried out by using Scheffé's or Tukey's method.

Assumptions

Four assumptions are made in the use of the F distribution in carrying out statistical tests with the fixed-effect SPANOVA. The first three you should be familiar with; the fourth is similar to the equal-correlation assumption of the RBANOVA.

1. *Independence:* Subjects are randomly sampled from their respective populations, and their scores are independent.
2. *Normality:* The populations from which the subjects were sampled are normal.
3. *Homogeneity of variances:* The populations from which subjects were sampled have equal variances.
4. *Homogeneity of covariances:* The population covariances for all pairs of the levels of the within-subjects factor (j and j') are equal, at each level of the between-subjects factor. If assumption 3 is true, assumption 4 can be restated as follows: The population correlations for all pairs of the levels of the within-subjects factor are equal, at each level of the between-subjects factor.

This last assumption needs clarification. As with the RBANOVA, we assume that in the population, the covariances between all pairs of the levels of the within-subjects factor are equal. This criterion must hold true at each level of the between-subjects factor. If the population variances are equal, this will also be true of the population correlations.[1] In terms of the moral judgment study, then, we assume that in the population, at each age level (the between-subjects factor), the correlations between ratings for all six pairwise combinations of scenarios are equal.

This assumption is shown schematically in Figure 16-2. In each cell of the between-subjects design, we observe the same subject's ratings under four different treatment conditions (scenarios). By correlating all pairs of these ratings, we produce a 4×4 (scenario $\times$ scenario) correlation matrix with ones on the main diagonal and (population) correlations

---

[1]This assumption may be violated in that correlations between adjacent measures (e.g., ρ_{12}) are typically higher than correlations between nonadjacent measures (e.g., ρ_{14}). For an accessible treatment of alternative approaches to analyzing mixed (split-plot) designs, see Obrien & Kaiser (1985). SPSS, for example, provides both split-plot and multivariate analysis of variance approaches in the same run. For additional technical considerations, see, for example, Schaalje, Zhang, Pantula, & Pollock (1991).

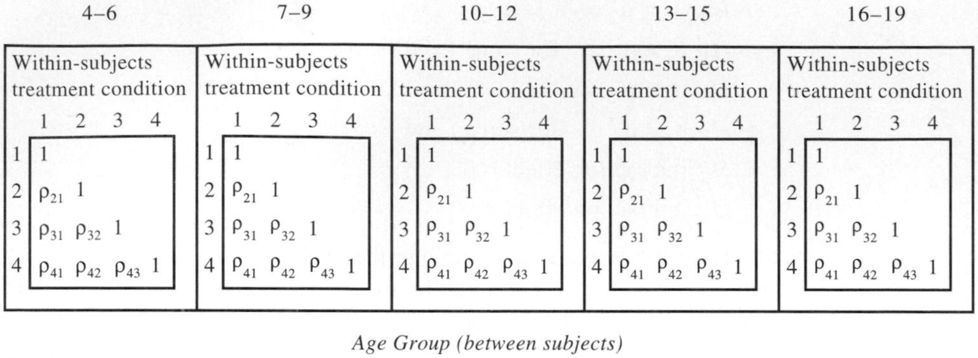

| | 4–6 | | | | 7–9 | | | | 10–12 | | | | 13–15 | | | | 16–19 | | | |

Age Group (between subjects)

FIGURE 16-2

Schematic representation of the assumption of homogeneity of covariances (when the assumption of homogeneity of variances is met; ρ = population correlation)

off the diagonal. That is, for any one between-subjects cell, we have a RBANOVA; and we assume that the population correlations are equal. Furthermore, in the SPANOVA, we assume that the correlation matrix for each cell of the between-subjects variable is equal to the correlation matrix in every other cell.[2]

Statistical tests of this assumption of equal correlations across the levels of the within-subjects variable ("symmetry") and equal-correlation matrices across the levels of the between-subjects variable ("homogeneity") are described by Kirk (1982) and available with major statistical packages. For example, SPSS provides a test of the equality of the variances and covariances within each cell of the between-subjects design (Mauchly's test of sphericity), and a test of the equivalence of the variance-covariance matrices across the cells of the between-subjects part of the design (Box's M test) (see Table 16-2). A rule of thumb exists for circumventing the formal (and complicated) tests of the assumption, as was the case with the RBANOVA. Consequently, these statistical tests are not presented here. The rule of thumb for testing this assumption about the within-subjects part of the SPANOVA is given in the section "Interpretation of the Results of the SPANOVA."

Computation of the SPANOVA

In the SPANOVA, total variability among scores can be partitioned into five sources of variation, two sources between subjects and three sources within subjects:

total variability = variability *between subjects* (variability due to treatment *A*
+ within-group variability between subjects) + variability *within
subjects* (variability due to treatment *B* + variability due to *AB*
+ variability due to the residual subjects
× treatment *B* interaction confounded with error)

[2]If we assume equal variances and covariances, then it follows that the correlations must also be equal because the correlation coefficient is equal to the covariance divided by the square root of the variance of variable 1 times the square root of the variance of variable 2. Actually, this assumption is a sufficient condition for the *F* test. See Kirk (1982) for a detailed exposition.

The SPANOVA provides sums of squares (*SS*) corresponding to each source of variation:

$$SS_T = SS_A + SS_{\text{subj.w.g.}} + SS_B + SS_{AB} + SS_{B \times \text{subj.w.g.}}$$

The formulas and computations for the sums of squares are given in Procedure 16-1 in the *Student Guide*.

Once the sums of squares are obtained, mean squares can be calculated by dividing by the conventional degrees of freedom (*df*) in Table 16-3. The degrees of freedom for the moral judgment study are given in Table 16-2. Finally, the degrees of freedom are additive, such that:

$$df_T = df_A + df_{\text{subj.w.g.}} + df_B + df_{AB} + df_{B \times \text{subj.w.g.}}$$

To calculate the mean squares, simply divide the sums of squares by their respective degrees of freedom. For example, $MS_A = 1.70/4 = .30$. The results of these calculations are shown in Table 16-2.

Finally, under the assumptions stated before, the *F* ratio for the between-subjects effect (*A*) is:

$$F(A) = \frac{MS_A}{MS_{\text{subj.w.g}}}$$

The *F* ratios for the within-subjects effects are:

$$F_B = \frac{MS_B}{MS_{B \times \text{subj.w.g}}} \qquad \text{and} \qquad F_{AB} = \frac{MS_{AB}}{MS_{B \times \text{subj.w.g}}}$$

The values of *F* can be found in Table 16-2 for the moral judgment study.

Decision Rules for Rejecting the Null Hypothesis

To determine whether or not to reject the null hypothesis for each of these hypotheses tested, we must compare F_{observed} (see Table 16-2) with F_{critical}. Values of F_{critical} can be found in Table E with these pieces of information in hand: α, df_{effect}, and df_{error}. Let's set $\alpha = .05$ and determine F_{critical} for the age effect in the moral judgment study (Table 16-2) with $df = 4$. The error term (subjects within groups) for this effect has $df = 20$. Then $F_{\text{critical}(.05,4,20)} = 2.87$, and $F_{\text{observed}} = .30$. From the SPANOVA, we cannot reject the null hypothesis.

The decision rules for testing hypotheses about the within-subjects effects are not so straightforward. Stringent assumptions had to be made regarding the homogeneity and symmetry of the within-subjects correlation matrices (Figure 16-2). We proceed using the following strategy:

- Conduct a conservative *F* test that protects against a violation of this assumption.[3] (The conservative *F* test adjusts the degrees of freedom for F_{critical} as explained in what

---

[3]The conservative test presented here is the simplest of the variety available. For an evaluation of this and other procedures, see Quintana & Maxwell, 1994.

follows.) If we reject the null hypothesis with the conservative test, stop and conclude that there is an effect.

- If the null hypothesis cannot be rejected, test the null hypothesis using the conventional degrees of freedom for $F_{critical}$. If the null hypothesis cannot be rejected, stop and conclude that there is insufficient evidence of an effect.
- If, however, $F_{observed}$ falls in between the conservative and conventional $F_{critical}$, a formal test of the assumption of homogeneity and symmetry of the covariance matrices is required before deciding whether to reject the null hypothesis (see Kirk, 1982, or Winer et al., 1991).

The conservative tests of the B and AB within-subjects effects are obtained by multiplying df_{effect} and $df_{B \times subj\ w.g.}$ by $1/(r - 1)$. For example, we multiply the conventional df for AB by $1/(r - 1)$ to obtain: $[1/(r - 1)](q - 1)(r - 1) = q - 1$. The results of carrying out this procedure on the degrees of freedom for the within-subjects sources of variation are shown in the last column of Table 16-3.

TABLE 16-3 Conventional and conservative degrees of freedom for the SPANOVA

Source	Conventional df	Conservative df
Between Subjects		
A	$q - 1$	Not applicable
Subjects w. Groups	$q(n - 1)$	Not applicable
Within Subjects		
B	$r - 1$	1
AB	$(q - 1)(r - 1)$	$q - 1$
B × Subjects w. Groups	$q(n - 1)(r - 1)$	$q(n - 1)$

INTERPRETATION OF THE RESULTS OF THE SPANOVA

As with the two-way ANOVA (Chapter 14), we begin with the interaction and ask if it is statistically significant. The rationale for this strategy is that a significant interaction may lead us to qualify our interpretation of the main effects. The age (A) × scenario (B) interaction in the moral judgment study is significant (Table 16-2). This result is encouraging because theory predicted this interaction, specifically, young children base their moral judgments on outcome information and young adults base their judgments on intent information. The means in Figure 16-1 reflect the interaction. Children 4–6 years of age appear to be influenced more by outcome than intent information; older children increasingly depend more on intent than outcome information. However, these observed differences may not all be reliable, and additional post hoc comparisons are needed to explore the age × treatment interaction.

The main effect of A is not statistically significant, indicating that moral judgment ratings, averaged over the four scenarios, are unrelated to age. We can see why in Figure 16-1. Positive and negative information balance one another so that the average rating at each grade level is close to zero. The main effect of B indicates that on average, positive information leads subjects to punish the actor, and intent information exerts a stronger influence than outcome information (except at ages 4–6 years). Again, a thorough analysis of the age × scenario interaction will elucidate this interpretation by comparing the differences among the four scenarios at each age.

RANDOM AND MIXED MODELS OF SPANOVA

In some applications of the SPANOVA, one or both factors may be random. Hypotheses are tested about the effects of factors A and B and of their interaction (AB). As usual, if B is random, the null and alternative hypotheses are stated as:

$$H_0: \sigma_B^2 = 0 \quad \text{and} \quad H_0: \sigma_{AB}^2 = 0$$
$$H_1: \sigma_B^2 \neq 0 \qquad\quad H_1: \sigma_{AB}^2 \neq 0$$

We assume that the levels of factor B were sampled randomly and that the effects of B and the interaction effect are jointly normal, each with mean zero and variance σ_B^2 and σ_{AB}^2, respectively.

Careful attention must be paid in forming the F test for either the random or mixed model (where A is fixed). In some cases, a quasi-F ratio must be used. It is a "kluge" in the sense that it combines two or more mean squares in the denominator to form the appropriate F ratio. To test the A effect in either a random- or mixed-model SPANOVA, the denominator turns out to be $MS_{\text{subj.w.g.}} + MS_{AB} - MS_{B \times \text{subj.w.g.}}$. The F test for the A effect is, then

$$F_A = \frac{MS_A}{MS_{\text{subj.w.g}} + MS_{AB} - MS_{B \times \text{subj.w.g}}}$$

Table 16-4 provides F ratios for the fixed-, random-, and mixed-effects (A fixed) SPANOVA.

TABLE 16-4 F ratios for fixed-, random-, and mixed-effects SPANOVA

Source	Fixed	Random	Mixed
Between Subjects			
A	$\dfrac{MA_A}{MS_{\text{subj.w.g.}}}$	$\dfrac{MS_A}{MS_{\text{subj.w.g.}} + MS_{AB} - MS_{B \times \text{subj.w.g.}}}$	$\dfrac{MS_A}{MS_{\text{subj.w.g.}} + MS_{AB} - MS_{B \times \text{subj.w.g.}}}$
Within Subjects			
B	$\dfrac{MS_B}{MS_{B \times \text{subj.w.g.}}}$	$\dfrac{MS_B}{MS_{AB}}$	$\dfrac{MS_B}{MS_{B \times \text{subj.w.g.}}}$
AB	$\dfrac{MS_{AB}}{MS_{B \times \text{subj.w.g.}}}$	$\dfrac{MS_{AB}}{MS_{B \times \text{subj.w.g.}}}$	$\dfrac{MS_{AB}}{MS_{B \times \text{subj.w.g.}}}$

Example Problem 16.1

Shavelson & Seminara (1968) reported a study of the effects of lunar and zero gravity on astronaut-like subjects' performance of basic maintenance tasks. Nine subjects were randomly assigned to one of three clothing conditions: shirt sleeve (street clothes; $n = 3$), unpressurized (vented) space suit ($n = 3$), or pressurized space suit ($n = 3$). Subjects in each clothing condition performed a maintenance task under two gravity conditions [earth's gravity (1 g) and lunar gravity (1/6 g)].[4] The hypothetical performance-time data based on the study are data shown in Table 16-5. A SPANOVA was run on the performance time data, and the findings are summarized in Table 16-6.

   Using these data, test whether there were significant effects due to clothing condition, gravity condition, and their interaction at the .05 level of significance. Include the following items in your answer.

a. Null and alternative hypotheses
b. Tests of assumptions or an explanation for not testing
c. $F_{critical}$ for each effect
d. Conclusions for each effect

TABLE 16-5 Performance times (seconds per torquing task)

Clothing Condition	Gravity Condition				Column Mean	$r_{1g, 1/6g}$
	1 g		$\frac{1}{6}$ g			
	Mean	Standard Deviation	Mean	Standard Deviation		
Shirt Sleeves	8.67	1.53	11.00	1.73	9.83	.95
Vented Suit	18.67	2.31	22.00	2.65	20.33	.98
Pressurized Suit	22.00	2.65	25.67	1.53	23.83	.99
Row Mean	16.44		19.56			

TABLE 16-6 SPANOVA results

Source	Sums of Squares	df	Mean Square	F
Between Subjects				
Clothing	637.00	2	318.50	36.74
Error	52.00	6	8.67	
Within Subjects				
Gravity	43.56	1	43.56	132.00
$C \times G$	1.44	2	.72	2.18
Error	2.00	6	.33	

[4]The design of the study has been simplified from the original, as have the data. Three gravity conditions were used: 1 g, 1/6 g, and a control condition in 1 g with the subject in the 1/6 g simulator harness. Moreover, three maintenance tasks were used in the original study. Here we use performance time data only from the torquing task, the task most likely to reflect differences in gravity conditions.

STRENGTH OF ASSOCIATION

Throughout I have stressed the importance of estimating the strength of association in conjunction with statistically significant effects in order to understand the magnitudes of the effects. Unfortunately, with all the possible options of between- and within-subjects factors possibly fixed or random, there is no straightforward approach to estimating strength of association (Winer et al., 1991). If you are interested in the topic, you might begin by reading Dodd & Schultz (1973).

POST HOC COMPARISONS

The overall F test for the between-subjects and within-subjects portions of the SPANOVA indicates whether or not there is a significant difference among population means, but it does not tell you just where that difference lies. For this reason, post hoc methods for testing hypotheses about mean differences are needed. In this section, Scheffé's and Tukey's methods for post hoc comparisons are presented.

The procedures for carrying them out are almost identical to those for factorial ANOVA (Chapter 14) with one exception—the choice of error term (denominator) for the statistical test. The general rule for choosing the error term for the post hoc statistical test, assuming A and B are fixed factors and subjects constitute a random factor, is as follows: To test differences among the A means, use the error term for A; to test differences among the B means, use the error term for B; to test differences among the cell means representing the AB interaction, *pool the between- and within-subjects error terms* (subjects within groups and $B \times$ subjects within groups; see Table 16-1).[5]

The formula for pooling the between-subjects and within-subjects error term is given in Formula 16-1.

$$MS_{PW} = \frac{SS_{\text{subj.w.g}} + SS_{B \times \text{subj.w.g}}}{q(n-1) + q(n-1)(r-1)} \qquad \textbf{(16-1)}$$

Pooling amounts to adding the sums of squares for the two error terms, and dividing by the sum of the degrees of freedom for the two error terms.

Scheffé's Method

Scheffé's method can be used to test pairwise and complex comparisons between means. The test for main effects of A and B in the SPANOVA is similar to the test for the factorial ANOVA. (The procedures for carrying out the test are given in Procedure 14-3 in the

---

[5]This approach is conservative. If A is the between-subjects factor and B is the within-subjects factor, some textbook authors recommend using the pooled error term whenever you compare cell means at difference levels of A—that is, compare a_i at b_j, or compare a_i at b_j with $a_{i'}$ at $b_{j'}$. When you compare cell means at different levels of B (b_j) for a given level of A (a_i), the within-subjects error term—$B \times$ subjects within groups—is recommended. I prefer simplicity when the consequence is conservatism.

Student Guide.) For the between-subjects factor (A), use subjects within groups and its corresponding *df;* and for the within-subjects factor (B), use $B \times$ subjects within groups and its corresponding *df* (see Formula 16-2).

$$t_{\text{obs.}(A)} = \frac{\hat{C}_A}{\sqrt{\dfrac{MS_{\text{subj.w.g}}}{nr}(w_1^2 + w_2^2 + \cdots + w_q^2)}}$$

$$t'_{\text{crit.}(A)} = \sqrt{df_A F_{\text{crit.}(\alpha, df_A, df_{\text{subj.w.g.}})}} \tag{16-2a}$$

$$t_{\text{obs.}(B)} = \frac{\hat{C}_B}{\sqrt{\dfrac{MS_{B \times \text{subj.w.g}}}{nq}(w_1^2 + w_2^2 + \cdots + w_r^2)}}$$

$$t'_{\text{crit.}(B)} = \sqrt{df_B F_{\text{crit.}(\alpha, df_B, df_{B \times \text{subj.w.g.}})}} \tag{16-2b}$$

Comparisons of cell means to examine an *interaction* are carried out in the usual way (see Chapter 14), but the error term used in the statistical test is the pooled within-group error. As an example, consider the hypothetical moral judgment study. The age $\times$ treatment interaction was statistically significant ($F = 6.43$; $df = 12, 60$; $\alpha = .05$), so that comparing cell means (Table 16-7) in order to interpret the interaction is appropriate. More specifically, let's compare mean judgments of young children (4–9 years old) with those of older children (10–19 years) when the actor's intent was positive but the outcome was negative. Theory predicts that the mean judgment (rating) of the older children will be higher than the younger children's. To test this hypothesis, we first write the appropriate contrast:

$$\hat{C} = (-3)(-1.40) + (-3)(1.40) + (2)(2.00) + (2)(2.60) + (2)(3.00) = 15.20$$

As predicted, the mean judgment of the older children was higher than the younger children's. But is this difference statistically significant? Formula 16-3 can be used to answer this question.

$$t_{\text{obs.}} = \frac{\hat{C}}{\sqrt{\dfrac{MS_{PW}}{n}(w_1^2 + w_2^2 + \cdots + w_k^2)}}$$

$$t'_{\text{crit.}} = \sqrt{(k-1)F_{\text{crit.}(\alpha, k-1, df_{PW})}} \tag{16-3}$$

where:

MS_{PW} is defined in Formula 16-1
$df_{PW} = q(n-1) + q(n-1)(r-1)$
$k =$ number of cells in the design

TABLE 16-7 Mean judgments from the hypothetical study of moral judgments

Treatment Condition[a]	Age (Years)					Row Mean
	4–6	7–9	10–12	13–15	16–19	
O+/I+	2.80	3.20	3.20	3.60	3.20	3.20
O+/I−	.40	−2.00	−2.20	−3.00	−2.80	−1.92
O−/I+	−1.40	1.40	2.00	2.60	3.00	1.52
O−/I−	−2.60	−3.60	−3.60	−3.00	−3.00	−3.16
Column Mean	−.20	−.25	−.15	.05	.10	−.09

[a]O =outcome (positive/negative); I = intent (positive/negative).

For the example, we have:

$$MS_{PW} = \frac{28.50 + 99.10}{20 + 60} = 1.60$$

$$t_{obs.} = \frac{15.20}{\sqrt{\frac{1.60}{5}[(-3)^2 + (-3)^2 + 2^2 + 2^2 + 2^2]}} = \frac{15.20}{3.10} = 4.90$$

$$t'_{crit.(.05)} = \sqrt{(20 - 1)F_{(.05,19,80)}} = \sqrt{(19)(1.70)} = 5.68$$

Since $t_{observed}$ does not exceed $t'_{critical}$, the null hypothesis, H_0: $C = 0$, cannot be rejected. We conclude that although the means are in the predicted direction, the observed difference may have arisen by chance. From Figure 16-1 and Table 16-7, the explanation seems clear. Subjects 7–9 years old behave more like the older subjects than the younger ones. If we regroup and compare 4–6-year-olds with all others, we have:

$$\hat{C} = (-4)(-1.40) + (1)(1.40) + (1)(2.00) + (1)(2.60) + (1)(3.00) = 14.60$$

$$t_{obs.} = \frac{14.60}{\sqrt{.32[(-4)^2 + 1^2 + 1^2 + 1^2 + 1^2]}} = \frac{14.60}{2.53} = 5.77$$

With this comparison, we reject the null hypothesis and conclude that very young children tend to use outcome information in morally judging an actor whereas older children tend to use intent information.

Tukey's Method

Tukey's HSD test is used to examine pairwise differences between means. Its application to the SPANOVA parallels its application to the between-subjects factorial ANOVA. The only difference lies in the error term that is used to determine the value of HSD:

1. To test the main effect for the between-subjects factor, use $MS_{subj.w.g.}$.
2. To test the main effect for the within-subjects factor, use $MS_{B \times subj.w.g.}$.

3. To test the interaction, use MS_{PW}.

For example, consider the moral judgment study. The overall SPANOVA indicated a statistically significant age × treatment interaction. To examine the interaction, we might examine all pairwise differences between cell means in Table 16-7. To do so, we need to determine the critical value of HSD. First, let $\alpha = .05$. Second, note that 20 means (5 age levels × 4 treatment conditions) enter into the pairwise differences. And finally, note that MS_{PW} is the appropriate error term with $df_{PW} = 20 + 60 = 80$.

We modify Formula 13-17 to:

$$HSD = q_{(\alpha, df_{PW}, k)} \sqrt{\frac{MS_{PW}}{n}} = q_{(.05, 80, 20)} \sqrt{\frac{1.60}{5}}$$

From Table F in Appendix II, we find that the value of $q_{(.05, 80, 20)}$ is approximately 5.24. So:

$$HSD = 5.24 \sqrt{\frac{1.60}{5}} = 2.93$$

Any pairwise difference between cell means in Table 16-7 that equals or exceeds 2.93 should lead us to reject the null hypothesis (i.e., $C = 0$) and conclude a difference between population means. For example, theory predicts that young adults (16–19 years) should reward more under condition $O-/I+$ than under condition $O+/I-$. The difference between these condition means is:

$$3.00 - (-2.80) = 5.80$$

Since this observed difference exceeds HSD, we reject H_0: $C = 0$ and conclude that in the population, the mean under condition $O-/I+$ is greater than under $O+/I-$, as theory predicts.

To examine the statistically significant treatment effect using Tukey's method, we might first calculate all pairwise differences, as indicated in Table 16-8.

TABLE 16-8 Pairwise differences

		Treatment Condition		
	O−/I−	*O+/I−*	*O−/I+*	*O+/I+*
Mean	*−3.16*	*−1.92*	*1.52*	*3.20*
−3.16	—	−1.24	−4.68	−6.36
−1.92		—	−3.44	−5.12
1.52			—	−1.68
3.20				—

Next, we determine the value of HSD. Note that we are interested in the pairwise differences among four means, based on 25 ($n = 5 \times$ age level = 5) observations. And note that the comparisons involve the within-subjects factor, so the appropriate error term is:

$MS_{B \times \text{subj.w.g.}}$ with $df = 60$

Thus we have

$$HSD = q_{(.05, 60, 4)} \sqrt{\frac{1.65}{25}} = 3.74(.26) = .97$$

Note that all pairwise differences exceed $|HSD|$. This result leads us to reject the null hypothesis in each case.

Example Problem 16.2

Using the data provided in Example Problem 16.1, test, statistically, the following comparisons: (1) shirt sleeves vs. suit (vented and pressurized) conditions and (2) vented vs. pressurized-suit conditions. In doing so, state the following:
- **a.** The null and alternative hypotheses for each comparison
- **b.** t_{critical} for each comparison at the .05 level
- **c.** The appropriate error term for each comparison
- **d.** Your conclusions

SUMMARY

This chapter presents the *split-plot analysis of variance* (SPANOVA), a statistical test used to examine differences between means collected from *mixed* designs (i.e., designs that combine both between-subjects and within-subjects factors). The purpose and underlying rationale and the procedures for computing and interpreting fixed-, random-, and mixed-effects SPANOVA are presented. Special attention is paid to stringent assumptions required for the F test with the SPANOVA. Procedures for conducting Scheffé's and Tukey's methods of post hoc comparison are presented and exemplified.

ANSWERS TO EXAMPLE PROBLEMS

1. **a.** Clothing Condition: H_0: $\mu_1 = \mu_2 = \mu_3$; H_1: $\mu_i \neq \mu_{i'}$.

   Gravity Condition: H_0: $\mu_1 = \mu_2$; H_1: $\mu_j \neq \mu_{j'}$.

   Clothing $\times$ Gravity: H_0: interaction effect $= 0$;

   $\qquad\qquad\qquad\qquad H_1$: interaction effect $\neq 0$.

   b. 1. *Independence:* Information is not given other than random assignment. (Subjects were run separately in the study.)
   2. *Normality:* Too few scores are available to examine this assumption. Often, time data are not normally distributed, but are log-normal. SPANOVA is robust.
   3. *Homogeneity of variances:* The variances in the six conditions range from 2.33 to 7.00, well within what would be expected due to sampling error.

4. *Homogeneity of covariances:* The covariances range from 2.50 to 6.00, well within the bounds of sampling expectation. Moreover, the correlations are all very high and roughly equivalent. If a question arose regarding the compound symmetry assumption, statistical tests are available on major computer packages. Or the sequence of conservative F testing can be used.

c. *Note:* When $r = 2$, the conservative and conventional *df* are the same.

   $F_{crit.}$: for clothing = 5.14; for gravity = 5.99; for $C \times G$ = 5.14

d. Conclusions: Reject the null hypothesis of equivalent performance times in the clothing condition populations. Conclude that clothing has an effect, and use post hoc comparisons to pinpoint that effect. Reject the null hypothesis of equivalent performance times in the gravity-condition populations. Performance in lunar gravity is slower than in earth gravity; performance time is increased by roughly 20 percent. Do not reject the null hypothesis of a clothing condition by gravity interaction.

2. a. Null and alternative hypotheses:

   1. Shirt sleeves vs. suit: H_0: $C = 0$; H_1: $C \neq 0$. Or more specifically, the null hypothesis is H_0: $\mu_1 = (\mu_2 + \mu_3)/2$.

   2. Vented vs. pressurized suit: H_0: $C = 0$; H_1: $C \neq 0$. More specifically,

      H_0: $\mu_2 = \mu_3$.

   b. $F_{crit.}$:

   1. Scheffé's method (.05, 2, 6): $[(2)(5.14)] = 10.28$, or in terms of t, 3.21.

   2. Tukey's method (.05, 6, 3): $(4.34)\{[8.67/(3 \times 2)]1/2]\} = (4.34)(1.20) = 5.22$.

   c. *Error term:* Subjects within groups are the error terms in both cases since both comparisons are between-groups comparisons.

   d. Conclusions:

   1. For comparison 1,

$$t_{obs.} = \frac{2(9.83) - (20.33 + 23.83)}{\sqrt{\dfrac{8.67}{(3)(2)}[(2)^2 + (-1)^2 + (-1)^2]}} = \frac{-24.50}{2.94} = -8.33$$

Since the absolute value of $t_{obs.}$ exceeds $t_{crit.}$, reject the null hypothesis and conclude that the suit conditions hamper performance time.

   2. For comparison 2,

      $23.83 - 20.33 = 3.50$

      Do not reject the null hypothesis. Apparently, the suit itself, whether or not inflated, hampers performance. (This finding is inconsistent with much of the literature. Most likely it is due to small sample size and lack of power.)

EXERCISES

In the exercises in Chapter 15, you examined the differences among treatments (experimental, attention control, no-treatment control) on aggressive boy's perceptions of an actor's negative intent at posttest. Use the data in Table 15-10 to test the effects of both treatment and test occasion (pretest, posttest) to further explore the hypothesis that aggressive boys in the experimental group would decrease their perceptions of negative intent from pre- to posttest compared to boys in the other two groups.

1. Present sample statistics that bear on the hypothesis. Do these statistics support the hypothesis?
2. Use the SPANOVA to determine whether the observed sample mean differences arose by chance.
   a. State the null and alternative hypotheses.
   b. State the assumptions underlying this statistical test. Which assumption(s) are particularly problematic? Why?
   c. Report the results in an SPANOVA summary table.
   d. Do you need to do post hoc comparisons? Why or why not? If you do, report the findings of the most telling comparison given the Hudley-Graham (H-G) hypothesis.
   e. Interpret all your findings. What do you conclude?

ANSWER TO EXERCISES

Analyses run with SPSS for MS WINDOWS Release 5.0.

1. Descriptive Statistics (Using SPSS Report Summaries in Rows)[a]

Treatment Group	Pretest	Posttest
Attribution Retraining		
Mean	4.67	1.83
StdDev	.82	.75
Attention Control		
Mean	5.33	5.00
StdDev	1.51	1.26
Control		
Mean	4.17	4.83
StdDev	.98	1.17
Grand Total		
Mean	4.72	3.89
StdDev	1.18	1.81

[a] Note: The three groups perceive, roughly on average, the same amount of negative intent at pretest. At posttest, the subjects in the experimental group perceived considerably less negative intent, on average. These descriptive statistics are consistent with the H-G hypothesis.

$H_0: \mu_E = \mu_A = \mu_C$; $H_1: \mu_i \neq \mu_{i'}$ for some i and i'

2. a. $H_0: \mu_{pretest} = \mu_{posttest}$; $H_1: \mu_{pretest} \neq \mu_{posttest}$

   $H_0:$ *interaction effect* $= 0$; $H_1:$ *interaction effect* $\neq 0$

   b. 1. *Independence*
      2. *Normality*
      3. *Homogeneity of Variance*
      4. *Homogeneity of Covariances*

      Particularly problematic are assumptions 3 and 4 combined, especially so because the assumption is that the variance and covariances are the same at each level of the between subjects variable (Group). These assumptions are problematic since sometimes the pattern of correlations is such that adjacent variables correlate more highly with each other than with more distant variables. By using the rule of thumb for the sequence of $F_{critical}$ values (conservative then conventional), the assumptions can usually be addressed. Moreover, statistical packages provide tests of these assumptions.

   c. SPANOVA Summary Table (Using SPSS Multivariate ANOVA Procedure)[6]

Analysis of Variance
Tests of Between-Subjects Effects

Source of Variation	SS	DF	MS	F	Sig of F
WITHIN + RESIDUAL	29.42	15	1.96		
GROUP	22.72	2	11.36	5.79	.014

Analysis of Variance–Design 1
Tests Involving 'OCCASION' Within-Subject Effect

Source of Variation	SS	DF	MS	F	Sig of F
WITHIN+RESIDUAL	7.75	15	.52		
OCCASION	6.25	1	6.25	12.10	.003
GROUP BY OCCASION	19.50	2	9.75	18.87	.000

Note: In a SPANOVA with only two levels of the within-subjects variable (pretest and posttest in the Example Problem), the conventional and conservative degrees of freedom are identical. (Go ahead and determine the conservative *df* for the within-

---

[6]SPSS Program Setup:
MANOVA PRETEST POSTTEST BY GROUP(1 3)
/WSFACTORS=OCCASION(2)
/CONTRAST(OCCASION)=DIFFERENCE
/RENAME=CONS DIFF
/PRINT SIGNIF(MULT UNIV AVERF) HOMOGENEITY(BOXM)
/NOPRINT PARAM(ESTIM)
/METHOD=UNIQUE
/ERROR WITHIN+RESIDUAL
/DESIGN GROUP.

subjects part of the design to convince yourself!). Hence, the assumption of equal variances and covariances is not problematic in this one, special case.

d. With a statistically significant interaction, post hoc comparisons are in order. One of the most telling comparisons, given the H-P hypothesis of a drop in perceptions of boys in the experimental group compared to the other two groups, would be Group 1 versus Groups 2 and 3 at posttest. This calls for a Scheffé test:

$$\hat{C} = -2(1.83) + 1(5) + 1(4.83) = 6.17$$

$$MS_{PW} = \frac{29.42 + 7.75}{15 + 15} = \frac{37.17}{30} = 1.24$$

$$t_{obs.} = \frac{6.17}{\sqrt{\frac{1.24}{6}[(-2)^2 + 1^2 + 1^2]}} = \frac{6.17}{\sqrt{.21(6)}} = \frac{6.17}{1.12} = 5.51$$

$$t_{crit.} = \sqrt{(3-1)F_{crit.(.05,2,30)}} = \sqrt{2(2.89)} = 2.40$$

Reject the null hypothesis and conclude that, in the population, experimental subjects perceive less negative intent at posttest than do subjects in the other two groups, on average. This finding supports the H-G hypothesis.

e. These data support the H-G hypothesis that attribution retraining lowers aggressive boys' perceptions of negative intent as compared to attention-control and no-treatment-control groups.

17 Analysis of Covariance

The analysis of covariance (ANCOVA) is a statistical method for examining data from one-way and factorial designs. It uses information provided by a continuous independent variable, called a *covariate,* to remove systematic individual differences among subjects from the estimate of experimental error. Hence the name *an*alysis of *cova*riance. The **covariate** contains information about differences among subjects that is collected before the experiment is conducted. This preexperiment information might be a pretest, or it might be some other individual-difference measure that is known to correlate highly with the posttest. Once the covariate has been measured, subjects are randomly assigned to treatment conditions, receive their respective treatments, and then receive a posttest.[1] The ANCOVA uses the covariate to remove systematic differences among subjects from the within-groups error term. The ANCOVA, then, is similar to the one-way and factorial ANOVA in that it can be used to test hypotheses about treatment effects and their interactions in between-subjects designs[2]; it is similar to within-subjects and mixed designs in that it uses information about individual differences to reduce the size of the error term. If used appropriately, the ANCOVA will be more powerful than the one-way or factorial ANOVA for between-subjects designs. And if the correlation between covariate and posttest is above .60, it will be more powerful than the within-subjects designs.

---

[1]This design fits Campbell & Stanley's (1963) pretest-posttest, true experimental design (see Chapter 1 in the *Student Guide*). The pretest might be the same as or parallel to the posttest, or a test whose scores are known to correlate highly with the posttest.

[2]The ANCOVA can also be used with within-subjects designs. See, for example, Kirk (1995).

As an example, consider the teacher expectancy study described in Chapter 1. Students in grades 1 through 6 were given a pretest (an ability measure), randomly assigned to a "bloomers" or control group, and at the end of the school year, given a posttest (the ability measure). If teacher expectancy operates as hypothesized, the randomly selected "bloomers" should score higher, on average, than the control group on the posttest.

Because of measurement problems at the lower grades, we will use data from grades 3 through 6 from Table 2-1 (reproduced in Table 17-1). Throughout this example, we ignore grade level and focus the analysis on the treatment (teacher expectancy) effect.[3]

From the descriptive statistics at the bottom of Table 17-1, what should we conclude? Should we expect mean ability differences between the bloomers and controls at pretest? What happened? Is the mean difference of 4.65 points at posttest due to chance or to population differences?

TABLE 17-1 Hypothetical data for the teacher expectancy study, grades 3–6

Grade Level	"Bloomers"			Control		
	Student	Pretest	Posttest	Student	Pretest	Posttest
3	11	90	98	41	80	102
	12	93	103	42	100	106
	13	104	107	43	105	107
	14	108	100	44	110	111
	15	125	125	45	119	119
4	16	95	95	46	95	102
	17	100	108	47	99	102
	18	104	108	48	104	107
	19	106	104	49	110	116
	20	110	116	50	120	120
5	21	75	106	51	85	112
	22	88	106	52	90	110
	23	90	95	53	100	115
	24	105	115	54	110	119
	25	120	124	55	115	125
6	26	80	97	56	79	96
	27	95	102	57	100	120
	28	100	110	58	105	117
	29	110	98	59	106	110
	30	120	122	60	110	116
Mean		100.90	106.95		102.10	111.60
Standard Deviation		13.05	9.30		11.68	7.64

In answering these questions, we might use a t test or a one-way ANOVA. At pretest, we conclude that the two groups have been drawn from the same population ($F = .09$; $df = 1,38$; $MS_{within} = 153.31$, $p > .05$). This conclusion is what we should expect, since sub-

---

[3]At the end of the chapter, we come back to the full grade-level × expectancy design.

jects were randomly assigned to the "bloomers" or control group. In contrast, if there is an expectancy effect, we should expect to find a statistically significant difference at posttest. But we do not find it ($F = 2.98$; $df = 1,38$; $MS_{within} = 72.43$; $p > .05$; see Table 17-2a).

At this point, we might conclude that there's no expectancy effect. Before reaching this conclusion, however, we should ask whether we have used all the information available to us in performing the most powerful statistical test possible. The answer to this question is no. We have information about individual differences among subjects at pretest, and a quick glance at Table 17-1 tells us that pretest scores go with or are correlated with posttest scores. Thus some of the variability within groups at posttest is predictable from variability at pretest. If we could remove this predictable variability from the within-group error term, we would have a more powerful test of the expectancy hypothesis.

Removing predictable variability in the error term is just what the ANCOVA does. The results of an analysis of covariance on the data in Table 17-1 are reported in Table 17-2b. Compared with the error term in the ANOVA, the error term for the ANCOVA is about half the size. The "cost" of obtaining this more precise estimate of error is shown in the source and *df* columns: The ANCOVA has one more source of variation—the *covariate*—than does the ANOVA, which costs 1 degree of freedom. But the price was worth it. With the additional power supplied by the ANCOVA, we are led to reject the null hypothesis and conclude a negative treatment effect: In the population, the mean ability score of bloomers at posttest is lower than that of subjects in the control condition!

TABLE 17-2   Analysis of variance on posttest scores (a) and of covariance on posttest scores with the pretest as covariate (b) for the teacher expectancy study (data in Table 17-1)

Source	Sum of Squares	df	Mean Square	F
(a) Analysis of Variance				
Groups	216.22	1	216.22	2.98
Error	2753.75	38	72.47	
Total	2969.97	39		
(b) Analysis of Covariance				
Group	164.67	1	164.67	4.48[a]
Covariate	1393.98	1	1393.98	37.93[a]
Error	1359.77	37	36.75	
Total	2918.42	39		

[a] $p < .05$.

In this chapter, the ANCOVA's conceptual underpinnings are presented along with techniques for statistically testing hypotheses. We focus on one-way designs with one covariate, but we briefly show the extension of the ANCOVA to factorial designs and designs with more than one covariate. Particular attention is paid to the ANCOVA's strong assumptions and its appropriate uses and its misuses.

DESCRIPTION OF THE ANCOVA

Purpose and Underlying Logic

The purpose of the ANCOVA is to help the researcher decide whether the observed differences between means may be due to chance or to systematic differences among treatment populations. It does so by statistically removing predictable individual differences from the dependent variable, thereby providing a more precise estimate of experimental error than a between-subjects design does and a very powerful statistical test of the null hypothesis.

To understand how the ANCOVA works, we will examine a picture. Figure 17-1a lets us look at two treatment populations, say, bloomers and controls, represented by scatterplots, where X is the covariate (e.g., pretest score in the expectancy study) and Y is the dependent variable (posttest score). Let's ignore the covariate for the moment and focus on the fact that scores in populations 1 (bloomers) and 2 (controls) are identically distributed—normally distributed with equal variances (see the ordinate in Figure 17-1a). The two populations, then, differ only in their location on the ordinate. Given sample data from populations 1 and 2, a t test or one-way ANOVA should lead us to reject the null hypothesis and conclude a mean difference in the populations.

Now consider the covariate (X) as well. The relation between X and Y within each treatment population is represented by a scatterplot. Except that one scatterplot is higher on the Y axis than the other, the two scatterplots are identical. This equivalence implies that the correlation between X and Y in one scatterplot (e.g., bloomers—scatterplot 1) is the same as in the other (control), and so are the regression lines ($\beta_1 = \beta_2 = \beta_W$; we write β_W for the pooled within-group regression line because in this figure, we are looking at the population). Judging from the slope and scatter of points about the regression lines, there is a strong relation between X and Y in Figure 17-1a. Indeed, the within-group regression of the dependent variable (Y) on the covariate (X) provides a measure of the variance in Y accounted for by X when treatment effects are removed (not present). Thus if β were known, we could remove the variability from the Y scores predictable from X—that is, for each subject in the experiment, we could take $Y_{pi} - \beta_W(X_{pi} - \bar{X}_G)$—and then carry out a one-way ANOVA on the adjusted Y scores. This strategy is, in fact, the goal of the ANCOVA. But since β_W is not known, a circuitous estimation route is taken (see what follows).

Before considering the ANCOVA in more detail, let us examine several other features of Figure 17-1a. Notice that in the populations, $\mu_{X_1} = \mu_{X_2} = \mu_X$. This result is a consequence of our assumption that except for treatment effects, subjects in the two populations are identical. In the long run, random sampling and assignment to treatment group will enable us to realize this result. Finally, within each scatterplot, the variance of the dependent variable for a given level of X is shown. This variance provides a measure of experimental error; the errors are normally distributed, and their variance is equal in both groups.

As mortal researchers, however, we are not privy to Figure 17-1a (the true state of affairs). Rather, on the basis of sample data, we have to decide whether Figure 17-1a or 17-1b represents the true situation. Suppose we take a random sample from the bloomer and control populations, and we organize our data as shown in Figure 17-1c. The question confronting the researcher is whether the two populations have identical means on Y (null hypothesis, Figure 17-1b) or different means (the alternative hypothesis, such as Figure 17-1a) as the true state of affairs.

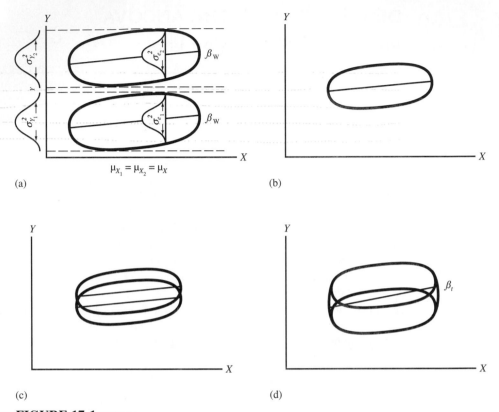

FIGURE 17-1

Conceptual underpinnings of the ANCOVA

To test the null hypothesis, we wish to make use of the pretest information and decide to run the ANCOVA. The ANCOVA permits us to remove the variability in the dependent variable (Y) that is predictable from X and to analyze the "residual" or "adjusted" scores. The benefit is a reduction in experimental error from σ_Y^2, shown on the ordinate of Figure 17-1a, to σ_e^2, shown for a given level of X within each scatterplot.

To remove the variability in Y predicted from X statistically, we recognize that information about the variability in Y predictable from X is contained in the regression coefficient (β_W).[4] That is, $Y_{\text{adj.}} = Y_{pi} - \beta_W(X_{pi} - \bar{X}_G)$. Then an analysis of variance could be run on $Y_{\text{adj.}}$ scores with variation due to systematic differences among subjects removed. That is, *if beta were known,* the analysis of covariance could be viewed as an analysis of variance on the adjusted or residual Y scores.

Unfortunately, β_W is not known and must be estimated. In doing so, our goal is to take the usual partitioning of the sums of squares in a one-way ANOVA—$SS_{T(Y)} = SS_{B(Y)} + SS_{W(Y)}$—and remove from these sums of squares the variability predictable from X to

---

[4]Recall from Chapter 7 that $Y = Y + b(X - \bar{X})$, or in deviation form, $\hat{y} = b(X - \bar{X})$. The working part of the prediction equation, then, is $b(X - \bar{X})$.

produce $SS_{T(Y)\text{adj.}} = SS_{B(Y)\text{adj.}} + SS_{W(Y)\text{adj.}}$. (*Note:* Instead of writing SS_T for "sum of squares total," we write $SS_{T(Y)}$ to make clear the distinction between the dependent variable and the covariate on which the adjustment is based.)

We begin by calculating $SS_{T(Y)\text{adj.}}$,[5] the total sum of squares adjusted for the predictability of Y from X, *ignoring,* for the moment, the particular treatment group the subject belongs to. Hence, we are interested in the regression line fitted to a scatterplot that ignores group membership (shown in Figure 17-1d). In this scatterplot, the regression line represents the predictability of Y from X, ignoring treatment condition, and is denoted β_t; we use b, a sample estimate of β_t, and t refers to the "total" scatterplot ignoring treatments. Once we have b_t, we can calculate $SS_{T(Y)}$ and remove the portion of variability predictable from variation on X. See Formula 17-1.

$$SS_{T(Y)\text{adj.}} = \sum_{p=1}^{n}\sum_{i=1}^{k}(Y_{pi} - \bar{Y}_G)^2 - b_t^2 \sum_{p=1}^{n}\sum_{i=1}^{k}(X_{pi} - \bar{X}_G)^2 \qquad (17\text{-}1)$$

where:

$$b_t = \frac{\displaystyle\sum_{p=1}^{n}\sum_{i=1}^{k}(X_{pi} - \bar{X}_G)(Y_{pi} - \bar{Y}_G)}{\displaystyle\sum_{p=1}^{n}\sum_{i=1}^{k}(X_{pi} - \bar{X}_G)^2}$$

Now, let's give $SS_{T(Y)\text{adj.}}$ some thought. What might account for this variability? Clearly, some of the variability in the adjusted total sum of squares is due to experimental error. However, if Figure 17-1a is correct, a substantial proportion of the variability is due to a treatment effect. The next step is to partition the $SS_{T(Y)\text{adj.}}$ into a component for experimental error and a component for treatment effects. We calculate the adjusted within-groups sum of squares by removing from the variability of Y in each group that portion predictable from X (b_W). See Formula 17-2.

$$SS_{W(Y)\text{adj.}} = \sum_{p=1}^{n}\sum_{i=1}^{k}(Y_{pi} - \bar{Y}_{.i})^2 - b_W^2 \sum_{p=1}^{n}\sum_{i=1}^{k}(X_{pi} - \bar{X}_{.i})^2 \qquad (17\text{-}2)$$

where b_W is the pooled, within-group regression of Y on X:

$$b_W = \frac{\displaystyle\sum_{p=1}^{n}\sum_{i=1}^{k}(X_{pi} - \bar{X}_{.i})(Y_{pi} - \bar{Y}_{.i})}{\displaystyle\sum_{p=1}^{n}\sum_{i=1}^{k}(X_{pi} - \bar{X}_{.i})^2}$$

---

[5]For derivations of the formulas that follow, see Kirk (1982, pp. 720–727).

The last step is to calculate $SS_{B(Y)\text{adj}.}$, which is done simply by subtraction. See Formula 17-3.

$$SS_{B(Y)\text{adj}.} = SS_{T(Y)\text{adj}.} - SS_{W(Y)\text{adj}.} \tag{17-3}$$

To directly adjust $SS_{B(Y)}$ runs into the following problem: The adjustment made to the dependent variable *must* be *independent* of the group differences to be tested (cf. Kirk, 1982)—hence the circuitous subtraction method.

Design Requirements

The one-way, fixed-effects ANCOVA presupposes that data have been collected as follows:

1. There is one independent variable with two or more levels. These levels may differ qualitatively or quantitatively.
2. A covariate is measured prior to the implementation of the treatment and control conditions.[6]
3. A subject is randomly assigned to one and only one group in the design.[7]

Hypotheses

The null and alternative hypotheses tested with the one-way, fixed-effects ANCOVA are:

$H_0: \mu_1 = \mu_2 = \cdots = \mu_i = \cdots = \mu_k$

$H_1: \mu_i \neq \mu_{i'}$ for some groups i and i'

In addition, the effect of the covariate can be tested statistically, although this test is of considerably less interest because the covariate was selected for its strong relation with the dependent variable:

$H_0: \beta_W = 0$

$H_1: \beta_W \neq 0$

---

[6]The covariate may also be measured after the treatments have been administered if we (1) measure the covariate before the treatments have affected it or (2) can assume that the treatments have no affect on the covariate. These conditions are fairly difficult to argue. The moral of the story is: *Measure the covariate before implementing the treatment conditions.*

[7]Nonrandom assignment presents serious difficulties in using the ANCOVA. Even when ANCOVA is carefully used, we can never be sure that the statistical adjustment accounts for all of the ways the intact groups differ from one another before the treatment and control conditions are implemented. Moreover, often when intact groups are used, the covariate and treatment are correlated so that adjusting for the covariate may remove part of the treatment effect. For these reasons, we specify random assignment as a design requirement. But you should know that advanced statistical techniques are available for making statistical adjustments in these cases. Discussion of them is beyond the scope of this textbook.

Assumptions

With the ANCOVA, we make the usual three assumptions common to the analysis of variance, but with a slightly different twist regarding normality and homogeneity of variances:

1. *Independence:* An individual's scores on the covariate and dependent variable are independent of the scores of all other subjects.
2. *Normality:* For individuals with the same score on the covariate (X) in the same group, the dependent variable (Y) has a normal distribution. If scores on the covariate are normally distributed, the ANCOVA is robust to this assumption (see, for example, Elashoff, 1969).
3. *Homogeneity of variances:* The variance of the Y scores for individuals with the same X score is the same for all groups and X scores. There are two pieces to this assumption. The first is homogeneity of variances across groups (assuming that the variances are the same at each level of X in each group). In this case, this assumption causes little problem with the ANCOVA if sample sizes are equal. The second is that the variance is the same at each level of the covariate X. If this assumption is violated, the data might be transformed (see Winer et al., 1991) to meet this assumption (e.g., by taking the logarithm of the scores).

But these assumptions are *not* all the assumptions made. (The price of power is always encumbered with commitments; the ANCOVA is no exception.) We make the following additional, stringent assumptions:

4. *Linearity:* We assume that in the population, the regression of the dependent variable (Y) on the covariate (X) is linear in each group. This assumption can and should be checked by examining the scatterplots for the X and Y scores in each group. Statistical packages such as BMDP, SAS, and SPSS provide statistical tests for linearity. If this assumption is violated, the statistical procedures presented in this chapter are inappropriate.
5. *Homogeneity of regression slopes:* We assume that in the population, the regression of the dependent variable (Y) on the covariate (X) is the same in each group:

$$\beta_1 = \beta_2 = \cdots = \beta_i = \cdots = \beta_k$$

A statistical test of this assumption is provided in statistical packages such as BMDP, SPSS, and SAS. If this assumption is violated, the ANCOVA is inappropriate. Attention should not focus on comparing group means. Rather, attention should focus on the effect of the independent variable on regression slopes (coefficients). For a discussion of theory and statistical modeling related to nonparallel regression slopes, see Cronbach & Snow (1977); see also Rogosa (1980).
6. *Independence of covariate and treatments:* This assumption amounts to assuming that by removing the variability in the dependent variable predictable from the covariate, we are *not* also removing part of the treatment effect. For example, often instructional treatments are adapted to individual differences in learners' ability. If subjects are not randomly assigned to treatments, using a measure of ability as a covariate might

lead us to remove part of the instructional treatment effect. Or if the covariate is measured after the experiment, the covariate itself, not just the dependent variable, may have been affected by the treatments. Again, by removing variability in the dependent variable using the covariate might lead to removing part of the treatment effect, too. The analysis of covariance is an inappropriate statistical technique when the covariate and treatment are not independent of one another.

7. *Covariate measured without error:* We assume that the covariate is measured without error or, alternatively, that the covariate is perfectly reliable (see the section "Reliability" in Chapter 15). Unreliability in the covariate decreases the precision of the ANCOVA by inflating the estimate of experimental error. The moral of this assumption is to measure the covariate as reliably as possible.

Computation of the ANCOVA

In the ANCOVA, the total variability among scores on the dependent variable can be partitioned into three sources of variability:

total variability (Y) = variability between treatments
+ systematic variability due to individual differences between subjects (relation between the covariate X and Y)
+ within-group error

Computationally, we can think of the ANCOVA as follows:

1. It calculates the sums of squares total and within groups just as is done with a one-way ANCOVA.
2. It calculates the regression coefficient corresponding to the total (ignoring group membership) and within-group relation between X and Y.
3. It removes this predictable variation from the sums of squares total to create sums of squares total (adjusted), and from sums of squares within groups to create sums of squares within (adjusted).
4. It calculates sums of squares treatment (adjusted) [or between groups (adjusted)] by subtracting sums of squares within (adjusted) from sums of squares total (adjusted).

In this way, the ANCOVA removes the variability due to individual differences (X) and has partitioned the *adjusted* total sums of squares as shown in Formula 17-4.

$$SSY_{total_{adj.}} = SSY_{treatment_{adj.}} + SSY_{within_{adj.}} \hspace{2cm} \textbf{(17-4)}$$

The rationale for making this adjustment is provided at the beginning of this chapter, as are the basic equations.

The degrees of freedom, corresponding to these sums of square, are additive as well. See Formula 17-5.

$$df_{total_{adj}} = df_{treatment_{adj}} + df_{within_{adj}} \qquad (17\text{--}5)$$

The steps in computing the ANCOVA and other statistics that are used to test its assumptions are enumerated in Procedure 17-1 in the *Student Guide*. In general, the computations go like this. The total and within-groups sums of squares for X and Y are calculated: SSX_{total}, SSY_{total}, SSX_{within}, and SSY_{within}. Then the total and pooled within-groups sums of crossproducts for X and Y (cf. correlation between X and Y) are calculated: SCP_{total} and SCP_{within}. The sums of crossproducts are used to adjust SSY_{total} and SSY_{within} to produce $SSY_{total_{adj}}$ and $SSY_{within_{adj}}$. Finally, $SSY_{treatment_{adj}}$ is obtained by subtraction to maintain its independence from the other two adjusted sums of squares: $SSY_{total_{adj}} - SSY_{within_{adj}}$.

The following example is used to illustrate the steps in Procedure 17-1 and to describe the consequences of these steps here. Consider a study in which (for ease of presentation) 15 subjects are randomly assigned to a control condition (group 1) or to one of two experimental groups (groups 2 and 3). The covariate is measured prior to implementing the treatments; after the treatments, the dependent variable is measured. Hypothetical data from the study are presented in Table 17-3. (The small sample sizes are for illustration; large samples, preferably over 50, should be used with ANCOVA, especially because regression slopes are being estimated.)

TABLE 17-3 Hypothetical data to illustrate the ANCOVA

			Condition			
	Control Group		*Experimental Group*			
			1		*2*	
	X	*Y*	*X*	*Y*	*X*	*Y*
	5	17	2	22	8	35
	8	16	7	26	5	28
	9	20	10	33	9	32
	3	14	11	30	3	27
	10	25	4	25	4	29
$\bar{X}$	7.00	18.40	6.80	27.20	5.80	30.20
s	2.92	4.28	2.59	3.27	2.97	6.36
b	1.21		1.04		1.09	

The ANCOVA formulas are presented in a source table format in Table 17-4. Table 17-5 applies these formulas to the computations using the data in Table 17-3.

Four items in Table 17-4 are noteworthy. First, as expected, we work with *adjusted* sums of squares and mean squares. Second, the degrees of freedom for the error (within groups) is one less than the degrees of freedom in a plain ANOVA: $k(n-1) - 1$. This value represents the 1 degree of freedom used in estimating the pooled within-group regression coefficient, b_W, that is used to adjust the dependent variable for its relation to the covariate. Third, the table includes a row for the covariate. This row provides a statistical test of whether the pooled within-groups regression coefficient equals zero. Since the covariate was selected because of its strong relation with the dependent variable, we expect to reject the null hypothesis. And, fourth, once we have the adjusted sums of squares and degrees of freedom, the calculations for mean squares and F are the same as with the ANOVA.

TABLE 17-4 Formulas used in completing the ANCOVA source table

Source of Variation	Sum of Squares	df	Mean Square	F
Treatment$_{adj.}$	$SSY_{treatment_{adj.}}$	$k-1$	$\dfrac{SSY_{treatment_{adj.}}}{df_{treatment_{adj.}}}$	$\dfrac{MSY_{treatment_{adj.}}}{MSY_{within_{adj.}}}$
Covariate	SS_{cov}	1	$\dfrac{SS_{cov}}{1}$	$\dfrac{MS_{cov}}{MSY_{within_{adj.}}}$
Within$_{adj.}$	$SSY_{within_{adj.}}$	$k(n-1)-1$	$\dfrac{SS_{within_{adj.}}}{df_{within_{adj.}}}$	
Total$_{adj.}$	$SSY_{total_{adj.}}$	$N-1$		

TABLE 17-5 ANCOVA summary table (data from Table 17-3)

Source of Variation	Sum of Squares	df	Mean Square	F
Treatment$_{adj.}$	439.89	2	219.95	52.10[a]
Covariate	(144.36)[b]	1	144.36	34.20[a]
Within$_{adj.}$	46.44	11	4.22	
Total$_{adj.}$	486.33	14		

[a] $F_{crit.(.01,2,11)} = 7.20$; $F_{crit.(.01,1,11)} = 9.65$.
[b] Recall that $SSY_{total_{adj.}} = SSY_{treatment_{adj.}} + SSY_{within_{adj.}}$; $SS_{cov} = SSY_{within} - SSY_{within_{adj.}}$; hence, the parentheses denote the fact that SS_{cov} does not enter into the calculation of the total adjusted SS.

From the ANCOVA summary table, we find, as expected, a significant relationship between the covariate and the dependent variable ($p < .01$). Moreover, we find a significant treatment effect. However, before interpreting these results, we must examine assumptions underlying the ANCOVA and calculate additional descriptive statistics. We turn to this task now.

Interpretation of the Results of the ANCOVA

The assumptions underlying the application of the ANCOVA are presented in the section "Assumptions." There are several logical assumptions that can be dealt with readily. One is the assumption of independence, and from the description of the preceding hypothetical study, we have reason to assert that the independence assumption has been met. The second assumption is that the covariate and treatments are independent. Measurement of the covariate before implementation of the treatments and random assignment of subjects to groups leads us to assert that this assumption has been met (see, in what follows, the check on random assignment).

To determine whether randomization worked, we compute a one-way ANOVA on the covariate. These results, shown in Table 17-6, lead us to conclude that subjects in the three groups were drawn from populations with identical means on the covariate and that randomization worked.

TABLE 17-6 One-way ANCOVA on the covariate
(data from Table 17-3)

Source of Variation	Sum of Squares	df	Mean Square	F
Treatment	4.13	2	2.07	0.21
Within	119.60	12	9.97	
Total	123.73	14		

There are too few subjects per group to examine the normality assumption. Nevertheless, the ANCOVA is robust if the distribution of scores on the covariate is normal, which is usually the case with covariates of ability.

With respect to the assumption of homogeneity of variances, we can examine variances from groups 1–3, respectively: 8.53, 14.67, and 6.71. There is nothing here to cause alarm. (BMDP, SAS and SPSS provide statistical tests.)

The assumption of linearity can be examined with scatterplots of X and Y within each group. This examination was done (but is not shown in this chapter), and a linear relation was found in each group, although sample size is very small and, consequently, this conclusion is tentative. (A statistical test could be carried out with BMDP, SAS, or SPSS.)

Homogeneity of regression slopes can be examined by inspecting the regression of Y on X in each of the three groups. The regression coefficients for groups 1–3 are 1.21, 1.04, and 1.09, respectively. [A statistical test was run with BMDP1V; the null hypothesis of homogeneity could not be rejected ($F - .06$, 2, 9; $p > .94$).]

Finally, we assume that the covariate is measured with perfect reliability. We are not provided the information needed to calculate reliability but note that the effect of the covariate was significant. So the reliability of the covariate had to be minimally satisfactory to predict the dependent variable.

At this point, we conclude that as best as we can tell, the assumptions of the ANCOVA have been met; and we move to the interpretation of the findings. For interpretation of the ANCOVA results, the means on Y and the means on Y adjusted for the covariate are presented in Table 17-7. We focus on adjusted means and find that the treatment groups scored, on average, higher than the control group, and treatment 2 scored higher than treatment 1. However, post hoc comparisons are needed to determine which of the observed mean differences are due to chance, and we turn to this task after explaining the mean adjustment procedure.

The adjusted mean for each group is calculated with Formula 17-6.

$$\bar{Y}_{.i_{\text{adj.}}} = \bar{Y}_{.i} - b_W(\bar{X}_{.j} - \bar{X}_G) \qquad\qquad\qquad (17\text{-}6)$$

TABLE 17-7 Means on the dependent variable

Group	Mean	Adjusted Mean
Control	18.40	17.83
Treatment 1	27.20	26.91
Treatment 2	30.20	31.01

The adjusted mean for the control group can be calculated by using descriptive statistics normally obtained in calculation of the ANCOVA (see Procedure 17-1): the unadjusted mean ($\bar{Y}_1 = 18.40$), the pooled within-groups regression coefficient ($b_W = 1.21$), the grand mean of the covariate ($\bar{X}_G = 6.53$), and the mean of the covariate for the group ($\bar{X}_1 = 7.00$):

$$\bar{Y}_{.1_{\text{adj.}}} = 18.40 - 1.21(7.00 - 6.53) = 17.83$$

Example Problem 17.1

The ANCOVA presented in Table 17-2 leads to the rejection of the null hypothesis. Before reaching the conclusion that the mean performance of the control group exceeded that of the expectancy group, you should check the assumptions.

a. For each assumption, present statistical evidence and an eyeball test of the tenability of that assumption. (By an eyeball test, I mean a presentation of appropriate descriptive statistics to see whether the assumption is tenable.)

b. Present the adjusted means for the control and bloomers groups. The descriptive statistics presented in Table 17-8 may prove useful.

TABLE 17-8 Descriptive statistics (data from Table 17-1)

	Group	
Descriptive Statistic	Control	Bloomers
Mean		
Covariate	102.10	100.90
Dependent	111.60	106.95
Standard Deviation		
Covariate	11.68	13.05
Dependent	7.64	9.30
Correlation of covariate		
with dependent variable	.72	.70
Within-group regression	.47	.50
Pooled within-group regression	.49	

Notice that in calculating the adjusted mean for the control group, we used the pooled within-groups regression coefficient (b_W) rather than b_1, the regression coefficient for the control group. Moreover, we used the grand mean on the covariate as the best estimate of the population mean for the control group. The use of the pooled statistics as the best estimates of the population parameters of interest follows from our statistical tests that led us to conclude that the population regression of the dependent variable on the covariate was the same across groups, and that the population means on the covariate were equal across groups.

POST HOC COMPARISON OF MEANS

Both Scheffé's test for complex comparisons and Tukey's test for pairwise comparisons can be used with the ANCOVA. Scheffé's test is the same as that for the one-way ANOVA, except that the comparison uses statistics adjusted for the covariate and the error term takes sampling differences among groups on the covariate into account. See Formula 17-7.

$$t_{obs.} = \frac{\hat{C}}{\sqrt{\dfrac{MS_{error}}{n}(w_1^2 + w_2^2 + \cdots + w_k^2)}} \qquad (17\text{-}7)$$

where:

$$\hat{C} = w_1\overline{Y}_{.1(adj.)} + w_2\overline{Y}_{.2(adj.)} + \cdots + w_k\overline{Y}_{.k(adj.)}, \text{ adapted from Formula 13-13a}$$

$$MS_{error} = MS_{within_{adj.}}\left(1 + \frac{\dfrac{SSX_{total} - SSX_{within}}{k-1}}{SSX_{within}}\right)$$

Suppose, for example, we decided to compare the control group with the two treatment groups. We have:

$$\hat{C} = (-2)(17.88) + (1)(26.91) + (1)(31.01) = 22.16$$

Before working with Formula 17-7, we also calculate MS_{error} using information from Tables 17-5 and 17-6:

$$MS_{error} = 4.22\left[1 + \frac{(123.73 - 119.60)/2}{119.60}\right] = 4.30$$

Substituting the mean difference (22.16) and MS_{error} (4.30) into Formula 17-7, along with the remaining statistics (from Procedure 17-1 in the *Student Guide*), we have:

$$t_{obs.} = \frac{22.16}{\sqrt{(4.30/5)[(-2)^2 + 1^2 + 1^2]}} = \frac{22.16}{2.27} = 9.76$$

The value of $t_{observed}$ is compared with the value of $t_{critical}$ with $k - 1$ and $k(n - 1) - 1$ degrees of freedom. Carrying out the test at the .01 level of significance, we find $t_{critical(.01,2,11)}$ (Formula 13-16):

$$t_{crit.(.01,2,11)} = \sqrt{(k - 1)F_{crit.(.01,2,11)}} = \sqrt{(2)(6.51)} = 3.61$$

Since $t_{observed}$ exceeds $t_{critical}$, we reject the null hypothesis of no difference among population means and conclude a treatment effect.

The next step is to examine the difference between the two treatment groups. For this pairwise comparison, Tukey's test can be used. However, the sampling distribution for Tukey's test with a covariate differs from the studentized range statistic we have been using up to this point. Because of the covariate, we use the generalized studentized range distribution and follow the Bryant-Paulson procedure (Bryant & Paulson, 1976; see also Kirk, 1995). The formula is presented in Formula 17-8.

$$q^*_{obs.} = \frac{w_1 \bar{Y}_{1adj.} - w_2 \bar{Y}_{2adj.}}{MS_{within_{adj.}} \left[\dfrac{2}{n} + \dfrac{(\bar{X}_{.i} - \bar{X}_{.i'})^2}{SSX_{total}} \right] \Big/ 2} \qquad (17\text{-}8)$$

where:

$q^* = $ Tukey's q with the Bryant-Paulson procedure

For our comparison of the two treatment groups, we have

$$q^*_{obs.} = \frac{31.01 - 26.91}{4.22 \left[\left(\dfrac{2}{5} \right) + \dfrac{(5.80 - 6.80)^2}{123.73} \right] \Big/ 2} = \frac{4.10}{.86} = 4.77$$

To determine whether to reject $q^*_{obs.}$, we refer to the generalized studentized range distribution in Table L. To use this table, we need the level of significance (.01 in the example), the number of groups ($k = 3$), the degrees of freedom for error ($df_{within_{adj.}} = 11$), and the number of covariates used in the analysis ($C = 1$):

$$q^*_{crit.(.01,3,11,1)} = 5.46$$

Because $q^*_{observed}$ does not exceed $q^*_{critical}$, we cannot reject the null hypothesis of equal population means.

We conclude, then, that the treatment groups exceed the control group in mean performance. The sample difference between the two treatment group means, however, may well have arisen by chance.

Example Problem 17.2

In Example Problem 17.1, a significant difference between the control and expectancy groups was found. No further post hoc comparisons need be carried out in this two-group case. But for practice, run Tukey's pairwise test for the difference in population means for these two groups ($SSX_{total} = 5840.00$ and $SSX_{within} = 5507.20$).

EXTENSIONS OF ANCOVA: FACTORIAL DESIGNS AND MORE THAN ONE COVARIATE

The analysis of covariance can be applied to factorial designs as well as one-way designs. In addition, it can be applied when more than one covariate has been measured in a study.

Application of ANCOVA to Factorial Designs

As an example of the application of the ANCOVA to a factorial design, data in Table 17-1 will be used. These hypothetical data, from the teacher expectancy study, were collected in a 4×2 (grade level × group) factorial design, with pretest ability scores as the covariate. If we conceive of this 4×2 design as a one-way design with $4 \times 2 = 8$ cells, then what we said about the one-way ANCOVA applies to the factorial ANCOVA.

Table 17-9 presents the results of the 4×2 ANCOVA. Both the grade level and the expectancy treatment effects are significant, and they need not be qualified because the grade × expectancy interaction was not significant. Moreover, as expected, the covariate accounted for a significant proportion of the variation in the dependent variable ($b_W = .55$).

TABLE 17-9 Grade level × expectancy group ANCOVA (data from Table 17-1)

Source of Variation	Sum of Squares	df	Mean Square	F
Grade	432.21	3	144.07	4.98[a]
Expectancy	158.92	1	158.92	5.49[a]
$G \times E$	31.68	3	10.56	.36
Covariate	1657.40	1	1657.40	57.28[a]
Error	897.00	31	28.94	

[a] $p < .05$.

Before interpreting these findings, however, we must check the assumptions underlying the ANCOVA. The equality of population means on the covariate ("randomization worked") was tested with a two-way ANOVA on the covariate. None of the effects was significant:

$$F_{grade} = .51 \qquad F_{expect.} = .08 \qquad F_{G \times E} = .11$$

The discussion of the assumptions of independence, normality, independence of covariate and treatment, and covariate reliability for the one-way ANCOVA apply here;

inspection of the variances indicated that the homogeneity assumption was not violated. Scatterplots, although based on only five observations per cell, indicated that linearity was tenable. And a test for homogeneity of regressions across the eight cells of the design led us to conclude that this assumption, too, was tenable ($F = .54$, $p > .79$).

For interpretation of the results of the factorial ANCOVA (Table 17-9), adjusted group means are presented in Table 17-10. We conclude that the expectancy treatment in grades 3–6 had a negative effect; the mean of the control group exceeds that of the bloomers. Moreover, the significant grade effect is due largely to the fifth graders and the sixth graders; at this point, post hoc comparisons would be appropriate (see Kirk, 1982).

TABLE 17-10 Adjusted means based on the grade × expectancy ANCOVA (Table 17-9)

| | Grade Level | | | | |
Group	3	4	5	6	Row
Expectancy	105.23	105.38	112.44	106.07	107.28
Control	108.29	107.15	117.02	112.62	111.27
Column	106.76	106.26	114.73	109.34	

Multiple Covariates

Often the researcher can identify a second covariate that is strongly related to the dependent variable and that is not strongly related to the first covariate. For example, in addition to the pretest covariate in the expectancy study, the researcher might have included grade-point average from the preceding semester. By removing the variability in posttest scores predictable from pretest scores and grades, the researcher can obtain an even more precise estimate of experimental error. The multiple-covariate case applies multiple regression (see Chapter 18) to remove the variability in Y predictable from the two (or more) covariates and is beyond the scope of this text. Kirk (1995) provides the details of this statistical test.

SUMMARY

This chapter presents the *analysis of covariance* (ANCOVA), a statistical test used to examine differences between means after adjusting for variability within groups predictable from an individual-difference variable measured before treatments are applied (covariate). The purpose and underlying rationale and the procedures for computing and interpreting a one-way, between-subjects, fixed-effects ANCOVA are presented. Special attention is paid to stringent assumptions required for the F test with the ANCOVA. Procedures for post hoc comparisons of *adjusted* posttest means are presented for Scheffé's and Tukey's methods. In addition, extensions of the ANCOVA to factorial, between-subjects, fixed-effects designs and to the multiple-covariate case are sketched.

ANSWERS TO EXAMPLE PROBLEMS

1. **a.** Assumptions:
   1. *Independence:* From the description of the study in Chapter 1, we suspect that there may be a problem if the teachers could not remember who were designated "bloomers" and who were not. We have insufficient information and would check on this before proceeding, if possible.
   2. *Normality:* Ability is typically symmetrically distributed, and the normal distribution usually is a good model of the sample distribution. By deleting first and second graders where there were measurement problems, we have reason to believe this assumption is tenable. Inspection of frequency distributions for each group supports this conclusion.
   3. *Homogeneity of variances:* The variance in the control group is 86.68 and is 58.37 in the expectancy group. This small difference is well within what would be expected from sampling variability.
   4. *Linearity:* Scatterplots indicate a linear relation between the covariate and the posttest in both groups.
   5. *Homogeneity of regression slopes:* The regression of posttest ability on pretest ability in the control group is $b_C = .50$ and in the expectancy group is $b_E = .47$. We conclude that this assumption has been met.
   6. *Covariate and treatment independence:* With measurement of the covariate prior to the application of the treatment and random assignment to groups, this assumption appears to have been met.
   7. *Covariate measured without error:* Having eliminated grades 1 and 2 where measurement problems arose, we assume that we now have sufficient reliability, as evidenced by detection of significant effects.

   b. $\bar{Y}_{.C_{adj.}} = \bar{Y}_{.C} - b_W(\bar{X}_{.C} - \bar{X}_G) = 111.60 - .49(102.1 - 101.5) = 111.60 - .29 = 111.31$

   $\bar{Y}_{.E_{adj.}} = 107.23$

2. Tukey's test is given in Formula 17-8:

$$q^* = \frac{(1)(111.60) - (-1)(106.95)}{37.93[.4 + (102.1 - 100.9)^2/5840]/2} - \frac{4.65}{2.75} = 1.69$$

$q^*_{crit.(.05,1,37,1)} \approx 2.89$

Do not reject H_0: $C = 0$.

EXERCISES

For the exercises in Chapter 16, you used treatment and test-occasion data (from Table 15-10) to explore further the hypothesis that aggressive boys in the experimental group would decrease their perceptions of negative intent from pre- to posttest compared to boys in the other two groups. Now let's use the pretest as a covariate and test the hypothesis on adjusted posttest scores.

1. Before conducting the ANCOVA, review the sample statistics from Chapter 16 exercises that bear on the hypothesis. Do these statistics support the hypothesis and assumptions?

2. Use the ANCOVA to determine whether the observed sample mean differences arose by chance.

   a. State the null and alternative hypotheses.

   b. State the assumptions underlying this statistical test. Calculate any statistics that might provide insight into the assumptions underlying the ANCOVA. Which assumption(s) are particularly problematic?

   c. Report the results in an ANCOVA summary table.

   d. Do you need to do post hoc comparisons? Why or why not? If you do, report the findings of the most telling comparison given the Hudley-Graham hypothesis.

   e. Interpret your findings. What do you conclude?

ANSWERS TO EXERCISES

1. The descriptive statistics (and past data analyses!) provide support for the Hudley-Graham (H-G) hypothesis about the effectiveness of attribution retraining in reducing aggressive boys' perceptions of negative intent in ambiguous situations. At pretest, the three groups perceive, on average, about the same amount of negative intent; at posttest, the experimental group's mean perception of negative intent dropped considerably more than did the other two groups' perceptions of negative intent.

2. a. H_0: $\mu_1 = \mu_2 = \mu_3$; H_1: $\mu_i \neq \mu_{i'}$ for some groups i and i'.

   H_1: $\beta_W = 0$; H_1: $\beta_W \neq 0$.

   b. *Independence:* We have concluded independence in past analyses. To check randomization, a oneway ANOVA[8] on pretest scores led to the decision not to reject the null hypothesis ($F = 1.58$; $df = 2,15$; $MS_W = 1.30$, $p < .24$):

   Normality: There are too few data points ($n = 6$ per group) to get a good handle on pre- and posttest distributions within each group, not to mention distributions of Y scores for each level of X within each of the three groups. Nevertheless, descriptive statistics for skewness and kurtosis at pre- and posttest (respectively), based on all 18 subjects (ignoring treatment group), are less than 1: kurtosis = $-.77$, $-.99$; skew-

---

[8]SPSS Program Setup:
ONEWAY pretest BY group(1 3)
/RANGES=TUKEY
/RANGES=SCHEFFE
/HARMONIC NONE
/STATISTICS DESCRIPTIVES HOMOGENEITY
/FORMAT NOLABELS
/MISSING ANALYSIS.

Source of Variation	SS	DF	MS	F	Sig of F
Between groups	4.1111	2	2.0556	1.5812	.2382
Within groups	19.5000	15	1.3000		
Total	23.6111	17			

ness = .12, −.08. These findings suggest that the ratings may be normally distributed.

Homogeneity of variances: We concluded in previous exercises with these data that variances are homogeneous across the three groups. There are too few data to check the assumption of homogeneity for each level of X.

The remaining assumptions are particularly crucial and potentially problematic for the ANCOVA:

Linearity: Again, with 6 data points in each group, even an "eyeball" test of this assumption lacks credibility.

Homogeneity of regression slopes: This assumption states that the regressions of posttest on pretest are equal in the 3 populations. Again, with 6 data points in each group, this assumption cannot be examined seriously. The regression coefficients for groups 1–3 are .50, .44, and .86, respectively. These statistics fall well within sampling variability and appear consistent with the assumption.

Independence of covariate and treatments: Subjects were pretested, and then randomly assigned to a treatment group. In the long run, this assures independence.

Covariate measured without error: We do not have reliability information on the pretest.

c. ANCOVA Source Table[9]

Source of Variation	SS	DF	MS	F	Sig of F
WITHIN+RESIDUAL	11.65	14	.83		
REGRESSION[Covariate]	6.02	1	6.02	7.23	.018
GROUP[a]	37.57	2	18.79	22.58	.000

[a]Group means are:

CELL	Obs. Mean	Adj. Mean
1	1.833	1.864
2	5.000	4.660
3	4.833	5.142

Note: SPSS does not report the ANCOVA summary table in conventional format.

---

[9]SPSS
Program Setup:
MANOVA posttest BY group(1 3) WITH pretest
/PRINT HOMOGENEITY (BARTLETT COCHRAN)
/NOPRINT PARAM(ESTIM)
/OMEANS TABLES(group)
/PMEANS TABLES(group)
/METHOD=UNIQUE
/ERROR WITHIN+RESIDUAL
/DESIGN.

d. With a statistically significant group effect, post hoc comparisons are in order. A comparison of the experimental group with the two control groups provides a direct test of the H-G hypothesis.

$$\hat{C} = (-2)(1.864) + (1)(4.660) + (1)(5.142) = 6.07$$

$$MS_{error} = .83 \left(1 + \frac{\frac{23.61 - 19.50}{3 - 1}}{19.50} \right) = .83(1.11) = .92$$

$$t_{obs.} = \frac{6.07}{\sqrt{\frac{.92}{6}[(-2)^2 + 1^2 + 1^2]}} = \frac{6.07}{\sqrt{(.15)(6)}} = \frac{6.07}{.95} = 6.39$$

$$t_{crit.(.05,2,14)} = \sqrt{(2)(3.74)} = 2.73$$

Reject the null hypothesis and conclude that the experimental group, on average, perceived less negative intent than did the other two groups.

e. The ANCOVA confirms previous analyses. The data support the H-G hypothesis.

VII

ADDITIONAL TOPICS: CORRELATIONAL AND NONPARAMETRIC STATISTICAL ANALYSIS

T he models for statistical inference presented so far apply mostly to experimental research. This research is characterized by the randomized factorial experiment. The analysis of variance provides a general statistical framework for testing hypotheses. The focus is often on theory testing, and the intent is to draw causal inferences.

There are correlational approaches to research that have the same goal: to test theory and to draw causal inferences. Such approaches are used especially when true experiments cannot be carried out due to cost, questionable external validity, or ethical considerations. For example, it is very unlikely that a credible experiment can be done to adequately address the causal relation between exposure to violence on television and aggressive behavior in society. The real treatment, years of exposure to TV, has already been administered before the behavioral scientist arrived on the scene. Any additional treatment pales in comparison to the natural experiment. Likewise, a resolution of the debate of the causal predominance of self-concept over academic or career achievements, or vice versa, is unlikely to be generally resolved by a true experiment for the same reasons. And the causal effects of educational resources and instructional methods on student achievement in the United States is unlikely to be resolved by a true experiment because such a design cannot be implemented.

The point is that many important research questions in the behavioral sciences have to be addressed with correlational designs, not experimental designs. In this section, **multiple regression analysis (MRA)** is presented as a statistical technique for modeling the linear relationship between a dependent variable (e.g., aggressive behavior) and a set of independent variables (e.g., time spent viewing violent TV shows, age, sex, socioeconomic status). I show how alternative models can be set forth to test hypotheses about which independent variables are related to the dependent variable. However, I do not go so far as to show how this technique can be used to test alternative causal models; such a demonstration is beyond the scope of this text.

This section concludes with two chapters on *nonparametric* statistical techniques. These techniques can be applied to experimental or correlational data. And many of these techniques parallel familiar *parametric* statistical techniques such as the *t* test and ANOVA.

Classical statistical methods such as the *t* test and ANOVA are called **parametric** statistical tests because they test hypotheses about parameters in the (usually normal) population. For example, both the *t* test and the ANOVA can be used to test the null hypothesis that the means of two populations underlying a control and experimental group are equal: H_0: $\mu_1 = \mu_2$. They are developed on the assumptions that scores are measured on at least an interval scale and are normally distributed in the populations, and that the score variances in the populations are all equal. Put another way, these statistical tests assume interval scales and that the populations are the same except for mean differences.

In contrast, **nonparametric** statistical tests do not (necessarily) test hypotheses about specific population parameters. Rather, they test hypotheses about, for example, the shapes of distributions or their central tendencies. Moreover, they do not necessarily assume interval measurement and normal populations with equal variances. Rather, nonparametric tests rest on weaker assumptions about the measurement scale and the nature of the parent populations. For example, nonparametric tests can be applied to ordinal scale data and modeled with discrete sampling distributions; the tests might assume that parent populations are symmetric in shape or only similar in shape.

Although the less stringent assumptions make nonparametric tests attractive to the behavioral scientist, a word of caution is appropriate. Nonparametric tests have been sold as a panacea. "In some miraculous way, using such a technique is supposed to solve all the problems raised by unknown measurement level, objectionable assumptions, and so on (including, some apparently believe, sloppy data). If this is true, this is the only known example of something for nothing in statistics or anywhere else" (Hays, 1973, p. 763).

When choosing between a parametric and a nonparametric test, then, the potential costs and benefits of each must be weighed. In situations in which certain of the assumptions of parametric tests are not met, the consequences of violating the assumptions should be taken into consideration. In many cases, the parametric tests are not seriously affected by a violation of their assumptions and may be more powerful than their nonparametric counterparts. In many other cases, however, parametric tests are not as powerful as their nonparametric counterparts when certain of their assumptions (e.g., homogeneity of variances) have been violated. And in some cases (e.g., unequal sample sizes and variances), assumptions of parametric tests are untenable, and so the accuracy of the statistical results is problematic. Furthermore, with small sample size ($n < 10$), assumptions underlying parametric tests tend to be untenable, and the nonparametric counterpart may be more appropriate. Finally, for computational ease, the nonparametric methods carry the day. With high-speed computers, however, computational ease is less of an advantage than it was, say, 20 years ago.

The choice of parametric or nonparametric tests is not always an easy one, and no simple rule of thumb exists for simplifying the decision. Yet there is a reasonable way out of the potential dilemma. Simply put, there's more than one way to skin a rabbit, or to analyze a set of data. Nonparametric techniques ask slightly different questions of the data than do parametric tests and encourage researchers to view their data from a different and enlightening perspective. The use of multiple perspectives in analyzing data, like triangulation in astronomy, is to be encouraged. With high-speed computing, both parametric and nonparametric analyses can be readily carried out and together may be more informative than either one alone. You are encouraged to do so.

18 Multiple Regression Analysis

- Description of MRA
- Interpretation of MRA Findings
- Summary
- Answers to Example Problems
- Exercises
- Answers to Exercises

$\mathbf{M}$*ultiple regression analysis* (MRA) is a statistical method for studying the relation between a dependent variable and two or more independent variables. The purpose for applying MRA might be prediction. For example, to decrease military personnel costs, policymakers seek to reduce attrition from the services. One way to do so is to select those young men and women who are least likely to drop out of military service during their first term of enlistment. Consequently, in the development of a selection policy, MRA might be used to predict first-term attrition from enlistees' aptitudes, amount of education, income, and marital status. The results would inform policymakers about selection variables, taken together, that are predictive of attrition. Or MRA might be used in an exploratory fashion in an attempt to identify those characteristics of individuals (e.g., creativity, intelligence, social skill, calmness) that are associated with ratings of leadership ability. Finally, MRA might be used to test a theory. For example, self-concept theory posits that school grades are influenced not only by students' achievement but also by self-concept, which underlies their behavior in the classroom. MRA can be used to determine whether self-concept ratings add anything to the prediction of grades beyond what can be predicted from achievement test scores.

The basic idea underlying MRA is the same as that for simple linear regression (Chapter 7). In simple regression, one variable, Y, is predicted from a second variable, X.[1] In MRA, the dependent variable (Y) is predicted from a set of independent variables, $X_1, X_2, \ldots, X_k$.

---

[1]Before proceeding with this chapter, you might want to review Chapter 7. Throughout this chapter, we assume you are comfortable with simple linear regression.

Like simple linear regression, MRA provides an index of the functional relationship between the dependent variable and each of the independent variables. The index takes the form of a regression coefficient; one coefficient is associated with each independent variable. Moreover, just as r^2 in simple regression analysis provides a measure of the proportion of variance in Y predictable from X, MRA generates R^2, an index of the proportion of variation in the dependent variable (Y) that is predictable from the set of independent variables (X's).[2] Finally, like simple regression, the method for predicting Y from a set of X's minimizes the (squared) errors in prediction. Or put a different way, the method estimates regression coefficients so as to minimize the squared difference between an individual's predicted score on Y and her actual score on Y. This method is known as the criterion of *least squares*.

As an example of an application of MRA, consider college administrators who are interested in selecting students who will succeed in their colleges (i.e., maintain an adequate grade-point average and graduate). As an aid in this selection process, often an MRA will be carried out. Typically, college GPA will be predicted from Scholastic Aptitude Test scores, high school grade-point average, and other information collected in the admission's process. The goal of the analysis is to establish a selection formula. This formula contains a weighted composite of those kinds of information about applicants that are most helpful in predicting success in the college. The analysis also provides an index how good the prediction is in terms of the proportion of variation in college GPA predicted from SAT scores, high school GPA, and the like.

This chapter presents the conceptual and statistical underpinnings of multiple regression analysis. Examples of the application and interpretation of MRA are provided.[3]

DESCRIPTION OF MRA
Purpose and Underlying Logic
The purposes of MRA are to help the researcher to predict some criterion or dependent variable (Y) from a set of predictor or independent variables ($X_1, X_2, \ldots, X_k$), to test hypotheses about alternative models of the relation between Y and the set of X's or to do some combination of these two things.

To see how MRA operates, we will consider an example. The data presented in Table 18-1 are from a study on the relation between academic achievement, grades, and general and academic self-concept. Before we turn to the data, however, an explanation of the self-concept variables is probably appropriate since you are already familiar with achievement tests and grades but might be less so with self-concept.

Self-concept, broadly defined, is one's perception of him or herself. It is structured in that people categorize the vast amount of information they have about themselves and relate the categories to one another. It is multifaceted, reflecting the categories people use. It is

---

[2] R^2 provides an index of the proportion of *variation* in the dependent variable that can be accounted for by the set of X's. That is, R^2 is a ratio of sums of squares: sum of squares predictable from the set of X's divided by the total sum of squares. Because it is not a ratio of variances, we do *not* formally talk of the proportion of variance in Y accounted for by the set of X's, even though "proportion of variance" is common parlance in MRA.

[3] This chapter presents the rudiments of MRA. For a complete presentation of the topic, see Draper & Smith (1981).

TABLE 18-1 Descriptive statistics for hypothetical data on self-concept, academic achievement, and grades ($N = 103$)

	Self-Concept		Academic Achievement (AA)	Grade Point Average (GPA)
Statistic	General (GSC)	Academic (ASC)		
Correlation				
GSC	1.00			
ASC	.45	1.00		
AA	.15	.40	1.00	
GPA	.25	.50	.62	1.00
Mean	5.20	5.60	54.30	2.50
Standard Deviation	.92	1.26	10.65	.50

hierarchical, with perceptions of behavior at the base moving to inferences about self in sub-areas (e.g., physical—appearance, ability; academic—math, history), then to inferences about self in nonacademic and academic areas, and then to inferences about self in general (see Shavelson et al., 1976).

Self-concept theory leads us to predict that academic achievement (AA) and academic self-concept (ASC) will be more closely related than AA and general self-concept (GSC). However, the relation between grades and these other variables is not so clear. Grades certainly reflect, to a good extent, academic achievement. But they also reflect students' efforts, improvement, participation, etc. Thus we hypothesize that the best predictors of grades might be academic achievement and general self-concept. Once AA and GSC have been used to predict grades, academic self-concept is not expected to improve the prediction of grades. That is, ASC is not expected to account for any additional variation in grades.

Basic Multiple Regression Equation.   MRA provides a technique for statistically examining these predictions from self-concept theory. To see how it works, let us begin with simple linear regression: one independent variable and one dependent variable. For example, using the information in Table 18-1, let's predict achievement from academic self-concept. We begin by writing an equation for the prediction:

$$\hat{Y} = a + bX$$

where $\hat{Y}$ denotes the predicted value of Y, and the least squares estimates of a and b are:

$$a = \bar{Y} - b\bar{X} \qquad \text{(Formula 7-5)}$$
$$b = r_{XY}\frac{s_Y}{s_X} \qquad \text{(Formula 7-6a)}$$

For our data, we have:

$$b = .40\left(\frac{10.65}{1.26}\right) = 3.38$$

$$a = 54.30 - 3.38(5.60) = 35.37$$
$$\hat{Y} = 35.37 + 3.38X$$

The working part of the equation is bX. The regression coefficient tells us that for every unit increase in academic self-concept, we should predict achievement to increase by more than $3\frac{1}{3}$ points (by 3.38 points). For an academic self-concept score of 4, we should predict an achievement score of $35.37 + 3.38(4) = 48.89$.

In an analogous fashion, we can write a linear equation for predicting a dependent variable from k independent variables. See Formula 18-1.

$$\hat{Y} = a + b_1X_1 + b_2X_2 + \cdots + b_kX_k \tag{18-1}$$

where a and b's are estimated by least squares.

Formula 18-1 says that the predicted value of Y is equal to a *linear combination of X's*. Moreover, it says that this combination is not just any old linear combination—such as simply adding variables X_1 through X_k and using the sum to predict Y. No, it says that a particular set of weights, the b's, are determined in such a way (according to the least squares criterion) so as to provide the mathematically best prediction of Y. No other linear combination of independent variables can beat it!

The multiple regression equation for predicting AA (Y) from, say, GSC (X_1) and ASC (X_2) is[4]:

$$\hat{Y} = a + b_1X_1 + b_2X_2$$

where the least squares estimates of a, b_1, and b_2 are given in Formulas 18-2a and 18-2b.

$$a = \bar{Y} - b_1\bar{X}_1 + b_2\bar{X}_2 \tag{18-2a}$$
$$b_1 = \frac{r_{Y1} - r_{Y2}r_{12}}{1 - r_{12}^2}\left(\frac{s_Y}{s_1}\right)$$
$$b_2 = \frac{r_{Y2} - r_{Y1}r_{12}}{1 - r_{12}^2}\left(\frac{s_Y}{s_2}\right) \tag{18-2b}$$

where:

r_{Y1} = correlation between Y and X_1
r_{Y2} = correlation between Y and X_2
r_{12} = correlation between X_1 and X_2

[4]Throughout this chapter, we provide formulas and computational examples for MRA with two independent variables. Although the concept of MRA with two independent variables generalizes to k independent variables, with more than two independent variables, the computational formulas get tedious and are best carried out with statistical packages like BMDP, SAS, or SPSS.

The coefficient a in Formula 18-2a is the intercept. It is analogous to the intercept in simple regression. The b's are *partial regression coefficients*. A partial regression coefficient shows the relationship between the dependent variable (Y) and one independent variable (e.g., X_1), controlling for the other independent variable (i.e., X_2 in our example). Or put another way, the partial regression coefficient shows the relationship between Y to X_1 for individuals with the same score on X_2.[5]

Before carrying out the calculations with Formula 18-2, let's take a closer look at the partial regression coefficient, b_1. In the numerator, we subtract from r_{Y1} the correlation between Y and X_2 and the correlation between X_1 and X_2. This manipulation allows us to estimate the relation between Y and X_1, holding X_2 constant. If the correlation between X_1 and X_2 is low, the adjustment to the relation between Y and X_1 is small. Of course, the limiting case for the partial regression coefficient occurs when X_1 and X_2 are uncorrelated. Then no adjustment to r_{Y1} is made—X_1 and X_2 are linearly independent of one another. Hence, there is no need to control for X_2 when we consider the relation between Y and X_1.[6] The moral of the story is that to maximize the prediction of Y, we should select predictors that are highly correlated with Y but are only modestly correlated with one another.

What we will find, however, just as in other things in life, is that this prescription often is too good to be true. A bunch of independent variables with low or zero correlations among each other and high correlations with the dependent variable is hard to find.

Indeed, we usually find that some of the independent variables are highly correlated. For example, we might predict college grades from SAT scores and achievement information; SAT and other achievement indicators are often highly correlated. Or we might predict college grades from SAT total, verbal, and quantitative scores (something that makes no sense but has been erroneously done). Since SAT total is a composite of the verbal and quantitative scores, the part-whole correlations ($r_{\text{total-verbal}}$ and $r_{\text{total-quantitative}}$) will be very high. *Multicollinearity*, the existence of high correlations among the independent variables, is a concern because it produces unstable estimates of the partial regression coefficients. That is, from one sample to the next, the partial regression coefficients can "bounce" considerably in magnitude and sometimes in sign (positive/negative).

Now, back to the calculations. Let's determine $\hat{Y}$ by inserting the appropriate descriptive statistics from Table 18-1 into Formula 18-2. We have:

$$a = 36.83$$
$$b_1 = -.44$$
$$b_2 = 3.52$$
$$\hat{Y} = 36.83 + (-.44)X_1 + (3.52)X_2$$

For a person with a general self-concept score of 4 and an academic self-concept score of 6, we predict her academic achievement to be:

---

[5]We assume that the relation between Y and X_1 is constant across all levels of X_2.

[6]Incidentally, multifactor experiments (with equal cell sizes) are *designed* to ensure that the factors (independent variables) are uncorrelated with one another. In this way, ANOVA can be applied to examine each factor and each interaction independently of all other factors and interactions. There is no ambiguity in interpreting the relation between the dependent variable and each of the independent variables and their interactions.

$$\hat{Y} = 36.83 + (-.44)4 + (3.52)6 = 56.23$$

Before we leave the topic of the multiple regression equation, note that the partial regression coefficient relating general self-concept to academic achievement looks strange. After all, the correlation between GSC and AA is positive (.15). How can the partial regression coefficient be negative? Recall that the partial regression coefficient tells you about the relation between AA and GSC, *holding ASC constant.* An inspection of the correlations in Table 18-1, then, may shed some light on this apparent anomaly. Notice that GSC and ASC are correlated at .45, but GSC's correlation with AA is quite low (.15) whereas ASC's correlation with AA is considerably higher (.40). Apparently, much of the variability shared in common between GSC and ASC ($r^2 = .202$) accounts for the predictability of AA from GSC. With ASC held constant, the relation between GSC and AA is negative, as indicated by b_1.

Multiple Correlation Coefficient.   In addition to obtaining information from the prediction equation (the predicted score and the estimates of a and the b's), we can estimate the magnitude of the relationship between the dependent variable and the best linear combination of independent variables. This estimate is called the *multiple correlation coefficient,* and it is denoted by R. Like the simple correlation coefficient r, the multiple coefficient R is a product-moment correlation. But unlike r, R ranges in value from 0 to 1.00. More formally, we define R as the correlation between the dependent variable Y and the predicted values on the dependent variable Y. See Formula 18-3.

$$R = \frac{\text{Cov}(Y, \hat{Y})}{s_Y s_{\hat{Y}}} \qquad (18\text{-}3)$$

Moreover, the square of the multiple correlation coefficient, R^2, has roughly the same interpretation as the square of the simple correlation coefficient r^2: R^2 provides a measure of the proportion of *variation* in Y accounted for by the set of independent variables (X's). More formally, R^2 is defined in Formula 18-4 in terms of readily available descriptive statistics.

$$R^2 = \frac{r_{Y1}^2 + r_{Y2}^2 - 2r_{Y1}r_{Y2}r_{12}}{1 - r_{12}^2} \qquad (18\text{-}4)$$

If we replace the symbols in Formula 18-4 with the correlations from Table 18-1, we find:

$$R^2 = \frac{(.15)^2 + (.40)^2 - 2(.15)(.40)(.45)}{1 - (.45)^2} = .16$$

In words, 16 percent of the variability in academic achievement is accounted for by the weighted composite of the independent variables, general and academic self-concept.

By taking the square root of R^2 in Formula 18-4, we have a handy formula for calculating R, rather than having to go through all the computations required by Formula 18-3:

$$R = \sqrt{.161} = .41$$

To provide additional insight into the nature of R^2, we can partition the variation of Y into two components: (1) variation in Y predictable from the set of X's and (2) variation in Y unpredictable from the set of X's. More formally, the sum of squares for Y (SS_Y) is equal to the sum of squares regression ($SS_{reg.}$), or *predictable* variation, plus the sum of squares residual ($SS_{res.}$) or *unpredictable* variation. See Formula 18-5.

$$SS_Y = SS_{reg.} + SS_{res.} \qquad \textbf{(18-5)}$$

Sum of squares SS_Y is defined in the usual manner:

$$\sum_{1}^{N} (Y - \bar{Y})^2$$

The sum $SS_{reg.}$ reflects the deviation of the predicted scores ($\hat{Y}$) about the mean of the predicted scores, which equals $\bar{Y}$. The greater the variability of $\hat{Y}$ about $\bar{Y}$, the greater the predictability of Y from the set (or composite) of X's. Finally, $SS_{res.}$ reflects the unpredictability of Y from the X's—the squared deviation of each Y from its predicted value $\hat{Y}$. Hence, we have the definitions given in Formulas 18-5a–c.

$$SS_Y = \sum_{p=1}^{N} (Y_p - \bar{Y})^2 \qquad \textbf{(18-5a)}$$

$$SS_{reg.} = \sum_{p=1}^{N} (\hat{Y}_p - \bar{Y})^2 \qquad \textbf{(18-5b)}$$

$$SS_{res.} = \sum_{p=1}^{N} (Y_p - \hat{Y}_p)^2 \qquad \textbf{(18-5c)}$$

Finally, if we divide both sides of Formula 18-5 by SS_Y, we can write the equation in terms of the proportion of variation in Y accounted for by the X's and the proportion of variation unaccounted for. See Formula 18-5d.

$$\frac{SS_Y}{SS_Y} = \frac{SS_{reg.}}{SS_Y} + \frac{SS_{res.}}{SS_Y} \qquad \textbf{(18-5d)}$$

or

$$1 = \text{proportion of variation in } Y \text{ predictable from } X\text{'s } (R^2)$$
$$+ \text{ proportion of variation in } Y \text{ unpredictable from } X\text{'s}$$

By definition, the proportion of variation in Y accounted for by the independent variables (X's) is R^2. By subtracting R^2 from both sides of the equation, we find that the proportion of variation in Y unaccounted for by X, the residual or *error in prediction*, is:

$1 - R^2$ = proportion of variation in Y unpredictable from X's

This partitioning of the total variation of Y into that proportion predictable from Y and that proportion due to error suggests that this information might be used to provide a statistical test of the prediction equation, using R^2 in an analogous fashion to the sum of squares between groups in a one-way ANOVA and $1 - R^2$ as the error term. This is, indeed, the case, and we turn our attention to the statistical test next.

Tests of Statistical Significance.   Statistical tests of significance for multiple regression address the question "Did R^2 arise by chance when its true value in the population is 0, or does it reflect a systematic relationship between Y and the independent variables?" As noted before, the statistical test in multiple regression compares the proportion of variation in Y predictable from a linear combination of the X's with the proportion of variation unpredictable from the X's.

The statistical test follows the F distribution and can be defined as in Formula 18-6.

$$F_{observed} = \frac{R^2/k}{(1 - R^2)/(N - k - 1)} \qquad (18\text{-}6)$$

with $df_{reg.} = k$, $df_{res.} = N - k - 1$, and

where:

R^2 = squared multiple correlation coefficient
k = number of independent variables
N = sample size

By substituting the values into the terms of Formula 18-6, we find:

$$F_{observed} = \frac{.16/2}{[(1 - .16)/(103 - 2 - 1)]} = \frac{.08}{.0084} = 9.52$$

Comparing $F_{observed}$ with $F_{critical(.05,2,100)} = 3.09$, we conclude that in the population, the observed relation is not due to chance; rather, it is due to a systematic relation between academic achievement and the two independent variables, general and academic self-concept.

Design Requirements

MRA employs a correlational design in which one group of subjects is measured on three or more continuous, individual-difference variables. Since causal ordering among the variables is usually not posited (but see the section "Correlation and Causality" in Chapter 6), causal interpretations are not warranted.

More specifically, the design requirements are as follows:

1. There is one dependent (or criterion) variable and two or more independent (or predictor) variables.
2. All variables are continuous.[7]
3. The minimal sample size needed to provide adequate estimates of the regression coefficients is something like 50 cases, and a general rule of thumb is that there should be at least about 10 times as many cases (subjects) as independent variables.

Hypotheses

In MRA, the null hypothesis tested is that in the population, the squared multiple correlation is equal to zero:

$$H_0: R^2 = 0$$

The alternative hypothesis is that the squared multiple correlation is not zero:

$$H_1: R^2 \neq 0$$

Assumptions

In order to use MRA to test hypotheses statistically, we make the following assumptions:

1. *Independence:* The scores for any particular subject are independent of the scores of all other subjects.
2. *Normality:* In the population, the scores on the dependent variable are normally distributed for each of the possible combinations of the levels of the X variables.
3. *Homoscedasticity:* In the population, the variances of the dependent variable for each of the possible combinations of the levels of the X variables are equal.
4. *Linearity:* In the population, the relation between the dependent variable and an independent variable is linear when all other independent variables are held constant.

The assumption of independence can be examined logically, as in the ANOVA. Did the procedures for collecting the data ensure independence of scores?

The remaining three assumptions can be examined by inspecting a scatterplot with the predicted Y scores ($\hat{Y}$) on the abscissa and the residuals ($Y - \hat{Y}$) on the ordinate. Figure 18-1 presents examples in which all three assumptions are met (Figure 18-1a), the assumption of normality is violated (Figure 18-1b), the assumption of linearity is violated (Figure 18-1c), and the assumption of homoscedasticity is violated (Figure 18-1d). Statistical packages such as SAS, SPSS, and BMDP offer statistical tests as well.

---

[7]MRA is not restricted to the continuous-variable case. One or more independent variables can be nominal. The nominal case is beyond the scope of this presentation (see, for example, Pedhazur, 1982). Incidentally, if all of the independent variables are nominal, MRA and ANOVA have identical statistical models.

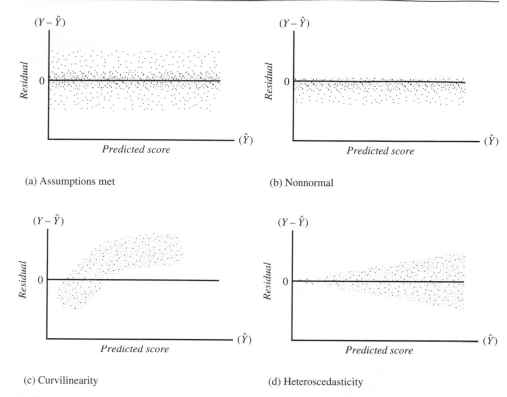

FIGURE 18-1

Scatterplots of residuals $(Y - \hat{Y})$ against predicted scores $(\hat{Y})$: (a) assumptions met; (b) nonnormality; (c) curvilinearity; and (d) heterosecadasticity

If the normality assumption is met, we should expect to see all of the points in the residual scatterplot clustered tightly in the center of the plot at each level of the predicted score. Moreover, there should be fewer and fewer points above and below reflecting a normal distribution of residuals at each level of the predicted score. The asymmetry in Figure 18-1b with a greater scatter of residuals below the center suggests violation of this assumption. If this assumption is violated, a transformation of the variables should be considered (e.g., see Draper & Smith, 1981).

If the assumption of linearity is met, we should expect to see a horizontal scatter of residuals. In Figure 18-1c, as the predicted values of Y increase, so do the residuals, suggesting violation of the assumption. If this assumption is violated, consideration should be given first to a transformation of the original data and then to fitting more complex, curvilinear multiple regression models (see Draper & Smith, 1981).

If the assumption of homoscedasticity is met, the scatter of the residuals about the center of the plot should be the same at each value of the predicted Y score. Figure 18-1d shows a characteristic fantail symptomatic of a violation of the assumption. In this case, as the predicted Y values increase, so does the variance of the residuals. In this case, a transformation of the original variables should be considered (e.g., see Draper & Smith, 1981).

Computations in MRA

In MRA, the multiple regression equation can be calculated directly from the raw scores in a data matrix with Formulas 18-5a–c. The coefficient R^2 can be calculated with Formula 18-5d. And a statistical test of R^2 can be made by using Formula 18-7.

$$F_{observed} = \frac{SS_{reg.}/k}{SS_{res.}/(N - k - 1)} \qquad (18\text{-}7)$$

with $df_{reg.} = k$ and $df_{res.} = N - k - 1$

Formula 18-7 can be cast in the familiar ANOVA source table, as shown in Table 18-2. This table demonstrates the use of ANOVA to partition the total variability in the dependent variable into two components, one predictable from the set of independent variables ($SS_{reg.}$) and the other unpredictable from the X's ($SS_{res.}$).

However, the use of Formula 18-2 for calculating the estimates of the parameters in the multiple regression equation and the use of Formula 18-6 for carrying out the statistical test are much less tedious to apply and can be used when only descriptive statistics are available. Consequently, we demonstrated MRA computations with those formulas. (Procedure 18-1 in the *Student Guide* provides the computations for predicting academic achievement (AA) from general self-concept (GSC) and academic self-concept (ASC) by using Formula 18-2. It applies Formula 18-4 to find R^2, and it also applies Formula 18-6 to provide a statistical test of the null hypothesis that R^2 equals zero.)

TABLE 18-2   ANOVA approach to statistical tests in MRA

Source	Sum of Squares	df	Mean Square	F
Regression	$SS_{reg.}$	k	$\dfrac{SS_{reg.}}{k}$	$\dfrac{SS_{reg.}/k}{SS_{res.}/(N - k - 1)}$
Residual	$SS_{res.}$	$N - k - 1$	$\dfrac{SS_{res.}}{N - k - 1}$	
Total	SS_{total}	$N - 1$		

Example Problem 18.1

There is reason to believe that school grades include student performance other than just academic achievement. Consequently, self-concept theory predicts that a combination of academic achievement and general self-concept will predict a significant proportion of the variability in GPA.
a. What proportion of variation in GPA can be predicted from AA and GSC?
b. Using data from Table 18-1, test this prediction statistically.
c. For a person with a score of 55 on academic achievement and a score of 5 on general self-concept, what is his predicted GPA?

INTERPRETATION OF MRA FINDINGS

Using hypothetical data from Table 18-1, we set out to see whether the hypothesis based on self-concept theory—that academic achievement (AA) could be predicted from general and academic self-concept (GSC and ASC, respectively), and more specifically, that ASC would be a better predictor of AA than GSC—could be supported empirically. Before we interpret the findings, however, the assumptions of independence, normality, homoscedasticity, and linearity should be checked.

Assumptions

Assume that the 103 subjects who participated in the hypothetical study were randomly sampled from some population and that the administration of the tests was carried out so as to ensure independent responses. Figure 18-2 presents a plot of residuals against predicted values of Y for GSC and ASC. The points in these two scatterplots appear to cluster about the zero residual line and to be spread equally above and below the line. These plots lead us to conclude that the assumptions underlying the MRA have been met.

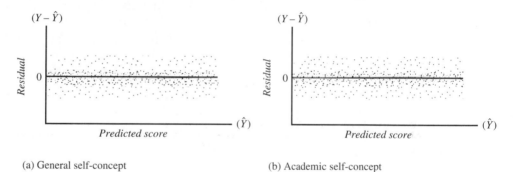

(a) General self-concept   (b) Academic self-concept

FIGURE 18-2
Scatterplots of residual academic achievement $(Y - \hat{Y})$ on predicted academic achievement $(\hat{Y})$: (a) for general self-concept; (b) for academic self-concept

Interpretation of Partial Regression Coefficients

To begin interpreting the results of our analysis, we start by examining the correlations in Table 18-1. As predicted, the correlation between ASC and AA (.40) is greater than the correlation between GSC and AA (.15). Moreover, the correlation between GSC and ASC (.45) suggests that these two measures share a variance in common ($r^2 = .20$), and this common variance might be based on the academic aspect of general self-concept. If so, we should expect ASC to be a stronger predictor of AA, as indexed by the partial regression coefficient, than GSC.

To examine this last prediction, we can compare the partial regression coefficients. For GSC, the coefficient is −.436; for ASC, it is 3.524. Before concluding that ASC is a more important predictor than GSC, however, we must recognize that the *magnitude of the par-*

tial regression coefficient is influenced by the variance of the predictor variable. So if the variance of ASC is substantially greater than that of GSC, we should expect the value of the partial regression coefficient for ASC to be larger, all other things being equal. An inspection of the standard deviations in Table 18-1 leads us to conclude that there is not a big enough difference in the variability of the two predictor measures to account for the large difference in coefficients. Hence, we conclude that, as expected, ASC is a stronger predictor of AA than GSC.

Suppose, however, that the variances of GSC and ASC were quite different. In this case, we would like to compare *standardized* partial regression coefficients—coefficients based on standard scores for GSC and ASC so that the variance of both (standardized) variables is set to 1.00. To transform the unstandardized coefficients b_1 and b_2 into standardized coefficients $\hat{\beta}_1$ and $\hat{\beta}_2$, we apply Formula 18-8.

$$\hat{\beta} = b\left(\frac{s_X}{s_Y}\right) \tag{18-8}$$

where:

$\hat{\beta}$ = standardized, partial regression coefficient
b = unstandardized coefficient
s_X, s_Y = standard deviation of the predictor of interest and the
        dependent variable, respectively

To transform the unstandardized coefficient for GSC into the standardized coefficient, we have:

$$\hat{\beta} = -.436\left(\frac{.92}{10.65}\right) = -.038$$

For ASC, we have:

$$\hat{\beta} = 3.524\left(\frac{1.26}{10.65}\right) = .417$$

As expected, the standardized partial regression coefficient for ASC is considerably larger than that for GSC, leading us to conclude that, as expected from self-concept theory, ASC is a stronger predictor than GSC.

Interpretation of R^2

The square of the multiple correlation coefficient, R^2, provides an index of the proportion (or percent) of variation in the dependent variable that can be accounted for by the linear composite of (regression-weighted) independent variables. That is, it is an index showing the percentage of variation in Y accounted for by the set of X's. In our example, $R = .41$ and $R^2 = .161$. In words, 16.1 percent of the variation in AA can be accounted for by the linear composite of GSC and ASC. Thus almost 84 percent of the variation in AA is unexplained, and consequently, other independent variables might be considered if our goal is not testing self-concept theory but improving the prediction of AA.

It turns out that R^2 is sensitive to sample size and the number of independent variables used in MRA. Recall that one of the design requirements for MRA is that sample size should exceed 50 cases and that there should be about 10 times more cases than independent variables. This design requirement reflects the fact that as the number of independent variables approaches the sample size (as k approaches N), R^2 approaches 1.00. Consequently, a statistical correction can be used to adjust R^2 and so reflect the "sensitivity" of R^2 to the number of independent variables (k) and sample size (N). See Formula 18-9.

$$R_*^2 = 1 - (1 - R^2)\left(\frac{N - 1}{N - k - 1}\right) \tag{18-9}$$

To adjust $R^2 = .161$ for $k = 2$ and $N = 103$, we replace the terms in Formula 18-9 as follows:

$$R_*^2 = 1 - (1 - .161)\left(\frac{103 - 1}{103 - 2 - 1}\right) = 1 - [.839(1.02)] = 1.44$$

The adjusted proportion of variation in AA accounted for by the linear composite of GSC and ASC, then, is .144. Thus, the adjustment procedure is a conservative one—as it should be, since as k tends toward N, R^2 tends toward 1.00.

Statistical Tests

Before placing too much credence in the partial regression coefficients and R^2, we should test whether the observed relationship between AA and the self-concept variables might have arisen just by chance. For this reason, we conduct a statistical test following the F distribution (see p. 373). From this test, we conclude that the observed relation (R^2) was not very likely to have arisen by chance and that the linear composite of GSC and ASC significantly predicts AA.

So far we have focused on testing the overall fit of the regression—that is, whether or not R^2 equals zero. A more important application of MRA lies in testing *competing models* of the relation between Y and a linear composite of X's. For example, self-concept theory leads to the hypothesis that once AA has been predicted from ASC, the addition of GSC will not significantly increase the predictability of ASC. To test this hypothesis statistically, we should test the increase in R^2 from a prediction equation with ASC to a prediction equation with ASC and GSC in it:

model 1:   predicted AA = $a + b$(ASC)

model 2:   predicted AA = $a + b_1$(ASC) + b_2(GSC)

For model 1, $R^2 = r^2 = .160$; and for model 2, $R^2 = .161$. A statistical test of the difference between R^2 for the two models, $.161 - .160 = .001$, is hardly needed. The hypothesis from self-concept theory appears to be supported in the hypothetical study.

Nevertheless, let's carry out the statistical test—if for no other reason than this gives me an excuse to present it. The F statistic is given in Formula 18-10.

$$F = \frac{(R^2_{Y \cdot 1,2,\ldots,k_1} - R^2_{Y \cdot 1,2,\ldots,k_2})/(k_1 - k_2)}{(1 - R^2_{Y \cdot 1,2,\ldots,k_1})/(N - k_1 - 1)} \tag{18-10}$$

with $df_1 = (k_1 - k_2)$, $df_2 = (N - k_1 - 1)$, and

where:

k_1 = number of independent variables in the larger set of independent variables
k_2 = number of independent variables in the smaller set of independent variables
N = number of cases

In our example, we have:

$$F_{\text{obs.}} = \frac{(.161 - .160)/(2 - 1)}{(1 - .161)/(103 - 2 - 1)} = \frac{.0010}{.0084} = .119$$

Since F_{observed} is less than $F_{\text{critical}(.05,1,100)} = 3.94$, we conclude that the addition of GSC to the prediction of AA does not add anything, as we hypothesized from self-concept theory.

The statistical comparison of the two models amounted to a test of the null hypothesis that the partial regression coefficient for GSC was zero. On the basis of the findings, we could not reject the null hypothesis.

The t test provides a more direct test of this null hypothesis than the statistical comparison of R^2's. And it has wide application, especially when there are more than two independent variables in MRA, as is usually the case. The researcher can use the t test to determine which of the independent variables, controlling for all others, are statistically related to the dependent variable.

The t test for a partial regression coefficient is no more than an application of the single-sample t test (Chapter 12). Just as we form the t test for a mean by dividing $(\bar{X} - \mu)$ by the standard error of the mean $(s_{\bar{x}})$, we form a t test for the partial regression coefficient by dividing $(b - \beta)$ by the standard error of the partial regression coefficient. See Formula 18-11.

$$t_{\text{observed}} = \frac{b - \beta}{\text{standard error of } b} \tag{18-11}$$

Under H_0:

$$t_{\text{observed}} = \frac{b - 0}{\text{standard error of } b}$$

with $N - k - 1 \; df$

The standard error of the partial regression coefficient provides an index of how much the estimated coefficient will "bounce" (vary) from one sample to another. Suppose, for example, we randomly sampled 100 subjects, measured X_1, X_2, and Y, and calculated the partial regression coefficient for X_1. Suppose we did these steps again. The partial regression coefficient from sample 2 would not equal the partial regression coefficient from sample 1. Now suppose we did these steps over and over again—oh, say, 10,000 times—and plotted a frequency distribution of the partial regression coefficients, with the values of the coefficient on the abscissa and the frequencies on the ordinate. This frequency distribution would tell us something about the bounce in the partial regression coefficient to be expected from one sample to the next. And the standard deviation of this distribution would tell us something about the *sampling error* of a partial regression coefficient. This standard deviation is analogous to the standard error of b. We define the standard error of a partial regression coefficient for b_1 and b_2 as in Formula 18-12.

$$s_{b_{Y1 \cdot 2}} = \sqrt{\frac{(\text{standard error of estimate})^2}{SS_{X_1}(\text{proportion of unpredictable variance in } Y)}} \tag{18-12}$$

$$s_{b_{Y1 \cdot 2}} = \sqrt{\frac{s_Y^2(1 - R_{Y.12}^2)}{s_{X_1}^2(1 - r_{12}^2)}} \tag{18-12a}$$

$$s_{b_{Y2 \cdot 1}} = \sqrt{\frac{s_Y'^2(1 - R_{Y.12}^2)}{s_{X_2}^2(1 - r_{12}^2)}} \tag{18-12b}$$

The numerator of Formula 18-12 contains the (squared) standard error of estimate—the error in estimating Y from a linear combination of X_1 and X_2. This term is analogous to the standard error of estimate presented in Chapter 7. And the denominator contains the proportion of variance not shared in common by the two predictors, adjusted for the variance in X_1 (Formula 18-12a) or adjusted for the variance in X_2 (Formula 18-12b). The only difference between the two formulas lies in the difference between the variance of each predictor. The greater the variance in the predictor (i.e., the less the restriction of range), the smaller the standard error of the partial regression coefficient will be.

One final point about the standard error of a partial regression coefficient is in order before we turn to the application of the t test. Notice in Formula 18-12 that as the correlation between the two predictors increases (r_{12}^2 increases), the denominator decreases in magnitude and the standard error increases. If $r^2 = 1.00$, the standard error is undefined. This result shows explicitly the problem of multicollinearity we pointed out earlier. As the correlation among the independent variables increases, the partial regression coefficients become increasingly unstable.

Now, let's turn our attention to the application of the t test. The comparison between model 1 and model 2 led us to conclude that including GSC in the equation did not improve matters. This conclusion is tantamount to saying that the null hypothesis—that the partial regression coefficient for GSC equaled zero—couldn't be rejected. We should obtain the same results applying a two-tail t test (Formula 18-11):

$$t = \frac{-.44 - 0}{[113.42(1 - .16)/.85(1 - .45)]^{1/2}} = \frac{-.44}{(95.26/.47)^{1/2}} = \frac{-.44}{14.24} = -.03$$

$$t_{\text{crit.}(.05, N-k-1=103-2-1=100)} \approx 1.97$$

Consistent with the statistical comparison of the two models, we should not reject the null hypothesis.

Finally, just as we could establish a confidence interval for a population mean, we can also establish a confidence interval for a population partial regression coefficient. To do so, we apply Formula 12-3, replacing $\bar{X}$ by b, μ by β, and the standard error of the mean $s_{\bar{X}}$ by the standard error of the partial regression coefficient, $S_{b_{Y1\cdot2}}$. See Formula 18-13.

$$\text{CI}_{1-\alpha}: \qquad b \pm t_{\text{crit.}(\alpha/2, df)} S_{b_{Y1\cdot2}} \tag{18-13}$$

In our example, we have:

$$\text{CI}_{.95}: \qquad -.44 \pm 1.97(14.24)$$
$$-.44 \pm 28.05$$
$$-28.49 \leq \beta_1 \leq 27.61$$

Consistent with our hypothesis-testing framework, the confidence interval obviously includes the value zero. We conclude that the probability is .95 that an interval formed in this manner will include the population partial regression coefficient. Or put another way, 95 percent of all intervals formed in this manner will include the parameter, but this particular interval may or may not include the parameter.

Example Problem 18.2

In Example Problem 18.1, the proportion of variation in GPAs that could be accounted for by AA and GSC was .41.

a. Adjust this proportion of variation to take into account the number of independent variables in the prediction equation and the sample size.

b. Self-concept theory hypotheses that GSC, in addition to AA, will contribute significantly to the prediction of GPA. Test this hypothesis statistically.

SUMMARY

This chapter presents *multiple regression analysis* (MRA), a statistical technique for predicting a dependent variable from two or more independent variables. The purpose and underlying rationale and the procedures for computing and interpreting the MRA are presented. Special attention is paid to assumptions and to interpretation of partial regression coefficients. Procedures for statistically testing R^2, the proportion of variation in the dependent variable accounted for by a set of independent variables, are presented and include testing alternative regression models. In addition, the t test for partial regression coefficients is presented along with interval estimation.

ANSWERS TO EXAMPLE PROBLEMS

1.

	GSC	AA	GPA
GSC	1		
AA	.15	1	
GPA	.25	.62	1
Mean	3.20	54.30	2.50
Standard Deviation	.92	10.65	.50

a. $R^2 = \dfrac{(.25)^2 + (.62)^2 - 2(.25)(.62)(.15)}{1 - (.15)^2} = \dfrac{.0625 + .3844 - .0465}{.9775} = \dfrac{.4004}{.9775} = .41$

$R = .64$

In words, 41 percent of the variation in GPA can be accounted for by the composite of GSC and AA, as theory predicted.

b. $F_{obs.} = \dfrac{.4004/2}{1 - .4004/(103 - 2 - 1)} = \dfrac{.2002}{.5996/100} = \dfrac{.2002}{.005996} = 33.689$

$F_{crit.(.05,2,100)} = 3.09$

Reject the null hypothesis. In the population, there is a significant relation between GPA and the linear composite of GSC and AA.

c. $b_1 = \dfrac{.25 - (.62)(.15)}{1 - (.15)^2} \left(\dfrac{.50}{.92}\right) = \dfrac{.157}{.9775}(.46) = .0739$

$b_2 = \dfrac{.62 - (.25)(.15)}{.9775} \left(\dfrac{.50}{10.65}\right) = \dfrac{.5825}{.9775}(.04695) = .028$

$a = 2.50 - (.0739)(5.20) - (.028)(54.30) = .595$

$\hat{Y} = .595 + .0739(5) + .028(55) = 2.5045$

The predicted GPA for a person with a GSC score of 5 and AA of 55 is 2.5045. Note that the GSC score (5) is near the mean of the GSC scores (5.20), and the AA score (55) is near the mean of the AA scores (54.30). So, as expected, the predicted GPA (2.5045) is quite close to the mean of the GPAs (2.50).

2. **a.** Formula 18-9 can be used to adjust R^2:

$$R_*^2 = 1 - (1 - R^2)\left(\dfrac{N-1}{N-k-1}\right) = 1 - (1 - .41)\left(\dfrac{103-1}{103-2-1}\right)$$

$$= (1 - .59)(1.02) = .402$$

b. Formula 18-10 can be used to test R^2 based on AA and GSC against $R^2 = r^2 = (.62)^2 = .384$:

$$F = \frac{(R^2_{Y.1,2,\ldots,k_1} - R^2_{Y.1,2,\ldots,k_2})/(k_1 - k_2)}{(1 - R^2_{Y.1,2,\ldots,k_1})/(N - k - 1)}$$

$$F_{obs.} = \frac{(.410 - .384)/(2 - 1)}{(1 - .410)/(103 - 2 - 1)} = \frac{.0260}{.0059} = 4.407$$

Since $F_{obs.}$ is greater than $F_{crit.(.05,1,100)} = 3.94$, we conclude that GSC, as hypothesized by self-concept theory, contributes to the prediction of GPA, even after AA is taken into account.

EXERCISES

To this point, we have found that academic self-concept (ASC) predicts academic achievement (AA) and that adding general self-concept (GSC) to the prediction equation does not improve the prediction. Other facets of self-concept might, however, improve prediction. Here let's explore what happens when social self-concept (SSC) is added to the prediction equation. Use the data in Tables 18-3 (a random sample of 30 subjects from the original 103) and 18-4 (descriptive statistics) to determine whether adding SSC to the equation increases our ability to predict AA beyond what is possible from ASC.

TABLE 18-3   Measures of academic self-concept (ASC), social self-concept (SSC), and academic achievement ($N = 30$)

ID	ASC	SSC	AA	ID	ASC	SSC	AA
1	4.40	5.04	56.40	16	6.13	5.83	70.46
2	6.43	5.71	64.88	17	5.05	2.87	61.91
3	5.86	4.28	65.04	18	4.69	3.85	48.89
4	6.33	7.78	56.50	19	4.88	4.57	62.58
5	5.15	5.84	47.06	20	6.11	7.92	63.78
6	4.06	5.87	37.37	21	6.33	4.93	62.46
7	7.94	7.95	64.75	22	3.48	4.96	56.93
8	4.03	6.31	44.49	23	5.60	5.32	52.98
9	6.67	7.63	59.88	24	6.86	5.85	52.81
10	3.72	6.39	41.22	25	4.59	5.91	60.37
11	3.85	5.30	52.66	26	4.92	6.09	50.41
12	5.64	7.09	45.57	27	6.44	5.67	54.92
13	5.16	8.92	46.80	28	7.11	7.71	45.96
14	6.66	6.61	60.40	29	6.13	7.17	41.91
15	7.45	6.95	48.98	30	4.61	4.93	44.24

1. Based on the descriptive statistics in Table 18-4, do you think that SSC will add to the prediction of AA? Why or why not? (*Hint:* Take a look at the formula for R^2.)

TABLE 18-4 Descriptive statistics for data in Table 18-2
($N = 30$)

| Statistic | Self-Concept | | Academic Achievement (AA) |
	Academic (ASC)	Social (SSC)	
Correlation			
ASC	1.00		
SSC	0.43	1.00	
AA	0.44	−0.20	1.00
Mean	5.51	6.04	54.24
Standard Deviation	1.13	1.36	8.29

2. In carrying out your statistical tests, you may either use the information in Table 18-4 and do your calculations by hand, or use the information in Table 18-3 and calculate sums of squares (etc.) either with a computer program or by hand.

   a. State the null and alternative hypotheses tested for predicting AA from ASC and SSC.
   b. State the assumptions underlying your statistical test and evaluate those assumptions either logically or empirically.
   c. Present the results of your statistical test.
   d. What do you conclude?
   e. Does the addition of SSC improve the prediction of AA? Present a statistical test. Why or why not?
   f. Overall, what do you conclude about the prediction of AA from self-concept measures?

ANSWERS TO EXERCISES

1. a. The random sample of 30 subjects looks very much like the larger sample in the correlation between ASC and AA (.44 vs. .45), and in means and standard deviations (except perhaps the somewhat smaller standard deviation for AA, which still is well within sampling error of what would be expected).

   b. At first blush, a low negative correlation between SSC and AA suggests that SSC would not contribute substantially to prediction. However, looking at Formula 18-4, we see that this negative correlation results in an increase in the numerator so that it just might improve prediction, perhaps even substantially.

2. a. H_0: $R^2 = 0$; H_1: $R^2 \neq 0$

   b. *Independence:* Assume measures of self-concept and achievement were obtained independently.
      Figure 18-3 will be used in discussing the remaining assumptions.

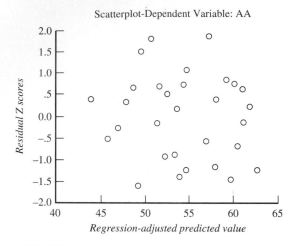

Scatterplot-Dependent Variable: AA

FIGURE 18-3

Normality, Homoscedasticity, and Linearity: Figure 18-3 suggests that all three assumptions have been met: residuals are symmetric about 0.

c. Results of Analysis (SPSS Output):[8]

Multiple R	.61853
R Square	.38258
Adjusted R Square	.33684
Standard Error	6.75440

	Analysis of Variance		
	DF	Sum of Squares	Mean Square
Regression	2	763.25997	381.62999
Residual	27	1231.79246	45.62194
F = 8.36505		*Signif F = .0015*	

[8]SPSS Program Setup
REGRESSION
/DESCRIPTIVES MEAN STDDEV CORR SIG N
/MISSING LISTWISE
/STATISTICS COEFF OUTS R ANOVA
/CRITERIA=PIN(.05)POUT(.10)
/NOORIGIN
/DEPENDENT aa
/METHOD=ENTER asc ssc
/SCATTERPLOT=(*ZRESID,*ADJPRED).

Variables in the Equation					
Variable	B	SE B	Beta	T	Sig T
SSC	−2.902773	1.017986	−0.476519	−2.851	.0082
ASC	4.740969	1.225939	0.646260	3.867	.0006
(Constant)	45.664488	7.041608		6.485	.0000

   d. The addition of SSC, correlated low and negatively with AA no less, substantially improved prediction over and above ASC (from $R^2_{AA\cdot ASC} = .16$ to $R^2_{AA\cdot ASC,SSC} = .38$)! But this finding remains to be tested statistically. See what follows.

   e. $F_{obs.} = \dfrac{(.38 - .16)(/(2 - 1)}{(1 - .38)/(30 - 2 - 1)} = \dfrac{.22}{.02} = 11$

The addition of SSC improves the prediction of AA statistically significantly. It operates as surmised in the earlier answer to 1.

   f. Overall, AA can be predicted from a combination of ASC and SSC. A linear combination of these variables predicts about 38 percent of the variation in achievement.

Chi-Square Tests

Chi-square tests are nonparametric statistical tests.[1] They are used with frequency data that have been collected in either a one-way or a factorial design. The chi-square test for one-way designs is called a *goodness-of-fit test* because it tests how closely observed frequencies from a sample fit theoretically expected frequencies based on a null hypothesis. Chi-square for factorial designs tests the null hypothesis that two variables are independent of one another in the population. This chapter presents the conceptual underpinnings of these tests, along with methods needed to apply them.

USES OF CHI-SQUARE TESTS

Chi-square tests are frequently used because behavioral researchers often are interested in counting the number of subjects falling into particular categories. The following example studies may give you some notion of how researchers come about counting frequencies.

In a study of political opinions, researchers conducting a poll might be interested in whether the number of Democrats, Republicans, etc., in their sample is proportional to the number of voters in each party in the precincts from which the sample was taken. Or a researcher developing a measure of self-concept might want to know whether subjects'

---

[1]See the description of nonparametric statistical tests in Section VII.

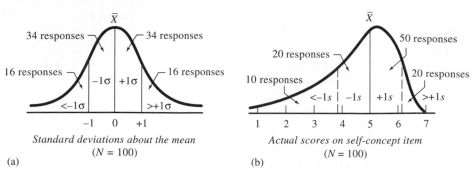

FIGURE 19-1
Theoretically expected and observed responses to a self-concept item: (a) theoretically expected frequency of scores if normally distributed; (b) observed responses

scores are normally distributed. For this study, the researcher would divide the theoretical normal distribution into categories such as those shown in Figure 19-1a. He would then build a frequency polygon of the observed responses and divide it into the same categories (see Figure 19-1b). The observed number of responses falling in each area of the frequency distribution could be compared with the expected frequency based on the normal distribution to see whether the responses were normally distributed.

Sometimes, interval measurements are converted to categories,[2] and the number of subjects falling into each category can be counted. For example, evaluators of remedial-reading programs in California received reading achievement data based on four different published reading tests. (Different schools used different reading tests.) Since the tests could not be equated with one another, subjects' scores on the tests were converted to categories. For example, subjects with scores one-half a standard deviation above the mean of their norm group were labeled as "high" on reading achievement, subjects one-half a standard deviation below the norm were labeled "low," and subjects in the middle were labeled, of course, "middle." The number of subjects in each of two different remedial-reading programs who fell in the "low," "middle," and "high" groups on reading achievement was counted and compared with the number in each category that would be expected if there were no relation between reading program and reading achievement.

Or a researcher might be interested in whether men with prior military experience have a different opinion about women in combat than men without military experience. Suppose that a random sample of 1000 men was drawn from the general population in the United States and asked two questions: (1) Have you served in the armed forces of the United States or any other country? (yes, no) and (2) should women serve in combat occupational specialties? (yes, no, no opinion). From these responses, the sample could be divided into six groups (2×3), and the number of respondents falling in each cell could be counted. The pattern of frequencies in the six cells could then be compared with the frequencies that

---

[2]For example, subjects might be divided into groups of low and high anxiety depending upon whether their score on an anxiety scale was below or above the median of an appropriate norm.

would be expected if there were no relationship between military experience and opinions about women in combat.

In all of these examples, the **chi-square statistic** (χ^2) is used to test whether the observed frequencies differed significantly from the expected frequencies. Since all of these examples have a couple of features in common, they can be used to illustrate the circumstances under which the chi-square statistic can be used. First, χ^2 compares observed frequencies with **expected frequencies.** The expected frequencies might be based on prior information such as the number of Democrats and Republicans in a precinct. Or they might be based on a (null) hypothesis such as that the responses to self-concept items are normally distributed. Or they might be based on what would be expected if chance assigned subjects to categories, as in the study of opinions about women in combat.

Second, χ^2 is used with data in the form of **counts** (in contrast, for example, to scores on a test). Thus χ^2 can be used with frequency data (f), proportion data $(f \div N)$, probability data (number of outcomes in event $\div$ total number of outcomes), and percentages (proportion $\times$ 100). In all of the example studies, observed frequencies were compared with expected frequencies. Nevertheless, if the data are in the form of proportions, the proportions can easily be converted to frequencies, and the χ^2 statistic can be used to test whether the observed proportions differed from the expected proportions $(f = N \times$ proportion$)$.

The third feature of the χ^2 test is the nature of the design in which the frequency data are collected. The independent variable or variables are in the form of **discrete categories.** For example, in the political opinion poll, the categories were defined by voter registration. They are discrete, nonoverlapping categories. Likewise, subjects in the study of the relationship between military experience and opinion about women in combat could be placed in nonoverlapping categories. Finally, in the example with reading achievement measures, subjects were placed in discrete categories: "low," "middle," and "high."

A fourth feature of the χ^2 test is that the data may be collected in a one-way design or in a two-way, factorial design.[3] In a one-way design, the independent variable may have two or more levels. For example, in the political opinion poll, the independent variable—party affiliation—had many possible levels. Likewise, in a two-way design, each independent variable may have two or more levels. For example, in the study on opinions about women in combat, the opinion variable had three levels and the military experience variable had two levels.

Finally, a subject or a subject's response can fall in one and only one cell of the design. Thus, a voter could be classified as affiliated with one and only one political party. Problems can arise when more than one observation is available on a subject. The first observation (e.g., pretest score) might fall in category *A,* and the second observation (e.g., posttest score) might fall in another category. This situation is not permitted in a χ^2 analysis.[4]

---

[3]Frequency data from more complicated factorial designs can be analyzed with log-linear models. For details, see Bishop et al. (1975).

[4]In this particular example, the problem can be overcome by reconceptualizing the pretest-posttest design. If the pretest is considered to be one independent variable with subjects categorized as low and high and the posttest is considered to be a second independent variable with two levels, a 2×2 (pretest $\times$ posttest) design is formed. In this case, subjects fall into one and only one cell of the design.

χ^2 FOR ONE-WAY DESIGNS: GOODNESS-OF-FIT TEST

In the chi-square test for a one-way design, there must be one independent variable with two or more levels. A subject may be counted in one and only one cell of the design. And the dependent variable is a count in the form of frequencies, proportions, probabilities, or percentages.

Purpose and Underlying Logic

Purpose.   The purpose of the χ^2 test for one-way designs is to determine whether the observed frequencies differ systematically from the theoretically expected frequencies, or whether the differences may be due to chance. Often the one-way χ^2 test is called a **goodness-of-fit test** because it examines how closely the observed frequencies fit the theoretically expected frequencies.

In order to use this statistical test, we must be able to specify, in advance, the theoretically expected frequencies. Although this task may seem monstrous, actually it is straightforward. In some cases, researchers wish to compare an observed frequency distribution with some theoretical frequency distribution like the normal distribution. The normal distribution, then, can be divided into discrete categories such as standard deviation units about the mean, and the theoretically expected frequency can be determined by multiplying the number of subjects in the sample by the proportion of cases expected in each area of the normal curve. For example, the proportion of cases falling between the mean and one standard deviation above it is approximately .34. So in a sample of 100 subjects, approximately 34 (100 × .34) should be found within 1 standard deviation above the mean if the sample data was drawn from a normal distribution (see Figure 19-1a).

In other cases, the theoretical frequencies can be specified by the researcher in much the same way the population mean μ was specified for case I research studies (see Chapters 8, 10, and 12). Here, the researcher has some prior notion about frequencies in some population, and she wants to compare the observed frequencies with some set of hypothesized frequencies in the population. For example, in the political opinion survey, the researcher wanted to compare the frequencies of Democrats, Republicans, etc., in the sample with the frequencies of registered voters in the precincts. The theoretical frequencies, then, can be determined by finding the proportion of Democrats, Republicans, etc., who are registered in the precincts. By multiplying the sample size by these proportions, the theoretically expected frequencies for the sample can be identified.

Or suppose a researcher wanted to determine whether the observed number of criminal homicides in a year differed from month to month. The expected frequencies can be determined by assuming that homicides are unrelated to time of year. Thus, in January with 31 days, the expected proportion of homicides would be 31/365 = .085. In February (if it's not a leap year), the expected proportion would be 28/365 = .077, and so on. The total number of criminal homicides in a year can be multiplied by these expected frequencies in order to determine the number of expected frequencies for each month. For example, if there were 100 homicides in a year, we should theoretically expect 8.5 homicides in January

(.085 × 100). In short, if the researcher specifies a null hypothesis such as "no relation between number of homicides and the month of the year," theoretical frequencies can be determined.

In developing the χ^2 statistic to measure how closely the observed frequencies (denoted by O) match the theoretically expected frequencies (denoted by E), we might subtract E from O in each category and then add the differences over all of the k categories. But, alas, if this summing is done, the result will always be zero. The result is zero because the sum of the observed frequencies equals the total number of subjects in the sample (N), as does the sum of the expected frequencies:

$$\sum_{i=1}^{k}(O_i - E_i) = \sum_{i=1}^{k}O_i - \sum_{i=1}^{k}E_i = N - N = 0$$

In order to avoid this problem—as before—we can square the difference between O and E:

$$(O - E)^2$$

The sum of the squared differences over all k categories will not be zero unless O equals E in every category. Thus, one possible statistic for comparing observed and expected frequencies is:

$$\sum_{i=1}^{k}(O_i - E_i)^2$$

However, one embellishment is needed to obtain the chi-square statistic. The chi-square statistic weights this squared difference (inversely) according to the expected frequency in each cell, as indicated in Formula 19-1.

$$\chi^2_{observed} = \sum_{i=1}^{k} \frac{(O_i - E_i)^2}{E_i} \qquad\qquad \textbf{(19-1)}$$

Because the squared difference within a cell is weighted inversely by the expected frequency (i.e., $1/E_i$), greater weight is given to those categories where we expect to find few subjects and *actually* find many. Intuitively, this technique seems appropriate, since we are more surprised to find many where few or none are expected than vice versa. This statistic, then, tells us how closely the observed and theoretical frequencies match each other. Notice that the closer the match between O and E, the smaller the value of the χ^2 statistic is.

Underlying Logic.   The chi-square statistic provides a measure of how much the observed and expected frequencies differ from one another. But how much difference should be tolerated before concluding that the observed frequencies were not sampled from a distribution represented by the expected frequencies? In other words, how large should $\chi^2_{observed}$ be in order to reject the null hypothesis that the observed frequencies were sampled from a distribution represented by the expected frequencies?

Since this decision of whether to reject the null hypothesis cannot be made with certainty, it is a probabilistic one. The problem, then, is to determine the probability of finding $\chi^2_{observed}$ as large as or larger than some value, assuming the null hypothesis is true. To do so, we need a sampling distribution for the χ^2. To get an intuitive feel for this distribution, consider the following situation: Suppose a researcher takes a random sample of 100 subjects from a normal population and constructs a frequency polygon. Then he divides the observed frequency distribution into four categories according to standard deviation units (see Figure 19-1). He then compares these observed frequencies with the theoretically expected frequencies based on the normal distribution. Since he is dealing with sample data, O will not agree with E in each category exactly. Rather, chance fluctuation should be expected. Thus, the value of χ^2 calculated with Formula 19-1 will not be zero for this sample. Suppose the researcher carries out this sampling procedure 2000 times. For each sample, χ^2 can be calculated; the 2000 χ^2 values will differ from one another. If the χ^2 values are placed in a frequency polygon with the value of χ^2 on the abscissa and the frequency with which each χ^2 value occurred on the ordinate, the frequency polygon will provide a *sampling distribution of chi-square* (see Figure 19-2). It tells us what to expect the chance fluctuations between O and E to be when, in fact, sampling was from a population specified by the theoretically expected frequencies. If the observed χ^2 value falls way out in the right-hand tail of the sampling distribution, its occurrence is quite improbable. In this case, the null hypothesis of no difference between the observed and expected frequencies should be rejected. If the observed value of χ^2 falls well within the sampling distribution of χ^2, the null hypothesis should not be rejected.

The chi-square distribution, like the t and F distributions, is a theoretical distribution—actually, a family of theoretical distributions. For one-way designs, the members of this family depend only on the number of distinct categories on which the statistic is based. Or more accurately, there is a different member of the family for each number of degrees of freedom, since:

$$df = \text{number of categories minus } 1 = k - 1$$

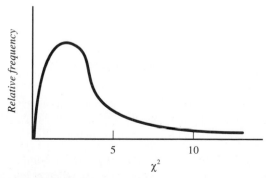

FIGURE 19-2
Sampling distribution of χ^2 when $df = 3$

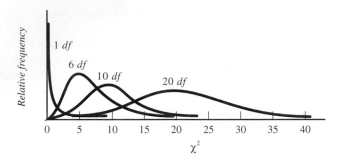

FIGURE 19-3

Sampling distributions of χ^2 for differing degrees of freedom

Notice that the degrees of freedom for the χ^2 distribution depend on the number of categories (k) and *not* the number of subjects in the sample (N). This result follows from the fact that the sum of the differences between O and E is zero (see the discussion in "Purpose"). So given $k - 1$ differences, the remaining difference is known.

Some important characteristics of the chi-square distribution can be seen in Figure 19-3, where several such distributions are shown, one for each of four numbers of degrees of freedom: 1, 6, 10, and 20. First, notice that as the number of categories (k) or degrees of freedom ($k - 1$) increases, the value of $\chi^2_{observed}$ is expected to increase. This result occurs because for each category, we calculate:

$$\frac{(O - E)^2}{E}$$

If there are two categories, $(O - E)^2/E$ will be summed twice; if there are 50 categories, . . . ; and so on.

Second, notice that the χ^2 distribution is unimodal. That is, it has one peak. And third, the χ^2 distribution is positively skewed. As the number of categories increases, however, the skewness decreases; and as the number of degrees of freedom grows infinitely large, the χ^2 distribution approaches the normal distribution.

In summary, the one-way χ^2 is used to test data in the form of frequency counts with each observation falling into one and only one category of a discrete, independent variable. The test is carried out by comparing the observed frequencies with the theoretically expected frequencies under the null hypothesis. Specifically, the χ^2 statistic is given by Formula 19-1:

$$\chi^2_{observed} = \sum_{i=1}^{k} \frac{(O_i - E_i)^2}{E_i}$$

with $k - 1$ degrees of freedom. The observed value of χ^2 can be compared with the critical value of χ^2 with $k - 1$ degrees of freedom in order to decide whether to reject the null hypothesis.

In order to get a feel for how the χ^2 test works, we can use the data in Figure 19-1. The data in Figure 19-1b represent the observed frequency of subjects' responses on an item from a self-concept scale. The observed distribution appears to be negatively skewed, but this appearance may be due to chance. Instead, these data might have been sampled from a normal distribution (the null hypothesis) with expected frequencies, as shown in Figure 19-1a. For each category in the two graphs, the observed and expected frequencies can be compared and $\chi^2_{observed}$ can be computed:

$$\chi^2_{observed} = \frac{(10-16)^2}{16} + \frac{(20-34)^2}{34} + \frac{(50-34)^2}{34} + \frac{(20-16)^2}{16}$$

$$= \frac{(-6)^2}{16} + \frac{(-14)^2}{34} + \frac{(16)^2}{34} + \frac{4^2}{16} = \frac{36}{16} + \frac{196}{34} + \frac{256}{34} + \frac{16}{16}$$

$$= 2.25 + 5.76 + 7.53 + 1 = 16.54$$

In order to determine whether to reject the null hypothesis, we compare $\chi^2_{observed}$ with $\chi^2_{critical}$ with $k - 1 = 4 - 1 = 3$ degrees of freedom.[5] From Table D at the end of the book, $\chi^2_{critical(\alpha=.05, df=3)} = 7.815$. Since $\chi^2_{observed}$ exceeds $\chi^2_{critical}$, the null hypothesis should be rejected, with the conclusion that the observed frequency distribution is nonnormal and negatively skewed.

At this point, we are ready to consider hypothesis testing with χ^2 more formally.

Hypotheses

Chi-square is typically used for nondirectional (two-tail) tests.[6] For such tests, the null and alternative hypotheses are as follows:

H_0: The observed distribution of frequencies equals the expected (hypothetical) distribution of frequencies in each category.

H_1: The observed distribution of frequencies does not equal the expected (hypothetical) distribution of frequencies.

Assumptions and Requirements

For testing whether the observed frequencies in two or more categories come from the hypothesized frequencies in these categories, we make five assumptions:

---

[5] Actually, the chi-square test for normality has $k - 3$ degrees of freedom. One degree of freedom is associated with the chi-square test, one is associated with estimating the mean of the normal distribution (μ), and the last is associated with estimating the variance of the normal distribution (σ^2). This technicality need not concern us here.

[6] The chi-square test is nondirectional (two-tail), because a negative deviation for $O - E$ is considered by the test just like a positive deviation. That is, the negative and positive deviations are squared and then combined. Thus, extremely negative values influence the value of χ^2 just like extremely positive values. A one-tail test makes sense only when we are dealing with a simple outcome (two categories) that can go in one of two possible directions. In this case, see Cochran (1954).

1. Each observation must fall in one and only one category.
2. The observations in the sample are independent of one another.
3. The observations are measured as frequencies.
4. The *expected* frequency for each category is not less than 5 for $df \geq 2$ and not less than 10 for $df = 1$. Note that this assumption is for expected, *not observed,* frequencies because the χ^2 distribution holds if the null hypothesis ("what's expected") is true.
5. The observed values of χ^2 with 1 degree of freedom must be corrected for continuity in order to use the table of values of χ^2_{critical}.

The first assumption can be checked by examining the categories to be used. The categories should be mutually exclusive so that each observation can belong to only one category. In the example of criminal homicides, the 12 months of the year served as categories. Each instance of criminal homicide could occur only in one particular month. A murder committed in May could not also occur in September. Assumption 2, independence, is discussed thoroughly in Chapter 12. Briefly, it can be examined by reviewing the sampling procedures.

Assumption 3 may be verified by examining the dependent variable to make sure that observations consist of frequencies or numbers of observations within each category. Observations in the form of proportions, probabilities, or percentages are also acceptable, since they are easily converted to frequencies.

Assumption 4 is required because the chi-square distribution is a theoretical distribution used to approximate the exact probability of the particular sampling distribution under assumptions 1 and 2. For large samples, probabilities from the χ^2 approximation are accurate. For small samples, they are not. Hence, assumption 4 provides a rule of thumb for identifying reasonably accurate probability values. This assumption can be checked by examining the *expected* frequencies for each category. If there are three or more categories, and if one or more of the categories has an expected frequency of less than 5, they may, in some cases, be combined in order to increase the expected frequency in a collapsed category. For example, in the homicide study, the incidence of criminal homicide could be examined for each 3-month period by collapsing sets of three adjacent month categories into single categories. This procedure is only recommended when combinations of categories can be made meaningfully (see "Collapsing Levels of a Variable" later in this chapter). Finally, assumption 5 is discussed later under "Correction for Continuity."

Computation of the One-Way χ^2 Test

The formula for testing whether an observed set of frequencies arose from an expected set of frequencies is given by Formula 19-1. The calculation of χ^2_{observed} is shown in Table 19-1, using data from Figure 19-1. (Note that $N = 100$ in the example data.) The computational procedure may be found in the *Student Guide.*

Decision Rules for Rejecting H_0

In order to decide whether to reject the null hypothesis, we must determine the critical value of χ^2. Since there is a different χ^2 distribution for each possible number of degrees of freedom, the first step is to determine $k - 1$, the number of degrees of freedom for the statistical

TABLE 19-1 Computational table for the data in Figure 19-1

(1) Category	(2) Observed Frequency (O)	(3) Expected Proportion	(4) Expected Frequency (E)	(5) O − E	(6) (O − E)²	(7) $\dfrac{(O-E)^2}{E}$
1	10	.16	16	−6	36	$\dfrac{36}{16} = 2.25$
2	20	.34	34	−14	196	$\dfrac{196}{34} = 5.76$
3	50	.34	34	16	256	$\dfrac{256}{34} = 7.53$
4	20	.16	16	4	16	$\dfrac{16}{16} = 1.00$
$\sum$	100	1.00	100	0		$\chi^2_{obs.} = 16.54$

test. In the example in Table 19-1, $k = 4$, so there are $k - 1 = 3$ degrees of freedom for the statistical test (see footnote 5). Next, the critical value of χ^2 at a specified level of α can be found in Table D. In order to find $\chi^2_{critical}$ with 3 df, suppose the researcher set α at .05 prior to collecting the data. Then, enter the table by finding the degrees of freedom along the rows and the level of α along the columns. For $df = 3$ and $\alpha = .05$, $\chi^2_{critical(.05,3)} = 7.815$. Since $\chi^2_{observed}$ (16.54) in this example exceeds $\chi^2_{critical}$, the null hypothesis should be rejected. Scores on the self-concept scale are not normally distributed. They are, in fact, negatively skewed; that is, people tended to rate themselves toward the high end of the scale. [This is a common, not so surprising, finding in research on self-concept; see Shavelson et al. (1976).] Recall that the chi-square test is nondirectional. The tabulated values at α provide the critical values for the two-tail test.

Numerical Example

Suppose a researcher is interested in whether there are monthly differences in the number of homicides in a middle-sized city in the United States. Police records are examined for a particular year, and the researcher finds that 100 such crimes have been recorded during the year of interest. The researcher records the number of homicides committed during each month; these data are displayed in Table 19-2.

The question is, "Do these observed frequencies of homicides differ from what might be expected if the number of homicides was unrelated to the month of the year?" In order to answer this question, we can use the χ^2 test. For this statistical test, the null and alternative hypotheses are:

H_0: no difference in the population between observed and expected frequencies

H_1: a difference in the population between observed and expected frequencies

And let's set $\alpha = .01$.

TABLE 19-2 Number of homicides committed each month over a 12-month period ($N = 100$)

Jan.	Feb.	Mar.	Apr.	May	June	July	Aug.	Sept.	Oct.	Nov.	Dec.
10	8	11	6	15	13	10	7	3	4	5	8

TABLE 19-3 Computation of $\chi^2_{observed}$ for the data on homicides provided in Table 19-2

(1) Category	(2) Observed Frequency (O)	(3) Expected Proportion	(4) Expected Frequency (E)	(5) O − E	(6) (O − E)²	(7) $\frac{(O - E)^2}{E}$
Jan.	10	.085	8.5	1.5	2.25	.26
Feb.	8	.077	7.7	.3	.09	.01
Mar.	11	.085	8.5	2.5	6.25	.74
Apr.	6	.082	8.2	−2.2	4.84	.59
May	15	.085	8.5	6.5	42.25	4.97
June	13	.082	8.2	4.8	23.04	2.81
July	10	.085	8.5	1.5	2.25	.26
Aug.	7	.085	8.5	−1.5	2.25	.26
Sept.	3	.082	8.2	−5.2	27.04	3.30
Oct.	4	.085	8.5	−4.5	20.25	2.38
Nov.	5	.082	8.2	−3.2	10.24	1.25
Dec.	8	.085	8.5	−.5	.25	.03
$\sum$	100	1.00	100	0		$\chi^2_{obs.} = 16.86$

Table 19-3 provides the necessary computations. The expected proportions were found as follows. If homicides are unrelated to the month of the year, then the number of such crimes in a month will depend only on the proportion of the 365 days in a year that occur in a particular month. For example, there are 31 days in January, so the proportion of days in a year occurring in January is $31 \div 365 = .085$. The expected frequencies are found by multiplying the expected proportion by the total number of homicides. So for January, the expected frequency is $.085 \times 100 = 8.5$. Since all of the *expected* frequencies in Table 19-3 exceed 5, we can proceed with the χ^2 test for the one-way design.

The remaining entries in Table 19-3 are straightforward. Note that as a computational check, the column sums are calculated.

To decide whether to reject the null hypothesis at $\alpha = .01$, we must obtain $\chi^2_{critical}$ from Table D. With $k - 1 = 12 - 1 = 11$ degrees of freedom,

$$\chi^2_{critical(.01, 11)} = 24.725$$

Since $\chi^2_{observed}$ (16.86) does not exceed $\chi^2_{critical}$, the null hypothesis should not be rejected. There is insufficient evidence to conclude that homicides occur more often in certain months than in others.

Example Problem 19.1

A weight control clinic was interested in the types of foods that dieters found most difficult to avoid. Sixty clients were randomly selected and individually asked the following question: Which of the following types of foods do you find *most* difficult to avoid when you are dieting?

1. Bread and rolls
2. Cookies and cakes
3. Ice cream and frozen desserts
4. Pastries and pies

The data in Table 19-4 were obtained.

TABLE 19-4 Number of clients responding

(1) Bread and Rolls	*(2)* Cookies and Cakes	*(3)* Ice Cream and Frozen Desserts	*(4)* Pastries and Pies
17	13	21	9

Conduct a χ^2 test at $\alpha = .01$ to determine whether these observed frequencies differ from what would be expected if these foods were all equally difficult to avoid. Include the following items in your answer.

a. Null and alternative hypotheses
b. Verification that the assumptions and requirements have been met
c. Computation of $\chi^2_{observed}$
d. $\chi^2_{critical}$
e. Conclusions

Correction for Continuity with 1 Degree of Freedom

The chi-square distribution, like the normal distribution, is a smooth, continuous curve. Observed frequencies, however, change discretely: from 1 to 2, from 2 to 3, etc. Thus, discrepancies may arise between the smooth curve of the values of the theoretical chi-square distribution and the bumpy distribution of observed values. This inconsistency between the theoretical and actual sampling distributions of chi-square is only serious enough to affect the outcome of a test with 1 degree of freedom. In this case, a correction is applied to the observed frequencies in order to smooth them.

The correction for the inconsistencies between the theoretical sampling distribution of χ^2 and the actual sampling distribution is called **Yates's correction for continuity.** It applies only when the number of degrees of freedom equals 1. The following strategy is used in applying Yates's correction:

1. Subtract .5 from the observed frequency if the observed frequency is greater than the expected frequency; that is, if $O > E$, subtract .5 from O.
2. Add .5 to the observed frequency if the observed frequency is less than the expected frequency; that is, if $O < E$, add .5 to O.

The net effect of this correction is to smooth the data and to reduce, slightly, the observed value of χ^2.

TABLE 19-5   Computational table for the statistics class example

(1) Category	(2) Observed Frequency (O)	(3) Expected Proportion	(4) Expected Frequency (E)	(5) O Corrected for Continuity (O*)	(6) $O^* - E$	(7) $(O^* - E)^2$	(8) $\dfrac{(O^* - E)^2}{E}$
Female	20	.33	16.67	19.5	2.83	8.01	$\dfrac{8.01}{16.67} = .48$
Male	30	.67	33.33	30.5	−2.83	8.01	$\dfrac{8.01}{33.33} = .24$
$\sum$	50	1.00	50	50	0		$\chi^2_{obs.} = .72$

As an example of how the correction is applied, consider the following study: A statistics class is required of all students in a psychology department in which two-thirds of the students are men and one-third are women. Consequently, the expected proportion of men and women in the statistics class is .67 and .33. An instructor observes that in a class of 50 students, 30 are men and 20 are women and wonders whether there are more men in the class than would be expected from the distribution of men and women in the department. In order to find out, the researcher conducts a χ^2 test at $\alpha = .05$. Since there are two groups, this test is a 1 df χ^2 test, and a correction for continuity must be made. The actual correction is shown in Table 19-5, using these example data. (See also Procedure 19-2 in the *Student Guide*.)

In order to decide whether to reject the null hypothesis, we must compare $\chi^2_{observed}$ with $\chi^2_{critical(.05,1)}$ (see Table D):

$$\chi^2_{critical(.05,1)} = 3.841$$

Since $\chi^2_{observed}$ (.72) does not exceed $\chi^2_{critical}$, the null hypothesis cannot be rejected. There is insufficient evidence to lead to the conclusion that more men than women enrolled in this statistics course than would be expected from the number of men and women in the department.

Example Problem 19.2

A large industrial company recently instituted a new type of management training program. Records of previous training programs showed that about 75 percent of the participants in these programs were rated as "successful" managers by their superiors. Three months after completing the new management training program, participants were rated as "successful" or "unsuccessful" managers by their superiors. The number of participants in each category is as follows:

Successful   37
Unsuccessful   3

Conduct a χ^2 test at $\alpha = .01$ to determine whether the number of participants rated as "successful" was greater than would be expected from previous experience. Include the following items in your answer.
a. Computation of χ^2
b. $\chi^2_{critical}$
c. Conclusions

χ^2 FOR TWO-WAY DESIGNS: CONTINGENCY TABLE ANALYSIS

In a chi-square test for a two-way design, there must be two independent variables, each with two or more levels, and a dependent variable in the form of a frequency count (namely, frequencies, proportions, probabilities, or percentages). As an example of a two-way design for which the χ^2 statistic is appropriate, recall the study of men's and women's achievement in college. Hewitt & Goldman (1975) found that the sex of the student and the student's choice of academic major were related; women tended to choose majors that gave higher grades. This result explained the apparent difference in achievement between men and women; it was not necessary to invoke certain masculine and feminine characteristics as hypothesized in the past. Table 19-6 presents data on choice of academic major for 897 male and female undergraduates at UCLA. The data are presented as a 2×4 (sex × major) design with frequencies entered in the cells of the design. Often such a table displaying a two-way design with frequencies in its cells is called a **contingency table.**

Purpose and Underlying Logic

The purpose of the χ^2 test for the two-way design is to determine whether the two variables in the design are independent of one another. In the study of men's and women's achievement, for example, a two-way χ^2 would test whether sex and academic major are independent.

The formula for calculating the two-way χ^2 is the same as for the one-way χ^2; only the degrees of freedom change. The degrees of freedom for the two-way χ^2 depend on the number of rows (r) and the number of columns (c) in the design:

$$df = (r - 1)(c - 1)$$

The chi-square statistic with $(r - 1)(c - 1)$ degrees of freedom is used to compare the observed and expected frequencies in a two-way contingency table. It is given in Formula 19-2.

TABLE 19-6 Major-field choices of male and female under-graduates at UCLA

	Academic Major				
Sex	*Physics*	*Engineering*	*English*	*Design*	*Total*
Male	108	345	94	17	564
Female	8	12	253	60	333
Total	116	357	347	77	897

Note: From Table 4-2.

$$\chi^2_{observed} = \sum_{i=1}^{k} \frac{(O_i - E_i)^2}{E_i} \qquad\qquad (19\text{-}2)$$

$$\text{with } df = (r - 1)(c - 1)$$

The observed values of χ^2 can be referred to the theoretical sampling distribution of χ^2 described under "Purpose" near the beginning of this chapter. In so doing, a decision on whether to reject the null hypothesis can be made.

Hypotheses

The null and alternative hypotheses for the two-way chi-square test are as follows:

H_0: Variables A and B are *independent* in the population.

H_1: Variables A and B are *related* in the population.

For the data in Table 19-6, the null and alternative hypotheses are as follows:

H_0: Sex and choice of academic major are independent in the population.

H_1: Sex and choice of academic major are related in the population.

Assumptions and Requirements

In the use of χ^2, the assumptions[7] and requirements are as follows:

1. Each observation must fall in one and only one cell of the design.
2. Each observation is independent of every other observation.
3. The observations are measured as frequencies.
4. The expected frequency for any cell is not less than 5 for $df \geq 2$ and not less than 10 for $df = 1$.
5. The observed values of χ^2 with 1 degree of freedom (i.e., a 2×2 contingency table) must be corrected for continuity in order to use the table of values of $\chi^2_{critical}$.

Since these assumptions and requirements are discussed under that heading near the beginning of this chapter, there need not be further discussion here.

Computation of the Two-Way χ^2 Test

Formula 19-2 is used for calculating the χ^2 statistic. The steps in calculating $\chi^2_{observed}$ for a two-way design are almost the same as for a one-way design. The major difference lies in the calculation of the expected frequencies.

In the two-way design, the expected frequencies represent the frequencies that would be expected if variables A and B were *independent*. Thus, regardless of the study, the expect-

---

[7]The requirements set forth here for 1 df contingency tables are conservative. See Camilli & Hopkins (1978).

ed frequencies for a two-way chi-square test are always calculated the same way, by using Formula 19-3.

$$E_{rc} = \frac{f_r f_c}{N}$$

(19-3)

where:

E_{rc} = expected frequency for a cell in row *r* and column *c*
f_r = number of observations (frequency) in the *r*th row
f_c = number of observations (frequency) in the *c*th column
N = total number of observations

More specifically, then, the value of E_{rc} is what we would expect if the row and column variables are independent.[8]

For example, the expected frequency of the cell corresponding to the first row and the first column in Table 19-6 can be found by multiplying the number of observations in the first row (564 males) by the number of observations in the first column (116 physics majors) and dividing this value by *N* (897 undergraduates):

$$E_{11} = \frac{564 \times 116}{897} = \frac{65{,}424}{897} = 72.94$$

This procedure for calculating the expected frequencies is carried out for all cells of the design. With this one exception, the procedures for calculating the χ^2 for a contingency table are the same as for calculating the one-way χ^2 as shown in Table 19-7 (see also Procedure 19-3 in the *Student Guide*).

Decision Rules for Rejecting H_0

In order to decide whether to reject H_0, we must compare $\chi^2_{observed}$ with $\chi^2_{critical(\alpha, df)}$. For a χ^2 contingency table, $df = (r - 1)(c - 1)$. With α and df known, Table D can be used to find $\chi^2_{critical}$. If $\chi^2_{observed}$ exceeds $\chi^2_{critical}$, we reject the null hypothesis and conclude that variables *A* and *B* are related. If $\chi^2_{observed}$ does not exceed $\chi^2_{critical}$, we conclude that there is insufficient evidence to say that variables *A* and *B* are not independent.

In the example problem with 2 rows and 4 columns (Table 19-6), $df = (2 - 1)(4 - 1)$ = 3. If the test is conducted at $\alpha = .01$,

$$\chi^2_{critical(.01,3)} = 11.345$$

---

[8]Here E_{rc} is actually based on joint probability. In order to illustrate, we will use E_{11} in Table 19-6—the expected number of males majoring in physics—will be used. In this case, E_{11} represents the probability of being male *and* being a physics major, assuming independence between sex and major. The probability of being male is the row total divided by *N*: 564 ÷ 897 = .629. The probability of being a physics major is the column total divided by *N*: 116 ÷ 897 = .129. The probability of being male *and* a physics major is p(male) $\times$ p(physics major) = .63 $\times$ .13 = .08. In order to convert the probability to a frequency, we multiply .08 by *N*: .08 $\times$ 897 $\approx$ 72.94 (rounding errors accumulated). See Chapter 9.

TABLE 19-7 Computational table for the data from Table 19-6

(1) Cell Row (Sex)	(1) Cell Column (Major)	(2) Observed Frequency (O)	(3) Expected Frequency[a] (E)	(4) O − E	(5) (O − E)²	(6) $\dfrac{(O-E)^2}{E}$
1	1	108	72.94	35.06	1,229.20	16.85
1	2	345	224.47	120.53	14,527.48	64.72
1	3	94	218.18	−124.18	15,420.67	70.68
1	4	17	48.42	−31.42	987.22	20.39
2	1	8	43.06	−35.06	1,229.20	28.55
2	2	12	132.53	−120.53	14,527.48	109.62
2	3	253	128.81	124.19	15,423.16	119.74
2	4	60	28.59	31.41	986.59	34.51
$\sum$		897	897.00	0		$\chi^2_{obs.} = 465.06$

$$^a E_{11} = \frac{564 \times 116}{897} = 72.94 \qquad E_{21} = \frac{333 \times 116}{897} = 43.06$$

$$E_{12} = \frac{564 \times 357}{897} = 224.47 \qquad E_{22} = \frac{333 \times 357}{897} = 132.53$$

$$E_{13} = \frac{564 \times 347}{897} = 218.18 \qquad E_{23} = \frac{333 \times 347}{897} = 128.82$$

$$E_{14} = \frac{564 \times 77}{897} = 48.42 \qquad E_{24} = \frac{333 \times 77}{897} = 28.59$$

Since in the example, $\chi^2_{observed}$ (465.06; see Procedure 19-3) exceeds $\chi^2_{critical}$, the null hypothesis should be rejected. Clearly, students' sex is related to choice of academic major. Specifically, women tend to choose majors in English and design, and men tend to choose majors in physics and engineering.

Numerical Example

A researcher wanted to determine whether there was any difference between boys' and girls' voting for president in a large school. The results of the election are shown in Table 19-8 for a random sample of 100 voters. To determine whether there was a relationship between the sex of the voter and the choice of candidate, we set forth the following hypotheses to be tested at $\alpha = .05$:

H_0: Sex and choice of candidate are independent in the population.

H_1: Sex and choice of candidate are related in the population.

To decide whether to reject the null hypothesis, we need $\chi^2_{critical}$ with $df = (2 - 1)$ $(3 - 1) = 2$ and $\alpha = .05$. From Table D,

$$\chi^2_{critical(.05,2)} = 5.991$$

If $\chi^2_{observed}$ equals or exceeds 5.991, the null hypothesis should be rejected.

TABLE 19-8 Votes cast by boys and girls for the three candidates running for class president

Sex	Candidate A	B	C	Total
Boys	30	20	10	60
Girls	15	10	15	40
Total	45	30	25	100

TABLE 19-9 Computation of $\chi^2_{observed}$ for data on the relation between sex and choice of candidate provided in Table 19-8

(1) Cell		(2)	(3)	(4)	(5)	(6)
Row (Sex)	Column (Candidate)	Observed Frequency (O)	Expected Frequency (E)	$O-E$	$(O-E)^2$	$\dfrac{(O-E)^2}{E}$
1	1	30	$\dfrac{60 \times 45}{100} = 27$	3	9	$\dfrac{9}{27} = .333$
1	2	20	$\dfrac{60 \times 30}{100} = 18$	2	4	$\dfrac{4}{18} = .222$
1	3	10	$\dfrac{60 \times 25}{100} = 15$	-5	25	$\dfrac{25}{15} = 1.667$
2	1	15	$\dfrac{40 \times 45}{100} = 18$	-3	9	$\dfrac{9}{18} = .50$
2	2	10	$\dfrac{40 \times 30}{100} = 12$	-2	4	$\dfrac{4}{12} = .333$
2	3	15	$\dfrac{40 \times 25}{100} = 10$	5	25	$\dfrac{25}{10} = 2.50$
$\sum$		100	100	0		$\chi^2_{obs.} = 5.55$

Table 19-9 provides the necessary computations. Since $df \geq 2$ and all *expected* frequencies exceed 5, we can proceed with the χ^2 test: $\chi^2_{observed} = 5.55$. Since $\chi^2_{observed}$ does not exceed $\chi^2_{critical}$, we conclude that there is insufficient evidence to reject the null hypothesis of independence.

Example Problem 19.3

In a public opinion survey, residents, sampled randomly in Los Angeles, were asked whether they supported the use of busing to desegregate city schools. The school board was interested in whether ethnic minority and nonminority residents felt differently about this issue. The data obtained are shown in Table 19-10. Conduct a χ^2 test at $\alpha = .05$ to test whether there is a relationship between minority group membership and opinion on school busing. Include the following items in your answer.

a. Null and alternative hypotheses
b. Verification that the assumptions and requirements have been met
c. Computation of $\chi^2_{observed}$

d. $\chi^2_{critical}$
e. Conclusions

TABLE 19-10 Public opinion survey results

	"Yes"	"No"	"No Opinion"	Total
Minority	50	35	15	100
Nonminority	65	100	35	200
Total	115	135	50	300

Correction for Continuity for the 2×2 χ^2

The 2×2 chi-square test is a statistical test with 1 degree of freedom: $(r - 1) \times (c - 1) = (2 - 1)(2 - 1) = 1$. Whenever the theoretical sampling distribution of chi-square is used with 1 *df*, Yate's correction for continuity should be used (see "Correction for Continuity" earlier for the rationale). This correction can be accomplished by subtracting .5 from the observed frequency whenever it exceeds the expected frequency, and adding .5 to the observed frequency whenever it is less than the expected frequency (see Table 19-5).

Since the 2×2 chi-square is the only two-way design with 1 degree of freedom, a simple computational formula that incorporates Yates's correction is available. Consider the following 2×2 contingency table:

a	b	$a + b$
c	d	$c + d$
$a + c$	$b + d$	N

The lowercase letters represent frequencies in each of the four cells. From this table, the value of chi-square can be found by using Formula 19-4.

$$\chi^2 = \frac{N\left(|ad - bc| - \frac{N}{2}\right)^2}{(a + b)(c + d)(a + c)(b + d)} \tag{19-4}$$

with $df = 1$

The correction for continuity is made by the term $N/2$.

To see how Formula 19-4 works, consider some data taken from a hypothetical survey (Table 19-11) of French and American businessmen about whether they preferred wine with lunch. In the statistical test, the usual hypotheses are set forth and $\alpha = .05$. The critical value of chi-square at $\alpha = .05$ with 1 degree of freedom, then, can be found in Table D:

$$\chi^2_{critical(.05,1)} = 3.841$$

If $\chi^2_{observed}$ is greater than or equal to 3.841, the null hypothesis should be rejected.

TABLE 19-11 Hypothetical survey of wine preferences of French and American businessmen

| Nationality | Do You Prefer Wine with Lunch? | | |
	Yes	No	Total
French	$a = 54$	$b = 6$	$a + b = 60$
American	$c = 16$	$d = 24$	$c + d = 40$
Total	$a + c = 70$	$b + d = 30$	$N = 100$

Before proceeding with the statistical test, we should check the smallest expected frequency to see whether it is at least 10 for this 1-degree-of-freedom test. The smallest expected frequency is $(30 \times 40) \div 100 = 12$. Now all that need be done is to insert the appropriate values from Table 19-11 into Formula 19-4 and solve:

$$\chi^2 = \frac{100\left[|(54)(24) - (6)(16)| - \frac{100}{2}\right]^2}{(60)(40)(70)(30)} = \frac{100(|1296 - 96| - 50)^2}{5{,}040{,}000} = \frac{100(1150)^2}{5{,}040{,}000}$$

$$= \frac{132{,}250{,}000}{5{,}040{,}000} = 26.24$$

Since $\chi^2_{observed}$ exceeds $\chi^2_{critical}$, the null hypothesis should be rejected. We conclude that there is a relation between nationality and wine preference. French businessmen tend to prefer wine at lunch, but American businessmen do not (see Table 19-11).

Example Problem 19.4

Half of the 44 students in a poetry class were assigned to hear a lecture on techniques that can be used to capture the unique qualities of the sea. The other half viewed a series of slides showing well-known seascapes painted by well-acclaimed artists. Then all students were assigned to write a poem on the sea. For a determination of which teaching technique was most effective, poems were categorized as to their quality. See Table 19-12. Conduct a χ^2 test at $\alpha = .01$ to determine whether teaching techniques and quality of poems are related. Include the following items in your answer.
a. Computation of χ^2
b. $\chi^2_{critical}$
c. Conclusions

TABLE 19-12 Results of poetry study

| Teaching Technique | Quality of Poem | | |
	Low	High	Total
Lecture	14	8	22
Slides	10	12	22
Total	24	20	44

Collapsing Levels of a Variable in a χ^2 Test

Sometimes, the *expected frequency* of one or more categories is less than 5 for χ^2 tests with $df \geq 2$ and less than 10 for a χ^2 test with $df = 1$, especially for small sample sizes. In these cases, the next step depends on the size of the contingency table. For a 2×2 contingency table, **Fisher's exact test** may be used. This test does not rely on the χ^2 distribution; rather, exact probabilities are computed (see, for example, Siegel, 1956). For larger contingency tables, it may be possible to use the χ^2 test by collapsing levels of a variable. In this way, expected frequencies at different levels are combined, thus boosting the expected frequency. Collapsing can be achieved by combining the frequencies in adjacent cells in a one-way design or by combining the frequencies in adjacent rows, columns, or both in a contingency table. However, there is also a conceptual issue in collapsing cells and this is most important. Simply stated, it must make sense to collapse categories. For example, in the absence of a good rationale, it might not make sense to collapse males with females, or physics majors with fine arts majors.

As an example of the procedure of collapsing levels, consider the following survey: A random sample of 100 subjects answered, among many questions, the following two items:

1. What is your sex?

   a. Male
   b. Female

2. How old were you on your last birthday?

   a. 17 or younger
   b. 18–23
   c. 24–29
   d. 30 or older

Hypothetical data from this study are presented in Table 19-13. To determine whether to collapse, we calculate the *smallest expected frequency*. Since the expected frequency depends on the row and column frequencies (Formula 19-3),

$$E_{rc} = \frac{f_r f_c}{N}$$

the smallest expected frequency will be found by multiplying the smallest f_r by the smallest f_c. In Table 19-13, the smallest f_r is 8 and the smallest f_c is 30:

$$E_{rc(\text{smallest})} = \frac{8 \times 30}{100} = \frac{240}{100} = 2.4$$

Since this expected frequency is less than 5 with $df = 3$, we should consider collapsing adjacent ages. The two oldest age categories could be combined quite logically, and the combination of the two might solve the problem. This combination has been done in Table 19-14. Now the smallest expected frequency is:

TABLE 19-13   Data on the relation between the sex and age of respondents in the survey ($N = 100$)

How Old Were You on Your Last Birthday?	What Is Your Sex?		Total
	Male	*Female*	
≤ 17	35	15	50
18–23	25	8	33
24–29	5	3	8
≥ 30	5	4	9
Total	70	30	100

TABLE 19-14   Data from Table 19-13 with the two highest age categories collapsed

How Old Were You on Your Last Birthday?	What Is Your Sex?		Total
	Male	*Female*	
≤ 17	35	15	50
18–23	25	8	33
≥ 24	10	7	17
Total	70	30	100

$$E_{rc(\text{smallest})} = \frac{17 \times 30}{100} = \frac{510}{100} = 5.10$$

Since $df \geq 2$ and the smallest expected frequency exceeds 5, χ^2 for contingency tables can be calculated. We would then proceed with the calculations as shown in Table 19-7.

In summary, one requirement of the χ^2 test is that the *expected frequencies* are all 5 or greater for $df \geq 2$ and that the expected frequencies are 10 or greater for $df = 1$. This require-ment applies to one-way and two-way designs. Sometimes, especially with small sample sizes, one or more expected frequencies do not meet these criteria. In this case, it might be possible to collapse adjacent cells (one-way designs) or to collapse adjacent rows, columns, or both (two-way designs) in order to increase the expected frequency to its minimally required value. In the collapsing, the combination of cells or rows (columns) must make conceptual sense.

Example Problem 19.5 ▬▬▬▬▬▬▬▬▬▬▬▬▬▬▬▬▬▬▬▬▬▬▬▬▬▬▬▬▬▬▬

Suppose that the data in Table 19-15 were collected in a survey of the relationship between average number of hours spent studying per day and performance in advanced chemistry courses at a par-ticular university.

Determine whether categories should be collapsed in order to do a χ^2 test. If so, combine cat-egories where appropriate. Include the following items in your answer.

a. Smallest E_{rc} in the noncollapsed data

b. Collapsed categories, if appropriate

c. Smallest E_{rc} of collapsed categories, if appropriate

TABLE 19-15 Data on study hours and performance

Hours of Study Per Day	Performance		Total
	Pass	Fail	
≤ 1	2	7	9
2	58	25	83
3	65	13	78
4	25	5	30
Total	150	50	200

SUMMARY

This chapter presents nonparametric statistical procedures for use in research designs in which data are collected in the form of counts (frequencies, proportions, probabilities, or percentages). In these designs, the independent variable takes the form of discrete categories, and a subject's response may fall in only one of these categories. The *chi-square* (χ^2) test is used to determine whether the observed frequencies in these categories differ from the *expected frequencies.* Procedures for conducting the χ^2 test for *one-way* and *two-way* designs are presented. Procedures for applying *Yates's correction for continuity* when the χ^2 test has only 1 degree of freedom are also discussed for both types of designs. Finally, procedures are given for collapsing levels of a variable when the expected frequency of one or more categories is less than a certain criterion.

ANSWERS TO EXAMPLE PROBLEMS

1. **a.** H_0: The observed distribution of frequencies equals the expected distribution of frequencies.

   H_1: The observed distribution of frequencies does not equal the expected distribution of frequencies.

   b. 1. *Mutually exclusive categories:* Each subject could choose only one response.

   2. *Independence:* Subjects were randomly selected and questioned individually.

   3. *Observations are measured as frequencies:* The data consist of the *number* of subjects making each response.

   4. *Expected frequencies greater than 5 and df $\geq$ 2:* If all types of foods were equally difficult to avoid, the expected frequency for each of the four categories would be $.25 \times 60 = 15$. Thus, no category has an expected frequency less than 5.

   5. *Correction for continuity:* Does not apply, since *df* are greater than 1.

c.

(1) Category	(2) Observed Frequency (O)	(3) Expected Proportion	(4) Expected Frequency (E)	(5) O − E	(6) (O − E)²	(7) $\dfrac{(O - E)^2}{E}$
a	17	.25	15	2	4	.27
b	13	.25	15	−2	4	.27
c	21	.25	15	6	36	2.40
d	9	.25	15	−6	36	2.40
Sum	60	1.00	60	0		$\chi^2_{obs.} = 5.34$

d. $\chi^2_{critical(.01,3)} = 11.345$

e. Since $\chi^2_{observed} < \chi^2_{critical}$, do not reject H_0. There is insufficient evidence to conclude that certain types of foods are more difficult for dieters to avoid than others.

2. a.

(1) Category	(2) Observed Frequency (O)	(3) Expected Proportion	(4) Expected Frequency (E)	(5) O Corrected for Continuity (O*)	(6) O* − E	(7) (O* − E)²	(8) $\dfrac{(O^* - E)^2}{E}$
Sucessful	37	.75	30	36.5	6.5	42.25	1.41
Nonsuccessful	3	.25	10	3.5	−6.5	42.25	4.23
Sum	40	1.00	40	40	0		$\chi^2_{obs.} = 5.64$

b. $\chi^2_{critical(.01,1)} = 6.635$

c. Since $\chi^2_{observed} < \chi^2_{critical}$, do not reject H_0. There is insufficient evidence to conclude that the number of "successful" managers is greater with the new training program than with previous programs.

3. a. H_0: Minority group membership and opinion on school busing are independent in the population.

H_1: Minority group membership and opinion on school busing are related in the population.

b. 1. *Mutually exclusive categories:* Each subject could choose only one response and belong to only one type of group.

2. *Independence:* Subjects were randomly selected and, presumably, polled individually.

3. *Observations are measured as frequencies:* The data consist of the *number* of subjects making each response.

4. *Expected frequencies less than 5 with df ≥ 2:* The smallest expected frequency is $(50 \times 100)/300 = 16.67$. Thus, no cell has an expected frequency less than 5.

5. *Correction for continuity:* Does not apply since *df* are greater than 1.

c.

(1) Cell		(2)	(3)	(4)	(5)	(6)
Row (Group)	*Column (Opinion)*	*Observed Frequency (O)*	*Expected Frequency[a] (E)*	*O − E*	*(O − E)²*	$\dfrac{(O-E)^2}{E}$
1	1	50	38.33	11.67	136.19	3.55
1	2	35	45.00	−10.00	100.00	2.22
1	3	15	16.67	−1.67	2.79	.17
2	1	65	76.67	−11.67	136.19	1.78
2	2	100	90.00	10.00	100.00	1.11
2	3	35	33.33	1.67	2.79	0.08
Sum		300	300	0		$\chi^2_{obs.} = 8.91$

$$^{a}E_{11} = 100 \times \frac{115}{300} = 38.33 \qquad E_{21} = 200 \times \frac{115}{300} = 76.67$$

$$E_{12} = \frac{100 \times 135}{300} = 45.00 \qquad E_{22} = \frac{200 \times 135}{300} = 90.00$$

$$E_{13(smallest)} = E_{13} = \frac{100 \times 50}{300} = 16.67 \qquad E_{23} = \frac{200 \times 50}{300} = 33.33$$

d. $\chi^2_{critical(.05,2)} = 5.99$

e. Since $\chi^2_{observed} > \chi^2_{critical}$, reject H_0. Conclude that minority group membership and opinion on school busing are related.

4. a.
$$\chi^2 = \frac{N\left(|ad - bc| - \dfrac{N}{2}\right)^2}{(a+b)(c+d)(a+c)(b+d)} = \frac{44\left[|(14)(12) - (8)(10)| - \dfrac{44}{2}\right]^2}{(22)(22)(24)(20)}$$

$$= \frac{191,644}{323,320} = .83$$

b. $\chi^2_{critical(.01,1)} = 6.635$

c. Since $\chi^2_{observed} < \chi^2_{critical}$, do not reject H_0. Conclude that teaching technique and quality of poems are independent.

5. a. $E_{rc} = \dfrac{9 \times 50}{200} = 2.25$

b.

Hours of Study per Day	Performance		Total
	Pass	Fail	
≤ 2	60	32	92
3	65	13	78
4	25	5	30
Total	150	50	200

c. $E_{rc(\text{smallest})} = \dfrac{(30)(50)}{200} = 7.5$ and $df = (3-1)(2-1) = 2$

EXERCISES

In the study of men's and women's college achievement, we found a statistically significant relationship between sex and academic major (see Table 19-7). The next piece of the puzzle is to see if there is a relationship between academic major and grade point average (GPA). If so, a plausible explanation for women's "overachievement" would be differences in major and not in gender characteristics. Hypothetical data on major and GPA are shown in Table 19-16. Use these data in the exercises that follow.

1. Out of curiosity (whose you ask?), do a statistical test to see if the GPA data are normally distributed. To this end, use a finer-grained analysis than I did at the beginning of the chapter: (I) Scores at or below -1.5 standard deviations (s) from the mean, (II) scores between -1.5 and $-1s$, (III) scores between -1 and $-.5s$, (IV) scores between $-.5s$ and the mean, (V) scores between the mean and $.5s$, (VI) scores between .5 and $1s$, (VII) scores between 1 and $1.5s$, and (VIII) scores at or above $1.5s$.

   a. State the null and alternative hypotheses for the statistical test.
   b. State the assumptions underlying the test and comment only if one is suspect. If it is, propose a strategy for dealing with it.
   c. Conduct a statistical test and report your findings.
   d. What do you conclude about the distribution of GPAs?

2. Carry out a statistical test to see if there is a relationship between academic major and GPA.

   a. State the null and alternative hypotheses for the analysis.
   b. State the assumptions underlying the test and comment only if one is suspect. If it is, propose a strategy for dealing with it.
   c. Conduct a statistical test and report your findings.
   d. What do you conclude about the relationship between major and GPA?

TABLE 19-16 Hypothetical data on academic major and grade point average (GPA)[9]

ID	Major	GPA		ID	Major	GPA		ID	Major	GPA
1	1.00	1.00	2.99	36	36.00	2.00	2.60	71	71.00	3.00	3.04
2	2.00	1.00	2.71	37	37.00	2.00	3.51	72	72.00	3.00	2.67
3	3.00	1.00	2.86	38	38.00	2.00	2.93	73	73.00	3.00	2.76
4	4.00	1.00	2.58	39	39.00	2.00	3.01	74	74.00	3.00	2.88
5	5.00	1.00	3.27	40	40.00	2.00	2.58	75	75.00	3.00	3.01
6	6.00	1.00	3.15	41	41.00	2.00	3.19	76	76.00	3.00	3.13
7	7.00	1.00	3.01	42	42.00	2.00	3.06	77	77.00	3.00	2.61
8	8.00	1.00	2.75	43	43.00	2.00	2.83	78	78.00	3.00	3.02
9	9.00	1.00	3.15	44	44.00	2.00	3.15	79	79.00	3.00	2.71
10	10.00	1.00	3.50	45	45.00	2.00	2.85	80	80.00	3.00	3.18
11	11.00	1.00	3.23	46	46.00	2.00	3.32	81	81.00	3.00	2.81
12	12.00	1.00	2.23	47	47.00	2.00	2.79	82	82.00	3.00	3.61
13	13.00	1.00	2.79	48	48.00	2.00	2.81	83	83.00	3.00	3.29
14	14.00	1.00	3.76	49	49.00	2.00	2.65	84	84.00	3.00	2.86
15	15.00	1.00	2.90	50	50.00	2.00	2.82	85	85.00	3.00	2.89
16	16.00	1.00	2.82	51	51.00	2.00	3.19	86	86.00	3.00	2.53
17	17.00	1.00	3.55	52	52.00	2.00	3.65	87	87.00	3.00	2.79
18	18.00	1.00	3.33	53	53.00	2.00	2.44	88	88.00	3.00	2.63
19	19.00	1.00	2.94	54	54.00	2.00	3.50	89	89.00	3.00	2.46
20	20.00	1.00	2.28	55	55.00	2.00	3.27	90	90.00	3.00	3.09
21	21.00	1.00	3.17	56	56.00	2.00	3.28	91	91.00	3.00	2.78
22	22.00	1.00	2.81	57	57.00	2.00	3.12	92	92.00	3.00	2.74
23	23.00	1.00	3.34	58	58.00	2.00	2.98	93	93.00	3.00	2.86
24	24.00	1.00	3.44	59	59.00	2.00	2.59	94	94.00	3.00	3.05
25	25.00	1.00	2.85	60	60.00	2.00	3.19	95	95.00	3.00	2.99
26	26.00	1.00	3.41	61	61.00	2.00	2.58	96	96.00	3.00	2.83
27	27.00	1.00	3.65	62	62.00	2.00	3.18	97	97.00	3.00	2.81
28	28.00	1.00	3.02	63	63.00	2.00	2.64	98	98.00	3.00	2.84
29	29.00	1.00	3.04	64	64.00	2.00	3.25	99	99.00	3.00	3.34
30	30.00	1.00	2.87	65	65.00	2.00	2.78	100	100.00	3.00	2.91
31	31.00	1.00	3.13	66	66.00	2.00	2.33	101	101.00	3.00	2.88
32	32.00	1.00	2.96	67	67.00	2.00	2.99	102	102.00	3.00	2.91
33	33.00	1.00	2.70	68	68.00	2.00	2.69	103	103.00	3.00	2.93
34	34.00	1.00	3.14	69	69.00	2.00	3.12	104	104.00	3.00	3.11
35	35.00	1.00	2.96	70	70.00	2.00	2.66	105	105.00	3.00	2.95

[9]SPSS data file

ANSWERS TO EXERCISES

1. a. H_0: The observed distribution of frequencies equals the expected (i.e., normal) distribution in each category.

   H_1: The observed distribution of frequencies does not equal the expected (i.e., normal) distribution in each category.

b. (1) Each observation falls in one and only one category, (2) observations are independent of one another, (3) observations are measured as frequencies, and (4) expected frequencies are at least 5. All assumptions are satisfied.

c. Cut Scores Used to Determine Categories I–VIII[10]:

Note: Mean = 2.97 and standard deviation = .30

(I)   Scores at or below −1.5 standard deviations (*s*): 2.52

(II)   Scores between −1.5 and −1*s*: 2.53 – 2.67

(III)   Scores between −1 and −.5*s*: 2.68 – 2.82

(IV)   Scores between −.5*s* and the mean: 2.83 – 2.97

(V)   Scores between the mean and .5*s*: 2.98 – 3.12

(VI)   Scores between .5 and 1*s*: 3.13 – 3.27

(VII)   Scores between 1 and 1.5*s*: 2.38 – 3.42

(VIII)   Scores at or above 1.5*s*: 3.43

Frequency distribution to "eyeball" shape:

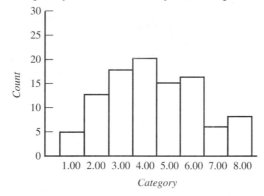

- - - - - Chi-Square Test[11]:

CATEGORY

	Cases		
Category	Observed	Expected	Residual
1.00	5	7.01	−2.01
2.00	12	9.65	2.35
3.00	18	15.73	2.27
4.00	21	20.11	.89
5.00	16	20.11	−4.11
6.00	17	15.73	1.27
7.00	7	9.65	−2.65
8.00	9	7.01	1.99
Total	105		

[10]Your cut points may have varied slightly by, say, .01 GPA.

[11]SPSS Program Setup:

NPAR TEST (*continued*)

Chi-Square	D.F.	Significance
3.7499	7	.8081

d. The null hypothesis of normality cannot be rejected. GPAs may very well have been drawn from a normal population.

2. a. H_0: Major and GPA category are independent in the population.

   H_1: Major and GPA category are related in the population.

   b. Each observation must fall in one and only one cell of the design, (b) each observation is independent of every other, (c) observations are measured as frequencies, and (e) the expected frequency in any cell is not less than 5. The last assumption is not met, as shown in the following SPSS run[12]:

MAJOR by CATEGORY

Page 1 of 2

CATEGORY						
Count Exp Val	Row					
MAJOR	1.00	2.00	3.00	4.00	5.00	Total
1.00	2 / 1.7	1 / 4.0	6 / 6.0	7 / 7.0	4 / 5.3	35 / 33.3%
2.00	2 / 1.7	7 / 4.0	5 / 6.0	3 / 7.0	5 / 5.3	35 / 33.3%
3.00	1 / 1.7	4 / 4.0	7 / 6.0	11 / 7.0	7 / 5.3	35 / 33.3%
Column (continued) Total	5 / 4.8%	12 / 11.4%	18 / 17.1%	21 / 20.0%	16 / 15.2%	105 / 100.0%

MAJOR by CATEGORY

Page 2 of 2

CATEGORY			
Count Exp Val	Row		
MAJOR	6.00	7.00	8.00	Total
1.00	7 / 5.7	3 / 2.3	5 / 3.0	35 / 33.3%
2.00	8 / 5.7	2 / 2.3	3 / 3.0	35 / 33.3%
3.00	2 / 5.7	2 / 2.3	1 / 3.0	35 / 33.3%
Column Total	17 / 16.2%	7 / 6.7%	9 / 8.6%	105 / 100.0%

Minimum Expected Frequency—1.667

Cells with Expected Frequency < 5—12 OF 24 (50.0%)

These findings indicated that collapsing the two lower and two upper categories is in order. This makes conceptual sense, so the CATEGORY data (1–8) were recoded to: 0=1 & 2, 3, 4, 5, 6, 9=7 & 8.

---

[11]CHISQUARE=category

/EXPECTED=6.68 9.19 14.98 19.15 19.15 14.98 9.19 6.68

/STATISTICS DESCRIPTIVES QUARTILES

/MISSING ANALYSIS.

[12]SPSS Program Setup:

CROSSTABS

/TABLES=major BY category

/FORMAT=AVALUE NOINDEX BOX LABELS TABLES

/STATISTIC=CHISQ

≥/CELLS=COUNT EXPECTED.

c. A statistical test was conducted on the COLLAPSED variable[13]:

MAJOR by COLLAPSE

COLLAPSE   Page 1 of 2

MAJOR	Count Exp Val	.00	3.00	Row 4.00	5.00	6.00	Total
1.00		3 5.7	6 6.0	7 7.0	4 5.3	7 5.7	35 33.3%
2.00		9 5.7	5 6.0	3 7.0	5 5.3	8 5.7	35 33.3%
3.00		5 5.7	7 6.0	11 7.0	7 5.3	2 5.7	35 33.3%
Column (continued) Total		17 16.2%	18 17.1%	21 20.0%	16 15.2%	17 16.2%	105 100.0%

MAJOR by COLLAPSE

COLLAPSE   Page 2 of 2

MAJOR	Count Exp Val	Row 9.00	Total
1.00		8 5.3	35 33.3%
2.00		5 5.3	35 33.3%
3.00		3 5.3	35 33.3%
Column Total		16 15.2%	105 100.0%

Chi-Square	Value	DF	Significance
Pearson	15.09594	10	.12860

Minimum Expected Frequency—5.333

d. Do not reject the null hypothesis of independence. Nevertheless, the pattern of observed frequencies is in the predicted direction. For the humanities (major=1), high frequencies are found above 5; for the sciences (major=3), higher frequencies are found below 5; and for the social sciences, the frequencies fall in between.

---

[13]SPSS Program Setup:
CROSSTABS
  /TABLES=major BY collapse
  /FORMAT=AVALUE NOINDEX BOX LABELS TABLES/STATISTIC = CHISQ
  /STATISTIC=CHISQ
  /CELLS=COUNT EXPECTED.

20

Additional Nonparametric Statistical Tests

- Wilcoxon (Mann-Whitney) t Test for Two Independent Groups
- Wilcoxon T Test for Dependent Samples
- Kruskal-Wallis One-Way Analysis of Variance by Ranks
- Summary
- Answers to Example Problems
- Exercises
- Answers to Exercises

In Section VII, you learned about the nature of nonparametric statistical tests and in the previous chapter you encountered the chi-square test for goodness of fit and for association.[1] This chapter rounds out the presentation of nonparametric techniques by presenting nonparametric statistics that test the difference in the *shape* or *location* (central tendency) of the populations underlying two or more groups. Specifically, three nonparametric statistical tests are presented:

1. Wilcoxon (Mann-Whitney) t test for two independent groups
2. Wilcoxon T test for two dependent groups
3. Kruskal-Wallis one-way analysis of variance by ranks

In doing so, I only scratch the surface of the panoply of nonparametric statistical tests available. If you become interested in nonparametrics, you might want to start with a classic: Siegel (1956).

WILCOXON (MANN-WHITNEY) t TEST FOR TWO INDEPENDENT GROUPS

Probably the most frequently used nonparametric analog to the parametric t test (Chapter 12) is the Wilcoxon (1949) test for differences between two independent groups. Various

---

[1]Indeed, you also encountered another nonparametric statistical test of association in Chapter 6, the Spearman rank correlation coefficient, although it was not called a nonparametric test.

forms of this nonparametric *t* test exist; here I present the test following Mann & Whitney (1947), which is referred to as the *Mann-Whitney U test.*

Purpose and Underlying Logic

The purpose of the Mann-Whitney *U* test is to help the researcher decide whether or not the distributions of scores in two independent groups were drawn from two identical population distributions. If the shapes of the population distributions are similar, the *U* test can be used to examine the null hypothesis that the two populations are identical with respect to their *central tendency.* In this case, the *U* test is a nonparametric analog to the *t* test for two independent groups. It may be used as an alternative to the *t* test or when the *t* test's assumptions of normality and equal variances are untenable.

The decision of whether or not to reject the null hypothesis cannot be made with certainty; it is a probabilistic one. The problem, then, is to determine the probability of observing differences between the distributions of scores in two independent groups assuming the null hypothesis is true.

The first step in coming up with a probability statement is to define a statistic that reflects differences between the two distributions of scores. This statistic is called the *U* statistic. It is based not on the raw scores but on the rank order of scores from lowest to highest, since these ranks adequately reflect differences between two distributions. In order to see this ranking, consider the data in Table 20-1 from the teacher expectancy study. (For details in computing *U,* see "Formula for the *U* Statistic" below.) Notice that most of the high scores are associated with the experimental group. So the ranks associated with the experimental group (4, 5, 7, 9, 10) are generally higher than those associated with the control group (1, 2, 3, 6, 8). The difference between the two distributions of scores, then, can be seen in the rank ordering of subjects' scores in the two groups: CCCEECECEE. The *U* statistic is simply the number of E scores preceding each C score. When we count the number of E scores preceding each C score, some E scores will be counted more than once. In the example, no E score precedes the first three C scores, two E scores precede the fourth C score, and a total of three E scores (counting the first two E scores for a second time) precede the fifth C score. So $U = 0 + 0 + 0 + 2 + 3 = 5$.

The next step is to determine the probability of observing *U* at or beyond some value, assuming the null hypothesis is true. With the *U* test, as with many nonparametric tests, this

TABLE 20-1 Using first graders' data from the study of teacher expectancy (see Table 2-1)

				Group					
C	*C*	*C*	*E*	*E*	*C*	*E*	*C*	*E*	*E*
Raw Score 90	99	102	107	111	114	117	121	122	125
Rank 1	2	3	4	5	6	7	8	9	10

Sum of Ranks
  Control group $1 + 2 + 3 + 6 + 8 = 20$
  Experimental group $4 + 5 + 7 + 9 + 10 = 35$

problem is solved by capitalizing on two pieces of information. First, all possible orderings of subjects' scores (e.g., all possible orderings of E's and C's) can be determined by knowing only the number of subjects in each of the two groups. Second, all possible random orderings, under the null hypothesis, are equally likely. From this information, the probability of a particular event (e.g., $U \leq$ some value) can be determined by the ratio of the number of ways subjects' scores can be rank-ordered in that event to the total possible orderings of subjects' scores.

Hypotheses

The hypotheses tested with the U statistic are somewhat different than the hypotheses presented so far. The null hypothesis is that the distributions of scores in the two populations from which the groups were drawn are identical. The alternative hypothesis is that the distributions of scores in the two populations from which the groups were drawn are different in some way. If the U statistic is used to test for differences between means, an additional restrictive assumption must be made: The population distributions are identical in all other respects. In this case, the null and alternative hypotheses can be written as in Table 20-2.

TABLE 20-2 Hypotheses for the U test

	Nondirectional Hypotheses	*Directional Hypotheses*
H_0	The distributions of scores in the two populations from which the groups were drawn are identical	The distributions of scores in the two populations from which the groups were drawn are identical
H_1	The distributions of scores in the two populations from which the groups were drawn differ in their means: $\mu_1 \neq \mu_2$	The distributions of scores in the two populations from which the groups were drawn differ in their means: $\mu_1 > \mu_2$ or $\mu_1 < \mu_2$

Design Requirements

The use of the U test implies that certain design requirements have been met. They are the same as for the t test for independent samples:

1. There is one independent variable with two levels (i.e., groups).
2. A subject appears in one and only one group.
3. The levels of the independent variable may differ from one another either qualitatively or quantitatively.

Assumptions

In the use of the Mann-Whitney U test, the assumption of independence of scores is made. If the U test is used to test hypotheses about central tendency, an additional assumption is made that the distributions of scores in the two populations are similar except for central tendency.

Computation of the U Statistic

Although we can use the counting method described before to calculate U, this method is tedious for fairly large samples. An alternative method that gives identical results is the following: First, the scores from both groups are pooled together so that there are $n_1 + n_2 = N$ scores considered together. Second, these N scores are arranged in order of their magnitude regardless of group. Each score, however, is labeled with the group from which it came. For example, the scores from the teacher expectancy study (Table 20-1) were pooled so that there are $5 + 5 = 10$ scores. These scores are arranged in order of their magnitude—lowest to highest—in the first row of Table 20-1. The group from which each score came—experimental (E) or control (C)—is identified in the column heading.

Third, a rank is assigned to each score according to its magnitude. A rank of 1 is assigned to the lowest score, a rank of 2 is assigned to the next highest score, and so on, until a rank of N is assigned to the highest score. In Table 20-1, the lowest score is 90 and a rank of 1 has been assigned to it. The highest score is 125 and a rank of 10 (because $N = 10$) has been assigned to it. In some cases, two or more scores may be tied for a particular rank. For example, suppose that in Table 20-1, the score of 102 was actually a score of 99. Now there would be two scores of 99 tied for ranks of 2 and 3. In this case, the average of the two ranks is assigned to both scores. For example, the two scores of 99 would each be assigned a rank of 2.5.[2]

Fourth, find the sum of the ranks for each of the two groups and then take the larger sum. In the example, the sum of the ranks for the experimental group would be taken, because it is larger than the sum of the ranks for the control group ($35 > 20$; see Table 20-1). This sum is called T_L:

$$T_L = \text{larger sum of the ranks} = 4 + 5 + 7 + 9 + 10 = 35$$

The fifth step is to calculate the Mann-Whitney U statistic from Formula 20-1.

$$U_1 = n_L n_S + \frac{n_L(n_L + 1)}{2} - T_L$$
$$U_2 = n_L n_S - U_1 \tag{20-1}$$

where:

n_L = number of subjects in the group with the larger sum of ranks
n_S = number of subjects in the other group
Mann-Whitney U = smaller of U_1 and U_2

Using the information from the example, we have

---

[2]The Mann-Whitney test assumes no two scores are exactly the same. In other words, there are no "ties" in theory. However, in practice, ties occur. If the ties occur between two observations *in the same group*, U is unaffected. If the ties occur between observations *in different groups*, U is affected. Usually this effect is negligible. For large samples ($n_L \geq 20$), a correction exists (see Siegel, 1956).

$$U_1 = (5)(5) + \frac{5(5+1)}{2} - 35 = 5$$
$$U_2 = (5)(5) - 5 = 20$$

The value of U_1, calculated with Formula 20-1, is the smaller of the two and is exactly the same as that obtained with the counting method, as expected.

Decision Rules for Rejecting the Null Hypothesis

In the decision of whether or not to reject the null hypothesis, the probability of observing a value of less than or equal to U (5 in the example) is needed. This decision is made one of three ways, depending on the size of the two groups. If $n \leq 8$, Table J at the end of the book can be used to determine the probability of U directly. If $9 \leq n \leq 20$, U must be compared with the critical value of U in Table K. These critical values of U designate the regions beyond which differences between the means of the two groups are unlikely to arise. Finally, if $n > 20$, the normal distribution (Table B) can be used to determine the critical value.

For $n \leq 8$. If the larger of the two samples is less than or equal to 8, Table J can be used to find the probability of $U_{observed}$. The following steps are taken in using this table to identify the critical values:

1. Locate the table corresponding to the larger of the two sample sizes (labeled N_2 in the table).
2. Locate the column of the table corresponding to the smaller of the two sample sizes (labeled N_1 in the table).
3. Locate the row of the table corresponding to $U_{observed}$.
4. Read the probability from the table that corresponds to the row and column appropriate to your data. This is the one-tail probability of observing the difference between means given the null hypothesis and should be used if the observed difference was in the predicted direction. The two-tail probability is obtained by doubling this value.
5. If a *directional* (one-tail) *alternative hypothesis* has been specified, reject the null hypothesis if the probability value in the table is less than or equal to α.
6. If a *nondirectional* (two-tail) *alternative hypothesis* has been specified, double the probability value in the table. Reject the null hypothesis if this value is less than or equal to α.

In the example, $n_1 = n_1 = 5$. So, first, locate the table for $n_L = 5$ in Table J. Next, find the column that indicates the value of n_S, which is 5. Finally, locate the row corresponding to $U_{observed} = 5$. Now, read the probability value corresponding to the row value of 5 and the column value of 5. This value is .075. Since this value is the one-tail probability of U, the null hypothesis cannot be rejected at $\alpha = .05$ for either a one-tail test ($p = .075$) or a two-tail test ($p = 2 \times .075 = .15$).

For $9 \leq n \leq 20$. If the larger of the two sample sizes falls in between 9 and 20, the critical values for U can be found in Table K. In the use of Table K, the following steps should be taken:

1. Locate the table corresponding to the level of significance (α)—one- or two-tail—that you have planned to use.
2. Locate the smaller sample size (n_S) along the rows of the table, and the larger (n_L) along the columns.
3. Read $U_{critical}$ that corresponds to the appropriate row (n_S) and column (n_L).
4. Reject the null hypothesis if $U_{observed}$ is *less than or equal to* $U_{critical}$ for a two-tail test, or if the observed group difference was in the predicted direction for a one-tail test.

For example, suppose that a researcher set $\alpha = .05$ (two-tail) and conducted a study in which $n_1 = 8$, $n_2 = 15$, and $U_{observed} = 12$. On the basis of $U_{observed} = 12$, should the null hypothesis be rejected? In order to answer this question, we must find $U_{critical}$ from Table K. First, we locate the table corresponding to $\alpha = .05$, two-tail. Next, we locate $n_S = 8$ among the rows of the table and $n_L = 15$ among the columns. Then, we read the critical value of U corresponding to the intersection of the row and column:

$$U_{critical} = 29$$

Since $U_{observed} = 12$ is less than $U_{critical} = 29$, the null hypothesis of identical population distributions should be rejected in favor of the alternative hypothesis of a difference in the central tendency of the two populations.

For $n > 20$. If the larger sample is greater than 20, the sampling distribution of U is approximately normal.[3] If we convert U into a z score, z_U, Table B can be used to decide whether or not to reject the null hypothesis. First, z_U is defined as in Formula 20-2.

$$z_U = \frac{U - \dfrac{n_1 n_2}{2}}{s_U} = \frac{U - \dfrac{n_1 n_2}{2}}{\sqrt{\dfrac{n_1 n_2 (n_1 + n_2 + 1)}{12}}} \qquad (20\text{-}2)$$

As an example of how to use and interpret the results of Formula 20-2, suppose that random samples of 30 "normals" and 30 "neurotics" were drawn from their respective populations in order to test the following hypotheses at $\alpha = .05$:

H_0: The distributions of self-concept scores in the two populations from which the samples were drawn are identical.

H_1: The distributions of self-concept scores in the two populations from which the samples were drawn differ only in their means, with $\mu_{normals} > \mu_{neurotics}$.

---

[3]The effect of sample size on the sampling distribution of the U statistic is analogous to that described for the sampling distribution of means in Chapter 10. As a consequence of the central limit theorem, the shape of the sampling distribution approaches normality as sample size increases. Note, however, that this statement does not imply that the distributions of scores on which the U statistic is computed are necessarily normal.

The original self-concept scores in the sample were converted to ranks. The larger sum of the ranks was, as predicted, associated with the normal sample: $T_L = 785$. And consequently, U was 580.[4] With this information, z_U can be found from Formula 20-2:

$$z_U = \frac{580 - \dfrac{(30)(30)}{2}}{\sqrt{\dfrac{(30)(30)(30 + 30 + 1)}{12}}} = \frac{580 - 450}{\sqrt{\dfrac{54,900}{12}}} = 1.92$$

From Table B, the probability of observing $z_U \geq 1.92$ is .027. Since this value is less than .05 (one-tail), the null hypothesis can be rejected. The mean self-concept score for normals is greater than for neurotics.

Procedure 20-1 in the *Student Guide* summarizes the steps in conducting the U test with sample sizes of less than 9, between 9 and 20, and greater than 20.

Example Problem 20.1

Using the data presented in Example Problem 12.2 in Chapter 12, test whether there are differences between the moral judgments of adults and children when given a short story in which the outcome is positive and the actor's intent is negative, using the Mann-Whitney U test ($\alpha = .05$, two-tail). Include the following items in your answer.
a. Null and alternative hypotheses
b. Test assumptions or explain if you do not conduct a test
c. Table showing conversion of scores to ranks
d. U
e. The probability of U given that H_0 is true
f. What do you conclude?

WILCOXON T TEST FOR DEPENDENT SAMPLES

The Wilcoxon T test for dependent samples provides an analog to the dependent t test presented in Chapter 12. It can be applied when data are collected on the same subjects observed in two treatment conditions or when data are collected on matched pairs of subjects, one member of the pair in treatment 1 and the other in treatment 2. (If within-subjects designs are unfamiliar to you, see Section VI.)

---

[4]In detail, with the use of Formula 20-1, we have

$$U = n_L n_S + \frac{n_L(n_L + 1)}{2} - T_L = (30)(30) + \frac{30(30 + 1)}{2} - 785$$

$$= 900 + \frac{930}{2} - 785 = 900 + 465 - 785 = 580$$

Purpose and Underlying Logic

The purpose of the Wilcoxon test for dependent samples is to help the researcher decide whether or not the distribution of scores obtained from the same subjects under two treatment conditions or obtained from matched pairs of subjects under two treatment conditions are drawn from identical treatment populations. If we assume that the treatment populations are identical except for their means, then the Wilcoxon test provides an analog to the dependent-samples t test presented in Chapter 12.

The Wilcoxon test works as follows: For each subject (or each matched pair of subjects), calculate a difference score: $d_p = X_{p1} - X_{p2}$. This difference score reflects the difference in scores earned in treatment 1 and 2 by a particular subject (or matched pair of subjects). Note that if the null hypothesis is true, we should expect about the same number of positive and negative differences, and the magnitudes of the positive and negative differences should be about the same.

Next, rank-order the differences, d_p's, *without* regard to sign—that is, rank-order the absolute value of the differences. Thus a score of -2 would be given a lower rank than either a score of -3 or $+3$. Then, attach a plus $(+)$ to each rank that arose from a positive differences (d_p), and a minus $(-)$ to each rank that arose from a negative difference. For example, if $d_p = -5$ and this corresponds to, say, a rank of 6, the final step would be to attach the sign of d_p $(-)$ to the rank (6): -6.

Now, if the null hypothesis is true—H_0: treatments 1 and 2 are identical in their effects—we should find some of the larger d_p's associated with treatment 1 (the pluses) and some associated with treatment 2 (the minuses), and some of the smaller d_p's associated with treatment 1 and some with treatment 2. If we summed the ranks associated with the pluses and summed the ranks associated with the minuses, except for sampling error, the two sums should be equal, assuming the null hypothesis is true.

However, if the sum of the positive ranks, for example, is considerably greater than the sum of the negative ranks, doubt would be cast on the null hypothesis. That is, we might decide to reject the null hypothesis and conclude a difference between treatment populations.

The decision hinges on the nature of the sampling distribution of these "sums." The sampling distribution of T provides the yardstick for making that decision (see Table N at the end of the book).

At this point, a concrete example may be helpful. Consider the moral judgment study. Piaget's theory of moral development leads us to predict that teenagers (13–18 years of age) will use information about an actor's *intent* to judge an actor morally, and they will tend to ignore information about the outcomes of an event in this judgment process. If the theory is correct, we should expect to see teenagers reward positive intent even if the outcome is negative but not to reward positive outcomes if the actor's intent is negative.

Table 20-3 presents the judgments of 10 teenagers under two treatment conditions: the actor's intent was positive but the outcome was negative, and the actor's intent was negative but the outcome was positive. If Piaget's theory is right, we should expect treatment 1 to yield higher ratings than treatment 2.

For each subject in Table 20-3, a difference score (d_p) has been calculated. Then, the d_p's were rank-ordered without regard to the direction (sign) of the difference. In the example, this ranking was easy because the signs of the differences were all the same. Notice

TABLE 20-3 Teenagers' moral judgments (data from Table 16-1)

| | Treatment | | | | |
| | (1) Positive Intent/ | (2) Negative Intent/ | | | |
Subject	Negative Outcome	Positive Outcome	d_p	Rank	Sign
1	+2	−3	5	3.5	+
2	+3	−2	5	3.5	+
3	+1	−4	5	3.5	+
4	+4	−1	5	3.5	+
5	+3	−5	8	10.0	+
6	+2	−5	7	9.0	+
7	+4	−2	6	7.5	+
8	+3	−2	5	3.5	+
9	+3	−2	5	3.5	+
10	+3	−3	6	7.5	+

that ties were handled as in the previous section. If two or more d_p's are the same size (in absolute value—i.e., ignoring sign), we assign to each the average of the ranks. For example, six subjects received a difference of 5. Hence, 5 corresponds to the first six ranks. The average of the ranks 1, 2, ... , 6 is $(1 + 2 + \cdots + 6)/6 = 3.5$.[5]

Next, the sign was attached to each difference score. Needless to say, this step was simple because treatment 1 always produced scores higher than those in treatment 2.

Finally, if we sum the ranks with positive signs (i.e., sum all of the ranks in this example), we get a sum of 55. The sum of the ranks with negative signs is, of course, zero in this example. This finding seems like a very unusual event if, in fact, the null hypothesis is true!

To determine whether, statistically, the data in Table 20-3 are highly unlikely under the null hypothesis, we need to know the sampling distribution of the *smaller sum, T.* Table N provides the sampling distributions for samples up to size 25. (Beyond this size, the normal distribution, Table B, provides a very good approximation; see what follows.)

In our example, the smaller sum is zero, or $T = 0$; and it is associated with the negative signs. This result indicates that treatment 1 always exceeded treatment 2 in the magnitude of moral judgment ratings. To determine whether a value of $T = 0$ could have arisen by chance when the null hypothesis is true, we refer to Table N and use a one-tail test at $\alpha = .01$. With $N = 10$ subjects, T must be less than or equal to 5 in order for us to reject the null hypothesis of identical population distributions. Since $T_{observed}$ is less than the table value of T, we should decide to reject the null hypothesis and conclude that the moral judgments of actors with positive intent are more positive than those of actors with negative intent.

---

[5]A tie may occur in another way. A subject (or matched pair of subjects) may receive exactly the same score in treatment 1 and treatment 2. In this case $d_p = 0$, and the subject's (or pair's) data are dropped from the analysis. I do not condone dropping data. However, given the pros and cons of alternatives (see Marascuilo & McSweeney, 1977), in this case dropping data is preferred.

Hypotheses

The null hypothesis tested with Wilcoxon's T test is that the distributions of scores in the two treatment populations are identical. This hypothesis is equivalent to saying that over repeated samples, the sum of the positive ranks equals the sum of the negative ranks. The nondirectional alternative hypothesis is that the population distributions are not equivalent. This hypothesis is tantamount to saying that the sum of the positive ranks is not equal to the sum of the negative ranks. The directional alternative states that the sum of the positive ranks, say, is greater than the sum of the negative ranks.

If we assume that the two population distributions are identical except in central tendency, the null and alternative hypotheses refer to the average (e.g., mean) scores in the two populations. Moreover, a directional alternative hypothesis states that the mean of treatment 1 exceeds the mean of treatment 2 in the population.

Design Requirements

The use of Wilcoxon's T test implies that certain design requirements have been met. These requirements are the same as for the dependent t test (Chapter 12):

1. There is one independent variable with two levels.
2. The same group of subjects is observed under both treatment conditions, or matched pairs of subjects are observed so that one member of the pair is observed under treatment 1 and the other member of the pair is observed under treatment 2.
3. The levels of the independent variable may differ from one another either quantitatively or qualitatively.

Assumptions

The following assumptions are made in use of the Wilcoxon test:

1. The scores of the N subjects are independently and randomly sampled from the two respective treatment populations.
2. The scores in the populations are continuously distributed.
3. The two populations have identical shapes or are both symmetric.

The last assumption is required only if the statistical test is concerned with differences in central tendency. Without the third assumption, the Wilcoxon T test is ambiguous. It will reflect differences between populations due to differences in their shapes, in means, in medians, or in both means and medians.

Computation of the T Statistic

For samples of less than or equal to 25 subjects, or matched pairs, $T_{observed}$ is defined simply as the smaller sum of the positive or negative rank differences between treatments 1 and 2 (Formula 20-3).

$$T_{obs.} = \text{smaller sum of the positive or negative rank differences}$$
$$\text{between treatments 1 and 2} \qquad \qquad \textbf{(20-3)}$$

Sample size is defined as the number of subjects or matched pairs with nonzero difference scores.

To obtain $T_{observed}$, follow these steps:

1. Obtain the signed difference between the scores for each subject or matched pair under the two treatment conditions (see Table 20-3), d_p.
2. Rank the absolute value of the d_p's (i.e., rank the d_p's without regard to sign).
3. Attach the sign of the difference (d_p) to the rank.
4. Find the sum of the positive ranks and the sum of the negative ranks.
5. Define $T_{observed}$ as the smaller sum.

In the example in Table 20-3, the sum of the positive ranks was 55 and the sum of the negative ranks was 0. Hence, $T_{observed} = 0$.

The value of $T_{observed}$ can be referred to the sampling distribution of T ($T_{critical}$) in Table N to determine whether or not the observed differences were likely to arise by chance when the population distributions (or means; see the earlier assumptions) are identical. If $T_{observed}$ is less than or equal to the table value, reject the null hypothesis. In our example (Table 20-3), $N = 10$; and a one-tail statistical test was conducted at the .01 level. From Table N, $T_{critical} = 5$. Since $T_{observed}$ (0) $< T_{critical}$ (5), we reject the null hypothesis and conclude support for Piaget's theory. (Procedure 20-2 in the *Student Guide* summarizes the steps in conducting the T test with samples less than or equal to 25.)

For samples greater than 25, the normal distribution (Table B) provides a reasonable approximation to the sampling distribution of T with mean and standard deviation (*SD*) as defined in Formulas 20-4a, b.

$$\text{mean} = \mu_T = \frac{N(N+1)}{4} \tag{20-4a}$$

$$SD = \sigma_T = \frac{N(N+1)(2N+1)}{24} \tag{20-4b}$$

With this information, $z_{observed}$ can be defined as $(T_{observed} - \mu_T)/\sigma_T$. For computational purposes, Formula 20-5 can be used.

$$z_{observed} = \frac{T_{observed} - \mu_T}{\sigma_T} = \frac{T - \dfrac{N(N+1)}{4}}{\dfrac{N(N+1)(2N+1)}{24}} \tag{20-5}$$

For example, suppose for a sample of 29 subjects, we found $T_{observed} = 50$. Using Formula 20-5, we find

$$z_{observed} = \frac{50 - \dfrac{29(30)}{4}}{\dfrac{29(30)[2(29)+1]}{24}} = \frac{-167.50}{2138.75} = -.08$$

For a two-tail test at the .01 level of significance, $z_{critical} = 2.58$ (see Table B). Since the absolute value of $z_{observed}$ does not exceed the table value, do not reject the null hypothesis.

Example Problem 20.2

Piaget's theory predicts that young children use outcome information, not intent information, to make moral judgments about an actor. This theory suggests that young children will reward positive outcomes even when the actor's intent is negative, and will punish negative outcomes even when the actor's intent is positive. To test this hypothesis ($\alpha = .05$, two-tail), data on 4–9 year olds from the hypothetical study of moral judgment can be used (Table 16-1). See Table 20-4.

TABLE 20-4 Data from the moral judgment study

Subject	Positive Outcome/ Negative Intent	Negative Outcome/ Positive Intent
1	+1	−2
2	−1	−3
3	−1	+1
4	+1	−1
5	+2	−2
6	−2	+2
7	2	−1
8	−3	+2
9	−4	+1
10	+1	+3

Provide the following information:

a. Null and alternative hypotheses
b. Discussion assumptions
c. Table showing calculations
d. $T_{observed}$ and $T_{critical}$
e. Conclusions

KRUSKAL-WALLIS ONE-WAY ANALYSIS OF VARIANCE BY RANKS

The Kruskal-Wallis one-way analysis of variance by ranks (KWANOVA) is the nonparametric analog to the one-way ANOVA (see Chapter 13). Indeed, Kruskal & Wallis (1952) constructed the KWANOVA by substituting ranks for the original data in the ANOVA.

The KWANOVA, then, is a nonparametric statistical test for analyzing data from two or more independent samples of subjects. It is used to test hypotheses about differences between two or more population averages. Sample data may be obtained from true experiments or criterion group designs.

TABLE 20-5   Students' belief scores in three classes of introductory psychology

	Instructor		
Subject	1 Humanist	2 ...	3 Behaviorist
1	3	2	8
2	4	5	7
3	6	7	3
4	5	6	5
5	8	9	7
6	9	3	2
7	6	7	4

As an example, consider the study of the correspondence between students' and instructors' beliefs about psychology and student achievement (see Chapter 6 for details). In this study, both students and instructors filled out a questionnaire regarding beliefs about psychology that arrayed respondents on a humanism-to-behaviorism scale. The study found that the closer students' beliefs were to their instructor's beliefs, the higher their achievement in psychology. One question that was not answered before is whether students chose their psychology classes on the basis of hearsay about the instructor's beliefs. That is, do students with humanistic beliefs tend to choose to take their psychology courses from instructors with humanistic beliefs, and do students with behavioristic beliefs tend to take courses from instructors with corresponding beliefs?

The KWANOVA can be used to analyze data from such a criterion group design. The data are presented in Table 20-5 for three instructors and their students. From these data, should we conclude self-selection based on compatibility of beliefs? That is, are the average scores of the students in the three instructors' classes significantly different from one another?

Purpose and Underlying Logic

The purpose of the KWANOVA is to help the researcher decide whether or not the average differences between independent groups are due to chance or to a treatment effect. The test assumes that the scores are measured on an ordinal scale but come from an underlying continuous distribution.

The KWANOVA works as follows: All scores in a table of data are rank-ordered regardless of group, from 1 (lowest) to N (highest). (Ties are treated in the usual way by taking the average of the ranks.) If the null hypothesis is true—that the distributions of scores in the populations underlying each group are identical—then the sum of the ranks in each group should be the same. If the sums are similar—well within what would be expected from sampling variability—the null hypothesis should not be rejected. If the sums are quite disparate, the null hypothesis should be rejected. To determine "how disparate is disparate" assuming the null hypothesis is true, we need a sampling distribution. For samples of size 6 per group or larger, the KWANOVA uses the chi-square sampling distribution.

The data in Table 20-5 can be used to illustrate the application of the KWANOVA. These data are presented again in Table 20-6 along with their corresponding ranks. The ranks are assigned without regard to group. Consequently, the score of 2, for example, appears once in group 2 and once in group 3. Taking the average of the first two rankings $[(1 + 2)/3 = 1.5]$, we assign a rank of 1.5 to each of the scores.

TABLE 20-6 Students' belief scores and ranks in three classes of introductory psychology

Subject	Instructor 1	Rank	Instructor 2	Rank	Instructor 3	Rank
1	3	4	2	1.5	8	18.5
2	4	6.5	5	9	7	15.5
3	6	12	7	15.5	3	4
4	5	9	6	12	5	9
5	8	18.5	9	20.5	7	15.5
6	9	20.5	3	4	2	1.5
7	6	12	7	15.5	4	6.5
Sum of ranks		82.5		78		70.5

Next, we take the sum of the ranks in each of the groups, as shown in the table. Under the null hypothesis, the sums should all be equal except for sampling error. The question remains, How likely are we to get the observed sums of 82.5, 78, and 70.5 when, in fact, we have sampled from identical populations? Before we determine the answer, the formalities of the KWANOVA are presented.

Hypotheses

The null hypothesis tested with the KWANOVA is that the distributions of scores in the populations underlying each group are identical. The alternative hypothesis is that the populations differ in their averages.

Design Requirements

The use of the KWANOVA presupposes that the following design requirements have been met:

1. There is one independent variable with two or more levels.
2. The levels of the independent variable may differ either qualitatively or quantitatively.
3. A subject may appear in one and only one cell of the design.
4. The minimum number of subjects in a group must be greater than or equal to 6 for the chi-square sampling distribution to hold.

Assumptions

The following assumptions are made in the use of the KWANOVA:

1. The scores are independently and randomly sampled from their respective treatment populations.
2. The scores in the population are continuously distributed.
3. The populations have identical shapes or are symmetric.

Computation of the KWANOVA

Assuming that the null hypothesis is true, the test statistic for the KWANOVA is defined by Formula 20-6.

$$H = \frac{12}{N(N+1)} \sum_{i=1}^{k} \frac{R_i^2}{n} - 3(N+1) \tag{20-6}$$

with $df = k - 1$ and

where:

R_i = sum of the ranks in group i
k = number of groups
n = number of subjects in a group
N = total sample size (kn)

From Table 20-6, we replace the terms in Formula 20-6 with the appropriate information and calculate H:

$$H = \frac{12}{21(21+1)} \left[\frac{(82.5)^2}{7} + \frac{(78)^2}{7} + \frac{(70.5)^2}{7} \right] - 3(21+1)$$

$$= \frac{12}{462} \left(\frac{17{,}860.5}{7} \right) - 66 = .025974(2551.5) - 66 = .27$$

The value of $H_{observed}$ can be compared with the chi-square distribution with $k - 1 = 3 - 1 = 2$ degrees of freedom in Table D. At the .05 level of significance, $H_{observed}$ would have to exceed or equal $H_{critical} = 5.99$ in order for us to reject the null hypothesis. We conclude, then, that the null hypothesis cannot be rejected. Students do not appear to be selecting instructors whose beliefs about psychology correspond to theirs.

It turns out that when there are a large number of ties, as there were in the example (see Table 20-6), $H_{observed}$ is conservative. A correction (C) can be applied to $H_{observed}$ to adjust for this conservatism. See Formula 20-7.

$$C = 1 - \frac{1}{N^3 - N} \sum_{s=1}^{N_s} (t_s^3 - t_s) \tag{20-7}$$

where:

k = number of groups
N = total sample size (kn)
t_s = frequency of the ties at score (S)
s = number of a particular tied score
N_s = number of tied scores $(s = 1, 2, \ldots, N_s)$

TABLE 20-7 Arrangement of data for the use of Formula 20-7

s	Tied Score	Frequency of Tied Scores
1	2	2
2	3	3
3	4	2
4	5	3
5	6	3
6	7	4
7	8	2
8	9	2

To use Formula 20-7, we first set up a table like Table 20-7. Then, the frequencies of the ties can be inserted into Formula 20-7 along with N, as follows:

$$C = 1 - \frac{1}{(21)^3 - 21}[(2^3 - 2) + (3^3 - 3) + \cdots + (2^3 - 2)]$$

$$= 1 - \frac{1}{9261}(6 + 24 + 6 + 24 + 24 + 60 + 6 + 6) = 1 - \left(\frac{156}{9261}\right) = .98$$

By dividing $H_{observed}$ by C, we obtain the corrected value, $H^*_{observed}$, given in Formula 20-8.

$$H^*_{observed} = \frac{H}{C} \tag{20-8}$$

From our example, we have

$$H^*_{observed} = \frac{.27}{.98} = .28$$

This result is not much of an improvement for all the work. Making this correction does not lead us to change our conclusion. In general, unless there are a great deal of ties with large frequencies, this correction will be negligible.

The steps in carrying out the KWANOVA are summarized in Procedure 20-3 in the *Student Guide*.

Example Problem 20.3

In the study of the correspondence between student achievement and students' and their instructor's beliefs about psychology, we have found that there was no relation between students' beliefs and their choice of instructor. The question remains, however, about whether there is a relation between instructors' beliefs and student achievement. For this question, data from the hypothetical study of psychological beliefs are presented in Table 20-8. Provide the following information:

a. Null and alternative hypotheses
b. Discuss assumptions
c. Table(s) showing computations
d. Observed test statistic and critical value
e. Conclusions

TABLE 20-8 Student final-exam scores in three classes (data from Table 6-1)

	Instructor		
	1	*2*	*3*
Subject	*Humanist*	· · ·	*Behaviorist*
1	7	1	10
2	6	7	8
3	9	10	2
4	10	9	6
5	2	3	9
6	3	4	2
7	10	9	5

Pairwise Post Hoc Comparisons

Just as a significant overall F test with the one-way ANOVA tells you that there is a significant difference among the k population means, a significant overall H test with the KWANOVA tells you that there is a significant difference to be found among the k populations. The next step in the analysis—if you reject the null hypothesis, that is—is to examine differences among groups by statistically testing differences between mean *ranks*.

Here we present a pairwise post hoc comparison procedure. It is none other than our old friend, Tukey's HSD test. In the case of the KWANOVA, Tukey's test is applied to mean ranks (see Mariscuilo & McSweeney, 1977). We define a mean rank as in Formula 20-9.

$$\bar{R}_i = \frac{1}{n}\sum_{p=1}^{n} r_{pi} = \frac{1}{n}(\text{sum of ranks in group } i) \qquad \textbf{(20-9)}$$

where:

$\bar{R}_i$ = mean of the ranks in group i
n = number of observations in group i (we assume equal sample sizes)
p = any unidentified observation
r_{pi} = rank assigned to observation p in group i

For example, the mean rank in group 1 in Table 20-6 is

$$\bar{R}_1 = \frac{82.5}{7} = 11.79$$

Table 20-9 contains the mean ranks for all three groups and the differences between all pairs of mean ranks. Notice that, as usual, we have ordered the mean ranks in the rows and columns according to their magnitude.

We define *HSD* in a manner similar to the definition given in Chapter 13 (Formula 13-17). The formula is presented in Formula 20-10.

$$HSD = \left(\frac{q_{(\alpha, k-1, \infty)}}{\sqrt{2}} \right) \sqrt{\text{error variance}}$$

$$= \left(\frac{q_{(\alpha, k-1, \infty)}}{\sqrt{2}} \right) \sqrt{\frac{N(N+1)}{6n}} \qquad \text{(20-10)}$$

where:

q = studentized range statistic (Table F)
N = total number of subjects in the study
n = number of subjects within each group (we assume equal sample sizes, so $N = kn$)

As an example of the use of Tukey's post hoc test for differences in mean ranks, we will use the data from Tables 20-6 and 20-9. However, a caveat is in order. Since we failed to reject the null hypotheses, we normally would not carry out post hoc comparisons. We do so here solely to illustrate the application of Tukey's procedure as applied to the KWANOVA.

TABLE 20-9 Differences among mean ranks from the hypothetical study of beliefs about psychology (data from Table 20-6)

Mean Rank (Group Number)	Mean Rank (Group Number)		
	10.07(3)	11.14(2)	11.79(1)
(3) 10.07	—	1.07	1.72
(2) 11.14		—	.65
(1) 11.79			—

A first step is to determine the value of q. In our example, with $\alpha = .05$ and $k = 3$, q would be:

$$q_{(.05, 3, \infty)} = 3.31$$

Next, we insert the value of q and the sample sizes (N and n) into Formula 20-10 and calculate the value of *HSD*:

$$HSD = \frac{3.31}{\sqrt{2}} \sqrt{\frac{21(21+1)}{6(7)}} = 2.34(3.32) = 7.76$$

We should reject the null hypothesis of no difference in pairwise population means for those differences in Table 20-9 that exceed 7.76. As expected (remember that the null hypothesis was not rejected), none of the differences in this table exceeds 7.76.

SUMMARY

This chapter presents three commonly used nonparametric statistical tests. The first, the *Mann-Whitney U test,* is the nonparametric analog to the *t* test for differences between the means of two independent groups (see Chapter 12). The second nonparametric test, the *Wilcoxon T test,* is the nonparametric analog to the dependent-samples *t* test presented in Chapter 12. And the third test, the *Kruskal-Wallis one-way analysis of variance by ranks,* is the nonparametric analog of the one-way ANOVA (Chapter 13). The purpose and underlying rationale and the procedures for computing and interpreting each of these statistical techniques are presented. Particular attention is paid to the hypotheses tested and the assumptions underlying these tests. Procedures for conducting post hoc tests using Tukey's method are presented for the KWANOVA.

ANSWERS TO EXAMPLE PROBLEMS

1. **a.** H_0: The distributions of moral judgments in the populations of children and adults from which these groups were drawn are identical.

   H_1: The moral judgments in the populations of children and adults from which these groups were drawn differ in their means:

   $\mu_C \neq \mu_A$

   b. 1. *Independent and random sampling:* Sampling procedures suggest that subjects were independently sampled from each population.

   2. *Distributions of similar shape:* We are unable to test with the frequency distribution, given the small number of scores.

   c.

	Group									
	A	*A*	*A*	*A*	*A*	*C*	*C*	*C*	*C*	*C*
Original	−5	−3	−2	−2	−2	−1	−1	+1	+1	+2
Moral Judgment Rank	1	2	4	4	4	6.5	6.5	8.5	8.5	10

   d. $U = 25 + 30/2 - 40 = 0$

   e. .004

   f. Reject H_0. Conclude that there is a relationship between age and the basis on which a moral judgment is made.

2. **a.** H_0: The distributions of scores in the two populations are identical.

   H_1: The distributions of scores differ only in their means, with $\mu_1 \neq \mu_2$.

   b. Assumptions:

   1. *Independence and random sampling:* Subjects were randomly sampled and received their treatments individually.
   2. *Underline continuous distribution:* We assume that the rating procedure reflects an underlying continuous dimension.
   3. *Equal distributions:* A sample size of 10 is too small to examine adequately the assumption of equal population distributions except for means. However, the variability of scores in the two conditions and the frequency of each score value suggest that this assumption may be tenable.

   c. Calculations:

   d. $T_{obs.} = 19.5$; $T_{crit.(.05/2, N=10)} = 8$

Subject	+Outcome −Intent	−Outcome +Intent	d_p	Rank	Sign
1	+1	−2	+3	6	+
2	−1	−3	+2	3.5	+
3	−1	+1	−2	3.5	−
4	+1	−1	+2	3.5	+
5	+2	−2	+4	7.5	+
6	−2	+2	−4	7.5	−
7	−2	−1	−1	1	−
8	−3	+2	−5	9.5	−
9	−4	+1	−5	9.5	−
10	+1	+3	−2	3.5	−

sum of $(+) = 6 + 3.5 + 3.5 + 7.5 = 19.5$

sum of $(-) = 3.5 + 7.5 + 1 + 9.5 + 9.5 + 3.5 = 34.5$

   e. Conclude that the null hypothesis cannot be rejected. Inspection of the data leads us to surmise that children aged 4-6 years (subjects 1–5) may very well base their judgments on outcomes: Children beyond 6 years of age apparently do not. However, larger samples are needed to investigate this further.

3. **a.** H_0: The distributions of achievement scores in the k populations are identical.

   H_1: The distributions of scores in the k populations differ only in their means.

   b. 1. The scores are independently and randomly sampled from their respective treatment populations. Insufficient information is given to evaluate independence. Subjects are self-selected into classes, so we infer to populations "like those represented by the students," at best.

   2. The scores in the population are continuously distributed. By the nature of achievement tests, we assume an underlying continuum. The observed scores are measured on at least an ordinal scale.

3. The populations have identical shapes or are both symmetric. By the nature of achievement test scores, we shall assume this to be true; sample sizes are too small to evaluate the assumption.

c. Computations:

Instructor 1	Rank	Instructor 2	Rank	Instructor 3	Rank
7	11.5	1	1	10	19.5
6	9.5	7	11.5	8	13
9	15.5	10	19.5	2	3
10	19.5	9	15.5	6	9.5
2	3	3	5.5	9	15.5
3	5.5	4	7	2	3
10	19.5	9	15.5	5	8
Sum	84.0		75.5		71.5

$$H = \frac{12}{21(21+1)} \left[\frac{(84)^2 + (75.5)^2 + (71.5)^2}{7} \right] - 3(21+1) = .025974 \left(\frac{17,868.5}{7} \right) - 66$$

$$= .025974(2552.64) - 66 = 66.30 - 66 = .30$$

$$C = 1 - \frac{1}{(21)^3 - 21}[(3^3 - 3) + (2^3 - 2) + \cdots + (4^3 - 4)]$$

$$= 1 - \frac{1}{9261}(24 + 6 + 6 + 6 + 60 + 60) = 1 - \left(\frac{162}{9261} \right) = 1 - .017 = .983$$

s	Tied Score	Frequency of Tied Scores
1	2	3
2	3	2
3	6	2
4	7	2
5	9	4
6	10	4

d. $H^*_{obs.} = .305$; $H_{crit.(.05, df=2)} = 5.99$

e. Do not reject the null hypothesis. There is insufficient evidence to conclude a relation between instructor beliefs about psychology and student achievement.

EXERCISES

Hudley & Graham (1993) examined the effects of attribution retraining (experimental group) with attention- and no-treatment control groups on aggressive and nonaggressive boys' perceptions of negative intent in ambiguous situations. They hypothesized that attribution retraining, but not the control conditions, would decrease aggressive boys' perceptions of negative intent. In the following exercises, test this hypothesis using data from Table

4-1. (Note: these exercises parallel those in Chapters 12 and 13. You might want to review your findings in these chapters before proceeding.)

1. Test the null hypothesis ($\alpha = .05$, one-tail) that the mean difference between pretest ratings of aggressive and nonaggressive boys is 0. Include the following.

   a. Null and alternative hypotheses
   b. Assumptions underlying your statistical test
   c. Statistical test
   d. Conclusions

2. Test the null hypothesis ($\alpha = .05$, one-tail) of no change in aggressive boys' perceptions of negative intent from pre- to posttest. Include the following.

   a. Null and alternative hypotheses
   b. Assumptions underlying your statistical test
   c. Statistical test
   d. Conclusions

3. Test the null hypothesis ($\alpha = .05$) that the mean differences between the three groups of aggressive boys (experimental, attention, no treatment) arose at posttest by chance. Include the following.

   a. Null and alternative hypotheses
   b. Assumptions underlying your statistical test
   c. Statistical test
   d. Particular comparisons of means if relevant
   e. Conclusions

ANSWERS TO EXERCISES

1. a. H_0: The distribution of intent ratings in the populations from which the two groups were drawn are identical.
   H_1: The distributions of ratings from the populations differ only in their means.

   b. *Independence and random sampling:* The procedures in this experiment suggest that this assumption was met.
   Distributions of similar shape: The sample sizes are small but the data tend to be symmetric.

   c. The Mann-Whitney U test (along with the Wilcoxon statistic and the z test provided by SPSS) yielded the following[6]:

---

[6]SPSS Program Setup:
NPAR TESTS
  /M-W=pretest BY aggress(1 2)
  /STATISTICS=DESCRIPTIVES QUARTILES [*Note:* Not shown in c above.]
  /MISSING ANALYSIS.

- - - - - Mann-Whitney U - Wilcoxon Rank Sum W Test

PRETEST
by AGGRESS Aggression

Mean Rank	Cases		
22.81	18	AGGRESS = 1.00	Aggressive
14.19	18	AGGRESS = 2.00	Nonaggressive
	36	Total	

Exact			Corrected for Ties	
U	W	2-Tailed P	Z	2-Tailed P
84.5	410.5	.0129	−2.5323	.0113

d. Consistent with the *t*-test findings (Exercise 2 in Chapter 12), the *U* test leads us to reject the null hypothesis. Conclude that nonaggressive boys perceive, on average, less negative intent in ambiguous situations than do aggressive boys.

2. a. H_0: The distributions of intent ratings in the populations from which the two groups were drawn are identical.
   H_1: The distributions of ratings from the populations differ only in their means.
   b. *Independence and random sampling:* The procedures in this experiment suggest that this assumption was met.
   Underlying continuous distribution: We assume the rating procedure reflects an underlying perceived negative-intent distribution.
   Distributions of similar shape: The sample sizes are small but the data tend to be symmetric.
   c. The Wilcoxon *T* test (using a *z* test provided by SPSS) yielded the following[7]:

- - - - - Wilcoxon Matched-Pairs Signed-Ranks Test

POSTTEST
with PRETEST

Mean Rank	Cases		
4.75	4	− Ranks	(PRETEST LT POSTTEST)
8.00	9	+ Ranks	(PRETEST GT POSTTEST)
	5	Ties	(PRETEST EQ POSTTEST)
	18	Total	

Z = −1.8520   2-Tailed P = .0640

---

[7]SPSS Program Setup:
NPAR TEST
 /WILCOXON=posttest WITH pretest (PAIRED)
 /STATISTICS=DESCRIPTIVES QUARTILES [*Note:* Not shown in c above.]
 /MISSING ANALYSIS.

For a one-tail test, $z_{critical} = 1.65$. Since there is some concern with using the normal distribution for samples of less than 25, I computed $T_{observed}$: 39. From Table N with $N = 18$ and $\alpha = .05$, $T_{critical} = 40$ (at .025).

    d. The T test leads us to reject the null hypothesis. Conclude that aggressive boys perceive, on average, less negative intent in ambiguous situations at posttest than at pretest. Note that this was a one-tail test. The two-tail test in Exercise 3 in Chapter 12 led us not to reject the null hypothesis as would a two-tail test with z above, but not with T (significant at .05 two-tail).

3. a. H_0: The distribution of intent ratings in the populations from which the three groups were drawn are identical.

      H_1: The distributions of ratings in the populations differ only in their means.

    b. *Independence and random sampling:* The procedures in this experiment suggest that this assumption was met.

      Underlying continuous distribution: We assume the rating procedure reflects an underlying perceived negative-intent distribution.

      Distributions of similar shape: The sample sizes are small but the data tend to be symmetric.

    c. The Kruskal-Wallis one-way ANOVA yielded the following[8]:

      - - - - - Kruskal-Wallis 1-Way ANOVA

      POSTTEST
      by GROUP   Treatment Group

Mean Rank	*Cases*		
3.58	6	GROUP = 1	Attribution Retraining
12.83	6	GROUP = 2	Attribution Control
12.08	6	GROUP = 3	Control
	18	Total	

Chi-Square	*D.F.*	*Significance*	*Chi-Square*	*D.F.*	*Significance*
			Corrected for Ties		
11.1140	2	.0039	11.3963	2	.0034

    d. The KWANOVA leads us to reject the null hypothesis. Post hoc comparisons using Tukey's method are in order:

$$HSD = \frac{3.31}{\sqrt{2}} \sqrt{\frac{18(19)}{6(6)}} = 2.34(3.08) = 7.21$$

---

[8]SPSS Program Setup:
NPAR TESTS
  /K-W=posttest BY group(1 3)
  /STATISTICS DESCRIPTIVES QUARTILES [*Note:* Not all shown.]
  /MISSING ANALYSIS.

The experimental group perceived, on average, less negative intent than did the other two groups.

e. Conclude that attribution retraining had a statistically significant impact, reducing aggressive boys' mean perception of negative intent in ambiguous situations as compared to control group peers. This conclusion is consistent with that in Exercise 2 in Chapter 13.

Appendix I: Review of Summation Notation

- Common Mathematical Notation
- Rules of Summation

This appendix is a brief review of some basic concepts in using summation notation. In particular, I present the concepts of simple and multiple summation notation along with some fundamental rules for working with summations. Since students in elementary statistics usually vary tremendously in their previous training in mathematics, this material will be more familiar to some students than others. Spend as much time as is necessary with this review, since mastery of these concepts is important to an understanding of the mathematical concepts and formulas presented throughout the textbook and proofs usually presented in footnotes.

COMMON MATHEMATICAL NOTATION

In most research, one or more variables are selected for study, and scores on these variables are collected on several subjects. Thus, the researcher typically wants to describe a set of scores or make inferences based on a group of scores rather than on single scores. When we compute statistics for these scores, then, it is useful to have some common symbols or notation to represent groups of scores and the arithmetic operations on them.

The capital letter X is often used to represent scores on a particular variable. (If one or more variables are collected in a study, the capital letters Y and Z are often used to denote these variables.) For example, suppose a researcher collected the scores for seven students on a measure of mathematical achievement—the McCormick Arithmetic Test (see Table

TABLE A1-1 Scores of students on the McCormick
Arithmetic Test

Student	Test Score (X)	Score Notation
1	48	X_1
2	35	X_2
3	50	X_3
4	19	X_4
5	43	X_5
6	47	X_6
7	21	X_7

A1-1). The capital letter X can be used to denote the variable mathematical achievement, as measured by the McCormick Arithmetic Test. The seven scores represent specific values of X earned by each of the seven students. So that we can distinguish one score from another, each value of X is customarily given a subscript corresponding to the identification number of the subject who received that score. Therefore, the scores in Table A1-1 can be denoted from X_1 to X_7 (see the third column).

In general, if there are N scores, the subscripts will range from 1 to N. Often, it is useful to refer to any single score in a distribution of X's. This single score is denoted in this textbook by the subscript p and is referred to as the pth score in the distribution—X_p (where p refers to persons). Note that X_p refers to the score of any unidentified person p, and it does not denote a particular person's score.

Simple Summation Notation

In order to compute many of the statistics in this book, we must sum all or a portion of the scores collected. The symbol Σ (an oversize Greek capital letter sigma) is used to denote the operation of summing or adding a group of numbers. Thus, ΣX means the sum of all values of X. In the example data in Table A1-1, $\Sigma X = 48 + 35 + 50 + 19 + 43 + 47 + 21 = 263$.

As noted earlier, sometimes we need to sum only a portion of the scores collected. The summation sign can be modified as follows to indicate more specifically the values that are to be added:

$$\sum_{p=1}^{N} X$$

The small notations above and below the summation sign are referred to as the "limits of the summation." The symbol is read as "sum of X from $p = 1$ to N." It means that the values of X_1 to X_n should be added:

$$\sum_{p=1}^{N} X = X_1 + X_2 + X_3 + \cdots + X_N$$

This notation can be used to indicate that only a portion of scores within a group are to be summed. For example $\sum_{p=3}^{6} X$ indicates that the sum of X_3, X_4, X_5, and X_6, should be taken. In the example data in Table A1-1:

$$\sum_{p=5}^{N} X = X_5 + X_6 + X_7 = 43 + 47 + 21 = 111$$

Multiple Summation Notation

In many research studies, data are available on more than one group of subjects. For example, subjects may be randomly assigned to a control or experimental group. The respective treatments are administered, and subjects in all groups are given a posttest upon completion of the treatment. Scores on the dependent variable are available on subjects in each group.

As an example, suppose a researcher studying verbal learning is investigating the type of strategies that produce the greatest learning of a list of words. She randomly assigns five college sophomores to one of three conditions. In one condition, subjects are presented with a list of 10 words (to keep the example data 10 or less) and instructed to learn the words by constructing a story using the list of words (meaningful strategy). In another condition, subjects are presented with the same list of words and instructed to learn the words by repeating them over and over (rote strategy). In the third condition, subjects are presented with the same list of words, but they were not instructed to use any particular strategy in learning the words (control group). At the end of the session, subjects are asked to recall as many of the words as they can remember. The data from the hypothetical experiment are presented in Table A1-2.

In research designs such as the one described earlier, it is often necessary to specify particular scores within a specific group. In this case, the notation must specify both the group and the subjects within the groups. Two subscripts are necessary to denote scores in such designs. By convention, any single score is denoted as X_{pi}, where p refers to the subject number and i refers to the group number. Thus X_{13} refers to subject 1 in group 3. Similarly, X_{51} refers to subject 5 in group 1. For the data in Table A1-2,

$$X_{13} = 5 \quad \text{and} \quad X_{51} = 6$$

The summation sign is also used to denote the operation of summing scores within a particular group in these more complex designs. For example, $\sum_{p=1}^{N} X_{p3}$ means that the scores

TABLE A1-2 Number of words recalled (X) in hypothetical verbal-learning study

Meaningful Strategy Group	Rote Strategy Group	Control Group
8	4	5
7	5	5
10	7	7
9	6	4
6	6	6

of subjects 1 to *N* in group 3 should be added. The limits of the summation identify the subjects' scores to be added, and the second subscript for *X* identifies the group. In the example study described before,

$$\sum_{p=1}^{N} X_{p3} = X_{13} + X_{23} + X_{33} + X_{43} + X_{53}$$

$$= 5 + 5 + 7 + 4 + 6 = 27$$

If the group number is specified only generally by an *i*, it means that the scores of the subjects identified by the limits of the summation should be summed separately within each group. Thus, $\sum_{p=1}^{n} X_{pi}$ is a direction to add each subject's scores within each group. This procedure will yield *i* sums. For example, for the data in Table A1-2, $\sum_{p=1}^{n} X_{pi}$ is a direction to take the sum of the scores of subjects within each group. This procedure will result in three sums:

$$\sum_{p=1}^{n} X_{p1} = 8 + 7 + 10 + 9 + 6 = 40$$

$$\sum_{p=1}^{n} X_{p2} = 4 + 5 + 7 + 6 + 6 = 28$$

$$\sum_{p=1}^{n} X_{p3} = 5 + 5 + 7 + 4 + 6 = 27$$

Now suppose we wished to add the sums of all subjects' scores within each group over the *i* groups. This operation is denoted as

$$\sum_{i=1}^{k} \left(\sum_{p=1}^{n} X_{pi} \right)$$

This symbol directs us to add the scores of subjects 1 to *N* within each group ($\sum_{p=1}^{n} X_{pi}$) and then add these sums over the *k* groups [$\sum_{i=1}^{k} (\sum_{p=1}^{n} X_{pi})$]. Note that this procedure yields the total sum of all scores.

For the example data shown in Table A1-2,

$$\sum_{i=1}^{k} \left(\sum_{p=1}^{n} X_{pi} \right) = \sum_{p=1}^{n} X_{p1} + \sum_{p=1}^{n} X_{p2} + \sum_{p=1}^{n} X_{p3} = 40 + 28 + 27 = 95$$

RULES OF SUMMATION

There are several rules that are helpful in using the summation sign in algebraic operation. These rules concern the summation of both variables and constants. (Constants are typically denoted by lowercase *a*, *b*, or *c*.)

Summation of a Constant

The rule for the summation of a constant is that if a is a constant value over N persons, then

$$\sum_{p=1}^{n} a_p = na$$

This expression says that the sum of a constant taken N times is N times the constant.
This equality can be loosely demonstrated as follows:

$$\sum_{p=1}^{n} a_p = a_1 + a_2 + \cdots + a_n = na$$

To take a specific example, suppose that $a = 2$. Then

$$\sum_{p=1}^{n=4} a_p = 2 + 2 + 2 + 2 = 4(2) = 8$$

This rule also applies to multiple summation notation. If a is a constant value over n persons and k groups, then $\sum_{i=1}^{k}\sum_{p=1}^{n} a = kna$. This expression says that the sum of a constant taken over n subjects and k groups is kn times the constant.
This equality can also be easily demonstrated:

$$\sum_{i=1}^{k}\sum_{p=1}^{n} a_{pi} = \sum_{i=1}^{k}(a_1 + a_2 + \cdots + a_n)_i = \sum_{i=1}^{k}(na)_i$$

$$= (na)_1 + (na)_2 + \cdots + (na)_k = k(na)$$

Suppose that $a = 4$. Then

$$\sum_{i-1}^{k=3}\sum_{p=1}^{n=5} a = 3 \times 5 \times 4 = 60$$

Summation of a Variable Multiplied by a Constant

The rule for the summation of a variable multiplied by a constant is that if a is a constant over N persons, then

$$\sum_{p=1}^{N} aX_p = a\sum_{p=1}^{N} X_p$$

That is, the sum of a constant times a variable equals the constant times the sum of the variable. This equality can be demonstrated as follows:

$$\sum_{p=1}^{N} aX_p = aX_1 + aX_2 + \cdots + aX_N$$

$$= a(X_1 + X_2 + \cdots + X_N) \qquad \text{(by the distributive law of multiplication)}$$

$$= a\sum_{p=1}^{N} X_p$$

Suppose $a = 2$. For the hypothetical data in Table A1-1, what is the value of $\sum_{p=1}^{N=7} aX_p$? Since $\sum_{p=1}^{N=7} X_p = 263$ (as computed before),

$$\sum_{p=2}^{N=7} aX_p = a\sum_{p=1}^{N=7} X_p = 2(263) = 526$$

This rule can also be applied to multiple summation notation. If a is a constant value over n persons in each group of k groups, then

$$\sum_{i=1}^{k}\sum_{p=1}^{n} aX = a\sum_{i=1}^{k}\sum_{p=1}^{n} X$$

That is, the sum over subjects and groups of a constant times a variable equals the constant times the sum of the variable over persons and groups.

This equality can be shown as follows:

$$\sum_{i=1}^{k}\sum_{p=1}^{n} aX_{pi} = \sum_{i=1}^{k}(aX_1 + aX_2 + \cdots + aX_n) = \sum_{i=1}^{k}[a(X_1 + X_2 + \cdots + X_n)]$$

$$= \sum_{i=1}^{k}\left(a\sum_{p=1}^{n} X_{pi}\right) = a\sum_{p=1}^{n} X_{p1} + a\sum_{p=1}^{n} X_{p2} + \cdots + a\sum_{p=1}^{n} X_{pk}$$

$$= a\sum_{i=1}^{k}\sum_{p=1}^{n} X_{pi}$$

Suppose $a = 3$. For the hypothetical data in Table A1-2, what is the value of $\sum_{i=1}^{k}\sum_{p=1}^{N} a X_{pi}$? Since $\sum_{i=1}^{k}\sum_{p=1}^{N} X_{pi} = 95$ (as computed before),

$$\sum_{i=1}^{k}\sum_{p=1}^{n} aX_{pi} = a\sum_{i=1}^{k}\sum_{p=1}^{n} X_{pi} = 3(95) = 285$$

Distributive Rule

The distributive rule for a summation sign is that if addition or subtraction of variables (or constants) is the only operation to be executed before summation, then

$$\sum_{p=1}^{N}(X_p + Y_p) = \sum_{p=1}^{N}X_p + \sum_{p=1}^{N}Y_p$$

Similarly,

$$\sum_{p=1}^{N}(X_p - Y_p) = \sum_{p=1}^{N}X_p - \sum_{p=1}^{N}Y_p$$

That is, the distributive rule states that the summation can be distributed across variables (or constants) when they are added or subtracted from one another. This equality can be shown as follows:

$$\sum_{p=1}^{N}(X_p + Y_p) = (X_1 + Y_1) + (X_2 + Y_2) + \cdots + (X_N + Y_N)$$
$$= X_1 + Y_1 + X_2 + Y_2 + \cdots + X_N + Y_N$$
$$= (X_1 + X_2 + \cdots + X_N) + (Y_1 + Y_2 + \cdots + Y_N)$$
$$= \sum_{p=1}^{N}X_p + \sum_{p=1}^{N}Y_p$$

(A similar proof can be given for subtraction.)

The summation sign can also be distributed across constants or the sum of differences of a variable and a constant. For example, suppose $a = 5$ and $\sum_{p=1}^{N-4}X_p = 8$. Then

$$\sum_{p=1}^{N=4}(X_p + a) = \sum_{p=1}^{N=4}X_p + \sum_{p=1}^{N=4}a$$

Since $\sum_{p=1}^{N}a = Na$, this is

$$\sum_{p=1}^{N}X_p + Na = 8 + 4(5) = 28$$

Appendix II
Miscellaneous Tables

TABLE A   Random numbers

49	80	44	40	17	36	34	42	39	88	73	94	16	26	68	13	65	41	03	27	29	57	51	23	85
71	41	61	58	85	31	20	67	55	96	55	49	29	71	24	95	03	97	08	53	37	55	99	29	19
30	93	07	46	85	87	87	55	96	83	66	69	90	47	32	86	80	17	84	97	30	75	81	87	42
40	07	20	48	57	20	98	65	37	11	35	92	39	54	81	33	67	23	97	09	89	60	81	94	25
46	41	72	26	06	88	75	62	89	68	61	26	95	10	12	35	53	94	97	02	48	39	72	97	35
10	17	03	63	01	80	47	36	12	35	32	73	84	24	00	83	94	11	86	74	73	11	64	43	54
62	26	23	24	03	86	82	81	67	22	57	64	92	39	12	90	09	82	70	98	24	30	76	50	90
50	39	48	14	26	63	75	14	53	66	27	20	49	24	77	02	44	51	42	11	19	33	15	42	59
64	63	91	00	31	64	43	94	43	39	15	48	76	74	14	17	95	14	74	11	13	97	04	04	13
39	25	52	69	73	69	93	07	69	37	56	71	27	33	43	33	91	31	55	64	40	26	38	43	40
43	36	57	16	53	27	42	48	99	46	72	53	53	93	66	46	86	23	06	34	55	35	37	67	24
41	02	06	51	42	75	22	46	96	51	63	43	01	10	62	03	40	88	99	95	32	12	84	10	45
54	26	22	92	54	74	96	90	04	77	99	96	33	82	92	44	44	99	88	44	97	59	39	07	36
68	99	03	52	80	83	06	20	33	72	06	19	79	88	78	04	33	98	55	87	90	12	49	91	67
62	70	79	56	96	92	90	11	82	75	64	64	78	34	90	12	89	24	68	21	97	04	46	20	89
82	40	59	90	46	07	88	80	91	80	95	16	48	38	00	03	89	14	78	47	49	02	74	11	13
34	82	79	57	23	06	60	90	93	03	36	30	99	01	02	35	52	61	42	24	28	11	58	56	94
78	88	89	81	84	88	50	83	16	26	40	17	87	22	03	58	54	40	40	75	07	96	93	35	36
26	45	11	29	68	49	80	75	95	67	99	88	15	73	70	11	60	72	57	35	94	70	42	64	99
73	32	97	51	44	85	39	97	11	59	70	47	36	64	63	58	78	76	11	32	14	24	27	99	22
89	06	96	86	15	24	68	32	48	27	98	64	57	36	63	21	91	95	99	64	99	50	43	34	27
09	31	15	54	12	64	99	43	34	73	62	89	39	09	18	56	92	52	77	41	67	60	84	35	07
76	05	02	55	08	84	64	24	02	57	07	16	44	22	66	73	72	04	85	26	13	53	10	55	98
33	36	23	95	22	29	92	46	98	53	74	17	99	28	04	10	08	94	67	50	92	60	89	88	47
62	71	09	60	07	02	51	85	10	01	05	41	79	56	13	29	75	27	00	95	77	51	74	61	25
99	87	91	83	51	87	10	32	16	56	37	47	79	72	63	14	85	78	93	51	05	03	60	13	77
61	68	57	26	37	55	49	88	18	86	16	57	17	52	46	44	83	12	99	88	32	52	81	55	42
19	68	38	77	23	04	83	60	01	33	92	83	13	22	90	47	80	55	61	47	24	54	44	54	83
06	45	91	25	34	46	65	31	91	72	27	61	17	09	58	55	13	70	57	06	36	97	24	09	04
05	54	42	00	96	03	22	08	71	01	23	76	21	34	93	47	99	65	70	57	53	13	84	09	65
47	68	34	99	99	86	24	96	58	43	61	76	80	53	04	83	70	29	84	59	55	37	64	89	65
71	53	16	31	16	48	09	53	16	87	40	65	70	98	63	06	75	56	63	87	26	03	34	06	27
96	10	13	29	15	66	65	82	89	33	49	89	02	89	51	76	11	48	06	48	46	02	24	77	32
35	56	71	27	37	02	88	55	44	67	31	88	75	77	86	19	05	32	65	29	76	16	14	07	79
09	74	16	98	95	67	50	90	12	37	71	83	51	71	50	68	76	40	42	02	09	25	03	20	28
66	33	45	26	19	03	47	24	43	95	35	32	26	17	95	57	34	62	07	78	13	91	86	91	31
91	17	40	84	49	21	39	22	43	61	49	79	78	18	53	05	41	23	17	25	84	48	76	11	61
53	48	84	07	83	50	54	83	73	07	99	20	53	86	59	90	80	96	86	50	47	10	06	84	45
02	61	52	76	02	85	24	87	46	71	10	49	96	29	49	67	27	13	22	72	19	78	70	81	37
33	41	27	63	80	19	53	38	15	28	75	82	36	05	74	52	02	78	95	26	30	23	61	64	60
35	78	69	34	38	90	50	65	76	87	94	29	64	89	95	94	56	87	09	19	98	40	02	03	81
72	07	31	82	08	62	64	83	02	32	57	08	37	17	37	42	86	51	42	57	19	42	46	13	95
72	87	34	16	47	89	51	73	07	84	00	95	44	55	66	06	33	34	34	48	33	73	66	06	64
39	71	06	66	46	01	06	01	52	68	29	52	64	46	70	48	43	96	74	49	55	92	34	09	29
32	74	72	84	15	53	53	47	60	82	64	01	17	84	58	14	79	91	48	42	80	74	89	51	00
60	53	30	82	01	54	39	19	06	11	91	78	06	08	70	47	36	75	39	37	07	56	85	33	20
10	34	29	05	06	08	10	96	00	86	89	79	11	08	35	65	06	17	47	66	43	72	09	86	03
12	14	45	04	52	07	86	40	98	94	60	76	39	50	65	90	25	92	28	13	39	58	80	43	85
16	23	80	78	88	49	12	69	20	48	51	89	28	76	03	46	17	29	18	57	43	00	47	47	85

TABLE A   Continued

30	22	46	03	21	27	72	04	62	69	98	38	28	58	61	04	66	21	95	89	41	09	39	42	58
08	35	97	29	04	44	36	49	66	06	35	42	62	87	46	10	22	89	76	22	99	94	86	30	61
91	12	55	30	10	87	52	67	31	03	87	26	54	50	94	18	70	88	65	41	36	18	34	66	37
64	22	05	51	61	87	94	69	22	21	29	63	90	17	84	28	89	57	73	84	50	66	80	69	70
27	70	20	11	18	35	40	41	62	74	89	77	89	66	42	61	85	48	56	45	28	32	37	55	47
74	99	31	63	57	24	02	69	87	73	16	94	68	09	58	10	21	23	55	81	84	16	02	90	98
23	97	94	37	13	67	20	02	69	13	97	62	08	50	14	77	33	71	89	03	68	85	74	05	09
64	95	46	98	67	66	47	13	20	33	65	45	70	14	74	00	49	35	61	07	76	60	71	43	72
21	01	00	87	49	56	67	58	41	49	86	85	69	19	41	79	79	68	47	72	93	71	81	91	36
65	82	97	65	71	21	30	84	84	76	02	15	48	85	32	44	80	77	26	87	84	51	23	47	13
77	35	18	33	69	38	84	94	80	28	72	03	96	70	28	97	74	36	48	38	84	57	71	43	90
48	32	29	81	42	38	07	53	69	56	78	05	66	81	24	69	04	95	80	66	12	58	97	78	97
60	90	60	81	94	01	20	85	25	83	34	09	74	26	39	16	85	48	56	99	61	46	80	34	40
25	89	80	80	60	30	10	56	01	57	08	44	35	05	96	94	23	80	59	46	37	85	67	00	92
28	78	79	95	51	68	53	12	03	30	50	76	80	53	00	11	91	31	06	06	29	91	41	32	53
61	56	13	41	34	26	82	52	53	17	70	84	40	59	29	07	89	01	32	39	96	00	71	60	11
34	98	67	81	85	59	17	73	00	14	90	37	78	80	91	84	38	25	31	79	24	75	60	43	42
52	44	08	36	02	00	21	93	24	02	69	28	37	90	58	87	42	13	00	23	70	34	42	30	32
85	10	12	24	05	65	60	56	27	70	56	50	97	11	16	49	24	83	32	68	16	84	71	33	35
69	96	88	30	84	23	49	90	29	36	73	70	52	71	86	68	27	70	58	88	82	17	24	68	53
36	23	26	32	29	46	29	52	42	49	59	22	74	29	72	70	44	21	76	35	43	80	41	51	47
78	98	22	94	62	75	77	03	92	66	90	71	70	45	38	58	50	33	62	42	52	04	02	40	16
46	49	49	64	58	59	15	57	81	16	12	85	53	85	54	16	72	21	99	11	57	10	87	90	44
22	52	34	57	24	38	66	45	88	33	34	57	94	64	96	94	02	23	83	50	12	85	81	93	94
34	05	19	39	69	53	41	96	20	72	37	38	93	65	05	11	27	44	06	45	46	22	66	62	08
89	78	89	51	56	90	71	19	35	96	92	75	08	44	54	04	98	62	12	02	38	04	94	73	41
66	50	53	86	58	99	76	51	57	25	11	44	85	94	95	71	96	02	87	08	74	46	16	84	45
80	04	56	65	27	80	33	83	83	38	45	38	02	29	92	09	33	71	95	74	94	48	08	68	10
16	81	21	96	08	92	18	66	72	55	17	21	17	01	42	39	61	27	98	77	86	49	58	53	40
26	82	01	14	90	49	61	45	24	96	33	27	30	15	41	41	51	29	23	96	68	19	37	59	41
63	26	98	22	45	12	65	59	52	08	50	99	37	00	98	98	51	09	14	49	02	18	01	88	62
45	27	28	09	62	88	67	82	88	55	90	54	85	69	89	96	34	88	27	47	73	22	71	38	79
50	51	74	78	90	07	30	98	49	91	36	14	92	39	81	76	36	78	89	80	80	08	32	18	81
45	66	04	40	01	79	79	64	18	85	08	23	15	84	00	33	05	75	13	34	46	89	62	02	23
84	87	93	01	33	33	12	96	85	16	12	44	89	42	73	79	93	25	48	37	64	14	52	25	48
22	13	16	96	98	94	74	19	83	79	24	00	65	39	63	70	37	64	96	18	56	58	06	67	27
78	62	46	06	01	17	15	78	42	76	43	08	22	21	97	80	50	26	42	32	77	55	84	11	99
37	11	46	97	33	94	70	42	62	30	44	68	69	25	55	55	35	64	49	92	23	92	73	04	87
68	28	09	51	12	92	15	85	34	96	06	66	26	38	24	76	56	78	65	89	06	88	53	99	65
80	89	76	02	33	48	80	09	95	74	97	01	75	90	23	36	80	65	45	18	20	67	06	14	04
12	42	69	85	28	06	99	64	24	24	89	22	67	45	90	26	23	01	58	43	52	97	94	24	16
27	28	10	80	58	75	16	92	18	95	54	50	00	85	08	74	29	90	73	21	12	01	93	47	48
62	92	52	02	30	11	31	02	95	49	21	50	46	53	72	53	75	10	38	55	01	72	14	16	22
75	68	68	48	30	08	23	10	88	88	38	73	41	88	42	01	12	65	77	81	17	87	72	58	70
95	87	66	67	61	53	94	73	82	56	68	26	74	96	33	99	08	80	84	27	04	91	77	57	57
79	93	68	75	78	10	77	98	93	67	81	59	53	82	79	79	57	86	44	67	15	41	01	02	65
58	04	29	41	30	87	96	49	84	29	82	80	45	37	04	70	48	43	50	60	33	73	70	86	16
76	07	90	92	74	74	16	80	41	64	25	94	13	26	68	88	82	68	43	23	44	33	51	27	04
88	25	38	94	34	29	91	12	72	63	04	65	22	20	73	84	09	49	68	68	33	04	06	29	46
84	50	15	11	24	27	86	97	53	01	69	59	74	42	92	02	09	32	96	00	80	55	60	64	21
32	94	52	54	14	44	04	96	98	92	39	80	96	36	84	63	46	39	06	31	05	75	70	49	33

Source: Generated with SPSS statistical package.

TABLE B   Proportions of area under the standard normal curve

(1) z	(2) area between mean and z	(3) area below z	(4) area above z	(1) z	(2) area between mean and z	(3) area below z	(4) area above z
0.00	0.0000	0.5000	0.5000	0.55	0.2088	0.7088	0.2912
0.01	0.0040	0.5040	0.4960	0.56	0.2123	0.7123	0.2877
0.02	0.0080	0.5080	0.4920	0.57	0.2157	0.7157	0.2843
0.03	0.0120	0.5120	0.4880	0.58	0.2190	0.7190	0.2810
0.04	0.0160	0.5160	0.4840	0.59	0.2224	0.7224	0.2776
0.05	0.0199	0.5199	0.4801	0.60	0.2257	0.7257	0.2743
0.06	0.0239	0.5239	0.4761	0.61	0.2291	0.7291	0.2709
0.07	0.0279	0.5279	0.4721	0.62	0.2324	0.7324	0.2676
0.08	0.0319	0.5319	0.4681	0.63	0.2357	0.7357	0.2643
0.09	0.0359	0.5359	0.4641	0.64	0.2389	0.7389	0.2611
0.10	0.0398	0.5398	0.4602	0.65	0.2422	0.7422	0.2578
0.11	0.0438	0.5438	0.4562	0.66	0.2454	0.7454	0.2546
0.12	0.0478	0.5478	0.4522	0.67	0.2486	0.7486	0.2514
0.13	0.0517	0.5517	0.4483	0.68	0.2517	0.7517	0.2483
0.14	0.0557	0.5557	0.4443	0.69	0.2549	0.7549	0.2451
0.15	0.0596	0.5596	0.4404	0.70	0.2580	0.7580	0.2420
0.16	0.0636	0.5636	0.4364	0.71	0.2611	0.7611	0.2389
0.17	0.0675	0.5675	0.4325	0.72	0.2642	0.7642	0.2358
0.18	0.0714	0.5714	0.4286	0.73	0.2673	0.7673	0.2327
0.19	0.0753	0.5753	0.4247	0.74	0.2704	0.7704	0.2296
0.20	0.0793	0.5793	0.4207	0.75	0.2734	0.7734	0.2266
0.21	0.0832	0.5832	0.4168	0.76	0.2764	0.7764	0.2236
0.22	0.0871	0.5871	0.4129	0.77	0.2794	0.7794	0.2206
0.23	0.0910	0.5910	0.4090	0.78	0.2823	0.7823	0.2177
0.24	0.0948	0.5948	0.4052	0.79	0.2852	0.7852	0.2148
0.25	0.0987	0.5987	0.4013	0.80	0.2881	0.7881	0.2119
0.26	0.1026	0.6026	0.3974	0.81	0.2910	0.7910	0.2090
0.27	0.1064	0.6064	0.3936	0.82	0.2939	0.7939	0.2061
0.28	0.1103	0.6103	0.3897	0.83	0.2967	0.7967	0.2033
0.29	0.1141	0.6141	0.3859	0.84	0.2995	0.7995	0.2005
0.30	0.1179	0.6179	0.3821	0.85	0.3023	0.8023	0.1977
0.31	0.1217	0.6217	0.3783	0.86	0.3051	0.8051	0.1949
0.32	0.1255	0.6255	0.3745	0.87	0.3078	0.8078	0.1922
0.33	0.1293	0.6293	0.3707	0.88	0.3106	0.8106	0.1894
0.34	0.1331	0.6331	0.3669	0.89	0.3133	0.8133	0.1867
0.35	0.1368	0.6368	0.3632	0.90	0.3159	0.8159	0.1841
0.36	0.1406	0.6406	0.3594	0.91	0.3186	0.8186	0.1814
0.37	0.1443	0.6443	0.3557	0.92	0.3212	0.8212	0.1788
0.38	0.1480	0.6480	0.3520	0.93	0.3238	0.8238	0.1762
0.39	0.1517	0.6517	0.3483	0.94	0.3264	0.8264	0.1736
0.40	0.1554	0.6554	0.3446	0.95	0.3289	0.8289	0.1711
0.41	0.1591	0.6591	0.3409	0.96	0.3315	0.8315	0.1685
0.42	0.1628	0.6628	0.3372	0.97	0.3340	0.8340	0.1660
0.43	0.1664	0.6664	0.3336	0.98	0.3365	0.8365	0.1635
0.44	0.1700	0.6700	0.3300	0.99	0.3389	0.8389	0.1611
0.45	0.1736	0.6736	0.3264	1.00	0.3413	0.8413	0.1587
0.46	0.1772	0.6772	0.3228	1.01	0.3438	0.8438	0.1562
0.47	0.1808	0.6808	0.3192	1.02	0.3461	0.8461	0.1539
0.48	0.1844	0.6844	0.3156	1.03	0.3485	0.8485	0.1515
0.49	0.1879	0.6879	0.3121	1.04	0.3508	0.8508	0.1492
0.50	0.1915	0.6915	0.3085	1.05	0.3531	0.8531	0.1469
0.51	0.1950	0.6950	0.3050	1.06	0.3554	0.8554	0.1446
0.52	0.1985	0.6985	0.3015	1.07	0.3577	0.8577	0.1423
0.53	0.2019	0.7019	0.2981	1.08	0.3599	0.8599	0.1401
0.54	0.2054	0.7054	0.2946	1.09	0.3621	0.8621	0.1379

TABLE B   Continued

(1)	(2) area between mean and	(3) area	(4) area	(1)	(2) area between mean and	(3) area	(4) area
z	z	below z	above z	z	z	below z	above z
1.10	0.3643	0.8643	0.1357	1.66	0.4515	0.9515	0.0485
1.11	0.3665	0.8665	0.1335	1.67	0.4525	0.9525	0.0475
1.12	0.3686	0.8686	0.1314	1.68	0.4535	0.9535	0.0465
1.13	0.3708	0.8708	0.1292	1.69	0.4545	0.9545	0.0455
1.14	0.3729	0.8729	0.1271	1.70	0.4554	0.9554	0.0446
1.15	0.3749	0.8749	0.1251	1.71	0.4564	0.9564	0.0436
1.16	0.3770	0.8770	0.1230	1.72	0.4573	0.9573	0.0427
1.17	0.3790	0.8790	0.1210	1.73	0.4582	0.9582	0.0418
1.18	0.3810	0.8810	0.1190	1.74	0.4591	0.9591	0.0409
1.19	0.3830	0.8830	0.1170	1.75	0.4599	0.9599	0.0401
1.20	0.3849	0.8849	0.1151	1.76	0.4608	0.9608	0.0392
1.21	0.3869	0.8869	0.1131	1.77	0.4616	0.9616	0.0384
1.22	0.3888	0.8888	0.1112	1.78	0.4625	0.9625	0.0375
1.23	0.3907	0.8907	0.1093	1.79	0.4633	0.9633	0.0367
1.24	0.3925	0.8925	0.1075	1.80	0.4641	0.9641	0.0359
1.25	0.3944	0.8944	0.1056	1.81	0.4649	0.9649	0.0351
1.26	0.3962	0.8962	0.1038	1.82	0.4656	0.9656	0.0344
1.27	0.3980	0.8980	0.1020	1.83	0.4664	0.9664	0.0336
1.28	0.3997	0.8997	0.1003	1.84	0.4671	0.9671	0.0329
1.29	0.4015	0.9015	0.0985	1.85	0.4678	0.9678	0.0322
1.30	0.4032	0.9032	0.0968	1.86	0.4686	0.9686	0.0314
1.31	0.4049	0.9049	0.0951	1.87	0.4693	0.9693	0.0307
1.32	0.4066	0.9066	0.0934	1.88	0.4699	0.9699	0.0301
1.33	0.4082	0.9082	0.0918	1.89	0.4706	0.9706	0.0294
1.34	0.4099	0.9099	0.0901	1.90	0.4713	0.9713	0.0287
1.35	0.4115	0.9115	0.0885	1.91	0.4719	0.9719	0.0281
1.36	0.4131	0.9131	0.0869	1.92	0.4726	0.9726	0.0274
1.37	0.4147	0.9147	0.0853	1.93	0.4732	0.9732	0.0268
1.38	0.4162	0.9162	0.0838	1.94	0.4738	0.9738	0.0262
1.39	0.4177	0.9177	0.0823	1.95	0.4744	0.9744	0.0256
1.40	0.4192	0.9192	0.0808	1.96	0.4750	0.9750	0.0250
1.41	0.4207	0.9207	0.0793	1.97	0.4756	0.9756	0.0244
1.42	0.4222	0.9222	0.0778	1.98	0.4761	0.9761	0.0239
1.43	0.4236	0.9236	0.0764	1.99	0.4767	0.9767	0.0233
1.44	0.4251	0.9251	0.0749	2.00	0.4772	0.9772	0.0228
1.45	0.4265	0.9265	0.0735	2.01	0.4778	0.9778	0.0222
1.46	0.4279	0.9279	0.0721	2.02	0.4783	0.9783	0.0217
1.47	0.4292	0.9292	0.0708	2.03	0.4788	0.9788	0.0212
1.48	0.4306	0.9306	0.0694	2.04	0.4793	0.9793	0.0207
1.49	0.4319	0.9319	0.0681	2.05	0.4798	0.9798	0.0202
1.50	0.4332	0.9332	0.0668	2.06	0.4803	0.9803	0.0197
1.51	0.4345	0.9345	0.0655	2.07	0.4808	0.9808	0.0192
1.52	0.4357	0.9357	0.0643	2.08	0.4812	0.9812	0.0188
1.53	0.4370	0.9370	0.0630	2.09	0.4817	0.9817	0.0183
1.54	0.4382	0.9382	0.0618	2.10	0.4821	0.9821	0.0179
1.55	0.4394	0.9394	0.0606	2.11	0.4826	0.9826	0.0174
1.56	0.4406	0.9406	0.0594	2.12	0.4830	0.9830	0.0170
1.57	0.4418	0.9418	0.0582	2.13	0.4834	0.9834	0.0166
1.58	0.4429	0.9429	0.0571	2.14	0.4838	0.9838	0.0162
1.59	0.4441	0.9441	0.0559	2.15	0.4842	0.9842	0.0158
1.60	0.4452	0.9452	0.0548	2.16	0.4846	0.9846	0.0154
1.61	0.4463	0.9463	0.0537	2.17	0.4850	0.9850	0.0150
1.62	0.4474	0.9474	0.0526	2.18	0.4854	0.9854	0.0146
1.63	0.4484	0.9484	0.0516	2.19	0.4857	0.9857	0.0143
1.64	0.4495	0.9495	0.0505	2.20	0.4861	0.9861	0.0139
1.65	0.4505	0.9505	0.0495	2.21	0.4864	0.9864	0.0136

Continues

TABLE B   Continued

(1)	(2) area between mean and z	(3) area below z	(4) area above z	(1)	(2) area between mean and z	(3) area below z	(4) area above z
z				z			
2.22	0.4868	0.9868	0.0132	2.76	0.4971	0.9971	0.0029
2.23	0.4871	0.9871	0.0129	2.77	0.4972	0.9972	0.0028
2.24	0.4875	0.9875	0.0125	2.78	0.4973	0.9973	0.0027
2.25	0.4878	0.9878	0.0122	2.79	0.4974	0.9974	0.0026
2.26	0.4881	0.9881	0.0119	2.80	0.4974	0.9974	0.0026
2.27	0.4884	0.9884	0.0116	2.81	0.4975	0.9975	0.0025
2.28	0.4887	0.9887	0.0113	2.82	0.4976	0.9976	0.0024
2.29	0.4890	0.9890	0.0110	2.83	0.4977	0.9977	0.0023
2.30	0.4893	0.9893	0.0107	2.84	0.4977	0.9977	0.0023
2.31	0.4896	0.9896	0.0104	2.85	0.4978	0.9978	0.0022
2.32	0.4898	0.9898	0.0102	2.86	0.4979	0.9979	0.0021
2.33	0.4901	0.9901	0.0099	2.87	0.4979	0.9979	0.0021
2.34	0.4904	0.9904	0.0096	2.88	0.4980	0.9980	0.0020
2.35	0.4906	0.9906	0.0094	2.89	0.4981	0.9981	0.0019
2.36	0.4909	0.9909	0.0091	2.90	0.4981	0.9981	0.0019
2.37	0.4911	0.9911	0.0089	2.91	0.4982	0.9982	0.0018
2.38	0.4913	0.9913	0.0087	2.92	0.4982	0.9982	0.0018
2.39	0.4916	0.9916	0.0084	2.93	0.4983	0.9983	0.0017
2.40	0.4918	0.9918	0.0082	2.94	0.4984	0.9984	0.0016
2.41	0.4920	0.9920	0.0080	2.95	0.4984	0.9984	0.0016
2.42	0.4922	0.9922	0.0078	2.96	0.4985	0.9985	0.0015
2.43	0.4925	0.9925	0.0075	2.97	0.4985	0.9985	0.0015
2.44	0.4927	0.9927	0.0073	2.98	0.4986	0.9986	0.0014
2.45	0.4929	0.9929	0.0071	2.99	0.4986	0.9986	0.0014
2.46	0.4931	0.9931	0.0069	3.00	0.4987	0.9987	0.0013
2.47	0.4932	0.9932	0.0068	3.01	0.4987	0.9987	0.0013
2.48	0.4934	0.9934	0.0066	3.02	0.4987	0.9987	0.0013
2.49	0.4936	0.9936	0.0064	3.03	0.4988	0.9988	0.0012
2.50	0.4938	0.9938	0.0062	3.04	0.4988	0.9988	0.0012
2.51	0.4940	0.9940	0.0060	3.05	0.4989	0.9989	0.0011
2.52	0.4941	0.9941	0.0059	3.06	0.4989	0.9989	0,0011
2.53	0.4943	0.9943	0.0057	3.07	0.4989	0.9989	0.0011
2.54	0.4945	0.9945	0.0055	3.08	0.4990	0.9990	0.0010
2.55	0.4946	0.9946	0.0054	3.09	0.4990	0.9990	0.0010
2.56	0.4948	0.9948	0.0052	3.10	0.4990	0.9990	0.0010
2.57	0.4949	0.9949	0.0051	3.11	0.4991	0.9991	0.0009
2.58	0.4951	0.9951	0.0049	3.12	0.4991	0.9991	0.0009
2.59	0.4952	0.9952	0.0048	3.13	0.4991	0.9991	0.0009
2.60	0.4953	0.9953	0.0047	3.14	0.4992	0.9992	0.0008
2.61	0.4955	0.9955	0.0045	3.15	0.4992	0.9992	0.0008
2.62	0.4956	0.9956	0.0044	3.16	0.4992	0.9992	0.0008
2.63	0.4957	0.9957	0.0043	3.17	0.4992	0.9992	0.0008
2.64	0.4959	0.9959	0.0041	3.18	0.4993	0.9993	0.0007
2.65	0.4960	0.9960	0.0040	3.19	0.4993	0.9993	0.0007
2.66	0.4961	0.9961	0.0039	3.20	0.4993	0.9993	0.0007
2.67	0.4962	0.9962	0.0038	3.21	0.4993	0.9993	0.0007
2.68	0.4963	0.9963	0.0037	3.22	0.4994	0.9994	0.0006
2.69	0.4964	0.9964	0.0036	3.23	0.4994	0.9994	0.0006
2.70	0.4965	0.9965	0.0035	3.24	0.4994	0.9994	0.0006
2.71	0.4966	0.9966	0.0034	3.30	0.4995	0.9995	0.0005
2.72	0.4967	0.9967	0.0033	3.40	0.4997	0.9997	0.0003
2.73	0.4968	0.9968	0.0032	3.50	0.4998	0.9998	0.0002
2.74	0.4969	0.9969	0.0031	3.60	0.4998	0.9998	0.0002
2.75	0.4970	0.9970	0.0030	3.70	0.4999	0.9999	0.0001

Source: Generated with SAS statistical package.

TABLE C   Critical values of t

DF	One-tail significance level					
	0.1000	0.0500	0.0250	0.0100	0.0050	0.0005
	Two-tail significance level					
	0.2000	0.1000	0.0500	0.0200	0.0100	0.0010
1	3.078	6.314	12.706	31.821	63.657	636.619
2	1.886	2.920	4.303	6.965	9.925	31.599
3	1.638	2.353	3.182	4.541	5.841	12.924
4	1.533	2.132	2.776	3.747	4.604	8.610
5	1.476	2.015	2.571	3.365	4.032	6.869
6	1.440	1.943	2.447	3.143	3.707	5.959
7	1.415	1.895	2.365	2.998	3.499	5.408
8	1.397	1.860	2.306	2.896	3.355	5.041
9	1.383	1.833	2.262	2.821	3.250	4.781
10	1.372	1.812	2.228	2.764	3.169	4.587
11	1.363	1.796	2.201	2.718	3.106	4.437
12	1.356	1.782	2.179	2.681	3.055	4.318
13	1.350	1.771	2.160	2.650	3.012	4.221
14	1.345	1.761	2.145	2.624	2.977	4.140
15	1.341	1.753	2.131	2.602	2.947	4.073
16	1.337	1.746	2.120	2.583	2.921	4.015
17	1.333	1.740	2.110	2.567	2.898	3.965
18	1.330	1.734	2.101	2.552	2.878	3.922
19	1.328	1.729	2.093	2.539	2.861	3.883
20	1.325	1.725	2.086	2.528	2.845	3.850
21	1.323	1.721	2.080	2.518	2.831	3.819
22	1.321	1.717	2.074	2.508	2.819	3.792
23	1.319	1.714	2.069	2.500	2.807	3.768
24	1.318	1.711	2.064	2.492	2.797	3.745
25	1.316	1.708	2.060	2.485	2.787	3.725
26	1.315	1.706	2.056	2.479	2.779	3.707
27	1.314	1.703	2.052	2.473	2.771	3.690
28	1.313	1.701	2.048	2.467	2.763	3.674
29	1.311	1.699	2.045	2.462	2.756	3.659
30	1.310	1.697	2.042	2.457	2.750	3.646
40	1.303	1.684	2.021	2.423	2.704	3.551
60	1.296	1.671	2.000	2.390	2.660	3.460
120	1.289	1.658	1.980	2.358	2.617	3.373
∞	1.282	1.645	1.960	2.327	2.576	3.291

Source: Generated with SAS statistical package.

TABLE D   Critical values of χ^2

DF	0.995	0.990	0.975	0.950	0.900	0.750	0.500
1	0.0000	0.0002	0.0010	0.0039	0.0158	0.1015	0.4549
2	0.0100	0.0201	0.0506	0.1026	0.2107	0.5754	1.3863
3	0.0717	0.1148	0.2158	0.3518	0.5844	1.2125	2.3660
4	0.2070	0.2971	0.4844	0.7107	1.0636	1.9226	3.3567
5	0.4117	0.5543	0.8312	1.1455	1.6103	2.6746	4.3515
6	0.6757	0.8721	1.2373	1.6354	2.2041	3.4546	5.3481
7	0.9893	1.2390	1.6899	2.1673	2.8331	4.2549	6.3458
8	1.3444	1.6465	2.1797	2.7326	3.4895	5.0706	7.3441
9	1.7349	2.0879	2.7004	3.3251	4.1682	5.8988	8.3428
10	2.1559	2.5582	3.2470	3.9403	4.8652	6.7372	9.3418
11	2.6032	3.0535	3.8157	4.5748	5.5778	7.5841	10.3410
12	3.0738	3.5706	4.4038	5.2260	6.3038	8.4384	11.3403
13	3.5650	4.1069	5.0088	5.8919	7.0415	9.2991	12.3398
14	4.0747	4.6604	5.6287	6.5706	7.7895	10.1653	13.3393
15	4.6009	5.2293	6.2621	7.2609	8.5468	11.0365	14.3389
16	5.1422	5.8122	6.9077	7.9616	9.3122	11.9122	15.3385
17	5.6972	6.4078	7.5642	8.6718	10.0852	12.7919	16.3382
18	6.2648	7.0149	8.2307	9.3905	10.8649	13.6753	17.3379
19	6.8440	7.6327	8.9065	10.1170	11.6509	14.5620	18.3377
20	7.4338	8.2604	9.5908	10.8508	12.4426	15.4518	19.3374
21	8.0337	8.8972	10.2829	11.5913	13.2396	16.3444	20.3372
22	8.6427	9.5425	10.9823	12.3380	14.0415	17.2396	21.3370
23	9.2604	10.1957	11.6886	13.0905	14.8480	18.1373	22.3369
24	9.8862	10.8564	12.4012	13.8484	15.6587	19.0373	23.3367
25	10.5197	11.5240	13.1197	14.6114	16.4734	19.9393	24.3366
26	11.1602	12.1981	13.8439	15.3792	17.2919	20.8434	25.3365
27	11.8076	12.8785	14.5734	16.1514	18.1139	21.7494	26.3363
28	12.4613	13.5617	15.3079	16.9279	18.9392	22.6572	27.3362
29	13.1211	14.2565	16.0471	17.7084	19.7677	23.5666	28.3361
30	13.7867	14.9535	16.7908	18.4927	20.5992	24.4776	29.3360
40	20.7065	22.1643	24.4330	26.5093	29.0505	33.6603	39.3353
50	27.9907	29.7067	32.3574	34.7643	37.6886	42.9421	49.3349
60	35.5345	37.4849	40.4817	43.1880	46.4589	52.2938	59.3347
70	43.2752	45.4417	48.7576	51.7393	55.3289	61.6983	69.3345
80	51.1719	53.5401	57.1532	60.3915	64.2778	71.1445	79.3343
90	59.1963	61.7541	65.6466	69.1260	73.2911	80.6247	89.3342
100	67.3276	70.0649	74.2219	77.9295	82.3581	90.1332	99.3341
z	−2.5758	−2.3263	−1.9600	−1.6449	−1.2816	−0.6745	0.0000

TABLE D   Continued

DF	0.250	0.100	0.050	0.025	0.010	0.005	0.001
1	1.3233	2.7055	3.8415	5.0239	6.6349	7.8794	10.8276
2	2.7726	4.6052	5.9915	7.3778	9.2103	10.5966	13.8155
3	4.1083	6.2514	7.8147	9.3484	11.3449	12.8382	16.2662
4	5.3853	7.7794	9.4877	11.1433	13.2767	14.8603	18.4668
5	6.6257	9.2364	11.0705	12.8325	15.0863	16.7496	20.5150
6	7.8408	10.6446	12.5916	14.4494	16.8119	18.5476	22.4577
7	9.0371	12.0170	14.0671	16.0128	18.4753	20.2777	24.3219
8	10.2189	13.3616	15.5073	17.5345	20.0902	21.9550	26.1245
9	11.3888	14.6837	16.9190	19.0228	21.6660	23.5894	27.8772
10	12.5489	15.9872	18.3070	20.4832	23.2093	25.1882	29.5883
11	13.7007	17.2750	19.6751	21.9200	24.7250	26.7568	31.2641
12	14.8454	18.5493	21.0261	23.3367	26.2170	28.2995	32.9095
13	15.9839	19.8119	22.3620	24.7356	27.6882	29.8195	34.5282
14	17.1169	21.0641	23.6848	26.1189	29.1412	31.3193	36.1233
15	18.2451	22.3071	24.9958	27.4884	30.5779	32.8013	37.6973
16	19.3689	23.5418	26.2962	28.8454	31.9999	34.2672	39.2524
17	20.4887	24.7690	27.5871	30.1910	33.4087	35.7185	40.7902
18	21.6049	25.9894	28.8693	31.5264	34.8053	37.1565	42.3124
19	22.7178	27.2036	30.1435	32.8523	36.1909	38.5823	43.8202
20	23.8277	28.4120	31.4104	34.1696	37.5662	39.9968	45.3147
21	24.9348	29.6151	32.6706	35.4789	38.9322	41.4011	46.7970
22	26.0393	30.8133	33.9244	36.7807	40.2894	42.7957	48.2679
23	27.1413	32.0069	35.1725	38.0756	41.6384	44.1813	49.7282
24	28.2412	33.1962	36.4150	39.3641	42.9798	45.5585	51.1786
25	29.3389	34.3816	37.6525	40.6465	44.3141	46.9279	52.6197
26	30.4346	35.5632	38.8851	41.9232	45.6417	48.2899	54.0520
27	31.5284	36.7412	40.1133	43.1945	46.9629	49.6449	55.4760
28	32.6205	37.9159	41.3371	44.4608	48.2782	50.9934	56.8923
29	33.7109	39.0875	42.5570	45.7223	49.5879	52.3356	58.3012
30	34.7997	40.2560	43.7730	46.9792	50.8922	53.6720	59.7031
40	45.6160	51.8051	55.7585	59.3417	63.6907	66.7660	73.4020
50	56.3336	63.1671	67.5048	71.4202	76.1539	79.4900	86.6608
60	66.9815	74.3970	79.0819	83.2977	88.3794	91.9517	99.6072
70	77.5767	85.5270	90.5312	95.0232	100.4252	104.2149	112.3169
80	88.1303	96.5782	101.8795	106.6286	112.3288	116.3211	124.8392
90	98.6499	107.5650	113.1453	118.1359	124.1163	128.2989	137.2084
100	109.1412	118.4980	124.3421	129.5612	135.8067	140.1695	149.4493
z	+0.6745	+1.2816	+1.6449	+1.9600	+2.3263	+2.5758	+3.0902

Source: Generated with SAS statistical package.

TABLE E   5% (upper values) and 1% (lower values) points for the distribution of F

df2 - SSb *(handwritten)*

df1	1	2	3	4	5	6	7	8
1	161	199	216	225	230	234	237	239
	4052	5000	5403	5625	5764	5859	5928	5981
2	18.51	19.00	19.16	19.25	19.30	19.33	19.35	19.37
	98.50	99.00	99.17	99.25	99.30	99.33	99.36	99.37
3	10.13	9.55	9.28	9.12	9.01	8.94	8.89	8.85
	34.12	30.82	29.46	28.71	28.24	27.91	27.67	27.49
4	7.71	6.94	6.59	6.39	6.26	6.16	6.09	6.04
	21.20	18.00	16.69	15.98	15.52	15.21	14.98	14.80
5	6.61	5.79	5.41	5.19	5.05	4.95	4.88	4.82
	16.26	13.27	12.06	11.39	10.97	10.67	10.46	10.29
6	5.99	5.14	4.76	4.53	4.39	4.28	4.21	4.15
	13.75	10.92	9.78	9.15	8.75	8.47	8.26	8.10
7	5.59	4.74	4.35	4.12	3.97	3.87	3.79	3.73
	12.25	9.55	8.45	7.85	7.46	7.19	6.99	6.84
8	5.32	4.46	4.07	3.84	3.69	3.58	3.50	3.44
	11.26	8.65	7.59	7.01	6.63	6.37	6.18	6.03
9	5.12	4.26	3.86	3.63	3.48	3.37	3.29	3.23
	10.56	8.02	6.99	6.42	6.06	5.80	5.61	5.47
10	4.96	4.10	3.71	3.48	3.33	3.22	3.14	3.07
	10.04	7.56	6.55	5.99	5.64	5.39	5.20	5.06
11	4.84	3.98	3.59	3.36	3.20	3.09	3.01	2.95
	9.65	7.21	6.22	5.67	5.32	5.07	4.89	4.74
12	4.75	3.89	3.49	3.26	3.11	3.00	2.91	2.85
	9.33	6.93	5.95	5.41	5.06	4.82	4.64	4.50
13	4.67	3.81	3.41	3.18	3.03	2.92	2.83	2.77
	9.07	6.70	5.74	5.21	4.86	4.62	4.44	4.30
14	4.60	3.74	3.34	3.11	2.96	2.85	2.76	2.70
	8.86	6.51	5.56	5.04	4.69	4.46	4.28	4.14
15	4.54	3.68	3.29	3.06	2.90	2.79	2.71	2.64
	8.68	6.36	5.42	4.89	4.56	4.32	4.14	4.00
16	4.49	3.63	3.24	3.01	2.85	2.74	2.66	2.59
	8.53	6.23	5.29	4.77	4.44	4.20	4.03	3.89
17	4.45	3.59	3.20	2.96	2.81	2.70	2.61	2.55
	8.40	6.11	5.18	4.67	4.34	4.10	3.93	3.79
18	4.41	3.55	3.16	2.93	2.77	2.66	2.58	2.51
	8.29	6.01	5.09	4.58	4.25	4.01	3.84	3.71
19	4.38	3.52	3.13	2.90	2.74	2.63	2.54	2.48
	8.18	5.93	5.01	4.50	4.17	3.94	3.77	3.63
20	4.35	3.49	3.10	2.87	2.71	2.60	2.51	2.45
	8.10	5.85	4.94	4.43	4.10	3.87	3.70	3.56
21	4.32	3.47	3.07	2.84	2.68	2.57	2.49	2.42
	8.02	5.78	4.87	4.37	4.04	3.81	3.64	3.51
22	4.30	3.44	3.05	2.82	2.66	2.55	2.46	2.40
	7.95	5.72	4.82	4.31	3.99	3.76	3.59	3.45
23	4.28	3.42	3.03	2.80	2.64	2.53	2.44	2.37
	7.88	5.66	4.76	4.26	3.94	3.71	3.54	3.41
24	4.26	3.40	3.01	2.78	2.62	2.51	2.42	2.36
	7.82	5.61	4.72	4.22	3.90	3.67	3.50	3.36
25	4.24	3.39	2.99	2.76	2.60	2.49	2.40	2.34
	7.77	5.57	4.68	4.18	3.85	3.63	3.46	3.32
26	4.23	3.37	2.98	2.74	2.59	2.47	2.39	2.32
	7.72	5.53	4.64	4.14	3.82	3.59	3.42	3.29
27	4.21	3.35	2.96	2.73	2.57	2.46	2.37	2.31
	7.68	5.49	4.60	4.11	3.78	3.56	3.39	3.26
28	4.20	3.34	2.95	2.71	2.56	2.45	2.36	2.29
	7.64	5.45	4.57	4.07	3.75	3.53	3.36	3.23
29	4.18	3.33	2.93	2.70	2.55	2.43	2.35	2.28
	7.60	5.42	4.54	4.04	3.73	3.50	3.33	3.20

SS_w *(handwritten, left margin)*

TABLE E Continued

df1	df2							
	1	2	3	4	5	6	7	8
30	4.17	3.32	2.92	2.69	2.53	2.42	2.33	2.27
	7.56	5.39	4.51	4.02	3.70	3.47	3.30	3.17
32	4.15	3.29	2.90	2.67	2.51	2.40	2.31	2.24
	7.50	5.34	4.46	3.97	3.65	3.43	3.26	3.13
34	4.13	3.28	2.88	2.65	2.49	2.38	2.29	2.23
	7.44	5.29	4.42	3.93	3.61	3.39	3.22	3.09
36	4.11	3.26	2.87	2.63	2.48	2.36	2.28	2.21
	7.40	5.25	4.38	3.89	3.57	3.35	3.18	3.05
38	4.10	3.24	2.85	2.62	2.46	2.35	2.26	2.19
	7.35	5.21	4.34	3.86	3.54	3.32	3.15	3.02
40	4.08	3.23	2.84	2.61	2.45	2.34	2.25	2.18
	7.31	5.18	4.31	3.83	3.51	3.29	3.12	2.99
42	4.07	3.22	2.83	2.59	2.44	2.32	2.24	2.17
	7.28	5.15	4.29	3.80	3.49	3.27	3.10	2.97
44	4.06	3.21	2.82	2.58	2.43	2.31	2.23	2.16
	7.25	5.12	4.26	3.78	3.47	3.24	3.08	2.95
46	4.05	3.20	2.81	2.57	2.42	2.30	2.22	2.15
	7.22	5.10	4.24	3.76	3.44	3.22	3.06	2.93
48	4.04	3.19	2.80	2.57	2.41	2.29	2.21	2.14
	7.19	5.08	4.22	3.74	3.43	3.20	3.04	2.91
50	4.03	3.18	2.79	2.56	2.40	2.29	2.20	2.13
	7.17	5.06	4.20	3.72	3.41	3.19	3.02	2.89
55	4.02	3.16	2.77	2.54	2.38	2.27	2.18	2.11
	7.12	5.01	4.16	3.68	3.37	3.15	2.98	2.85
60	4.00	3.15	2.76	2.53	2.37	2.25	2.17	2.10
	7.08	4.98	4.13	3.65	3.34	3.12	2.95	2.82
65	3.99	3.14	2.75	2.51	2.36	2.24	2.15	2.08
	7.04	4.95	4.10	3.62	3.31	3.09	2.93	2.80
70	3.98	3.13	2.74	2.50	2.35	2.23	2.14	2.07
	7.01	4.92	4.07	3.60	3.29	3.07	2.91	2.78
80	3.96	3.11	2.72	2.49	2.33	2.21	2.13	2.06
	6.96	4.88	4.04	3.56	3.26	3.04	2.87	2.74
100	3.94	3.09	2.70	2.46	2.31	2.19	2.10	2.03
	6.90	4.82	3.98	3.51	3.21	2.99	2.82	2.69
125	3.92	3.07	2.68	2.44	2.29	2.17	2.08	2.01
	6.84	4.78	3.94	3.47	3.17	2.95	2.79	2.66
150	3.90	3.06	2.66	2.43	2.27	2.16	2.07	2.00
	6.81	4.75	3.91	3.45	3.14	2.92	2.76	2.63
200	3.89	3.04	2.65	2.42	2.26	2.14	2.06	1.98
	6.76	4.71	3.88	3.41	3.11	2.89	2.73	2.60
400	3.86	3.02	2.63	2.39	2.24	2.12	2.03	1.96
	6.70	4.66	3.83	3.37	3.06	2.85	2.68	2.56
1000	3.85	3.00	2.61	2.38	2.22	2.11	2.02	1.95
	6.66	4.63	3.80	3.34	3.04	2.82	2.66	2.53
∞	3.84	3.00	2.61	2.37	2.21	2.10	2.01	1.94
	6.64	4.61	3.78	3.32	3.02	2.80	2.64	2.51

Continues

TABLE E   Continued

df1	df2 9	10	11	12	14	16	20	24
1	241	242	243	244	245	246	248	249
	6022	6056	6083	6106	6143	6170	6209	6235
2	19.38	19.40	19.40	19.41	19.42	19.43	19.45	19.45
	99.39	99.40	99.41	99.42	99.43	99.44	99.45	99.46
3	8.81	8.79	8.76	8.74	8.71	8.69	8.66	8.64
	27.35	27.23	27.13	27.05	26.92	26.83	26.69	26.60
4	6.00	5.96	5.94	5.91	5.87	5.84	5.80	5.77
	14.66	14.55	14.45	14.37	14.25	14.15	14.02	13.93
5	4.77	4.74	4.70	4.68	4.64	4.60	4.56	4.53
	10.16	10.05	9.96	9.89	9.77	9.68	9.55	9.47
6	4.10	4.06	4.03	4.00	3.96	3.92	3.87	3.84
	7.98	7.87	7.79	7.72	7.60	7.52	7.40	7.31
7	3.68	3.64	3.60	3.57	3.53	3.49	3.44	3.41
	6.72	6.62	6.54	6.47	6.36	6.28	6.16	6.07
8	3.39	3.35	3.31	3.28	3.24	3.20	3.15	3.12
	5.91	5.81	5.73	5.67	5.56	5.48	5.36	5.28
9	3.18	3.14	3.10	3.07	3.03	2.99	2.94	2.90
	5.35	5.26	5.18	5.11	5.01	4.92	4.81	4.73
10	3.02	2.98	2.94	2.91	2.86	2.83	2.77	2.74
	4.94	4.85	4.77	4.71	4.60	4.52	4.41	4.33
11	2.90	2.85	2.82	2.79	2.74	2.70	2.65	2.61
	4.63	4.54	4.46	4.40	4.29	4.21	4.10	4.02
12	2.80	2.75	2.72	2.69	2.64	2.60	2.54	2.51
	4.39	4.30	4.22	4.16	4.05	3.97	3.86	3.78
13	2.71	2.67	2.63	2.60	2.55	2.51	2.46	2.42
	4.19	4.10	4.02	3.96	3.86	3.78	3.66	3.59
14	2.65	2.60	2.57	2.53	2.48	2.44	2.39	2.35
	4.03	3.94	3.86	3.80	3.70	3.62	3.51	3.43
15	2.59	2.54	2.51	2.48	2.42	2.38	2.33	2.29
	3.89	3.80	3.73	3.67	3.56	3.49	3.37	3.29
16	2.54	2.49	2.46	2.42	2.37	2.33	2.28	2.24
	3.78	3.69	3.62	3.55	3.45	3.37	3.26	3.18
17	2.49	2.45	2.41	2.38	2.33	2.29	2.23	2.19
	3.68	3.59	3.52	3.46	3.35	3.27	3.16	3.08
18	2.46	2.41	2.37	2.34	2.29	2.25	2.19	2.15
	3.60	3.51	3.43	3.37	3.27	3.19	3.08	3.00
19	2.42	2.38	2.34	2.31	2.26	2.21	2.16	2.11
	3.52	3.43	3.36	3.30	3.19	3.12	3.00	2.92
20	2.39	2.35	2.31	2.28	2.22	2.18	2.12	2.08
	3.46	3.37	3.29	3.23	3.13	3.05	2.94	2.86
21	2.37	2.32	2.28	2.25	2.20	2.16	2.10	2.05
	3.40	3.31	3.24	3.17	3.07	2.99	2.88	2.80
22	2.34	2.30	2.26	2.23	2.17	2.13	2.07	2.03
	3.35	3.26	3.18	3.12	3.02	2.94	2.83	2.75
23	2.32	2.27	2.24	2.20	2.15	2.11	2.05	2.01
	3.30	3.21	3.14	3.07	2.97	2.89	2.78	2.70
24	2.30	2.25	2.22	2.18	2.13	2.09	2.03	1.98
	3.26	3.17	3.09	3.03	2.93	2.85	2.74	2.66
25	2.28	2.24	2.20	2.16	2.11	2.07	2.01	1.96
	3.22	3.13	3.06	2.99	2.89	2.81	2.70	2.62
26	2.27	2.22	2.18	2.15	2.09	2.05	1.99	1.95
	3.18	3.09	3.02	2.96	2.86	2.78	2.66	2.58
27	2.25	2.20	2.17	2.13	2.08	2.04	1.97	1.93
	3.15	3.06	2.99	2.93	2.82	2.75	2.63	2.55
28	2.24	2.19	2.15	2.12	2.06	2.02	1.96	1.91
	3.12	3.03	2.96	2.90	2.79	2.72	2.60	2.52
29	2.22	2.18	2.14	2.10	2.05	2.01	1.94	1.90
	3.09	3.00	2.93	2.87	2.77	2.69	2.57	2.49

TABLE E   Continued

df1	df2							
	9	10	11	12	14	16	20	24
30	2.21	2.16	2.13	2.09	2.04	1.99	1.93	1.89
	3.07	2.98	2.91	2.84	2.74	2.66	2.55	2.47
32	2.19	2.14	2.10	2.07	2.01	1.97	1.91	1.86
	3.02	2.93	2.86	2.80	2.70	2.62	2.50	2.42
34	2.17	2.12	2.08	2.05	1.99	1.95	1.89	1.84
	2.98	2.89	2.82	2.76	2.66	2.58	2.46	2.38
36	2.15	2.11	2.07	2.03	1.98	1.93	1.87	1.82
	2.95	2.86	2.79	2.72	2.62	2.54	2.43	2.35
38	2.14	2.09	2.05	2.02	1.96	1.92	1.85	1.81
	2.92	2.83	2.75	2.69	2.59	2.51	2.40	2.32
40	2.12	2.08	2.04	2.00	1.95	1.90	1.84	1.79
	2.89	2.80	2.73	2.66	2.56	2.48	2.37	2.29
42	2.11	2.06	2.03	1.99	1.94	1.89	1.83	1.78
	2.86	2.78	2.70	2.64	2.54	2.46	2.34	2.26
44	2.10	2.05	2.01	1.98	1.92	1.88	1.81	1.77
	2.84	2.75	2.68	2.62	2.52	2.44	2.32	2.24
46	2.09	2.04	2.00	1.97	1.91	1.87	1.80	1.76
	2.82	2.73	2.66	2.60	2.50	2.42	2.30	2.22
48	2.08	2.03	1.99	1.96	1.90	1.86	1.79	1.75
	2.80	2.71	2.64	2.58	2.48	2.40	2.28	2.20
50	2.07	2.03	1.99	1.95	1.89	1.85	1.78	1.74
	2.78	2.70	2.63	2.56	2.46	2.38	2.27	2.18
55	2.06	2.01	1.97	1.93	1.88	1.83	1.76	1.72
	2.75	2.66	2.59	2.53	2.42	2.34	2.23	2.15
60	2.04	1.99	1.95	1.92	1.86	1.82	1.75	1.70
	2.72	2.63	2.56	2.50	2.39	2.31	2.20	2.12
65	2.03	1.98	1.94	1.90	1.85	1.80	1.73	1.69
	2.69	2.61	2.53	2.47	2.37	2.29	2.17	2.09
70	2.02	1.97	1.93	1.89	1.84	1.79	1.72	1.67
	2.67	2.59	2.51	2.45	2.35	2.27	2.15	2.07
80	2.00	1.95	1.91	1.88	1.82	1.77	1.70	1.65
	2.64	2.55	2.48	2.42	2.31	2.23	2.12	2.03
100	1.97	1.93	1.89	1.85	1.79	1.75	1.68	1.63
	2.59	2.50	2.43	2.37	2.27	2.19	2.07	1.98
125	1.96	1.91	1.87	1.83	1.77	1.73	1.66	1.60
	2.55	2.47	2.39	2.33	2.23	2.15	2.03	1.94
150	1.94	1.89	1.85	1.82	1.76	1.71	1.64	1.59
	2.53	2.44	2.37	2.31	2.20	2.12	2.00	1.92
200	1.93	1.88	1.84	1.80	1.74	1.69	1.62	1.57
	2.50	2.41	2.34	2.27	2.17	2.09	1.97	1.89
400	1.90	1.85	1.81	1.78	1.72	1.67	1.60	1.54
	2.45	2.37	2.29	2.23	2.13	2.05	1.92	1.84
1000	1.89	1.84	1.80	1.76	1.70	1.65	1.58	1.53
	2.43	2.34	2.27	2.20	2.10	2.02	1.90	1.81
∞	1.88	1.83	1.79	1.75	1.69	1.64	1.57	1.52
	2.41	2.32	2.25	2.19	2.08	2.00	1.88	1.79

Continues

TABLE E   Continued

df1	30	40	50	75	100	200	500	∞
				df2				
1	250	251	252	253	253	254	254	254
	6261	6287	6303	6324	6334	6350	6360	6366
2	19.46	19.47	19.48	19.48	19.49	19.49	19.49	19.50
	99.47	99.47	99.48	99.49	99.49	99.49	99.50	99.50
3	8.62	8.59	8.58	8.56	8.55	8.54	8.53	8.53
	26.50	26.41	26.35	26.28	26.24	26.18	26.15	26.13
4	5.75	5.72	5.70	5.68	5.66	5.65	5.64	5.63
	13.84	13.75	13.69	13.61	13.58	13.52	13.49	13.46
5	4.50	4.46	4.44	4.42	4.41	4.39	4.37	4.37
	9.38	9.29	9.24	9.17	9.13	9.08	9.04	9.02
6	3.81	3.77	3.75	3.73	3.71	3.69	3.68	3.67
	7.23	7.14	7.09	7.02	6.99	6.93	6.90	6.88
7	3.38	3.34	3.32	3.29	3.27	3.25	3.24	3.23
	5.99	5.91	5.86	5.79	5.75	5.70	5.67	5.65
8	3.08	3.04	3.02	2.99	2.97	2.95	2.94	2.93
	5.20	5.12	5.07	5.00	4.96	4.91	4.88	4.86
9	2.86	2.83	2.80	2.77	2.76	2.73	2.72	2.71
	4.65	4.57	4.52	4.45	4.41	4.36	4.33	4.31
10	2.70	2.66	2.64	2.60	2.59	2.56	2.55	2.54
	4.25	4.17	4.12	4.05	4.01	3.96	3.93	3.91
11	2.57	2.53	2.51	2.47	2.46	2.43	2.42	2.41
	3.94	3.86	3.81	3.74	3.71	3.66	3.62	3.60
12	2.47	2.43	2.40	2.37	2.35	2.32	2.31	2.30
	3.70	3.62	3.57	3.50	3.47	3.41	3.38	3.36
13	2.38	2.34	2.31	2.28	2.26	2.23	2.22	2.21
	3.51	3.43	3.38	3.31	3.27	3.22	3.19	3.17
14	2.31	2.27	2.24	2.21	2.19	2.16	2.14	2.13
	3.35	3.27	3.22	3.15	3.11	3.06	3.03	3.01
15	2.25	2.20	2.18	2.14	2.12	2.10	2.08	2.07
	3.21	3.13	3.08	3.01	2.98	2.92	2.89	2.87
16	2.19	2.15	2.12	2.09	2.07	2.04	2.02	2.01
	3.10	3.02	2.97	2.90	2.86	2.81	2.78	2.75
17	2.15	2.10	2.08	2.04	2.02	1.99	1.97	1.96
	3.00	2.92	2.87	2.80	2.76	2.71	2.68	2.65
18	2.11	2.06	2.04	2.00	1.98	1.95	1.93	1.92
	2.92	2.84	2.78	2.71	2.68	2.62	2.59	2.57
19	2.07	2.03	2.00	1.96	1.94	1.91	1.89	1.88
	2.84	2.76	2.71	2.64	2.60	2.55	2.51	2.49
20	2.04	1.99	1.97	1.93	1.91	1.88	1.86	1.84
	2.78	2.69	2.64	2.57	2.54	2.48	2.44	2.42
21	2.01	1.96	1.94	1.90	1.88	1.84	1.83	1.81
	2.72	2.64	2.58	2.51	2.48	2.42	2.38	2.36
22	1.98	1.94	1.91	1.87	1.85	1.82	1.80	1.78
	2.67	2.58	2.53	2.46	2.42	2.36	2.33	2.31
23	1.96	1.91	1.88	1.84	1.82	1.79	1.77	1.76
	2.62	2.54	2.48	2.41	2.37	2.32	2.28	2.26
24	1.94	1.89	1.86	1.82	1.80	1.77	1.75	1.73
	2.58	2.49	2.44	2.37	2.33	2.27	2.24	2.21
25	1.92	1.87	1.84	1.80	1.78	1.75	1.73	1.71
	2.54	2.45	2.40	2.33	2.29	2.23	2.19	2.17
26	1.90	1.85	1.82	1.78	1.76	1.73	1.71	1.69
	2.50	2.42	2.36	2.29	2.25	2.19	2.16	2.13
27	1.88	1.84	1.81	1.76	1.74	1.71	1.69	1.67
	2.47	2.38	2.33	2.26	2.22	2.16	2.12	2.10
28	1.87	1.82	1.79	1.75	1.73	1.69	1.67	1.65
	2.44	2.35	2.30	2.23	2.19	2.13	2.09	2.07
29	1.85	1.81	1.77	1.73	1.71	1.67	1.65	1.64
	2.41	2.33	2.27	2.20	2.16	2.10	2.06	2.04

TABLE E   Continued

df1	30	40	50	75	100	200	500	∞
				df2				
30	1.84	1.79	1.76	1.72	1.70	1.66	1.64	1.62
	2.39	2.30	2.25	2.17	2.13	2.07	2.03	2.01
32	1.82	1.77	1.74	1.69	1.67	1.63	1.61	1.60
	2.34	2.25	2.20	2.12	2.08	2.02	1.98	1.96
34	1.80	1.75	1.71	1.67	1.65	1.61	1.59	1.57
	2.30	2.21	2.16	2.08	2.04	1.98	1.94	1.91
36	1.78	1.73	1.69	1.65	1.62	1.59	1.56	1.55
	2.26	2.18	2.12	2.04	2.00	1.94	1.90	1.87
38	1.76	1.71	1.68	1.63	1.61	1.57	1.54	1.53
	2.23	2.14	2.09	2.01	1.97	1.90	1.86	1.84
40	1.74	1.69	1.66	1.61	1.59	1.55	1.53	1.51
	2.20	2.11	2.06	1.98	1.94	1.87	1.83	1.81
42	1.73	1.68	1.65	1.60	1.57	1.53	1.51	1.49
	2.18	2.09	2.03	1.95	1.91	1.85	1.80	1.78
44	1.72	1.67	1.63	1.59	1.56	1.52	1.49	1.48
	2.15	2.07	2.01	1.93	1.89	1.82	1.78	1.75
46	1.71	1.65	1.62	1.57	1.55	1.51	1.48	1.46
	2.13	2.04	1.99	1.91	1.86	1.80	1.76	1.73
48	1.70	1.64	1.61	1.56	1.54	1.49	1.47	1.45
	2.12	2.02	1.97	1.89	1.84	1.78	1.73	1.71
50	1.69	1.63	1.60	1.55	1.52	1.48	1.46	1.44
	2.10	2.01	1.95	1.87	1.82	1.76	1.71	1.68
55	1.67	1.61	1.58	1.53	1.50	1.46	1.43	1.41
	2.06	1.97	1.91	1.83	1.78	1.71	1.67	1.64
60	1.65	1.59	1.56	1.51	1.48	1.44	1.41	1.39
	2.03	1.94	1.88	1.79	1.75	1.68	1.63	1.60
65	1.63	1.58	1.54	1.49	1.46	1.42	1.39	1.37
	2.00	1.91	1.85	1.77	1.72	1.65	1.60	1.57
70	1.62	1.57	1.53	1.48	1.45	1.40	1.37	1.35
	1.98	1.89	1.83	1.74	1.70	1.62	1.57	1.54
80	1.60	1.54	1.51	1.45	1.43	1.38	1.35	1.33
	1.94	1.85	1.79	1.70	1.65	1.58	1.53	1.50
100	1.57	1.52	1.48	1.42	1.39	1.34	1.31	1.28
	1.89	1.80	1.74	1.65	1.60	1.52	1.47	1.43
125	1.55	1.49	1.45	1.40	1.36	1.31	1.27	1.25
	1.85	1.76	1.69	1.60	1.55	1.47	1.41	1.37
150	1.54	1.48	1.44	1.38	1.34	1.29	1.25	1.22
	1.83	1.73	1.66	1.57	1.52	1.43	1.38	1.33
200	1.52	1.46	1.41	1.35	1.32	1.26	1.22	1.19
	1.79	1.69	1.63	1.53	1.48	1.39	1.33	1.28
400	1.49	1.42	1.38	1.32	1.28	1.22	1.17	1.13
	1.75	1.64	1.58	1.48	1.42	1.32	1.25	1.19
1000	1.47	1.41	1.36	1.30	1.26	1.19	1.13	1.08
	1.72	1.61	1.54	1.44	1.38	1.28	1.19	1.12
∞	1.46	1.40	1.35	1.28	1.25	1.17	1.11	1.03
	1.70	1.59	1.53	1.42	1.36	1.25	1.16	1.05

Source: Generated with SAS statistical package.

TABLE F Percentage points of the studentized range statistics

Error df	α	2	3	4	5	6	7	8	9	10	11
		\multicolumn{10}{c}{r = number of means or number of steps between ordered means}									
5	.05	3.64	4.60	5.22	5.67	6.03	6.33	6.58	6.80	6.99	7.17
	.01	5.70	6.98	7.80	8.42	8.91	9.32	9.67	9.97	10.24	10.48
6	.05	3.46	4.34	4.90	5.30	5.63	5.90	6.12	6.32	6.49	6.65
	.01	5.24	6.33	7.03	7.56	7.97	8.32	8.61	8.87	9.10	9.30
7	.05	3.34	4.16	4.68	5.06	5.36	5.61	5.82	6.00	6.16	6.30
	.01	4.95	5.92	6.54	7.01	7.37	7.68	7.94	8.17	8.37	8.55
8	.05	3.26	4.04	4.53	4.89	5.17	5.40	5.60	5.77	5.92	6.05
	.01	4.75	5.64	6.20	6.62	6.96	7.24	7.47	7.68	7.86	8.03
9	.05	3.20	3.95	4.41	4.76	5.02	5.24	5.43	5.59	5.74	5.87
	.01	4.60	5.43	5.96	6.35	6.66	6.91	7.13	7.33	7.49	7.65
10	.05	3.15	3.88	4.33	4.65	4.91	5.12	5.30	5.46	5.60	5.72
	.01	4.48	5.27	5.77	6.14	6.43	6.67	6.87	7.05	7.21	7.36
11	.05	3.11	3.82	4.26	4.57	4.82	5.03	5.20	5.35	5.49	5.61
	.01	4.39	5.15	5.62	5.97	6.25	6.48	6.67	6.84	6.99	7.13
12	.05	3.08	3.77	4.20	4.51	4.75	4.95	5.12	5.27	5.39	5.51
	.01	4.32	5.05	5.50	5.84	6.10	6.32	6.51	6.67	6.81	6.94
13	.05	3.06	3.73	4.15	4.45	4.69	4.88	5.05	5.19	5.32	5.43
	.01	4.26	4.96	5.40	5.73	5.98	6.19	6.37	6.53	6.67	6.79
14	.05	3.03	3.70	4.11	4.41	4.64	4.83	4.99	5.13	5.25	5.36
	.01	4.21	4.89	5.32	5.63	5.88	6.08	6.26	6.41	6.54	6.66
15	.05	3.01	3.67	4.08	4.37	4.59	4.78	4.94	5.08	5.20	5.31
	.01	4.17	4.84	5.25	5.56	5.80	5.99	6.16	6.31	6.44	6.55
16	.05	3.00	3.65	4.05	4.33	4.56	4.74	4.90	5.03	5.15	5.26
	.01	4.13	4.79	5.19	5.49	5.72	5.92	6.08	6.22	6.35	6.46
17	.05	2.98	3.63	4.02	4.30	4.52	4.70	4.86	4.99	5.11	5.21
	.01	4.10	4.74	5.14	5.43	5.66	5.85	6.01	6.15	6.27	6.38
18	.05	2.97	3.61	4.00	4.28	4.49	4.67	4.82	4.96	5.07	5.17
	.01	4.07	4.70	5.09	5.38	5.60	5.79	5.94	6.08	6.20	6.31
19	.05	2.96	3.59	3.98	4.25	4.47	4.65	4.79	4.92	5.04	5.14
	.01	4.05	4.67	5.05	5.33	5.55	5.73	5.89	6.02	6.14	6.25
20	.05	2.95	3.58	3.96	4.23	4.45	4.62	4.77	4.90	5.01	5.11
	.01	4.02	4.64	5.02	5.29	5.51	5.69	5.84	5.97	6.09	6.19
24	.05	2.92	3.53	3.90	4.17	4.37	4.54	4.68	4.81	4.92	5.01
	.01	3.96	4.55	4.91	5.17	5.37	5.54	5.69	5.81	5.92	6.02
30	.05	2.89	3.49	3.85	4.10	4.30	4.46	4.60	4.72	4.82	4.92
	.01	3.89	4.45	4.80	5.05	5.24	5.40	5.54	5.65	5.76	5.85
40	.05	2.86	3.44	3.79	4.04	4.23	4.39	4.52	4.63	4.73	4.82
	.01	3.82	4.37	4.70	4.93	5.11	5.26	5.39	5.50	5.60	5.69
60	.05	2.83	3.40	3.74	3.98	4.16	4.31	4.44	4.55	4.65	4.73
	.01	3.76	4.28	4.59	4.82	4.99	5.13	5.25	5.36	5.45	5.53
120	.05	2.80	3.36	3.68	3.92	4.10	4.24	4.36	4.47	4.56	4.64
	.01	3.70	4.20	4.50	4.71	4.87	5.01	5.12	5.21	5.30	5.37
∞	.05	2.77	3.31	3.63	3.86	4.03	4.17	4.29	4.39	4.47	4.55
	.01	3.64	4.12	4.40	4.60	4.76	4.88	4.99	5.08	5.16	5.23

TABLE F   Continued

12	13	14	15	16	17	18	19	20	α	Error df
\multicolumn{11}{c}{*r = number of means or number of steps between ordered means*}										*Error df*
7.32	7.47	7.60	7.72	7.83	7.93	8.03	8.12	8.21	.05	5
10.70	10.89	11.08	11.24	11.40	11.55	11.68	11.81	11.93	.01	
6.79	6.92	7.03	7.14	7.24	7.34	7.43	7.51	7.59	.05	6
9.48	9.65	9.81	9.95	10.08	10.21	10.32	10.43	10.54	.01	
6.43	6.55	6.66	6.76	6.85	6.94	7.02	7.10	7.17	.05	7
8.71	8.86	9.00	9.12	9.24	9.35	9.46	9.55	9.65	.01	
6.18	6.29	6.39	6.48	6.57	6.65	6.73	6.80	6.87	.05	8
8.18	8.31	8.44	8.55	8.66	8.76	8.85	8.94	9.03	.01	
5.98	6.09	6.19	6.28	6.36	6.44	6.51	6.58	6.64	.05	9
7.78	7.91	8.03	8.13	8.23	8.33	8.41	8.49	8.57	.01	
5.83	5.93	6.03	6.11	6.19	6.27	6.34	6.40	6.47	.05	10
7.49	7.60	7.71	8.81	7.91	7.99	8.08	8.15	8.23	.01	
5.71	5.81	5.90	5.98	6.06	6.13	6.20	6.27	6.33	.05	11
7.25	7.36	7.46	7.56	7.65	7.73	7.81	7.88	7.95	.01	
5.61	5.71	5.80	5.88	5.95	6.02	6.09	6.15	6.21	.05	12
7.06	7.17	7.26	7.36	7.44	7.52	7.59	7.66	7.73	.01	
5.53	5.63	5.71	5.79	5.86	5.93	5.99	6.05	6.11	.05	13
6.90	7.01	7.10	7.19	7.27	7.35	7.42	7.48	7.55	.01	
5.46	5.55	5.64	5.71	5.79	5.85	5.91	5.97	6.03	.05	14
6.77	6.87	6.96	7.05	7.13	7.20	7.27	7.33	7.39	.01	
5.40	5.49	5.57	5.65	5.72	5.78	5.85	5.90	5.96	.05	15
6.66	6.76	6.84	6.93	7.00	7.07	7.14	7.20	7.26	.01	
5.35	5.44	5.52	5.59	5.66	5.73	5.79	5.84	5.90	.05	16
6.56	6.66	6.74	6.82	6.90	6.97	7.03	7.09	7.15	.01	
5.31	5.39	5.47	5.54	5.61	5.67	5.73	5.79	5.84	.05	17
6.48	6.57	6.66	6.73	6.81	6.87	6.94	7.00	7.05	.01	
5.27	5.35	5.43	5.50	5.57	5.63	5.69	5.74	5.79	.05	18
6.41	6.50	6.58	6.65	6.73	6.79	6.85	6.91	6.97	.01	
5.23	5.31	5.39	5.46	5.53	5.59	5.65	5.70	5.75	.05	19
6.34	6.43	6.51	6.58	6.65	6.72	6.78	6.84	6.89	.01	
5.20	5.28	5.36	5.43	5.49	5.55	5.61	5.66	5.71	.05	20
6.28	6.37	6.45	6.52	6.59	6.65	6.71	6.77	6.82	.01	
5.10	5.18	5.25	5.32	5.38	5.44	5.49	5.55	5.59	.05	24
6.11	6.19	6.26	6.33	6.39	6.45	6.51	6.56	6.61	.01	
5.00	5.08	5.15	5.21	5.27	5.33	5.38	5.43	5.47	.05	30
5.93	6.01	6.08	6.14	6.20	6.26	6.31	6.36	6.41	.01	
4.90	4.98	5.04	5.11	5.16	5.22	5.27	5.31	5.36	.05	40
5.76	5.83	5.90	5.96	6.02	6.07	6.12	6.16	6.21	.01	
4.81	4.88	4.94	5.00	5.06	5.11	5.15	5.20	5.24	.05	60
5.60	5.67	5.73	5.78	5.84	5.89	5.93	5.97	6.01	.01	
4.71	4.78	4.84	4.90	4.95	5.00	5.04	5.09	5.13	.05	120
5.44	5.50	5.56	5.61	5.66	5.71	5.75	5.79	5.83	.01	
4.62	4.68	4.74	4.80	4.85	4.89	4.93	4.97	5.01	.05	∞
5.29	5.35	5.40	5.45	5.49	5.54	5.57	5.61	5.65	.01	

Source: Table F is abridged from Table 29 in *Biometrika tables for statisticians.* Vol. 1 (2nd ed.), edited by E. S. Pearson & H.O. Hartley. New York: Cambridge, 1958. Reproduced with the kind permission of the editors and the trustees of *Biometrika*.

TABLE G   Critical values of the Pearson product-moment correlation
If the observed value of *r* is *greater than or equal to* the tabulated value for the appropriate level of significance (columns) and degrees of freedom (rows), then reject H_0. The degrees of freedom are the number of pairs of scores minus two, or $N - 2$. The critical values in the table are both + and − for nondirectional (two-tail) tests.

	Level of significance for a directional (one-tailed) test				
	.05	*.025*	*.01*	*.005*	*.0005*
	Level of significance for a nondirectional (two-tailed) test				
df = N − 2	*.10*	*.05*	*.02*	*.01*	*.001*
1	.9877	.9969	.9995	.9999	1.0000
2	.9000	.9500	.9800	.9900	.9990
3	.8054	.8783	.9343	.9587	.9912
4	.7293	.8114	.8822	.9172	.9741
5	.6694	.7545	.8329	.8745	.9507
6	.6215	.7067	.7887	.8343	.9249
7	.5822	.6664	.7498	.7977	.8982
8	.5494	.6319	.7155	.7646	.8721
9	.5214	.6021	.6851	.7348	.8471
10	.4973	.5760	.6581	.7079	.8233
11	.4762	.5529	.6339	.6835	.8010
12	.4575	.5324	.6120	.6614	.7800
13	.4409	.5139	.5923	.6411	.7603
14	.4259	.4973	.5742	.6226	.7420
15	.4124	.4821	.5577	.6055	.7246
16	.4000	.4683	.5425	.5897	.7084
17	.3887	.4555	.5285	.5751	.6932
18	.3783	.4438	.5155	.5614	.6787
19	.3687	.4329	.5034	.5487	.6652
20	.3598	.4227	.4921	.5368	.6524
25	.3233	.3809	.4451	.4869	.5974
30	.2960	.3494	.4093	.4487	.5541
35	.2746	.3246	.3810	.4182	.5189
40	.2573	.3044	.3578	.3932	.4896
45	.2428	.2875	.3384	.3721	.4648
50	.2306	.2732	.3218	.3541	.4433
60	.2108	.2500	.2948	.3248	.4078
70	.1954	.2319	.2737	.3017	.3799
80	.1829	.2172	.2565	.2830	.3568
90	.1726	.2050	.2422	.2673	.3375
100	.1638	.1946	.2301	.2540	.3211

Source: Table G is taken from Table VII of Fisher & Yates, *Statistical tables for biological, agricultural and medical research,* published by Longman Group UK Ltd., London (previously published by Oliver and Boyd Ltd., Edinburgh), with permission of the authors and the publishers.

TABLE H   Coefficients of correlation significant at the .05 level (upper values) and at the .01
level (lower values) for varying degrees of freedom (two-tail test).

Degrees of Freedom	\multicolumn{9}{c}{*Number of variables*}	
	2	*3*	*4*	*5*	*6*	*7*	*9*	*13*	*25*	*t*
1	.997	.999	.999	.999	1.000	1.000	1.000	1.000	1.000	12.706
	1.000	1.000	1.000	1.000	1.000	1.000	1.000	1.000	1.000	63.657
2	.950	.975	.983	.987	.990	.992	.994	.996	.998	4.303
	.990	.995	.997	.998	.998	.998	.999	.999	1.000	9.925
3	.878	.930	.950	.961	.968	.973	.979	.986	.993	3.182
	.959	.976	.983	.987	.990	.991	.993	.995	.998	5.841
4	.811	.881	.912	.930	.942	.950	.961	.973	.986	2.776
	.917	.949	.962	.970	.975	.979	.984	.989	.994	4.604
5	.754	.836	.874	.898	.914	.925	.941	.958	.978	2.571
	.874	.917	.937	.949	.957	.963	.971	.980	.989	4.032
6	.707	.795	.839	.867	.886	.900	.920	.943	.969	2.447
	.834	.886	.911	.927	.938	.946	.957	.969	.983	3.707
7	.666	.758	.807	.838	.860	.876	.900	.927	.960	2.365
	.798	.855	.885	.904	.918	.928	.942	.958	.977	3.499
8	.632	.726	.777	.811	.835	.854	.880	.912	.950	2.306
	.765	.827	.860	.882	.898	.909	.926	.949	.970	3.355
9	.602	.697	.750	.786	.812	.832	.861	.897	.941	2.262
	.735	.800	.836	.861	.878	.891	.911	.934	.963	3.250
10	.576	.671	.726	.763	.790	.812	.843	.882	.932	2.228
	.708	.776	.814	.840	.859	.874	.895	.922	.955	3.169
11	.553	.648	.703	.741	.770	.792	.826	.868	.922	2.201
	.684	.753	.793	.821	.841	.857	.880	.910	.948	3.106
12	.532	.627	.683	.722	.751	.774	.809	.854	.913	2.179
	.661	.732	.773	.802	.824	.841	.866	.898	.940	3.055
13	.514	.608	.664	.703	.733	.757	.794	.840	.904	2.160
	.641	.712	.755	.785	.807	.825	.852	.886	.932	3.012
14	.497	.590	.646	.686	.717	.741	.779	.828	.895	2.145
	.623	.694	.737	.768	.792	.810	.838	.875	.924	2.977
15	.482	.574	.630	.670	.701	.726	.765	.815	.886	2.131
	.606	.677	.721	.752	.776	.796	.825	.864	.917	2.947
16	.468	.559	.615	.655	.686	.712	.751	.803	.878	2.120
	.590	.662	.706	.738	.762	.782	.813	.853	.909	2.921
17	.456	.545	.601	.641	.673	.698	.738	.792	.869	2.110
	.575	.647	.691	.724	.749	.769	.800	.842	.902	2.898
18	.444	.532	.587	.628	.660	.686	.726	.781	.861	2.101
	.561	.633	.678	.710	.736	.756	.789	.832	.894	2.878
19	.433	.520	.575	.615	.647	.674	.714	.770	.853	2.093
	.549	.620	.665	.698	.723	.744	.778	.822	.887	2.861
20	.423	.509	.563	.604	.636	.662	.703	.760	.845	2.086
	.537	.608	.652	.685	.712	.733	.767	.812	.880	2.845
21	.413	.498	.552	.592	.624	.651	.693	.750	.837	2.080
	.526	.596	.641	.674	.700	.722	.756	.803	.873	2.831
22	.404	.488	.542	.582	.614	.640	.682	.740	.830	2.074
	.515	.585	.630	.663	.690	.712	.746	.794	.866	2.819
23	.396	.479	.532	.572	.604	.630	.673	.731	.823	2.069
	.505	.574	.619	.652	.679	.701	.736	.785	.859	2.807

Continues

TABLE H   Continued

Degrees of freedom	Number of variables									t
	2	3	4	5	6	7	9	13	25	
24	.388	.470	.523	.562	.594	.621	.663	.722	.815	2.064
	.496	.565	.609	.642	.669	.692	.727	.776	.852	2.797
25	.381	.462	.514	.553	.585	.612	.654	.714	.808	2.060
	.487	.555	.600	.633	.660	.682	.718	.768	.846	2.787
26	.374	.454	.506	.545	.576	.603	.645	.706	.802	2.056
	.478	.546	.590	.624	.651	.673	.709	.760	.839	2.779
27	.367	.446	.498	.536	.568	.594	.637	.698	.795	2.052
	.470	.538	.582	.615	.642	.664	.701	.752	.833	2.771
28	.361	.439	.490	.529	.560	.586	.629	.690	.788	2.048
	.463	.530	.573	.606	.634	.656	.692	.744	.827	2.763
29	.355	.432	.482	.521	.552	.579	.621	.682	.782	2.045
	.456	.522	.565	.598	.625	.648	.685	.737	.821	2.756
30	.349	.426	.476	.514	.545	.571	.614	.675	.776	2.042
	.449	.514	.558	.591	.618	.640	.677	.729	.815	2.750
35	.325	.397	.445	.482	.512	.538	.580	.642	.746	2.030
	.418	.481	.523	.556	.582	.605	.642	.696	.786	2.724
40	.304	.373	.419	.455	.484	.509	.551	.613	.720	2.021
	.393	.454	.494	.526	.552	.575	.612	.667	.761	2.704
45	.288	.353	.397	.432	.460	.485	.526	.587	.696	2.014
	.372	.430	.470	.501	.527	.549	.586	.640	.737	2.690
50	.273	.336	.379	.412	.440	.464	.504	.565	.674	2.008
	.354	.410	.449	.479	.504	.526	.562	.617	.715	2.678
60	.250	.308	.348	.380	.406	.429	.467	.526	.636	2.000
	.325	.377	.414	.442	.466	.488	.523	.577	.677	2.660
70	.233	.286	.324	.354	.379	.401	.438	.495	.604	1.994
	.302	.351	.386	.413	.436	.456	.491	.544	.644	2.648
80	.217	.269	.304	.332	.356	.377	.413	.469	.576	1.990
	.283	.330	.362	.389	.411	.431	.464	.516	.615	2.638
90	.205	.254	.288	.315	.338	.358	.392	.446	.552	1.987
	.267	.312	.343	.368	.390	.409	.441	.492	.590	2.632
100	.195	.241	.274	.300	.322	.341	.374	.426	.530	1.984
	.254	.297	.327	.351	.372	.390	.421	.470	.568	2.626
125	.174	.216	.246	.269	.290	.307	.338	.387	.485	1.979
	.228	.266	.294	.316	.335	.352	.381	.428	.521	2.616
150	.159	.198	.225	.247	.266	.282	.310	.356	.450	1.976
	.208	.244	.270	.290	.308	.324	.351	.395	.484	2.609
200	.138	.172	.196	.215	.231	.246	.271	.312	.398	1.972
	.181	.212	.234	.253	.269	.283	.307	.347	.430	2.601
300	.113	.141	.160	.176	.190	.202	.223	.258	.332	1.968
	.148	.174	.192	.208	.221	.233	.253	.287	.359	2.592
400	.098	.122	.139	.153	.165	.176	.194	.225	.291	1.966
	.128	.151	.167	.180	.192	.202	.220	.250	.315	2.588
500	.088	.109	.124	.137	.148	.157	.174	.202	.262	1.965
	.115	.135	.150	.162	.172	.182	.198	.225	.284	2.586
1.000	.062	.077	.088	.097	.105	.112	.124	.144	.188	1.962
	.081	.096	.106	.115	.122	.129	.141	.160	.204	2.581
∞										1.960
										2.576

Source: Table H is adapted from Wallace, H.A., & Snedecor, G.W. *Correlation and machine calculation.* Ames, Iowa: Iowa State College, 1931. Courtesy of the authors and the publisher.

TABLE I   Conversion of a Pearson r into a Fisher Z coefficient

r	Z	r	Z	r	Z	r	Z	r	Z
.000	.000	.200	.203	.400	.424	.600	.693	.800	1.099
.005	.005	.205	.208	.405	.430	.605	.701	.805	1.113
.010	.010	.210	.213	.410	.436	.610	.709	.810	1.127
.015	.015	.215	.218	.415	.442	.615	.717	.815	1.142
.020	.020	.220	.224	.420	.448	.620	.725	.820	1.157
.025	.025	.225	.229	.425	.454	.625	.733	.825	1.172
.030	.030	.230	.234	.430	.460	.630	.741	.830	1.188
.035	.035	.235	.239	.435	.466	.635	.750	.835	1.204
.040	.040	.240	.245	.440	.472	.640	.758	.840	1.221
.045	.045	.245	.250	.445	.478	.645	.767	.845	1.238
.050	.050	.250	.255	.450	.485	.650	.775	.850	1.256
.055	.055	.255	.261	.455	.491	.655	.784	.855	1.274
.060	.060	.260	.266	.460	.497	.660	.793	.860	1.293
.065	.065	.265	.271	.465	.504	.665	.802	.865	1.313
.070	.070	.270	.277	.470	.510	.670	.811	.870	1.333
.075	.075	.275	.281	.475	.517	.675	.820	.875	1.354
.080	.080	.280	.288	.480	.523	.680	.829	.880	1.376
.085	.085	.285	.293	.485	.530	.685	.838	.885	1.398
.090	.090	.290	.299	.490	.536	.690	.848	.890	1.422
.095	.095	.295	.304	.495	.543	.695	.858	.895	1.447
.100	.100	.300	.310	.500	.549	.700	.867	.900	1.472
.105	.105	.305	.315	.505	.556	.705	.877	.905	1.499
.110	.110	.310	.321	.510	.563	.710	.887	.910	1.528
.115	.116	.315	.326	.515	.570	.715	.897	.915	1.557
.120	.121	.320	.332	.520	.576	.720	.908	.920	1.589
.125	.126	.325	.337	.525	.583	.725	.918	.925	1.623
.130	.131	.330	.343	.530	.590	.730	.929	.930	1.658
.135	.136	.335	.348	.535	.597	.735	.940	.935	1.697
.140	.141	.340	.354	.540	.604	.740	.950	.940	1.738
.145	.146	.345	.360	.545	.611	.745	.962	.945	1.783
.150	.151	.350	.365	.550	.618	.750	.973	.950	1.832
.155	.156	.355	.371	.555	.626	.755	.984	.955	1.886
.160	.161	.360	.377	.560	.633	.760	.996	.960	1.946
.165	.167	.365	.383	.565	.640	.765	1.008	.965	2.014
.170	.172	.370	.388	.570	.648	.770	1.020	.970	2.092
.175	.177	.375	.394	.575	.655	.775	1.033	.975	2.185
.180	.182	.380	.400	.580	.662	.780	1.045	.980	2.298
.185	.187	.385	.406	.585	.670	.785	1.058	.985	2.443
.190	.192	.390	.412	.590	.678	.790	1.071	.990	2.647
.195	.198	.395	.418	.595	.685	.795	1.085	.995	2.994

Source: Table I is taken from Table V.B. of Fisher, *Statistical methods for research workers.*
Published by Longman Group UK Ltd., London (previously published by Oliver and Boyd Ltd.,
Edinburgh, 1932), with permission of the author and the publishers.

TABLE J   Probabilities associated with values as small as observed values of U in the Mann-Whitney test ($3 \leq n_L \leq 8$)

$N_2 = 3$

U	N_1		
	1	2	3
0	.250	.100	.050
1	.500	.200	.100
2	.750	.400	.200
3		.600	.350
4			.500
5			.650

$N_2 = 4$

U	N_1			
	1	2	3	4
0	.200	.067	.028	.014
1	.400	.133	.057	.029
2	.600	.267	.114	.057
3		.400	.200	.100
4		.600	.314	.171
5			.429	.243
6			.571	.343
7				.443
8				.557

$N_2 = 5$

U	N_1				
	1	2	3	4	5
0	.167	.047	.018	.008	.004
1	.333	.095	.036	.016	.008
2	.500	.190	.071	.032	.016
3	.667	.286	.125	.056	.028
4		.429	.196	.095	.048
5		.571	.286	.143	.075
6			.393	.206	.111
7			.500	.278	.155
8			.607	.365	.210
9				.452	.274
10				.548	.345
11					.421
12					.500
13					.579

$N_2 = 6$

U	N_1					
	1	2	3	4	5	6
0	.143	.036	.012	.005	.002	.001
1	.286	.071	.024	.010	.004	.002
2	.428	.143	.048	.019	.009	.004
3	.571	.214	.083	.033	.015	.008
4		.321	.131	.057	.026	.013
5		.429	.190	.086	.041	.021
6		.571	.274	.129	.063	.032
7			.357	.176	.089	.047
8			.452	.238	.123	.066
9			.548	.305	.165	.090
10				.381	.214	.120
11				.457	.268	.155
12				.545	.331	.197
13					.396	.242
14					.465	.294
15					.535	.350
16						.409
17						.469
18						.531

TABLE J Continued

$N_2 = 7$

				N_1			
U	1	2	3	4	5	6	7
0	.125	.028	.008	.003	.001	.001	.000
1	.250	.056	.017	.006	.003	.001	.001
2	.375	.111	.033	.012	.005	.002	.001
3	.500	.167	.058	.021	.009	.004	.002
4	.625	.250	.092	.036	.015	.007	.003
5		.333	.133	.055	.024	.011	.006
6		.444	.192	.082	.037	.017	.009
7		.556	.258	.115	.053	.026	.013
8			.333	.158	.074	.037	.019
9			.417	.206	.101	.051	.027
10			.500	.264	.134	.069	.036
11			.583	.324	.172	.090	.049
12				.394	.216	.117	.064
13				.464	.265	.147	.082
14				.538	.319	.183	.104
15					.378	.223	.130
16					.438	.267	.159
17					.500	.314	.191
18					.562	.365	.228
19						.418	.267
20						.473	.310
21						.527	.355
22							.402
23							.451
24							.500
25							.549

Continues

TABLE J   Continued

$N_2 = 8$

U	1	2	3	4	5	6	7	8	t	*Normal*
0	.111	.022	.006	.002	.001	.000	.000	.000	3.308	.001
1	.222	.044	.012	.004	.002	.001	.000	.000	3.203	.001
2	.333	.089	.024	.008	.003	.001	.001	.000	3.098	.001
3	.444	.133	.042	.014	.005	.002	.001	.001	2.993	.001
4	.556	.200	.067	.024	.009	.004	.002	.001	2.888	.002
5		.267	.097	.036	.015	.006	.003	.001	2.783	.003
6		.356	.139	.055	.023	.010	.005	.002	2.678	.004
7		.444	.188	.077	.033	.015	.007	.003	2.573	.005
8		.556	.248	.107	.047	.021	.010	.005	2.468	.007
9			.315	.141	.064	.030	.014	.007	2.363	.009
10			.387	.184	.085	.041	.020	.010	2.258	.012
11			.461	.230	.111	.054	.027	.014	2.153	.016
12			.539	.285	.142	.071	.036	.019	2.048	.020
13				.341	.177	.091	.047	.025	1.943	.026
14				.404	.217	.114	.060	.032	1.838	.033
15				.467	.262	.141	.076	.041	1.733	.041
16				.533	.311	.172	.095	.052	1.628	.052
17					.362	.207	.116	.065	1.523	.064
18					.416	.245	.140	.080	1.418	.078
19					.472	.286	.168	.097	1.313	.094
20					.528	.331	.198	.117	1.208	.113
21						.377	.232	.139	1.102	.135
22						.426	.268	.164	.998	.159
23						.475	.306	.191	.893	.185
24						.525	.347	.221	.788	.215
25							.389	.253	.683	.247
26							.433	.287	.578	.282
27							.478	.323	.473	.318
28							.522	.360	.368	.356
29								.399	.263	.396
30								.439	.158	.437
31								.480	.052	.481
32								.520		

Source: Table J is from Mann, H.B., & Whitney, D.R. On a test of whether one of two random variables is stochastically larger than the other. *Annals of Mathematical Statistics,* 1947. **18,** 52–54. Reprinted by permission of the authors and the publisher.

TABLE K   Critical values of U in the Mann-Whitney test ($9 \leq n_L \leq 20$)

Critical Values of U for a One-tailed Test at $\alpha = .001$ or for a Two-tail Test at $\alpha = .002$

N_1	9	10	11	12	13	14	15	16	17	18	19	20
1												
2												
3								0	0	0	0	0
4		0	0	0	1	1	1	2	2	3	3	3
5	1	1	2	2	3	3	4	5	5	6	7	7
6	2	3	4	4	5	6	7	8	9	10	11	12
7	3	5	6	7	8	9	10	11	13	14	15	16
8	5	6	8	9	11	12	14	15	17	18	20	21
9	7	8	10	12	14	15	17	19	21	23	25	26
10	8	10	12	14	17	19	21	23	25	27	29	32
11	10	12	15	17	20	22	24	27	29	32	34	37
12	12	14	17	20	23	25	28	31	34	37	40	42
13	14	17	20	23	26	29	32	35	38	42	45	48
14	15	19	22	25	29	32	36	39	43	46	50	54
15	17	21	24	28	32	36	40	43	47	51	55	59
16	19	23	27	31	35	39	43	48	52	56	60	65
17	21	25	29	34	38	43	47	52	57	61	66	70
18	23	27	32	37	42	46	51	56	61	66	71	76
19	25	29	34	40	45	50	55	60	66	71	77	82
20	26	32	37	42	48	54	59	65	70	76	82	88

Critical Values of U for a One-tailed Test at $\alpha = .01$ or for a Two-tail Test at $\alpha = .02$

N_1	9	10	11	12	13	14	15	16	17	18	19	20
1												
2				0	0	0	0	0	0	0	1	1
3	1	1	1	2	2	2	3	3	4	4	4	5
4	3	3	4	5	5	6	7	7	8	9	9	10
5	5	6	7	8	9	10	11	12	13	14	15	16
6	7	8	9	11	12	13	15	16	18	19	20	22
7	9	11	12	14	16	17	19	21	23	24	26	28
8	11	13	15	17	20	22	24	26	28	30	32	34
9	14	16	18	21	23	26	28	31	33	36	38	40
10	16	19	22	24	27	30	33	36	38	41	44	47
11	18	22	25	28	31	34	37	41	44	47	50	53
12	21	24	28	31	35	38	42	46	49	53	56	60
13	23	27	31	35	39	43	47	51	55	59	63	67
14	26	30	34	38	43	47	51	56	60	65	69	73
15	28	33	37	42	47	51	56	61	66	70	75	80
16	31	36	41	46	51	56	61	66	71	76	82	87
17	33	38	44	49	55	60	66	71	77	82	88	93
18	36	41	47	53	59	65	70	76	82	88	94	100
19	38	44	50	56	63	69	75	82	88	94	101	107
20	40	47	53	60	67	73	80	87	93	100	107	114

Critical Values of U for a One-tailed Test at $\alpha = .025$ or for a Two-tail Test at $\alpha = .05$

N_1	9	10	11	12	13	14	15	16	17	18	19	20
1												
2	0	0	0	1	1	1	1	1	2	2	2	2
3	2	3	3	4	4	5	5	6	6	7	7	8
4	4	5	6	7	8	9	10	11	11	12	13	13
5	7	8	9	11	12	13	14	15	17	18	19	20
6	10	11	13	14	16	17	19	21	22	24	25	27
7	12	14	16	18	20	22	24	26	28	30	32	34
8	15	17	19	22	24	26	29	31	34	36	38	41
9	17	20	23	26	28	31	34	37	39	42	45	48
10	20	23	26	29	33	36	39	42	45	48	52	55
11	23	26	30	33	37	40	44	47	51	55	58	62
12	26	29	33	37	41	45	49	53	57	61	65	69
13	28	33	37	41	45	50	54	59	63	67	72	76
14	31	36	40	45	50	55	59	64	67	74	78	83
15	34	39	44	49	54	59	64	70	75	80	85	90
16	37	42	47	53	59	64	70	75	81	86	92	98
17	39	45	51	57	63	67	75	81	87	93	99	105
18	42	48	55	61	67	74	80	86	93	99	106	112
19	45	52	58	65	72	78	85	92	99	106	113	119
20	48	55	62	69	76	83	90	98	105	112	119	127

Critical Values of U for a One-tailed Test at $\alpha = .05$ or for a Two-tail Test at $\alpha = .10$

N_1	9	10	11	12	13	14	15	16	17	18	19	20
1											0	0
2	1	1	1	2	2	2	3	3	3	4	4	4
3	3	4	5	5	6	7	7	8	9	9	10	11
4	6	7	8	9	10	11	12	14	15	16	17	18
5	9	11	12	13	15	16	18	19	20	22	23	25
6	12	14	16	17	19	21	23	25	26	28	30	32
7	15	17	19	21	24	26	28	30	33	35	37	39
8	18	20	23	26	28	31	33	36	39	41	44	47
9	21	24	27	30	33	36	39	42	45	48	51	54
10	24	27	31	34	37	41	44	48	51	55	58	62
11	27	31	34	38	42	46	50	54	57	61	65	69
12	30	34	38	42	47	51	55	60	64	68	72	77
13	33	37	42	47	51	56	61	65	70	75	80	84
14	36	41	46	51	56	61	66	71	77	82	87	92
15	39	44	50	55	61	66	72	77	83	88	94	100
16	42	48	54	60	65	71	77	83	89	95	101	107
17	45	51	57	64	70	77	83	89	96	102	109	115
18	48	55	61	68	75	82	88	95	102	109	116	123
19	51	58	65	72	80	87	94	101	109	116	123	130
20	54	62	69	77	84	92	100	107	115	123	130	138

Source: Table K is adapted and abridged from Tables 1, 3, 5, and 7 of Auble, D. Extended tables for the Mann-Whitney statistic. *Bulletin of the Institute of Educational Research at Indiana University,* 1953, **1**, 2. Reprinted by the kind permission of the author and the publisher.

TABLE L   Percentage points of the Bryant-Paulson generalized studentized range statistic

Error df	Number of Covariates (C)	α	Number of Means (k)										
			2	3	4	5	6	7	8	10	11	12	16
3	1	.05	5.42	7.18	8.32	9.17	9.84	10.39	10.86	11.62	12.22	13.14	13.83
		.01	10.28	13.32	15.32	16.80	17.98	18.95	19.77	21.12	22.19	23.82	25.05
	2	.05	6.21	8.27	9.60	10.59	11.37	12.01	12.56	13.44	14.15	15.22	16.02
		.01	11.97	15.56	17.91	19.66	21.05	22.19	23.16	24.75	26.01	27.93	29.38
	3	.05	6.92	9.23	10.73	11.84	12.72	12.44	14.06	15.05	15.84	17.05	17.95
		.01	13.45	17.51	20.17	22.15	23.72	25.01	26.11	27.90	29.32	31.50	33.13
4	1	.05	4.51	5.84	6.69	7.32	8.23	8.58	9.15	9.61	10.30	10.82	
		.01	7.68	9.64	10.93	11.89	12.65	13.28	13.82	14.70	15.40	16.48	17.29
	2	.05	5.04	6.54	7.51	8.23	8.80	9.26	9.66	10.31	10.83	11.61	12.21
		.01	8.69	10.95	12.43	13.54	14.41	15.14	15.76	16.77	17.58	18.81	19.74
	3	.05	5.51	7.18	8.25	9.05	9.67	10.19	10.63	11.35	11.92	12.79	13.45
		.01	9.59	12.11	13.77	15.00	15.98	16.79	17.47	18.60	19.50	20.87	21.91
5	1	.05	4.06	5.17	5.88	6.40	6.82	7.16	7.45	7.93	8.30	8.88	9.32
		.01	6.49	7.99	8.97	9.70	10.28	10.76	11.17	11.84	12.38	13.20	13.83
	2	.05	4.45	5.68	6.48	7.06	7.52	7.90	8.23	8.76	9.18	9.83	10.31
		.01	7.20	8.89	9.99	10.81	11.47	12.01	12.47	13.23	13.84	14.77	15.47
	3	.05	4.81	6.16	7.02	7.66	8.17	8.58	8.94	9.52	9.98	10.69	11.22
		.01	7.83	9.70	10.92	11.82	12.54	13.14	13.65	14.48	15.15	16.17	16.95
6	1	.05	3.79	4.78	5.40	5.86	6.23	6.53	6.78	7.20	7.53	8.04	8.43
		.01	5.83	7.08	7.88	8.48	8.96	9.36	9.70	10.25	10.70	11.38	11.90
	2	.05	4.10	5.18	5.87	6.37	6.77	7.10	7.38	7.84	8.21	8.77	9.20
		.01	6.36	7.75	8.64	9.31	9.85	10.29	10.66	11.28	11.77	12.51	13.11
	3	.05	4.38	5.55	6.30	6.84	7.28	7.64	7.94	8.44	8.83	9.44	9.90
		.01	6.85	8.36	9.34	10.07	10.65	11.13	11.54	12.22	12.75	13.59	14.21
7	1	.05	3.62	4.52	5.09	5.51	5.84	6.11	6.34	6.72	7.03	7.49	7.84
		.01	5.41	6.50	7.20	7.72	8.14	8.48	8.77	9.26	9.64	10.24	10.69
	2	.05	3.87	4.85	5.47	5.92	6.28	6.58	6.83	7.24	7.57	8.08	8.46
		.01	5.84	7.03	7.80	8.37	8.83	9.21	9.53	10.06	10.49	11.14	11.64
	3	.05	4.11	5.16	5.82	6.31	6.70	7.01	7.29	7.73	8.08	8.63	9.03
		.01	6.23	7.52	8.36	8.98	9.47	9.47	9.88	10.23	10.80	11.26	11.97
8	1	.05	3.49	4.34	4.87	5.26	5.57	5.82	6.03	6.39	6.67	7.10	7.43
		.01	5.12	6.11	6.74	7.20	7.58	7.88	8.15	8.58	8.92	9.46	9.87
	2	.05	3.70	4.61	5.19	5.61	5.94	6.21	6.44	6.82	7.12	7.59	7.94
		.01	5.48	6.54	7.23	7.74	8.14	8.48	8.76	9.23	9.61	10.19	10.63
	3	.05	3.91	4.88	5.49	5.93	6.29	6.58	6.83	7.23	7.55	8.05	8.42
		.01	5.81	6.95	7.69	8.23	8.67	9.03	9.33	9.84	10.24	10.87	11.34
10	1	.05	3.32	4.10	4.58	4.93	5.21	5.43	5.63	5.94	6.19	6.58	6.87
		.01	4.76	5.61	6.15	6.55	6.86	7.13	7.35	7.72	8.01	8.47	8.82
	2	.05	3.49	4.31	4.82	5.19	5.49	5.73	5.93	6.27	6.54	6.95	7.26
		.01	5.02	5.93	6.51	6.93	7.27	7.55	7.79	8.19	8.50	8.99	9.36
	3	.05	3.65	4.51	5.05	5.44	5.75	6.01	6.22	6.58	6.86	7.29	7.62
		.01	5.27	6.23	6.84	7.30	7.66	7.96	8.21	8.63	8.96	9.48	9.88
12	1	.05	3.22	3.95	4.40	4.73	4.98	5.19	5.37	5.67	5.90	6.26	6.53
		.01	4.54	5.31	5.79	6.15	6.43	6.67	6.87	7.20	7.46	7.87	8.18
	2	.05	3.35	4.12	4.59	4.93	5.20	5.43	5.62	5.92	6.17	6.55	6.83
		.01	4.74	5.56	6.07	6.35	6.75	7.00	7.21	7.56	7.84	8.27	8.60
	3	.05	3.48	4.28	4.78	5.14	5.42	5.65	5.85	6.17	6.43	6.82	7.12
		.01	4.94	5.80	6.34	6.74	7.05	7.31	7.54	7.90	8.20	8.65	9.00

TABLE L Continued

Error df	Number of Covariates (C)	α	2	3	4	5	6	7	8	10	12	16	20
							Number of Means (k)						
14	1	.05	3.15	3.85	4.28	4.59	4.83	5.03	5.20	5.48	5.70	6.03	6.29
		.01	4.39	5.11	5.56	5.89	6.15	6.36	6.55	6.85	7.09	7.47	7.75
	2	.05	3.26	3.99	4.44	4.76	5.01	5.22	5.40	5.69	5.92	6.27	6.54
		.01	4.56	5.31	5.78	6.13	6.40	6.63	6.82	7.14	7.40	7.79	8.09
	3	.05	3.37	4.13	4.59	4.93	4.93	5.19	5.41	5.59	5.89	6.13	6.50
		.01	4.72	5.51	6.00	6.36	6.65	6.89	7.09	7.42	7.69	8.10	8.41
16	1	.05	3.10	3.77	4.19	4.49	4.72	4.91	5.07	5.34	5.55	5.87	6.12
		.01	4.28	4.96	5.39	5.70	5.95	6.15	6.32	6.60	6.83	7.18	7.45
	2	.05	3.19	3.90	4.32	4.63	4.88	5.07	5.24	5.52	5.74	6.07	6.33
		.01	4.42	5.14	5.58	5.90	6.16	6.37	6.55	6.85	7.08	7.45	7.73
	3	.05	3.29	4.01	4.46	4.78	5.03	5.23	5.41	5.69	5.92	6.27	6.53
		.01	4.56	5.30	5.76	6.10	6.37	6.59	6.77	7.08	7.33	7.71	8.00
18	1	.05	3.06	3.72	4.41	4.63	4.82	4.98	5.23	5.44	5.75	5.98	6.00
		.01	4.20	4.86	5.26	5.56	5.79	5.99	6.15	6.42	6.63	6.96	7.22
	2	.05	3.14	3.82	4.24	4.54	4.77	4.96	5.13	5.39	5.60	5.92	6.17
		.01	4.32	5.00	5.43	5.73	5.98	6.18	6.35	6.63	6.85	7.19	7.46
	3	.05	3.23	3.93	4.35	4.66	4.90	5.10	5.27	5.54	5.76	6.09	6.34
		.01	4.44	5.15	5.59	5.90	6.16	6.36	6.54	6.83	7.06	7.42	7.69
20	1	.05	3.03	3.67	4.07	4.35	4.57	4.75	4.90	5.15	5.35	5.65	5.88
		.01	4.14	4.77	5.17	5.45	5.68	5.86	6.02	6.27	6.48	6.80	7.04
	2	.05	3.10	3.77	4.17	4.46	4.69	4.88	5.03	5.29	5.49	5.81	6.04
		.01	4.25	4.90	5.31	5.60	5.84	6.03	6.19	6.46	6.67	7.00	7.25
	3	.05	3.18	3.86	4.28	4.57	4.81	5.00	5.16	5.42	5.63	5.96	6.20
		.01	4.35	5.03	5.45	5.75	5.99	6.19	6.36	6.63	6.85	7.19	7.45
24	1	.05	2.98	3.61	3.99	4.26	4.47	4.65	4.79	5.03	5.22	5.51	5.73
		.01	4.05	4.65	5.02	5.29	5.50	5.68	5.83	6.07	6.26	6.56	6.78
	2	.05	3.04	3.69	4.08	4.35	4.57	4.75	4.90	5.14	5.34	5.63	5.86
		.01	4.14	4.76	5.14	5.42	5.63	5.81	5.96	6.21	6.41	6.71	6.95
	3	.05	3.11	3.76	4.16	4.44	4.67	4.85	5.00	5.25	5.45	5.75	5.98
		.01	4.22	4.86	5.25	5.54	5.76	5.94	6.10	6.35	6.55	6.87	7.11
30	1	.05	2.94	3.55	3.91	4.18	4.38	4.54	4.69	4.91	5.09	5.37	5.58
		.01	3.96	4.54	4.89	5.14	5.34	5.50	5.64	5.87	6.05	6.32	6.53
	2	.05	2.99	3.61	3.98	4.25	4.46	4.62	4.77	5.00	5.18	5.46	5.68
		.01	4.03	4.62	4.98	5.24	5.44	5.61	5.75	5.98	6.16	6.44	6.66
	3	.05	3.04	3.67	4.05	4.32	4.53	4.70	4.85	5.08	5.27	5.56	5.78
		.01	4.10	4.70	5.06	5.33	5.54	5.71	5.85	6.08	6.27	6.56	6.78
40	1	.05	2.89	3.49	3.84	4.09	4.29	4.45	4.58	4.80	4.97	5.23	5.43
		.01	3.88	4.43	4.76	5.00	5.19	5.34	5.47	5.68	5.85	6.10	6.30
	2	.05	2.93	3.53	3.89	4.15	4.34	4.50	4.64	4.86	5.04	5.30	5.50
		.01	3.93	4.48	4.82	5.07	5.26	5.41	5.54	5.76	5.93	6.19	6.38
	3	.05	2.97	3.57	3.94	4.20	4.40	4.56	4.70	4.92	5.10	5.37	5.57
		.01	3.98	4.54	4.88	5.13	5.32	5.48	5.61	5.83	6.00	6.27	6.47
60	1	.05	2.85	3.43	3.77	4.01	4.20	4.35	4.48	4.69	4.85	5.10	5.29
		.01	3.79	4.32	4.64	4.86	5.04	5.18	5.30	5.50	5.65	5.89	6.07
	2	.05	2.88	3.46	3.80	4.05	4.24	4.39	4.52	4.73	4.89	5.14	5.33
		.01	3.83	4.36	4.68	4.90	5.08	5.22	5.35	5.54	5.70	5.94	6.12
	3	.05	2.90	3.49	3.83	4.08	4.27	4.43	4.56	4.77	4.93	5.19	5.38
		.01	3.86	4.39	4.72	4.95	5.12	5.27	5.39	5.59	5.75	6.00	6.18

Continues

TABLE L   Continued

Error df	Number of Covariates (C)	α	\multicolumn{11}{c}{Number of Means (k)}
			2	3	4	5	6	7	8	10	12	16	20
120	1	.05	2.81	3.37	3.70	3.93	4.11	4.26	4.38	4.58	4.73	4.97	5.15
		.01	3.72	4.22	4.52	4.73	4.89	5.03	5.14	5.32	5.47	5.69	5.85
	2	.05	2.82	3.38	3.72	3.95	4.13	4.28	4.40	4.60	4.75	4.99	5.17
		.01	3.73	4.24	4.54	4.75	4.91	5.05	5.16	5.35	5.49	5.71	5.88
	3	.05	2.84	3.40	3.73	3.97	4.15	4.30	4.42	4.62	4.77	5.01	5.19
		.01	3.75	4.25	4.55	4.77	4.94	5.07	5.18	5.37	5.51	5.74	5.90

Source: Table L is from Bryant, J.L., & Paulson, A.S. An extension of Tukey's method of multiple comparisons to experimental designs with designs with random concomitant variables. *Biometrika*, 1976, **63**, 631–638. Reprinted by the kind permission of the editors and the trustees.

TABLE M   Approximate power and sample size for various levels of significance (α) and effect size: case I, one- and two-tail tests; and case II, one- and two-tail tests

(a) Case I: One-Tail Significance Test

	Power	\multicolumn{14}{c}{Effect Size (Δ_I)}
		.15	.20	.25	.30	.35	.40	.45	.50	.55	.60	.65	.70	.75	.80
α = .10	.60	104	59	37	*										
	.70	144	81	52	36	*									
	.80	200	112	72	50	37	*								
	.90	291	164	105	73	54	91	32	*						
α = .05	.60	160	90	58	40	30	*								
	.70	209	118	75	52	38	*								
	.80	276	155	99	69	51	39	31	*						
	.90	382	215	137	95	70	54	42	34	*					
α = .01	.60	296	166	107	74	54	42	33	*						
	.70	361	203	130	90	66	51	40	32	*					
	.80	447	251	161	112	82	63	50	40	33	*				
	.90	579	326	209	145	106	81	64	52	43	36	31	*		

(b) Case I: Two-Tail Significance Test

	Power	\multicolumn{14}{c}{Effect Size (Δ_I)}
		.15	.20	.25	.30	.35	.40	.45	.50	.55	.60	.65	.70	.75	.80
α = .10	.60	160	90	58	40	30	*								
	.70	209	118	75	52	38	*								
	.80	276	155	99	69	51	39	31	*						
	.90	382	215	137	95	70	54	42	34	*					
α = .05	.60	217	122	78	54	40	31	*							
	.70	273	154	98	68	50	38	30	*						
	.80	348	196	125	87	64	49	39	31	*					
	.90	467	262	168	117	86	66	52	42	35	*				
α = .01	.60	356	200	128	89	65	50	40	32	*					
	.70	427	240	154	107	78	60	48	38	32	*				
	.80	520	292	187	130	96	73	58	47	39	33	*			
	.90	662	373	238	166	122	93	74	60	49	41	35	30	*	

TABLE M Continued

(c) Case II: One-Tail Significance Test (Sample Size for Each Group)

Effect Size (Δ_{II})

	Power	.15	.20	.25	.30	.35	.40	.45	.50	.55	.60	.65	.70	.75	.80
$\alpha = .10$	.60	208	117	75	52	38	*								
	.70	288	162	104	72	53	41	32	*						
	.80	400	225	144	100	73	56	44	36	30	*				
	.90	583	328	210	146	107	82	65	52	43	36	31	*		
$\alpha = .05$	.60	321	181	116	80	59	45	36	*						
	.70	419	235	151	105	77	59	47	38	31	*				
	.80	551	310	198	138	101	78	61	50	41	34	*			
	.90	763	429	274	191	140	107	85	69	57	48	41	35	31	*
$\alpha = .01$	.60	592	333	213	148	109	83	66	53	44	37	32	*		
	.70	722	406	260	181	133	102	80	65	54	45	38	33	*	
	.80	893	502	322	223	164	126	99	80	66	56	48	41	36	31
	.90	1158	651	417	290	213	163	129	104	86	72	62	53	46	41

(d) Case II: Two-Tail Significance Test (Sample Size for Each Group)

Effect Size (Δ_{II})

	Power	.15	.20	.25	.30	.35	.40	.45	.50	.55	.60	.65	.70	.75	.80
$\alpha = .10$	.60	321	181	116	80	59	45	36	*						
	.70	419	235	151	105	77	59	47	38	31	*				
	.80	551	310	198	138	101	78	61	50	41	34	*			
	.90	763	429	275	191	140	107	85	69	57	48	41	35	31	*
$\alpha = .05$	.60	434	244	156	109	80	61	48	39	32	*				
	.70	547	308	197	137	100	77	61	49	41	34	*			
	.80	697	392	251	174	128	98	77	63	52	44	37	32	*	
	.90	933	525	336	233	171	131	104	84	69	58	50	43	37	33
$\alpha = .01$	.60	712	400	256	178	131	100	79	64	53	44	38	33	*	
	.70	854	481	308	214	157	120	95	77	64	53	45	39	34	30
	.80	1040	585	374	260	191	146	116	94	77	65	55	48	42	37
	.90	1324	745	477	331	243	186	147	119	99	83	71	61	53	47

*Sample size is below 30.

TABLE N   Critical values of T in the Wilcoxon dependent-samples test

N	Level of Significance One-Tail Test		
	.025	.01	.005
	Two-Tail Test		
	.05	.02	.01
6	0	—	—
7	2	0	—
8	4	2	0
9	6	3	2
10	8	5	3
11	11	7	5
12	14	10	7
13	17	13	10
14	21	16	13
15	25	20	16
16	30	24	20
17	35	28	23
18	40	33	28
19	46	38	32
20	52	43	38
21	59	49	43
22	66	56	49
23	73	62	55
24	81	69	61
25	89	77	68

Source: Table N is taken from Table G of Siegel, S. *Nonparametric Statistics for the Behavioral Sciences.* New York: McGraw-Hill, 1956 (p. 254). Adapted from Table I of Wilcoxon, F. *Some rapid approximate statistical procedures.* New York: American Cyanamid Company, 1949, (p. 13). Reprinted by permission of the authors and the publishers.

Appendix III:
Glossary of Formulas

- Chi-square
- Correlation
- Covariance
- Effect size
- F test
- Intraclass correlation ($\hat{\rho}_I$)
- Linear regression equation
- Mean
- Mean Square (*MS*)
- Median
- Mode
- Multiple correlation coefficient
- Multiple correlation square
- Omega square ($\hat{\omega}^2$)
- Percentile score
- Probability of an event
- Range
- Regression slope
- Reliability
- Scheffé's test
- Semi-interquartile range
- Spearman rank correlation
- Standard deviation
- Standard error of estimate
- Standard error of the difference between means
- Standard error of the mean
- Sum of squares (*SS*)
- t test (single sample, independent samples, dependent samples)
- Tukey's HSD test
- Variance
- Weighted mean
- z score
- $z_{\bar{X}}$ test
- $z_{\bar{X}_1-\bar{X}_2}$ test

Chi square

$$\chi^2_{observed} = \sum_{i=1}^{k} \frac{(O_i - E_i)^2}{E_i} \tag{19-1}$$

where: O = observed frequency
E = expected frequency

Correlation

$$r_{XY} = \frac{\text{Cov}_{XY}}{s_X s_Y} \tag{6-2}$$

where: Cov_{XY} = covariance
s_X = standard deviation of X
s_Y = standard deviation of Y

Covariance

$$\text{Cov}_{XY} = \frac{\sum (X - \bar{X})(Y - \bar{Y})}{N - 1} = \frac{\sum xy}{N - 1} \tag{6-1}$$

where: $\bar{X}$ = mean of a set of scores on variable X
$\bar{Y}$ = mean of a set of scores on variable Y
$x = X - \bar{X}$
$y = Y - \bar{Y}$
N = total number of scores entering the sum

Effect size
(a) Case I research:

$$\Delta_{\text{I}} = \frac{|\mu_1 - \mu_0|}{\sigma} \tag{11-1}$$

where: μ_1 = population mean under alternative hypothesis
μ_0 = population mean under null hypothesis
σ = population standard deviation

(b) Case II research:

$$\Delta_{\text{II}} = \frac{|\mu_1 - \mu_2|}{\sigma} \tag{11-2}$$

where: μ_1 = population mean of group 1
μ_2 = population mean of group 2
σ = population standard deviation

F test
One way ANOVA

$$F_{\text{observed}} = \frac{MS_{\text{between}}}{MS_{\text{within}}}$$

(13-10)

where: MS = mean square

In general

$$F_{\text{observed}} = \frac{MS_{\text{effect}}}{MS_{\text{appropriate error term}}}$$

where: MS = mean square

Intraclass correlation ($\hat{\rho}_{\text{I}}$)
One-way ANOVA

$$\hat{\rho}_{\text{I}} = \frac{MS_B - MS_W}{MS_B + (n-1)MS_W}$$

(13-12)

where: MS_B = mean square between groups
              MS_W = mean square within groups
              n = number of subjects within a group

Linear regression equation
One predictor

$$\hat{Y} = \bar{Y} + b_{YX}(X - \bar{X})$$

(7-7)

where: $\hat{Y}$ = predicted Y score
              $\bar{Y}$ = mean of a set of scores on variable Y
              b_{YX} = regression slope for predicting Y from X
              $\bar{X}$ = mean of a set of scores on variable X

Two predictors

$$\hat{Y} = a + b_1X_1 + b_2X_2$$

(18-1)

where: $\hat{Y}$ = predicted Y score
              a = intercept (see Formula 18–2a)
              b_1 = partial regression coefficient for variable 1 (see Formula 18–2b)
              b_2 = partial regression coefficient for variable 2 (see Formula 18–2b)

Mean

$$\bar{X} = \frac{\sum X}{N}$$

(4-2)

where: $\bar{X}$ = mean of a set of scores on variable X
              N = total number of scores entering the sum

Mean Square (*MS*)

$$MS = \frac{SS}{df}$$

where: SS = sum of squares
            df = degrees of freedom

Median

$$\text{Median} = X_{ll} + \frac{1\left(\dfrac{n}{2} - cf_{ll}\right)}{f_i} \qquad \text{(4-1)}$$

where: X_{ll} = lower real limit of the interval that contains the median
            i = interval size
            N = total number of scores
            cf_{ll} = cumulative frequency of the interval below the interval
                   containing the median
            f_{ll} = frequency of the interval containing the median

Mode

The most frequently earned score in a distribution.

Multiple correlation coefficient

$$R = \frac{\text{Cov}(Y, \hat{Y})}{s_Y s_{\hat{Y}}} \qquad \text{(18-3)}$$

where: $\text{Cov}(Y, \hat{Y})$ = covariance of Y and predicted Y
                     s = standard deviation

Multiple correlation square

$$R^2 = \frac{r_{Y1}^2 + r_{Y2}^2 - 2r_{Y1}r_{Y2}r_{12}}{1 - r_{12}^2} \qquad \text{(18-4)}$$

where: r = correlation
            $1, 2$ = predictor 1 and 2

Omega square ($\hat{\omega}^2$)
One-Way ANOVA

$$\hat{\omega}^2 = \frac{SS_B - (k-1)MS_W}{SS_T + MS_W} \qquad \text{(13-11)}$$

where: SS_B = sum of squares between groups
            MS_W = mean square within groups
            SS_T = total sum of squares

Percentile score

$$\text{Score at percentile } Q = X_{ll} + \frac{i(cf - cf_{ul})}{f_i} \tag{4-7}$$

where: X_{ll} = value of the lower real limit of the interval containing the *cf* of interest
i = size of the interval
cf = cumulative frequency corresponding to the percentile of interest
cf_{ul} = cumulative frequency at the upper real limit of the interval below the interval containing *cf*

Probability of an event

$$p(E) = \frac{\#E}{\#OS} = \text{relative frequency of } E \tag{9-1}$$

where: p = probability
$\#E$ = number of outcomes in event
$\#OS$ = number of outcomes in outcome space

Range

$$X_{\text{highest}} - X_{\text{lowest}} \tag{4-5}$$

Regression slope

$$b_{YX} = \frac{\text{Cov}_{XY}}{s_X^2} = r_{XY}\frac{s_Y}{s_X} \tag{7-6}$$

where: Cov_{XY} = covariance
s_X^2 = variance of X
r_{XY} = correlation
s = standard deviation

Reliability

$$r_{XX'} = \frac{\hat{\sigma}_s^2}{\hat{\sigma}_s^2 + \dfrac{\hat{\sigma}_e^2}{k}} \tag{15-5a}$$

where: $\hat{\sigma}_s^2$ = estimated variance for subjects
$\hat{\sigma}_e^2$ = estimated variance for error
k = number of repeated measures

Scheffé's test
  One-way ANOVA

$$t_{observed} = \frac{\hat{C}}{\sqrt{MS_W \left(\dfrac{w_1^2}{n_1} + \dfrac{w_2^2}{n_2} + \cdots + \dfrac{w_k^2}{n_k} \right)}} \qquad \text{(13-15)}$$

$$t_{critical} = \sqrt{(k-1)F_{critical(\alpha, k-1, df_W)}} \qquad \text{(13-16)}$$

where: $\hat{C}$ = comparison of interest
          MS_W = mean square within group
          w = weight
          n = number of subjects within a group
          k = number of groups
          df_W = degrees of freedom within groups

Semi-interquartile range

$$SIQR = \frac{Q_3 - Q_1}{2} \qquad \text{(4-6)}$$

where: Q_3 = score at the 75th percentile
          Q_1 = score at the 25th percentile

Spearman rank correlation

$$r_s = \frac{\text{Cov}_{XY}}{s_X s_Y} \qquad \text{(6-5)}$$

where: X and Y = ranks
          Cov_{XY} = covariance
          s_X = standard deviation of X
          s_Y = standard deviation of Y

Standard deviation

$$s = \sqrt{\frac{\sum(X - \bar{X})^2}{N - 1}} = \sqrt{\frac{\sum x^2}{N - 1}} \qquad \text{(4-8)}$$

where: $x = X - \bar{X}$
          N = total number of cases entering sum

Standard error of estimate

$$s_{YX} = s_Y \sqrt{1 - r_{XY}^2}$$

(7-8)

where: s = standard deviation

r = correlation

Standard error of the difference between means
Population

$$\sigma_{\bar{X}_1 - \bar{X}_2} = \sqrt{\sigma_{\bar{X}_1}^2 + \sigma_{\bar{X}_2}^2}$$

(10-1)

where: $\sigma_{\bar{X}}$ = standard error of the mean

Independent samples

$$s_{\bar{X}_1 - \bar{X}_2} = \sqrt{s_{\bar{X}_1}^2 + s_{\bar{X}_2}^2} = \sqrt{\left[\frac{(n_1 - 1)s_1^2 + (n_2 - 1)s_2^2}{n_1 + n_2 - 2}\right]\left(\frac{1}{n_1} + \frac{1}{n_2}\right)}$$

(12-4, 5)

where: $s_{\bar{X}}$ = standard error of the mean

s — standard deviation

n = number of subjects in a group

Dependent samples

$$s_{\bar{X}_1 - \bar{X}_2}^* \sqrt{s_{\bar{X}_1}^2 + s_{\bar{X}_2}^2 - 2r_{12}s_{\bar{X}_1}s_{\bar{X}_2}}$$

(12-6)

where: $s_{\bar{X}}$ = standard error of the mean

s = standard deviation

r = correlation

Standard error of the mean
Population

$$\sigma_{\bar{X}} = \frac{\sigma}{\sqrt{N}}$$

(10-1)

where: σ = standard deviation

N = number of subjects

Sample

$$s_{\bar{X}} = \frac{s}{\sqrt{N}}$$

(12-1)

where: s = standard deviation

N = number of subjects

Sum of squares (SS)
One-way ANOVA (between groups)

$$SS_B = \sum_i n_1(\bar{X}_i - \bar{X}_G)^2 \tag{13-6}$$

where: $\bar{X}_i$ = mean of group i
$\bar{X}_G$ = grand mean

In general: Sum of squared deviations such as sum of squared deviations of group or cell means about a grand mean, or sum of squared deviations of scores about a group or cell mean.

t test (single sample)

$$t_{observed} = \frac{\bar{X} - \mu}{s_{\bar{X}}} \tag{12-2}$$

where: μ = population mean
$\bar{X}$ = sample mean
$s_{\bar{X}}$ = standard error of the mean

t test (independent samples)

$$t_{observed} = \frac{\bar{X}_1 - \bar{X}_2}{\sqrt{\left[\dfrac{(n_1 - 1)s_1^2 + (n_2 - 1)s_2^2}{n_1 + n_2 - 2}\right]\left(\dfrac{1}{n_1} + \dfrac{1}{n_2}\right)}} \tag{12-5}$$

where: n = number of subjects in a group
s = standard deviation
$\bar{X}$ = standard mean

t test (dependent samples)

$$t_{observed}^* = \frac{\bar{X}_1 - \bar{X}_2}{\sqrt{s_{\bar{X}_1}^2 + s_{\bar{X}_1}^2 - 2r_{12}s_{\bar{X}_1}s_{\bar{X}_2}}} \tag{12-7}$$

where: $\bar{X}$ = standard mean
$s_{\bar{X}}$ = standard error of the mean
r = correlation

Tukey's HSD test
One-way ANOVA

$$HSD = q_{(\alpha, df_W, k)} \sqrt{\frac{MS_W}{n}} \qquad \text{(13-17)}$$

where: q = value of studentized range statistic (Table F)
α = probability of a Type I error
df_W = degrees of freedom within groups
k = number of groups
n = number of subjects within a group

Variance

$$s^2 = \frac{\sum(X - \bar{X})^2}{N - 1} = \frac{\sum x^2}{N - 1} \qquad \text{(4-10)}$$

where: $x = X - \bar{X}$
N = total number of cases entering a sum

Weighted mean

$$\bar{X}_W = \sum_{i=1}^{k} N_i \bar{X}_i \qquad \text{(4-4)}$$

where: $\bar{X}_W$ = weighted mean
k = number of means being combined
N = number of scores entering into the mean
$\bar{X}_i$ = sample mean for the group i

z score

$$z = \frac{X - \bar{X}}{s} = \frac{x}{s} \qquad \text{(5-1)}$$

where: $\bar{X}$ = mean
s = standard deviation
$x = X - \bar{X}$

$z_{\bar{X}}$ test

$$z_{\bar{X}} = \frac{\bar{X} - \mu}{\sigma_{\bar{X}}} \qquad \text{(10-2)}$$

where: $\bar{X}$ = sample mean
μ = population mean
$\sigma_{\bar{X}}$ = standard error of the mean

$z_{\bar{X}_1 - \bar{X}_2}$ **test**

$$z_{\bar{X}_1 - \bar{X}_2} = \frac{\bar{X}_1 - \bar{X}_2}{\sigma_{\bar{X}_1 - \bar{X}_2}}$$

(10-5)

where: $\bar{X}$ = sample mean

$\sigma_{\bar{X}_1 - \bar{X}_2}$ = standard error of the difference between means

References

Bem, D.J., & Honorton, C. (1994). Does psi exist? Replicable evidence for an anomalous process of information transfer. *Psychological Bulletin, 115,* 4–18.

Bishop, Y.M.M., Fienberg, S.E., & Holland, P.W. (1975). *Discrete multivariate analysis: Theory and practice.* Cambridge, MA: MIT Press.

Blalock, H.M. (1964). *Causal inferences in nonexperimental research.* Chapel Hill: University of North Carolina Press.

Brunswik, E. (1955). Representative design and probabilistic theory in a functional psychology. *Psychological Review, 62,* 193–217.

Braun, C. (1976). Teacher expectations: Sociopsychological dynamics. *Review of Educational Research, 46,* 185–213.

Braun, C. (1987). Teachers' expectations. In M.J. Dunkin (ed.), *International Encyclopedia of Teaching and Teacher Education.* New York: Pergamon Press, pp. 598–605.

Brilliant, A. (1994). Dreaming is believing. *The Santa Barbara Independent, 8,* April 14–21, p. 11.

Bryant, L.J., & Paulson, A.S. (1976). An extension of Tukey's method of multiple comparisons to experimental designs with random concomitant variables. *Biometrika, 63,* 631–638.

Camilli, G., & Hopkins, K.D. (1978). Applicability of chi square to 2×2 contingency tables with small expected frequencies. *Psychological Bulletin, 85,* 163–167.

Campbell, D.T., & Stanley, J.C. (1963). Experimental and quasi-experimental designs for research on teaching. In N.L. Gage (ed.), *Handbook of research on teaching.* Chicago: Rand McNally.

Campbell, D.T., & Stanley, J.C. (1966). *Experimental and quasi-experimental designs for research on teaching.* Chicago: Rand McNally.

Cochran, W.G. (1954). Some methods for strengthening the common χ^2 tests. *Biometrics, 10,* 417–451.

Cochran, W.G. (1966). *Sampling techniques* (2nd ed.). New York: Wiley.

Cohen, J. (1988). *Statistical power analysis for the behavioral sciences* (2nd ed.). Hillsdale, NJ: Erlbaum.

Cohen, J. (1992a). A power primer. *Psychological Bulletin, 112,* 155–159.

Cohen, J. (1992b). Statistical power analysis. *Current Directions in Psychological Science, 1,* 98–101.

Cook, T.D., & Campbell, D.T. (1979). *Quasi-experimentation: Design & Analysis issues for field settings.* Chicago: Rand McNally.

Cornfield, J., & Tukey, J.W. (1956). Average values of mean squares in factorials. *Annals of Mathematical Statistics, 27,* 907–949.

Cronbach, L.J. (1975). Beyond two disciplines of scientific psychology. *American Psychologist, 30,* 116–127.

Cronbach, L.J., Gleser, G.C., Nanda, H., & Rajaratnam, N. (1972). *The dependability of behavioral measurements: Theory of generalizability for scores and profiles.* New York: Wiley.

Cronbach, L.J., & Snow, R.E. (1977). *Aptitudes and instructional methods: A handbook for research on interactions.* New York: Irvington.

Davis, J.A. (1985). *The logic of causal order.* In J.L. Sullivan & R.G. Niemi (eds.), *Quantitative applications in the social sciences.* Beverly Hills, CA: Sage.

Dodd, D.H., & Schultz, R.F., Jr. (1973). Computational procedures for estimating magnitude of effect for some analysis of variance designs. *Psychological Bulletin, 79,* 391–395.

Draper, N.R., & Smith, H. (1981). *Applied regression analysis.* New York: Wiley.

Duncan, O.D. (1975). *Introduction to structural equation models.* New York: Academic Press.

Elashoff, J.D. (1969). Analysis of covariance: A delicate instrument. *American Educational Research Journal, 6,* 383–401.

Elashoff, J.D., & Snow, R.E. (1971). *Pygmalion reconsidered: A case study in statistical inference: Reconsideration of the Rosenthal-Jacobson data on teacher expectancy.* Belmont, CA: Wadsworth.

Friedman, H. (1982). Simplified determinations of statistical power, magnitude of effect and research sample sizes. *Educational and Psychological Measurement, 42,* 521–526.

Gagnè, E.D., Yekovich, C.W., & Yekovich, F.R. (1993). *The cognitive psychology of school subjects* (2nd ed.). New York: HarperCollins.

Glass, GV, & Stanley, J.C. (1970). *Statistical methods in education and psychology.* Englewood Cliffs, NJ: Prentice Hall.

Goldman, R.D., Schmidt, D.E., Hewitt, B.N., & Fisher, R. (1974). Grading practices in different major fields. *American Educational Research Journal, 11,* 343–357.

Hahn & Meeker (1993). Assumptions for statistical inference. *The American Statistician, 47,* 1–11.

Hays, W.L. (1973). *Statistics for the social sciences* (2nd ed.), New York: Holt, Rinehart and Winston.

Hays, W.L. (1988). *Statistics* (4th ed.), New York: Holt, Rinehart and Winston.

Hays, W. (1994). *Statistics* (5th ed.), New York: Harcourt, Brace, Jovanovich.

Hewitt, B.N., & Goldman, R.D. (1975). Occam's razor slices through the myth that college women overachieve. *Journal of Educational Psychology, 67,* 325–330.

Hudley, C., & Graham, S. (1993). An attributional intervention to reduce peer-directed aggression among African-American boys. *Child Development, 64,* 124–138.

Jones, L.V. (1971). The nature of measurement. In R.L. Thorndike (ed.). *Educational measurement* (2nd ed.). Washington, D.C.: American Council of Education.

Keller, D., Crouse, J., & Trusheim, D. (1993). Relationships among gender differences in freshman course grades and course characteristics. *Journal of Educational Psychology, 85,* 702–709.

Kirk, R.E. (1982). *Experimental design* (2nd ed.). Belmont, CA: Brooks/Cole.

Kirk, R.E. (1995). *Experimental design* (3rd ed.). Belmont, CA: Brooks/Cole.

Kruskal, W.H., & Wallis, W.A. (1952). Use of ranks in one-criterion variance analysis. *Journal of the American Statistical Association, 47,* 583–621.

Levin, J.R. (1993). Statistical significance testing from three perspectives. *Journal of Experimental Education, 61,* 378–382.

Lord, F.M., & Novick, M. (1971). *Statistical theories of mental test scores.* Reading, MA: Addison-Wesley.

Majasan, J.K. (1972). College students' achievement as a function of the congruence between their beliefs and their instructor's beliefs. Unpublished doctoral dissertation, Stanford University.

Mann, H.B., & Whitney, D.R. (1947). On a test of whether one of two random variables is stochastically larger than the other. *Annals of Mathematical Statistics, 18,* 50–60.

Marascuilo, L.A., & McSweeney. M. (1977). *Nonparametric and distribution free methods for the social sciences.* Belmont, CA: Wadsworth.

Marsh, H.W., & Shavelson, R.J. (1985). Self-concept: Its multifaceted, hierarchical structure. *Educational Psychologist, 20,* 107–125.

Maxwell, S.E., & Delaney, H.D. (1993). Bivariate median splits and spurious statistical significance. *Psychological Bulletin, 113,* 181–190.

Mitchell, J. (1986). Measurement scales and statistics: A clash of paradigms. *Psychological Bulletin, 100,* 398–407.

Mook, D.G. (1983). In defense of external invalidity. *American Psychologist, 38,* 379–387.

Neisser, U. (1976). *Cognition and reality.* San Francisco: W.H. Freeman.

Obrien, R.G., & Kaiser, M.K. (1985). MANOVA method for analyzing repeated measures designs: An extensive primer. *Psychological Bulletin 97,* 316–333.

Pedhazur, E.J. (1982). *Multiple regression in behavioral research: Explanation and prediction* (2nd ed). New York: Holt, Rinehart and Winston.

Quintana, S.M., & Maxwell, S.E. (1994). A Monte Carlo comparison of seven ε-adjustment procedures in repeated measures designs with small sample sizes. *Journal of Educational Statistics 19,* 57–71.

Ramsey, P.H. (1994). Testing variances in psychological and educational research. *Journal of Educational Statistics, 19,* 23–42.

Rogosa, D. (1980). Comparing parallel regression lines. *Psychological Bulletin, 88,* 307–321.

Rosenthal, R. (1966). *Experimenter effects in behavioral research.* New York: Appleton-Century-Crofts.

Rosenthal, R. (1973). The Pygmalion effect lives. *Psychology Today, 7,* 56–63.

Rosenthal, R., & Jacobson, L. (1968). *Pygmalion in the classroom.* New York: Holt, Rinehart and Winston.

Runkel, P.J. (1956). Cognitive similarity in facilitating communication. *Sociometry, 19,* 178–191.

Schaalje, B., Zhang J., Pantula, S.G., & Pollock, K.H. (1991). Analysis of repeated-measures data from randomized block experiments. *Biometrics, 47,* 813–824.

Schacter, S, & Singer, J.E. (1962). Cognitive, social, and physiological determinants of emotional state. *Psychological Review, 69,* 379–399.

Scheffé, H. (1959). *Analysis of variance.* New York: Wiley.

Seebach, L. (1993). Low SAT scores reflect much more than a gender gap. *Santa Barbara News Press,* Thursday, July 15, p. A13.

Shavelson, R.J., Cadwell, J., & Izu, T. (1977). Teachers' sensitivity to the reliability of information in making pedagogical decisions. *American Educational Research Journal, 14,* 83–97.

Shavelson, R.J., Hubner, J.J., & Stanton, G.C. (1976). Self-concept: Validation of construct interpretations. *Review of Educational Research, 46,* 407–441.

Shavelson, R.J., & Seminara, J.L. (1968). Effect of lunar gravity on man's performance of basic maintenance tasks. *Journal of Applied Psychology, 52,* 177–183.

Shavelson, R.J., & Webb, N.M. (1991). *Generalizability theory: A primer.* Thousand Oaks, CA: Sage.

Siegel, S. (1956). *Nonparametric statistics for the behavioral sciences.* New York: McGraw-Hill.

Sinclair, R.C., Hoffman, C., Mark, M.M., Martin, L.L., & Pickering, T.L. (1994). Construct accessibility and the misattribution off arousal: Schachter and Singer Revisited, *5,* 15–19.

Smith, M.L., & Glass, GV (1977). Meta-analysis of psychotherapy outcomes studies. *American Psychologist, 32,* 752–760.

Tatsuoka, M.M. (1992). Statistical methods. In M.C. Alkin (ed.), *Encyclopedia of educational research, Volume 4* (6th ed.). New York: Macmillan, pp. 1275–1303.

Thorndyke, P.W. (1977). Cognitive structures in comprehension and memory of narrative discourse. *Cognitive Psychology, 9,* 77–110.

Toothaker, L.E. (1993). *Multiple comparison procedures.* Newbury Park, CA: Sage.

Tukey, J.W. (1949). One degree of freedom for nonadditivity. *Biometrics, 5,* 232–242.

Tukey, J.W. (1977). *Exploratory data analysis.* Reading, MA: Addison-Wesley.

Tversky, A., & Kahneman, D. (1974). Judgment under uncertainty: Heuristics and biases. *Science, 185,* 1124–1131.

Vellman, P.F., & Wilkinson, L. (1993). Nominal, ordinal, interval, and ratio typologies are misleading. *American Statistician, 47*(1), 65–72.

Weiner, B. (1986). *An attributional theory of motivation and emotion.* New York: Springer-Verlag.

Weiner, B. (1991). Metaphors in motivation and attribution. *American Psychologist, 46,* 921–930.

Weiner, B., & Peter, N. (1973). A cognitive-developmental analysis of achievement and moral judgments. *Developmental psychology, 9,* 290–309.

Wigdor, A.K. & Green, B.F., Jr. (eds.). (1991). *Performance assessment for the workplace* (Vol. I). Washington, D.C.: National Academy Press.

Wilcox, R. (1992). *New statistical procedures for the social sciences: Median solutions to basic problems.* Hillsdale, NJ: Erlbaum Associates.

Wilcoxon, F. (1949). *Some rapid approximate statistical procedures.* Stamford, CT: Stamford Research Laboratories, American Cyanamid Company.

Winer, B.J., Brown, D.R., & Michels, K.M. (1991). *Statistical principles in experimental design* (3rd ed.). New York: McGraw-Hill.

Index